Part of JIST's Top Careers™ Series

Top 100

CAREERS for
College Graduates™

Your Complete Guidebook to Major Jobs
in Many Fields

SEVENTH EDITION

Michael Farr

JIST®
Works
America's Career Publisher™

Top 100 Careers for College Graduates, Seventh Edition
Your Complete Guidebook to Major Jobs in Many Fields

Previous edition was titled *America's Top 101 Jobs for College Graduates.*

© 2007 by JIST Publishing, Inc.

Published by JIST Works, an imprint of JIST Publishing, Inc.
8902 Otis Avenue
Indianapolis, IN 46216-1033
Phone: 1-800-648-JIST   Fax: 1-800-JIST-FAX
E-mail: info@jist.com   Web site: www.jist.com

Some books by Michael Farr:	JIST's Top Careers™ Series:
Best Jobs for the 21st Century	*Top 300 Careers*
Overnight Career Choice	*Top 100 Health-Care Careers*
Same-Day Resume	*100 Fastest-Growing Jobs*
Next-Day Job Interview	*Top 100 Careers Without a Four-Year Degree*
The Quick Resume & Cover Letter Book	*Top 100 Careers for College Graduates*
The Very Quick Job Search	*Top 100 Computer and Technical Careers*

Visit www.jist.com for free job search information, book excerpts, and ordering information on our many products. For free information on 14,000 job titles, visit www.careeroink.com.

Quantity discounts are available for JIST products. Have future editions of JIST books automatically delivered to you on publication through our convenient standing order program. Please call 1-800-648-JIST or visit www.jist.com for a free catalog and more information.

Acquisitions Editor: Susan Pines
Development Editors: Stephanie Koutek, Jill Mazurczyk
Database Work: Laurence Shatkin
Cover Layout: Trudy Coler
Cover Photo: Copyright 2007 Jupiter Images Corporation
Interior Design and Layout: Marie Kristine Parial-Leonardo
Proofreader: Jeanne Clark

Printed in the United States of America

09 08 07 06   9 8 7 6 5 4 3 2 1

Library of Congress Cataloging in Publication data is on file with the Library of Congress

We have been careful to provide accurate information throughout this book, but it is possible that errors and omissions have been introduced. Please consider this in making any career plans or other important decisions. Trust your own judgment above all else and in all things.

Trademarks: All brand names and product names used in this book are trade names, service marks, trademarks, or registered trademarks of their respective owners.

ISBN-13: 978-1-59357-318-8
ISBN-10: 1-59357-318-9

Relax. You Don't Have to Read This Whole Book!

You don't need to read this entire book. I've organized it into easy-to-use sections so you can get just the information you want. You will find everything you need to

★ Learn about the 100 top careers for college graduates, including their daily tasks, pay, outlook, and required education and skills.

★ Match your personal skills to the careers.

★ Take seven steps to land a good job in less time.

To get started, simply scan the table of contents to learn more about these sections and to see a list of the jobs described in this book. Really, this book is easy to use, and I hope it helps you.

Who Should Use This Book?

This is more than a book of job descriptions. I've spent quite a bit of time thinking about how to make its contents useful for a variety of situations, including

★ **Exploring career options.** The job descriptions in Part II give a wealth of information on many of the most desirable jobs in the labor market. The assessment in Part I can help you focus your career options.

★ **Considering more education or training.** The information helps you avoid costly mistakes in choosing a career or deciding on additional training or education—and it increases your chances of planning a bright future.

★ **Job seeking.** This book helps you identify new job targets, prepare for interviews, and write targeted resumes. The advice in Part III has been proven to cut job search time in half.

★ **Career planning.** The job descriptions help you explore your options, and Parts III and IV provide career planning advice and other useful information.

Source of Information

The job descriptions come from the good people at the U.S. Department of Labor, as published in the most recent edition of the *Occupational Outlook Handbook*. The *OOH* is the best source of career information available, and the descriptions include the most current, accurate data on jobs. Thank you to all the people at the Department of Labor who gather, compile, analyze, and make sense of this information. It's good stuff, and I hope you can make good use of it.

Mike Farr

Contents

Summary of Major Sections

Introduction. Provides an explanation of the job descriptions, how best to use the book, and other details. *Begins on page 1.*

Part I: Using the Job-Match Grid to Choose a Career. Match your skills and preferences to the jobs in this book. *Begins on page 13.*

Part II: Descriptions of the Top 100 Careers for College Graduates. Presents thorough descriptions of the top 100 careers for college graduates. These jobs typically require a four-year college degree or more. Some of the jobs can be obtained by those without a four-year or higher degree but are most often held by college graduates. Each description gives information on the nature of the work, working conditions, employment, training, other qualifications, advancement, job outlook, earnings, related occupations, and sources of additional information. The jobs are presented in alphabetical order within educational groups. The page numbers where specific descriptions begin are listed in the detailed contents. *Begins on page 29.*

Part III: Quick Job Search—Seven Steps to Getting a Good Job in Less Time. This relatively brief but important section offers results-oriented career planning and job search techniques. It includes tips on identifying your key skills, defining your ideal job, using effective job search methods, writing resumes, organizing your time, improving your interviewing skills, and following up on leads. The last part of this section features professionally written and designed resumes for some of the top jobs for college graduates. *Begins on page 325.*

Part IV: Important Trends in Jobs and Industries. This section includes 3 well-written articles on labor market trends. The articles are worth your time. Titles of the articles are "Tomorrow's Jobs," "Employment Trends in Major Industries," and "Job Outlook for College Graduates." *Begins on page 389.*

Detailed Contents

v

Introduction

This book is about improving your life, not just about selecting a job. The career you choose will have an enormous impact on how you live your life.

While a huge amount of information is available on occupations, most people don't know where to find accurate, reliable facts to help them make good career decisions—or they don't take the time to look. Important choices such as what to do with your career or whether to get additional training or education deserve your time.

If you are considering more training or education—whether additional coursework, a college degree, or an advanced degree—this book will help with solid information. Training or education beyond high school is now typically required to get better jobs, and the education and training needed for the jobs in this book vary enormously. This book is designed to give you facts to help you explore your options.

A certain type of work or workplace may interest you as much as a certain type of job. If your interests and values lead you to work in healthcare, for example, you can do this in a variety of work environments, in a variety of industries, and in a variety of jobs. For this reason, I suggest you begin exploring alternatives by following your interests and finding a career path that allows you to use your talents doing something you enjoy.

Also, remember that money is not everything. The time you spend in career planning can pay off in higher earnings, but being satisfied with your work—and your life—is often more important than how much you earn. This book can help you find the work that suits you best.

Keep in Mind That Your Situation Is Not "Average"

Projected employment growth and earnings trends are quite positive for many occupations and industries. Keep in mind, however, that the averages in this book will not be true for many individuals. Within any field, many people earn more and many earn less than the average.

My point is that *your* situation is probably not average. Some people do better than others, and some are willing to accept less pay for a more desirable work environment. Earnings vary enormously in different parts of the country, in different occupations, and in different industries. But this book's solid information is a great place to start. Good information will give you a strong foundation for good decisions.

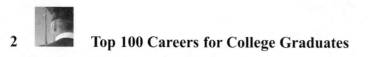

Four Important Labor Market Trends That Will Affect Your Career

Our economy has changed in dramatic ways over the past 10 years, with profound effects on how we work and live. Part IV of this book provides more information on labor market trends but, in case you don't read it, here are four trends that you simply *must* consider.

1. Education Pays

I'm sure you won't be surprised to learn that people with higher levels of education and training have higher average earnings. The data that follows comes from the U.S. Department of Labor. I've selected data to show you the median earnings for people with various levels of education. (The median is the point where half earn more and half earn less.) Based on this information, I computed the earnings advantage of people at various education levels over those who did not graduate from high school. I've also included information showing the average percentage of people at that educational level who are unemployed.

Earnings for Year-Round, Full-Time Workers Age 25 and Over, by Educational Attainment

Level of Education	Median Annual Earnings	Premium Over High School Dropouts	Unemployment Rate
Master's degree	$53,200	$33,400	2.9
Bachelor's degree	45,000	25,200	3.3
Associate degree	33,600	13,800	4.0
Some college, no degree	31,100	11,300	5.2
High school graduate	27,700	7,900	5.5
High school dropout	19,800	—	8.8

Source: Bureau of Labor Statistics

As you can see in the table, the earnings difference between a college graduate and someone with a high school education is $17,300 a year—enough to buy a nice car, make a down payment on a house, or even take a few months' vacation for two to Europe. As you see, over a lifetime, this earnings difference will make an enormous difference in lifestyle.

The table makes it very clear that those with more training and education earn more than those with less and experience lower levels of unemployment. Jobs that require education and training beyond high school are projected to grow significantly faster than jobs that do not. People with higher levels of education and training are less likely to be unemployed, and when they are, they remain unemployed for shorter periods of time. There are always exceptions, but it is quite clear that a college education results in higher earnings and lower rates of unemployment.

2. Knowledge of Computer and Other Technologies Is Increasingly Important

As you look over the list of jobs in the table of contents, you may notice that many require computer or technical skills. Even jobs that do not appear to be technical often call for computer literacy. Managers, for example, are often expected to understand and use spreadsheet, word-processing, and database software.

In all fields, those without job-related technical and computer skills will have a more difficult time finding good opportunities because they are competing with those who have these skills. Older workers, by the way, often do not have the computer skills that younger workers do. Employers tend to hire people who have the skills they need, and people without these abilities won't get the best jobs. So, whatever your age, consider upgrading your job-related computer and technology skills if you need to—and plan to stay up to date on your current and future jobs.

3. Ongoing Education and Training Are Essential

School and work once were separate activities, and most people did not go back to school after they began working. But with rapid changes in technology, most people are now required to learn throughout their work lives. Jobs are constantly upgraded, and today's jobs often cannot be handled by people who have only the knowledge and skills that were adequate for workers a few years ago.

To remain competitive, you will need to constantly upgrade your technology and other job-related skills. This may include taking formal courses, reading work-related magazines at home, signing up for on-the-job training, or participating in other forms of education. Upgrading your work-related skills on an ongoing basis is no longer optional for most jobs, and you ignore doing so at your peril.

4. Good Career Planning Has Increased in Importance

Most people spend more time watching TV in a week than they spend on career planning during an entire year. Yet most people will change their jobs many times and make major career changes five to seven times. For this reason, it is important for you to spend time considering your career options and preparing to advance.

While you probably picked up this book for its information on jobs, it also provides a great deal of information on career planning. For example, Part III gives good career and job search advice, and Part IV has useful information on labor market trends. I urge you to read these and related materials because career-planning and job-seeking skills are the keys to surviving in this new economy.

Tips on Using This Book

This book is based on information from a variety of government sources and includes the most up-to-date and accurate data available. The entries are well written and pack a lot of information into short descriptions. *Top 100 Careers for College Graduates* can be used in many ways, and I've provided tips for these four major uses:

★ For people exploring career, education, or training alternatives

★ For job seekers

★ For employers and business people

★ For counselors, instructors, and other career specialists

Tips for People Exploring Career, Education, or Training Alternatives

Top 100 Careers for College Graduates is an excellent resource for anyone exploring career, education, or training alternatives. Many people do not have a good idea of what they want to do in their careers. They may be considering additional training or education but may not know what sort they should get. If you are one of these people, this book can help in several ways. Here are a few pointers.

Review the list of jobs. Trust yourself. Research studies indicate that most people have a good sense of their interests. Your interests can be used to guide you to career options you should consider in more detail.

Begin by looking over the occupations listed in the table of contents. Look at all the jobs, because you may identify previously overlooked possibilities. If other people will be using this book, please don't mark in it. Instead, on a

separate sheet of paper, list the jobs that interest you. Or make a photocopy of the table of contents and use it to mark the jobs that interest you.

Next, look up and carefully read the descriptions of the jobs that most interest you in Part II. A quick review will often eliminate one or more of these jobs based on pay, working conditions, education required, or other considerations. After you have identified the three or four jobs that seem most interesting, research each one more thoroughly before making any important decisions.

Match your skills to the jobs in this book using the Job-Match Grid. Another way to identify possible job options is to answer questions about your skills and job preferences in Part I, "Using the Job-Match Grid to Choose a Career." This section will help you focus your job options and concentrate your research on a handful of job descriptions.

Study the jobs and their training and education requirements. Too many people decide to obtain additional training or education without knowing much about the jobs the training will lead to. Reviewing the descriptions in this book is one way to learn more about an occupation before you enroll in an education or training program. If you are currently a student, the job descriptions in this book can also help you decide on a major course of study or learn more about the jobs for which your studies are preparing you.

Do not be too quick to eliminate a job that interests you. If a job requires more education or training than you currently have, you can obtain this training in many ways.

Don't abandon your past experience and education too quickly. If you have significant work experience, training, or education, these should not be abandoned too quickly. Many times, after people carefully consider what they want to do, they change careers and find that they can still use the skills they already have.

Top 100 Careers for College Graduates can help you explore career options in several ways. First, carefully review descriptions for jobs you have held in the past. On a separate sheet of paper, list the skills needed in those jobs. Then do the same for jobs that interest you now. By comparing the lists, you will be able to identify skills you used in previous jobs that you could also use in jobs that interest you for the future. These "transferable" skills form the basis for moving to a new career.

You can also identify skills you have developed or used in nonwork activities, such as hobbies, family responsibilities, volunteer work, school, military, and extracurricular interests. If you want to stay with your current employer, the job descriptions can also help. For example, you may identify jobs within your organization that offer more rewarding work, higher pay, or other advantages over your present job. Read the descriptions related to these jobs, as you may be able to transfer into another job rather than leave the organization.

Tips for Job Seekers

You can use the job descriptions in this book to give you an edge in finding job openings and in getting job offers—even when you are competing with people who have better credentials. Here are some ways *Top 100 Careers for College Graduates* can help you in the job search.

Identify related job targets. You may be limiting your job search to a small number of jobs for which you feel qualified, but by doing so you eliminate many jobs you could do and enjoy. Your search for a new job should be broadened to include more possibilities.

Go through the entire list of jobs in the table of contents and check any that require skills similar to those you have. Look at all the jobs, since doing so sometimes helps you identify targets you would otherwise overlook.

You may want to answer questions about your skills and job preferences in Part I, "Using the Job-Match Grid to Choose a Career." Your results can help you identify career options that may suit you.

Many people are not aware of the many specialized jobs related to their training or experience. The descriptions in *Top 100 Careers for College Graduates* are for major job titles, but a variety of more-specialized jobs may require similar skills. The "Other Major Career Information Sources" section later in this introduction lists sources you can use to find out about more-specialized jobs.

The descriptions can also point out jobs that interest you but that have higher responsibility or compensation levels. While you may not consider yourself qualified for such jobs now, you should think about seeking jobs that are above your previous levels but within your ability to handle.

Prepare for interviews. This book's job descriptions are an essential source of information to help you prepare for interviews. If you carefully review the description of a job before an interview, you will be much better prepared to emphasize your key skills. You should also review descriptions for past jobs and identify skills needed in the new job.

Negotiate pay. The job descriptions in this book will help you know what pay range to expect. Note that local pay and other details can differ substantially from the national averages in the descriptions.

Tips for Employers and Business People

Employers, human resource professionals, and other business users can use this book's information to write job descriptions, study pay ranges, and set criteria for new employees. The information can also help you conduct more-effective interviews by providing a list of key skills needed by new hires.

Tips for Counselors, Instructors, and Other Career Specialists

Counselors, instructors, and other career specialists will find this book helpful for their clients or students exploring career options or job targets. My best suggestion to professionals is to get this book off the shelf and into the hands of the people who need it. Leave it on a table or desk and show people how the information can help them. Wear this book out—its real value is as a tool used often and well.

Additional Information About the Projections

For more information about employment change, job openings, earnings, unemployment rates, and training requirements by occupation, consult *Occupational Projections and Training Data*, published by the Bureau of Labor Statistics. For occupational information from an industry perspective, including some occupations and career paths that *Top 100 Careers for College Graduates* does not cover, consult another BLS publication, *Career Guide to Industries*. This book is also available from JIST with enhanced content under the title *40 Best Fields for Your Career*.

Information on the Major Sections of This Book

This book was designed to be easy to use. The table of contents provides brief comments on each section, and that may be all you need. If not, here are some additional details you may find useful in getting the most out of this book.

Part I: Using the Job-Match Grid to Choose a Career

Part I features an assessment with checklists and questions to match your skills and preferences to the jobs in this book. The seven skills covered in the assessment are artistic, communication, interpersonal, managerial, mathematics, mechanical, and science. The five job characteristics covered in the assessment are economically sensitive, geographically concentrated, hazardous conditions, outdoor work, and physically demanding.

Part II: Descriptions of Top 100 Careers for College Graduates

Part II is the main part of the book and probably the reason you picked it up. It contains brief, well-written descriptions for 100 major jobs typically held by people with college degrees. A list of the jobs is provided in the table of contents. The content for each of these job descriptions comes from the U.S. Department of Labor and is considered by many to be the most accurate and up-to-date data available. These jobs are presented in alphabetical order within five educational categories:

Jobs Typically Requiring a Professional or Doctoral Degree. This group includes such jobs as dentists, veterinarians, physicians and surgeons, lawyers, and medical scientists.

Jobs Typically Requiring a Master's Degree. Jobs such as psychologists, librarians, mathematicians, and operations research analysts are included in this category.

Jobs Typically Requiring a Bachelor's Degree Plus Work Experience. This group includes jobs such as actuaries, various management positions, education administrators, and top executives.

Jobs Typically Requiring a Bachelor's Degree. Some of the jobs here include engineers, accountants and auditors, teachers, physician assistants, budget analysts, public relations specialists, and computer programmers.

Jobs That May Not Require a Bachelor's Degree But Are Often Held by College Graduates. I included a variety of desirable jobs that are often held by college graduates but that don't require a four-year degree for entry. Having a degree will, of course, be a plus for many of these jobs, including aircraft pilots and flight engineers, interpreters and translators, police and detectives, registered nurses, and respiratory therapists.

Together, the jobs in Part II provide enormous variety at all levels of earnings and interest. One way to explore career options is to go to the table of contents and identify those jobs that seem interesting. If you are interested in medical jobs, for example, you can quickly spot those you will want to learn more about. You may also see other jobs that look interesting, and you should consider these as well.

Your next step would be to read the descriptions for the jobs that interest you and, based on what you learn, identify those that *most* interest you. These are the jobs you should consider, and Parts III and IV will give you additional information on how you might best do so.

How the 100 Jobs Were Selected

The jobs included in this book are selected from the nearly 270 jobs covered in detail by the *Occupational Outlook Handbook,* published by the U.S. Department of Labor. They are jobs that normally require at least a bachelor's degree or in which a bachelor's degree is found among many new hires. The size of the workforce varies from a high of 3.8 million (sales representatives, wholesale and manufacturing) to a low of 2,500 (mathematicians). Most of the jobs have a workforce over 100,000 and therefore account for a lot of job openings. Even if overall employment in such a job is shrinking, the large workforce guarantees many job opportunities because of retirements and turnover, so such jobs are worth your consideration for that reason alone. Jobs in this book that have a small workforce generally have high entry requirements (for example, mathematicians need at least a master's degree), so there usually is less competition for the limited number of openings.

Details on Each Section of the Job Descriptions

Each occupational description in this book follows a standard format, making it easier for you to compare jobs. The following overview describes the kinds of information found in each part of a description and offers tips on how to interpret the information.

Job Title

This is the title used for the job in the *Occupational Outlook Handbook*.

O*NET Codes

This section of each job description lists one or more code numbers (for example: 11-9031.00, 11-9032.00) for related jobs in a major occupational information system used by the U.S. Department of Labor. This system, named the Occupational Information Network (or O*NET), is used by a variety of state and federal programs to classify applicants and job openings and by a variety of career information systems. You can use the O*NET code numbers to get additional information on the related O*NET titles on the Internet at www.onetcenter.org or at www.careeroink.com. Reference books that provide O*NET descriptions include the *O*NET Dictionary of Occupational Titles* and the *Enhanced Occupational Outlook Handbook*, both published by JIST Publishing. Your librarian can help you find these books.

Significant Points

The bullet points in this part of the description highlight key characteristics for each job, such as recent trends or education and training requirements.

Nature of the Work

This part of the description discusses what workers typically do in a particular job. Individual job duties may vary by industry or employer. For instance, workers in larger firms tend to be more specialized, whereas those in smaller firms often have a wider variety of duties. Most occupations have several levels of skills and responsibilities through which workers may progress. Beginners may start as trainees performing routine tasks under close supervision. Experienced workers usually undertake more difficult tasks and are expected to perform with less supervision.

In this part of the description, you will also find information about the influence of technological advancements on the way work is done. For example, because of the Internet, reporters are now able to submit stories from remote locations with just a click of the mouse.

This part also discusses emerging specialties. For instance, Webmasters—who are responsible for all the technical aspects involved in operating a Web site—comprise a specialty within computer scientists and database administrators.

Working Conditions

This part of the description identifies the typical hours worked, the workplace environment, physical activities, risk of injury, special equipment, and the extent of travel required. For example, conservation scientists and foresters are susceptible to injury, while paralegals and legal assistants have high job-related stress. Radiologic technologists and technicians may wear protective clothing or equipment; police and detectives may do physically demanding work; and some top executives travel frequently.

In many occupations, people work regular business hours—40 hours a week, Monday through Friday. In other occupations, they do not. For example, registered nurses often work evenings and weekends. The work setting can range from a hospital to a mall to an off-shore oil rig.

Information on various worker characteristics, such as the average number of hours worked per week, is obtained from the Current Population Survey (CPS), a survey of households conducted by the U.S. Census Bureau for the Bureau of Labor Statistics (BLS).

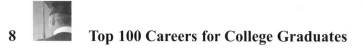

Training, Other Qualifications, and Advancement

After finding out what a job is all about, you probably want to understand how to train for it. This section describes the most significant sources of education and training, including the education or training preferred by employers, the typical length of training, and the possibilities for advancement. Job skills sometimes are acquired through high school, informal on-the-job training, formal training (including apprenticeships), the U.S. Armed Forces, home study, hobbies, or previous work experience. For example, sales experience is particularly important for many sales jobs. Many professional and technical jobs, on the other hand, require formal postsecondary education—postsecondary vocational or technical training or college, postgraduate, or professional education.

This section also mentions desirable skills, aptitudes, and personal characteristics. For some entry-level jobs, personal characteristics are more important than formal training. Employers generally seek people who read, write, and speak well; compute accurately; think logically; learn quickly; get along with others; and demonstrate dependability.

Some occupations require certification or licensing to enter the field, to advance in the occupation, or to practice independently. Certification or licensing generally involves completing courses and passing examinations. Many occupations increasingly are requiring workers to participate in continuing education or training in relevant skills, either to keep up with the changes in their jobs or to improve their advancement opportunities.

Employment

This section reports the number of jobs the occupation recently provided; the key industries where these jobs are found; and the number or proportion of self-employed workers in the occupation, if significant. Self-employed workers accounted for about 8 percent of the workforce in 2004; however, they were concentrated in a small number of occupations, such as farmers and ranchers, childcare workers, lawyers, health practitioners, and the construction trades.

When significant, the geographic distribution of jobs and the proportion of part-time (less than 35 hours a week) workers in the occupation are mentioned.

Job Outlook

In planning for the future, you need to consider potential job opportunities. This section describes the factors that will result in employment growth or decline. A number of factors are examined in developing employment projections. One factor is job growth or decline in industries that employ a significant percentage of workers in the occupation. If workers are concentrated in a rapidly growing industry, their employment will likely also grow quickly. For example, the growing need for business expertise is fueling demand for consulting services. Hence, management, scientific, and technical consulting services are projected to be among the fastest-growing industries through 2014.

Demographic changes, which affect what services are required, can influence occupational growth or decline. For example, an aging population demands more healthcare workers, from registered nurses to pharmacists. Technological change is another key factor. New technology can either create new job opportunities or eliminate jobs by making workers obsolete. The Internet has increased the demand for workers in the computer and information technology fields, such as computer support specialists and systems administrators. However, the Internet also has adversely affected travel agents, because many people now book tickets, hotels, and rental cars online.

Another factor affecting job growth or decline is changes in business practices, such as the outsourcing of work or the restructuring of businesses. In the past few years, insurance carriers have been outsourcing sales and claims adjuster jobs to large 24-hour call centers in order to reduce costs. Corporate restructuring also has made many organizations "flatter," resulting in fewer middle management positions.

The substitution of one product or service for another can affect employment projections. For example, consumption of plastic products has grown as they have been substituted for metal goods in many consumer and manufactured products in recent years. The process is likely to continue and should result in stronger demand for machine operators in plastics than in metal.

Competition from foreign trade usually has a negative impact on employment. Often, foreign manufacturers can produce goods more cheaply than they can be produced in the United States, and the cost savings can be passed on in the form of lower prices with which U.S. manufacturers cannot compete.

In some cases, this book mentions that an occupation is likely to provide numerous job openings or, in others, that an occupation likely will afford relatively few openings. This information reflects the projected change in employment as well as replacement needs. Large occupations that have high turnover generally provide the most job openings, reflecting the need to replace workers who transfer to other occupations or who stop working.

Some job descriptions discuss the relationship between the number of job seekers and the number of job openings. In some occupations, there is a rough balance between job seekers and job openings, resulting in good opportunities. In other occupations, employers may report difficulty finding qualified applicants, resulting in excellent job opportunities. Still other occupations are characterized by a surplus of applicants, leading to keen competition for jobs. On the one hand, limited training facilities, salary regulations, or undesirable aspects of the work—as in the case of private household workers—can result in an insufficient number of entrants to fill all job openings. On the other hand, glamorous or potentially high-paying occupations, such as actors or musicians, generally have surpluses of job seekers. Variation in job opportunities by industry, educational attainment, size of firm, or geographic location also may be discussed. Even in crowded fields, job openings do exist. Good students or highly qualified individuals should not be deterred from undertaking training for, or seeking entry into, those occupations.

Key Phrases Used in the Job Descriptions

This table explains how to interpret the key phrases that describe projected changes in employment. It also explains the terms for the relationship between the number of job openings and the number of job seekers.

Changing Employment Between 2004 and 2014

If the statement reads	Employment is projected to
Grow much faster than average	Increase 27 percent or more
Grow faster than average	Increase 18 to 26 percent
Grow about as fast as average	Increase 9 to 17 percent
Grow more slowly than average	Increase 0 to 8 percent
Decline	Decrease any amount

Opportunities and Competition for Jobs

If the statement reads	Job openings compared to job seekers may be
Very good to excellent opportunities	More numerous
Good or favorable opportunities	In rough balance
May face or can expect keen competition	Fewer

Earnings

This section discusses typical earnings and how workers are compensated—by means of annual salaries, hourly wages, commissions, piece rates, tips, or bonuses. Within every occupation, earnings vary by experience, responsibility, performance, tenure, and geographic area. Information on earnings in the major industries in which the occupation is employed may be given. Some statements contain additional earnings data from non-BLS sources. Starting and average salaries of federal workers are based on 2005 data from the U.S. Office of Personnel Management. The National Association of Colleges and Employers supplies information on average salary offers in 2005 for students graduating with a bachelor's, master's, or Ph.D. degree in certain fields. A few statements contain additional earnings information from other sources, such as unions, professional associations, and private companies. These data sources are cited in the text.

Benefits account for a significant portion of total compensation costs to employers. Benefits such as paid vacation, health insurance, and sick leave may not be mentioned because they are so widespread. Although not as common as traditional benefits, flexible hours and profit-sharing plans may be offered to attract and retain highly qualified workers. Less-common benefits also include childcare, tuition for dependents, housing assistance, summers off, and free or discounted merchandise or services. For certain occupations, the percentage of workers affiliated with a union is listed.

Related Occupations

Occupations involving similar duties, skills, interests, education, and training are listed here. This allows you to look up these jobs if they also interest you.

Sources of Additional Information

No single publication can describe all aspects of an occupation. Thus, this section lists the mailing addresses of associations, government agencies, unions, and other organizations that can provide occupational information. In some cases, toll-free telephone numbers and Internet addresses also are listed. Free or relatively inexpensive publications offering more information may be mentioned; some of these publications also may be available in libraries, in school career centers, in guidance offices, or on the Internet.

Part III: Quick Job Search—Seven Steps to Getting a Good Job in Less Time

For more than 25 years, I've been helping people find better jobs in less time. If you have ever experienced unemployment, you know it is not pleasant. Unemployment is something most people want to get over quickly—in fact, the quicker the better. Part III will give you some techniques to help.

I know that most of you who read this book want to improve yourselves. You want to consider career and training options that lead to a better job and life in whatever way you define this—better pay, more flexibility, work that is more enjoyable or more meaningful, proving to your mom that you really can do anything you set your mind to, and other reasons. That is why I include advice on career planning and job search in Part III. It's a short section, but it includes the basics that are most important in planning your career and in reducing the time it takes to get a job. I hope it will make you think about what is important to you in the long run.

The second section of Part III showcases professionally written resumes for some of the top jobs for college graduates. Use these as examples when creating your own resume.

I know you will resist completing the activities in Part III, but consider this: It is often not the best person who gets the job, but the best job seeker. People who do their career planning and job search homework often get jobs over those with better credentials, because they have these distinct advantages:

1. **They get more interviews,** including many for jobs that will never be advertised.

2. **They do better in interviews.**

People who understand what they want and what they have to offer employers present their skills more convincingly and are much better at answering problem questions. And, because they have learned more about job search techniques, they are likely to get more interviews with employers who need the skills they have.

Doing better in interviews often makes the difference between getting a job offer and sitting at home. And spending time planning your career can make an enormous difference to your happiness and lifestyle over time. So please consider reading Part III and completing its activities. I suggest you schedule a time right now to at least read Part III. An hour or so spent there can help you do just enough better in your career planning, job seeking, and interviewing to make the difference.

One other thing: If you work through Part III and it helps you in some significant way, I'd like to hear from you. Please write or e-mail me via the publisher, whose contact information appears elsewhere in this book.

Part IV: Important Trends in Jobs and Industries

This section is made up of three very good articles on labor market trends. These articles come directly from U.S. Department of Labor sources and are interesting, well written, and short. One is on overall trends, with an emphasis on occupational groups; another is on employment trends in major industry groups; and the third is on opportunities for college graduates. I know they sound boring, but the articles are quick reads and will give you a good idea of factors that will impact your career in the years to come.

The first article is titled "Tomorrow's Jobs." It highlights many important trends in employment and includes information on the fastest-growing jobs, jobs with high pay at various levels of education, and other details.

The second article is titled "Employment Trends in Major Industries." I included this information because you may find that you can use your skills or training in industries you have not considered. The article provides a good review of major trends with an emphasis on helping you make good employment decisions. This information can help you seek jobs in industries that offer higher pay or that are more likely to interest you. Many people overlook one important fact—the industry you work in is as important as the occupation you choose.

The third article, "Job Outlook for College Graduates," explores the advantages that college graduates have in the workforce.

Other Major Career Information Sources

The information in this book will be very useful, but you may want or need additional information. Keep in mind that the job descriptions here cover major jobs and not the many more-specialized jobs that are often related to them. Each job description in this book provides some sources of information related to that job, but here are additional resources to consider.

The *Occupational Outlook Handbook* (or the *OOH*): Updated every two years by the U.S. Department of Labor, this book provides descriptions for almost 270 major jobs covering more than 85 percent of the workforce. The *OOH* is the source of the job descriptions used in this book, and the book *Top 300 Careers* includes all the *OOH* content plus additional information.

The *Enhanced Occupational Outlook Handbook:* Includes all descriptions in the *OOH* plus descriptions of more than 6,300 more-specialized jobs that are related to them.

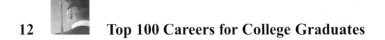

The *O*NET Dictionary of Occupational Titles:* The only printed source of the more than 950 jobs described in the U.S. Department of Labor's Occupational Information Network database (O*NET).

The *New Guide for Occupational Exploration:* An important career reference that allows you to explore all major O*NET jobs based on your interests.

www.careeroink.com: This Web site provides more than 14,000 job descriptions, including those mentioned in the previous books, and a variety of useful ways to explore them.

Best Jobs for the 21st Century: Includes descriptions for the 500 jobs (out of more than 1,100) with the best combination of earnings, growth, and number of openings. Useful lists make jobs easy to explore (examples: highest-paying jobs by level of education or training; best jobs overall; and best jobs for different ages, personality types, interests, and many more).

Exploring Careers—A Young Person's Guide to 1,000 Jobs: For youth exploring career and education opportunities, this book covers 1,000 job options in an interesting and useful format.

Using the Job-Match Grid to Choose a Career

By the Editors at JIST

This book describes so many occupations—how can you choose the best job for you? This section is your answer! It can help you to identify the jobs where your abilities will be valued, and you can rule out jobs that have certain characteristics you'd rather avoid. You will respond to a series of statements and use the Job-Match Grid to match your skills and preferences to the most appropriate jobs in this book.

So grab a pencil and get ready to mark up the following sections. Or, if someone else will be using this book, find a sheet of paper and get ready to take notes.

Thinking About Your Skills

Everybody knows that skills are important for getting and keeping a job. Employers expect you to list relevant skills on your resume. They ask about your skills in interviews. And they expect you to develop skills on the job so that you will remain productive as new technologies and new work situations emerge.

But maybe you haven't thought about how closely skills are related to job satisfaction. For example, let's say you have enough communication skills to hold a certain job where these skills are used heavily, but you wouldn't really *enjoy* using them. In that case, this job probably would be a bad choice for you. You need to identify a job that will use the skills that you *do* enjoy using.

That's why you need to take a few minutes to think about your skills: the ones you're good at and the ones you like using. The checklists that follow can help you do this. On each of the seven skills checklists that follow, use numbers to indicate how much you agree with each statement:

> 3 = I strongly agree
>
> 2 = I agree
>
> 1 = There's some truth to this
>
> 0 = This doesn't apply to me

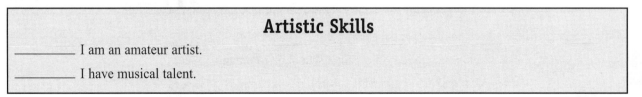

Artistic Skills

_____ I am an amateur artist.

_____ I have musical talent.

(continued)

(continued)

_____ I enjoy planning home makeovers.

_____ I am good at performing onstage.

_____ I enjoy taking photos or shooting videos.

_____ I am good at writing stories, poems, articles, or essays.

_____ I have enjoyed taking ballet or other dance lessons.

_____ I like to cook and plan meals.

_____ I can sketch a good likeness of something or somebody.

_____ Playing music or singing is a hobby of mine.

_____ I have a good sense of visual style.

_____ I have participated in amateur theater.

_____ I like to express myself through writing.

_____ I can prepare tasty meals better than most people.

_____ I have a flair for creating attractive designs.

_____ I learn new dance steps or routines easily.

_____ **Total for Artistic Skills**

A note for those determined to work in the arts: Before you move on to the next skill, take a moment to decide whether working in some form of art is essential to you. Some people have exceptional talent and interest in a certain art form and are unhappy unless they are working in that art form—or until they have given their best shot at trying to break into it. If you are that kind of person, the total score shown above doesn't really matter. In fact, you may have given a 3 to just *one* of the statements above, but if you care passionately about your art form, you should toss out ordinary arithmetic and change the total to 100.

Communication Skills

_____ I am good at explaining complicated things to people.

_____ I like to take notes and write up minutes for meetings.

_____ I have a flair for public speaking.

_____ I am good at writing directions for using a computer or machine.

_____ I enjoy investigating facts and showing other people what they indicate.

_____ People consider me a good listener.

_____ I like to write letters to newspaper editors or political representatives.

_____ I have been an effective debater.

_____ I like developing publicity fliers for a school or community event.

_____ I am good at making diagrams that break down complex processes.

_____ I like teaching people how to drive a car or play a sport.

_____ I have been successful as the secretary of a club.

_____ I enjoy speaking at group meetings or worship services.

_____ I have a knack for choosing the most effective word.

_____ I enjoy tutoring young people.

_____ Technical manuals are not hard for me to understand.

_____ **Total for Communication Skills**

Interpersonal Skills

_____ I am able to make people feel that I understand their point of view.

_____ I enjoy working collaboratively.

_____ I often can make suggestions to people without sounding critical of them.

_____ I enjoy soliciting clothes, food, and other supplies for needy people.

_____ I am good at "reading" people to tell what's on their minds.

_____ I have a lot of patience with people who are doing something for the first time.

_____ People consider me outgoing.

_____ I enjoy taking care of sick relatives, friends, or neighbors.

_____ I am good at working out conflicts between friends or family members.

_____ I enjoy serving as a host or hostess for houseguests.

_____ People consider me a team player.

_____ I enjoy meeting new people and finding common interests.

_____ I am good at fundraising for school groups, teams, or community organizations.

_____ I like to train or care for animals.

_____ I often know what to say to defuse a tense situation.

_____ I have enjoyed being an officer or advisor for a youth group.

_____ **Total for Interpersonal Skills**

Managerial Skills

_____ I am good at inspiring people to work together toward a goal.

_____ I tend to use time wisely and not procrastinate.

_____ I usually know when I have enough information to make a decision.

_____ I enjoy planning and arranging programs for school or a community organization.

_____ I am not reluctant to take responsibility when things turn out wrong.

_____ I have enjoyed being a leader of a scout troop or other such group.

_____ I often can figure out what motivates somebody.

_____ People trust me to speak on their behalf and represent them fairly.

_____ I like to help organize things at home, such as shopping lists and budgets.

(continued)

(continued)

_____ I have been successful at recruiting members for a club or other organization.

_____ I have enjoyed helping run a school or community fair or carnival.

_____ People find me persuasive.

_____ I enjoy buying large quantities of food or other products for an organization.

_____ I have a knack for identifying abilities in other people.

_____ I am able to get past details and look at the big picture.

_____ I am good at delegating authority rather than trying to do everything myself.

_____ **Total for Managerial Skills**

Mathematics Skills

_____ I have always done well in math classes.

_____ I enjoy balancing checkbooks for family members.

_____ I can make mental calculations quickly.

_____ I enjoy calculating sports statistics or keeping score.

_____ Preparing family income tax returns is not hard for me.

_____ I like to tutor young people in math.

_____ I have taken or plan to take courses in statistics or calculus.

_____ I enjoy budgeting the family expenditures.

_____ **Subtotal for Mathematics Skills**

x 2   **Multiply by 2**

_____ **Total for Mathematics Skills**

Mechanical Skills

_____ I have a good sense of how mechanical devices work.

_____ I like to tinker with my car or motorcycle.

_____ I can understand diagrams of machinery or electrical wiring.

_____ I enjoy installing and repairing home stereo or computer equipment.

_____ I like looking at the merchandise in a building-supply warehouse store.

_____ I can sometimes fix household appliances when they break down.

_____ I have enjoyed building model airplanes, automobiles, or boats.

_____ I can do minor plumbing and electrical installations in the home.

_____ **Subtotal for Mechanical Skills**

x 2   **Multiply by 2**

_____ **Total for Mechanical Skills**

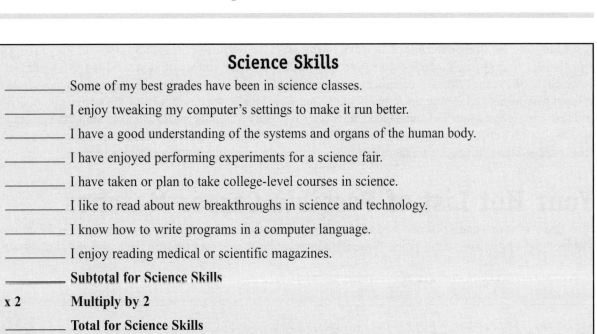

Science Skills

_____ Some of my best grades have been in science classes.

_____ I enjoy tweaking my computer's settings to make it run better.

_____ I have a good understanding of the systems and organs of the human body.

_____ I have enjoyed performing experiments for a science fair.

_____ I have taken or plan to take college-level courses in science.

_____ I like to read about new breakthroughs in science and technology.

_____ I know how to write programs in a computer language.

_____ I enjoy reading medical or scientific magazines.

_____ **Subtotal for Science Skills**

x 2   **Multiply by 2**

_____ **Total for Science Skills**

Finding Your Skills on the Job-Match Grid

Okay, you've made a lot of progress so far. Now it's time to review what you've said about skills so you can use these insights to sort through the jobs listed on the Job-Match Grid.

Look at your totals for the seven skills listed previously. Enter your totals in the left column on this scorecard:

Total	Skill	Rank
_____	Artistic	_____
_____	Communication	_____
_____	Interpersonal	_____
_____	Managerial	_____
_____	Mathematics	_____
_____	Mechanical	_____
_____	Science	_____

Next, enter the rank of each skill in the right column—that is, the highest-scored skill gets ranked #1, the next-highest #2, and so forth. **Important:** Keep in mind that *the numbers in the Total column are only a rough guideline.* If you feel that a skill should be ranked higher or lower than its numerical total would suggest, *go by your impressions rather than just by the numbers.*

Now turn to the Job-Match Grid and find the columns for your #1-ranked and #2-ranked skills. Move down through the grid, going from page to page, and notice what symbols appear in those columns. If a row of the grid has a black circle (●) in *both* columns, circle the occupation name—or, if someone else will be using this book, jot down the name on a piece of paper. These occupations use a high level of both skills, or the skills are essential to these jobs.

Go through the Job-Match Grid a second time, looking at the column for your #3-ranked skill. If a *job you have already circled* has a black circle (●) or a bull's-eye (◉) in the column for your #3-ranked skill, put a check mark next to the occupation name. If none of your selected jobs has a black circle or a bull's-eye in this column, look for a white circle (○) and mark these jobs with check marks.

A second note for those determined to work in the arts: If a *particular* art form is essential for you to work in, you almost certainly know which occupations involve that art form and which don't. So not every job that has a black circle (●) in the "Artistic" column is going to interest you. Circle only the jobs that have a black circle in this column that *are* related to your art form (if you're not sure, look at the description of the occupation in this book) and that also have a symbol of some kind (●, ◉, or ○) in the column for your #2-ranked skill. As you circle each job, also give it a check mark, because there will be so few of them that you won't need to go through the Job-Match Grid a second time. If you have a more general interest in the arts, follow the general instructions.

Your Hot List of Possible Career Matches

Now that you have made a first and second cut of the jobs on the Job-Match Grid, you can focus on the occupations that look most promising at this point. Write the names of the occupations that are both *circled* and *checked:*

_____   _____

_____   _____

_____   _____

_____   _____

_____   _____

_____   _____

This is your Hot List of occupations that you are going to explore in detail *if* they are not eliminated by certain important job-related factors that you'll consider next.

Thinking About Other Job-Related Factors

Next, you need to consider four other job-related factors:

- ★ Economic sensitivity
- ★ Outdoor work
- ★ Physically demanding work
- ★ Hazardous conditions

Economic Sensitivity

You've read about how our nation's economy has gone up and down over the years. When the economy is on an upswing, there are more job openings, but when it veers downward toward recession, jobs are harder to find.

Are you aware that these trends affect some occupations more than others? For example, during an economic upswing, people do more vacation traveling and businesses send more workers on business trips. This keeps travel agencies very busy, so they need to hire more travel agents. When the economy is going down, people cut back on their vacation travel, businesses tell their workers to use teleconferencing instead of business trips, and travel agents are not in demand. Some may be laid off, and people who want to enter this field may find very few openings. By contrast, most jobs in the health-care field are not sensitive to the economy, and automotive mechanics are just as busy as ever during economic slowdowns because people want to keep their old cars running.

So this issue of economic sensitivity (and its opposite, job security) is one that may affect which occupation you choose. Some people want to avoid economically sensitive occupations because they don't want to risk losing their job (or having difficulty finding a job) during times of recession. Other people are willing to risk being in an economically sensitive occupation because they want to profit from the periods when both the economy and the occupation are booming.

> How important is it to you to be in an occupation that *doesn't* go through periods of boom and bust along with the nation's economy? Check one:
>
> _____ It doesn't matter to me.
>
> _____ It's not important, but I'd consider it.
>
> _____ It's somewhat important to me.
>
> _____ It's very important to me.

If you answered "It doesn't matter to me," skip to the next section, "Outdoor Work." Otherwise, turn back to the Job-Match Grid and find the column for "Economically Sensitive."

If you answered "It's not important, but I'd consider it," see whether any of the jobs on your Hot List have a black circle (●) in this column. If so, cross them off and write an "E" next to them.

If you answered "It's somewhat important to me," see whether any of the jobs on your Hot List have a black circle (●) or a bull's-eye (◉) in this column. If so, cross them off and write an "E" next to them.

If you answered "It's very important to me," see whether any of the jobs on your Hot List have *any* symbol (●, ◉, or ○) in this column. If so, cross them off and write an "E" next to them.

Outdoor Work

Some people prefer to work indoors in a climate-controlled setting, such as an office, a classroom, a factory floor, a laboratory, or a hospital room. Other people would rather work primarily in an outdoor setting, such as a forest, an athletic field, or a city street. And some would enjoy a job that alternates between indoor and outdoor activities.

> What is *your* preference for working indoors or outdoors? Check one:
>
> _____ It's very important to me to work **indoors.**
>
> _____ I'd prefer to work mostly **indoors.**
>
> _____ Either indoors or outdoors is okay with me.
>
> _____ I'd prefer to work mostly **outdoors.**
>
> _____ It's very important to me to work **outdoors.**

If you answered "Either indoors or outdoors is okay with me," skip to the next section, "Physically Demanding Work." Otherwise, turn to the Job-Match Grid and find the column for "Outdoor Work."

If you answered "It's very important to me to work **indoors,**" see whether any of the jobs on your Hot List have *any* symbol (●, ◉, or ○) in this column. If so, cross them off and write an "O" next to them.

If you answered "I'd prefer to work mostly **indoors,**" see whether any of the jobs on your Hot List have a black circle (●) in this column. If so, cross them off and write an "O" next to them.

If you answered "I'd prefer to work mostly **outdoors,**" see whether any of the jobs on your Hot List have *no* symbol—just a blank—in this column. If so, cross them off and write an "O" next to them. All the jobs remaining on your Hot List should have some kind of symbol (●, ◉, or ○) in this column.

If you answered "It's very important to me to work **outdoors,**" see whether any of the jobs on your Hot List have either *no* symbol or just a white circle (○) in this column. If so, cross them off and write an "O" next to them. All the jobs remaining on your Hot List should have either a black circle (●) or a bull's-eye (◉) in this column.

Physically Demanding Work

Jobs vary by how much muscle power they require you to use. Some jobs require a lot of lifting heavy loads, standing for long times, climbing, or stooping. On other jobs, the heaviest thing you lift is a notebook or telephone handset, and most of the time you are sitting. Still other jobs require only a moderate amount of physical exertion.

What is *your* preference for the physical demands of work? Check one:

_____ I don't care whether my work requires heavy or light physical exertion.

_____ I want my work to require only light physical exertion.

_____ I want my work to require no more than occasional moderate physical exertion.

_____ I want my work to require moderate physical exertion, with occasional heavy exertion.

_____ I want my work to require a lot of heavy physical exertion.

If you answered "I don't care whether my work requires heavy or light physical exertion," skip to the next section, "Hazardous Conditions." Otherwise, turn to the Job-Match Grid and find the column for "Physically Demanding Work."

If you answered "I want my work to require only light physical exertion," see whether any of the jobs on your Hot List have *any* symbol (●, ◉, or ○) in this column. If so, cross them off and write a "P" next to them.

If you answered "I want my work to require no more than occasional moderate physical exertion," see whether any of the jobs on your Hot List have either a black circle (●) or a bull's-eye (◉) in this column. If so, cross them off and write a "P" next to them.

If you answered "I want my work to require moderate physical exertion, with occasional heavy exertion," see whether any of the jobs on your Hot List have either a black circle (●), a white circle (○), or *no* symbol in this column. If so, cross them off and write a "P" next to them. All the jobs remaining on your Hot List should have a bull's-eye (◉) in this column.

If you answered "I want my work to require a lot of heavy physical exertion," see whether any of the jobs on your Hot List have either *no* symbol or just a white circle (○) or a bull's-eye (◉) in this column. If so, cross them off and write a "P" next to them. All the jobs remaining on your Hot List should have a black circle (●) in this column.

Hazardous Conditions

Every day about 9,000 Americans sustain a disabling injury on the job. Many workers have jobs that require them to deal with hazardous conditions, such as heat, noise, radiation, germs, toxins, or dangerous machinery. These workers need to wear protective clothing or follow safety procedures to avoid injury.

What is *your* preference regarding hazardous conditions on the job? Check one:

_____ I want hazardous workplace conditions to be very unlikely.

_____ I want hazardous conditions to be unlikely or minor.

_____ I am willing to accept some major workplace hazards.

If you answered "I am willing to accept some major workplace hazards," skip to the section "Geographically Concentrated Jobs." Otherwise, turn to the Job-Match Grid and find the column for "Hazardous Conditions."

If you answered "I want hazardous workplace conditions to be very unlikely," see whether any of the jobs on your Hot List have *any* symbol (●, ◉, or ○) in this column. If so, cross them off and write an "H" next to them.

If you answered "I want hazardous conditions to be unlikely or minor," see whether any of the jobs on your Hot List have a black circle (●) in this column. If so, cross them off and write an "H" next to them.

If Every Job on Your Hot List Is Now Crossed Off

It's possible that you have crossed off *all* the occupations on your Hot List. If so, consider these two options:

★ You may want to relax some of your requirements. Maybe you were too hasty in crossing off some of the jobs. Take another look at the four job-related factors and decide whether you could accept work that doesn't meet the requirements you set previously—for example, work that is not as much indoors or outdoors as you specified. If you change your mind now, you can tell by the letters in the margin which jobs you crossed off for which reasons.

★ You may want to add to your Hot List by considering additional skills. So far you have considered only occupations that involve your top three skills. You may want to add jobs that have a black circle (●) or a bull's-eye (◉) in the column for your #4-ranked skill and possibly for your #5-ranked skill. If you do add any jobs, be sure to repeat your review of the four job-related factors.

Evaluating Occupations Described in This Book

You are now ready to make the jump from the checklists to the detailed information about jobs in this book. The first detailed issue you need to consider is whether you will be able to find work in your area or have to relocate.

Geographically Concentrated Jobs

Turn to the Job-Match Grid one more time and find the column for "Geographically Concentrated." Look at all the occupations on your Hot List that haven't been crossed off. If there is a symbol in this column, especially a bull's-eye (◉) or a black circle (●), it means that employment for this occupation tends to be concentrated in certain geographic areas. For example, most acting jobs are found in big cities because that's where you'll find most theaters, TV studios, and movie studios. Most water transportation jobs are found on the coasts and beside major lakes and rivers.

If a symbol shows that a Hot List occupation *is* geographically concentrated, the location of the jobs may be obvious, as in the examples of acting and water transportation. If it's not clear to you where the jobs may be found, find the occupation in Part II and look for the facts under the heading "Employment" in the description. Once you understand where most of the jobs are, you have to make some decisions:

★ **Are most of the job openings in a geographic location where I am now or would enjoy living?** If you answered "yes" to this question, repeat this exercise for all the other occupations still on your Hot List. Then jump to the next heading, "Nature of the Work." If you answered "no," proceed to the next bulleted question.

★ **If most of the job openings are in a distant place where I don't want to relocate, am I willing to take a chance and hope to be one of the few workers who get hired in an *uncommon* location?** If you answered "yes," take a good look at the Job Outlook information in the job description. If the outlook for the occupation is very good and if you expect to have some of the advantages mentioned

there (such as the right degree, in some cases), taking a chance on being hired in an unusual location may be a reasonable decision. On the other hand, if the outlook is only so-so or not good and if you have no special qualifications, you probably are setting yourself up for disappointment. You should seriously consider changing your mind about this decision. At least speak to people in your area who are knowledgeable about the occupation to determine whether you have any chance of success. If you answered "no"—you are not willing to take a chance—cross off this occupation and write a "G" next to it. (If you now have no jobs left on your Hot List, see the previous section titled "If Every Job on Your Hot List Is Now Crossed Off.")

Nature of the Work

When you read the job description for an occupation on your Hot List, you will see that the "Nature of the Work" section discusses what workers do on the job, what tools and equipment they use, and how closely they are supervised. Keep in mind that this is an overview of a diverse collection of workers, and in fact few workers perform the full set of tasks itemized here. In fact, in many cases the work force covered by the job description is so diverse that it actually divides into several occupational specialties, which are italicized.

Here are some things to think about as you read this section:

★ Note the kinds of problems, materials, and tools you will encounter on the job. Are these are a good match for your interests?

★ Also note the work activities mentioned here. Do you think they will be rewarding? Are there many that stand out as unpleasant or boring?

Working Conditions

This section in each job description identifies the typical hours worked, the workplace environment (both physical and psychological), physical activities and susceptibility to injury, special equipment, and the extent of travel required. If conditions vary between the occupational specialties, that is mentioned here. Here are some things to look for in the Working Conditions section:

★ If you have a disability, note the physical requirements that are mentioned here and consider whether you can meet these requirements with or without suitable accommodations.

★ If you're bothered by conditions such as heights, stress, or a cramped workspace, see whether this section mentions any conditions that would discourage you.

★ Note what this section says about the work schedule and the need for travel, if any. This information may be good to know if you have pressing family responsibilities or, on the other hand, a desire for unusual hours or travel.

★ If you find a working condition that bothers you, be sure to check the wording to see whether it *always* applies to the occupation or whether it only *may* apply. Even if it seems to be a condition that you cannot avoid, find out for sure by talking to people in the occupation or educators who teach related courses. Maybe you can carve out a niche that avoids the unappealing working condition.

Training, Other Qualifications, and Advancement

In the "Training, Other Qualifications, and Advancement" section, you can see how to prepare for the occupation and how to advance in it. It identifies the significant entry routes—those that are most popular and that are preferred by employers. It mentions any licensure or certification that may be necessary for entry or advancement. It also identifies the particular skills, aptitudes, and work habits that employers value. Look for these topics in this section:

★ Compare the entry requirements to your background and to the educational and training opportunities that are available to you. Be sure to consider nontraditional and informal entry routes, if any are possible, as well as the formal routes. Ask yourself, Am I willing to get the additional education or training that will be necessary? Do I have the time, money, ability, interest, and commitment?

★ Maybe you're already partway down the road to job entry. In general, you should try to use your previous education, training, and work experience rather than abandon it. Look for specifics that are already on your resume—educational accomplishments, skills, work habits—that will meet employers' expectations. If you have some of these qualifications already, this occupation may be a better career choice than some others.

Employment

The "Employment" section in the job description reports how many jobs the occupation currently provides, the industries that provide the most jobs, and the number or proportion of self-employed or part-time workers in the occupation, if significant. In this section, you'll want to pay attention to these facts:

★ Note the industries that provide most of the employment for the occupation. This knowledge can help you identify contacts who can tell you more about the work, and later it can help in your job hunting.

★ If you're interested in self-employment or part-time work, see whether these work arrangements are mentioned here.

Job Outlook

The "Job Outlook" section describes the economic forces that will affect future employment in the occupation. Here are some things to look for in this section:

★ The information here can help you identify occupations with a good job outlook so that you will have a better-than-average chance of finding work. Be alert for any mention of an advantage that you may have over other job seekers (for example, a college degree) or any other factor that might make your chances better or worse.

★ If you are highly motivated and highly qualified for a particular occupation, don't be discouraged by a bad employment outlook. Job openings occur even in shrinking or overcrowded occupations, and with exceptional talent or good personal connections, you may go on to great success.

★ These projections are the most definitive ones available, but they are not foolproof and apply only to a 10-year time span. No matter what occupation you choose, you will need to adapt to changes.

Earnings

The "Earnings" section discusses the wages for the occupation. Here are some things to keep in mind:

★ The wage figures are national averages. Actual wages in your geographic region may be considerably higher or lower. Also, an average figure means that half of the workers earn more and half earn less, and the actual salary any one worker earns can vary greatly from that average.

★ Remember to consider *all* the pluses and minuses of the job. Not every day of the work week is payday, so make your choice based on the whole occupation, not just the paycheck.

Related Occupations

The "Related Occupations" section identifies occupations that are similar to the one featured in the job description in terms of tasks, interests, skills, education, or training. You may find this section interesting for these reasons:

★ If you're interested in an occupation but not strongly committed to pursuing it, this section may suggest another occupation with similar rewards that may turn out to be a better fit. Try to research these related occupations, but keep in mind that they may not all be included in this book.

★ You may want to choose one of these occupations as your Plan B goal if your original goal should not work out. In that case, it helps to identify an occupation that involves similar kinds of problems and work settings but requires *less* education or training.

Sources of Additional Information

This section in each job description lists several sources and resources you can turn to for more information about the occupation. Try to consult at least some of these sources. This book should be only the beginning of your career decision-making process. You need more detailed information from several viewpoints to make an informed decision.

Don't rely entirely on the Web sites listed here. You especially need to talk to and observe individual workers to learn what their workdays are like, what the workers enjoy and dislike about the job, how they got hired, and what effects the job has had on other aspects of their lives. Maybe you can make contact with local workers through the local chapter of an organization listed here.

Narrowing Down Your Choices

The information in the job descriptions should help you cross more jobs off your Hot List. And what you learn by turning to other resources should help you narrow down your Hot List jobs to a few promising choices and maybe one best bet. Here are some final considerations: Have I talked to people who are actually doing this work? Am I fully aware of the pluses and minuses of this job? If there are aspects of the job that I don't like, how do I expect to avoid them or overcome them? If the odds of finding a job opening are not good, why do I expect to beat the odds? What is my Plan B goal if I lose interest in my original goal or don't succeed at it?

The Job-Match Grid

The grid on the following pages provides information about the personal skills and job characteristics for occupations covered in this book. Use the directions and questions that start at the beginning of this section to help you get the most from this grid.

Below is what the symbols on the grid represent. If a job has no symbol in a column, it means that the skill or job characteristic is not important or relevant to the job.

Personal Skills

● Essential or high skill level

◉ Somewhat essential or moderate skill level

○ Basic skill level

Job Characteristics

● Highly likely

◉ Somewhat likely

○ A little likely

Job-Match Grid

	Personal Skills							Job Characteristics				
	Artistic	Communication	Interpersonal	Managerial	Mathematics	Mechanical	Science	Economically Sensitive	Outdoor Work	Physically Demanding Work	Hazardous Conditions	Geographically Concentrated
Jobs Typically Requiring a Professional or Doctoral Degree												
Biological scientists		◉	○	◉	●	●	●	○	◉	○	○	
Chiropractors		●	◉	●	◉	○	●				○	
Dentists	○	●	●	●	◉	●	●			○	◉	
Lawyers		●	●	●	○		○	◉				
Medical scientists		◉	○	◉	●	●	●	○			○	
Optometrists	○	●	◉	●	◉	◉	●				◉	
Pharmacists		●	◉	◉	●	○	●				○	
Physicians and surgeons	◉	●	●	●	◉	●	●			◉	◉	
Physicists and astronomers	○	◉	○	○	●	●	●	○	○			○
Podiatrists	○	●	●	●	◉	◉	●					
Veterinarians	○	●	●	●	●	●	●		○	●	●	
Jobs Typically Requiring a Master's Degree												
Archivists, curators, and museum technicians	●	◉	○	○	◉	●	●			○		◉
Audiologists		●	◉	●	◉	○	●					
Counselors		●	●	○	○		○					
Economists		◉	○	◉	●							
Environmental scientists and hydrologists	○	◉	○	◉	●	●	●	○	●	○		
Geoscientists	○	◉	○	◉	●	●	●	○	●	○		
Instructional coordinators	○	●	●	◉	◉	◉	◉					
Librarians	○	●	◉	●	○	◉	○					
Market and survey researchers		●	●	○	●			◉				
Mathematicians		○	○	○	●		◉					
Operations research analysts		○	○	○	●		◉	○				
Physical therapists		●	●	○	◉	○	●			●	◉	
Psychologists		●	●	○	◉		◉					
Social scientists, other		◉	◉	○	◉	○	○					
Social workers		●	●	○	○		○					
Speech-language pathologists	○	●	●	○	●	○	●					
Statisticians		○	○	○	●		◉					
Teachers—postsecondary	◉	●	●	●	●		◉					
Urban and regional planners	◉	◉	◉	◉	●		○	○	○			
Jobs Typically Requiring a Bachelor's Degree, Plus Work Experience												
Actuaries		○	○	○	●		◉					
Administrative services managers	○	●	●	●	◉			○				
Advertising, marketing, promotions, public relations, and sales managers	●	●	●	●	●	◉		●				

(continued)

Personal Skills: ●—Essential or high skill level; ◉—Somewhat essential or moderate skill level; ○—Basic skill level
Job Characteristics: ●—Highly likely; ◉—Somewhat likely; ○—A little likely

© JIST Works

(continued)

	Personal Skills							Job Characteristics				
	Artistic	Communication	Interpersonal	Managerial	Mathematics	Mechanical	Science	Economically Sensitive	Outdoor Work	Physically Demanding Work	Hazardous Conditions	Geographically Concentrated
Computer and information systems managers		●	●	●	●	●	●	●				
Education administrators		●	●	●	◉		○					
Engineering and natural sciences managers		●	●	●	●	●	●	◉				
Financial managers		●	●	●	●		○	◉				
Judges, magistrates, and other judicial workers		●	○	○	○		○					
Management analysts		●	◉	○	●			○				
Medical and health services managers		●	●	●	◉	◉	◉					
Top executives	○	●	●	●	●			◉	○			
Jobs Typically Requiring a Bachelor's Degree												
Accountants and auditors		○	○	◉	●			○				
Agricultural and food scientists		◉	○	◉	●	●	●		◉	○	○	
Architects, except landscape and naval	●	◉	◉	◉	●	●	◉	◉	◉	○		
Athletic trainers		◉	○				●		●	○		◉
Atmospheric scientists		◉	○	◉	●	●	●	○	◉			
Budget analysts		○	○	○	●							
Chemists and materials scientists	○	◉	○	◉	●	●	●	◉			○	
Commercial and industrial designers		○	◉	◉	●	●	○	●		○		◉
Computer programmers		◉	○	○	●	◉	●	○				
Computer scientists and database administrators		◉	○	○	●		●	○				
Computer software engineers		◉	◉	◉	●	●	●	○				
Computer systems analysts		◉	○	○	●		●	○				
Conservation scientists and foresters		◉	○	◉	●	●	●	○	●	◉	○	●
Construction managers	○	●	●	●	●	●	◉	●	●	○	◉	
Dietitians and nutritionists		●	●	○	◉	○	●					
Engineers	◉	◉	○	◉	●	●	●	◉	○	○	○	◉
Fashion designers	●	○	◉	◉				●		○		●
Financial analysts and personal financial advisors		●	●	○	●		○	●				
Graphic designers	●	◉	◉	◉				○		○		○
Human resources, training, and labor relations managers and specialists		●	●	●	○			○				
Insurance sales agents		●	●		◉			◉				
Insurance underwriters		○	○	○	●							
Interior designers	●	○	○	◉	●		◉	●		○		○
Landscape architects	●	◉	◉	◉	◉	●	◉	◉	●	○		
Loan officers		◉	●	○	◉			◉				
Meeting and convention planners		●	●	●	◉			◉		○		◉
News analysts, reporters, and correspondents	◉	●	●	○	○	○	◉		◉			

Personal Skills: ●—Essential or high skill level; ◉—Somewhat essential or moderate skill level; ○—Basic skill level
Job Characteristics: ●—Highly likely; ◉—Somewhat likely; ○—A little likely

| | Personal Skills | | | | | | | Job Characteristics | | | | |
	Artistic	Communication	Interpersonal	Managerial	Mathematics	Mechanical	Science	Economically Sensitive	Outdoor Work	Physically Demanding Work	Hazardous Conditions	Geographically Concentrated
Occupational therapists		●	●	◉	◉	◉	◉			○	◉	
Physician assistants		●	●	○	●	◉	●			◉	◉	
Probation officers and correctional treatment specialists		◉	◉	○	○	○	○				●	
Property, real estate, and community association managers	○	●	●	●	○	○		○	○			
Public relations specialists	◉	●	●	○	○							◉
Recreation workers	○	●	●	○	○	○	○	◉	◉	●		
Recreational therapists	●	●	●	○	○	○	○		●	◉		
Sales engineers	○	●	●		◉	○	◉	●				
Securities, commodities, and financial services sales agents		●	●	●	●			●				●
Tax examiners, collectors, and revenue agents		○	○	○	●							
Teachers—adult literacy and remedial education	◉	●	●	●	◉		◉					
Teachers—preschool, kindergarten, elementary, middle, and secondary	◉	●	●	●	◉	○	◉					
Teachers—special education	◉	●	●	●	◉	○	◉					
Jobs That May Not Require a Bachelor's Degree But Are Often Held by College Graduates												
Actors, producers, and directors	●	●	●	◉		◉	○	○	○	●		●
Aircraft pilots and flight engineers		●	●	●	●	◉	●	●	○	◉	●	○
Armed forces		◉	◉	◉	○	○	○		◉	●	◉	◉
Artists and related workers	●	○	○	○	○	◉	○	◉	○	○		
Computer support specialists and systems administrators		◉	◉	○	◉	●	◉	○				
Interpreters and translators	●	●	○									
Musicians, singers, and related workers	●	◉	◉	○		○	○			○		○
Nuclear medicine technologists		◉	○	○	●	●	●				◉	
Occupational health and safety specialists and technicians		◉	○	◉	◉	◉	◉		○	◉	◉	
Paralegals and legal assistants		●	●	○	○		○	◉				
Police and detectives		●	○	◉	○	●	○			●	●	●
Purchasing managers, buyers, and purchasing agents		●	●	●	◉		○	○				
Radiologic technologists and technicians		◉	◉	○	●	●	◉			◉	◉	
Real estate brokers and sales agents	○	●	●	◉	◉			◉	○			
Registered nurses		●	●	◉	●	●	●			◉	◉	
Respiratory therapists		●	●	○	●	●	●			○	◉	

(continued)

Personal Skills: ●—Essential or high skill level; ◉—Somewhat essential or moderate skill level; ○—Basic skill level
Job Characteristics: ●—Highly likely; ◉—Somewhat likely; ○—A little likely

(continued)

	Personal Skills							Job Characteristics				
	Artistic	Communication	Interpersonal	Managerial	Mathematics	Mechanical	Science	Economically Sensitive	Outdoor Work	Physically Demanding Work	Hazardous Conditions	Geographically Concentrated
Sales representatives, wholesale and manufacturing	○	●	●		◉		○	●				
Surveyors, cartographers, photogrammetrists, and surveying technicians	◉	◉	◉	○	◉	◉	◉	◉	◉	◉		
Television, video, and motion picture camera operators and editors	●	○	○	○	○	●	○		◉	◉		●

Personal Skills: ●—Essential or high skill level; ◉—Somewhat essential or moderate skill level; ○—Basic skill level
Job Characteristics: ●—Highly likely; ◉—Somewhat likely; ○—A little likely

Descriptions of the Top 100 Careers for College Graduates

This is the book's main section. It contains helpful descriptions of the 100 major occupations for college graduates. To learn a job's ranking, see the introduction.

The jobs are arranged in alphabetical order within groupings by education required. Refer to the table of contents for a list of the jobs and the page numbers where their descriptions begin. Review the table of contents to discover occupations that interest you and then find out more about them in this section. If you are interested in medical careers, for example, you can go through the list and quickly pinpoint those you want to learn more about. Or use the assessment in Part I to identify several possible career matches.

While the job descriptions in this part are easy to understand, the introduction provides additional information for interpreting them. Keep in mind that the descriptions present information that is average for the country. Conditions in your area and with specific employers may be quite different.

Also, you may come across jobs that sound interesting but require more education and training than you have or are considering. Don't eliminate them too soon. There are many ways to obtain education, and most people change careers many times. You probably have more skills than you realize that can transfer to new jobs. People often have more opportunities than barriers. Use the descriptions to learn more about possible jobs and look into the suggested resources to help you take the next step.

Jobs Typically Requiring a Professional or Doctoral Degree

Biological Scientists

Chiropractors

Dentists

Lawyers

Medical Scientists

Optometrists

Pharmacists

Physicians and Surgeons

Physicists and Astronomers

Podiatrists

Veterinarians

Biological Scientists

(O*NET 19-1020.01, 19-1021.01, 19-1021.02, 19-1022.00, 19-1023.00, and 19-1029.99)

Significant Points

■ A Ph.D. degree usually is required for independent research, but a master's degree is sufficient for some jobs in applied research or product development; a bachelor's degree is adequate for some nonresearch jobs.

■ Doctoral degree holders face competition for basic research positions; holders of bachelor's or master's degrees in biological science can expect better opportunities in nonresearch positions.

■ Biotechnological research and development will continue to drive employment growth.

Nature of the Work

Biological scientists study living organisms and their relationship to their environment. They research problems dealing with life processes and living organisms. Most specialize in some area of biology, such as zoology (the study of animals) or microbiology (the study of microscopic organisms). (Medical scientists, whose work is closely related to that of biological scientists, are discussed elsewhere in this book.)

Many biological scientists work in research and development. Some conduct basic research to advance knowledge of living organisms, including viruses, bacteria, and other infectious agents. Basic biological research continues to provide the building blocks necessary to develop solutions to human health problems and to preserve and repair the natural environment. Biological scientists mostly work independently in private industry, university, or government laboratories, often exploring new areas of research or expanding on specialized research started in graduate school. Those who are not wage and salary workers in private industry typically submit grant proposals to obtain funding for their projects. Colleges and universities, private industry, and federal government agencies such as the National Institutes of Health and the National Science Foundation contribute to the support of scientists whose research proposals are determined to be financially feasible and to have the potential to advance new ideas or processes.

Biological scientists who work in applied research or product development use knowledge provided by basic research to develop new drugs, treatments, and medical diagnostic tests; increase crop yields; and protect and clean up the environment by developing new biofuels. They usually have less autonomy than basic researchers to choose the emphasis of their research, relying instead on market-driven directions based on their firms' products and goals. Because biological scientists doing applied research and product development in private industry may be required to describe their research plans or results to nonscientists who are in a position to veto or approve their ideas, they must understand the potential cost of their work and its impact on business. Scientists often work in teams, interacting with engineers, scientists of other disciplines, business managers, and technicians. Some biological scientists also work with customers or suppliers and manage budgets.

Those who conduct research usually work in laboratories and use electron microscopes, computers, thermal cyclers, and a wide variety of other equipment. Some conduct experiments using laboratory animals or greenhouse plants. This is particularly true of botanists, physiologists, and zoologists. For some biological scientists, research also is performed outside of laboratories. For example, a botanist might do research in tropical rain forests to see what plants grow there, or an ecologist might study how a forest area recovers after a fire. Some marine biologists also work outdoors, often on research vessels from which they study various marine organisms such as marine plankton or fish.

Some biological scientists work in managerial or administrative positions, usually after spending some time doing research and learning about a particular firm, agency, or project. They may plan and administer programs for testing foods and drugs, for example, or direct activities at zoos or botanical gardens. Some work as consultants to businesses or to government agencies.

Recent advances in biotechnology and information technology are transforming the industries in which biological scientists work. In the 1980s, swift advances in basic biological knowledge related to genetics and molecules spurred growth in the field of biotechnology. Biological scientists using this technology manipulate the genetic material of animals or plants, attempting to make organisms more productive or resistant to disease. Research using biotechnology techniques, such as recombining DNA, has led to the production of important substances, including human insulin and growth hormone. Many other substances not previously available in large quantities are starting to be produced by biotechnological means; some may be useful in treating cancer and other diseases. Today, many biological scientists are involved in biotechnology. Those who work on the Human Genome Project isolate genes and determine their function. This work continues to lead to the discovery of the genes associated with specific diseases and inherited traits, such as certain types of cancer or obesity. These advances in biotechnology have created research opportunities in almost all areas of biology, with commercial applications in the food industry, agriculture, and environmental remediation and in other emerging areas such as DNA fingerprinting.

Most biological scientists are further classified by the type of organism they study or by the specific activity they perform, although recent advances in the understanding of basic life processes at the molecular and cellular levels have blurred some traditional classifications.

Aquatic biologists study micro-organisms, plants, and animals living in water. *Marine biologists* study saltwater organisms, and *limnologists* study freshwater organisms. Much of the work of marine biology centers on molecular biology, the study of the biochemical processes that take place inside living cells. Marine biologists sometimes are mistakenly called oceanographers, but oceanography is the study of the physical characteristics of oceans and the ocean floor. (See this book's descriptions of environmental scientists and hydrologists and of geoscientists.)

Biochemists study the chemical composition of living things. They analyze the complex chemical combinations and reactions involved in metabolism, reproduction, growth, and heredity. Biochemists and molecular biologists do most of their work in biotechnology, which involves understanding the complex chemistry of life.

Botanists study plants and their environment. Some study all aspects of plant life, including algae, fungi, lichens, mosses, ferns, conifers, and flowering plants; others specialize in areas such as identification and classification of plants, the structure and function of plant parts, the biochemistry of plant processes, the causes and cures of plant diseases, the interaction of plants with other organisms and the environment, and the geological record of plants.

Microbiologists investigate the growth and characteristics of microscopic organisms such as bacteria, algae, or fungi. Most microbiologists specialize in environmental, food, agricultural, or industrial microbiology; virology (the study of viruses); immunology (the study of mechanisms that fight infections); or bioinformatics (the process of integrating molecular biology and information science). Many microbiologists use biotechnology to advance knowledge of cell reproduction and human disease.

Physiologists study life functions of plants and animals, both in the whole organism and at the cellular or molecular level, under normal and abnormal conditions. Physiologists often specialize in functions such as growth, reproduction, photosynthesis, respiration, or movement or in the physiology of a certain area or system of the organism.

Biophysicists study the application of principles of physics, such as electrical and mechanical energy and related phenomena, to living cells and organisms.

Zoologists and wildlife biologists study animals and wildlife—their origin, behavior, diseases, and life processes. Some experiment with live animals in controlled or natural surroundings, while others dissect dead animals to study their structure. Zoologists and wildlife biologists also may collect and analyze biological data to determine the environmental effects of current and potential use of land and water areas. Zoologists usually are identified by the animal group studied—*ornithologists* (birds), *mammalogists* (mammals), *herpetologists* (reptiles), and *ichthyologists* (fish).

Ecologists study the relationships among organisms and between organisms and their environments, examining the effects of population size, pollutants, rainfall, temperature, and altitude. Using knowledge of various scientific disciplines, ecologists may collect, study, and report data on the quality of air, food, soil, and water.

Agricultural and food scientists, sometimes referred to as biological scientists, are discussed elsewhere in this book.

Working Conditions

Biological scientists usually work regular hours in offices or laboratories and usually are not exposed to unsafe or unhealthy conditions. Those who work with dangerous organisms or toxic substances in the laboratory must follow strict safety procedures to avoid contamination. Many biological scientists such as botanists, ecologists, and zoologists take field trips that involve strenuous physical activity and primitive living conditions. Biological scientists in the field may work in warm or cold climates in all kinds of weather. In their research, they may dig, chip with a hammer, scoop with a net, and carry equipment in a backpack. They also may climb, stand, kneel, or dive.

Marine biologists encounter a variety of working conditions. Some marine biologists work in laboratories; others work on research ships. Marine biologists who work underwater must practice safe diving while working around sharp coral reefs and hazardous marine life. Although some marine biologists obtain their specimens from the sea, many still spend a good deal of their time in laboratories and offices, conducting tests, running experiments, recording results, and compiling data.

Some biological scientists depend on grant money to support their research. They may be under pressure to meet deadlines and to conform to rigid grant-writing specifications when preparing proposals to seek new or extended funding.

Training, Other Qualifications, and Advancement

A Ph.D. degree usually is necessary for independent research, industrial research, and college teaching, as well as for advancement to administrative positions. A master's degree is sufficient for some jobs in basic research, applied research or product development, management, or inspection; it also may qualify one to work as a research technician or as a teacher in an aquarium. A bachelor's degree is adequate for some nonresearch jobs. For example, some graduates with a bachelor's degree start as biological scientists in testing and inspection or get jobs related to biological science, such as technical sales or service representatives. In some cases, graduates with a bachelor's degree are able to work in a laboratory environment on their own projects, but this is unusual. Some may work as research assistants, whereas others become biological laboratory technicians or, with courses in education, high school biology teachers. Many with a bachelor's degree in biology enter medical, dental, veterinary, or other health profession schools.

In addition to required courses in chemistry and biology, undergraduate biological science majors usually study allied disciplines such as mathematics, physics, engineering, and computer science. Computer courses are essential because employers prefer job applicants who are able to apply computer skills to modeling and simulation tasks and to operate computerized laboratory equipment, particularly in emerging fields such as bioinformatics. Those interested in studying the environment also should take courses in environmental studies and become familiar with current legislation and regulations. Prospective biological scientists who hope to work as marine biologists should have at least a bachelor's degree in a biological or marine science. However, students should not overspecialize in undergraduate study, as knowledge of marine biology often is acquired in graduate study. Most colleges and universities offer bachelor's degrees in biological science, and many offer advanced degrees. Curriculums for advanced degrees often emphasize a subfield such as microbiology or botany, but not all universities offer all curriculums. Larger universities frequently have separate departments specializing in different areas of biological science. For example, a program in botany might cover agronomy, horticulture, or plant pathology. Advanced degree programs include classroom and fieldwork, laboratory research, and a thesis or dissertation.

Biological scientists with a Ph.D. often take temporary postdoctoral research positions that provide specialized research experience. Postdoctoral positions may offer the opportunity to publish research findings. A solid record of published research is essential in obtaining a permanent position involving basic research, especially for those seeking a permanent college or university faculty position. In private industry, some may become managers or administrators within the field of biology; others leave biology for nontechnical managerial, administrative, or sales jobs.

Biological scientists should be able to work independently or as part of a team and be able to communicate clearly and concisely, both orally and in writing. Those in private industry, especially those who aspire to management or administrative positions, should possess strong business and communication skills and be familiar with regulatory issues and marketing and management techniques. Those doing field research in remote areas must have physical stamina. Biological scientists also must have patience and self-discipline to conduct long and detailed research projects.

Employment

Biological scientists held about 77,000 jobs in 2004. Slightly more than half of all biological scientists were employed by federal, state, and local governments. Federal biological scientists worked mainly for the U.S. Departments of Agriculture, Interior, and Defense and for the National Institutes of Health. Most of the rest worked in scientific research and testing laboratories, the pharmaceutical and medicine manufacturing industry, or hospitals.

In addition, many biological scientists held biology faculty positions in colleges and universities. (See the description of teachers—postsecondary elsewhere in this book.)

Job Outlook

Employment of biological scientists is projected to grow about as fast as average for all occupations over the 2004–2014 period, as biotechnological research and development continues to drive job growth. However, doctoral degree holders face competition for basic research positions. The federal government funds much basic research and development, including many areas of medical research that relate to biological science. Recent budget increases at the National Institutes of Health have led to large increases in federal basic research and development expenditures, with research grants growing both in number and in dollar amount. Nevertheless, the increase in expenditures is expected to slow significantly over the 2004–2014 projection period, resulting in a highly competitive environment for winning and renewing research grants. Furthermore, should the number of advanced degrees awarded continue to grow, applicants for research grants are likely to face even more competition. Currently, about 1 in 3 grant proposals are approved for long-term research projects. In addition, applied research positions in private industry may become more difficult to obtain if increasing numbers of scientists seek jobs in private industry because of the competitive job market for independent research positions in universities and for college and university faculty.

Opportunities for those with a bachelor's or master's degree in biological science are expected to be better. The number of science-related jobs in sales, marketing, and research management for which non-Ph.D.s usually qualify is expected to exceed the number of independent research positions. Non-Ph.D.s also may fill positions as science or engineering technicians or as medical health technologists and technicians. Some may become high school biology teachers.

Biological scientists enjoyed very rapid gains in employment between the mid-1980s and mid-1990s—reflecting, in part, increased staffing requirements in new biotechnology companies. Employment growth should slow somewhat, along with a slow-down in the number of new biotechnology firms; some existing firms will merge or be absorbed by larger biotechnology or pharmaceutical firms. However, much of the basic biological research done in recent years has resulted in new knowledge, including the isolation and identification of genes. Biological scientists will be needed to take this knowledge to the next stage, which is understanding how certain genes function within an entire organism, so that gene therapies can be developed to treat diseases. Even pharmaceutical and other firms not solely engaged in biotechnology use biotechnology techniques extensively, spurring employment increases for biological scientists. For example, biological scientists are continuing to help farmers increase crop yields by pinpointing genes that can help crops such as wheat grow worldwide in areas that currently are hostile to the crop. Expected expansion of research related to health issues such as AIDS, cancer, and Alzheimer's disease also should create more jobs for these scientists. In addition, efforts to discover new and improved ways to clean up and preserve the environment will continue to add to job growth. More biological scientists will be needed to determine the environmental impact of industry and government actions and to prevent or correct environmental problems such as the negative effects of pesticide use. Some biological scientists will find opportunities in environmental regulatory agencies; others will use their expertise to advise lawmakers on legislation to save environmentally sensitive areas. There will continue to be demand for biological scientists specializing in botany, zoology, and marine biology, but opportunities will be limited because of the small size of these fields. New industrial applications of biotechnology, such as changing how companies make ethanol for transportation fuel, also will spur demand for biological scientists.

Marine biology, despite its attractiveness as a career, is a very small specialty within biological science. Prospective marine biology students should be aware that those who would like to enter this specialty far outnumber the very few openings that occur each year for the type of glamorous research jobs that many would like to obtain. Almost all marine biologists who do basic research have a Ph.D.

Biological scientists are less likely to lose their jobs during recessions than are those in many other occupations because many are employed on long-term research projects. However, an economic downturn could influence the amount of money allocated to new research and development efforts, particularly in areas of risky or innovative research. An economic downturn also could limit the possibility of extension or renewal of existing projects.

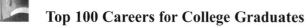

Earnings

Median annual earnings of biochemists and biophysicists were $68,950 in May 2004. The middle 50 percent earned between $49,430 and $88,540. The lowest 10 percent earned less than $38,710, and the highest 10 percent earned more than $110,660. Median annual earnings of microbiologists were $54,840 in May 2004. The middle 50 percent earned between $41,000 and $74,260. The lowest 10 percent earned less than $32,630, and the highest 10 percent earned more than $101,720. Median annual earnings of zoologists and wildlife biologists were $50,330 in May 2004. The middle 50 percent earned between $39,150 and $63,800. The lowest 10 percent earned less than $31,450, and the highest 10 percent earned more than $81,200. Median annual earnings of biochemists and biophysicists employed in scientific research and development services were $73,900 in May 2004.

According to the National Association of Colleges and Employers, beginning salary offers in July 2005 averaged $31,258 a year for bachelor's degree recipients in biological and life sciences.

In the federal government in 2005, general biological scientists in nonsupervisory, supervisory, and managerial positions earned an average salary of $69,908; microbiologists, $80,798; ecologists, $72,021; physiologists, $93,208; geneticists, $85,170; zoologists, $101,601; and botanists, $62,207.

Related Occupations

Many other occupations deal with living organisms and require a level of training similar to that of biological scientists. These include medical scientists, agricultural and food scientists, and conservation scientists and foresters as well as health occupations such as physicians and surgeons, dentists, and veterinarians.

Sources of Additional Information

For information on careers in the biological sciences, contact

▶ American Institute of Biological Sciences, 1444 I St. NW, Suite 200, Washington, DC 20005. Internet: http://www.aibs.org

For information on careers in biochemistry or biological sciences, contact

▶ Federation of American Societies for Experimental Biology, 9650 Rockville Pike, Bethesda, MD 20814. Internet: http://www.faseb.org

For a brochure titled *Careers in Botany*, contact

▶ The Botanical Society of America, 4475 Castleman Ave., P.O. Box 299, St. Louis, MI 63166. Internet: http://www.botany.org

For information on careers in microbiology, contact

▶ American Society for Microbiology, Career Information–Education Department, 1752 N St. NW, Washington, DC 20036. Internet: http://www.asm.org

Information on obtaining a biological scientist position with the federal government is available from the Office of Personnel Management through USAJOBS, the federal government's official employment information system. This resource for locating and applying for job opportunities can be accessed through the Internet at http://www.usajobs.opm.gov or through an interactive voice response telephone system at (703) 724-1850 or TDD (978) 461-8404. These numbers are not toll free, and charges may result.

Chiropractors

(O*NET 29-1011.00)

Significant Points

■ Job prospects should be good; employment is expected to increase faster than average as consumer demand for alternative health care grows.

■ Chiropractors must be licensed, requiring 2 to 4 years of undergraduate education, the completion of a 4-year chiropractic college course, and passing scores on national and state examinations.

■ About 58 percent of chiropractors are self-employed.

■ Earnings are relatively low in the beginning, but increase as the practice grows.

Nature of the Work

Chiropractors, also known as *doctors of chiropractic* or *chiropractic physicians*, diagnose and treat patients whose health problems are associated with the body's muscular, nervous, and skeletal systems, especially the spine. Chiropractors believe that interference with these systems impairs the body's normal functions and lowers its resistance to disease. They also hold that spinal or vertebral dysfunction alters many important body functions by affecting the nervous system and that skeletal imbalance through joint or articular dysfunction, especially in the spine, can cause pain.

The chiropractic approach to health care is holistic, stressing the patient's overall health and wellness. It recognizes that many factors affect health, including exercise, diet, rest, environment, and heredity. Chiropractors provide natural, drugless, nonsurgical health treatments and rely on the body's inherent recuperative abilities. They also recommend changes in lifestyle—in eating, exercise, and sleeping habits, for example—to their patients. When appropriate, chiropractors consult with and refer patients to other health practitioners.

Like other health practitioners, chiropractors follow a standard routine to secure the information they need for diagnosis and treatment. They take the patient's medical history; conduct physical, neurological, and orthopedic examinations; and may order laboratory tests. X rays and other diagnostic images are important tools because of the chiropractor's emphasis on the spine and its proper function. Chiropractors also employ a postural and spinal analysis common to chiropractic diagnosis.

In cases in which difficulties can be traced to the involvement of musculoskeletal structures, chiropractors manually adjust the spinal column. Some chiropractors use water, light, massage, ultrasound, electric, acupuncture, and heat therapy. They also may apply supports such as straps, tapes, and braces. Chiropractors counsel patients about wellness concepts such as nutrition, exercise, changes in lifestyle, and stress management, but do not prescribe drugs or perform surgery.

Some chiropractors specialize in sports injuries, neurology, orthopedics, pediatrics, nutrition, internal disorders, or diagnostic imaging.

Many chiropractors are solo or group practitioners who also have the administrative responsibilities of running a practice. In larger offices, chiropractors delegate these tasks to office managers and chiropractic assistants. Chiropractors in private practice are responsible for developing a patient base, hiring employees, and keeping records.

Working Conditions

Chiropractors work in clean, comfortable offices. Their average workweek is about 40 hours, although longer hours are not uncommon. Solo practitioners set their own hours, but may work evenings or weekends to accommodate patients.

Like other health practitioners, chiropractors are sometimes on their feet for long periods. Chiropractors who take X rays must employ appropriate precautions against the dangers of repeated exposure to radiation.

Training, Other Qualifications, and Advancement

All states and the District of Columbia regulate the practice of chiropractic and grant licenses to chiropractors who meet the educational and examination requirements established by the state. Chiropractors can practice only in states where they are licensed. Some states have agreements permitting chiropractors licensed in one state to obtain a license in another without further examination, provided that their educational, examination, and practice credentials meet state specifications.

Most state boards require at least 2 years of undergraduate education; an increasing number are requiring a 4-year bachelor's degree. All boards require the completion of a 4-year program at an accredited chiropractic college leading to the Doctor of Chiropractic degree.

For licensure, most state boards recognize either all or part of the four-part test administered by the National Board of Chiropractic Examiners. State examinations may supplement the National Board tests, depending on state requirements. All states except New Jersey require the completion of a specified number of hours of continuing education each year in order to maintain licensure. Chiropractic associations and accredited chiropractic programs and institutions offer continuing education programs.

In 2005, 15 chiropractic programs and 2 chiropractic institutions in the United States were accredited by the Council on Chiropractic Education. Applicants are required to have at least 90 semester hours of undergraduate study leading toward a bachelor's degree, including courses in English, the social sciences or humanities, organic and inorganic chemistry, biology, physics, and psychology. Many applicants have a bachelor's degree, which may eventually become the minimum entry requirement. Several chiropractic colleges offer prechiropractic study as well as a bachelor's degree program. Recognition of prechiropractic education offered by chiropractic colleges varies among the state boards.

Chiropractic programs require a minimum of 4,200 hours of combined classroom, laboratory, and clinical experience. During the first 2 years, most chiropractic programs emphasize classroom and laboratory work in basic science subjects such as anatomy, physiology, public health, microbiology, pathology, and biochemistry. The last 2 years stress courses in manipulation and spinal adjustment and

provide clinical experience in physical and laboratory diagnosis, neurology, orthopedics, geriatrics, physiotherapy, and nutrition. Chiropractic programs and institutions grant the degree of Doctor of Chiropractic.

Chiropractic colleges also offer postdoctoral training in orthopedics, neurology, sports injuries, nutrition, rehabilitation, radiology, industrial consulting, family practice, pediatrics, and applied chiropractic sciences. Once such training is complete, chiropractors may take specialty exams leading to "diplomate" status in a given specialty. Exams are administered by specialty chiropractic associations.

Chiropractic requires keen observation to detect physical abnormalities. It also takes considerable manual dexterity, but not unusual strength or endurance, to perform adjustments. Chiropractors should be able to work independently and handle responsibility. As in other health-related occupations, empathy, understanding, and the desire to help others are good qualities for dealing effectively with patients.

Newly licensed chiropractors can set up a new practice, purchase an established one, or enter into partnership with an established practitioner. They also may take a salaried position with an established chiropractor, a group practice, or a health care facility.

Employment

Chiropractors held about 53,000 jobs in 2004. Approximately 58 percent of chiropractors are self-employed. Most chiropractors are in solo practice, although some are in group practice or work for other chiropractors. A small number teach, conduct research at chiropractic institutions, or work in hospitals and clinics.

Many chiropractors are located in small communities. However, there still often are geographic imbalances in the distribution of chiropractors, in part because many establish practices close to one of the few chiropractic institutions.

Job Outlook

Job prospects are expected to be good for persons who enter the practice of chiropractic. Employment of chiropractors is expected to grow faster than the average for all occupations through the year 2014 as consumer demand for alternative health care grows. Because chiropractors emphasize the importance of healthy lifestyles and do not prescribe drugs or perform surgery, chiropractic care is appealing to many health-conscious Americans. Chiropractic treatment of the back, neck, extremities, and joints has become more accepted as a result of research and changing attitudes about alternative, noninvasive health care practices. The rapidly expanding older population, with its increased likelihood of mechanical and structural problems, also will increase demand for chiropractors.

Demand for chiropractic treatment, however, is related as well to the ability of patients to pay, either directly or through health insurance. Although more insurance plans now cover chiropractic services, the extent of such coverage varies among plans. Increasingly, chiropractors must educate communities about the benefits of chiropractic care in order to establish a successful practice.

In this occupation, replacement needs arise almost entirely from retirements. Chiropractors usually remain in the occupation until they retire; few transfer to other occupations. Establishing a new practice will be easiest in areas with a low concentration of chiropractors.

Earnings

Median annual earnings of salaried chiropractors were $69,910 in May 2004. The middle 50 percent earned between $46,710 and $118,280 a year.

In 2005, the mean salary for chiropractors was $104,363, according to a survey conducted by *Chiropractic Economics* magazine.

In chiropractic, as in other types of independent practice, earnings are relatively low in the beginning and increase as the practice grows. Geographic location and the characteristics and qualifications of the practitioner also may influence earnings. Self-employed chiropractors must provide their own health insurance and retirement.

Related Occupations

Chiropractors treat patients and work to prevent bodily disorders and injuries. So do athletic trainers, massage therapists, occupational therapists, physical therapists, physicians and surgeons, podiatrists, and veterinarians.

Sources of Additional Information

General information on a career as a chiropractor is available from the following organizations:

▸ American Chiropractic Association, 1701 Clarendon Blvd., Arlington, VA 22209. Internet: http://www.amerchiro.org

▸ International Chiropractors Association, 1110 North Glebe Rd., Suite 1000, Arlington, VA 22201. Internet: http://www.chiropractic.org

For a list of chiropractic programs and institutions, as well as general information on chiropractic education, contact

▸ Council on Chiropractic Education, 8049 North 85th Way, Scottsdale, AZ 85258-4321. Internet: http://www.cce-usa.org

For information on state education and licensure requirements, contact

▸ Federation of Chiropractic Licensing Boards, 5401 W. 10th St., Suite 101, Greeley, CO 80634-4400. Internet: http://www.fclb.org

For more information on the national chiropractic licensing exam, contact

▸ National Board of Chiropractic Examiners, 901 54th Ave., Suite 101, Greeley, CO 80634-4400. Internet: http://www.nbce.org

For information on admission requirements to a specific chiropractic college, as well as scholarship and loan information, contact the college's admissions office.

Dentists

(O*NET 29-1021.00, 29-1022.00, 29-1023.00, 29-1024.00, and 29-1029.99)

Significant Points

■ Most dentists are solo practitioners.

■ Dentists usually complete at least 8 years of education beyond high school.

■ Employment is projected to grow about as fast as average, and most job openings will result from the need to replace the large number of dentists expected to retire.

■ Job prospects should be good.

Nature of the Work

Dentists diagnose, prevent, and treat problems with teeth or mouth tissue. They remove decay, fill cavities, examine X rays, place protective plastic sealants on children's teeth, straighten teeth, and repair fractured teeth. They also perform corrective surgery on gums and supporting bones to treat gum diseases. Dentists extract teeth and make models and measurements for dentures to replace missing teeth. They provide instruction on diet, brushing, flossing, the use of fluorides, and other aspects of dental care. They also administer anesthetics and write prescriptions for antibiotics and other medications.

Dentists use a variety of equipment, including X-ray machines; drills; and instruments such as mouth mirrors, probes, forceps, brushes, and scalpels. They wear masks, gloves, and safety glasses to protect themselves and their patients from infectious diseases.

Dentists in private practice oversee a variety of administrative tasks, including bookkeeping and buying equipment and supplies. They may employ and supervise dental hygienists and dental assistants.

Most dentists are general practitioners, handling a variety of dental needs. Other dentists practice in any of nine specialty areas. *Orthodontists*, the largest group of specialists, straighten teeth by applying pressure to the teeth with braces or retainers. The next largest group, *oral and maxillofacial surgeons*, operates on the mouth and jaws. The remainder may specialize as *pediatric dentists* (focusing on dentistry for children); *periodontists* (treating gums and bone supporting the teeth); *prosthodontists* (replacing missing teeth with permanent fixtures, such as crowns and bridges, or with removable fixtures such as dentures); *endodontists* (performing root canal therapy); *public health dentists* (promoting good dental health and preventing dental diseases within the community); *oral pathologists* (studying oral diseases); or *oral and maxillofacial radiologists* (diagnosing diseases in the head and neck through the use of imaging technologies).

Working Conditions

Most dentists work 4 or 5 days a week. Some work evenings and weekends to meet their patients' needs. Most full-time dentists work between 35 and 40 hours a week, but others work more. Initially, dentists may work more hours as they establish their practice. Experienced dentists often work fewer hours. Many continue in part-time practice well beyond the usual retirement age.

Most dentists are solo practitioners, meaning that they own their own businesses and work alone or with a small staff. Some dentists have partners, and a few work for other dentists as associate dentists.

Training, Other Qualifications, and Advancement

All 50 states and the District of Columbia require dentists to be licensed. To qualify for a license in most states, candidates must graduate from 1 of the 56 dental schools accredited by the American Dental Association's (ADA's) Commission on Dental Accreditation in 2004 and then must pass written and practical examinations. Candidates may fulfill the written part of the state licensing requirements by passing the National Board Dental Examinations. Individual states or regional testing agencies administer the written or practical examinations.

Dental schools require a minimum of 2 years of college-level predental education, regardless of the major chosen. However, most dental students have at least a bachelor's degree. Predental education emphasizes coursework in science, and many applicants to dental school major in a science such as biology or chemistry, while other applicants major in another subject and take many science courses as well. A few applicants are accepted to dental school after 2 or 3 years of college and complete their bachelor's degree while attending dental school.

All dental schools require applicants to take the Dental Admissions Test (DAT). When selecting students, schools consider scores earned on the DAT, applicants' grade point averages, and information gathered through recommendations and interviews. Competition for admission to dental school is keen.

Dental school usually lasts 4 academic years. Studies begin with classroom instruction and laboratory work in basic sciences, including anatomy, microbiology, biochemistry, and physiology. Beginning courses in clinical sciences, including laboratory techniques, also are provided at this time. During the last 2 years, students treat patients, usually in dental clinics, under the supervision of licensed dentists. Most dental schools award the degree of Doctor of Dental Surgery (DDS). The rest award an equivalent degree, Doctor of Dental Medicine (DMD).

Some dental school graduates work for established dentists as associates for 1 to 2 years to gain experience and save money to equip an office of their own. Most dental school graduates, however, purchase an established practice or open a new one immediately after graduation.

In 2004, 17 states licensed or certified dentists who intended to practice in a specialty area. Requirements include 2 to 4 years of postgraduate education and, in some cases, the completion of a special state examination. Most state licenses permit dentists to engage in both general and specialized practice. Dentists who want to teach or conduct research usually spend an additional 2 to 5 years in advanced dental training in programs operated by dental schools or hospitals. According to the ADA, each year about 12 percent of new graduates enroll in postgraduate training programs to prepare for a dental specialty.

Dentistry requires diagnostic ability and manual skills. Dentists should have good visual memory, excellent judgment regarding space and shape, a high degree of manual dexterity, and scientific ability. Good business sense, self-discipline, and good communication skills are helpful for success in private practice. High school

and college students who want to become dentists should take courses in biology, chemistry, physics, health, and mathematics.

Employment

Dentists held about 150,000 jobs in 2004. Employment was distributed among general practitioners and specialists as follows:

Dentists, general	128,000
Orthodontists	10,000
Oral and maxillofacial surgeons	6,000
Prosthodontists	1,000
Dentists, all other specialists	5,000

About one third of dentists were self-employed and not incorporated. Almost all dentists work in private practice. According to ADA, 78 percent of dentists in private practice are sole proprietors, and 14 percent belong to a partnership. A few salaried dentists work in hospitals and offices of physicians.

Job Outlook

Employment of dentists is projected to grow about as fast as average for all occupations through 2014. Although employment growth will provide some job opportunities, most jobs will result from the need to replace the large number of dentists expected to retire. Job prospects should be good as new dentists take over established practices or start their own.

Demand for dental care should grow substantially through 2014. As members of the baby-boom generation advance into middle age, a large number will need complicated dental work, such as bridges. In addition, elderly people are more likely to retain their teeth than were their predecessors, so they will require much more care than in the past. The younger generation will continue to need preventive checkups despite treatments such as fluoridation of the water supply, which decreases the incidence of tooth decay. However, employment of dentists is not expected to grow as rapidly as the demand for dental services. As their practices expand, dentists are likely to hire more dental hygienists and dental assistants to handle routine services.

Dentists will increasingly provide care and instruction aimed at preventing the loss of teeth rather than simply providing treatments such as fillings. Improvements in dental technology also will allow dentists to offer more effective and less painful treatment to their patients.

Earnings

Median annual earnings of salaried dentists were $129,920 in May 2004. Earnings vary according to number of years in practice, location, hours worked, and specialty.

Self-employed dentists in private practice tend to earn more than do salaried dentists, and a relatively large proportion of dentists is self-employed. Like other business owners, these dentists must provide their own health insurance, life insurance, and retirement benefits.

Related Occupations

Dentists examine, diagnose, prevent, and treat diseases and abnormalities. Chiropractors, optometrists, physicians and surgeons, podiatrists, psychologists, and veterinarians do related work.

Sources of Additional Information

For information on dentistry as a career, a list of accredited dental schools, and a list of state boards of dental examiners, contact

▸ American Dental Association, Commission on Dental Accreditation, 211 E. Chicago Ave., Chicago, IL 60611. Internet: http://www.ada.org

For information on admission to dental schools, contact

▸ American Dental Education Association, 1400 K St. NW, Suite 1100, Washington, DC 20005. Internet: http://www.adea.org

Persons interested in practicing dentistry should obtain the requirements for licensure from the board of dental examiners of the state in which they plan to work.

To obtain information on scholarships, grants, and loans, including federal financial aid, prospective dental students should contact the office of student financial aid at the schools to which they apply.

Lawyers

(O*NET 23-1011.00)

Significant Points

- Competition for job openings should be keen because of the large number of students graduating from law school each year.

- Formal requirements to become a lawyer generally include a 4-year college degree, 3 years of law school, and passing a written bar examination; however, some requirements may vary by state.

- Competition for admission to most law schools is intense.

- About 3 out of 4 lawyers practiced privately, either as partners in law firms or in solo practices.

Nature of the Work

The legal system affects nearly every aspect of our society, from buying a home to crossing the street. Lawyers form the backbone of this vital system, linking it to society in numerous ways. For that reason, they hold positions of great responsibility and are obligated to adhere to a strict code of ethics.

Lawyers, also called *attorneys*, act as both advocates and advisors in our society. As advocates, they represent one of the parties in criminal and civil trials by presenting evidence and arguing in court to support their client. As advisors, lawyers counsel their clients concerning their legal rights and obligations and suggest particular courses of action in business and personal matters. Whether acting as an advocate or an advisor, all attorneys research the intent of laws and judicial decisions and apply the law to the specific circumstances faced by their client.

The more detailed aspects of a lawyer's job depend upon his or her field of specialization and position. Although all lawyers are licensed to represent parties in court, some appear in court more frequently than others. Trial lawyers, who specialize in trial work, must be able to think quickly and speak with ease and authority. In addition, familiarity with courtroom rules and strategy is particularly important in trial work. Still, trial lawyers spend the majority of their time outside the courtroom, conducting research, interviewing clients and witnesses, and handling other details in preparation for a trial.

Lawyers may specialize in a number of areas, such as bankruptcy, probate, international, or elder law. Those specializing in environmental law, for example, may represent interest groups, waste disposal companies, or construction firms in their dealings with the U.S. Environmental Protection Agency (EPA) and other federal and state agencies. These lawyers help clients prepare and file for licenses and applications for approval before certain activities may occur. In addition, they represent clients' interests in administrative adjudications.

Some lawyers specialize in the growing field of intellectual property, helping to protect clients' claims to copyrights, artwork under contract, product designs, and computer programs. Still other lawyers advise insurance companies about the legality of insurance transactions, guiding the company in writing insurance policies to conform with the law and to protect the companies from unwarranted claims. When claims are filed against insurance companies, these attorneys review the claims and represent the companies in court.

Most lawyers are in private practice, concentrating on criminal or civil law. In criminal law, lawyers represent individuals who have been charged with crimes and argue their cases in courts of law. Attorneys dealing with civil law assist clients with litigation, wills, trusts, contracts, mortgages, titles, and leases. Other lawyers handle only public-interest cases—civil or criminal—which may have an impact extending well beyond the individual client.

Lawyers are sometimes employed full time by a single client. If the client is a corporation, the lawyer is known as "house counsel" and usually advises the company concerning legal issues related to its business activities. These issues might involve patents, government regulations, contracts with other companies, property interests, or collective bargaining agreements with unions.

A significant number of attorneys are employed at the various levels of government. Lawyers who work for state attorneys general, prosecutors, public defenders, and courts play a key role in the criminal justice system. At the federal level, attorneys investigate cases for the U.S. Department of Justice and other agencies. Government lawyers also help develop programs, draft and interpret laws and legislation, establish enforcement procedures, and argue civil and criminal cases on behalf of the government.

Other lawyers work for legal aid societies—private, nonprofit organizations established to serve disadvantaged people. These lawyers generally handle civil, rather than criminal, cases. A relatively small number of trained attorneys work in law schools. Most are faculty members who specialize in one or more subjects; however, some serve as administrators. Others work full time in nonacademic settings and teach part time. (For additional information, see the job description for teachers—postsecondary elsewhere in this book.)

Lawyers are increasingly using various forms of technology to perform their varied tasks more efficiently. Although all lawyers continue to use law libraries to prepare cases, some supplement conventional printed sources with computer sources, such as the Internet and legal databases. Software is used to search this legal literature automatically and to identify legal texts relevant to a specific case. In litigation involving many supporting documents, lawyers may use computers to organize and index material. Lawyers also utilize electronic filing, videoconferencing, and voice-recognition technology to share information more effectively with other parties involved in a case.

Working Conditions

Lawyers do most of their work in offices, law libraries, and courtrooms. They sometimes meet in clients' homes or places of business and, when necessary, in hospitals or prisons. They may travel to attend meetings; gather evidence; and appear before courts, legislative bodies, and other authorities.

Salaried lawyers usually have structured work schedules. Lawyers who are in private practice may work irregular hours while conducting research, conferring with clients, or preparing briefs during nonoffice hours. Lawyers often work long hours, and of those who regularly work full time, about half work 50 hours or more per week. They may face particularly heavy pressure when a case is being tried. Preparation for court includes keeping abreast of the latest laws and judicial decisions.

Although legal work generally is not seasonal, the work of tax lawyers and other specialists may be an exception. Because lawyers in private practice often can determine their own workload and the point at which they will retire, many stay in practice well beyond the usual retirement age.

Training, Other Qualifications, and Advancement

To practice law in the courts of any state or other jurisdiction, a person must be licensed, or admitted to its bar, under rules established by the jurisdiction's highest court. All states require that applicants for admission to the bar pass a written bar examination; most states also require applicants to pass a separate written ethics examination. Lawyers who have been admitted to the bar in one state occasionally may be admitted to the bar in another without taking an examination if they meet the latter jurisdiction's standards of good moral character and a specified period of legal experience. In most cases, however, lawyers must pass the bar examination in each state in which they plan to practice. Federal courts and agencies set their own qualifications for those practicing before or in them.

To qualify for the bar examination in most states, an applicant usually must earn a college degree and graduate from a law school accredited by the American Bar Association (ABA) or the proper state authorities. ABA accreditation signifies that the law school—particularly its library and faculty—meets certain standards developed to promote quality legal education. As of 2005, there were 191

ABA-accredited law schools; others were approved by state authorities only. With certain exceptions, graduates of schools not approved by the ABA are restricted to taking the bar examination and practicing in the state or other jurisdiction in which the school is located; most of these schools are in California. In 2005, seven states—California, Maine, New York, Vermont, Virginia, Washington, and Wyoming—accepted the study of law in a law office as qualification for taking the bar examination; three jurisdictions—California, the District of Columbia, and New Mexico—now accept the study of law by correspondence. Several states require registration and approval of students by the State Board of Law Examiners, either before the students enter law school or during their early years of legal study.

Although there is no nationwide bar examination, 48 states, the District of Columbia, Guam, the Northern Mariana Islands, Puerto Rico, and the Virgin Islands require the 6-hour Multistate Bar Examination (MBE) as part of the overall bar examination; the MBE is not required in Louisiana or Washington. The MBE covers a broad range of issues, and sometimes a locally prepared state bar examination is given in addition to it. The 3-hour Multistate Essay Examination (MEE) is used as part of the bar examination in several states. States vary in their use of MBE and MEE scores.

Many states also require Multistate Performance Testing (MPT) to test the practical skills of beginning lawyers. Requirements vary by state, although the test usually is taken at the same time as the bar exam and is a one-time requirement.

The required college and law school education usually takes 7 years of full-time study after high school—4 years of undergraduate study followed by 3 years of law school. Law school applicants must have a bachelor's degree to qualify for admission. To meet the needs of students who can attend only part time, a number of law schools have night or part-time divisions, which usually require 4 years of study; about 1 in 10 graduates from ABA-approved schools attended part time.

Although there is no recommended "prelaw" major, prospective lawyers should develop proficiency in writing and speaking, reading, researching, analyzing, and thinking logically—skills needed to succeed both in law school and in the profession. Regardless of major, a multidisciplinary background is recommended. Courses in English, foreign languages, public speaking, government, philosophy, history, economics, mathematics, and computer science, among others, are useful. Students interested in a particular aspect of law may find related courses helpful. For example, prospective patent lawyers need a strong background in engineering or science, and future tax lawyers must have extensive knowledge of accounting.

Acceptance by most law schools depends on the applicant's ability to demonstrate an aptitude for the study of law, usually through good undergraduate grades, the Law School Admission Test (LSAT), the quality of the applicant's undergraduate school, any prior work experience, and sometimes a personal interview. However, law schools vary in the weight they place on each of these and other factors.

All law schools approved by the ABA require applicants to take the LSAT. Nearly all law schools require applicants to have certified transcripts sent to the Law School Data Assembly Service, which then submits the applicants' LSAT scores and their standardized

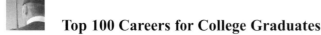

records of college grades to the law schools of their choice. Both this service and the LSAT are administered by the Law School Admission Council. Competition for admission to many law schools—especially the most prestigious ones—generally is intense, with the number of applicants greatly exceeding the number that can be admitted.

During the first year or year and a half of law school, students usually study core courses, such as constitutional law, contracts, property law, torts, civil procedure, and legal writing. In the remaining time, they may elect specialized courses in fields such as tax, labor, or corporate law. Law students often acquire practical experience by participating in school-sponsored legal clinic activities; in the school's moot court competitions, in which students conduct appellate arguments; in practice trials under the supervision of experienced lawyers and judges; and through research and writing on legal issues for the school's law journal.

A number of law schools have clinical programs in which students gain legal experience through practice trials and projects under the supervision of practicing lawyers and law school faculty. Law school clinical programs might include work in legal aid clinics, for example, or on the staff of legislative committees. Part-time or summer clerkships in law firms, government agencies, and corporate legal departments also provide valuable experience. Such training can lead directly to a job after graduation and can help students decide what kind of practice best suits them. Clerkships also may be an important source of financial aid.

In 2004, law school graduates in 52 jurisdictions were required to pass the Multistate Professional Responsibility Examination (MPRE), which tests their knowledge of the ABA codes on professional responsibility and judicial conduct. In some states, the MPRE may be taken during law school, usually after completing a course on legal ethics.

Law school graduates receive the degree of *juris doctor* (J.D.) as the first professional degree. Advanced law degrees may be desirable for those planning to specialize, research, or teach. Some law students pursue joint degree programs, which usually require an additional semester or year of study. Joint degree programs are offered in a number of areas, including law and business administration or public administration.

After graduation, lawyers must keep informed about legal and nonlegal developments that affect their practices. Currently, 40 states and jurisdictions mandate continuing legal education (CLE). Many law schools and state and local bar associations provide continuing education courses that help lawyers stay abreast of recent developments. Some states allow CLE credits to be obtained through participation in seminars on the Internet.

The practice of law involves a great deal of responsibility. Individuals planning careers in law should like to work with people and be able to win the respect and confidence of their clients, associates, and the public. Perseverance, creativity, and reasoning ability also are essential to lawyers, who often analyze complex cases and handle new and unique legal problems.

Most beginning lawyers start in salaried positions. Newly hired salaried attorneys usually start as associates and work with more experienced lawyers or judges. After several years of gaining more responsibilities, some lawyers are admitted to partnership in their firm or go into practice for themselves. Some experienced lawyers are nominated or elected to judgeships. (See the section on judges, magistrates, and other judicial workers elsewhere in this book.) Others become full-time law school faculty or administrators; a growing number of these lawyers have advanced degrees in other fields as well.

Some attorneys use their legal training in administrative or managerial positions in various departments of large corporations. A transfer from a corporation's legal department to another department often is viewed as a way to gain administrative experience and rise in the ranks of management.

Employment

Lawyers held about 735,000 jobs in 2004. Approximately 3 out of 4 lawyers practiced privately, either as partners in law firms or in solo practices. Most salaried lawyers held positions in government or with corporations or nonprofit organizations. The greatest number of lawyers working in government were employed at the local level. In the federal government, lawyers work for many different agencies, but are concentrated in the Departments of Justice, Treasury, and Defense. Many salaried lawyers working outside of government are employed as house counsel by public utilities, banks, insurance companies, real estate agencies, manufacturing firms, and other business firms and nonprofit organizations. Some also have part-time independent practices, while others work part time as lawyers and full time in another occupation.

Job Outlook

Employment of lawyers is expected to grow about as fast as the average for all occupations through 2014, primarily as a result of growth in the population and in the general level of business activities. Job growth among lawyers also will result from increasing demand for legal services in such areas as health care, intellectual property, venture capital, energy, elder, antitrust, and environmental law. In addition, the wider availability and affordability of legal clinics should result in increased use of legal services by middle-income people. However, growth in demand for lawyers will be limited as businesses, in an effort to reduce costs, increasingly use large accounting firms and paralegals to perform some of the same functions that lawyers do. For example, accounting firms may provide employee-benefit counseling, process documents, or handle various other services previously performed by a law firm. Also, mediation and dispute resolution increasingly are being used as alternatives to litigation.

Competition for job openings should continue to be keen because of the large number of students graduating from law school each year. Graduates with superior academic records from highly regarded law schools will have the best job opportunities. Perhaps as a result of competition for attorney positions, lawyers are increasingly finding work in nontraditional areas for which legal training is an asset, but not normally a requirement—for example, administrative, managerial, and business positions in banks, insurance firms, real estate companies, government agencies, and other organizations. Employment opportunities are expected to continue to arise in these organizations at a growing rate.

As in the past, some graduates may have to accept positions in areas outside of their field of interest or for which they feel overqualified. Some recent law school graduates who have been unable to find permanent positions are turning to the growing number of temporary staffing firms that place attorneys in short-term jobs until they are able to secure full-time positions. This service allows companies to hire lawyers on an "as-needed" basis and permits beginning lawyers to develop practical skills while looking for permanent positions.

Because of the keen competition for jobs, a law graduate's geographic mobility and work experience assume greater importance. The willingness to relocate may be an advantage in getting a job, but to be licensed in another state, a lawyer may have to take an additional state bar examination. In addition, employers are increasingly seeking graduates who have advanced law degrees and experience in a specialty, such as tax, patent, or admiralty law.

Employment growth for lawyers will continue to be concentrated in salaried jobs as businesses and all levels of government employ a growing number of staff attorneys and as employment in the legal services industry grows. Most salaried positions are in urban areas where government agencies, law firms, and big corporations are concentrated. The number of self-employed lawyers is expected to decrease slowly, reflecting the difficulty of establishing a profitable new practice in the face of competition from larger, established law firms. Moreover, the growing complexity of law, which encourages specialization, along with the cost of maintaining up-to-date legal research materials, favors larger firms.

For lawyers who wish to work independently, establishing a new practice will probably be easiest in small towns and expanding suburban areas. In such communities, competition from larger, established law firms is likely to be less keen than in big cities, and new lawyers may find it easier to become known to potential clients.

Some lawyers are adversely affected by cyclical swings in the economy. During recessions, demand declines for some discretionary legal services, such as planning estates, drafting wills, and handling real estate transactions. Also, corporations are less likely to litigate cases when declining sales and profits result in budgetary restrictions. Some corporations and law firms will not hire new attorneys until business improves, and these establishments may even cut staff to contain costs. Several factors, however, mitigate the overall impact of recessions on lawyers; during recessions, for example, individuals and corporations face other legal problems, such as bankruptcies, foreclosures, and divorces requiring legal action.

Earnings

In May 2004, the median annual earnings of all lawyers were $94,930. The middle half of the occupation earned between $64,620 and $143,620. Median annual earnings in the industries employing the largest numbers of lawyers in May 2004 were as follows:

Management of companies and enterprises	$126,250
Federal government	108,090
Legal services	99,580
Local government	73,410
State government	70,280

Median salaries of lawyers 9 months after graduation from law school in 2004 varied by type of work, as indicated in table 1.

Table 1. Median salaries of lawyers 9 months after graduation, 2004

Type of work	Salary
All graduates	$55,000
Private practice	80,000
Business/industry	60,000
Judicial clerkship and government	44,700
Academe	40,000

Source: National Association of Law Placement

Salaries of experienced attorneys vary widely according to the type, size, and location of their employer. Lawyers who own their own practices usually earn less than those who are partners in law firms. Lawyers starting their own practice may need to work part time in other occupations to supplement their income until their practice is well established.

Most salaried lawyers are provided health and life insurance, and contributions are made to retirement plans on their behalf. Lawyers who practice independently are covered only if they arrange and pay for such benefits themselves.

Related Occupations

Legal training is necessary in many other occupations, including paralegals and legal assistants; law clerks; title examiners, abstractors, and searchers; and judges, magistrates, and other judicial workers.

Sources of Additional Information

Information on law schools and a career in law may be obtained from the following organizations:

▶ American Bar Association, 321 North Clark St., Chicago, IL 60610. Internet: http://www.abanet.org

▶ National Association for Law Placement, 1025 Connecticut Ave. NW, Suite 1110, Washington, DC 20036. Internet: http://www.nalp.org

Information on the LSAT, the Law School Data Assembly Service, the law school application process, and financial aid available to law students may be obtained from

▶ Law School Admission Council, P.O. Box 40, Newtown, PA 18940. Internet: http://www.lsac.org

Information on obtaining positions as occupational health and safety specialists and technicians with the federal government is available from the Office of Personnel Management through USAJOBS, the federal government's official employment information system. This resource for locating and applying for job opportunities can be accessed through the Internet at http://www.usajobs.opm.gov or through an interactive voice response telephone system at (703) 724-1850 or TDD (978) 461-8404. These numbers are not toll free, and charges may result.

The requirements for admission to the bar in a particular state or other jurisdiction also may be obtained at the state capital, from the clerk of the Supreme Court, or from the administrator of the State Board of Bar Examiners.

Medical Scientists

(O*NET 19-1041.00 and 19-1042.00)

Significant Points

- Most medical scientists work in research and development.

- Most medical scientists need a Ph.D. degree in a biological science; however, epidemiologists typically require a master's degree in public health or, in some cases, a Ph.D. or medical degree.

- Despite projected rapid job growth, competition is expected for most positions.

Nature of the Work

Medical scientists research human diseases in order to improve human health. Most medical scientists conduct biomedical research and development to advance knowledge of life processes and living organisms, including viruses, bacteria, and other infectious agents. Past research has resulted in advances in diagnosis, treatment, and prevention of many diseases. Basic medical research continues to provide the building blocks necessary to develop solutions to human health problems, such as vaccines and medicines. Medical scientists also engage in clinical investigation, technical writing, drug application review, patent examination, and related activities.

Medical scientists study biological systems to understand the causes of disease and other health problems and to develop treatments and research tools and techniques, many of which have medical applications. These scientists try to identify changes in a cell or in chromosomes that signal the development of medical problems, such as different types of cancer. For example, medical scientists involved in cancer research may formulate a combination of drugs that will lessen the effects of the disease. Medical scientists who are also physicians can administer these drugs to patients in clinical trials, monitor their reactions, and observe the results. Those who are not physicians normally collaborate with a physician who deals directly with patients. Medical scientists examine the results of clinical trials and, if necessary, adjust the dosage levels to reduce negative side effects or to try to induce even better results. In addition to developing treatments for health problems, medical scientists attempt to discover ways to prevent health problems—for example, by affirming the link between smoking and lung cancer or between alcoholism and liver disease.

Many medical scientists work independently in private industry, university, or government laboratories, often exploring new areas of research or expanding on specialized research that they began in graduate school. Medical scientists working in colleges and universities, hospitals, and nonprofit medical research organizations typically submit grant proposals to obtain funding for their projects. Colleges and universities; private industry; and federal government agencies, such as the National Institutes of Health and the National Science Foundation, contribute greatly to the support of scientists whose research proposals are determined to be financially feasible and to have the potential to advance new ideas or processes.

Medical scientists who work in applied research or product development use knowledge discovered through basic research to develop new drugs and medical treatments. They usually have less autonomy than basic medical researchers to choose the emphasis of their research, relying instead on market-driven forces arising from their firm's products and goals. Medical scientists doing applied research and product development in private industry may be required to express their research plans or results to nonscientists who are in a position to reject or approve their ideas; thus, they must understand the impact of their work on business. Scientists increasingly work as part of teams, interacting with engineers, scientists of other disciplines, business managers, and technicians.

Medical scientists who conduct research usually work in laboratories and use electron microscopes, computers, thermal cyclers, or a wide variety of other equipment. Some may work directly with individual patients or larger groups as they administer drugs and monitor and observe the patients during clinical trials. Medical scientists who are also physicians may administer gene therapy to human patients, draw blood, excise tissue, or perform other invasive procedures.

Some medical scientists work in managerial, consulting, or administrative positions, usually after spending some time doing research and learning about the firm, agency, or project. In the 1980s, swift advances in basic medical knowledge related to genetics and molecules spurred growth in the field of biotechnology. Medical scientists using this technology manipulate the genetic material of animals, attempting to make organisms more productive or resistant to disease. Research using biotechnology techniques, such as recombining DNA, has led to the discovery of important drugs, including human insulin and growth hormone. Many other substances not previously available in large quantities are now produced by biotechnological means; some may one day be useful in treating diseases such as Parkinson's or Alzheimer's. Today, many medical scientists are involved in the science of genetic engineering—isolating, identifying, and sequencing human genes and then determining their function. This work continues to lead to the discovery of the genes associated with specific diseases and inherited traits, such as certain types of cancer or obesity. These advances in biotechnology have opened up research opportunities in almost all areas of medical science.

Some medical scientists specialize in epidemiology. This branch of medical science investigates and describes the determinants of disease, disability, and other health outcomes and develops the means for prevention and control. Epidemiologists may study many different diseases, such as tuberculosis, influenza, or cholera, often focusing on epidemics.

Epidemiologists can be separated into two groups—research and clinical. *Research epidemiologists* conduct research in an effort to eradicate or control infectious diseases that affect the entire body, such as AIDS or typhus. Others may focus only on localized infections of the brain, lungs, or digestive tract, for example. Research epidemiologists work at colleges and universities, schools of public health, medical schools, and research and development services firms. For example, federal government agencies, such as the U.S. Department of Defense, may contract with a research firm's epidemiologists to evaluate the incidence of malaria in certain parts of the world. While some perform consulting services, other research epidemiologists may work as college and university faculty.

Clinical epidemiologists work primarily in consulting roles at hospitals, informing the medical staff of infectious outbreaks and providing containment solutions. These epidemiologists sometimes are referred to as infection control professionals, and some of them are also physicians. Epidemiologists who are not physicians often collaborate with physicians to find ways to contain diseases and outbreaks. In addition to traditional duties of studying and controlling diseases, clinical epidemiologists also may be required to develop standards and guidelines for the treatment and control of communicable diseases. Some clinical epidemiologists may work in outpatient settings.

Working Conditions

Medical scientists typically work regular hours in offices or laboratories and usually are not exposed to unsafe or unhealthy conditions. However, those scientists who work with dangerous organisms or toxic substances in the laboratory must follow strict safety procedures to avoid contamination. Medical scientists also spend time working in clinics and hospitals administering drugs and treatments to patients in clinical trials. On occasion, epidemiologists may be required to work evenings and weekends to attend meetings and hearings for medical investigations.

Some medical scientists depend on grant money to support their research. They may be under pressure to meet deadlines and to conform to rigid grant-writing specifications when preparing proposals to seek new or extended funding.

Training, Other Qualifications, and Advancement

A Ph.D. degree in a biological science is the minimum education required for most prospective medical scientists, except epidemiologists, because the work of medical scientists is almost entirely research oriented. A Ph.D. degree qualifies one to do research on basic life processes or on particular medical problems or diseases and to analyze and interpret the results of experiments on patients. Some medical scientists obtain a medical degree instead of a Ph.D., but may not be licensed physicians because they have not taken the state licensing examination or completed a residency program, typically because they prefer research to clinical practice. Medical scientists who administer drug or gene therapy to human patients, or who otherwise interact medically with patients—drawing blood, excising tissue, or performing other invasive procedures—must be licensed physicians. To be licensed, physicians must graduate from an accredited medical school, pass a licensing examination, and complete 1 to 7 years of graduate medical education. (See the description of physicians and surgeons elsewhere in this book.) It is particularly helpful for medical scientists to earn both Ph.D. and medical degrees.

Students planning careers as medical scientists should have a bachelor's degree in a biological science. In addition to required courses in chemistry and biology, undergraduates should study allied disciplines, such as mathematics, engineering, physics, and computer science, or courses in their field of interest. Once they have completed

undergraduate studies, they can then select a specialty area for their advanced degree, such as cytology, bioinformatics, genomics, or pathology. In addition to formal education, medical scientists usually spend several years in a postdoctoral position before they apply for permanent jobs. Postdoctoral work provides valuable laboratory experience, including experience in specific processes and techniques such as gene splicing, which is transferable to other research projects. In some institutions, the postdoctoral position can lead to a permanent job.

Medical scientists should be able to work independently or as part of a team and be able to communicate clearly and concisely, both orally and in writing. Those in private industry, especially those who aspire to consulting and administrative positions, should possess strong communication skills so that they can provide instruction and advice to physicians and other health care professionals.

The minimum educational requirement for epidemiology is a master's degree from a school of public health. Some jobs require a Ph.D. or medical degree, depending on the work performed. Epidemiologists who work in hospitals and health care centers often must have a medical degree with specific training in infectious diseases. Currently, about 140 infectious disease training programs exist in 42 states. Some employees in research epidemiology positions are required to be licensed physicians because they must administer drugs in clinical trials.

Epidemiologists who perform laboratory tests often require the knowledge and expertise of a licensed physician in order to administer drugs to patients in clinical trials. Epidemiologists who are not physicians frequently work closely with one.

Few students select epidemiology for undergraduate study. Undergraduates, nonetheless, should study biological sciences and should have a solid background in chemistry, mathematics, and computer science. Once a student is prepared for graduate studies, he or she can choose a specialty within epidemiology. For example, those interested in studying environmental epidemiology should focus on environmental coursework, such as water pollution, air pollution, or pesticide use. The core work of environmental studies includes toxicology and molecular biology, and students may continue with advanced coursework in environmental or occupational epidemiology. Other specialty areas that students can pursue include infectious process, infection control precautions, surveillance methodology, and outbreak investigation. Some epidemiologists begin their careers in other health care occupations, such as registered nurse and medical technologist.

The Association for Professionals in Infection Control and Epidemiology (APIC) offers continuing-education courses and certification programs in infection prevention and control and applied epidemiology. To become certified as an infection control professional, applicants are required by a certified board to pass an examination for a one-time fee. Certification is recommended for those seeking advancement and for those seeking to continually upgrade their knowledge in a rapidly evolving field.

Employment

Medical scientists held about 77,000 jobs in 2004. Epidemiologists accounted for only 4,800 of that total. In addition, many medical scientists held faculty positions in colleges and universities, but they are classified as college or university faculty. (See teachers—postsecondary elsewhere in this book.)

About 24 percent of medical scientists were employed in government; 24 percent were employed in scientific research and development services firms; 14 percent were employed in pharmaceutical and medicine manufacturing; 9 percent were employed in private hospitals; and most of the remainder were employed in private educational services and ambulatory health care services.

Among epidemiologists, 50 percent were employed in government; 23 percent were employed in management, scientific, and technical consulting services; 12 percent were employed in scientific research and development services; and 8 percent were employed in private hospitals.

Job Outlook

Employment of medical scientists is expected to grow much faster than average for all occupations through 2014. Despite projected rapid job growth, doctoral degree holders can expect to face considerable competition for basic research positions. The federal government funds much basic research and development, including many areas of medical research. Recent budget increases at the National Institutes of Health have led to large increases in federal basic research and development expenditures, with the number of grants awarded to researchers growing in number and dollar amount. However, the increase in expenditures is expected to slow significantly over the 2004–2014 projection period, resulting in a highly competitive environment for winning and renewing research grants. In addition, if the number of advanced degrees awarded continues to grow, applicants are likely to face even more competition.

Medical scientists enjoyed rapid gains in employment between the mid-1980s and mid-1990s—reflecting, in part, increased staffing requirements in new biotechnology companies. Job growth should be dampened somewhat as increases in the number of new biotechnology firms slow down and as existing firms merge or are absorbed by larger, more established biotechnology or pharmaceutical firms. However, much of the basic medical research done in recent years has resulted in new knowledge, including the isolation and identification of new genes. Medical scientists will be needed to take this knowledge to the next stage—understanding how certain genes function within an entire organism—so that gene therapies can be developed to treat diseases. Even pharmaceutical and other firms not solely engaged in biotechnology are expected to increasingly use biotechnology techniques, thus creating employment for medical scientists.

Expected expansion in research related to health issues such as AIDS, cancer, and Alzheimer's disease, along with treating growing threats such as the increase in antibiotic resistance, also should result in employment growth. Moreover, environmental conditions such as overcrowding and the increasing frequency of international travel will tend to spread existing diseases and give rise to new ones. Medical scientists will continue to be needed because they greatly contribute to the development of many treatments and medicines that improve human health.

Opportunities in epidemiology also should be highly competitive, as the number of available positions remains limited. However, an increasing focus on monitoring patients at hospitals and health care centers to ensure positive patient outcomes will contribute to job growth. In addition, a heightened awareness of bioterrorism and rare, but infectious, diseases such as West Nile Virus or severe acute respiratory syndrome (SARS) should spur demand for these workers. As hospitals enhance their infection control programs, many will seek to boost the quality and quantity of their staff. Besides job openings due to employment growth, additional openings will result as workers leave the labor force or transfer to other occupations.

Medical scientists and some epidemiologists are less likely to lose their jobs during recessions than are those in many other occupations because they are employed on long-term research projects. However, a recession could influence the amount of money allocated to new research and development, particularly in areas of risky or innovative medical research. A recession also could limit extensions or renewals of existing projects.

Earnings

Median annual earnings of medical scientists, except epidemiologists, were $61,320 in May 2004. The middle 50 percent of these workers earned between $44,120 and $86,830. The lowest 10 percent earned less than $33,030, and the highest 10 percent earned more than $114,360. Median annual earnings in the industries employing the largest numbers of medical scientists in May 2004 were

Pharmaceutical and medicine manufacturing $76,800

Scientific research and development services 65,110

General medical and surgical hospitals 55,410

Colleges, universities, and professional schools 45,600

Median annual earnings of epidemiologists were $54,800 in May 2004. The middle 50 percent earned between $45,320 and $67,160. The lowest 10 percent earned less than $36,130, and the highest 10 percent earned more than $82,310.

Related Occupations

Many other occupations deal with living organisms and require a level of training similar to that of medical scientists. These occupations include biological scientists; agricultural and food scientists; and health occupations such as physicians and surgeons, dentists, and veterinarians.

Sources of Additional Information

For a brochure entitled *Is a Career in the Pharmaceutical Sciences Right for Me,* contact

‣ American Association of Pharmaceutical Scientists (AAPS), 2107 Wilson Blvd., Suite 700, Arlington, VA 22201.

For a career brochure entitled *A Million and One,* contact

‣ American Society for Microbiology, Career Information—Education Department, 1752 N St. NW, Washington, DC 20036-2804. Internet: http://www.asm.org

For information on infectious diseases training programs, contact

‣ Infectious Diseases Society of America, Guide to Training Programs, 66 Canal Center Plaza, Suite 600, Alexandria, VA 22314. Internet: http://www.idsociety.org

Information on obtaining a medical scientist position with the federal government is available from the Office of Personnel Management through USAJOBS, the federal government's official employment information system. This resource for locating and applying for job opportunities can be accessed through the Internet at http://www.usajobs.opm.gov or through an interactive voice response telephone system at (703) 724-1850 or TDD (978) 461-8404. These numbers are not toll free, and charges may result.

Optometrists

(O*NET 29-1041.00)

Significant Points

- Admission to optometry school is competitive.

- To be licensed, optometrists must earn a Doctor of Optometry degree from an accredited optometry school and pass a written National Board exam and a clinical examination.

- Employment is expected to grow faster than average in response to the vision care needs of a growing and aging population.

Nature of the Work

Optometrists, also known as *doctors of optometry,* or *ODs,* provide most primary vision care. They examine people's eyes to diagnose vision problems and eye diseases, and they test patients' visual acuity, depth and color perception, and ability to focus and coordinate the eyes. Optometrists prescribe eyeglasses and contact lenses and provide vision therapy and low-vision rehabilitation. Optometrists analyze test results and develop a treatment plan. They administer drugs to patients to aid in the diagnosis of vision problems and prescribe drugs to treat some eye diseases. Optometrists often provide preoperative and postoperative care to cataract patients as well as to patients who have had laser vision correction or other eye surgery. They also diagnose conditions caused by systemic diseases such as diabetes and high blood pressure, referring patients to other health practitioners as needed.

Optometrists should not be confused with *ophthalmologists* or *dispensing opticians. Ophthalmologists* are physicians who perform eye surgery, as well as diagnose and treat eye diseases and injuries. Like optometrists, they also examine eyes and prescribe eyeglasses and contact lenses. *Dispensing opticians* fit and adjust eyeglasses and, in some states, may fit contact lenses according to prescriptions written by ophthalmologists or optometrists. (See the description of physicians and surgeons elsewhere in this book.)

Most optometrists are in general practice. Some specialize in work with the elderly, children, or partially sighted persons who need specialized visual devices. Others develop and implement ways to protect workers' eyes from on-the-job strain or injury. Some specialize in contact lenses, sports vision, or vision therapy. A few teach optometry, perform research, or consult.

Most optometrists are private practitioners who also handle the business aspects of running an office, such as developing a patient base, hiring employees, keeping paper and electronic records, and

ordering equipment and supplies. Optometrists who operate franchise optical stores also may have some of these duties.

Working Conditions

Optometrists work in places—usually their own offices—that are clean, well lighted, and comfortable. Most full-time optometrists work about 40 hours a week. Many work weekends and evenings to suit the needs of patients. Emergency calls, once uncommon, have increased with the passage of therapeutic-drug laws expanding optometrists' ability to prescribe medications.

Training, Other Qualifications, and Advancement

All states and the District of Columbia require that optometrists be licensed. Applicants for a license must have a Doctor of Optometry degree from an accredited optometry school and must pass both a written National Board examination and a national, regional, or state clinical board examination. The written and clinical examinations of the National Board of Examiners in Optometry usually are taken during the student's academic career. Many states also require applicants to pass an examination on relevant state laws. Licenses are renewed every 1 to 3 years and, in all states, continuing education credits are needed for renewal.

The Doctor of Optometry degree requires the completion of a 4-year program at an accredited optometry school, preceded by at least 3 years of preoptometric study at an accredited college or university. Most optometry students hold a bachelor's or higher degree. In 2004, 17 U.S. schools and colleges of optometry offered programs accredited by the Accreditation Council on Optometric Education of the American Optometric Association.

Requirements for admission to schools of optometry include courses in English, mathematics, physics, chemistry, and biology. A few schools also require or recommend courses in psychology, history, sociology, speech, or business. Because a strong background in science is important, many applicants to optometry school major in a science such as biology or chemistry, while other applicants major in another subject and take many science courses offering laboratory experience. Applicants must take the Optometry Admissions Test, which measures academic ability and scientific comprehension. Admission to optometry school is competitive. As a result, most applicants take the test after their sophomore or junior year, allowing them an opportunity to take the test again and raise their score. A few applicants are accepted to optometry school after 3 years of college and complete their bachelor's degree while attending optometry school.

Optometry programs include classroom and laboratory study of health and visual sciences, as well as clinical training in the diagnosis and treatment of eye disorders. Courses in pharmacology, optics, vision science, biochemistry, and systemic disease are included.

Business ability, self-discipline, and the ability to deal tactfully with patients are important for success. The work of optometrists requires attention to detail and manual dexterity.

Optometrists wishing to teach or conduct research may study for a master's or Ph.D. degree in visual science, physiological optics, neurophysiology, public health, health administration, health information and communication, or health education. One-year postgraduate clinical residency programs are available for optometrists who wish to obtain advanced clinical competence. Specialty areas for residency programs include family practice optometry, pediatric optometry, geriatric optometry, vision therapy and rehabilitation, low-vision rehabilitation, cornea and contact lenses, refractive and ocular surgery, primary eye care optometry, and ocular disease.

Employment

Optometrists held about 34,000 jobs in 2004. The number of jobs is greater than the number of practicing optometrists because some optometrists hold two or more jobs. For example, an optometrist may have a private practice but also work in another practice, in a clinic, or in a vision care center. According to the American Optometric Association, about three-fourths of practicing optometrists are in private practice. Although many practice alone, optometrists increasingly are in a partnership or group practice.

Salaried jobs for optometrists were primarily in offices of optometrists; offices of physicians, including ophthalmologists; and health and personal care stores, including optical goods stores. A few salaried jobs for optometrists were in hospitals, the federal government, or outpatient care centers, including health maintenance organizations. Almost one third of optometrists were self-employed and not incorporated.

Job Outlook

Employment of optometrists is expected to grow faster than the average for all occupations through 2014 in response to the vision care needs of a growing and aging population. As baby boomers age, they will be more likely to visit optometrists and ophthalmologists because of the onset of vision problems in middle age, including those resulting from the extensive use of computers. The demand for optometric services also will increase because of growth in the oldest age group, with its increased likelihood of cataracts, glaucoma, diabetes, and hypertension. Greater recognition of the importance of vision care, along with rising personal incomes and growth in employee vision care plans, also will spur job growth.

Employment of optometrists would grow more rapidly were it not for anticipated productivity gains that will allow each optometrist to see more patients. These expected gains stem from greater use of optometric assistants and other support personnel, who will reduce the amount of time optometrists need with each patient. Also, laser surgery that can correct some vision problems is available, and although optometrists still will be needed to provide preoperative and postoperative care for laser surgery patients, patients who successfully undergo this surgery may not require optometrists to prescribe glasses or contacts for several years.

In addition to growth, the need to replace optometrists who retire or leave the occupation for another reason will create employment opportunities.

Earnings

Median annual earnings of salaried optometrists were $88,410 in May 2004. The middle 50 percent earned between $63,840 and $118,320. Median annual earnings of salaried optometrists in May 2004 were $87,430 in offices of optometrists. Salaried optometrists tend to earn more initially than do optometrists who set up their own practices. In the long run, however, those in private practice usually earn more.

According to the American Optometric Association, median net annual income for all optometrists, including the self-employed, was $114,000 in 2004. The middle 50 percent earned between $84,000 and $166,000.

Related Occupations

Other workers who apply scientific knowledge to prevent, diagnose, and treat disorders and injuries are chiropractors, dentists, physicians and surgeons, psychologists, podiatrists, and veterinarians.

Sources of Additional Information

For information on optometry as a career and a list of accredited optometric institutions of education, contact

▸ Association of Schools and Colleges of Optometry, 6110 Executive Blvd., Suite 510, Rockville, MD 20852. Internet: http://www.opted.org

Additional career information is available from

▸ American Optometric Association, Educational Services, 243 North Lindbergh Blvd., St. Louis, MO 63141. Internet: http://www.aoanet.org

The board of optometry in each state can supply information on licensing requirements.

For information on specific admission requirements and sources of financial aid, contact the admissions officers of individual optometry schools.

Pharmacists

(O*NET 29-1051.00)

Significant Points

■ Very good employment opportunities are expected for pharmacists.

■ Earnings are high, but some pharmacists work long hours, nights, weekends, and holidays.

■ Pharmacists are becoming more involved in making decisions regarding drug therapy and in counseling patients.

■ A license is required; the prospective pharmacist must graduate from an accredited college of pharmacy and pass a state examination.

Nature of the Work

Pharmacists distribute drugs prescribed by physicians and other health practitioners and provide information to patients about medications and their use. They advise physicians and other health practitioners on the selection, dosages, interactions, and side effects of medications. Pharmacists also monitor the health and progress of patients in response to drug therapy to ensure the safe and effective use of medication. Pharmacists must understand the use, clinical effects, and composition of drugs, including their chemical, biological, and physical properties. Compounding—the actual mixing of ingredients to form powders, tablets, capsules, ointments, and solutions—is a small part of a pharmacist's practice because most medicines are produced by pharmaceutical companies in a standard dosage and drug delivery form. Most pharmacists work in a community setting, such as a retail drugstore, or in a health care facility, such as a hospital, nursing home, mental health institution, or neighborhood health clinic.

Pharmacists in community and retail pharmacies counsel patients and answer questions about prescription drugs, including questions regarding possible side effects or interactions among various drugs. They provide information about over-the-counter drugs and make recommendations after talking with the patient. They also may give advice about the patient's diet, exercise, or stress management or about durable medical equipment and home health care supplies. In addition, they also may complete third-party insurance forms and other paperwork. Those who own or manage community pharmacies may sell non-health-related merchandise, hire and supervise personnel, and oversee the general operation of the pharmacy. Some community pharmacists provide specialized services to help patients manage conditions such as diabetes, asthma, smoking cessation, or high blood pressure. Some community pharmacists also are trained to administer vaccinations.

Pharmacists in health care facilities dispense medications and advise the medical staff on the selection and effects of drugs. They may make sterile solutions to be administered intravenously. They also assess, plan, and monitor drug programs or regimens. Pharmacists counsel hospitalized patients on the use of drugs and on their use at home when the patients are discharged. Pharmacists also may evaluate drug-use patterns and outcomes for patients in hospitals or managed care organizations.

Pharmacists who work in home health care monitor drug therapy and prepare infusions—solutions that are injected into patients—and other medications for use in the home.

Some pharmacists specialize in specific drug therapy areas, such as intravenous nutrition support, oncology (cancer), nuclear pharmacy (used for chemotherapy), geriatric pharmacy, and psychopharmacotherapy (the treatment of mental disorders by means of drugs).

Most pharmacists keep confidential computerized records of patients' drug therapies to prevent harmful drug interactions. Pharmacists are responsible for the accuracy of every prescription that is filled, but they often rely upon pharmacy technicians and pharmacy aides to assist them in the dispensing process. Thus, the pharmacist may delegate prescription-filling and administrative tasks and supervise their completion. Pharmacists also frequently oversee pharmacy students serving as interns in preparation for graduation and licensure.

Increasingly, pharmacists are pursuing nontraditional pharmacy work. Some are involved in research for pharmaceutical manufacturers, developing new drugs and therapies and testing their effects on people. Others work in marketing or sales, providing expertise to

clients on a drug's use, effectiveness, and possible side effects. Some pharmacists work for health insurance companies, developing pharmacy benefit packages and carrying out cost-benefit analyses on certain drugs. Other pharmacists work for the government, public health care services, the armed services, and pharmacy associations. Finally, some pharmacists are employed full time or part time as college faculty, teaching classes and performing research in a wide range of areas.

Working Conditions

Pharmacists work in clean, well-lighted, and well-ventilated areas. Many pharmacists spend most of their workday on their feet. When working with sterile or dangerous pharmaceutical products, pharmacists wear gloves and masks and work with other special protective equipment. Many community and hospital pharmacies are open for extended hours or around the clock, so pharmacists may work nights, weekends, and holidays. Consultant pharmacists may travel to nursing homes or other facilities to monitor patients' drug therapy.

About 21 percent of pharmacists worked part time in 2004. Most full-time salaried pharmacists worked approximately 40 hours a week. Some, including many self-employed pharmacists, worked more than 50 hours a week.

Training, Other Qualifications, and Advancement

A license to practice pharmacy is required in all states, the District of Columbia, and all U.S. territories. To obtain a license, the prospective pharmacist must graduate from a college of pharmacy that is accredited by the Accreditation Council for Pharmacy Education (ACPE) and pass an examination. All states require the North American Pharmacist Licensure Exam (NAPLEX), which tests pharmacy skills and knowledge, and 43 states and the District of Columbia require the Multistate Pharmacy Jurisprudence Exam (MPJE), which tests pharmacy law. Both exams are administered by the National Association of Boards of Pharmacy. Pharmacists in the eight states that do not require the MPJE must pass a state-specific exam that is similar to the MPJE. In addition to the NAPLEX and MPJE, some states require additional exams unique to their state. All states except California currently grant a license without extensive reexamination to qualified pharmacists who already are licensed by another state. In Florida, reexamination is not required if a pharmacist has passed the NAPLEX and MPJE within 12 years of his or her application for a license transfer. Many pharmacists are licensed to practice in more than one state. Most states require continuing education for license renewal. Persons interested in a career as a pharmacist should check with individual state boards of pharmacy for details on examination requirements, license renewal requirements, and license transfer procedures.

In 2004, 89 colleges of pharmacy were accredited to confer degrees by the Accreditation Council for Pharmacy Education. Pharmacy programs grant the degree of Doctor of Pharmacy (Pharm.D.), which requires at least 6 years of postsecondary study and the passing of a state board of pharmacy's licensure examination. Courses offered at colleges of pharmacy are designed to teach students about all aspects of drug therapy. In addition, schools teach students how to communicate with patients and other health care providers about drug information and patient care. Students also learn professional ethics, how to develop and manage medication distribution systems, and concepts of public health. In addition to receiving classroom instruction, students in Pharm.D. programs spend about one-fourth of their time learning in a variety of pharmacy practice settings under the supervision of licensed pharmacists. The Pharm.D. degree has replaced the Bachelor of Pharmacy (B.Pharm.) degree, which is no longer being awarded.

The Pharm.D. is a 4-year program that requires at least 2 years of college study prior to admittance, although most applicants have completed 3 years. Entry requirements usually include courses in mathematics and natural sciences, such as chemistry, biology, and physics, as well as courses in the humanities and social sciences. Approximately two-thirds of all colleges require applicants to take the Pharmacy College Admissions Test (PCAT).

In 2003, the American Association of Colleges of Pharmacy (AACP) launched the Pharmacy College Application Service, known as PharmCAS, for students who are interested in applying to schools and colleges of pharmacy. This centralized service allows applicants to use a single Web-based application and one set of transcripts to apply to multiple schools of pharmacy. A total of 43 schools participated in 2003.

In the 2003–2004 academic year, 67 colleges of pharmacy awarded the master of science degree or the Ph.D. degree. Both degrees are awarded after the completion of a Pharm.D. degree and are designed for those who want more laboratory and research experience. Many master's and Ph.D. degree holders do research for a drug company or teach at a university. Other options for pharmacy graduates who are interested in further training include 1-year or 2-year residency programs or fellowships. Pharmacy residencies are postgraduate training programs in pharmacy practice and usually require the completion of a research study. There currently are more than 700 residency training programs nationwide. Pharmacy fellowships are highly individualized programs that are designed to prepare participants to work in a specialized area of pharmacy, such as clinical practice or research laboratories. Some pharmacists who run their own pharmacy obtain a master's degree in business administration (MBA). Others may obtain a degree in public administration or public health.

Areas of graduate study include pharmaceutics and pharmaceutical chemistry (physical and chemical properties of drugs and dosage forms), pharmacology (effects of drugs on the body), toxicology, and pharmacy administration.

Prospective pharmacists should have scientific aptitude, good communication skills, and a desire to help others. They also must be conscientious and pay close attention to detail because the decisions they make affect human lives.

In community pharmacies, pharmacists usually begin at the staff level. In independent pharmacies, after they gain experience and secure the necessary capital, some become owners or part owners of pharmacies. Pharmacists in chain drugstores may be promoted to pharmacy supervisor or manager at the store level, then to manager at the district or regional level, and later to an executive position within the chain's headquarters.

Hospital pharmacists may advance to supervisory or administrative positions. Pharmacists in the pharmaceutical industry may advance in marketing, sales, research, quality control, production, packaging, or other areas.

Employment

Pharmacists held about 230,000 jobs in 2004. About 61 percent work in community pharmacies that are either independently owned or part of a drugstore chain, grocery store, department store, or mass merchandiser. Most community pharmacists are salaried employees, but some are self-employed owners. About 24 percent of salaried pharmacists work in hospitals. Others work in clinics, mail-order pharmacies, pharmaceutical wholesalers, home health care agencies, or the federal government.

Job Outlook

Very good employment opportunities are expected for pharmacists over the 2004–2014 period because the number of job openings created by employment growth and the need to replace pharmacists who leave the occupation or retire are expected to exceed the number of degrees granted in pharmacy. Enrollments in pharmacy programs are rising as more students are attracted by high salaries and good job prospects. Despite this increase in enrollments, job openings should still be more numerous than those seeking employment.

Employment of pharmacists is expected to grow faster than the average for all occupations through the year 2014 because of the increasing demand for pharmaceuticals, particularly from the growing elderly population. The increasing numbers of middle-aged and elderly people—who use more prescription drugs than younger people—will continue to spur demand for pharmacists in all employment settings. Other factors likely to increase the demand for pharmacists include scientific advances that will make more drug products available, new developments in genome research and medication distribution systems, increasingly sophisticated consumers seeking more information about drugs, and coverage of prescription drugs by a greater number of health insurance plans and Medicare.

Community pharmacies are taking steps to manage an increasing volume of prescriptions. Automation of drug dispensing and greater employment of pharmacy technicians and pharmacy aides will help these establishments to dispense more prescriptions.

With its emphasis on cost control, managed care encourages the use of lower-cost prescription drug distributors, such as mail-order firms and online pharmacies, for purchases of certain medications. Prescriptions ordered through the mail and via the Internet are filled in a central location and shipped to the patient at a lower cost. Mail-order and online pharmacies typically use automated technology to dispense medication and employ fewer pharmacists. If the utilization of mail-order pharmacies increases rapidly, job growth among pharmacists could be limited.

Employment of pharmacists will not grow as fast in hospitals as in other industries because hospitals are reducing inpatient stays, downsizing, and consolidating departments. The number of outpatient surgeries is increasing, so more patients are being discharged and purchasing their medications through retail, supermarket, or mail-order pharmacies rather than through hospitals. An aging population means that more pharmacy services will be required in nursing homes, assisted-living facilities, and home care settings. The most rapid job growth among pharmacists is expected in these 3 settings.

New opportunities are emerging for pharmacists in managed care organizations where they analyze trends and patterns in medication use and in pharmacoeconomics—the cost and benefit analysis of different drug therapies. Opportunities also are emerging for pharmacists trained in research and disease management—the development of new methods for curing and controlling diseases. Pharmacists also are finding jobs in research and development and in sales and marketing for pharmaceutical manufacturing firms. New breakthroughs in biotechnology will increase the potential for drugs to treat diseases and expand the opportunities for pharmacists to conduct research and sell medications. In addition, pharmacists are finding employment opportunities in pharmacy informatics, which uses information technology to improve patient care.

Job opportunities for pharmacists in patient care will arise as cost-conscious insurers and health systems continue to emphasize the role of pharmacists in primary and preventive health care. Health insurance companies realize that the expense of using medication to treat diseases and various health conditions often is considerably less than the costs for patients whose conditions go untreated. Pharmacists also can reduce the expenses resulting from unexpected complications due to allergic reactions or interactions among medications.

Earnings

Median annual wage and salary earnings of pharmacists in May 2004 were $84,900. The middle 50 percent earned between $75,720 and $94,850 a year. The lowest 10 percent earned less than $61,200, and the highest 10 percent earned more than $109,850 a year. Median annual earnings in the industries employing the largest numbers of pharmacists in May 2004 were

Department stores	$86,720
Grocery stores	85,680
Health and personal care stores	85,380
General medical and surgical hospitals	84,560
Other general merchandise stores	84,170

Related Occupations

Pharmacy technicians and pharmacy aides also work in pharmacies. Persons in other professions who may work with pharmaceutical compounds include biological scientists, medical scientists, and chemists and materials scientists. Increasingly, pharmacists are involved in patient care and therapy, work that they have in common with physicians and surgeons.

Sources of Additional Information

For information on pharmacy as a career, preprofessional and professional requirements, programs offered by colleges of pharmacy, and student financial aid, contact

▸ American Association of Colleges of Pharmacy, 1426 Prince St., Alexandria, VA 22314. Internet: http://www.aacp.org

General information on careers in pharmacy is available from

▸ American Society of Health-System Pharmacists, 7272 Wisconsin Ave., Bethesda, MD 20814. Internet: http://www.ashp.org

▸ National Association of Chain Drug Stores, 413 N. Lee St., P.O. Box 1417-D49, Alexandria, VA 22313-1480. Internet: http://www.nacds.org

▸ Academy of Managed Care Pharmacy, 100 North Pitt St., Suite 400, Alexandria, VA 22314. Internet: http://www.amcp.org

▸ American Pharmacists Association, 2215 Constitution Ave. NW, Washington, DC 20037-2985. Internet: http://www.aphanet.org

Information on the North American Pharmacist Licensure Exam (NAPLEX) and the Multistate Pharmacy Jurisprudence Exam (MPJE) is available from

▸ National Association of Boards of Pharmacy, 1600 Feehanville Dr., Mount Prospect, IL 60056. Internet: http://www.nabp.net

State licensure requirements are available from each state's board of pharmacy. Information on specific college entrance requirements, curriculums, and financial aid is available from any college of pharmacy.

Physicians and Surgeons

(O*NET 29-1061.00, 29-1062.00, 29-1063.00, 29-1064.00, 29-1065.00, 29-1066.00, 29-1067.00, and 29-1069.99)

Significant Points

■ Many physicians and surgeons work long, irregular hours; over one-third of full-time physicians worked 60 or more hours a week in 2004.

■ Formal education and training requirements are among the most demanding of any occupation, but earnings are among the highest.

■ Job opportunities should be very good, particularly in rural and low-income areas.

■ New physicians are much less likely to enter solo practice and more likely to work as salaried employees of group medical practices, clinics, hospitals, or health networks.

Nature of the Work

Physicians and surgeons serve a fundamental role in our society and have an effect upon all our lives. They diagnose illnesses and prescribe and administer treatment for people suffering from injury or disease. Physicians examine patients; obtain medical histories; and order, perform, and interpret diagnostic tests. They counsel patients on diet, hygiene, and preventive health care.

There are two types of physicians: M.D.—*Doctor of Medicine*—and D.O.—*Doctor of Osteopathic Medicine.* M.D.s also are known as *allopathic physicians.* While both M.D.s and D.O.s may use all accepted methods of treatment, including drugs and surgery, D.O.s place special emphasis on the body's musculoskeletal system, preventive medicine, and holistic patient care. D.O.s are more likely than M.D.s to be primary care specialists, although they can be found in all specialties. About half of D.O.s practice general or family medicine, general internal medicine, or general pediatrics.

Physicians work in one or more of several specialties, including, but not limited to, anesthesiology, family and general medicine, general internal medicine, general pediatrics, obstetrics and gynecology, psychiatry, and surgery.

Anesthesiologists. Anesthesiologists focus on the care of surgical patients and pain relief. Like other physicians, they evaluate and treat patients and direct the efforts of those on their staffs. Anesthesiologists confer with other physicians and surgeons about appropriate treatments and procedures before, during, and after operations. These critical-care specialists are responsible for maintenance of the patient's vital life functions—heart rate, body temperature, blood pressure, breathing—through continual monitoring and assessment during surgery. They often work outside of the operating room, providing pain relief in the intensive care unit, during labor and delivery, and for those who suffer from chronic pain.

Family and general practitioners. Family and general practitioners are often the first point of contact for people seeking health care, acting as the traditional family doctor. They assess and treat a wide range of conditions, ailments, and injuries, from sinus and respiratory infections to broken bones and scrapes. Family and general practitioners typically have a patient base of regular, long-term visitors. Patients with more serious conditions are referred to specialists or other health care facilities for more intensive care.

General internists. General internists diagnose and provide non-surgical treatment for diseases and injuries of internal organ systems. They provide care mainly for adults who have a wide range of problems associated with the internal organs, such as the stomach, kidneys, liver, and digestive tract. Internists use a variety of diagnostic techniques to treat patients through medication or hospitalization. Like general practitioners, general internists are commonly looked upon as primary care specialists. They have patients referred to them by other specialists, in turn referring patients to those and yet other specialists when more complex care is required.

General pediatricians. Providing care from birth to early adulthood, pediatricians are concerned with the health of infants, children, and teenagers. They specialize in the diagnosis and treatment of a variety of ailments specific to young people and track their patients' growth to adulthood. Like most physicians, pediatricians work with different health care workers, such as nurses and other physicians, to assess and treat children with various ailments, such as muscular dystrophy. Most of the work of pediatricians, however, involves treating day-to-day illnesses that are common to children—minor injuries, infectious diseases, and immunizations—much as a general practitioner treats adults. Some pediatricians specialize in serious medical conditions and pediatric surgery, treating autoimmune disorders or serious chronic ailments.

Obstetricians and gynecologists. Obstetricians and gynecologists (OB/GYNs) are specialists whose focus is women's health. They are responsible for general medical care for women, but also provide care related to pregnancy and the reproductive system. Like general practitioners, OB/GYNs are concerned with the prevention, diagnosis, and treatment of general health problems, but they focus on ailments specific to the female anatomy, such as breast and cervical cancer, urinary tract and pelvic disorders, and hormonal disorders. OB/GYNs also specialize in childbirth, treating and counseling women throughout their pregnancy, from giving prenatal diagnoses to delivery and postpartum care. OB/GYNs track the health of, and treat, both mother and fetus as the pregnancy progresses.

Psychiatrists. Psychiatrists are the primary caregivers in the area of mental health. They assess and treat mental illnesses through a combination of psychotherapy, psychoanalysis, hospitalization, and medication. Psychotherapy involves regular discussions with patients about their problems; the psychiatrist helps them find solutions through changes in their behavioral patterns, the exploration of their past experiences, and group and family therapy sessions. Psychoanalysis involves long-term psychotherapy and counseling for patients. In many cases, medications are administered to correct chemical imbalances that may be causing emotional problems. Psychiatrists may also administer electroconvulsive therapy to those of their patients who do not respond to, or who cannot take, medications.

Surgeons. Surgeons are physicians who specialize in the treatment of injury, disease, and deformity through operations. Using a variety of instruments, and with patients under general or local anesthesia, a surgeon corrects physical deformities, repairs bone and tissue after injuries, or performs preventive surgeries on patients with debilitating diseases or disorders. Although a large number perform general surgery, many surgeons choose to specialize in a specific area. One of the most prevalent specialties is orthopedic surgery: the treatment of the musculoskeletal system. Others include neurological surgery (treatment of the brain and nervous system), cardiovascular surgery, otolaryngology (treatment of the ear, nose, and throat), and plastic or reconstructive surgery. Like primary care and other specialist physicians, surgeons also examine patients, perform and interpret diagnostic tests, and counsel patients on preventive health care.

A number of other medical specialists, including allergists, cardiologists, dermatologists, emergency physicians, gastroenterologists, ophthalmologists, pathologists, and radiologists, also work in clinics, hospitals, and private offices.

Working Conditions

Many physicians—primarily general and family practitioners, general internists, pediatricians, OB/GYNs, and psychiatrists—work in small private offices or clinics, often assisted by a small staff of nurses and other administrative personnel. Increasingly, physicians are practicing in groups or health care organizations that provide backup coverage and allow for more time off. These physicians often work as part of a team coordinating care for a population of patients; they are less independent than solo practitioners of the past.

Surgeons and anesthesiologists typically work in well-lighted, sterile environments while performing surgery and often stand for long periods. Most work in hospitals or in surgical outpatient centers. Many physicians and surgeons work long, irregular hours. Over one-third of full-time physicians and surgeons worked 60 hours or more a week in 2004. Only 8 percent of all physicians and surgeons worked part time, compared with 16 percent for all occupations. Physicians and surgeons must travel frequently between office and hospital to care for their patients. Those who are on call deal with many patients' concerns over the phone and may make emergency visits to hospitals or nursing homes.

Training, Other Qualifications, and Advancement

Formal education and training requirements for physicians are among the most demanding of any occupation—4 years of undergraduate school, 4 years of medical school, and 3 to 8 years of internship and residency, depending on the specialty selected. A few medical schools offer combined undergraduate and medical school programs that last 6 rather than the customary 8 years.

Premedical students must complete undergraduate work in physics, biology, mathematics, English, and inorganic and organic chemistry. Students also take courses in the humanities and the social sciences. Some students volunteer at local hospitals or clinics to gain practical experience in the health professions.

The minimum educational requirement for entry into a medical school is 3 years of college; most applicants, however, have at least a bachelor's degree, and many have advanced degrees. There are 146 medical schools in the United States—126 teach allopathic medicine and award a Doctor of Medicine (M.D.) degree; 20 teach osteopathic medicine and award the Doctor of Osteopathic Medicine (D.O.) degree. Acceptance to medical school is highly competitive. Applicants must submit transcripts, scores from the Medical College Admission Test, and letters of recommendation. Schools also consider an applicant's character, personality, leadership qualities, and participation in extracurricular activities. Most schools require an interview with members of the admissions committee.

Students spend most of the first 2 years of medical school in laboratories and classrooms, taking courses such as anatomy, biochemistry, physiology, pharmacology, psychology, microbiology, pathology, medical ethics, and laws governing medicine. They also learn to take medical histories, examine patients, and diagnose illnesses. During their last 2 years, students work with patients under the supervision of experienced physicians in hospitals and clinics, learning acute, chronic, preventive, and rehabilitative care. Through rotations in internal medicine, family practice, obstetrics and gynecology, pediatrics, psychiatry, and surgery, they gain experience in the diagnosis and treatment of illness.

Following medical school, almost all M.D.s enter a residency—graduate medical education in a specialty that takes the form of paid on-the-job training, usually in a hospital. Most D.O.s serve a 12-month rotating internship after graduation and before entering a residency, which may last 2 to 6 years.

All states, the District of Columbia, and U.S. territories license physicians. To be licensed, physicians must graduate from an accredited medical school, pass a licensing examination, and complete 1 to 7 years of graduate medical education. Although physicians licensed in one state usually can get a license to practice in another without further examination, some states limit reciprocity. Graduates of foreign medical schools generally can qualify for licensure after passing an examination and completing a U.S. residency.

M.D.s and D.O.s seeking board certification in a specialty may spend up to 7 years in residency training, depending on the specialty. A final examination immediately after residency or after 1 or 2 years of practice also is necessary for certification by a member board of the American Board of Medical Specialists (ABMS) or the American Osteopathic Association (AOA). The ABMS represents 24 specialty boards, ranging from allergy and immunology to urology. The AOA has approved 18 specialty boards, ranging from anesthesiology to surgery. For certification in a subspecialty, physicians usually need another 1 to 2 years of residency.

A physician's training is costly. According to the Association of American Medical Colleges, in 2004 more than 80 percent of medical school graduates were in debt for educational expenses.

People who wish to become physicians must have a desire to serve patients, be self-motivated, and be able to survive the pressures and long hours of medical education and practice. Physicians also must have a good bedside manner, emotional stability, and the ability to make decisions in emergencies. Prospective physicians must be willing to study throughout their career in order to keep up with medical advances.

Employment

Physicians and surgeons held about 567,000 jobs in 2004; approximately 1 out of 7 was self-employed and not incorporated. About 60 percent of salaried physicians and surgeons were in office of physicians, and 16 percent were employed by private hospitals. Others practiced in federal, state, and local governments, including hospitals, colleges, universities, and professional schools; private colleges, universities, and professional schools; and outpatient care centers.

According to the American Medical Association (AMA), in 2003 about 2 out 5 physicians in patient care were in primary care, but not in a subspecialty of primary care (table 1).

Table 1. Percent distribution of physicians by specialty, 2003

	Percent
Total	100.0
Primary care	40.8
Family medicine and general practice	12.8
Internal medicine	15.1
Obstetrics & gynecology	5.3
Pediatrics	7.6
Specialties	59.2
Anesthesiology	5.4
Psychiatry	5.4
Surgical specialties, selected	14.6
All other specialties	33.9

Source: American Medical Association, Physician Characteristics and Distribution in the U.S., 2005.

A growing number of physicians are partners or salaried employees of group practices. Organized as clinics or as associations of physicians, medical groups can afford expensive medical equipment and realize other business advantages.

According to the AMA, the New England and Middle Atlantic states have the highest ratio of physicians to population; the South Central and Mountain states have the lowest. D.O.s are more likely than M.D.s to practice in small cities and towns and in rural areas. M.D.s tend to locate in urban areas, close to hospital and education centers.

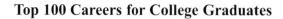
Job Outlook

Employment of physicians and surgeons is projected to grow faster than the average for all occupations through the year 2014 due to the continued expansion of health care industries. The growing and aging population will drive overall growth in the demand for physician services as consumers continue to demand high levels of care using the latest technologies, diagnostic tests, and therapies. In addition to employment growth, job openings will result from the need to replace physicians and surgeons who retire over the 2004–2014 period.

Demand for physicians' services is highly sensitive to changes in consumer preferences, health care reimbursement policies, and legislation. For example, if changes to health coverage result in consumers facing higher out-of-pocket costs, they may demand fewer physician services. Demand for physician services may also be tempered by patients relying more on other health care providers—such as physician assistants, nurse practitioners, optometrists, and nurse anesthetists—for some health care services. In addition, new technologies will increase physician productivity. Telemedicine will allow physicians to treat patients or consult with other providers remotely. Increasing use of electronic medical records, test and prescription orders, billing, and scheduling will also improve physician productivity.

Opportunities for individuals interested in becoming physicians and surgeons are expected to be very good. Reports of shortages in some specialties or geographic areas should attract new entrants, encouraging schools to expand programs and hospitals to expand available residency slots. However, because physician training is so lengthy, employment change happens gradually. In the short term, to meet increased demand, experienced physicians may work longer hours; delay retirement; or take measures to increase productivity, such as using more support staff to provide services. Opportunities should be particularly good in rural and low-income areas because some physicians find these areas unattractive due to less control over work hours, isolation from medical colleagues, or other reasons.

Unlike their predecessors, newly trained physicians face radically different choices of where and how to practice. New physicians are much less likely to enter solo practice and more likely to take salaried jobs in group medical practices, clinics, and health networks.

Earnings

Earnings of physicians and surgeons are among the highest of any occupation. According to the Medical Group Management Association's Physician Compensation and Production Survey, median total compensation for physicians in 2004 varied by specialty, as shown in table 2. Total compensation for physicians reflects the amount reported as direct compensation for tax purposes, plus all voluntary salary reductions. Salary, bonus and/or incentive payments, research stipends, honoraria, and distribution of profits were included in total compensation.

Table 2. Median total compensation of physicians by specialty, 2004

	Less than two years in specialty	More than one year in specialty
Anesthesiology	$259,948	$321,686
Surgery: General	228,839	282,504
Obstetrics/gynecology: General	203,270	247,348
Psychiatry: General	173,922	180,000
Internal medicine: General	141,912	166,420
Pediatrics: General	132,953	161,331
Family practice (without obstetrics)	137,119	156,010

Source: Medical Group Management Association, Physician Compensation and Production Report, 2005.

Self-employed physicians—those who own or are part owners of their medical practice—generally have higher median incomes than salaried physicians. Earnings vary according to number of years in practice; geographic region; hours worked; and skill, personality, and professional reputation. Self-employed physicians and surgeons must provide for their own health insurance and retirement.

Related Occupations

Physicians work to prevent, diagnose, and treat diseases, disorders, and injuries. Other health care practitioners who need similar skills and who exercise critical judgment include chiropractors, dentists, optometrists, physician assistants, podiatrists, registered nurses, and veterinarians.

Sources of Additional Information

For a list of medical schools and residency programs, as well as general information on premedical education, financial aid, and medicine as a career, contact

▸ Association of American Medical Colleges, Section for Student Services, 2450 N St. NW, Washington, DC 20037-1126. Internet: http://www.aamc.org

▸ American Association of Colleges of Osteopathic Medicine, 5550 Friendship Blvd., Suite 310, Chevy Chase, MD 20815-7231. Internet: http://www.aacom.org

For general information on physicians, contact

▸ American Medical Association, 515 N. State St., Chicago, IL 60610. Internet: http://www.ama-assn.org

▸ American Osteopathic Association, Division of Communications, 142 East Ontario St., Chicago, IL 60611. Internet: http://www.osteopathic.org

For information about various medical specialties, contact

▸ American Board of Medical Specialties, 1007 Church St., Suite 404, Evanston, IL 60201-5913. Internet: http://www.abms.org

▸ American Society of Anesthesiologists, 520 N. Northwest Hwy., Park Ridge, IL 60068-2573. Internet: http://www.asahq.org

▸ American Academy of Family Physicians, Resident Student Activities Department, 11400 Tomahawk Creek Pkwy., Leawood, KS 66211-2672. Internet: http://fmignet.aafp.org

▶ American College of Physicians, 190 North Independence Mall West, Philadelphia, PA 19106. Internet: http://www.acponline.org

▶ American College of Obstetricians and Gynecologists, 409 12th St. SW, P.O. Box 96920, Washington, DC 20090-6920. Internet: http://www.acog.org

▶ American Academy of Pediatrics, 141 Northwest Point Blvd., Elk Grove Village, IL 60007-1098. Internet: http://www.aap.org

▶ American Psychiatric Association, 1000 Wilson Blvd., Suite 1825, Arlington, VA 22209-3901. Internet: http://www.psych.org

▶ American College of Surgeons, Division of Education, 633 North Saint Clair St., Chicago, IL 60611-3211. Internet: http://www.facs.org

Information on federal scholarships and loans is available from the directors of student financial aid at schools of medicine.

Information on licensing is available from state boards of examiners.

Physicists and Astronomers

(O*NET 19-2011.00 and 19-2012.00)

Significant Points

■ Scientific research and development services firms and the federal government employ 3 out of 5 physicists and astronomers.

■ Most jobs are in basic research and development, usually requiring a doctoral degree; master's degree holders qualify for many jobs in applied research and development, while bachelor's degree holders often qualify as technicians, research assistants, or other types of jobs.

■ Employment is expected to grow more slowly than average.

■ Competition for jobs is expected; however, graduates with a physics or astronomy degree at any level will find their knowledge of science and mathematics useful for entry to many other occupations.

Nature of the Work

Physicists explore and identify basic principles and laws governing motion and gravitation; the macroscopic and microscopic behavior of gases; and the structure and behavior of matter, the generation and transfer between energy, and the interaction of matter and energy. Some physicists use these principles in theoretical areas, such as the nature of time and the origin of the universe; others apply their knowledge of physics to practical areas, such as the development of advanced materials, electronic and optical devices, and medical equipment.

Physicists design and perform experiments with lasers, particle accelerators, telescopes, mass spectrometers, and other equipment. On the basis of their observations and analysis, they attempt to discover and explain laws describing the forces of nature, such as gravity, electromagnetism, and nuclear interactions. Physicists also find ways to apply physical laws and theories to problems in nuclear energy, electronics, optics, materials, communications, aerospace technology, and medical instrumentation.

Astronomy is sometimes considered a subfield of physics. *Astronomers* use the principles of physics and mathematics to learn about the fundamental nature of the universe, including the sun, moon, planets, stars, and galaxies. They also apply their knowledge to solve problems in navigation, space flight, and satellite communications and to develop the instrumentation and techniques used to observe and collect astronomical data.

Most physicists work in research and development. Some do basic research to increase scientific knowledge. Physicists who conduct applied research build upon the discoveries made through basic research and work to develop new devices, products, and processes. For example, basic research in solid-state physics led to the development of transistors and then integrated circuits used in computers.

Physicists also design research equipment, which often has additional unanticipated uses. For example, lasers are used in surgery, microwave devices function in ovens, and measuring instruments can analyze blood or the chemical content of foods. A small number of physicists work in inspection, testing, quality control, and other production-related jobs in industry.

Much physics research is done in small or medium-sized laboratories. However, experiments in plasma, nuclear, and high-energy physics, as well as in some other areas of physics, require extremely large, expensive equipment, such as particle accelerators. Physicists in these subfields often work in large teams. Although physics research may require extensive experimentation in laboratories, research physicists still spend time in offices planning, recording, analyzing, and reporting on research.

Almost all astronomers do research. Some are theoreticians, working on the laws governing the structure and evolution of astronomical objects. Others analyze large quantities of data gathered by observatories and satellites and write scientific papers or reports on their findings. Some astronomers actually operate large space- or ground-based telescopes, usually as part of a team. However, astronomers may spend only a few weeks each year making observations with optical telescopes, radio telescopes, and other instruments. For many years, satellites and other space-based instruments, such as the Hubble space telescope, have provided prodigious amounts of astronomical data. New technology resulting in improvements in analytical techniques and instruments, such as computers and optical telescopes and mounts, is leading to a resurgence in ground-based research. A small number of astronomers work in museums housing planetariums. These astronomers develop and revise programs presented to the public and may direct planetarium operations.

Physicists generally specialize in one of many subfields: elementary particle physics, nuclear physics, atomic and molecular physics, physics of condensed matter (solid-state physics), optics, acoustics, space physics, plasma physics, or the physics of fluids. Some specialize in a subdivision of one of these subfields. For example, within condensed-matter physics, specialties include superconductivity, crystallography, and semiconductors. However, all physics involves the same fundamental principles, so specialties may overlap and physicists may switch from one subfield to another. Also, growing numbers of physicists work in interdisciplinary fields, such as biophysics, chemical physics, and geophysics.

Working Conditions

Physicists often work regular hours in laboratories and offices. At times, however, those who are deeply involved in research may work long or irregular hours. Most do not encounter unusual hazards in their work. Some physicists temporarily work away from home at national or international facilities with unique equipment, such as particle accelerators. Astronomers who make observations with ground-based telescopes may spend long periods in observatories; this work usually involves travel to remote locations and may require long hours, including night work.

Physicists and astronomers whose work depends on grant money often are under pressure to write grant proposals to keep their work funded.

Training, Other Qualifications, and Advancement

Because most jobs are in basic research and development, a doctoral degree is the usual educational requirement for physicists and astronomers. Additional experience and training in a postdoctoral research appointment, although not required, is important for physicists and astronomers aspiring to permanent positions in basic research in universities and government laboratories. Many physics and astronomy Ph.D. holders ultimately teach at the college or university level.

Master's degree holders usually do not qualify for basic research positions, but do qualify for many kinds of jobs requiring a physics background, including positions in manufacturing and applied research and development. Increasingly, many master's degree programs are specifically preparing students for physics-related research and development that does not require a Ph.D. degree. These programs teach students specific research skills that can be used in private-industry jobs. In addition, a master's degree coupled with state certification usually qualifies one for teaching jobs in high schools or at 2-year colleges.

Those with bachelor's degrees in physics are rarely qualified to fill positions in research or in teaching at the college level. They are, however, usually qualified to work as technicians or research assistants in engineering-related areas, in software development and other scientific fields, or in setting up computer networks and sophisticated laboratory equipment. Increasingly, some may qualify for applied research jobs in private industry or take on nontraditional physics roles, often in computer science, such as a systems analyst or database administrator. Some become science teachers in secondary schools. Holders of a bachelor's or master's degree in astronomy often enter an unrelated field. In addition, they are qualified to work in planetariums running science shows, to assist astronomers doing research, and to operate space-based and ground-based telescopes and other astronomical instrumentation. (See the descriptions of engineers, geoscientists, computer programmers, computer scientists and database administrators, computer software engineers, and computer systems analysts elsewhere in this book.)

About 510 colleges and universities offer a bachelor's degree in physics. Undergraduate programs provide a broad background in the natural sciences and mathematics. Typical physics courses include electromagnetism, optics, thermodynamics, atomic physics, and quantum mechanics.

Approximately 185 colleges and universities have departments offering Ph.D. degrees in physics; an additional 68 colleges offer a master's as their highest degree in physics. Graduate students usually concentrate in a subfield of physics, such as elementary particles or condensed matter. Many begin studying for their doctorate immediately after receiving their bachelor's degree.

About 80 universities grant degrees in astronomy, either through an astronomy, physics, or combined physics-astronomy department. Currently, about 40 departments are combined with the physics department and the same number are administered separately. With fewer than 40 doctoral programs in astronomy, applicants face considerable competition for available slots. Those planning a career in the subject should have a very strong physics background. In fact, an undergraduate degree in either physics or astronomy is excellent preparation, followed by a Ph.D. in astronomy.

Mathematical ability, problem-solving and analytical skills, an inquisitive mind, imagination, and initiative are important traits for anyone planning a career in physics or astronomy. Prospective physicists who hope to work in industrial laboratories applying physics knowledge to practical problems should broaden their educational background to include courses outside of physics, such as economics, information technology, and business management. Good oral and written communication skills also are important because many physicists work as part of a team, write research papers or proposals, or have contact with clients or customers with nonphysics backgrounds.

Many physics and astronomy Ph.D. holders begin their careers in a postdoctoral research position, in which they may work with experienced physicists as they continue to learn about their specialty and develop ideas and results to be used in later work. Initial work may be under the close supervision of senior scientists. After some experience, physicists perform increasingly complex tasks and work more independently. Those who develop new products or processes sometimes form their own companies or join new firms to exploit their own ideas. Experience, either in academic laboratories or through internships, fellowships, or work-study programs in industry, also is useful. Some employers of research physicists, particularly in the information technology industry, prefer to hire individuals with several years of postdoctoral experience.

Employment

Physicists and astronomers held about 16,000 jobs in 2004. Jobs for astronomers accounted for only 5 percent of the total. About 33 percent of physicists and astronomers worked for scientific research and development services firms. The federal government employed 25 percent, mostly in the U.S. Department of Defense, but also in the National Aeronautics and Space Administration (NASA) and in the U.S. Departments of Commerce, Health and Human Services, and Energy. Other physicists and astronomers worked in colleges and universities in nonfaculty—usually research—positions or for state governments, information technology companies, pharmaceutical and medicine manufacturing companies, or electronic equipment manufacturers.

In 2004, many physicists and astronomers held faculty positions in colleges and universities. (See the description of teachers—postsecondary elsewhere in this book.)

Although physicists and astronomers are employed in all parts of the country, most work in areas in which universities, large research and development laboratories, or observatories are located.

Job Outlook

Employment of physicists and astronomers is expected to grow more slowly than average for all occupations through 2014. Federal research expenditures are the major source of physics-related and astronomy-related research funds, especially for basic research. Although these expenditures are expected to increase over the 2004–2014 projection period, resulting in some growth in employment and opportunities, the limited science research funds available still will result in competition for basic research jobs among Ph.D. holders. The need to replace physicists and astronomers who retire or otherwise leave the occupation permanently will account for most expected job openings.

Although research and development expenditures in private industry will continue to grow, many research laboratories in private industry are expected to continue to reduce basic research, which includes much physics research, in favor of applied or manufacturing research and product and software development. Nevertheless, persons with a physics background continue to be in demand in the areas of information technology, semiconductor technology, and other applied sciences. This trend is expected to continue; however, many of the new workers will have job titles such as computer software engineer, computer programmer, or systems analyst or developer rather than physicist.

Throughout the 1990s, the number of doctorates granted in physics was much greater than the number of job openings for physicists, resulting in keen competition, particularly for research positions in colleges and universities and in research and development centers. Recent increases in undergraduate physics enrollments, however, may lead to growth in enrollments in graduate physics programs so that toward the end of the projection period, there may be an increase in the number of doctoral degrees granted that will intensify the competition for job openings.

Opportunities may be more numerous for those with a master's degree, particularly graduates from programs preparing students for applied research and development, product design, and manufacturing positions in private industry. Many of these positions, however, will have titles other than physicist, such as engineer or computer scientist.

Persons with only a bachelor's degree in physics or astronomy are not qualified to enter most physicist or astronomer research jobs, but may qualify for a wide range of positions related to engineering; mathematics; computer science; environmental science; and—for those with the appropriate background—some nonscience fields, such as finance. Those who meet state certification requirements can become high school physics teachers, an occupation in strong demand in many school districts. Most states require new teachers to obtain a master's degree in education within a certain time. Despite competition for traditional physics and astronomy

research jobs, graduates with a physics or astronomy degree at any level will find their knowledge of science and mathematics useful for entry into many other occupations.

Earnings

Median annual earnings of physicists were $87,450 in May 2004. The middle 50 percent earned between $66,590 and $109,420. The lowest 10 percent earned less than $49,450, and the highest 10 percent earned more than $132,780.

Median annual earnings of astronomers were $97,320 in May 2004. The middle 50 percent earned between $66,190 and $120,350, the lowest 10 percent less than $43,410, and the highest 10 percent more than $137,860.

According to a 2005 National Association of Colleges and Employers survey, the average annual starting salary offer to physics doctoral degree candidates was $56,070.

The American Institute of Physics reported a median annual salary of $104,000 in 2004 for its full-time members with Ph.D.s (excluding those in postdoctoral positions); the median was $94,000 for those with master's degrees and $72,000 for bachelor's degree holders. Those working in temporary postdoctoral positions earned significantly less.

The average annual salary for physicists employed by the federal government was $104,917 in 2005; for astronomy and space scientists, it was $110,195.

Related Occupations

The work of physicists and astronomers relates closely to that of engineers, chemists and materials scientists, atmospheric scientists, environmental scientists, geoscientists, computer systems analysts, computer scientists and database administrators, computer programmers, and mathematicians.

Sources of Additional Information

General information on career opportunities in physics is available from the following organizations:

▸ American Institute of Physics, Career Services Division and Education and Employment Division, One Physics Ellipse, College Park, MD 20740-3843. Internet: http://www.aip.org

▸ The American Physical Society, One Physics Ellipse, College Park, MD 20740-3844. Internet: http://www.aps.org

Podiatrists

(O*NET 29-1081.00)

Significant Points

■ Despite increasing demand for podiatric care, job openings for podiatrists are expected to be limited because the occupation is small and most podiatrists remain in it until they retire.

■ Opportunities for newly trained podiatrists will be better in group medical practices, clinics, and health networks than in traditional, solo practices.

■ Podiatrists need a state license that requires the completion of at least 90 hours of undergraduate study; a 4-year post-graduate program at a college of podiatric medicine; and, in most states, a postdoctoral residency program lasting at least 2 years.

■ Podiatrists enjoy very high earnings.

Nature of the Work

Americans spend a great deal of time on their feet. As the nation becomes more active across all age groups, the need for foot care will become increasingly important to maintaining a healthy lifestyle.

The human foot is a complex structure. It contains 26 bones—plus muscles, nerves, ligaments, and blood vessels—and is designed for balance and mobility. The 52 bones in the feet make up about one-fourth of all the bones in the human body. *Podiatrists,* also known as *doctors of podiatric medicine* (DPMs), diagnose and treat disorders, diseases, and injuries of the foot and lower leg.

Podiatrists treat corns, calluses, ingrown toenails, bunions, heel spurs, and arch problems; ankle and foot injuries, deformities, and infections; and foot complaints associated with diseases such as diabetes. To treat these problems, podiatrists prescribe drugs, order physical therapy, set fractures, and perform surgery. They also fit corrective inserts called orthotics, design plaster casts and strappings to correct deformities, and design custom-made shoes. Podiatrists may use a force plate or scanner to help design the orthotics: patients walk across a plate connected to a computer that "reads" their feet, picking up pressure points and weight distribution. From the computer readout, podiatrists order the correct design or recommend another kind of treatment.

To diagnose a foot problem, podiatrists also order X rays and laboratory tests. The foot may be the first area to show signs of serious conditions such as arthritis, diabetes, and heart disease. For example, patients with diabetes are prone to foot ulcers and infections due to poor circulation. Podiatrists consult with and refer patients to other health practitioners when they detect symptoms of these disorders.

Most podiatrists have a solo practice, although more are forming group practices with other podiatrists or health practitioners. Some specialize in surgery, orthopedics, primary care, or public health. Besides these board-certified specialties, podiatrists may practice other specialties, such as sports medicine, pediatrics, dermatology, radiology, geriatrics, or diabetic foot care.

Podiatrists who are in private practice are responsible for running a small business. They may hire employees, order supplies, and keep records, among other tasks. In addition, some educate the community on the benefits of foot care through speaking engagements and advertising.

Working Conditions

Podiatrists usually work in their own offices. They also may spend time visiting patients in nursing homes or performing surgery at hospitals or ambulatory surgical centers, but usually have fewer after-hours emergencies than other doctors have. Those with private practices set their own hours, but may work evenings and weekends to accommodate their patients.

Training, Other Qualifications, and Advancement

All states and the District of Columbia require a license for the practice of podiatric medicine. Each state defines its own licensing requirements, although many states grant reciprocity to podiatrists who are licensed in another state. Applicants for licensure must be graduates of an accredited college of podiatric medicine and must pass written and oral examinations. Some states permit applicants to substitute the examination of the National Board of Podiatric Medical Examiners, given in the second and fourth years of podiatric medical college, for part or all of the written state examination. Most states also require the completion of a postdoctoral residency program of at least 2 years and continuing education for license renewal.

Prerequisites for admission to a college of podiatric medicine include the completion of at least 90 semester hours of undergraduate study, an acceptable grade point average, and suitable scores on the Medical College Admission Test (some colleges also may accept the Dental Admission Test or the Graduate Record Exam). All of the colleges require 8 semester hours each of biology, inorganic chemistry, organic chemistry, and physics, as well as 6 hours of English. The science courses should be those designed for premedical students. Potential podiatric medical students also are evaluated on the basis of extracurricular and community activities, personal interviews, and letters of recommendation. About 95 percent of podiatric students have at least a bachelor's degree.

In 2005, there were seven colleges of podiatric medicine accredited by the Council on Podiatric Medical Education. Colleges of podiatric medicine offer a 4-year program whose core curriculum is similar to that in other schools of medicine. During the first 2 years, students receive classroom instruction in basic sciences, including anatomy, chemistry, pathology, and pharmacology. Third- and fourth-year students have clinical rotations in private practices, hospitals, and clinics. During these rotations, they learn how to take general and podiatric histories, perform routine physical examinations, interpret tests and findings, make diagnoses, and perform therapeutic procedures. Graduates receive the degree of Doctor of Podiatric Medicine (DPM).

Most graduates complete a hospital-based residency program after receiving a DPM. Residency programs last from 2 to 4 years. Residents receive advanced training in podiatric medicine and surgery and serve clinical rotations in anesthesiology, internal medicine, pathology, radiology, emergency medicine, and orthopedic and general surgery. Residencies lasting more than 1 year provide more extensive training in specialty areas.

There are a number of certifying boards for the podiatric specialties of orthopedics, primary medicine, and surgery. Certification means that the DPM meets higher standards than those required for licensure. Each board requires advanced training, the completion of written and oral examinations, and experience as a practicing podiatrist. Most managed-care organizations prefer board-certified podiatrists.

People planning a career in podiatry should have scientific aptitude, manual dexterity, interpersonal skills, and good business sense.

Podiatrists may advance to become professors at colleges of podiatric medicine, department chiefs in hospitals, or general health administrators.

Employment

Podiatrists held about 10,000 jobs in 2004. About 23 percent of podiatrists are self-employed. Most podiatrists were solo practitioners, although more are entering group practices with other podiatrists or other health practitioners. Solo practitioners primarily were unincorporated self-employed workers, although some also were incorporated wage and salary workers in offices of other health practitioners. Other podiatrists are employed in hospitals and by the federal government.

Job Outlook

Employment of podiatrists is expected to grow about as fast as the average for all occupations through 2014. More people will turn to podiatrists for foot care because of the rising number of injuries sustained by a more active and increasingly older population. Additional job openings will result from podiatrists who retire from the occupation, particularly members of the baby-boom generation. However, relatively few job openings from this source are expected because the occupation is small and most podiatrists remain in it until they retire.

Medicare and most private health insurance programs cover acute medical and surgical foot services, as well as diagnostic X rays and leg braces. Details of such coverage vary among plans. However, routine foot care, including the removal of corns and calluses, ordinarily is not covered unless the patient has a systemic condition that has resulted in severe circulatory problems or areas of desensitization in the legs or feet. Like dental services, podiatric care is often discretionary and, therefore, more dependent on disposable income than some other medical services.

Employment of podiatrists would grow even faster were it not for continued emphasis on controlling the costs of specialty health care. Insurers will balance the cost of sending patients to podiatrists against the cost and availability of substitute practitioners, such as physicians and physical therapists. Opportunities will be better for board-certified podiatrists because many managed-care organizations require board certification. Opportunities for newly trained podiatrists will be better in group medical practices, clinics, and health networks than in traditional solo practices. Establishing a practice will be most difficult in the areas surrounding colleges of podiatric medicine, where podiatrists are concentrated.

Earnings

Podiatrists enjoy very high earnings. Median annual earnings of salaried podiatrists were $94,400 in 2004. Additionally, a survey by *Podiatry Management Magazine* reported median net income of $113,000 in 2004. Podiatrists in partnerships tended to earn higher net incomes than those in solo practice. Self-employed podiatrists must provide for their own health insurance and retirement.

Related Occupations

Other workers who apply medical knowledge to prevent, diagnose, and treat lower-body muscle and bone disorders and injuries include athletic trainers, chiropractors, massage therapists, occupational therapists, physical therapists, and physicians and surgeons. Workers who specialize in developing orthopedic shoe inserts, braces, and prosthetic limbs are orthotists and prosthetists.

Sources of Additional Information

For information on a career in podiatric medicine, contact

▸ American Podiatric Medical Association, 9312 Old Georgetown Rd., Bethesda, MD 20814-1621. Internet: http://www.apma.org

Information on the colleges of podiatric medicine and their entrance requirements, curricula, and student financial aid is available from

▸ American Association of Colleges of Podiatric Medicine, 15850 Crabbs Branch Way, Suite 320, Rockville, MD 20855-2622. Internet: http://www.aacpm.org

Veterinarians

(O*NET 29-1131.00)

Significant Points

■ Veterinarians should have an affinity for animals and the ability to get along with their owners.

■ Graduation from an accredited college of veterinary medicine and a state license are required.

■ Competition for admission to veterinary school is keen; however, graduates should have very good job opportunities.

■ About 1 out of 5 veterinarians is self-employed; self-employed veterinarians usually have to work hard and long to build a sufficient client base.

Nature of the Work

Veterinarians play a major role in the health care of pets; livestock; and zoo, sporting, and laboratory animals. Some veterinarians use their skills to protect humans against diseases carried by animals and conduct clinical research on human and animal health problems. Others work in basic research, broadening the scope of fundamental theoretical knowledge, and in applied research, developing new ways to use knowledge.

Most veterinarians perform clinical work in private practices. More than 50 percent of these veterinarians predominantly or exclusively treat small animals. Small-animal practitioners usually care for companion animals, such as dogs and cats, but also treat birds, reptiles, rabbits, and other animals that can be kept as pets. About one-fourth of all veterinarians work in mixed animal practices, where they see pigs, goats, sheep, and some nondomestic animals in addition to companion animals. Veterinarians in clinical practice diagnose animal health problems; vaccinate against diseases, such as distemper and rabies; medicate animals suffering from infections or illnesses; treat and dress wounds; set fractures; perform surgery; and advise owners about animal feeding, behavior, and breeding.

A small number of private-practice veterinarians work exclusively with large animals, mostly horses or cows; some also care for various kinds of food animals. These veterinarians usually drive to farms or ranches to provide veterinary services for herds or individual animals. Much of this work involves preventive care to maintain the health of the animals. These veterinarians test for and vaccinate against diseases and consult with farm or ranch owners and managers regarding animal production, feeding, and housing issues. They also treat and dress wounds; set fractures; and perform surgery, including cesarean sections on birthing animals. Veterinarians euthanize animals when necessary. Other veterinarians care for zoo, aquarium, or laboratory animals.

Veterinarians who treat animals use medical equipment such as stethoscopes; surgical instruments; and diagnostic equipment, including radiographic and ultrasound equipment. Veterinarians working in research use a full range of sophisticated laboratory equipment.

Veterinarians can contribute to human as well as animal health. A number of veterinarians work with physicians and scientists as they research ways to prevent and treat various human health problems. For example, veterinarians contributed greatly in conquering malaria and yellow fever; solved the mystery of botulism; produced an anticoagulant used to treat some people with heart disease; and defined and developed surgical techniques for humans, such as hip and knee joint replacements and limb and organ transplants. Today, some determine the effects of drug therapies, antibiotics, or new surgical techniques by testing them on animals.

Some veterinarians are involved in food safety at various levels. Veterinarians who are livestock inspectors check animals for transmissible diseases, advise owners on the treatment of their animals, and may quarantine animals. Veterinarians who are meat, poultry, or egg product inspectors examine slaughtering and processing plants, check live animals and carcasses for disease, and enforce government regulations regarding food purity and sanitation.

Working Conditions

Veterinarians often work long hours. Those in group practices may take turns being on call for evening, night, or weekend work; solo practitioners may work extended and weekend hours, responding to emergencies or squeezing in unexpected appointments. The work setting often can be noisy.

Veterinarians in large-animal practices spend time driving between their office and farms or ranches. They work outdoors in all kinds of weather and may have to treat animals or perform surgery under unsanitary conditions. When working with animals that are frightened or in pain, veterinarians risk being bitten, kicked, or scratched.

Veterinarians working in nonclinical areas, such as public health and research, have working conditions similar to those of other professionals in those lines of work. In these cases, veterinarians enjoy clean, well-lit offices or laboratories and spend much of their time dealing with people rather than animals.

Training, Other Qualifications, and Advancement

Prospective veterinarians must graduate with a Doctor of Veterinary Medicine (D.V.M. or V.M.D.) degree from a 4-year program at an accredited college of veterinary medicine and must obtain a license to practice. There are 28 colleges in 26 states that meet accreditation standards set by the Council on Education of the American Veterinary Medical Association (AVMA). The prerequisites for admission vary. Many of these colleges do not require a bachelor's degree for entrance, but all require a significant number of credit hours—ranging from 45 to 90 semester hours—at the undergraduate level. However, most of the students admitted have completed an undergraduate program. Applicants without a bachelor's degree face a difficult task gaining admittance.

Preveterinary courses emphasize the sciences. Veterinary medical colleges typically require classes in organic and inorganic chemistry, physics, biochemistry, general biology, animal biology, animal nutrition, genetics, vertebrate embryology, cellular biology, microbiology, zoology, and systemic physiology. Some programs require calculus; some require only statistics, college algebra and trigonometry, or precalculus. Most veterinary medical colleges also require core courses, including some in English or literature, the social sciences, and the humanities. Increasingly, courses in practice management and career development are becoming a standard part of the curriculum to provide a foundation of general business knowledge for new graduates.

In addition to satisfying preveterinary course requirements, applicants must submit test scores from the Graduate Record Examination (GRE), the Veterinary College Admission Test (VCAT), or the Medical College Admission Test (MCAT), depending on the preference of the college to which they are applying. Currently, 22 schools require the GRE, 4 require the VCAT, and 2 accept the MCAT.

In admittance decisions, some veterinary medical colleges place heavy consideration on a candidate's veterinary and animal experience. Formal experience, such as work with veterinarians or scientists in clinics, agribusiness, research, or some area of health science, is particularly advantageous. Less formal experience, such as working with animals on a farm or ranch or at a stable or animal shelter, also is helpful. Students must demonstrate ambition and an eagerness to work with animals.

There is keen competition for admission to veterinary school. The number of accredited veterinary colleges has remained largely the same since 1983, whereas the number of applicants has risen significantly. Only about 1 in 3 applicants was accepted in 2004. AVMA-recognized veterinary specialties—such as pathology, internal medicine, dentistry, nutrition, ophthalmology, surgery, radiology, preventive medicine, and laboratory animal medicine—are usually in the form of a 2-year internship. Interns receive a small salary but usually find that their internship experience leads to a higher beginning salary relative to those of other starting veterinarians. Veterinarians who seek board certification in a specialty also must complete a 3- to 4-year residency program that provides intensive training in specialties such as internal medicine, oncology, radiology, surgery, dermatology, anesthesiology, neurology, cardiology, ophthalmology, and exotic small-animal medicine.

All states and the District of Columbia require that veterinarians be licensed before they can practice. The only exemptions are for veterinarians working for some federal agencies and some state governments. Licensing is controlled by the states and is not strictly uniform, although all states require the successful completion of the D.V.M. degree—or equivalent education—and a passing grade on a national board examination. The Educational Commission for Foreign Veterinary Graduates (ECFVG) grants certification to individuals trained outside the United States who demonstrate that they meet specified requirements for the English language and for clinical proficiency. ECFVG certification fulfills the educational requirement for licensure in all states. Applicants for licensure satisfy the examination requirement by passing the North American Veterinary Licensing Exam (NAVLE), an 8-hour computer-based examination consisting of 360 multiple-choice questions covering all aspects of veterinary medicine. Administered by the National Board of Veterinary Medical Examiners (NBVME), the NAVLE includes visual materials designed to test diagnostic skills that constitute 10 percent of the total examination.

The majority of states also require candidates to pass a state jurisprudence examination covering state laws and regulations. Some states do additional testing on clinical competency as well. There are few reciprocal agreements between states, making it difficult for a veterinarian to practice in a different state without first taking that state's examination.

Nearly all states have continuing education requirements for licensed veterinarians. Requirements differ by state and may involve attending a class or otherwise demonstrating knowledge of recent medical and veterinary advances.

Most veterinarians begin as employees in established practices. Despite the substantial financial investment in equipment, office space, and staff, many veterinarians with experience set up their own practice or purchase an established one.

Newly trained veterinarians can become U.S. Government meat and poultry inspectors, disease-control workers, animal welfare and safety workers, epidemiologists, research assistants, or commissioned officers in the U.S. Public Health Service or various branches of the U.S. Armed Forces. A state license may be required.

Prospective veterinarians must have good manual dexterity. They should have an affinity for animals and the ability to get along with their owners, especially pet owners, who tend to form a strong bond with their pet. Veterinarians who intend to go into private practice should possess excellent communication and business skills because they will need to manage their practice and employees successfully and promote, market, and sell their services.

Employment

Veterinarians held about 61,000 jobs in 2004. About 1 out of 5 veterinarians was self-employed in a solo or group practice. Most others were salaried employees of another veterinary practice. The federal government employed about 1,200 civilian veterinarians, chiefly in the U.S. Departments of Agriculture, Health and Human Services, and, increasingly, Homeland Security. Other employers of veterinarians are state and local governments, colleges of veterinary medicine, medical schools, research laboratories, animal food companies, and pharmaceutical companies. A few veterinarians work for

zoos, but most veterinarians caring for zoo animals are private practitioners who contract with the zoos to provide services, usually on a part-time basis.

In addition, many veterinarians hold veterinary faculty positions in colleges and universities. (See the description of teachers—postsecondary elsewhere in this book.)

Job Outlook

Employment of veterinarians is expected to increase as fast as average for all occupations over the 2004–2014 projection period. Despite this average growth, very good job opportunities are expected because the 28 schools of veterinary medicine, even at full capacity, result in a limited number of graduates each year. However, as mentioned earlier, there is keen competition for admission to veterinary school. As pets are increasingly viewed as a member of the family, pet owners will be more willing to spend on advanced veterinary medical care, creating further demand for veterinarians.

Most veterinarians practice in animal hospitals or clinics and care primarily for companion animals. Recent trends indicate particularly strong interest in cats as pets. Faster growth of the cat population is expected to increase the demand for feline medicine and veterinary services, while demand for veterinary care for dogs should continue to grow at a more modest pace.

Pet owners are becoming more aware of the availability of advanced care and are more willing to pay for intensive veterinary care than in the past because many pet owners are more affluent and because they consider their pet part of the family. More pet owners even purchase pet insurance, increasing the likelihood that a considerable amount of money will be spent on veterinary care for their pets. More pet owners also will take advantage of nontraditional veterinary services, such as preventive dental care.

New graduates continue to be attracted to companion-animal medicine because they prefer to deal with pets and to live and work near heavily populated areas. This situation will not necessarily limit the ability of veterinarians to find employment or to set up and maintain a practice in a particular area. Rather, beginning veterinarians may take positions requiring evening or weekend work to accommodate the extended hours of operation that many practices are offering. Some veterinarians take salaried positions in retail stores offering veterinary services. Self-employed veterinarians usually have to work hard and long to build a sufficient client base.

The number of jobs for large-animal veterinarians is likely to grow more slowly than that for veterinarians in private practice who care for companion animals. Nevertheless, job prospects may be better for veterinarians who specialize in farm animals than for companion-animal practitioners because of low earnings in the former specialty and because many veterinarians do not want to work in rural or isolated areas.

Continued support for public health and food safety, national disease control programs, and biomedical research on human health problems will contribute to the demand for veterinarians, although positions in these areas of interest are few in number. Homeland security also may provide opportunities for veterinarians involved in efforts to minimize animal diseases and prevent them from entering the country. Veterinarians with training in food safety, animal health and welfare, and public health and epidemiology should have the best opportunities for a career in the federal government.

Earnings

Median annual earnings of veterinarians were $66,590 in May 2004. The middle 50 percent earned between $51,420 and $88,060. The lowest 10 percent earned less than $39,020, and the highest 10 percent earned more than $118,430.

According to a survey by the American Veterinary Medical Association, average starting salaries of veterinary medical college graduates in 2004 varied by type of practice as follows:

Small animals, predominantly	$50,878
Small animals, exclusively	50,703
Large animals, exclusively	50,403
Private clinical practice	49,635
Large animals, predominantly	48,529
Mixed animals	47,704
Equine (horses)	38,628

The average annual salary for veterinarians in the federal government in nonsupervisory, supervisory, and managerial positions was $78,769 in 2005.

Related Occupations

Veterinarians prevent, diagnose, and treat diseases, disorders, and injuries in animals. Those who do similar work for humans include chiropractors, dentists, optometrists, physicians and surgeons, and podiatrists. Veterinarians have extensive training in physical and life sciences, and some do scientific and medical research, similar to the work of biological scientists and medical scientists.

Animal care and service workers and veterinary technologists and technicians work extensively with animals. Like veterinarians, they must have patience and feel comfortable with animals. However, the level of training required for these occupations is substantially less than that needed by veterinarians.

Sources of Additional Information

For additional information on careers in veterinary medicine, a list of U.S. schools and colleges of veterinary medicine, and accreditation policies, send a letter-size, self-addressed, stamped envelope to

▶ American Veterinary Medical Association, 1931 N. Meacham Rd., Suite 100, Schaumburg, IL 60173-4360. Internet: http://www.avma.org

For information on veterinary education, write to

▶ Association of American Veterinary Medical Colleges, 1101 Vermont Ave. NW, Suite 710, Washington, DC 20005. Internet: http://www.aavmc.org

For information on scholarships, grants, and loans, contact the financial aid officer at the veterinary schools to which you wish to apply.

Information on obtaining a veterinary position with the federal government is available from the Office of Personnel Management through USAJOBS, the federal government's official employment information system. This resource for locating and applying for job opportunities can be accessed through the Internet at http://www.usajobs.opm.gov or through an interactive voice response telephone system at (703) 724-1850 or TDD (978) 461-8404. These numbers are not toll free, and charges may result.

Jobs Typically Requiring a Master's Degree

Archivists, Curators, and Museum Technicians

Audiologists

Counselors

Economists

Environmental Scientists and Hydrologists

Geoscientists

Instructional Coordinators

Librarians

Market and Survey Researchers

Mathematicians

Operations Research Analysts

Physical Therapists

Psychologists

Social Scientists, Other

Social Workers

Speech-Language Pathologists

Statisticians

Teachers—Postsecondary

Urban and Regional Planners

Archivists, Curators, and Museum Technicians

(O*NET 25-4011.00, 25-4012.00, and 25-4013.00)

Significant Points

■ Most work in museums, historical sites, and similar institutions; educational institutions; or in federal, state, or local government.

■ A graduate degree and related work experience generally are required.

■ Keen competition is expected for most jobs because qualified applicants generally outnumber job openings.

Nature of the Work

Archivists, curators, and museum technicians acquire and preserve important documents and other valuable items for permanent storage or display. They work for museums, governments, zoos, colleges and universities, corporations, and other institutions that require experts to preserve important records. They also describe, catalogue, analyze, exhibit, and maintain valuable objects and collections for the benefit of researchers and the public. These documents and collections may include works of art; transcripts of meetings; coins and stamps; living and preserved plants and animals; and historic objects, buildings, and sites.

Archivists and curators plan and oversee the arrangement, cataloguing, and exhibition of collections and, along with technicians and conservators, maintain collections. Archivists and curators may coordinate educational and public outreach programs, such as tours, workshops, lectures, and classes, and may work with the boards of institutions to administer plans and policies. They also may research topics or items relevant to their collections. Although some duties of archivists and curators are similar, the types of items they deal with differ: Curators usually handle objects with cultural, biological, or historical significance, such as sculptures, textiles, and paintings, while archivists handle mainly records and documents that are retained because of their importance and potential value in the future.

Archivists collect, organize, and maintain control over a wide range of information deemed important enough for permanent safekeeping. This information takes many forms: photographs, films, video and sound recordings, computer tapes, and video and optical disks, as well as more traditional paper records, letters, and documents. Archivists work for a variety of organizations, including government agencies, museums, historical societies, corporations, and educational institutions that use or generate records of great potential value to researchers, exhibitors, genealogists, and others who would benefit from having access to original source material.

Archivists maintain records in accordance with accepted standards and practices that ensure the long-term preservation and easy retrieval of the documents. Records may be saved on any medium, including paper, film, videotape, audiotape, electronic disk, or computer. They also may be copied onto some other format to protect the original and to make the records more accessible to researchers who use them. As various storage media evolve, archivists must keep abreast of technological advances in electronic information storage.

Archivists often specialize in an area of history or technology so they can more accurately determine which records in that area qualify for retention and should become part of the archives. Archivists also may work with specialized forms of records, such as manuscripts, electronic records, photographs, cartographic records, motion pictures, and sound recordings.

Computers are increasingly being used to generate and maintain archival records. Professional standards for the use of computers in handling archival records are still evolving. Expanding computer capabilities that allow more records to be stored and exhibited electronically have transformed, and are expected to continue to transform, many aspects of archival collections.

Curators administer the affairs of museums, zoos, aquariums, botanical gardens, nature centers, and historic sites. The head curator of the museum is usually called the *museum director*. Curators direct the acquisition, storage, and exhibition of collections, including negotiating and authorizing the purchase, sale, exchange, or loan of collections. They are also responsible for authenticating, evaluating, and categorizing the specimens in a collection. Curators oversee and help conduct the institution's research projects and related educational programs. Today, an increasing part of a curator's duties involves fundraising and promotion, which may include the writing and reviewing of grant proposals, journal articles, and publicity materials, as well as attendance at meetings, conventions, and civic events.

Most curators specialize in a particular field, such as botany, art, paleontology, or history. Those working in large institutions may be highly specialized. A large natural-history museum, for example, would employ separate curators for its collections of birds, fishes, insects, and mammals. Some curators maintain their collections, others do research, and others perform administrative tasks. In small institutions with only one or a few curators, one curator may be responsible for a number of tasks, from maintaining collections to directing the affairs of the museum.

Conservators manage, care for, preserve, treat, and document works of art, artifacts, and specimens—work that may require substantial historical, scientific, and archaeological research. They use X rays, chemical testing, microscopes, special lights, and other laboratory equipment and techniques to examine objects and determine their condition, their need for treatment or restoration, and the appropriate method for preserving them. Conservators document their findings and treat items to minimize their deterioration or to restore them to their original state. Conservators usually specialize in a particular material or group of objects, such as documents and books, paintings, decorative arts, textiles, metals, or architectural material.

Museum technicians assist curators by performing various preparatory and maintenance tasks on museum items. Some museum technicians also may assist curators with research. Archives technicians help archivists organize, maintain, and provide access to historical documentary materials.

Working Conditions

The working conditions of archivists and curators vary. Some spend most of their time working with the public, providing reference assistance and educational services. Others perform research or process records, which often means working alone or in offices with only a few people. Those who restore and install exhibits or work with bulky, heavy record containers may lift objects, climb, or stretch. Those in zoos, botanical gardens, and other outdoor museums and historic sites frequently walk great distances.

Curators who work in large institutions may travel extensively to evaluate potential additions to the collection, organize exhibitions, and conduct research in their area of expertise. However, travel is rare for curators employed in small institutions.

Training, Other Qualifications, and Advancement

Employment as an archivist, conservator, or curator usually requires graduate education and related work experience. While completing their formal education, many archivists and curators work in archives or museums to gain the "hands-on" experience that many employers seek.

Although archivists earn a variety of undergraduate degrees, a graduate degree in history or library science, with courses in archival science, is preferred by most employers. Also, a few institutions now offer master's degrees in archival studies. Some positions may require knowledge of the discipline related to the collection, such as business or medicine. Many colleges and universities offer courses or practical training in archival science as part of their history, library science, or other curriculum. The Academy of Certified Archivists offers voluntary certification for archivists. The designation "Certified Archivist" is obtained by those with at least a master's degree and a year of appropriate archival experience. The certification process requires candidates to pass a written examination, and they must renew their certification periodically.

Archivists need research and analytical ability to understand the content of documents and the context in which they were created and to decipher deteriorated or poor-quality printed matter, handwritten manuscripts, photographs, or films. A background in preservation management is often required of archivists because they are responsible for taking proper care of their records. Archivists also must be able to organize large amounts of information and write clear instructions for its retrieval and use. In addition, computer skills and the ability to work with electronic records and databases are very important. Because electronic records are becoming the prevalent form of recordkeeping and archivists must create searchable databases, a knowledge of Web technology is increasingly being required.

Many archives, including one-person shops, are very small and have limited opportunities for promotion. Archivists typically advance by transferring to a larger unit that has supervisory positions. A doctorate in history, library science, or a related field may be needed for some advanced positions, such as director of a state archive.

For employment as a curator, most museums require a master's degree in an appropriate discipline of the museum's specialty—art, history, or archaeology—or in museum studies. Many employers prefer a doctoral degree, particularly for curators in natural history or science museums. Earning two graduate degrees—in museum studies (museology) and a specialized subject—gives a candidate a distinct advantage in this competitive job market. In small museums, curatorial positions may be available to individuals with a bachelor's degree. For some positions, an internship of full-time museum work supplemented by courses in museum practices is needed.

Curatorial positions often require knowledge in a number of fields. For historic and artistic conservation, courses in chemistry, physics, and art are desirable. Because curators—particularly those in small museums—may have administrative and managerial responsibilities, courses in business administration, public relations, marketing, and fundraising also are recommended. Like archivists, curators need computer skills and the ability to work with electronic databases. Many curators are responsible for posting information on the Internet, so they also need to be familiar with digital imaging, scanning technology, and copyright law.

Curators must be flexible because of their wide variety of duties, among which are the design and presentation of exhibits. In small museums, curators need manual dexterity to build exhibits or restore objects. Leadership ability and business skills are important for museum directors, while marketing skills are valuable in increasing museum attendance and fundraising.

In large museums, curators may advance through several levels of responsibility, eventually becoming the museum director. Curators in smaller museums often advance to larger ones. Individual research and publications are important for advancement in larger institutions.

When hiring conservators, employers look for a master's degree in conservation or in a closely related field together with substantial experience. There are only a few graduate programs in museum conservation techniques in the United States. Competition for entry to these programs is keen; to qualify, a student must have a background in chemistry, archaeology or studio art, and art history, as well as work experience. For some programs, knowledge of a foreign language also is helpful. Conservation apprenticeships or internships as an undergraduate can enhance one's admission prospects. Graduate programs last 2 to 4 years, the latter years of which include internship training. A few individuals enter conservation through apprenticeships with museums, nonprofit organizations, and conservators in private practice. Apprenticeships should be supplemented with courses in chemistry, studio art, and history. Apprenticeship training, although accepted, is a more difficult route into the conservation profession.

Museum technicians usually need a bachelor's degree in an appropriate discipline of the museum's specialty; training in museum studies; or previous experience working in museums, particularly in the design of exhibits. Similarly, archives technicians usually need a bachelor's degree in library science or history or relevant work experience. Technician positions often serve as a stepping-stone for individuals interested in archival and curatorial work. Except in small museums, a master's degree is needed for advancement.

Relatively few schools grant a bachelor's degree in museum studies. More common are undergraduate minors or tracks of study that are part of an undergraduate degree in a related field, such as art history, history, or archaeology. Students interested in further study may

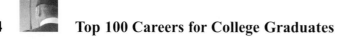

obtain a master's degree in museum studies, offered in colleges and universities throughout the country. However, many employers feel that, while museum studies are helpful, a thorough knowledge of the museum's specialty and museum work experience are more important.

Continuing education, which enables archivists, curators, and museum technicians to keep up with developments in the field, is available through meetings, conferences, and workshops sponsored by archival, historical, and museum associations. Some larger organizations, such as the National Archives, offer such training in-house.

Employment

Archivists, curators, and museum technicians held about 27,000 jobs in 2004. About 34 percent were employed in museums, historical sites, and similar institutions, and 16 percent worked for state and private educational institutions, mainly college and university libraries. Nearly 28 percent worked in federal, state, and local government, excluding educational institutions. Most federal archivists work for the National Archives and Records Administration; others manage military archives in the U.S. Department of Defense. Most federal government curators work at the Smithsonian Institution, in the military museums of the Department of Defense, and in archaeological and other museums and historic sites managed by the U.S. Department of the Interior. All state governments have archival or historical-record sections employing archivists. State and local governments also have numerous historical museums, parks, libraries, and zoos employing curators.

Some large corporations that have archives or record centers employ archivists to manage the growing volume of records created or maintained as required by law or necessary to the firms' operations. Religious and fraternal organizations, professional associations, conservation organizations, major private collectors, and research firms also employ archivists and curators.

Conservators may work under contract to treat particular items rather than as regular employees of a museum or other institution. These conservators may work on their own as private contractors, or they may work as an employee of a conservation laboratory or regional conservation center that contracts their services to museums.

Job Outlook

Keen competition is expected for most jobs as archivists, curators, and museum technicians because qualified applicants generally outnumber job openings. Graduates with highly specialized training, such as master's degrees in both library science and history with a concentration in archives or records management and extensive computer skills, should have the best opportunities for jobs as archivists. A curator job also is attractive to many people, and many applicants have the necessary training and knowledge of the subject, but there are only a few openings. Consequently, candidates may have to work part time, as an intern, or even as a volunteer assistant curator or research associate after completing their formal education. Substantial work experience in collection management, research, exhibit design, or restoration, as well as

database management skills, will be necessary for permanent status.

The job outlook for conservators may be more favorable, particularly for graduates of conservation programs. However, competition is stiff for the limited number of openings in these programs, and applicants need a technical background. Conservation program graduates with knowledge of a foreign language and a willingness to relocate will have an advantage over less-qualified candidates.

Employment of archivists, curators, and museum technicians is expected to increase about as fast as the average for all occupations through 2014. Jobs are expected to grow as public and private organizations emphasize establishing archives and organizing records and information and as public interest in science, art, history, and technology increases. Museum and zoo attendance has experienced a drop in recent years because of a weak economy, but the long-term trend has been a rise in attendance, and this trend is expected to continue. There is healthy public and private support for and interest in museums, which will generate demand for archivists, curators, and museum technicians. However, museums and other cultural institutions can be subject to cuts in funding during recessions or periods of budget tightening, reducing demand for these workers. Although the rate of turnover among archivists and curators is relatively low, the need to replace workers who leave the occupation or stop working will create some additional job openings.

Earnings

Median annual earnings of archivists in May 2004 were $36,470. The middle 50 percent earned between $28,900 and $46,480. The lowest 10 percent earned less than $21,780, and the highest 10 percent earned more than $61,260. Median annual earnings of curators in May 2004 were $43,620. The middle 50 percent earned between $32,790 and $58,280. The lowest 10 percent earned less than $25,360, and the highest 10 percent earned more than $77,490. Median annual earnings of museum technicians and conservators in May 2004 were $31,820. The middle 50 percent earned between $23,770 and $43,020. The lowest 10 percent earned less than $18,210, and the highest 10 percent earned more than $58,260.

In 2005, the average annual salary for archivists in the federal government in nonsupervisory, supervisory, and managerial positions was $75,876; for museum curators, $76,126; for museum specialists and technicians, $55,291; and for archives technicians, $41,347.

Related Occupations

The skills that archivists, curators, and museum technicians use in preserving, organizing, and displaying objects or information of historical interest are shared by artists and related workers; librarians; and anthropologists and archeologists, historians, and other social scientists.

Sources of Additional Information

For information on archivists and on schools offering courses in archival studies, contact

▶ Society of American Archivists, 527 South Wells St., 5th Floor, Chicago, IL 60607-3922. Internet: http://www.archivists.org

For general information about careers as a curator and schools offering courses in museum studies, contact

▶ American Association of Museums, 1575 Eye St. NW, Suite 400, Washington, DC 20005. Internet: http://www.aam-us.org

For information about careers and education programs in conservation and preservation, contact

▶ American Institute for Conservation of Historic and Artistic Works, 1717 K St. NW, Suite 200, Washington, DC 20006. Internet: http://aic.stanford.edu

For information about archivists and archivist certification, contact

▶ Academy of Certified Archivists, 48 Howard St., Albany, NY 12207. Internet: http://www.certifiedarchivists.org

For information about government archivists, contact

▶ National Association of Government Archivists and Records Administrators, 48 Howard St., Albany, NY 12207. Internet: http://www.nagara.org

Information on obtaining positions as archivists, curators, and museum technicians with the federal government is available from the Office of Personnel Management through USAJOBS, the federal government's official employment information system. This resource for locating and applying for job opportunities can be accessed through the Internet at http://www.usajobs.opm.gov or through an interactive voice response telephone system at (703) 724-1850 or TDD (978) 461-8404. These numbers are not toll free, and charges may result.

Audiologists

(O*NET 29-1121.00)

Significant Points

■ Employment growth will be spurred by the expanding population in older age groups that are prone to medical conditions that result in hearing problems.

■ More than half work in health care facilities; many others are employed by educational services.

■ A master's degree in audiology has been the standard credential; however, a clinical doctoral degree is becoming more common for new entrants and is expected to become the new standard for the profession.

Nature of the Work

Audiologists work with people who have hearing, balance, and related ear problems. They examine individuals of all ages and identify those with the symptoms of hearing loss and other auditory, balance, and related sensory and neural problems. They then assess the nature and extent of the problems and help the individuals manage them. Using audiometers, computers, and other testing devices, they measure the loudness at which a person begins to hear sounds, the ability to distinguish between sounds, and the impact of hearing loss on an individual's daily life. In addition, audiologists use computer equipment to evaluate and diagnose balance disorders. Audiologists interpret these results and may coordinate them with medical, educational, and psychological information to make a diagnosis and determine a course of treatment.

Hearing disorders can result from a variety of causes, including trauma at birth, viral infections, genetic disorders, exposure to loud noise, certain medications, or aging. Treatment may include examining and cleaning the ear canal, fitting and dispensing hearing aids, and fitting and programming cochlear implants. Audiologic treatment also includes counseling on adjusting to hearing loss, training on the use of hearing instruments, and teaching communication strategies for use in a variety of environments. For example, they may provide instruction in listening strategies. Audiologists also may recommend, fit, and dispense personal or large-area amplification systems and alerting devices.

In audiology (hearing) clinics, audiologists may independently develop and carry out treatment programs. They keep records on the initial evaluation, progress, and discharge of patients. In other settings, audiologists may work with other health and education providers as part of a team in planning and implementing services for children and adults, from birth to old age. Audiologists who diagnose and treat balance disorders often work in collaboration with physicians and physical and occupational therapists.

Some audiologists specialize in work with the elderly, children, or hearing-impaired individuals who need special treatment programs. Others develop and implement ways to protect workers' hearing from on-the-job injuries. They measure noise levels in workplaces and conduct hearing protection programs in factories, as well as in schools and communities.

Audiologists who work in private practice also manage the business aspects of running an office, such as developing a patient base, hiring employees, keeping records, and ordering equipment and supplies.

A few audiologists conduct research on types of—and treatment for—hearing, balance, and related disorders. Others design and develop equipment or techniques for diagnosing and treating these disorders.

Working Conditions

Audiologists usually work at a desk or table in clean, comfortable surroundings. The job is not physically demanding but does require attention to detail and intense concentration. The emotional needs of patients and their families may be demanding. Most full-time audiologists work about 40 hours per week, which may include weekends and evenings to meet the needs of patients. Some work part time. Those who work on a contract basis may spend a substantial amount of time traveling between facilities.

Training, Other Qualifications, and Advancement

Audiologists are regulated in 49 states; all require that individuals have at least a master's degree in audiology. However, a clinical doctoral degree is expected to become the new standard, and several states are currently in the process of changing their regulations to require the Doctor of Audiology (Au.D.) degree or equivalent. A passing score on the national examination on audiology offered through the Praxis Series of the Educational Testing Service also is needed. Other requirements typically are 300 to 375 hours of supervised clinical experience and 9 months of postgraduate professional clinical experience. Forty-one states have continuing education requirements for licensure renewal. An additional examination and license is required in order to dispense hearing aids in some states. Medicaid, Medicare, and private health insurers generally require practitioners to be licensed to qualify for reimbursement.

In 2005, there were 24 master's degree programs and 62 clinical doctoral programs offered at accredited colleges and universities. Graduation from an accredited program may be required to obtain a license. Requirements for admission to programs in audiology include courses in English, mathematics, physics, chemistry, biology, psychology, and communication. Graduate course work in audiology includes anatomy; physiology; physics; genetics; normal and abnormal communication development; auditory, balance, and neural systems assessment and treatment; diagnosis and treatment; pharmacology; and ethics.

Audiologists can acquire the Certificate of Clinical Competence in Audiology (CCC-A) offered by the American Speech-Language-Hearing Association. To earn a CCC, a person must have a graduate degree and 375 hours of supervised clinical experience, complete a 36-week postgraduate clinical fellowship, and pass the Praxis Series examination in audiology, administered by the Educational Testing Service. According to the American Speech-Language-Hearing Association, as of 2007, audiologists will need to have a bachelor's degree and complete 75 hours of credit toward a doctoral degree in order to seek certification. As of 2012, audiologists will have to earn a doctoral degree in order to be certified.

Audiologists may also be certified through the American Board of Audiology. Applicants must earn a master's or doctoral degree in audiology from a regionally accredited college or university, achieve a passing score on a national examination in audiology, and demonstrate that they have completed a minimum of 2,000 hours of mentored professional practice in a two-year period with a qualified audiologist. Certificants must apply for renewal every three years. They must demonstrate that they have earned 45 hours of approved continuing education within the three-year period. Beginning in 2007, all applicants must earn a doctoral degree in audiology.

Audiologists should be able to effectively communicate diagnostic test results, diagnoses, and proposed treatments in a manner easily understood by their patients. They must be able to approach problems objectively and provide support to patients and their families. Because a patient's progress may be slow, patience, compassion, and good listening skills are necessary.

Employment

Audiologists held about 10,000 jobs in 2004. More than half of all jobs were in offices of physicians or other health practitioners, including audiologists; in hospitals; and in outpatient care centers. About 1 in 7 jobs was in educational services, including elementary and secondary schools. Other jobs for audiologists were in health and personal care stores, including hearing aid stores; scientific research and development services; and state and local governments.

A small number of audiologists were self-employed in private practice. They provided hearing health care services in their own offices or worked under contract for schools, health care facilities, or other establishments.

Job Outlook

Employment of audiologists is expected to grow about as fast as the average for all occupations through the year 2014. Because hearing loss is strongly associated with aging, rapid growth in older population groups will cause the number of persons with hearing and balance impairments to increase markedly. Medical advances are also improving the survival rate of premature infants and trauma victims, who then need assessment and possible treatment. Greater awareness of the importance of early identification and diagnosis of hearing disorders in infants also will increase employment. Most states now require that all newborns be screened for hearing loss and receive appropriate early intervention services.

Employment in educational services will increase along with growth in elementary and secondary school enrollments, including enrollment of special education students. The number of audiologists in private practice will rise due to the increasing demand for direct services to individuals as well as increasing use of contract services by hospitals, schools, and nursing care facilities.

Growth in employment of audiologists will be moderated by limitations on insurance reimbursements for the services they provide. Additionally, increased educational requirements may limit the pool of workers entering the profession and any resulting higher salaries may cause doctors to hire more lower-paid ear technicians to perform the functions that audiologists held in doctor's offices. Only a few job openings for audiologists will arise from the need to replace those who leave the occupation, because the occupation is small.

Earnings

Median annual earnings of audiologists were $51,470 in May 2004. The middle 50 percent earned between $42,160 and $62,210. The lowest 10 percent earned less than $34,990, and the highest 10 percent earned more than $75,990.

According to a 2004 survey by the American Speech-Language-Hearing Association, the median annual salary for full-time certified audiologists who worked on a calendar-year basis, generally 11 or 12 months annually, was $56,000. For those who worked on an academic-year basis, usually 9 or 10 months annually, the median annual salary was $53,000. The median starting salary for certified audiologists with one to three years of experience was $45,000 on a calendar-year basis.

Related Occupations

Audiologists specialize in the prevention, diagnosis, and treatment of hearing problems. Workers in related occupations include occupational therapists, optometrists, physical therapists, psychologists, recreational therapists, rehabilitation counselors, and speech-language pathologists.

Sources of Additional Information

State licensing boards can provide information on licensure requirements. State departments of education can supply information on certification requirements for those who wish to work in public schools.

General information on careers in audiology is available from

▸ American Academy of Audiology, 11730 Plaza America Dr., Suite 300, Reston, VA 20190. Internet: http://www.audiology.org

Career information, a description of the CCC-A credential, and a listing of accredited graduate programs is available from

▸ American Speech-Language-Hearing Association, 10801 Rockville Pike, Rockville, MD 20852. Internet: http://www.asha.org

Information on American Board of Audiology certification is available from

▸ American Board of Audiology, 11730 Plaza America Dr., Suite 300, Reston, VA 20190. Internet: http://www.americanboardofaudiology.org

Counselors

(O*NET 21-1011.00, 21-1012.00, 21-1013.00, 21-1014.00, 21-1015.00, and 21-1019.99)

Significant Points

■ School counselors must be certified, and other counselors must be licensed to practice in all but two states. A master's degree generally is needed to become a licensed counselor.

■ Job opportunities for counselors should be very good because job openings are expected to exceed the number of graduates from counseling programs.

■ State and local governments employ about 4 in 10 counselors, and the health services industry employs most of the others.

Nature of the Work

Counselors assist people with personal, family, educational, mental health, and career decisions and problems. Their duties depend on the individuals they serve and on the settings in which they work.

Educational, vocational, and school counselors provide individuals and groups with career and educational counseling. In school settings—elementary through postsecondary—they usually are called school counselors, and they work with students, including those with academic and social development problems and those with special needs. They advocate for students and work with other individuals and organizations to promote the academic, career, personal, and social development of children and youths. School counselors help students evaluate their abilities, interests, talents, and personality characteristics in order to develop realistic academic and career goals. Counselors use interviews, counseling sessions, interest and aptitude assessment tests, and other methods to evaluate and advise students. They also operate career information centers and career education programs. High school counselors advise students regarding college majors, admission requirements, entrance exams,

financial aid, trade or technical schools, and apprenticeship programs. They help students develop job search skills, such as resume writing and interviewing techniques. College career planning and placement counselors assist alumni or students with career development and job-hunting techniques.

Elementary school counselors observe younger children during classroom and play activities and confer with their teachers and parents to evaluate the children's strengths, problems, or special needs. In conjunction with teachers and administrators, they make sure that the curriculum addresses both the academic and the emotional development needs of students. Elementary school counselors do less vocational and academic counseling than do secondary school counselors.

School counselors at all levels help students to understand and deal with social, behavioral, and personal problems. These counselors emphasize preventive and developmental counseling to provide students with the life skills needed to deal with problems before they occur and to enhance students' personal, social, and academic growth. Counselors provide special services, including alcohol and drug prevention programs and conflict resolution classes. They also try to identify cases of domestic abuse and other family problems that can affect a student's development. Counselors interact with students individually, in small groups, or with entire classes. They consult and collaborate with parents, teachers, school administrators, school psychologists, medical professionals, and social workers in order to develop and implement strategies to help students be successful in the education system.

Vocational counselors who provide mainly career counseling outside the school setting are also referred to as *employment counselors* or *career counselors*. Their chief focus is helping individuals with career decisions. Vocational counselors explore and evaluate the client's education, training, work history, interests, skills, and personality traits and arrange for aptitude and achievement tests to assist the client in making career decisions. They also work with individuals to develop their job-search skills, and they assist clients in locating and applying for jobs. In addition, career counselors provide support to persons experiencing job loss, job stress, or other career transition issues.

Rehabilitation counselors help people deal with the personal, social, and vocational effects of disabilities. They counsel people with disabilities resulting from birth defects, illness or disease, accidents, or the stress of daily life. They evaluate the strengths and limitations of individuals; provide personal and vocational counseling; and arrange for medical care, vocational training, and job placement. Rehabilitation counselors interview both individuals with disabilities and their families; evaluate school and medical reports; and confer and plan with physicians, psychologists, occupational therapists, and employers to determine the capabilities and skills of the individual. Conferring with the client, they develop a rehabilitation program that often includes training to help the person develop job skills. Rehabilitation counselors also work toward increasing the client's capacity to live independently.

Mental health counselors work with individuals, families, and groups to address and treat mental and emotional disorders and to promote optimum mental health. They are trained in a variety of therapeutic techniques used to address a wide range of issues, including depression; addiction and substance abuse; suicidal impulses; stress management; problems with self-esteem; issues associated with aging; job and career concerns; educational decisions; issues related to mental and emotional health; and family, parenting, and marital or other relationship problems. Mental health counselors often work closely with other mental health specialists, such as psychiatrists, psychologists, clinical social workers, psychiatric nurses, and school counselors. (Descriptions of physicians and surgeons, psychologists, registered nurses, and social workers appear elsewhere in this book.)

Substance abuse and behavioral disorder counselors help people who have problems with alcohol, drugs, gambling, and eating disorders. They counsel individuals who are addicted to drugs, helping them to identify behaviors and problems related to their addiction. They also conduct programs aimed at preventing addictions from occurring in the first place. These counselors hold sessions designed for individuals, families, or groups.

Marriage and family therapists apply principles, methods, and therapeutic techniques to individuals, families, couples, or organizations in order to resolve emotional conflicts. In doing so, they modify people's perceptions and behaviors, enhance communication and understanding among family members, and help to prevent family and individual crises. Marriage and family therapists also may engage in psychotherapy of a nonmedical nature, make appropriate referrals to psychiatric resources, perform research, and teach courses about human development and interpersonal relationships.

Other counseling specialties include gerontological, multicultural, and genetic counseling. A gerontological counselor provides services to elderly persons and their families when they face changing lifestyles as they grow older. A multicultural counselor helps employers adjust to an increasingly diverse workforce. Genetic counselors provide information and support to families who have members with birth defects or genetic disorders and to families who may be at risk for a variety of inherited conditions. These counselors identify families at risk, investigate the problem that is present in the family, interpret information about the disorder, analyze inheritance patterns and risks of recurrence, and review available options with the family.

Working Conditions

Some school counselors work the traditional 9- to 10-month school year with a 2- to 3-month vacation, but increasing numbers, especially those working in middle and high schools, are employed on 11-month or full-year contracts. They usually work the same hours as teachers, but may travel more frequently to attend conferences and conventions. College career planning and placement counselors work long and irregular hours during student recruiting periods.

Rehabilitation counselors usually work a standard 40-hour week. Self-employed counselors and those working in mental health and community agencies, such as substance abuse and behavioral disorder counselors, frequently work evenings in order to counsel clients who work during the day. Both mental health counselors and marriage and family therapists also often work flexible hours to accommodate families in crisis or working couples who must have evening or weekend appointments.

Counselors must possess high physical and emotional energy to handle the array of problems that they address. Dealing daily with these problems can cause stress. Although the risk of litigation is relatively low, it is still prudent for counselors in all fields to hold some form of personal liability insurance. Because privacy is essential for confidential and frank discussions with clients, counselors usually have private offices.

Training, Other Qualifications, and Advancement

All states require school counselors to hold a state school counseling certification and to have completed at least some graduate course work; most require the completion of a master's degree. Some states require public school counselors to have both counseling and teaching certificates and to have had some teaching experience before receiving certification. For counselors based outside of schools, 48 states and the District of Columbia have some form of counselor licensure that governs their practice of counseling. Requirements typically include the completion of a master's degree in counseling, the accumulation of 2 years or 3,000 hours of supervised clinical experience beyond the master's degree level, the passage of a state-recognized exam, adherence to ethical codes and standards, and the completion of annual continuing education requirements.

Counselors must be aware of educational and training requirements that are often very detailed and that vary by area and by counseling specialty. Prospective counselors should check with state and local governments, employers, and national voluntary certification organizations in order to determine which requirements apply.

As mentioned, a master's degree is typically required to be licensed as a counselor. A bachelor's degree often qualifies a person to work as a counseling aide, rehabilitation aide, or social service worker. Some states require counselors in public employment to have a master's degree; others accept a bachelor's degree with appropriate counseling courses. Counselor education programs in colleges and universities usually are found in departments of education or psychology. Fields of study include college student affairs, elementary or secondary school counseling, education, gerontological counseling, marriage and family counseling, substance abuse counseling, rehabilitation counseling, agency or community counseling, clinical mental health counseling, counseling psychology, career counseling, and related fields. Courses are grouped into eight core areas: human growth and development, social and cultural diversity, relationships, group work, career development, assessment, research and program evaluation, and professional identity. In an accredited master's degree program, 48 to 60 semester hours of graduate study, including a period of supervised clinical experience in counseling, are required.

Graduate programs in career, community, gerontological, mental health, school, student affairs, and marriage and family counseling are accredited by the Council for Accreditation of Counseling and Related Educational Programs (CACREP). While completion of a CACREP-accredited program is not necessary to become a counselor, it makes it easier to fulfill the requirements for state licensing. Another organization, the Council on Rehabilitation Education (CORE), accredits graduate programs in rehabilitation counseling.

Accredited master's degree programs include a minimum of 2 years of full-time study, including 600 hours of supervised clinical internship experience.

Some counselors elect to be nationally certified by the National Board for Certified Counselors, Inc. (NBCC), which grants the general practice credential "National Certified Counselor." To be certified, a counselor must hold a master's degree with a concentration in counseling from a regionally accredited college or university; must have at least 2 years of supervised field experience in a counseling setting (graduates from counselor education programs accredited by CACREP are exempted); must provide two professional endorsements, one of which must be from a recent supervisor; and must have a passing score on the NBCC's National Counselor Examination for Licensure and Certification (NCE). This national certification is voluntary and is distinct from state licensing. However, in some states, those who pass the national exam are exempted from taking a state certification exam. NBCC also offers specialty certifications in school, clinical mental health, and addiction counseling, which supplement the national certified counselor designation. These specialty certifications require passage of a supplemental exam. To maintain their certification, counselors retake and pass the NCE or complete 100 credit hours of acceptable continuing education every 5 years.

Another organization, the Commission on Rehabilitation Counselor Certification, offers voluntary national certification for rehabilitation counselors. Some employers may require rehabilitation counselors to be nationally certified. To become certified, rehabilitation counselors usually must graduate from an accredited educational program, complete an internship, and pass a written examination. (Certification requirements vary according to an applicant's educational history. Employment experience, for example, is required for those with a counseling degree in a specialty other than rehabilitation.) After meeting these requirements, candidates are designated "Certified Rehabilitation Counselors." To maintain their certification, counselors must successfully retake the certification exam or complete 100 credit hours of acceptable continuing education every 5 years.

Other counseling organizations also offer certification in particular counseling specialties. Usually, becoming certified is voluntary, but having certification may enhance one's job prospects.

Some employers provide training for newly hired counselors. Others may offer time off or provide help with tuition if it is needed to complete a graduate degree. Counselors must participate in graduate studies, workshops, and personal studies to maintain their certificates and licenses.

Persons interested in counseling should have a strong desire to help others and should possess the ability to inspire respect, trust, and confidence. They should be able to work independently or as part of a team. Counselors must follow the code of ethics associated with their respective certifications and licenses.

Prospects for advancement vary by counseling field. School counselors can move to a larger school; become directors or supervisors of counseling, guidance, or pupil personnel services; or, usually with further graduate education, become counselor educators, counseling psychologists, or school administrators. (Psychologists and education administrators are covered elsewhere in this book.) Some counselors choose to work for a state's department of education. For marriage and family therapists, doctoral education in family therapy emphasizes the training of supervisors, teachers, researchers, and clinicians in the discipline.

Counselors can become supervisors or administrators in their agencies. Some counselors move into research, consulting, or college teaching or go into private or group practice.

Employment

Counselors held about 601,000 jobs in 2004. Employment was distributed among the counseling specialties as follows:

Educational, vocational, and school counselors	248,000
Rehabilitation counselors	131,000
Mental health counselors	96,000
Substance abuse and behavioral disorder counselors	76,000
Marriage and family therapists	24,000
Counselors, all other	25,000

Educational, vocational, and school counselors work primarily in elementary and secondary schools and colleges and universities. Other types of counselors work in a wide variety of public and private establishments, including health care facilities; job training, career development, and vocational rehabilitation centers; social agencies; correctional institutions; and residential care facilities, such as halfway houses for criminal offenders and group homes for children, the elderly, and the disabled. Some substance abuse and behavioral disorder counselors work in therapeutic communities where addicts live while undergoing treatment. Counselors also work in organizations engaged in community improvement and social change, drug and alcohol rehabilitation programs, and state and local government agencies. A growing number of counselors are self-employed and work in group practices or private practice, due in part to new laws allowing counselors to be paid for their services by insurance companies and to the growing recognition that counselors are well-trained, effective professionals.

Job Outlook

Overall employment of counselors is expected to grow faster than the average for all occupations through 2014. In addition, numerous job openings will occur as many counselors retire or leave the profession. While job prospects will vary with location and specialization, opportunities generally should be very good because the number of job openings that arise should exceed the number of graduates of counseling programs. Rehabilitation counselors and substance abuse and behavioral disorder counselors, in particular, should experience excellent prospects.

Employment of school counselors is expected to grow with increases in student enrollments at postsecondary schools and colleges and as more states require elementary schools to employ counselors. Expansion of the responsibilities of school counselors should also lead to increases in their employment. For example, counselors are becoming more involved in crisis and preventive counseling, helping students deal with issues ranging from drug and alcohol abuse to death and suicide. Although schools and governments realize the value of counselors in helping their students to achieve academic success, budget constraints at every school level will dampen job growth of school counselors. However, federal grants and subsidies may help to offset tight budgets and allow the reduction in student-to-counselor ratios to continue. Job prospects should be more favorable in rural and inner-city schools.

Demand for vocational or career counselors should grow as multiple job and career changes become common for workers and as workers become increasingly aware of the counselors' services. In addition, state and local governments will employ growing numbers of counselors to assist beneficiaries of welfare programs who exhaust their eligibility and must find jobs. Other opportunities for employment counselors will arise in private job-training centers that provide training and other services to laid-off workers and others seeking to acquire new skills or new careers.

Demand is expected to be strong for substance abuse and behavioral disorder counselors because drug offenders are increasingly being sent to treatment programs rather than to jail. Mental health counselors will be needed to staff statewide networks that are being established to improve services for children and adolescents with serious emotional disturbances and for their family members. Under managed care systems, insurance companies are increasingly providing for reimbursement of counselors as a less costly alternative to psychiatrists and psychologists.

The number of people who will need rehabilitation counseling is expected to grow as advances in medical technology allow more people to survive injury or illness and live independently again. In addition, legislation requiring equal employment rights for people with disabilities will spur demand for counselors, who not only help these people make a transition into the workforce but also help companies to comply with the law.

Employment of mental health counselors and marriage and family therapists will grow as more people become comfortable with seeking professional help for a variety of health, personal, and family problems. Employers are also increasingly offering employee assistance programs that provide mental health and alcohol and drug abuse counseling. More people are expected to use these services as society focuses on ways of developing mental well-being, such as controlling stress associated with job and family responsibilities.

Earnings

Median annual earnings of educational, vocational, and school counselors in May 2004 were $45,570. The middle 50 percent earned between $34,530 and $58,400. The lowest 10 percent earned less than $26,260, and the highest 10 percent earned more than $72,390. School counselors can earn additional income working summers in the school system or in other jobs. Median annual earnings in the industries employing the largest numbers of educational, vocational, and school counselors in 2004 were as follows:

Elementary and secondary schools	$51,160
Junior colleges	45,730
Colleges, universities, and professional schools	39,110

Individual and family services	30,240
Vocational rehabilitation services	27,800

Median annual earnings of substance abuse and behavioral disorder counselors in May 2004 were $32,130. The middle 50 percent earned between $25,840 and $40,130. The lowest 10 percent earned less than $21,060, and the highest 10 percent earned more than $49,600.

Median annual earnings of mental health counselors in May 2004 were $32,960. The middle 50 percent earned between $25,660 and $43,370. The lowest 10 percent earned less than $20,880, and the highest 10 percent earned more than $55,810.

Median annual earnings of rehabilitation counselors in May 2004 were $27,870. The middle 50 percent earned between $22,110 and $36,120. The lowest 10 percent earned less than $18,560, and the highest 10 percent earned more than $48,130.

For substance abuse, mental health, and rehabilitation counselors, government employers generally pay the highest wages, followed by hospitals and social service agencies. Residential care facilities often pay the lowest wages.

Median annual earnings of marriage and family therapists in May 2004 were $38,980. The middle 50 percent earned between $30,260 and $49,990. The lowest 10 percent earned less than $23,460, and the highest 10 percent earned more than $65,080. Median annual earnings in May 2004 were $33,620 in individual and family social services, the industry employing the largest number of marriage and family therapists.

Self-employed counselors who have well-established practices, as well as counselors employed in group practices, usually have the highest earnings.

Related Occupations

Counselors help people evaluate their interests, abilities, and disabilities and deal with personal, social, academic, and career problems. Others who help people in similar ways include teachers; social and human service assistants; social workers; psychologists; physicians and surgeons; registered nurses; members of the clergy; occupational therapists; and human resources, training, and labor relations managers and specialists.

Sources of Additional Information

For general information about counseling, as well as information on specialties such as college, mental health, rehabilitation, multicultural, career, marriage and family, and gerontological counseling, contact

▸ American Counseling Association, 5999 Stevenson Ave., Alexandria, VA 22304-3300. Internet: http://www.counseling.org

For information on school counselors, contact

▸ American School Counselors Association, 1101 King St., Suite 625, Alexandria, VA 22314. Internet: http://www.schoolcounselor.org

For information on accredited counseling and related training programs, contact

▸ Council for Accreditation of Counseling and Related Educational Programs, American Counseling Association, 5999 Stevenson Ave., 4th Floor, Alexandria, VA 22304. Internet: http://www.cacrep.org

For information on national certification requirements for counselors, contact

▸ National Board for Certified Counselors, Inc., 3 Terrace Way, Suite D, Greensboro, NC 27403-3660. Internet: http://www.nbcc.org

State departments of education can supply information on those colleges and universities offering guidance and counseling training that meets state certification and licensure requirements.

State employment service offices have information about job opportunities and entrance requirements for counselors.

Economists

(O*NET 19-3011.00)

Significant Points

■ Slower-than-average job growth is expected as firms increasingly employ workers to perform more-specialized tasks with titles that reflect the specific duties of the job rather than the general title of economist.

■ Jobseekers with a background in economics should have good opportunities, although some of these opportunities will be in related occupations.

■ Candidates who hold a master's or Ph.D. degree in economics will have the best employment prospects and advancement opportunities.

■ Quantitative skills are important in all economics specialties.

Nature of the Work

Economists study how society distributes scarce resources, such as land, labor, raw materials, and machinery, to produce goods and services. They conduct research, collect and analyze data, monitor economic trends, and develop forecasts. They research issues such as energy costs, inflation, interest rates, exchange rates, business cycles, taxes, or employment levels.

Economists devise methods and procedures for obtaining the data they need. For example, sampling techniques may be used to conduct a survey, and various mathematical modeling techniques may be used to develop forecasts. Preparing reports, including tables and charts, on research results is an important part of an economist's job. Presenting economic and statistical concepts in a clear and meaningful way is particularly important for economists whose research is directed toward making policies for an organization. Some economists also might perform economic analysis for the media.

Many economists specialize in a particular area of economics, although general knowledge of basic economic principles is useful in each area. *Microeconomists* study the supply and demand decisions of individuals and firms, such as how profits can be maximized and how much of a good or service consumers will demand at a certain price. *Industrial economists* or *organizational economists* study the market structure of particular industries in terms of

the number of competitors within those industries and examine the market decisions of competitive firms and monopolies. These economists also may be concerned with antitrust policy and its impact on market structure. *Macroeconomists* study historical trends in the whole economy and forecast future trends in areas such as unemployment, inflation, economic growth, productivity, and investment. Closely related to macroeconomists are *monetary economists* or *financial economists*, who study the money and banking system and the effects of changing interest rates. *International economists* study international financial markets, exchange rates, and the effects of various trade policies such as tariffs. *Labor economists* or *demographic economists* study the supply and demand for labor and the determination of wages. These economists also try to explain the reasons for unemployment and the effects of changing demographic trends, such as an aging population and increasing immigration, on labor markets. *Public finance economists* are involved primarily in studying the role of the government in the economy and the effects of tax cuts, budget deficits, and welfare policies. *Econometricians* investigate all areas of economics and use mathematical techniques such as calculus, game theory, and regression analysis to formulate economic models that help to explain economic relationships and that are used to develop forecasts related to the nature and length of business cycles, the effects of a specific rate of inflation on the economy, the effects of tax legislation on unemployment levels, and other economic phenomena. Many economists have applied these fundamental areas of economics to specific applications such as health, education, agriculture, urban and regional economics, law, history, energy, and the environment.

Most economists are concerned with practical applications of economic policy and work for a variety of organizations. Economists working for corporations are involved primarily in microeconomic issues, such as forecasting consumer demand and sales of the firm's products. Some analyze their competitors' growth and market share and advise their company on how to handle the competition. Others monitor legislation passed by Congress, such as environmental and worker safety regulations, and assess its impact on their business. Corporations with many international branches or subsidiaries might employ economists to monitor the economic situations in countries where they do business or to provide a risk assessment of a country into which the company might expand.

Economists working in economic consulting or research firms may perform the same tasks as economists working for corporations. Economists in consulting firms also perform much of the macroeconomic analysis and forecasting that is conducted in the United States. These economists collect data on various indicators; maintain databases; analyze historical trends; and develop models to forecast growth, inflation, unemployment, or interest rates. Their analyses and forecasts are frequently published in newspapers and journal articles.

Another large employer of economists is the government. Economists in the federal government administer most of the surveys and collect the majority of the economic data characterizing the United States. For example, economists in the U.S. Department of Commerce collect and analyze data on the production, distribution, and consumption of commodities produced in the United States and overseas, while economists employed by the U.S. Department of Labor collect and analyze data on the domestic economy, including

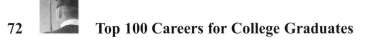

data on prices, wages, employment, productivity, and safety and health. Economists who work for government agencies also assess economic conditions in the United States or abroad in order to estimate the economic effects of specific changes in legislation or public policy. Government economists advise policy makers in areas such as telecommunications deregulation, Social Security revamping, the effects of tax cuts on the budget deficit, and the effectiveness of imposing tariffs on imported steel. An economist working in state or local government might analyze data on the growth of school-age or prison populations and on employment and unemployment rates in order to project future spending needs.

Working Conditions

Economists have structured work schedules. They often work alone, writing reports, preparing statistical charts, and using computers, but they also may be an integral part of a research team. Most work under pressure of deadlines and tight schedules, which may require overtime. Their routine may be interrupted by special requests for data and by the need to attend meetings or conferences. Frequent travel may be necessary.

Training, Other Qualifications, and Advancement

A master's or Ph.D. degree in economics is required for many private-sector economist jobs and for advancement to more responsible positions. Economics includes numerous specialties at the graduate level, such as advanced economic theory, econometrics, international economics, and labor economics. Students should select graduate schools that are strong in specialties in which they are interested. Undergraduate economics majors can choose from a variety of courses ranging from microeconomics, macroeconomics, and econometrics to more philosophical courses, such as the history of economic thought. Because of the importance of quantitative skills to economists, courses in mathematics, statistics, econometrics, sampling theory and survey design, and computer science are extremely helpful. Some schools help graduate students find internships or part-time employment in government agencies, economic consulting or research firms, or financial institutions prior to graduation.

In the federal government, candidates for entry-level economist positions must have a bachelor's degree with a minimum of 21 semester hours of economics and 3 hours of statistics, accounting, or calculus.

Whether working in government, industry, research organizations, or consulting firms, economists with a bachelor's degree usually qualify for most entry-level positions as a research assistant, for administrative or management trainee positions, or for various sales jobs. A master's degree usually is required to qualify for more responsible research and administrative positions. Many businesses, research and consulting firms, and government agencies seek individuals who have strong computer and quantitative skills and can perform complex research. A Ph.D. is necessary for top economist positions in many organizations. Many corporation and government executives have a strong background in economics.

A master's degree usually is the minimum requirement for a job as an instructor in a junior or community college. In most colleges and universities, however, a Ph.D. is necessary for appointment as an instructor. A Ph.D. and extensive publications in academic journals are required for a professorship, tenure, and promotion.

Aspiring economists should gain experience gathering and analyzing data, conducting interviews or surveys, and writing reports on their findings while in college. This experience can prove invaluable later in obtaining a full-time position in the field because much of the economist's work, especially in the beginning, may center on these duties. With experience, economists eventually are assigned their own research projects. Related job experience, such as work as a stock or bond trader, might be advantageous.

Those considering careers as economists should be able to pay attention to details because much time is spent on precise data analysis. Patience and persistence are necessary qualities, given that economists must spend long hours on independent study and problem solving. Good communication skills also are useful, as economists must be able to present their findings, both orally and in writing, in a clear, concise manner.

Employment

Economists held about 13,000 jobs in 2004. The government employed 58 percent of economists in a wide range of government agencies, with 34 percent in federal government and 24 percent in state and local government. The U.S. Departments of Labor, Agriculture, and State are the largest federal employers of economists. The remaining jobs were spread throughout private industry, particularly in scientific research and development services and management, scientific, and technical consulting services. A number of economists combine a full-time job in government, academia, or business with part-time or consulting work in another setting.

Employment of economists is concentrated in large cities. Some work abroad for companies with major international operations; for U.S. government agencies; and for international organizations, such as the World Bank, International Monetary Fund, and United Nations.

In addition to the previously mentioned jobs, economists hold faculty positions in colleges and universities. Economics faculties have flexible work schedules and may divide their time among teaching, research, consulting, and administration. (See the description of teachers—postsecondary elsewhere in this book.)

Job Outlook

Employment of economists is expected to grow more slowly than average for all occupations through 2014. Employment growth should be the fastest in private industry, especially in management, scientific, and technical consulting services. Rising demand for economic analysis in virtually every industry should stem from the growing complexity of the global economy; the effects of competition on businesses; and increased reliance on quantitative methods for analyzing and forecasting business, sales, and other economic trends. Some corporations choose to hire economic consultants to fill these needs rather than keeping an economist on staff. This practice should result in more economists being employed in consulting services. However, job growth will be limited as firms increasingly employ workers to perform more-specialized tasks with titles that reflect the specific duties of the job instead of the general title of economist. In addition, few new jobs are expected in government, but the need to replace experienced workers who transfer to other occupations or who retire or leave the labor force for other reasons will lead to job openings for economists across all industries in which they are employed.

Individuals with a background in economics should have job opportunities, although some of these opportunities will be in related occupations. As firms increasingly employ workers to perform more-specialized tasks, the best opportunities for individuals with backgrounds in economics are expected to be in positions that have titles other than economist. Some examples of job titles often held by those with an economics background are financial analyst, market analyst, public policy consultant, researcher or research assistant, and econometrician.

A master's or Ph.D. degree, coupled with a strong background in economic theory, mathematics, statistics, and econometrics, provides the basis for acquiring any specialty within the economics field. Economists who are skilled in quantitative techniques and their application to economic modeling and forecasting, and who also have good communications skills, should have the best job opportunities. Like those in many other disciplines, however, Ph.D. holders are likely to face keen competition for tenured teaching positions in colleges and universities.

Bachelor's degree holders may face competition for the limited number of economist positions for which they qualify. However, they will qualify for a number of other positions in which they can take advantage of their economic knowledge by conducting research, developing surveys, or analyzing data. Many graduates with bachelor's degrees will find jobs in industry and business as management or sales trainees or as administrative assistants. Bachelor's degree holders with good quantitative skills and a strong background in mathematics, statistics, survey design, and computer science also may be hired by private firms as researchers. Some will find jobs in government.

Candidates who meet state certification requirements may become high school economics teachers. The demand for secondary school economics teachers is expected to grow as economics becomes an increasingly important and popular course.

Earnings

Median annual wage and salary earnings of economists were $72,780 in May 2004. The middle 50 percent earned between $53,650 and $96,240. The lowest 10 percent earned less than $41,040, and the highest 10 percent earned more than $129,170.

The federal government recognizes education and experience in certifying applicants for entry-level positions. The starting salary for economists having a bachelor's degree was about $24,667 a year in 2005; however, those with superior academic records could begin at $30,567. Those having a master's degree could qualify for positions at an annual salary of $37,390. Those with a Ph.D. could begin at $45,239, while some individuals with experience and an advanced degree could start at $54,221. Starting salaries

were slightly higher in selected geographical areas where the prevailing local pay was higher. The average annual salary for economists employed by the federal government was $89,441 a year in 2005.

Related Occupations

Economists are concerned with understanding and interpreting financial matters, among other subjects. Other occupations in this area include accountants and auditors; actuaries; budget analysts; financial analysts and personal financial advisors; financial managers; insurance underwriters; loan officers; and purchasing managers, buyers, and purchasing agents. Other occupations involved in market research and data collection are management analysts and market and survey researchers.

Sources of Additional Information

For information on careers in business economics, contact

▸ National Association for Business Economics, 1233 20th St. NW, Suite 505, Washington, DC 20036.

Information on obtaining positions as economists with the federal government is available from the Office of Personnel Management through USAJOBS, the federal government's official employment information system. This resource for locating and applying for job opportunities can be accessed through the Internet at http://www.usajobs.opm.gov or through an interactive voice response telephone system at (703) 724-1850 or TDD (978) 461-8404. These numbers are not toll free, and charges may result.

Environmental Scientists and Hydrologists

(O*NET 19-2041.00 and 19-2043.00)

Significant Points

■ Environmental scientists and hydrologists often split their work between offices, laboratories, and field sites.

■ Federal, state, and local governments employ over half of all environmental scientists and hydrologists.

■ Although a bachelor's degree in an earth science is adequate for a few entry-level jobs, employers increasingly prefer a master's degree; a Ph.D. degree is required for most high-level research or college teaching positions.

■ The strongest job growth should be in private-sector consulting firms.

Nature of the Work

Environmental scientists and hydrologists use their knowledge of the physical makeup and history of the Earth to protect the environment, study the properties of underground and surface waters, locate water and energy resources, predict water-related geologic hazards, and offer environmental site assessments and advice on indoor air quality and hazardous-waste-site remediation.

Environmental scientists conduct research to identify and abate or eliminate sources of pollutants or hazards that affect people, wildlife, and their environments. These workers analyze and report measurements or observations of air, food, water, soil, and other sources and make recommendations on how best to clean and preserve the environment. Understanding the issues involved in protecting the environment—degradation, conservation, recycling, and replenishment—is central to the work of environmental scientists, who often use their skills and knowledge to design and monitor waste disposal sites, preserve water supplies, and reclaim contaminated land and water to comply with federal environmental regulations.

Many environmental scientists do work and have training that is similar to other physical or life scientists, but is applied to environmental areas. Many specialize in some specific area, such as environmental ecology and conservation, environmental chemistry, environmental biology, or fisheries science. Most environmental scientists are further classified by the specific activity they perform, although recent advances in the understanding of basic life processes within the ecosystem have blurred some traditional classifications. For example, environmental ecologists study the relationships between organisms and their environments and the effects of influences such as population size, pollutants, rainfall, temperature, and altitude. Utilizing their knowledge of various scientific disciplines, they may collect, study, and report data on air, food, soil, and water. Ecological modelers study ecosystems, the control of environmental pollution, and the management of resources. These environmental scientists may use mathematical modeling, systems analysis, thermodynamics, and computer techniques. Environmental chemists may study the toxicity of various chemicals—how those chemicals affect plants, animals, and people.

Hydrologists study the quantity, distribution, circulation, and physical properties of underground and surface waters. Often, they specialize in either underground water or surface water. They examine the form and intensity of precipitation, its rate of infiltration into the soil, its movement through the earth, and its return to the ocean and atmosphere. Hydrologists use sophisticated techniques and instruments. For example, they may use remote sensing technology, data assimilation, and numerical modeling to monitor the change in regional and global water cycles. Some surface-water hydrologists use sensitive stream-measuring devices to assess flow rates and the quality of water. The work hydrologists do is particularly important in flood control and environmental preservation, including groundwater decontamination.

Many environmental scientists and hydrologists work at consulting firms, advising and helping businesses and government agencies comply with environmental policy, particularly with regard to groundwater decontamination and flood control. Environmental scientists and hydrologists at consulting firms are generally hired to solve problems. Most firms fall into two categories: large multidisciplinary engineering companies, the largest of which may employ more than 15,000 workers, and small niche firms that may employ fewer than 50 workers. When entering the field, prospects should consider the type of firm and the scope of the projects it undertakes. In larger firms, environmental scientists are more likely to engage in large, long-term projects in which their role will mesh with those of workers in other scientific disciplines. In smaller specialty firms,

however, they may be responsible for many skills beyond traditional environmental disciplines, such as working with environmental laws and regulations; making environmental risk assessments; writing technical proposals; giving presentations to managers and regulators; and working with other specialists on a variety of issues, including engineering remediation.

Environmental scientists who determine policy may help identify how human behavior can be modified in the future to avoid such problems as groundwater contamination and depletion of the ozone layer. Some environmental scientists work in managerial positions, usually after spending some time performing research or learning about environmental laws and regulations. (Information on geoscientists, whose work is closely related to that of environmental scientists and hydrologists, is located elsewhere in this book.)

Working Conditions

Most entry-level environmental scientists and hydrologists spend the majority of their time in the field, while more experienced workers generally devote more of their time to office or laboratory work. Many beginning hydrologists and some environmental scientists, such as environmental ecologists and environmental chemists, often take field trips that involve physical activity. Environmental scientists and hydrologists in the field may work in warm or cold climates in all kinds of weather. In their research, they may dig or chip with a hammer, scoop with a net, come in contact with water, and carry equipment in a backpack. Travel often is required to meet with prospective clients or investors. Those in laboratories may conduct tests, run experiments, record results, and compile data.

Environmental scientists and hydrologists in research positions with the federal government or in colleges and universities frequently are required to design programs and write grant proposals in order to continue their data collection and research. Environmental scientists and hydrologists in consulting jobs face similar pressures to market their skills and write proposals so that they will have steady work. Occasionally, those who write technical reports to business clients and regulators may be under pressure to meet deadlines.

Training, Other Qualifications, and Advancement

A bachelor's degree is adequate for a few entry-level positions, but environmental scientists are increasingly needing a master's degree in a natural science. A master's degree also is the minimum educational requirement for most entry-level applied research positions in private industry, in state and federal agencies, and at state geological surveys. A doctoral degree is necessary for college teaching and most high-level research positions.

Many environmental scientists earn degrees in life science, chemistry, geology, geophysics, atmospheric science, or physics and then, either through further education or through their research interests and work experience, apply their education to environmental areas. Others earn a degree in environmental science. A bachelor's degree in environmental science offers an interdisciplinary approach to the natural sciences with an emphasis on biology, chemistry, and geology. In addition, undergraduate environmental science majors should focus on data analysis and physical geography, particularly if

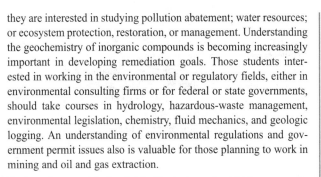
they are interested in studying pollution abatement; water resources; or ecosystem protection, restoration, or management. Understanding the geochemistry of inorganic compounds is becoming increasingly important in developing remediation goals. Those students interested in working in the environmental or regulatory fields, either in environmental consulting firms or for federal or state governments, should take courses in hydrology, hazardous-waste management, environmental legislation, chemistry, fluid mechanics, and geologic logging. An understanding of environmental regulations and government permit issues also is valuable for those planning to work in mining and oil and gas extraction.

Students interested in the field of hydrology should take courses in the physical sciences, geophysics, chemistry, engineering science, soil science, mathematics, aquatic biology, atmospheric science, geology, oceanography, hydrogeology, and the management or conservation of water resources. In some cases, graduates with a bachelor's degree in a hydrologic science are qualified for positions in environmental consulting and planning regarding water quality or wastewater treatment. Curricula for advanced degrees often emphasize the natural sciences, but not all universities offer all curricula.

The American Institute of Hydrology offers certification programs in professional hydrology. Certification is recommended for those seeking advancement and for those seeking to upgrade their knowledge.

For environmental scientists and hydrologists who enter the field of consulting, courses in business, finance, marketing, or economics may be useful. In addition, combining environmental science training with other disciplines such as engineering, or a technical degree coupled with a master's degree in business administration, qualifies these scientists for the widest range of jobs. Environmental scientists and hydrologists also should have some knowledge of the potential liabilities associated with some environmental work.

Computer skills are essential for prospective environmental scientists and hydrologists. Students who have some experience with computer modeling, data analysis and integration, digital mapping, remote sensing, and geographic information systems will be the most prepared to enter the job market. A knowledge of the Geographic Information System (GIS) and Global Positioning System (GPS)—a locator system that uses satellites—is vital.

Environmental scientists and hydrologists must have excellent interpersonal skills because they usually work as part of a team with other scientists, engineers, and technicians. Strong oral and written communication skills also are essential because writing technical reports and research proposals and communicating technical and research results to company managers, regulators, and the public are important aspects of the work. Those involved in fieldwork must have physical stamina.

Environmental scientists and hydrologists often begin their careers in field exploration or, occasionally, as research assistants or technicians in laboratories or offices. They are given more difficult assignments as they gain experience. Eventually, they may be promoted to project leader, program manager, or some other management and research position.

Because international work is becoming increasingly pervasive, knowledge of a second language can be a valuable skill to employers.

Employment

Environmental scientists and hydrologists held about 81,000 jobs in 2004. Jobs for hydrologists accounted for only 10 percent of the total. Many more individuals held environmental science faculty positions in colleges and universities, but they are classified as college and university faculty. (See the description of teachers—postsecondary elsewhere in this book.)

About 44 percent of environmental scientists were employed in state and local governments; 15 percent in management, scientific, and technical consulting services; 14 percent in architectural, engineering and related services; and 8 percent in the federal government. About 5 percent were self-employed.

Among hydrologists, 22 percent were employed in architectural, engineering, and related services, and 18 percent worked for management, scientific, and technical consulting services. In 2004, the federal government employed about 2,500 hydrologists, mostly within the U.S. Department of the Interior for the U.S. Geological Survey (USGS) and within the U.S. Department of Defense. Another 15 percent worked for state agencies, such as state geological surveys and state departments of conservation. About 5 percent of hydrologists were self-employed, most as consultants to industry or government.

Job Outlook

Employment of environmental scientists is expected to grow about as fast as the average for all occupations through 2014, while employment of hydrologists should grow much faster than average. Job growth for environmental scientists and hydrologists should be strongest at private-sector consulting firms. Demand for environmental scientists and hydrologists will be spurred largely by public policy, which will oblige companies and organizations to comply with complex environmental laws and regulations, particularly those regarding groundwater decontamination, clean air, and flood control.

Job opportunities also will be spurred by a continued general awareness regarding the need to monitor the quality of the environment, to interpret the impact of human actions on terrestrial and aquatic ecosystems, and to develop strategies for restoring ecosystems.

Many environmental scientists and hydrologists work in consulting. Consulting firms have hired these scientists to advise and help businesses and government comply with new regulations on issues related to underground tanks, land disposal areas, and other hazardous-waste-management facilities. Currently, environmental consulting is maturing and evolving from investigations to remediation and engineering solutions. At the same time, the regulatory climate is evolving from a rigid structure to a more flexible risk-based approach. These factors, coupled with new federal and state initiatives that integrate environmental activities into the business process itself, will result in a greater focus on waste minimization, resource recovery, pollution prevention, and the consideration of environmental effects during product development. This shift in focus from reactive solutions to preventive management will provide many new opportunities for environmental scientists and hydrologists in consulting roles.

Some opportunities are expected for environmental scientists at state geological surveys, stemming from the need to conduct environmental site assessments for local governments to help improve the flow of railroad and automobile traffic in urban areas. In addition, environmental scientists will be needed to help planners and communities develop and construct buildings, transportation corridors, and utilities that protect water resources and reflect efficient and beneficial land use.

Opportunities will be better for hydrologists as the population increases and moves to more environmentally sensitive locations. For example, as people increasingly migrate toward coastal regions, hydrologists will be needed to assess building sites for potential geologic hazards and to mitigate the effects of natural hazards such as floods and landslides. Hydrologists also will be needed to conduct research on hazardous-waste sites in order to determine the impact of hazardous pollutants on soil and groundwater so that engineers can design remediation systems. Demand is growing for hydrologists who understand both the scientific and engineering aspects of waste remediation. As states design initiatives to improve water resources by preventing pollution, there should be opportunities for hydrologists in state government. Increased government regulations, such as those regarding the management of storm water, and issues related to water conservation, deteriorating coastal environments, and rising sea levels also will stimulate employment growth for these workers.

Federal and state geological surveys depend to a large extent on the public climate and the current budget. Thus, job security for environmental scientists and hydrologists within a state survey may be cyclical. During periods of economic recession, layoffs of environmental scientists and hydrologists may occur in consulting firms; layoffs are much less likely in government.

Earnings

Median annual earnings of environmental scientists were $51,080 in May 2004. The middle 50 percent earned between $39,100 and $67,360. The lowest 10 percent earned less than $31,610, and the highest 10 percent earned more than $85,940.

Median annual earnings of hydrologists were $61,510 in May 2004, with the middle 50 percent earning between $47,080 and $77,910, the lowest 10 percent earning less than $38,580, and the highest 10 percent earning more than $94,460.

Median annual earnings in the industries employing the largest number of environmental scientists in May 2004 were as follows:

Federal government	$73,530
Management, scientific, and technical consulting services	51,190
Architectural, engineering, and related services	49,160
Local government	48,870
State government	46,850

According to the National Association of Colleges and Employers, beginning salary offers in July 2005 for graduates with bachelor's degrees in a environmental science averaged $31,366 a year.

In 2005, the federal government's average salary for hydrologists in managerial, supervisory, and nonsupervisory positions was $77,182.

Related Occupations

Environmental scientists and hydrologists perform investigations for the purpose of abating or eliminating sources of pollutants or hazards that affect the environment or some population—plant, animal, or human. Many other occupations deal with preserving or researching the natural environment, including conservation scientists and foresters, atmospheric scientists, and some biological scientists and science and engineering technicians.

Environmental scientists and hydrologists have extensive training in physical sciences, and many apply their knowledge of chemistry, physics, biology, and mathematics to explain certain phenomena closely related to the work of geoscientists.

Using their qualitative and quantitative problem-solving skills, physicists; chemists; engineers; mathematicians; surveyors, cartographers, photogrammetrists, and surveying technicians; computer systems analysts; and computer scientists and database administrators may perform similar work in environment-related activities.

Sources of Additional Information

Information on training and career opportunities for environmental scientists is available from

▸ American Geological Institute, 4220 King St., Alexandria, VA 22302-1502. Internet: http://www.agiweb.org

For information on careers in hydrology, contact

▸ American Institute of Hydrology, 300 Village Green Circle, Suite #201, Smyrna, GA 30080. Internet: http://www.aihydro.org

For career information and a list of education and training programs in oceanography and related fields, contact

▸ Marine Technology Society, 5565 Sterrett Place, Suite 108, Columbia, MD 21004. Internet: http://www.mtsociety.org

Information on obtaining a position as a hydrologist or an environmental protection specialist with the federal government is available from the Office of Personnel Management through USAJOBS, the federal government's official employment information system. This resource for locating and applying for job opportunities can be accessed through the Internet at http://www.usajobs.opm.gov or through an interactive voice response telephone system at (703) 724-1850 or TDD (978) 461-8404. These numbers are not toll free, and charges may result.

Geoscientists

(O*NET 19-2041.00, 19-2042.01, and 19-2043.00)

Significant Points

■ Work at remote field sites is common.

■ Federal, state, and local governments employ 24 percent of all geoscientists.

■ A master's degree is usually the minimum educational requirement; a Ph.D. degree is required for most high-level research and college teaching positions.

■ Although employment of geoscientists is expected to grow more slowly than average, good job opportunities are expected in most areas of geoscience.

Nature of the Work

Geoscientists study the composition, structure, and other physical aspects of the Earth. With the use of sophisticated instruments and by analyzing the composition of the earth and water, geoscientists study the Earth's geologic past and present. Many geoscientists are involved in searching for adequate supplies of natural resources such as groundwater, metals, and petroleum, while others work closely with environmental and other scientists in preserving and cleaning up the environment.

Geoscientists usually study, and are subsequently classified into, one of several closely related fields of geoscience. *Geologists* study the composition, processes, and history of the Earth. They try to find out how rocks were formed and what has happened to them since their formation. They also study the evolution of life by analyzing plant and animal fossils. *Geophysicists* use the principles of physics, mathematics, and chemistry to study not only the Earth's surface, but also its internal composition; ground and surface waters; atmosphere; oceans; and magnetic, electrical, and gravitational forces.

Oceanographers use their knowledge of geology and geophysics, in addition to biology and chemistry, to study the world's oceans and coastal waters. They study the motion and circulation of the ocean waters; the physical and chemical properties of the oceans; and how these properties affect coastal areas, climate, and weather. Oceanographers are further broken down according to their areas of expertise. For example, *physical oceanographers* study the tides, waves, currents, temperatures, density, and salinity of the ocean. They examine the interaction of various forms of energy, such as light, radar, sound, heat, and wind, with the sea, in addition to investigating the relationship between the sea, weather, and climate. *Chemical oceanographers* study the distribution of chemical compounds and chemical interactions that occur in the ocean and on the sea floor. They may investigate how pollution affects the chemistry of the ocean. *Geological and geophysical oceanographers* study the topographic features and the physical makeup of the ocean floor. Their knowledge can help companies find oil and gas off coastal waters. (*Biological oceanographers,* often called marine biologists, study the distribution and migration patterns of the many diverse forms of sea life in the ocean, but because they are considered biological scientists, they are not covered in this description of geoscientists. See the description of biological scientists elsewhere in this book.)

Geoscientists can spend a large part of their time in the field identifying and examining rocks, studying information collected by remote sensing instruments in satellites, conducting geological surveys, constructing field maps, and using instruments to measure the Earth's gravity and magnetic field. For example, they often perform seismic studies, which involve bouncing energy waves off buried layers of rock, to search for oil and gas or to understand the structure of the subsurface layers. Seismic signals generated by an earthquake are used to determine the earthquake's location and intensity. In laboratories, geologists and geophysicists examine the chemical and physical properties of specimens. They study fossil remains of animal and plant life or experiment with the flow of water and oil through rocks.

Numerous specialties that further differentiate the type of work geoscientists do fall under the two major disciplines of geology and geophysics. For example, *petroleum geologists* map the subsurface of the ocean or land as they explore the terrain for oil and gas deposits. They use sophisticated geophysical instrumentation and computers to interpret geological information. *Engineering geologists* apply geologic principles to the fields of civil and environmental engineering, offering advice on major construction projects and assisting in environmental remediation and natural hazard-reduction projects. *Mineralogists* analyze and classify minerals and precious stones according to their composition and structure. They study the environment surrounding rocks in order to find new mineral resources. *Sedimentologists* study the nature, origin, distribution, and alteration of sediments, such as sand, silt, and mud. These sediments may contain oil, gas, coal, and many other mineral deposits. *Paleontologists* study fossils found in geological formations to trace the evolution of plant and animal life and the geologic history of the Earth. *Stratigraphers* examine the formation and layering of rocks to understand the environment in which they were formed. *Volcanologists* investigate volcanoes and volcanic phenomena to try to predict the potential for future eruptions and hazards to human health and welfare. *Glacial geologists* study the physical properties and movement of glaciers and ice sheets. *Geochemists* study the nature and distribution of chemical elements in groundwater and earth materials.

Geophysicists specialize in areas such as geodesy, seismology, and magnetic geophysics. *Geodesists* study the Earth's size, shape, gravitational field, tides, polar motion, and rotation. *Seismologists* interpret data from seismographs and other geophysical instruments to detect earthquakes and locate earthquake-related faults. *Geomagnetists* measure the Earth's magnetic field and use measurements taken over the past few centuries to devise theoretical models that explain the Earth's origin. *Paleomagnetists* interpret fossil magnetization in rocks and sediments from the continents and oceans to record the spreading of the sea floor, the wandering of the continents, and the many reversals of polarity that the Earth's magnetic field has undergone through time. Other geophysicists study atmospheric sciences and space physics. (See the descriptions of atmospheric scientists and of physicists and astronomers elsewhere in this book.)

Working Conditions

Some geoscientists spend the majority of their time in an office, but many others divide their time between fieldwork and office or laboratory work. Work at remote field sites is common. Many geoscientists, such as volcanologists, often take field trips that involve physical activity. Geoscientists in the field may work in warm or cold climates and in all kinds of weather. In their research, they may dig or chip with a hammer, scoop with a net, and carry equipment in a backpack. Oceanographers may spend considerable time at sea on academic research ships. Fieldwork often requires working long hours. Geologists frequently travel to remote field sites by helicopter or four-wheel-drive vehicle and cover large areas on foot. An increasing number of exploration geologists and geophysicists work in foreign countries, sometimes in remote areas and under difficult conditions. Travel often is required to meet with prospective clients or investors.

Geoscientists in research positions with the federal government or in colleges and universities frequently are required to design programs and write grant proposals in order to continue their data collection and research. Geoscientists in consulting jobs face similar pressures to market their skills and write proposals so that they will have steady work.

Training, Other Qualifications, and Advancement

A bachelor's degree is adequate for a few entry-level positions, but most geoscientists need at least a master's degree in general geology or earth science. A master's degree also is the minimum educational requirement for most entry-level research positions in private industry, federal agencies, and state geological surveys. A Ph.D. degree is necessary for most high-level research and college teaching positions.

Many colleges and universities offer a bachelor's or higher degree in a geoscience. In 2005, more than 100 universities offered accredited bachelor's degree programs in geoscience, about 80 universities had master's degree programs, and about 60 offered doctoral degree programs.

Traditional geoscience courses emphasizing classical geologic methods and topics (such as mineralogy, petrology, paleontology, stratigraphy, and structural geology) are important for all geoscientists. Persons studying physics, chemistry, biology, mathematics, engineering, or computer science may also qualify for some geoscience positions if their course work includes study in geology or natural sciences.

Computer skills are essential for prospective geoscientists; students who have experience with computer modeling, data analysis and integration, digital mapping, remote sensing, and geographic information systems will be the most prepared entering the job market. A knowledge of the Global Information System (GIS) and Global Positioning System (GPS)—a locator system that uses satellites—has also become essential. Some employers seek applicants with field experience, so a summer internship may be beneficial to prospective geoscientists.

Geoscientists must have excellent interpersonal skills because they usually work as part of a team with other geoscientists and with environmental scientists, engineers, and technicians. Strong oral and written communication skills also are important because writing technical reports and research proposals, as well as communicating research results to others, are important aspects of the work. Because many jobs require foreign travel, knowledge of a second language is becoming an important attribute to employers. Geoscientists must be inquisitive; be able to think logically; and be capable of complex analytical thinking, including spatial visualization and the ability to develop comprehensive conclusions, often from sparse data. Those involved in fieldwork must have physical stamina.

Geoscientists often begin their careers in field exploration or as research assistants or technicians in laboratories or offices. They are given more difficult assignments as they gain experience. Eventually, they may be promoted to project leader, program manager, or some other management or research position.

Employment

Geoscientists held about 28,000 jobs in 2004. Many more individuals held geoscience faculty positions in colleges and universities, but they are classified as college and university faculty. (See the description of teachers—postsecondary elsewhere in this book.)

About 25 percent of geoscientists were employed in architectural, engineering, and related services, and 20 percent worked for oil and gas extraction companies. In 2004, state agencies such as state geological surveys and state departments of conservation employed about 3,600 geoscientists. Another 2,900 worked for the federal government, including geologists, geophysicists, and oceanographers, mostly within the U.S. Department of the Interior for the U.S. Geological Survey (USGS) and within the U.S. Department of Defense. About 5 percent of geoscientists were self-employed, most as consultants to industry or government.

Job Outlook

Although employment growth will vary by occupational specialty, overall employment of geoscientists is expected to grow more slowly than the average for all occupations through 2014. However, due to the relatively low number of qualified geoscience graduates and the large number of expected retirements, opportunities are expected to be good in most areas of geoscience.

Graduates with a master's degree may have the best opportunities. Those with a Ph.D. who wish to become college and university faculty or to do advanced research may face competition. There are few openings for graduates with only a bachelor's degree in geoscience, but these graduates may find excellent opportunities as high school science teachers. They also can become science technicians or enter a wide variety of related occupations.

Few opportunities for geoscientists are expected in federal and state government, mostly because of budgetary constraints at key agencies, such as the USGS, and the trend among governments toward contracting out to consulting firms. However, departures of geoscientists who retire or leave the government for other reasons will result in some job openings over the next decade. A small number of new jobs will result from the need for oceanographers to conduct research for the military or for federal agencies such as the National Oceanic and Atmospheric Administration (NOAA) on issues related to maintaining healthy and productive oceans.

Many geoscientists work in the exploration and production of oil and gas. Historically, employment of petroleum geologists, geophysicists, and some other geoscientists has been cyclical and affected considerably by the price of oil and gas. When prices were low, oil and gas producers curtailed exploration activities and laid off geologists. When prices were higher, companies had the funds and incentive to renew exploration efforts and hire geoscientists in larger numbers. In recent years, a growing worldwide demand for oil and gas and for new exploration and recovery techniques—particularly in deep water and previously inaccessible sites in Alaska and the Gulf of Mexico—has returned some stability to the petroleum industry. Growth in this area, though, will be limited due to increasing efficiencies in finding oil and gas. Geoscientists who speak a foreign language and who are willing to work abroad should enjoy the best opportunities as the need for energy, construction materials, and a broad range of geoscience expertise grows in developing nations.

Job growth is expected within management, scientific, and technical consulting services. Demand will be spurred by a continuing emphasis on the need for energy, environmental protection, responsible land management, and water-related issues. Management, scientific, and technical consulting services have increased their hiring of many geoscientists in recent years due to increased government contracting and also in response to demand for professionals to provide technical assistance and management plans to corporations. Moreover, many of these workers will be needed to monitor the quality of the environment, including aquatic ecosystems, issues related to water conservation, deteriorating coastal environments, and rising sea levels—all of which will stimulate employment growth of geoscientists.

An expected increase in highway building and other infrastructure projects will be a source of jobs for engineering geologists.

During periods of economic recession, geoscientists may be laid off. Especially vulnerable to layoffs are those in consulting and, to a lesser extent, workers in government. Employment for those working in the production of oil and gas, however, will largely be dictated by the cyclical nature of the energy sector and changes in government policy.

Earnings

Median annual earnings of geoscientists were $68,730 in May 2004. The middle 50 percent earned between $49,260 and $98,380; the lowest 10 percent earned less than $37,700, the highest 10 percent more than $130,750.

According to the National Association of Colleges and Employers, beginning salary offers in July 2005 for graduates with bachelor's degrees in geology and related sciences averaged $39,365 a year.

In 2005, the federal government's average salary for geologists in managerial, supervisory, and nonsupervisory positions was $83,178 for geologists, $94,836 for geophysicists, and $87,007 for oceanographers.

The petroleum, mineral, and mining industries are vulnerable to recessions and to changes in oil and gas prices, among other factors, and usually release workers when exploration and drilling slow down. Consequently, they offer higher salaries, but less job security, than other industries.

Related Occupations

Many geoscientists work in the petroleum and natural-gas industry, an industry that also employs numerous other workers whose jobs deal with the scientific and technical aspects of the exploration and extraction of petroleum and natural gas. Among these other workers are engineering technicians, science technicians, petroleum engineers, surveyors, cartographers, photogrammetrists, and surveying technicians. Also, some physicists, chemists, atmospheric scientists, biological scientists, and environmental scientists and hydrologists—as well as mathematicians, computer systems analysts, computer scientists and database administrators—perform related work both in the exploration and extraction of petroleum and natural gas and in activities having to do with the environment.

Sources of Additional Information

Information on training and career opportunities for geologists is available from either of the following organizations:

▸ American Geological Institute, 4220 King St., Alexandria, VA 22302-1502. Internet: http://www.agiweb.org

▸ American Association of Petroleum Geologists, P.O. Box 979, Tulsa, OK 74101. Internet: http://www.aapg.org

Information on oceanography and related fields is available from

▸ Marine Technology Society, 5565 Sterrett Place, Suite 108, Columbia, MD 21004. Internet: http://www.mtsociety.org

Information on obtaining a position as a geologist, geophysicist, or oceanographer with the federal government is available from the Office of Personnel Management through USAJOBS, the federal government's official employment information system. This resource for locating and applying for job opportunities can be accessed through the Internet at http://www.usajobs.opm.gov or through an interactive voice response telephone system at (703) 724-1850 or TDD (978) 461-8404. These numbers are not toll free, and charges may result.

Instructional Coordinators

(O*NET 25-9031.00)

Significant Points

■ Many instructional coordinators have experience as teachers or education administrators.

■ A bachelor's degree is the minimum educational requirement, but a graduate degree is preferred.

■ The need to meet new educational standards will create more demand for instructional coordinators to train teachers and develop new materials.

Nature of the Work

Instructional coordinators, also known as *curriculum specialists, staff development specialists,* or *directors of instructional material,* play a large role in improving the quality of education in the classroom. They develop curricula, select textbooks and other materials, train teachers, and assess educational programs in terms of quality and adherence to regulations and standards. They also assist in implementing new technology in the classroom. Instructional coordinators often specialize in specific subjects, such as reading, language arts, mathematics, or social studies.

Instructional coordinators evaluate how well a school or training program's curriculum, or plan of study, meets students' needs. They research teaching methods and techniques and develop procedures to determine whether program goals are being met. To aid in their evaluation, they may meet with members of educational committees and advisory groups to learn about subjects—English, history, or mathematics, for example—and to relate curriculum materials to these subjects, to students' needs, and to occupations for which these subjects are good preparation. They also may develop question-naires and interview school staff about the curriculum. Based on their research and observations of instructional practice, they recommend instruction and curriculum improvements.

Another duty some instructional coordinators have is to review text-books, software, and other educational materials and make recommendations on purchases. They monitor materials ordered and the ways in which teachers use them in the classroom. They also supervise workers who catalogue, distribute, and maintain a school's educational materials and equipment.

Instructional coordinators develop effective ways to use technology to enhance student learning. They monitor the introduction of new technology, including the Internet, into a school's curriculum. In addition, instructional coordinators might recommend installing educational computer software, such as interactive books and exercises designed to enhance student literacy and develop math skills. Instructional coordinators may invite experts—such as computer hardware, software, and library or media specialists—into the classroom to help integrate technological materials into a school's curriculum.

Many instructional coordinators plan and provide onsite education for teachers and administrators. They may train teachers about the use of materials and equipment or help them to improve their skills. Instructional coordinators also mentor new teachers and train experienced ones in the latest instructional methods. This role becomes especially important when a school district introduces new content, program innovations, or a different organizational structure. For example, when a state or school district introduces standards or tests that must be met by students in order to pass to the next grade, instructional coordinators often must advise teachers on the content of the standards and provide instruction on implementing the standards in the classroom.

Working Conditions

Instructional coordinators, including those employed by school districts, often work year round, usually in offices or classrooms. Some spend much of their time traveling between schools meeting with teachers and administrators. The opportunity to shape and improve instructional curricula and work in an academic environment can be satisfying. However, some instructional coordinators find the work stressful because the occupation requires continual accountability to school administrators and it is not uncommon for people in this occupation to work long hours.

Training, Other Qualifications, and Advancement

The minimum educational requirement for instructional coordinators is a bachelor's degree, usually in education. Most employers, however, prefer candidates with a master's or higher degree. State licensing is necessary for instructional coordinators in public school systems, although specific requirements vary by state. In some states, a teaching license is needed, while in others instructional coordinators need an education administrator license. Instructional coordinators should have training in curriculum development and instruction or in the specific field for which they are responsible, such as mathematics or history. Instructional coordinators must have a good understanding of how to teach specific groups of students in addition to expertise in developing educational materials. As a result, many persons transfer into instructional coordinator jobs after working for several years as teachers. Work experience in an education administrator position, such as principal or assistant principal, also can be beneficial.

Helpful college courses may include those in curriculum development and evaluation, instructional approaches, or research design, which teaches how to create and implement research studies to determine the effectiveness of a given method of instruction or curriculum or to measure and improve student performance. Moreover, instructional coordinators usually are required to take continuing education courses to keep their skills current. Topics for continuing education courses may include teacher evaluation techniques, curriculum training, new teacher induction, consulting and teacher support, and observation and analysis of teaching.

Instructional coordinators must be able to make sound decisions about curriculum options and to organize and coordinate work efficiently. They should have strong interpersonal and communication skills. Familiarity with computer technology also is important for instructional coordinators, who are increasingly involved in gathering and coordinating technical information for students and teachers.

Depending on experience and educational attainment, instructional coordinators may advance to higher administrative positions in a school system or to management or executive positions in private industry.

Employment

Instructional coordinators held about 117,000 jobs in 2004. More than 2 in 5 worked for local governments, mainly in public schools and school district offices. One in 5 worked in private education, primarily in private elementary, secondary, and postsecondary schools and educational consulting firms. About 1 in 5 worked for state governments in public colleges and universities or state departments of education. The remainder worked mostly in the following industries: individual and family services; child day care services; scientific research and development services; and management, scientific, and technical consulting services.

Job Outlook

Employment of instructional coordinators is expected to grow much faster than the average for all occupations through the year 2014. Over the next decade, instructional coordinators will be instrumental in developing new curricula to meet the demands of a changing society and in training the teacher workforce. Although budget constraints may limit employment growth to some extent, a continuing emphasis on improving the quality of education is expected to result in an increasing demand for these workers. Also, as an increased emphasis on accountability at all levels of government causes more schools to focus on improving educational quality and student performance, growing numbers of coordinators will be needed to incorporate the standards into existing curricula and make sure teachers and administrators are informed of the changes. Opportunities are expected to be best for those who specialize in subject areas that have been targeted for improvement by the No Child Left Behind Act—namely, reading, math, and science.

Instructional coordinators also will be needed to provide classes on using technology in the classroom, to keep teachers up to date on changes in their fields, and to demonstrate new teaching techniques. Additional job growth for instructional coordinators will stem from the increasing emphasis on lifelong learning and on programs for students with special needs, including those for whom English is a second language. These students often require more educational resources and consolidated planning and management within the educational system.

Earnings

Median annual earnings of instructional coordinators in May 2004 were $48,790. The middle 50 percent earned between $35,940 and $65,040. The lowest 10 percent earned less than $27,300, and the highest 10 percent earned more than $81,210.

Related Occupations

Instructional coordinators are professionals involved in education and training and development, which requires organizational, administrative, teaching, research, and communication skills. Occupations with similar characteristics include preschool, kindergarten, elementary, middle, and secondary school teachers; postsecondary teachers; education administrators; counselors; and human resources, training, and labor relations managers and specialists.

Sources of Additional Information

Information on requirements and job opportunities for instructional coordinators is available from local school systems and state departments of education.

Librarians

(O*NET 25-4021.00)

Significant Points

■ A master's degree in library science usually is required; special librarians may need an additional graduate or professional degree.

■ A large number of retirements in the next decade is expected to result in many job openings for librarians to replace those who leave.

■ Librarians increasingly use information technology to perform research, classify materials, and help students and library patrons seek information.

Nature of the Work

The traditional concept of a library is being redefined from a place to access paper records or books to one that also houses the most advanced media, including CD-ROM, the Internet, virtual libraries, and remote access to a wide range of resources. Consequently, *librarians,* or *information professionals,* increasingly are combining traditional duties with tasks involving quickly changing technology. Librarians assist people in finding information and using it effectively for personal and professional purposes. Librarians must have knowledge of a wide variety of scholarly and public information sources and must follow trends related to publishing, computers, and the media in order to oversee the selection and organization of library materials. Librarians manage staff and develop and direct information programs and systems for the public to ensure that information is organized in a manner that meets users' needs.

Most librarian positions incorporate three aspects of library work: user services, technical services, and administrative services. Still, even librarians specializing in one of these areas have other responsibilities. Librarians in user services, such as reference and children's librarians, work with patrons to help them find the information they need. The job involves analyzing users' needs to determine what information is appropriate, as well as searching for, acquiring, and providing the information. The job also includes an instructional role, such as showing users how to access information. For example, librarians commonly help users navigate the Internet so they can search for relevant information efficiently. Librarians in technical services, such as acquisitions and cataloguing, acquire and prepare materials for use and often do not deal directly with the public. Librarians in administrative services oversee the management and planning of libraries: They negotiate contracts for services, materials, and equipment; supervise library employees; perform public-relations and fundraising duties; prepare budgets; and direct activities to ensure that everything functions properly.

In small libraries or information centers, librarians usually handle all aspects of the work. They read book reviews, publishers' announcements, and catalogues to keep up with current literature and other available resources, and they select and purchase materials from publishers, wholesalers, and distributors. Librarians prepare new materials by classifying them by subject matter and describe books and other library materials to make them easy to find. Librarians supervise assistants, who prepare cards, computer records, or other access tools that direct users to resources. In large libraries, librarians often specialize in a single area, such as acquisitions, cataloguing, bibliography, reference, special collections, or administration. Teamwork is increasingly important to ensure quality service to the public.

Librarians also compile lists of books, periodicals, articles, and audiovisual materials on particular subjects; analyze collections; and recommend materials. They collect and organize books, pamphlets, manuscripts, and other materials in a specific field, such as rare books, genealogy, or music. In addition, they coordinate programs such as storytelling for children and literacy skills and book talks for adults, conduct classes, publicize services, provide reference help, write grants, and oversee other administrative matters.

Librarians are classified according to the type of library in which they work: a public library; school library media center; college, university, or other academic library; or special library. Some librarians work with specific groups, such as children, young adults, adults, or the disadvantaged. In school library media centers, librarians—often called *school media specialists*—help teachers develop curricula, acquire materials for classroom instruction, and sometimes team teach.

Librarians also work in information centers or libraries maintained by government agencies, corporations, law firms, advertising agencies, museums, professional associations, unions, medical centers, hospitals, religious organizations, and research laboratories. They acquire and arrange an organization's information resources, which usually are limited to subjects of special interest to the organization. These special librarians can provide vital information services by preparing abstracts and indexes of current periodicals, organizing bibliographies, or analyzing background information and preparing reports on areas of particular interest. For example, a special librarian working for a corporation could provide the sales department with information on competitors or new developments affecting the field. A *medical librarian* may provide information about new medical treatments, clinical trials, and standard procedures to health professionals, patients, consumers, and corporations. *Government document librarians,* who work for government agencies and depository libraries in each of the states, preserve government publications, records, and other documents that make up a historical record of government actions.

Many libraries have access to remote databases and maintain their own computerized databases. The widespread use of automation in libraries makes database-searching skills important to librarians. Librarians develop and index databases and help train users to develop searching skills for the information they need. Some libraries are forming consortiums with other libraries to allow patrons to access a wider range of databases and to submit information requests to several libraries simultaneously. The Internet also has greatly expanded the amount of available reference information. Librarians must be aware of how to use these resources in order to locate information.

Librarians with computer and information systems skills can work as *automated-systems librarians,* planning and operating computer systems, and as *information architects,* designing information storage and retrieval systems and developing procedures for collecting, organizing, interpreting, and classifying information. These librarians analyze and plan for future information needs. (See the description of computer scientists and database administrators elsewhere in this book.) The increasing use of automated information systems is enabling librarians to focus on administrative and budgeting responsibilities, grant writing, and specialized research requests while delegating more technical and user services responsibilities to technicians.

More and more, librarians are applying their information management and research skills to arenas outside of libraries—for example, database development, reference tool development, information systems, publishing, Internet coordination, marketing, Web content management and design, and training of database users. *Entrepreneurial librarians* sometimes start their own consulting practices, acting as freelance librarians or information brokers and providing services to other libraries, businesses, or government agencies.

Working Conditions

Librarians spend a significant portion of time at their desks or in front of computer terminals; extended work at video display terminals can cause eyestrain and headaches. Assisting users in obtaining information or books for their jobs, homework, or recreational reading can be challenging and satisfying, but working with users under deadlines can be demanding and stressful. Some librarians lift and carry books and some climb ladders to reach high stacks, although most modern libraries have readily accessible stacks. Librarians in small organizations sometimes shelve books themselves.

More than 2 out of 10 librarians work part time. Public and college librarians often work weekends and evenings, as well as some holidays. School librarians usually have the same workday and vacation schedules as classroom teachers. Special librarians usually work normal business hours, but in fast-paced industries—such as advertising or legal services—they can work longer hours when needed.

Training, Other Qualifications, and Advancement

A master's degree in library science (MLS) is necessary for librarian positions in most public, academic, and special libraries and in some school libraries. The federal government requires that the librarians it employs have an MLS or the equivalent in education and experience. Many colleges and universities offer MLS programs, but employers often prefer graduates of the approximately 56 schools accredited by the American Library Association. Most MLS programs require a bachelor's degree, but no specific undergraduate program is required.

Most MLS programs take one year to complete; some take two. A typical graduate program includes courses in the foundations of library and information science, including the history of books and printing, intellectual freedom and censorship, and the role of libraries and information in society. Other basic courses cover the selection and processing of materials, the organization of information, reference tools and strategies, and user services. Courses are adapted to educate librarians to use new resources brought about by advancing technology, such as online reference systems, Internet search methods, and automated circulation systems. Course options can include resources for children or young adults; classification, cataloguing, indexing, and abstracting; library administration; and library automation. Computer-related course work is an increasingly important part of an MLS degree. Some programs offer interdisciplinary degrees combining technical courses in information science with traditional training in library science.

The MLS degree provides general preparation for library work, but some individuals specialize in a particular area, such as reference, technical services, or children's services. A Ph.D. degree in library and information science is advantageous for a college teaching position or for a top administrative job in a college or university library or large library system.

In addition to an MLS degree, most special librarians supplement their education with knowledge of the field in which they are specializing, sometimes earning a master's, doctoral, or professional degree in the subject. Areas of specialization include medicine, law, business, engineering, and the natural and social sciences. For example, a librarian working for a law firm may also be a licensed attorney, holding both library science and law degrees, while medical librarians should have a strong background in the sciences. In some jobs, knowledge of a foreign language is needed.

States generally have certification requirements for librarians in public schools and local libraries, though there are wide variations among states. Many require school librarians, often called library media specialists, to be certified as teachers in addition to having courses in library science. An MLS is needed in some states, often with a library media specialization, while in others a master's in education with a specialty in school library media or educational media is needed. Twenty-four states also require certification of librarians employed in local library systems, while several others have voluntary certification guidelines.

Librarians participate in continuing education and training, once they are on the job, in order to keep abreast of new information systems brought about by changing technology.

Experienced librarians can advance to administrative positions, such as department head, library director, or chief information officer.

Employment

Librarians held about 159,000 jobs in 2004. Most worked in school and academic libraries, but one-fourth worked in public libraries. The remainder worked in special libraries or as information professionals for companies and other organizations.

Job Outlook

Employment of librarians is expected to grow more slowly than the average for all occupations over the 2004–2014 period. However, job opportunities are expected to be very good because a large number of librarians are expected to retire in the coming decade. More than 3 in 5 librarians are aged 45 or older and will become eligible for retirement in the next 10 years, which will result in many job openings. Also, the number of people going into this profession has fallen in recent years, resulting in more jobs than applicants in some cases.

Growth in the number of librarians will be limited by government budget constraints and the increasing use of computerized information storage and retrieval systems. Both will result in the hiring of fewer librarians and the replacement of librarians with less costly library technicians and assistants. Computerized systems make cataloguing easier, allowing library technicians to perform the work. In addition, many libraries are equipped for users to access library computers directly from their homes or offices. That way, users can bypass librarians altogether and conduct research on their own. However, librarians will still be needed to manage staff, help users develop database-searching techniques, address complicated reference requests, and define users' needs.

Jobs for librarians outside traditional settings will grow the fastest over the decade. Nontraditional librarian jobs include working as information brokers and working for private corporations, nonprofit organizations, and consulting firms. Many companies are turning to librarians because of their research and organizational skills and their knowledge of computer databases and library automation systems. Librarians can review vast amounts of information and analyze, evaluate, and organize it according to a company's specific needs. Librarians also are hired by organizations to set up information on the Internet. Librarians working in these settings may be classified as systems analysts, database specialists and trainers, Webmasters or Web developers, or local area network (LAN) coordinators.

Earnings

Salaries of librarians vary according to the individual's qualifications and the type, size, and location of the library. Librarians with primarily administrative duties often have greater earnings. Median annual earnings of librarians in May 2004 were $45,900. The middle 50 percent earned between $36,980 and $56,960. The lowest 10 percent earned less than $28,930, and the highest 10 percent earned more than $70,200. Median annual earnings in the industries employing the largest numbers of librarians in May 2004 were as follows:

Colleges, universities, and professional schools	$47,830
Elementary and secondary schools	47,580
Local government	42,500
Other information services	40,000

The average annual salary for all librarians in the federal government in nonsupervisory, supervisory, and managerial positions was $74,630 in 2005.

About three in ten librarians are a member of a union or are covered under a union contract.

Related Occupations

Librarians play an important role in the transfer of knowledge and ideas by providing people with access to the information they need and want. Jobs requiring similar analytical, organizational, and communication skills include archivists, curators, and museum technicians and computer and information scientists, research. School librarians have many duties similar to those of school teachers. Librarians are increasingly storing, cataloguing, and accessing information with computers. Other jobs that use similar computer skills include computer systems analysts and computer scientists and database administrators.

Sources of Additional Information

For information on a career as a librarian and information on accredited library education programs and scholarships, contact

▸ American Library Association, Office for Human Resource Development and Recruitment, 50 East Huron St., Chicago, IL 60611. Internet: http://www.ala.org

For information on a career as a special librarian, contact

▸ Special Libraries Association, 331 South Patrick St., Alexandria, VA 22314. Internet: http://www.sla.org

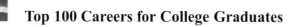

For information on a career as a law librarian, scholarship information, and a list of ALA-accredited schools offering programs in law librarianship, contact

▸ American Association of Law Libraries, 53 West Jackson Blvd., Suite 940, Chicago, IL 60604. Internet: http://www.aallnet.org

For information on employment opportunities for health sciences librarians and for scholarship information, credentialing information, and a list of MLA-accredited schools offering programs in health sciences librarianship, contact

▸ Medical Library Association, 65 East Wacker Place, Suite 1900, Chicago, IL 60601. Internet: http://www.mlanet.org

Information concerning requirements and application procedures for positions in the Library of Congress can be obtained directly from

▸ Human Resources Office, Library of Congress, 101 Independence Ave. SE, Washington, DC 20540-2231. Internet: http://www.loc.gov/hr

State library agencies can furnish information on scholarships available through their offices, requirements for certification, and general information about career prospects in the particular state of interest. Several of these agencies maintain job hotlines reporting openings for librarians.

State departments of education can furnish information on certification requirements and job opportunities for school librarians.

Market and Survey Researchers

(O*NET 19-3021.00 and 19-3022.00)

Significant Points

■ Market and survey researchers need at least a bachelor's degree, but a master's degree may be required for employment; continuing education also is important.

■ Employment is expected to grow faster than average.

■ Job opportunities should be best for those with a master's or Ph.D. degree in marketing or a related field and strong quantitative skills.

Nature of the Work

Market, or *marketing, research analysts* are concerned with the potential sales of a product or service. Gathering statistical data on competitors and examining prices, sales, and methods of marketing and distribution, they analyze data on past sales to predict future sales. Market research analysts devise methods and procedures for obtaining the data they need. Often, they design telephone, mail, or Internet surveys to assess consumer preferences. They conduct some surveys as personal interviews, going door-to-door, leading focus group discussions, or setting up booths in public places such as shopping malls. Trained interviewers usually conduct the surveys under the market research analyst's direction.

After compiling and evaluating the data, market research analysts make recommendations to their client or employer on the basis of their findings. They provide a company's management with information needed to make decisions on the promotion, distribution, design, and pricing of products or services. The information also may be used to determine the advisability of adding new lines of merchandise, opening new branches, or otherwise diversifying the company's operations. Market research analysts also might develop advertising brochures and commercials, sales plans, and product promotions such as rebates and giveaways.

Survey researchers design and conduct surveys for a variety of clients, such as corporations, government agencies, political candidates, and providers of various services. The surveys collect information that is used for performing research, making fiscal or policy decisions, measuring the effectiveness of those decisions, or improving customer satisfaction. Analysts may conduct opinion research to determine public attitudes on various issues; the research results may help political or business leaders and others assess public support for their electoral prospects or social policies. Like market research analysts, survey researchers may use a variety of mediums to conduct surveys, such as the Internet, personal or telephone interviews, or questionnaires sent through the mail. They also may supervise interviewers who conduct surveys in person or over the telephone.

Survey researchers design surveys in many different formats, depending upon the scope of their research and the method of collection. Interview surveys, for example, are common because they can increase participation rates. Survey researchers may consult with economists, statisticians, market research analysts, or other data users in order to design surveys. They also may present survey results to clients.

Working Conditions

Market and survey researchers generally have structured work schedules. Some often work alone, writing reports, preparing statistical charts, and using computers, but they also may be an integral part of a research team. Market researchers who conduct personal interviews have frequent contact with the public. Most work under pressure of deadlines and tight schedules, which may require overtime. Their routine may be interrupted by special requests for data as well as by the need to attend meetings or conferences. Travel may be necessary.

Training, Other Qualifications, and Advancement

A bachelor's degree is the minimum educational requirement for many market and survey research jobs. However, a master's degree may be required, especially for technical positions, and increases opportunities for advancement to more responsible positions. Also, continuing education is important in order to keep current with the latest methods of developing, conducting, and analyzing surveys and other data. Market and survey researchers may earn advanced degrees in business administration, marketing, statistics, communications, or some closely related discipline. Some schools help graduate students find internships or part-time employment in government agencies, consulting firms, financial institutions, or marketing research firms prior to graduation.

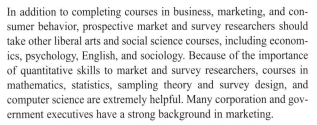

In addition to completing courses in business, marketing, and consumer behavior, prospective market and survey researchers should take other liberal arts and social science courses, including economics, psychology, English, and sociology. Because of the importance of quantitative skills to market and survey researchers, courses in mathematics, statistics, sampling theory and survey design, and computer science are extremely helpful. Many corporation and government executives have a strong background in marketing.

A master's degree is usually the minimum educational requirement for a job as a marketing or survey research instructor in junior and community colleges. In most colleges and universities, however, a Ph.D. is necessary for appointment as an instructor. A Ph.D. and extensive publications in academic journals are required for a professorship, tenure, and promotion.

While in college, aspiring market and survey researchers should gain experience gathering and analyzing data, conducting interviews or surveys, and writing reports on their findings. This experience can prove invaluable later in obtaining a full-time position in the field because much of the initial work may center on these duties. With experience, market and survey researchers eventually are assigned their own research projects.

Much of the market and survey researcher's time is spent on precise data analysis, so those considering careers in the occupation should be able to pay attention to detail. Patience and persistence are necessary qualities because these workers must spend long hours on independent study and problem solving. At the same time, they must work well with others: often, market and survey researchers oversee interviews of a wide variety of individuals. Communication skills are important, too, because researchers must be able to present their findings both orally and in writing in a clear, concise manner.

While certification currently is not required for market and survey researchers, the Marketing Research Association (MRA) offers a certification program for professional researchers. Certification is based on education and experience requirements as well as on continuing education.

Employment

Market and survey researchers held about 212,000 jobs in 2004, most of which—190,000—were held by market research analysts. Because of the applicability of market research to many industries, market research analysts are employed throughout the economy. The industries that employ the largest number of market research analysts were management of companies and enterprises; management, scientific, and technical consulting services; insurance carriers; credit intermediation and related activities; computer systems design and related services; marketing research and public opinion polling; software publishers; professional and commercial equipment and supplies merchant wholesalers; securities and commodity contracts intermediation and brokerage; and advertising and related services.

Survey researchers held about 22,000 jobs in 2004. Survey researchers were employed mainly by professional, scientific, and technical services firms, especially in market research and public opinion polling; scientific research and development services; and management, scientific, and technical consulting services. State government also provided many jobs for survey researchers.

A number of market and survey researchers combine a full-time job in government, academia, or business with part-time or consulting work in another setting. About nine percent of market and survey researchers are self-employed.

Besides holding the previously mentioned jobs, many market and survey researchers held faculty positions in colleges and universities. Marketing faculties have flexible work schedules and may divide their time among teaching, research, consulting, and administration. (See the description of teachers—postsecondary elsewhere in this book.)

Job Outlook

Employment of market and survey researchers is expected to grow faster than the average for all occupations through 2014. Many job openings are likely to result from the need to replace experienced workers who transfer to other occupations or who retire or leave the labor force for other reasons.

Job opportunities should be best for those with a master's or Ph.D. degree in marketing or a related field and strong quantitative skills. Bachelor's degree holders may face competition, as many positions, especially the more technical ones, require a master's or higher degree. Among bachelor's degree holders, those with good quantitative skills, including a strong background in mathematics, statistics, survey design, and computer science, will have the best opportunities. Ph.D. degree holders in marketing and related fields should have a range of opportunities in industry and consulting firms. Like those in many other disciplines, however, Ph.D. holders probably will face keen competition for tenured teaching positions in colleges and universities.

Demand for market research analysts should be strong because of an increasingly competitive economy. Marketing research provides organizations with valuable feedback from purchasers, allowing companies to evaluate consumer satisfaction and plan more effectively for the future. As companies seek to expand their market and as consumers become better informed, the need for marketing professionals will increase. In addition, as globalization of the marketplace continues, market researchers will increasingly be utilized to analyze foreign markets and competition for goods and services.

Market research analysts should have the best opportunities in consulting firms and marketing research firms as companies find it more profitable to contract for market research services rather than support their own marketing department. Increasingly, market research analysts not only are collecting and analyzing information, but also are helping clients implement the analysts' ideas and recommendations. Other organizations, including computer systems design companies, software publishers, financial services organizations, health care institutions, advertising firms, and insurance companies, may offer job opportunities for market research analysts. Survey researchers will be needed to meet the growing demand for market and opinion research as an increasingly competitive economy requires businesses to allocate advertising funds more effectively and efficiently.

Earnings

Median annual earnings of market research analysts in May 2004 were $56,140. The middle 50 percent earned between $40,510 and $79,990. The lowest 10 percent earned less than $30,890, and the highest 10 percent earned more than $105,870. Median annual earnings in the industries employing the largest numbers of market research analysts in May 2004 were

Management of companies and enterprises $58,440

Computer systems design and related services 58,100

Insurance carriers 51,030

Other professional, scientific, and technical
services 50,950

Management, scientific, and technical
consulting services 49,080

Median annual earnings of survey researchers in May 2004 were $26,490. The middle 50 percent earned between $17,920 and $41,390. The lowest 10 percent earned less than $15,330, and the highest 10 percent earned more than $56,740. Median annual earnings of survey researchers in other professional, scientific, and technical services were $22,880.

Related Occupations

Market and survey researchers perform research to find out how well the market receives products or services. Such research may include planning, implementing, and analyzing surveys to determine the needs and preferences of people. Other jobs using these skills include economists, psychologists, sociologists, statisticians, and urban and regional planners.

Sources of Additional Information

For information about careers and certification in market research, contact

▸ Marketing Research Association, 110 National Dr., Glastonbury, CT 06033. Internet: http://www.mra-net.org

For information about careers in survey research, contact

▸ Council of American Survey Research Organizations, 170 North Country Rd., Suite 4, Port Jefferson, NY 11777. Internet: http://www.casro.org

Mathematicians

(O*NET 15-2021.00)

Significant Points

■ A Ph.D. degree in mathematics usually is the minimum educational requirement, except in the federal government.

■ The number of jobs with the title "mathematician" is declining as the workforce becomes increasingly specialized; competition will be keen for the limited number of available jobs.

■ Master's and Ph.D. degree holders with a strong background in mathematics and a related field, such as computer science or engineering, should have better employment opportunities in related occupations.

Nature of the Work

Mathematics is one of the oldest and most fundamental sciences. Mathematicians use mathematical theory, computational techniques, algorithms, and the latest computer technology to solve economic, scientific, engineering, physics, and business problems. The work of mathematicians falls into two broad classes—theoretical (pure) mathematics and applied mathematics. These classes, however, are not sharply defined and often overlap.

Theoretical mathematicians advance mathematical knowledge by developing new principles and recognizing previously unknown relationships between existing principles of mathematics. Although these workers seek to increase basic knowledge without necessarily considering its practical use, such pure and abstract knowledge has been instrumental in producing or furthering many scientific and engineering achievements. Many theoretical mathematicians are employed as university faculty, dividing their time between teaching and conducting research. (See the description of teachers—postsecondary elsewhere in this book.)

Applied mathematicians, on the other hand, use theories and techniques, such as mathematical modeling and computational methods, to formulate and solve practical problems in business, government, and engineering and in the physical, life, and social sciences. For example, they may analyze the most efficient way to schedule airline routes between cities, the effects and safety of new drugs, the aerodynamic characteristics of an experimental automobile, or the cost-effectiveness of alternative manufacturing processes. Applied mathematicians working in industrial research and development may develop or enhance mathematical methods when solving a difficult problem. Some mathematicians, called *cryptanalysts,* analyze and decipher encryption systems designed to transmit military, political, financial, or law enforcement-related information in code.

Applied mathematicians start with a practical problem, envision the separate elements of the process under consideration, and then reduce the elements to mathematical variables. They often use computers to analyze relationships among the variables and solve complex problems by developing models with alternative solutions.

Much of the work in applied mathematics is done by individuals with titles other than mathematician. In fact, because mathematics is the foundation on which so many other academic disciplines are built, the number of workers using mathematical techniques is much greater than the number formally designated as mathematicians. For example, engineers, computer scientists, physicists, and economists are among those who use mathematics extensively. Some professionals, including statisticians, actuaries, and operations research analysts, actually are specialists in a particular branch of mathematics. Frequently, applied mathematicians are required to collaborate with other workers in their organizations to achieve common solutions to problems. (For more information, see the descriptions of actuaries, operations research analysts, and statisticians elsewhere in this book.)

Working Conditions

Mathematicians usually work in comfortable offices. They often are part of interdisciplinary teams that may include economists, engineers, computer scientists, physicists, technicians, and others. Deadlines, overtime work, special requests for information or analysis, and prolonged travel to attend seminars or conferences may be part of their jobs. Mathematicians who work in academia usually have a mix of teaching and research responsibilities. These mathematicians may conduct research alone or in close collaboration with other mathematicians. Collaborators may work together at the same institution or from different locations, using technology such as e-mail to communicate. Mathematicians in academia also may be aided by graduate students.

Training, Other Qualifications, and Advancement

A Ph.D. degree in mathematics usually is the minimum educational requirement for prospective mathematicians, except in the federal government. In the federal government, entry-level job candidates usually must have a 4-year degree with a major in mathematics or a 4-year degree with the equivalent of a mathematics major—24 semester hours of mathematics courses.

In private industry, candidates for mathematician jobs typically need a Ph.D., although there may be opportunities for those with a master's degree. Most of the positions designated for mathematicians are in research and development laboratories as part of technical teams. In such settings, mathematicians engage either in basic research on pure mathematical principles or in applied research on developing or improving specific products or processes. The majority of those with a bachelor's or master's degree in mathematics who work in private industry do so not as mathematicians but in related fields such as computer science, where they have titles such as computer programmer, systems analyst, or systems engineer.

A bachelor's degree in mathematics is offered by most colleges and universities. Mathematics courses usually required for this degree include calculus, differential equations, and linear and abstract algebra. Additional courses might include probability theory and statistics, mathematical analysis, numerical analysis, topology, discrete mathematics, and mathematical logic. Many colleges and universities urge or require students majoring in mathematics to take courses in a field that is closely related to mathematics, such as computer science, engineering, life science, physical science, or economics. A double major in mathematics and another related discipline is particularly desirable to many employers. High school students who are prospective college mathematics majors should take as many mathematics courses as possible while in high school.

In 2004, about 200 colleges and universities offered a master's degree as the highest degree in either pure or applied mathematics; about 200 offered a Ph.D. degree in pure or applied mathematics. In graduate school, students conduct research and take advanced courses, usually specializing in a subfield of mathematics.

For jobs in applied mathematics, training in the field in which the mathematics will be used is very important. Mathematics is used extensively in physics, actuarial science, statistics, engineering, and operations research. Computer science, business and industrial management, economics, finance, chemistry, geology, life sciences, and behavioral sciences are likewise dependent on applied mathematics. Mathematicians also should have substantial knowledge of computer programming because most complex mathematical computation and much mathematical modeling are done on a computer.

Mathematicians need good reasoning ability and persistence to identify, analyze, and apply basic principles to technical problems. Communication skills also are important, as mathematicians must be able to interact and discuss proposed solutions with people who may not have extensive knowledge of mathematics.

Employment

Mathematicians held about 2,500 jobs in 2004. Many people with mathematical backgrounds also worked in other occupations. For example, about 53,000 persons held positions as postsecondary mathematical science teachers in 2004.

Many mathematicians work for federal or state governments. The U.S. Department of Defense is the primary federal employer, accounting for about three-fourths of the mathematicians employed by the federal government. Many of the other mathematicians employed by the federal government work for the National Aeronautics and Space Administration (NASA). In the private sector, major employers include scientific research and development services and management, scientific, and technical consulting services. Some mathematicians also work for software publishers, for insurance companies, and in aerospace or pharmaceutical manufacturing.

Job Outlook

Employment of mathematicians is expected to decline through 2014, reflecting the reduction in the number of jobs with the title "mathematician." As a result, competition is expected to be keen for the limited number of jobs as mathematicians. Master's and Ph.D. degree holders with a strong background in mathematics and a related discipline, such as engineering or computer science, should have the best opportunities. Many of these workers have job titles that reflect their occupation, such as systems analyst, rather than the title mathematician, reflecting their primary educational background.

Advancements in technology usually lead to expanding applications of mathematics, and more workers with knowledge of mathematics will be required in the future. However, jobs in industry and government often require advanced knowledge of related scientific disciplines in addition to mathematics. The most common fields in which mathematicians study and find work are computer science and software development, physics, engineering, and operations research. More mathematicians also are becoming involved in financial analysis. Mathematicians must compete for jobs, however, with people who have degrees in these other disciplines. The most successful jobseekers will be able to apply mathematical theory to real-world problems and will possess good communication, teamwork, and computer skills.

Private industry jobs require at least a master's degree in mathematics or in a related field. Bachelor's degree holders in mathematics usually are not qualified for most jobs, and many seek advanced degrees in mathematics or a related discipline. However, bachelor's degree holders who meet state certification requirements may become primary or secondary school mathematics teachers.

Holders of a master's degree in mathematics will face very strong competition for jobs in theoretical research. Because the number of Ph.D. degrees awarded in mathematics continues to exceed the number of university positions available, many of these graduates will need to find employment in industry and government.

Earnings

Median annual earnings of mathematicians were $81,240 in May 2004. The middle 50 percent earned between $60,050 and $101,360. The lowest 10 percent had earnings of less than $43,160, while the highest 10 percent earned over $120,900.

In early 2005, the average annual salary for mathematicians employed by the federal government in supervisory, nonsupervisory, and managerial positions was $88,194; that for mathematical statisticians was $91,446; and for cryptanalysts the average was $70,774.

Related Occupations

Other occupations that require extensive knowledge of mathematics or, in some cases, a degree in mathematics include actuaries, statisticians, computer programmers, computer systems analysts, computer scientists and database administrators, computer software engineers, and operations research analysts. A strong background in mathematics also facilitates employment as teachers—postsecondary; teachers—preschool, kindergarten, elementary, middle, and secondary; engineers; economists; market and survey researchers; financial analysts and personal financial advisors; and physicists and astronomers.

Sources of Additional Information

For more information about careers and training in mathematics, especially for doctoral-level employment, contact

▶ American Mathematical Society, 201 Charles St., Providence, RI 02904-2294. Internet: http://www.ams.org

For specific information on careers in applied mathematics, contact

▶ Society for Industrial and Applied Mathematics, 3600 University City Science Center, Philadelphia, PA 19104-2688. Internet: http://www.siam.org

Information on obtaining positions as mathematicians with the federal government is available from the Office of Personnel Management through USAJOBS, the federal government's official employment information system. This resource for locating and applying for job opportunities can be accessed through the Internet at http://www.usajobs.opm.gov or through an interactive voice response telephone system at (703) 724-1850 or TDD (978) 461-8404. These numbers are not toll free, and charges may result.

Operations Research Analysts

(O*NET 15-2031.00)

Significant Points

■ Employers generally prefer applicants with at least a master's degree in operations research or management science or a closely related field such as computer science, engineering, business, mathematics, or information systems.

■ Employment growth is projected to be slower than average, reflecting slow growth in the number of jobs with the title "operations research analyst."

■ Individuals with a master's or Ph.D. degree in management science, operations research, or equivalent should have good job opportunities as operations research analysts or in closely related occupations such as systems analysts, computer scientists, or management analysts.

Nature of the Work

"Operations research" and "management science" are terms that are used interchangeably to describe the discipline of applying advanced analytical techniques to help make better decisions and to solve problems. The procedures of operations research have been used effectively during wartime in areas such as deploying radar, searching for enemy submarines, and getting supplies to where they were needed most. New analytical methods have been developed and numerous peacetime applications have emerged, leading to the use of operations research in many industries and occupations.

The prevalence of operations research in the nation's economy reflects the growing complexity of managing large organizations that require the effective use of money, materials, equipment, and people. *Operations research analysts* help determine better ways to coordinate these elements by applying analytical methods from mathematics, science, and engineering. Analysts often find multiple possible solutions for meeting the particular goals of a project. These potential solutions are then presented to managers, who choose the course of action that they perceive to be best for the organization.

Operations research analysts often have one area of specialization, such as working in the transportation or the financial services industry, but the issues and industries in which operations research can be used are many. In general, operations research analysts may be involved in top-level strategizing, planning, forecasting, allocating resources, measuring performance, scheduling, designing production facilities and systems, managing the supply chain, pricing, coordinating transportation and distribution, or analyzing large databases.

The duties of the operations research analyst vary according to the structure and management of the employer's or client's organization. Some firms centralize operations research in one department; others use operations research in each division. Operations research analysts also may work closely with senior managers to identify and solve a variety of problems. Some organizations contract with consulting firms to provide operations research services. Economists, computer systems analysts, mathematicians, and others may apply operations research techniques to address problems in their respective fields. (These occupations are discussed elsewhere in this book.)

Regardless of the type or structure of the client organization, operations research entails following a standard set of procedures and conducting analysis to help managers improve performance. Managers begin the process by describing the symptoms of a problem to the analyst, who then formally defines the problem. For example, an operations research analyst for an auto manufacturer may be asked to determine the best inventory level for each of the parts needed on a production line and to ascertain the optimal number of windshields to be kept in stock. Too many windshields would be wasteful and expensive, whereas too few could result in an unintended halt in production.

Operations research analysts study such problems, breaking them into their components. Analysts then gather information about each of the components from a variety of sources. To determine the optimal inventory, for example, operations research analysts might talk with engineers about production levels, discuss purchasing arrangements with buyers, and examine storage-cost data provided by the accounting department.

With the relevant information in hand, the analyst determines the most appropriate analytical technique. Techniques used may include Monte Carlo simulation, linear and nonlinear programming, dynamic programming, queuing and other stochastic-process models, Markov decision processes, econometric methods, data envelopment analysis, neural networks, expert systems, decision analysis, and the analytic hierarchy process. Nearly all of these techniques involve the construction of a mathematical model that attempts to describe the system being studied. The use of models enables the analyst to explicitly describe the different components and clarify the relationships among them. The descriptions can be altered to examine what may happen to the system under different circumstances. In most cases, a computer program is developed to numerically evaluate the model.

Usually the model chosen is modified and run repeatedly to obtain different solutions. A model for airline flight scheduling, for example, might stipulate such things as connecting cities, the amount of fuel required to fly the routes, projected levels of passenger demand, varying ticket and fuel prices, pilot scheduling, and maintenance costs. By assessing different possible schedules, the analyst is able to determine the best flight schedule consistent with particular assumptions.

Based on the results of the analysis, the operations research analyst presents recommendations to managers. The analyst may need to modify and rerun the computer program to consider different assumptions before presenting the final recommendation. Once managers reach a decision, the analyst usually works with others in the organization to ensure the plan's successful implementation.

Working Conditions

Operations research analysts generally work regular hours in an office environment. However, because they work on projects that are of immediate interest to top managers, operations research analysts often are under pressure to meet deadlines and may work more than a 40-hour week.

Training, Other Qualifications, and Advancement

Employers generally prefer applicants with at least a master's degree in operations research or a closely related field, such as computer science, engineering, business, mathematics, information systems, or management science, coupled with a bachelor's degree in computer science or a quantitative discipline such as economics, mathematics, or statistics. Dual graduate degrees in operations research and computer science are especially attractive to employers. Operations research analysts must be able to think logically, use computers proficiently, work well with people, and demonstrate good oral and written communication skills.

In addition to supporting formal education in one manner or another, employers often sponsor training for experienced workers, helping them keep up with new developments in operations research techniques and computer science. Some analysts attend advanced university classes on these subjects at their employer's expense.

Computers are the most important tools used by operations research analysts for performing in-depth analysis. As a result, training and experience in programming are required. Analysts typically need to be proficient in database collection and management, programming, and the development and use of sophisticated software packages.

Beginning analysts usually perform routine work under the supervision of more experienced analysts. As the novices gain knowledge and experience, they are assigned more complex tasks and are given greater autonomy to design models and solve problems. Operations research analysts can advance by assuming positions as technical specialists or supervisors. Analysts also gain valuable insights into the industry or field in which they specialize and may assume higher-level nontechnical managerial or administrative positions. Operations research analysts with significant experience may become consultants, and some may even open their own consulting practices.

Employment

Operations research analysts held about 58,000 jobs in 2004. Major employers include computer systems design firms; insurance carriers and other financial institutions; telecommunications companies; management, scientific, and technical consulting services firms; and federal, state, and local governments. More than 4 out of 5 operations research analysts in the federal government work for the Department of Defense, and many in private industry work directly or indirectly on national defense.

Job Outlook

Employment of operations research analysts is expected to grow more slowly than average for all occupations through 2014, reflecting slow growth in the number of jobs with the title "operations research analyst." Job opportunities in operations research should be good, however, because organizations throughout the economy will strive to improve their productivity, effectiveness, and competitiveness and because of the extensive availability of data, computers, and software. Many jobs in operations research have other titles, such as operations analyst, management analyst, systems analyst, and computer scientist. Individuals who hold a master's or Ph.D. degree in operations research, management science, or a closely related field should find good job opportunities because the number of openings generated by employment growth and the need to replace those leaving the occupation is expected to exceed the number of persons graduating with these credentials.

Organizations face pressure today from growing domestic and international competition and must work to make their operations as effective as possible. As a result, businesses increasingly will rely on operations research analysts to optimize profits by improving productivity and reducing costs. As new technology is introduced into the marketplace, operations research analysts will be needed to determine how to utilize the technology in the best way.

Opportunities for operations research analysts exist in almost every industry because of the diversity of applications for their work. As businesses and government agencies continue to contract out jobs to cut costs, opportunities for operations research analysts will be best in management, scientific, and technical consulting firms. Opportunities in the military will exist as well, but will depend on the size of future military budgets. Military leaders will rely on operations research analysts to test and evaluate the accuracy and effectiveness of new weapons systems and strategies. (See this book's description of job opportunities in the Armed Forces.)

Earnings

Median annual earnings of operations research analysts were $60,190 in May 2004. The middle 50 percent earned between $45,640 and $78,420. The lowest 10 percent had earnings of less than $36,180, while the highest 10 percent earned more than $95,990.

The average annual salary for operations research analysts in the federal government in nonsupervisory, supervisory, and managerial positions was $89,882 in 2005.

Related Occupations

Operations research analysts apply advanced analytical methods to large, complicated problems. Workers in other occupations that stress advanced analysis include computer systems analysts, computer scientists and database administrators, computer programmers, engineers, mathematicians, statisticians, economists, and market and survey researchers. Because its goal is improved organizational effectiveness, operations research also is closely allied to managerial occupations such as computer and information systems managers and management analysts.

Sources of Additional Information

Information on career opportunities for operations research analysts is available from

▸ Institute for Operations Research and the Management Sciences, 7240 Parkway Dr., Suite 310, Hanover, MD 21076. Internet: http://www.informs.org

For information on operations research careers in the Armed Forces and the U.S. Department of Defense, contact

▸ Military Operations Research Society, 1703 N. Beauregard St., Suite 450, Alexandria, VA 22311. Internet: http://www.mors.org

Information on obtaining positions as operations research analysts with the federal government is available from the Office of Personnel Management through USAJOBS, the federal government's official employment information system. This resource for locating and applying for job opportunities can be accessed through the Internet at http://www.usajobs.opm.gov or through an interactive voice response telephone system at (703) 724-1850 or TDD (978) 461-8404. These numbers are not toll free, and charges may result.

Physical Therapists

(O*NET 29-1123.00)

Significant Points

■ Employment is expected to increase much faster than the average as growth in the number of individuals with disabilities or limited functioning spurs demand for therapy services.

■ Job opportunities should be particularly good in acute hospital, rehabilitation, and orthopedic settings.

■ After graduating from an accredited physical therapist educational program, therapists must pass a licensure exam before they can practice.

■ Nearly 6 out of 10 physical therapists work in hospitals or in offices of physical therapists.

Nature of the Work

Physical therapists provide services that help restore function, improve mobility, relieve pain, and prevent or limit permanent physical disabilities of patients suffering from injuries or disease. They restore, maintain, and promote overall fitness and health. Their patients include accident victims and individuals with disabling conditions such as low-back pain, arthritis, heart disease, fractures, head injuries, and cerebral palsy.

Therapists examine patients' medical histories and then test and measure the patients' strength, range of motion, balance and coordination, posture, muscle performance, respiration, and motor function. They also determine patients' ability to be independent and reintegrate into the community or workplace after injury or illness. Next, physical therapists develop plans describing a treatment strategy, its purpose, and its anticipated outcome. Physical therapist assistants, under the direction and supervision of a physical therapist, may be involved in implementing treatment plans with patients. Physical therapist aides perform routine support tasks, as directed by the therapist.

Treatment often includes exercise for patients who have been immobilized and lack flexibility, strength, or endurance. Physical therapists encourage patients to use their own muscles to increase their flexibility and range of motion before finally advancing to other exercises that improve strength, balance, coordination, and endurance. The goal is to improve how an individual functions at work and at home.

Physical therapists also use electrical stimulation, hot packs or cold compresses, and ultrasound to relieve pain and reduce swelling. They may use traction or deep-tissue massage to relieve pain. Therapists also teach patients to use assistive and adaptive devices, such as crutches, prostheses, and wheelchairs. They also may show patients exercises to do at home to expedite their recovery.

As treatment continues, physical therapists document the patient's progress, conduct periodic examinations, and modify treatments when necessary. Besides tracking the patient's progress, such documentation identifies areas requiring more or less attention.

Physical therapists often consult and practice with a variety of other professionals, such as physicians, dentists, nurses, educators, social workers, occupational therapists, speech-language pathologists, and audiologists.

Some physical therapists treat a wide range of ailments; others specialize in areas such as pediatrics, geriatrics, orthopedics, sports medicine, neurology, and cardiopulmonary physical therapy.

Working Conditions

Physical therapists practice in hospitals, clinics, and private offices that have specially equipped facilities, or they treat patients in hospital rooms, homes, or schools.

In 2004, most full-time physical therapists worked a 40-hour week; some worked evenings and weekends to fit their patients' schedules. About 1 in 4 physical therapists worked part time. The job can be physically demanding because therapists often have to stoop, kneel, crouch, lift, and stand for long periods. In addition, physical therapists move heavy equipment and lift patients or help them turn, stand, or walk.

Training, Other Qualifications, and Advancement

All states require physical therapists to pass a licensure exam before they can practice and after graduating from an accredited physical therapist educational program.

According to the American Physical Therapy Association, there were 205 accredited physical therapist programs in 2004. Of the accredited programs, 94 offered master's degrees and 111 offered doctoral degrees. All physical therapist programs seeking accreditation are required to offer degrees at the master's degree level and above in accordance with the Commission on Accreditation in Physical Therapy Education.

Physical therapist programs start with basic science courses such as biology, chemistry, and physics and then introduce specialized courses, including biomechanics, neuroanatomy, human growth and development, manifestations of disease, examination techniques, and therapeutic procedures. Besides getting classroom and laboratory instruction, students receive supervised clinical experience. Among the courses that are useful when one applies to a physical therapist educational program are anatomy, biology, chemistry, social science, mathematics, and physics. Before granting admission, many professional education programs require experience as a volunteer in a physical therapy department of a hospital or clinic. For high school students, volunteering with the school athletic trainer is a good way to gain experience.

Physical therapists should have strong interpersonal skills in order to be able to educate patients about their physical therapy treatments. Physical therapists also should be compassionate and possess a desire to help patients. Similar traits are needed to interact with the patient's family.

Physical therapists are expected to continue their professional development by participating in continuing education courses and workshops. In fact, a number of states require continuing education as a condition of maintaining licensure.

Employment

Physical therapists held about 155,000 jobs in 2004. The number of jobs is greater than the number of practicing physical therapists because some physical therapists hold two or more jobs. For example, some may work in a private practice, but also work part time in another health care facility.

Nearly 6 out of 10 physical therapists worked in hospitals or in offices of physical therapists. Other jobs were in home health care services, nursing care facilities, outpatient care centers, and offices of physicians.

Some physical therapists were self-employed in private practices, seeing individual patients and contracting to provide services in hospitals, rehabilitation centers, nursing care facilities, home health care agencies, adult day care programs, and schools. Physical therapists also teach in academic institutions and conduct research.

Job Outlook

Employment of physical therapists is expected to grow much faster than the average for all occupations through 2014. The impact of proposed federal legislation imposing limits on reimbursement for therapy services may adversely affect the short-term job outlook for physical therapists. However, over the long run, the demand for physical therapists should continue to rise as growth in the number of individuals with disabilities or limited function spurs demand for therapy services. Job opportunities should be particularly good in acute hospital, rehabilitation, and orthopedic settings because the elderly receive the most treatment in these settings. The growing elderly population is particularly vulnerable to chronic and debilitating conditions that require therapeutic services. Also, the baby-boom generation is entering the prime age for heart attacks and strokes, increasing the demand for cardiac and physical rehabilitation. Further, young people will need physical therapy as technological advances save the lives of a larger proportion of newborns with severe birth defects.

Future medical developments also should permit a higher percentage of trauma victims to survive, creating additional demand for rehabilitative care. In addition, growth may result from advances in medical technology that could permit the treatment of more disabling conditions.

Widespread interest in health promotion also should increase demand for physical therapy services. A growing number of employers are using physical therapists to evaluate worksites, develop exercise programs, and teach safe work habits to employees in the hope of reducing injuries in the workplace.

Earnings

Median annual earnings of physical therapists were $60,180 in May 2004. The middle 50 percent earned between $50,330 and $71,760. The lowest 10 percent earned less than $42,010, and the highest 10 percent earned more than $88,580. Median annual earnings in the industries employing the largest numbers of physical therapists in May 2004 were

Home health care services...................................$64,650

Nursing care facilities 61,720

Offices of physicians 61,270

General medical and surgical hospitals 60,350

Offices of other health practitioners.....................60,130

Related Occupations

Physical therapists rehabilitate persons with physical disabilities. Others who work in the rehabilitation field include audiologists, chiropractors, occupational therapists, recreational therapists, rehabilitation counselors, respiratory therapists, and speech-language pathologists.

Sources of Additional Information

Additional career information and a list of accredited educational programs in physical therapy are available from

▸ American Physical Therapy Association, 1111 North Fairfax St., Alexandria, VA 22314-1488. Internet: http://www.apta.org

Psychologists

(O*NET 19-3031.01, 19-3031.02, 19-3031.03, 19-3032.00, and 19-3039.99)

Significant Points

■ About 4 out of 10 psychologists are self-employed, compared with less than 1 out of 10 among all professional workers.

■ Most specialists, including clinical and counseling psychologists, need a doctoral degree; school psychologists need an educational specialist degree, and industrial-organizational psychologists need a master's degree.

■ Competition for admission to graduate psychology programs is keen.

■ Overall employment of psychologists is expected to grow faster than the average for all occupations through 2014.

Nature of the Work

Psychologists study the human mind and human behavior. Research psychologists investigate the physical, cognitive, emotional, or social aspects of human behavior. Psychologists in health service provider fields provide mental health care in hospitals, clinics, schools, or private settings. Psychologists employed in applied settings, such as business, industry, government, or nonprofits, provide training, conduct research, design systems, and act as advocates for psychology.

Like other social scientists, psychologists formulate hypotheses and collect data to test their validity. Research methods vary with the topic under study. Psychologists sometimes gather information through controlled laboratory experiments or by administering personality, performance, aptitude, or intelligence tests. Other methods include observation, interviews, questionnaires, clinical studies, and surveys.

Psychologists apply their knowledge to a wide range of endeavors, including health and human services, management, education, law, and sports. In addition to working in a variety of settings, psychologists usually specialize in one of a number of different areas.

Clinical psychologists—who constitute the largest specialty—work most often in counseling centers, independent or group practices, hospitals, or clinics. They help mentally and emotionally disturbed clients adjust to life and may assist medical and surgical patients in dealing with illnesses or injuries. Some clinical psychologists work in physical rehabilitation settings, treating patients with spinal cord injuries, chronic pain or illness, stroke, arthritis, and neurological conditions. Others help people deal with times of personal crisis, such as divorce or the death of a loved one.

Clinical psychologists often interview patients and give diagnostic tests. They may provide individual, family, or group psychotherapy and may design and implement behavior modification programs. Some clinical psychologists collaborate with physicians and other specialists to develop and implement treatment and intervention programs that patients can understand and comply with. Other clinical psychologists work in universities and medical schools, where they train graduate students in the delivery of mental health and behavioral medicine services. Some administer community mental health programs.

Areas of specialization within clinical psychology include health psychology, neuropsychology, and geropsychology. *Health psychologists* promote good health through health maintenance counseling programs designed to help people achieve goals, such as stopping smoking or losing weight. *Neuropsychologists* study the relation between the brain and behavior. They often work in stroke and head injury programs. *Geropsychologists* deal with the special problems faced by the elderly. The emergence and growth of these specialties reflects the increasing participation of psychologists in providing direct services to special patient populations.

Often, clinical psychologists will consult with other medical personnel regarding the best treatment for patients, especially treatment that includes medication. Clinical psychologists generally are not permitted to prescribe medication to treat patients; only psychiatrists and other medical doctors may prescribe certain medications. (See the description of physicians and surgeons elsewhere in this book.) However, two states—Louisiana and New Mexico—currently allow clinical psychologists to prescribe medication with some limitations, and similar proposals have been made in other states.

Counseling psychologists use various techniques, including interviewing and testing, to advise people on how to deal with problems of everyday living. They work in settings such as university counseling centers, hospitals, and individual or group practices.

School psychologists work with students in elementary and secondary schools. They collaborate with teachers, parents, and school personnel to create safe, healthy, and supportive learning environments for all students; address students' learning and behavior problems; improve classroom management strategies or parenting skills; counter substance abuse; assess students with learning disabilities and gifted and talented students to help determine the best way to educate them; and improve teaching, learning, and socialization strategies. They also may evaluate the effectiveness of academic programs, prevention programs, behavior management procedures, and other services provided in the school setting.

Industrial-organizational psychologists apply psychological principles and research methods to the workplace in the interest of improving productivity and the quality of work life. They also are involved in research on management and marketing problems. They screen, train, and counsel applicants for jobs, as well as perform organizational development and analysis. An industrial psychologist might work with management to reorganize the work setting in order to improve productivity or quality of life in the workplace. Industrial psychologists frequently act as consultants brought in by management to solve a particular problem.

Developmental psychologists study the physiological, cognitive, and social development that takes place throughout life. Some specialize in behavior during infancy, childhood, and adolescence or changes that occur during maturity or old age. Developmental psychologists also may study developmental disabilities and their effects. Increasingly, research is developing ways to help elderly people remain independent as long as possible.

Social psychologists examine people's interactions with others and with the social environment. They work in organizational consultation, marketing research, systems design, or other applied psychology fields. Prominent areas of study include group behavior, leadership, attitudes, and perception.

Experimental or *research psychologists* work in university and private research centers and in business, nonprofit, and governmental organizations. They study the behavior of both human beings and animals, such as rats, monkeys, and pigeons. Prominent areas of study in experimental research include motivation, thought, attention, learning and memory, sensory and perceptual processes, effects of substance abuse, and genetic and neurological factors affecting behavior.

Working Conditions

A psychologist's subfield and place of employment determine his or her working conditions. Clinical, school, and counseling psychologists in private practice have their own offices and set their own hours. However, they often offer evening and weekend hours to accommodate their clients. Those employed in hospitals, nursing homes, and other health care facilities may work shifts that include evenings and weekends, while those who work in schools and clinics generally work regular hours.

Psychologists employed as faculty by colleges and universities divide their time between teaching and research and also may have administrative responsibilities; many have part-time consulting practices. Most psychologists in government and industry have structured schedules.

Increasingly, many psychologists are working as part of a team, consulting with other psychologists and professionals. Many experience pressures because of deadlines, tight schedules, and overtime. Their

routine may be interrupted frequently. Travel may be required in order to attend conferences or conduct research.

Training, Other Qualifications, and Advancement

A doctoral degree usually is required for employment as an independent licensed clinical or counseling psychologist. Psychologists with a Ph.D. qualify for a wide range of teaching, research, clinical, and counseling positions in universities, health care services, elementary and secondary schools, private industry, and government. Psychologists with a Doctor of Psychology (Psy.D.) degree usually work in clinical positions or in private practices, but they also sometimes teach, conduct research, or carry out administrative responsibilities.

A doctoral degree generally requires 5 to 7 years of graduate study. The Ph.D. degree culminates in a dissertation based on original research. Courses in quantitative research methods, which include the use of computer-based analysis, are an integral part of graduate study and are necessary to complete the dissertation. The Psy.D. may be based on practical work and examinations rather than a dissertation. In clinical or counseling psychology, the requirements for the doctoral degree include at least a 1-year internship.

A specialist degree is required in most states for an individual to work as a school psychologist, although a few states still credential school psychologists with master's degrees. A specialist (Ed.S.) degree in school psychology requires a minimum of 3 years of full-time graduate study (at least 60 graduate semester hours) and a 1-year internship. Because their professional practice addresses educational and mental health components of students' development, school psychologists' training includes coursework in both education and psychology.

Persons with a master's degree in psychology may work as industrial-organizational psychologists. They also may work as psychological assistants under the supervision of doctoral-level psychologists and may conduct research or psychological evaluations. A master's degree in psychology requires at least 2 years of full-time graduate study. Requirements usually include practical experience in an applied setting and a master's thesis based on an original research project.

Competition for admission to graduate psychology programs is keen. Some universities require applicants to have an undergraduate major in psychology. Others prefer only coursework in basic psychology with courses in the biological, physical, and social sciences and in statistics and mathematics.

A bachelor's degree in psychology qualifies a person to assist psychologists and other professionals in community mental health centers, vocational rehabilitation offices, and correctional programs. Bachelor's degree holders may work as research or administrative assistants for psychologists. Some work as technicians in related fields, such as marketing research. Many find employment in other areas, such as sales or business management.

In the federal government, candidates having at least 24 semester hours in psychology and one course in statistics qualify for entry-level positions. However, competition for these jobs is keen because this is one of the few areas in which one can work as a psychologist without an advanced degree.

The American Psychological Association (APA) presently accredits doctoral training programs in clinical, counseling, and school psychology, as well as accrediting institutions that provide internships for doctoral students in school, clinical, and counseling psychology. The National Association of School Psychologists, with the assistance of the National Council for Accreditation of Teacher Education, also is involved in the accreditation of advanced-degree programs in school psychology.

Psychologists in independent practice or those who offer any type of patient care—including clinical, counseling, and school psychologists—must meet certification or licensing requirements in all states and the District of Columbia. Licensing laws vary by state and by type of position and require licensed or certified psychologists to limit their practice to areas in which they have developed professional competence through training and experience. Clinical and counseling psychologists usually require a doctorate in psychology, the completion of an approved internship, and 1 to 2 years of professional experience. In addition, all states require that applicants pass an examination. Most state licensing boards administer a standardized test, and many supplement that with additional oral or essay questions. Some states require continuing education for renewal of the license.

The National Association of School Psychologists (NASP) awards the Nationally Certified School Psychologist (NCSP) designation, which recognizes professional competency in school psychology at a national, rather than state, level. Currently, 26 states recognize the NCSP and allow those with the certification to transfer credentials from one state to another without taking a new certification exam. In states that recognize the NCSP, the requirements for certification or licensure and those for the NCSP often are the same or similar. Requirements for the NCSP include the completion of 60 graduate semester hours in school psychology; a 1,200-hour internship, 600 hours of which must be completed in a school setting; and a passing score on the National School Psychology Examination.

The American Board of Professional Psychology (ABPP) recognizes professional achievement by awarding specialty certification, primarily in clinical psychology; clinical neuropsychology; and counseling, forensic, industrial-organizational, and school psychology. Candidates for ABPP certification need a doctorate in psychology, postdoctoral training in their specialty, five years of experience, professional endorsements, and a passing grade on an examination.

Aspiring psychologists who are interested in direct patient care must be emotionally stable, mature, and able to deal effectively with people. Sensitivity, compassion, good communication skills, and the ability to lead and inspire others are particularly important qualities for persons wishing to do clinical work and counseling. Research psychologists should be able to do detailed work both independently and as part of a team. Patience and perseverance are vital qualities because achieving results in the psychological treatment of patients or in research may take a long time.

Employment

Psychologists held about 179,000 jobs in 2004. Educational institutions employed about 1 out of 4 psychologists in positions other than teaching, such as counseling, testing, research, and administration. Almost 2 out of 10 were employed in health care, primarily in offices of mental health practitioners, physicians' offices, outpatient mental health and substance abuse centers, and private hospitals. Government agencies at the state and local levels employed psychologists in public hospitals, clinics, correctional facilities, and other settings.

After several years of experience, some psychologists—usually those with doctoral degrees—enter private practice or set up private research or consulting firms. About 4 out of 10 psychologists were self-employed in 2004, compared with less than 1 out of 10 among all professional workers.

In addition to the previously mentioned jobs, many psychologists held faculty positions at colleges and universities and as high school psychology teachers. (See the description of teachers—postsecondary elsewhere in this book.)

Job Outlook

Employment of psychologists is expected to grow faster than average for all occupations through 2014 because of increased demand for psychological services in schools, hospitals, social service agencies, mental health centers, substance abuse treatment clinics, consulting firms, and private companies.

Among the specialties in this field, school psychologists—especially those with a specialist degree or higher—may enjoy the best job opportunities. Growing awareness of how students' mental health and behavioral problems, such as bullying, affect learning is increasing demand for school psychologists to offer student counseling and mental health services. Clinical and counseling psychologists will be needed to help people deal with depression and other mental disorders, marriage and family problems, job stress, and addiction. The rise in health care costs associated with unhealthy lifestyles, such as smoking, alcoholism, and obesity, has made prevention and treatment more critical. An increase in the number of employee assistance programs, which help workers deal with personal problems, also should spur job growth in clinical and counseling specialties. Industrial-organizational psychologists will be in demand to help to boost worker productivity and retention rates in a wide range of businesses. Industrial-organizational psychologists will help companies deal with issues such as workplace diversity and antidiscrimination policies. Companies also will use psychologists' expertise in survey design, analysis, and research to develop tools for marketing evaluation and statistical analysis.

Demand should be particularly strong for persons holding doctorates from leading universities in applied specialties, such as counseling, health, and school psychology. Psychologists with extensive training in quantitative research methods and computer science may have a competitive edge over applicants without background.

Master's degree holders in fields other than industrial-organizational psychology will face keen competition for jobs because of the limited number of positions that require only a master's degree. Master's degree holders may find jobs as psychological assistants or counselors, providing mental health services under the direct supervision of a licensed psychologist. Still others may find jobs involving research and data collection and analysis in universities, government, or private companies.

Opportunities directly related to psychology will be limited for bachelor's degree holders. Some may find jobs as assistants in rehabilitation centers or in other jobs involving data collection and analysis. Those who meet state certification requirements may become high school psychology teachers.

Earnings

Median annual earnings of wage and salary clinical, counseling, and school psychologists in May 2004 were $54,950. The middle 50 percent earned between $41,850 and $71,880. The lowest 10 percent earned less than $32,280, and the highest 10 percent earned more than $92,250. Median annual earnings in the industries employing the largest numbers of clinical, counseling, and school psychologists in May 2004 were

Offices of other health practitioners	$64,460
Elementary and secondary schools	58,360
Outpatient care centers	46,850
Individual and family services	42,640

Median annual earnings of wage and salary industrial-organizational psychologists in May 2004 were $71,400. The middle 50 percent earned between $56,880 and $93,210. The lowest 10 percent earned less than $45,620, and the highest 10 percent earned more than $125,560.

Related Occupations

Psychologists are trained to conduct research and teach, evaluate, counsel, and advise individuals and groups with special needs. Others who do this kind of work include clergy, counselors, physicians and surgeons, social workers, sociologists, and special education teachers.

Sources of Additional Information

For information on careers, educational requirements, financial assistance, and licensing in all fields of psychology, contact

▸ American Psychological Association, Research Office and Education Directorate, 750 1st St. NE, Washington, DC 20002-4242. Internet: http://www.apa.org/students

For information on careers, educational requirements, certification, and licensing of school psychologists, contact

▸ National Association of School Psychologists, 4340 East West Hwy., Suite 402, Bethesda, MD 20814. Internet: http://www.nasponline.org

Information about state licensing requirements is available from

▸ Association of State and Provincial Psychology Boards, P.O. Box 241245, Montgomery, AL 36124-1245. Internet: http://www.asppb.org

Information about psychology specialty certifications is available from

▸ American Board of Professional Psychology, Inc., 300 Drayton St., 3rd Floor, Savannah, GA 31401. Internet: http://www.abpp.org

Social Scientists, Other

(O*NET 19-3041.00, 19-3091.01, 19-3091.02, 19-3092.00, 19-3093.00, and 19-3094.00)

Significant Points

■ About half work for federal, state, and local governments, mostly for the federal government.

■ The educational attainment of social scientists is among the highest of all occupations.

■ Anthropologists and archaeologists will experience average growth, but slower-than-average employment growth is expected for geographers, historians, political scientists, and sociologists because they enjoy fewer opportunities outside of government and academic settings.

■ Competition for jobs will remain keen for all specialties because many of these social scientists compete for jobs with other workers, such as psychologists, statisticians, and market and survey researchers.

Nature of the Work

The major social science occupations covered in this job description include anthropologists, archaeologists, geographers, historians, political scientists, and sociologists. (Economists, market and survey researchers, psychologists, and urban and regional planners are covered elsewhere in this book.)

Social scientists study all aspects of society—from past events and achievements to human behavior and relationships among groups. Their research provides insights that help us understand different ways in which individuals and groups make decisions, exercise power, and respond to change. Through their studies and analyses, social scientists suggest solutions to social, business, personal, governmental, and environmental problems.

Research is a major activity of many social scientists, who use a variety of methods to assemble facts and construct theories. Applied research usually is designed to produce information that will enable people to make better decisions or manage their affairs more effectively. Collecting information takes many forms, including interviews and questionnaires to gather demographic and opinion data, living and working among the population being studied, performing field investigations, analyzing historical records and documents, experimenting with human or animal subjects in a laboratory, and preparing and interpreting maps and computer graphics. The work of specialists in social science varies greatly, although specialists in one field may find that their research overlaps work being conducted in another discipline.

Anthropologists study the origin and the physical, social, and cultural development and behavior of humans. They may examine the way of life, archaeological remains, language, or physical characteristics of people in various parts of the world. Some compare the customs, values, and social patterns of different cultures. Anthropologists usually concentrate in sociocultural anthropology, archaeology, linguistics, or biophysical anthropology. *Sociocultural anthropologists* study the customs, cultures, and social lives of groups in settings that range from unindustrialized societies to modern urban centers. *Linguistic anthropologists* investigate the role of, and changes to, language over time in various cultures. *Biophysical anthropologists* research the evolution of the human body, look for the earliest evidences of human life, and analyze how culture and biology influence one another. *Physical anthropologists* examine human remains found at archaeological sites in order to understand population demographics and factors that affected these populations, such as nutrition and disease.

Archaeologists examine and recover material evidence such as the ruins of buildings, tools, pottery, and other objects remaining from past human cultures in order to determine the chronology, history, customs, and living habits of earlier civilizations. Most anthropologists and archaeologists specialize in a particular region of the world.

Geographers analyze distributions of physical and cultural phenomena on local, regional, continental, and global scales. *Economic geographers* study the distribution of resources and economic activities. *Political geographers* are concerned with the relationship of geography to political phenomena, whereas cultural geographers study the geography of cultural phenomena. *Physical geographers* examine variations in climate, vegetation, soil, and landforms and their implications for human activity. *Urban and transportation geographers* study cities and metropolitan areas, while *regional geographers* study the physical, economic, political, and cultural characteristics of regions ranging in size from a congressional district to entire continents. *Medical geographers* investigate health care delivery systems, epidemiology (the study of the causes and control of epidemics), and the effect of the environment on health. Most geographers use geographic information systems (GIS) technology to assist with their work. For example, they may use GIS to create computerized maps that can track information such as population growth, traffic patterns, environmental hazards, natural resources, and weather patterns, after which they use the information to advise governments on the development of houses, roads, or landfills.

Historians research, analyze, and interpret the past. They use many sources of additional information in their research, including government and institutional records, newspapers and other periodicals, photographs, interviews, films, and unpublished manuscripts such as personal diaries and letters. Historians usually specialize in a country or region; a particular period; or a particular field, such as social, intellectual, cultural, political, or diplomatic history. Biographers collect detailed information on individuals. Other historians help study and preserve archival materials, artifacts, and historic buildings and sites.

Political scientists study the origin, development, and operation of political systems and public policy. They conduct research on a wide range of subjects, such as relations between the United States and other countries, the institutions and political life of nations, the politics of small towns or a major metropolis, and the decisions of the U.S. Supreme Court. Studying topics such as public opinion, political decision making, ideology, and public policy, they analyze the structure and operation of governments, as well as various political entities. Depending on the topic, a political scientist might conduct a public-opinion survey, analyze election results or public documents, or interview public officials.

Sociologists study society and social behavior by examining the groups and social institutions people form, as well as various social, religious, political, and business organizations. They also study the behavior of and interaction among groups, trace their origin and growth, and analyze the influence of group activities on individual members. Sociologists are concerned with the characteristics of social groups, organizations, and institutions; the ways individuals are affected by each other and by the groups to which they belong; and the effect of social traits such as gender, age, or race on a person's daily life. The results of sociological research aid educators, lawmakers, administrators, and others who are interested in resolving social problems and formulating public policy.

Most sociologists work in one or more specialties, such as social organization, stratification, and mobility; racial and ethnic relations; education; the family; social psychology; urban, rural, political, and comparative sociology; gender relations; demography; gerontology; criminology; and sociological practice.

Working Conditions

Most social scientists have regular hours. Generally working behind a desk, either alone or in collaboration with other social scientists, they read and write research articles or reports. Many experience the pressures of writing and publishing, as well as those associated with deadlines and tight schedules. Sometimes they must work overtime, for which they usually are not compensated. Social scientists often work as an integral part of a research team, among whose members good communications skills are important. Travel may be necessary to collect information or attend meetings. Social scientists on foreign assignment must adjust to unfamiliar cultures, climates, and languages.

Some social scientists do fieldwork. For example, anthropologists, archaeologists, and geographers may travel to remote areas, live among the people they study, learn their languages, and stay for long periods at the site of their investigations. They may work under rugged conditions, and their work may involve strenuous physical exertion.

Social scientists employed by colleges and universities usually have flexible work schedules, often dividing their time among teaching, research, writing, consulting, and administrative responsibilities.

Training, Other Qualifications, and Advancement

The educational attainment of social scientists is among the highest of all occupations. The Ph.D. or an equivalent degree is a minimum requirement for most positions in colleges and universities and is important for advancement to many top-level nonacademic research and administrative posts. Graduates with master's degrees in applied specialties usually have better opportunities outside of colleges and universities, although the situation varies by field. Graduates with a master's degree in a social science may qualify for teaching positions in community colleges. Bachelor's degree holders have limited opportunities and, in most social science occupations, do not qualify for "professional" positions. The bachelor's degree does, however, provide a suitable background for many different kinds of entry-level jobs, such as research assistant, administrative aide, or management or sales trainee. With the addition of sufficient education courses, social science graduates also can qualify for teaching positions in secondary and elementary schools.

Training in statistics and mathematics is essential for many social scientists. Mathematical and quantitative research methods increasingly are being used in geography, political science, and other fields. The ability to utilize computers for research purposes is mandatory in most disciplines. Most geographers—and increasing numbers of archaeologists—also will need to be familiar with GIS technology.

Many social science students find that internships or field experience is beneficial. Numerous local museums, historical societies, government agencies, and other organizations offer internships or volunteer research opportunities. Archaeological field schools instruct future anthropologists, archaeologists, and historians in how to excavate, record, and interpret historical sites.

Depending on their jobs, social scientists may need a wide range of personal characteristics. Intellectual curiosity and creativity are fundamental personal traits because social scientists constantly seek new information about people, things, and ideas. The ability to think logically and methodically is important to a political scientist comparing, for example, the merits of various forms of government. Objectivity, having an open mind, and systematic work habits are important in all kinds of social science research. Perseverance is essential for an anthropologist, who might have to spend years studying artifacts from an ancient civilization before making a final analysis and interpretation. Excellent written and oral communication skills also are necessary for all these professionals.

Employment

Social scientists held about 18,000 jobs in 2004. Many worked as researchers, administrators, and counselors for a wide range of employers. About half worked for federal, state, and local governments, mostly in the federal government. Other employers included scientific research and development services; management, scientific, and technical consulting services; business, professional, labor, political, and similar organizations; and architectural, engineering, and related firms.

Many individuals with training in a social science discipline teach in colleges and universities and in secondary and elementary schools. (For more information, see teachers—postsecondary elsewhere in this book.) The proportion of social scientists who teach varies by specialty: For example, the academic world usually is a more important source of jobs for graduates in history than for graduates in most other social science fields.

Job Outlook

Overall employment of social scientists is expected to grow more slowly than average for all occupations through 2014. However, projected growth rates vary by specialty. Anthropologists and archaeologists will experience average employment growth. Employment of geographers, historians, political scientists, and sociologists will grow more slowly than average, mainly because these workers enjoy fewer opportunities outside of government and academic settings.

Competition will remain keen for social science positions. Many jobs in policy, research, or marketing for which social scientists qualify are not advertised exclusively as social scientist positions. Because of the wide range of skills and knowledge possessed by the social scientists discussed here, many compete for jobs with other workers, such as market and survey researchers, psychologists, engineers, urban and regional planners, and statisticians.

A few social scientists will find opportunities as university faculty, although competition for these jobs also will remain keen. Usually, there are more graduates than available faculty positions, although retirements among faculty are expected to rise in the next few years. The growing importance and popularity of social science subjects in secondary schools is strengthening the demand for social science teachers at that level.

Anthropologists and archaeologists will see the majority of their employment growth in the management, scientific, and technical consulting services industry. Anthropologists who work as consultants often apply anthropological knowledge and methods to problems ranging from economic development issues to forensics. Also, as construction projects increase, archaeologists will be needed to perform preliminary excavations in order to preserve historical sites and artifacts.

Geographers will have opportunities to utilize their skills to advise government, real estate developers, utilities, and telecommunications firms on where to build new roads, buildings, power plants, and cable lines. Geographers also will advise on environmental matters, such as where to build a landfill or preserve wetland habitats. Geographers with a background in GIS will find numerous job opportunities applying GIS technology in nontraditional areas, such as emergency assistance, where GIS can track locations of ambulances, police, and fire rescue units and their proximity to the emergency. Workers in these jobs may not necessarily be called "geographers," but instead may be referred to by a different title, such as "GIS analyst" or "GIS specialist." GIS technology also will be utilized in areas of growing importance, such as homeland security and defense.

Historians, political scientists, and sociologists will find jobs in policy or research. Historians may find opportunities with historic preservation societies as public interest in preserving and restoring historical sites increases. Political scientists will be able to utilize their knowledge of political institutions to further the interests of nonprofit, political lobbying, and social organizations. Sociologists may find work conducting policy research for consulting firms and nonprofit organizations, and their knowledge of society and social behavior may be used by a variety of companies in product development, marketing, and advertising. Job growth will be very slow in the federal government, a key employer of social scientists.

Earnings

In May 2004, anthropologists and archaeologists had median annual earnings of $43,890; geographers, $58,970; historians, $44,490; political scientists, $86,750; and sociologists, $57,870.

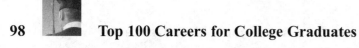

In the federal government, social scientists with a bachelor's degree and no experience could start at a yearly salary of $24,677 or $30,567 in 2005, depending on their college records. Those with a master's degree could start at $37,390, and those with a Ph.D. degree could begin at $45,239, while some individuals with experience and an advanced degree could start at $54,221. Beginning salaries were slightly higher in selected areas of the country where the prevailing local pay level was higher.

Related Occupations

Social scientists' duties and training outlined in this job description are similar to those of other occupations covered elsewhere in this book, including other social science occupations: economists, market and survey researchers, psychologists, and urban and regional planners. Many social scientists conduct surveys, study social problems, teach, and work in museums, performing tasks similar to those of statisticians; counselors; social workers; teachers—postsecondary; teachers—preschool, kindergarten, elementary, middle, and secondary; and archivists, curators, and museum technicians.

Political scientists are concerned with the function of government, including the legal system, as are lawyers; paralegals and legal assistants; and judges, magistrates, and other judicial workers. Many political scientists analyze and report on current events, much as do news analysts, reporters, and correspondents.

Along with conservation scientists and foresters, atmospheric scientists, and environmental scientists and hydrologists, geographers are concerned with the earth's environment and natural resources. Geographers also use GIS computer technology to make maps. Other occupations with similar duties are surveyors, cartographers, photogrammetrists, and surveying technicians; computer systems analysts; and computer scientists and database administrators.

Detailed information about economists, market and survey researchers, psychologists, and urban and regional planners is presented elsewhere in this book.

Sources of Additional Information

For information about careers in anthropology, contact

▶ American Anthropological Association, 2200 Wilson Blvd., Suite 600, Arlington, VA 22201. Internet: http://www.aaanet.org

For information about careers in archaeology, contact

▶ Society for American Archaeology, 900 2nd St. NE, Suite 12, Washington, DC 20002-3560. Internet: http://www.saa.org

▶ Archaeological Institute of America, 656 Beacon St., 6th Floor, Boston, MA 02215-2006. Internet: http://www.archaeological.org

For information about careers in geography, contact

▶ Association of American Geographers, 1710 16th St. NW, Washington, DC 20009-3198. Internet: http://www.aag.org

Information on careers for historians is available from

▶ American Historical Association, 400 A St. SE, Washington, DC 20003-3889. Internet: http://www.historians.org

For information about careers in political science, contact

▶ American Political Science Association, 1527 New Hampshire Ave. NW, Washington, DC 20036-1206. Internet: http://www.apsanet.org

▶ National Association of Schools of Public Affairs and Administration, 1120 G St. NW, Suite 730, Washington, DC 20005-3869. Internet: http://www.naspaa.org

Information about careers in sociology is available from

▶ American Sociological Association, 1307 New York Ave. NW, Suite 700, Washington, DC 20005-4712. Internet: http://www.asanet.org

Social Workers

(O*NET 21-1021.00, 21-1022.00, 21-1023.00, and 21-1029.99)

Significant Points

■ About 9 out of 10 jobs are in health care and social assistance industries, as well as state and local government agencies.

■ While a bachelor's degree is the minimum requirement, a master's degree in social work or a related field has become the standard for many positions.

■ Employment is projected to grow faster than average.

■ Competition for jobs is expected in cities, but opportunities should be good in rural areas.

Nature of the Work

Social work is a profession for those with a strong desire to help improve people's lives. *Social workers* help people function the best way they can in their environment, deal with their relationships, and solve personal and family problems. Social workers often see clients who face a life-threatening disease or a social problem, such as inadequate housing, unemployment, a serious illness, a disability, or substance abuse. Social workers also assist families that have serious domestic conflicts, sometimes involving child or spousal abuse.

Social workers often provide social services in health-related settings that now are governed by managed care organizations. To contain costs, these organizations emphasize short-term intervention, ambulatory and community-based care, and greater decentralization of services.

Most social workers specialize. Although some conduct research or are involved in planning or policy development, most social workers prefer an area of practice in which they interact with clients.

Child, family, and school social workers provide social services and assistance to improve the social and psychological functioning of children and their families and to maximize the family well-being and academic functioning of children. Some social workers assist single parents; arrange adoptions; or help find foster homes for neglected, abandoned, or abused children. In schools, they address such problems as teenage pregnancy, misbehavior, and truancy and advise teachers on how to cope with problem students. Increasingly, school social workers are teaching workshops to an entire class. Some social workers specialize in services for senior citizens, running support groups for family caregivers or for the adult children of aging parents; advising elderly people or family members about choices in areas such as housing, transportation, and long-term care; and coordinating and monitoring these services. Through employee assistance programs, they may help workers cope with job-related pressures or with personal problems that affect the quality of their work. Child, family, and school social workers typically work for individual and family services agencies, schools, or state or local governments. These social workers may be known as child welfare social workers, family services social workers, child protective services social workers, occupational social workers, or gerontology social workers.

Medical and public health social workers provide persons, families, or vulnerable populations with the psychosocial support needed to cope with chronic, acute, or terminal illnesses, such as Alzheimer's disease, cancer, or AIDS. They also advise family caregivers, counsel patients, and help plan for patients' needs after discharge by arranging for at-home services, from meals-on-wheels to oxygen equipment. Some work on interdisciplinary teams that evaluate certain kinds of patients—geriatric or organ transplant patients, for example. Medical and public health social workers may work for hospitals, nursing and personal care facilities, individual and family services agencies, or local governments.

Mental health and substance abuse social workers assess and treat individuals with mental illness or substance abuse problems, including abuse of alcohol, tobacco, or other drugs. Such services include individual and group therapy, outreach, crisis intervention, social rehabilitation, and training in skills of everyday living. They also may help plan for supportive services to ease patients' return to the community. Mental health and substance abuse social workers are likely to work in hospitals, substance abuse treatment centers, individual and family services agencies, or local governments. These social workers may be known as clinical social workers. (Counselors and psychologists, who may provide similar services, are discussed elsewhere in this book.)

Other types of social workers include *social work planners and policymakers*, who develop programs to address such issues as child abuse, homelessness, substance abuse, poverty, and violence. These workers research and analyze policies, programs, and regulations. They identify social problems and suggest legislative and other solutions. They may help raise funds or write grants to support these programs.

Working Conditions

Full-time social workers usually work a standard 40-hour week; however, some occasionally work evenings and weekends to meet with clients, attend community meetings, and handle emergencies. Some, particularly in voluntary nonprofit agencies, work part time. Social workers usually spend most of their time in an office or residential facility, but also may travel locally to visit clients, meet with service providers, or attend meetings. Some may use one of several offices within a local area in which to meet with clients. The work, while satisfying, can be emotionally draining. Understaffing and large caseloads add to the pressure in some agencies. To tend to patient care or client needs, many hospitals and long-term care facilities are employing social workers on teams with a broad mix of occupations, including clinical specialists, registered nurses, and health aides.

Training, Other Qualifications, and Advancement

A bachelor's degree in social work (BSW) degree is the most common minimum requirement to qualify for a job as a social worker; however, majors in psychology, sociology, and related fields may qualify for some entry-level jobs, especially in small community agencies. Although a bachelor's degree is sufficient for entry into the field, an advanced degree has become the standard for many positions. A master's degree in social work (MSW) is typically required for positions in health settings and is required for clinical work as well. Some jobs in public and private agencies also may require an advanced degree, such as a master's degree in social services policy or administration. Supervisory, administrative, and staff training positions usually require an advanced degree. College and university teaching positions and most research appointments normally require a doctorate in social work (DSW or Ph.D.).

As of 2004, the Council on Social Work Education (CSWE) accredited 442 BSW programs and 168 MSW programs. The Group for the Advancement of Doctoral Education (GADE) listed 80 doctoral programs in social work (DSW or Ph.D.). BSW programs prepare graduates for direct service positions, such as caseworker, and include courses in social work values and ethics, dealing with a culturally diverse clientele, at-risk populations, promotion of social and economic justice, human behavior and the social environment, social welfare policy and services, social work practice, social research methods, and field education. Accredited BSW programs require a minimum of 400 hours of supervised field experience.

Master's degree programs prepare graduates for work in their chosen field of concentration and continue to develop the skills required to perform clinical assessments, manage large caseloads, take on supervisory roles, and explore new ways of drawing upon social services to meet the needs of clients. Master's programs last 2 years and include a minimum of 900 hours of supervised field instruction or internship. A part-time program may take 4 years. Entry into a master's program does not require a bachelor's degree in social work, but courses in psychology, biology, sociology, economics, political science, and social work are recommended. In addition, a second language can be very helpful. Most master's programs offer advanced standing for those with a bachelor's degree from an accredited social work program.

All states and the District of Columbia have licensing, certification, or registration requirements regarding social work practice and the use of professional titles. Although standards for licensing vary by state, a growing number of states are placing greater emphasis on communications skills, professional ethics, and sensitivity to cultural diversity issues. Most states require two years (3,000 hours) of supervised clinical experience for licensure of clinical social workers. In addition, the National Association of Social Workers (NASW) offers voluntary credentials. Social workers with an MSW may be eligible for the Academy of Certified Social Workers (ACSW), the Qualified Clinical Social Worker (QCSW), or the Diplomate in Clinical Social Work (DCSW) credential, based on their professional experience. Credentials are particularly important for those in private practice; some health insurance providers require social workers to have them in order to be reimbursed for services.

Social workers should be emotionally mature, objective, and sensitive to people and their problems. They must be able to handle responsibility, work independently, and maintain good working relationships with clients and co-workers. Volunteer or paid jobs as a social work aide offer ways of testing one's interest in this field.

Advancement to supervisor, program manager, assistant director, or executive director of a social service agency or department is possible, but usually requires an advanced degree and related work experience. Other career options for social workers include teaching, research, and consulting. Some of these workers also help formulate government policies by analyzing and advocating policy positions in government agencies, in research institutions, and on legislators' staffs.

Some social workers go into private practice. Most private practitioners are clinical social workers who provide psychotherapy, usually paid for through health insurance or by the client themselves. Private practitioners must have at least a master's degree and a period of supervised work experience. A network of contacts for referrals also is essential. Many private practitioners split their time between working for an agency or hospital and working in their private practice. They may continue to hold a position at a hospital or agency in order to receive health and life insurance.

Employment

Social workers held about 562,000 jobs in 2004. About 9 out of 10 jobs were in health care and social assistance industries, as well as state and local government agencies, primarily in departments of health and human services. Although most social workers are employed in cities or suburbs, some work in rural areas. The following tabulation shows 2004 employment by type of social worker:

Child, family, and school social workers 272,000

Mental health and substance abuse
   social workers 116,000

Medical and public health social workers..............110,000

Social workers, all other 64,000

Job Outlook

Competition for social worker jobs is expected in cities, where demand for services often is highest and training programs for social workers are prevalent. However, opportunities should be good in rural areas, which often find it difficult to attract and retain qualified staff. By specialty, job prospects may be best for those social workers with a background in gerontology and substance abuse treatment.

Employment of social workers is expected to increase faster than the average for all occupations through 2014. The rapidly growing elderly population and the aging baby-boom generation will create greater demand for health and social services, resulting in particularly rapid job growth among gerontology social workers. Many job openings also will stem from the need to replace social workers who leave the occupation.

As hospitals continue to limit the length of patient stays, the demand for social workers in hospitals will grow more slowly than in other areas. Because hospitals are releasing patients earlier than in the past, social worker employment in home health care services is growing. However, the expanding senior population is an even larger factor. Employment opportunities for social workers with backgrounds in gerontology should be good in the growing numbers of assisted-living and senior-living communities. The expanding senior population also will spur demand for social workers in nursing homes, long-term care facilities, and hospices.

Strong demand is expected for substance abuse social workers over the 2004–2014 projection period. Substance abusers are increasingly being placed into treatment programs instead of being sentenced to prison. Because of the increasing numbers of individuals sentenced to prison or probation who are substance abusers, correctional systems are increasingly requiring substance abuse treatment as a condition added to their sentencing or probation. As this trend grows, demand will increase for treatment programs and social workers to assist abusers on the road to recovery.

Employment of social workers in private social service agencies also will increase. However, agencies increasingly will restructure services and hire more lower-paid social and human service assistants instead of social workers. Employment in state and local government agencies may grow somewhat in response to increasing needs for public welfare, family services, and child protection services; however, many of these services will be contracted out to private agencies. Employment levels in public and private social services agencies may fluctuate, depending on need and government funding levels.

Employment of school social workers also is expected to grow as expanded efforts to respond to rising student enrollments and continued emphasis on integrating disabled children into the general school population lead to more jobs. There could be competition for school social work jobs in some areas because of the limited number of openings. The availability of federal, state, and local funding will be a major factor in determining the actual job growth in schools.

Opportunities for social workers in private practice will expand, but growth may be somewhat hindered by restrictions that managed care organizations put on mental health services. The growing popularity of employee assistance programs is expected to spur demand for private practitioners, some of whom provide social work services to corporations on a contractual basis. However, the popularity of employee assistance programs will fluctuate with the business cycle because businesses are not likely to offer these services during recessions.

Earnings

Median annual earnings of child, family, and school social workers were $34,820 in May 2004. The middle 50 percent earned between $27,840 and $45,140. The lowest 10 percent earned less than $23,130, and the top 10 percent earned more than $57,860. Median annual earnings in the industries employing the largest numbers of child, family, and school social workers in May 2004 were

Elementary and secondary schools $44,300

Local government 40,620

State government 35,070

Individual and family services 30,680

Other residential care facilities 30,550

Median annual earnings of medical and public health social workers were $40,080 in May 2004. The middle 50 percent earned between $31,620 and $50,080. The lowest 10 percent earned less than $25,390, and the top 10 percent earned more than $58,740. Median annual earnings in the industries employing the largest numbers of medical and public health social workers in May 2004 were

General medical and surgical hospitals $44,920

Home health care services 42,710

Local government 39,390

Nursing care facilities 35,680

Individual and family services 32,100

Median annual earnings of mental health and substance abuse social workers were $33,920 in May 2004. The middle 50 percent earned between $26,730 and $43,430. The lowest 10 percent earned less than $21,590, and the top 10 percent earned more than $54,180. Median annual earnings in the industries employing the largest numbers of mental health and substance abuse social workers in May 2004 were

Psychiatric and substance abuse hospitals............$36,170

Local government 35,720

Outpatient care centers 33,220

Individual and family services 32,810

Residential mental retardation, mental health
and substance abuse facilities...........................29,110

Median annual earnings of social workers, all other were $39,440 in May 2004. The middle 50 percent earned between $30,350 and $51,530. The lowest 10 percent earned less than $24,080, and the top 10 percent earned more than $62,720. Median annual earnings in the industries employing the largest numbers of social workers, all other in May 2004 were

Local government $42,570

State government 40,940

Individual and family services 32,280

About 1 out of 5 social workers is a member of a union. Many belong to the union associated with their place of employment.

Related Occupations

Through direct counseling or referral to other services, social workers help people solve a range of personal problems. Workers in occupations with similar duties include counselors, probation officers and correctional treatment specialists, psychologists, and social and human services assistants.

Sources of Additional Information

For information about career opportunities in social work and voluntary credentials for social workers, contact

▶ National Association of Social Workers, 750 First St. NE, Suite 700, Washington, DC 20002-4241. Internet: http://www.socialworkers.org

For a listing of accredited social work programs, contact

▶ Council on Social Work Education, 1725 Duke St., Suite 500, Alexandria, VA 22314-3457. Internet: http://www.cswe.org

Information on licensing requirements and testing procedures for each state may be obtained from state licensing authorities or from

▶ Association of Social Work Boards, 400 South Ridge Pkwy., Suite B, Culpeper, VA 22701. Internet: http://www.aswb.org

Speech-Language Pathologists

(O*NET 29-1127.00)

Significant Points

■ About half work in educational services, and most others are employed by health care and social assistance facilities.

■ A master's degree in speech-language pathology is the standard credential required for licensing in most states.

■ Employment is expected to grow because the expanding population in older age groups is prone to medical conditions that result in speech, language, and swallowing problems.

■ Excellent job opportunities are expected.

Nature of the Work

Speech-language pathologists, sometimes called *speech therapists,* assess, diagnose, treat, and help to prevent speech, language, cognitive-communication, voice, swallowing, fluency, and other related disorders.

Speech-language pathologists work with people who cannot produce speech sounds or cannot produce them clearly; those with speech rhythm and fluency problems, such as stuttering; people with voice disorders, such as inappropriate pitch or harsh voice; those with problems understanding and producing language; those who wish to improve their communication skills by modifying an accent; and those with cognitive communication impairments, such as attention, memory, and problem-solving disorders. They also work with people who have swallowing difficulties.

Speech, language, and swallowing difficulties can result from a variety of causes, including stroke, brain injury or deterioration, developmental delays or disorders, learning disabilities, cerebral palsy, cleft palate, voice pathology, mental retardation, hearing loss, or emotional problems. Problems can be congenital, developmental, or acquired. Speech-language pathologists use qualitative and quantitative assessment methods, including standardized tests, as well as special instruments, to analyze and diagnose the nature and extent of speech, language, and swallowing impairments. Speech-language pathologists develop an individualized plan of care tailored to each patient's needs. For individuals with little or no speech capability, speech-language pathologists may select augmentative or alternative communication methods, including automated devices and sign language, and teach their use. They teach these individuals how to make sounds, improve their voices, or increase their oral or written language skills to communicate more effectively. They also teach individuals how to strengthen muscles or use compensatory strategies to swallow without choking or inhaling food or liquid. Speech-language pathologists help patients develop, or recover, reliable communication and swallowing skills so patients can fulfill their educational, vocational, and social roles.

Speech-language pathologists keep records on the initial evaluation, progress, and discharge of clients. This helps pinpoint problems, tracks client progress, and justifies the cost of treatment when applying for reimbursement. They counsel individuals and their families concerning communication disorders and how to cope with the stress and misunderstanding that often accompany them. They also work with family members to recognize and change behavior patterns that impede communication and treatment and show them communication-enhancing techniques to use at home.

Most speech-language pathologists provide direct clinical services to individuals with communication or swallowing disorders. In medical facilities, they may perform their job in conjunction with physicians, social workers, psychologists, and other therapists. Speech-language pathologists in schools collaborate with teachers, special educators, interpreters, other school personnel, and parents to develop and implement individual or group programs, provide counseling, and support classroom activities. Some speech-language pathologists conduct research on how people communicate. Others design and develop equipment or techniques for diagnosing and treating speech problems.

Working Conditions

Speech-language pathologists usually work at a desk or table in clean comfortable surroundings. In medical settings, they may work at the patient's bedside and assist in positioning the patient. In school settings, they may work with students in an office or classroom. Some deliver services in the client's home. While the job is not physically demanding, it requires attention to detail and intense concentration. The emotional needs of clients and their families may be demanding. Most full-time speech-language pathologists work 40 hours per week; about 1 in 5 work part time. Those who work on a contract basis may spend a substantial amount of time traveling between facilities.

Training, Other Qualifications, and Advancement

In 2005, 47 states required speech-language pathologists to be licensed if they worked in a health care setting, and all states required a master's degree or equivalent. A passing score on the national examination on speech-language pathology, offered through the Praxis Series of the Educational Testing Service, is needed as well. Other requirements typically are 300 to 375 hours of supervised clinical experience and 9 months of postgraduate professional clinical experience. Forty-one states have continuing education requirements for licensure renewal. Medicaid, Medicare, and private health insurers generally require a practitioner to be licensed to qualify for reimbursement.

Only 11 states require this same license to practice in the public schools. The other states issue a teaching license or certificate that typically requires a master's degree from an approved college or university. Some states will grant a temporary teaching license or

certificate to bachelor's degree applicants, but a master's degree must be earned in 3 to 5 years. A few states grant a full teacher's certificate or license to bachelor's degree applicants.

In 2004, 239 colleges and universities offered graduate programs in speech-language pathology that are accredited by the Council on Academic Accreditation in Audiology and Speech-Language Pathology. While graduation from an accredited program is not always required to become a speech-language pathologist, it may be helpful in obtaining a license or may be required to obtain a license in some states. Courses cover the anatomy, physiology, and development of the areas of the body involved in speech, language, and swallowing; the nature of disorders; acoustics; and psychological aspects of communication. Graduate students also learn to evaluate and treat speech, language, and swallowing disorders and receive supervised clinical training in communication disorders.

Speech-language pathologists can acquire the Certificate of Clinical Competence in Speech-Language Pathology (CCC-SLP) offered by the American Speech-Language-Hearing Association. To earn a CCC, a person must have a graduate degree and 400 hours of supervised clinical experience, complete a 36-week postgraduate clinical fellowship, and pass the Praxis Series examination in speech-language pathology administered by the Educational Testing Service (ETS).

Speech-language pathologists should be able to effectively communicate diagnostic test results, diagnoses, and proposed treatment in a manner easily understood by their patients and their families. They must be able to approach problems objectively and be supportive. Because a patient's progress may be slow, patience, compassion, and good listening skills are necessary.

As speech-language pathologists gain clinical experience and engage in continuing professional education, many develop expertise with certain populations, such as preschoolers and adolescents, or disorders, such as aphasia and learning disabilities. Some may obtain board recognition in a specialty area, such as child language, fluency, or feeding and swallowing. Experienced clinicians may become mentors or supervisors of other therapists or be promoted to administrative positions.

Employment

Speech-language pathologists held about 96,000 jobs in 2004. About half were employed in educational services, primarily in preschools and elementary and secondary schools. Others were employed in hospitals; offices of other health practitioners, including speech-language pathologists; nursing care facilities; home health care services; individual and family services; outpatient care centers; and child day care centers.

A few speech-language pathologists are self-employed in private practice. They contract to provide services in schools, offices of physicians, hospitals, or nursing care facilities or work as consultants to industry.

Job Outlook

Employment of speech-language pathologists is expected to grow about as fast as the average for all occupations through the year 2014. As the members of the baby boom generation continue to age, the possibility of neurological disorders and associated speech, language, and swallowing impairments increases. Medical advances are also improving the survival rate of premature infants and trauma and stroke victims, who then need assessment and possible treatment. An increased emphasis also has been placed on early identification of speech and language problems in young children. The combination of growth in the occupation and an expected increase in retirements over the coming years should create excellent job opportunities for speech-language pathologists. Opportunities should be particularly favorable for those with the ability to speak a second language, such as Spanish.

In health care facilities, restrictions on reimbursement for therapy services may limit the growth of speech-language pathologists in the near term. However, over the long run, the demand for therapists should continue to rise as growth in the number of individuals with disabilities or limited function spurs demand for therapy services.

Employment in educational services will increase along with growth in elementary and secondary school enrollments, including enrollment of special education students. Federal law guarantees special education and related services to all eligible children with disabilities. Greater awareness of the importance of early identification and diagnosis of speech and language disorders will also increase employment.

The number of speech-language pathologists in private practice will rise due to the increasing use of contract services by hospitals, schools, and nursing care facilities.

Earnings

Median annual earnings of speech-language pathologists were $52,410 in May 2004. The middle 50 percent earned between $42,090 and $65,750. The lowest 10 percent earned less than $34,720, and the highest 10 percent earned more than $82,420. Median annual earnings in the industries employing the largest numbers of speech-language pathologists in May 2004 were

Offices of other health practitioners $57,240

General medical and surgical hospitals 55,900

Elementary and secondary schools 48,320

According to a 2003 survey by the American Speech-Language-Hearing Association, the median annual salary for full-time certified speech-language pathologists who worked on a calendar-year basis, generally 11 or 12 months annually, was $48,000. Certified speech-language pathologists who worked 25 or fewer hours per week had a median hourly salary of $40.00. Starting salaries for certified speech-language pathologists with one to three years of experience were $42,000 for those who worked on a calendar-year basis. According to a 2004 survey by the American Speech-Language-Hearing Association, the median annual salary for speech-language pathologists in schools was $50,000 for those employed on an academic-year basis (usually 9 or 10 months).

Related Occupations

Speech-language pathologists specialize in the prevention, diagnosis, and treatment of speech and language problems. Workers in related occupations include audiologists, occupational therapists,

optometrists, physical therapists, psychologists, and recreational therapists. Speech-language pathologists in school systems often work closely with special education teachers in assisting students with disabilities.

Sources of Additional Information

State licensing boards can provide information on licensure requirements. State departments of education can supply information on certification requirements for those who wish to work in public schools.

For information on careers in speech-language pathology, a description of the CCC-SLP credential, and a listing of accredited graduate programs in speech-language pathology, contact

▸ American Speech-Language-Hearing Association, 10801 Rockville Pike, Rockville, MD 20852. Internet: http://www.asha.org

Statisticians

(O*NET 15-2041.00)

Significant Points

■ About 41 percent of statisticians work for federal, state, and local governments; other employers include scientific research and development services and finance and insurance firms.

■ A master's degree in statistics or mathematics is the minimum educational requirement for most jobs as a statistician.

■ Employment of statisticians is projected to grow more slowly than average because many jobs that require a degree in statistics will not carry the title "statistician."

■ Individuals with a degree in statistics should have favorable job opportunities in a variety of disciplines.

Nature of the Work

Statistics is the scientific application of mathematical principles to the collection, analysis, and presentation of numerical data. *Statisticians* contribute to scientific inquiry by applying their mathematical and statistical knowledge to the design of surveys and experiments; the collection, processing, and analysis of data; and the interpretation of the results. Statisticians may apply their knowledge of statistical methods to a variety of subject areas, such as biology, economics, engineering, medicine, public health, psychology, marketing, education, and sports. Many economic, social, political, and military decisions cannot be made without statistical techniques, such as the design of experiments to gain federal approval of a newly manufactured drug.

One technique that is especially useful to statisticians is sampling—obtaining information about a population of people or group of things by surveying a small portion of the total. For example, to determine the size of the audience for particular programs, television-rating services survey only a few thousand families rather than all viewers. Statisticians decide where and how to gather the data, determine the type and size of the sample group, and develop the survey questionnaire or reporting form. They also prepare instructions for workers who will collect and tabulate the data. Finally, statisticians analyze, interpret, and summarize the data, using computer software.

In business and industry, statisticians play an important role in quality control and in product development and improvement. In an automobile company, for example, statisticians might design experiments to determine the failure time of engines exposed to extreme weather conditions by running individual engines until failure and breakdown. Working for a pharmaceutical company, statisticians might develop and evaluate the results of clinical trials to determine the safety and effectiveness of new medications. And, at a computer software firm, statisticians might help construct new statistical software packages to analyze data more accurately and efficiently. In addition to product development and testing, some statisticians also are involved in deciding what products to manufacture, how much to charge for them, and to whom the products should be marketed. Statisticians also may manage assets and liabilities, determining the risks and returns of certain investments.

Statisticians also are employed by nearly every government agency. Some government statisticians develop surveys that measure population growth, consumer prices, or unemployment. Other statisticians work for scientific, environmental, and agricultural agencies and may help determine the level of pesticides in drinking water, the number of endangered species living in a particular area, or the number of people afflicted with a particular disease. Statisticians also are employed in national defense agencies, determining the accuracy of new weapons and the likely effectiveness of defense strategies.

Because statistical specialists are employed in so many work areas, specialists who use statistics often have different professional designations. For example, a person using statistical methods to analyze economic data may have the title econometrician, while statisticians in public health and medicine may hold titles such as biostatistician, biometrician, or epidemiologist.

Working Conditions

Statisticians usually work regular hours in comfortable offices. Some statisticians travel to provide advice on research projects, supervise and set up surveys, or gather statistical data. While advanced communications devices such as e-mail and teleconferencing are making it easier for statisticians to work with clients in different areas, there still are situations that require the statistician to be present, such as during meetings or while gathering data. Some in this occupation may have duties that vary widely, such as designing experiments or performing fieldwork in various communities. Statisticians who work in academia generally have a mix of teaching and research responsibilities.

Training, Other Qualifications, and Advancement

Although employment opportunities exist for individuals with a bachelor's degree, a master's degree in statistics or mathematics is usually the minimum educational requirement for most statistician jobs. Research and academic positions in institutions of higher education, for example, require at least a master's degree, and usually a Ph.D., in statistics. Beginning positions in industrial research often require a master's degree combined with several years of experience.

The training required for employment as an entry-level statistician in the federal government, however, is a bachelor's degree, including at least 15 semester hours of statistics or a combination of 15 hours of mathematics and statistics if at least 6 semester hours are in statistics. Qualifying as a mathematical statistician in the federal government requires 24 semester hours of mathematics and statistics, with a minimum of 6 semester hours in statistics and 12 semester hours in an area of advanced mathematics, such as calculus, differential equations, or vector analysis.

In 2004, approximately 230 universities offered a degree program in statistics, biostatistics, or mathematics. Many other schools also offered graduate-level courses in applied statistics for students majoring in biology, business, economics, education, engineering, psychology, and other fields. Acceptance into graduate statistics programs does not require an undergraduate degree in statistics, although good training in mathematics is essential.

Many schools also offered degrees in mathematics, operations research, and other fields that include a sufficient number of courses in statistics to qualify graduates for some entry-level positions with the federal government. Required subjects for statistics majors include differential and integral calculus, statistical methods, mathematical modeling, and probability theory. Additional courses that undergraduates should take include linear algebra, design and analysis of experiments, applied multivariate analysis, and mathematical statistics.

Because computers are used extensively for statistical applications, a strong background in computer science is highly recommended. For positions involving quality and productivity improvement, training in engineering or physical science is useful. A background in biological, chemical, or health science is important for positions involving the preparation and testing of pharmaceutical or agricultural products. Courses in economics and business administration are helpful for many jobs in market research, business analysis, and forecasting.

Good communications skills are important for prospective statisticians in industry, who often need to explain technical matters to persons without statistical expertise. An understanding of business and the economy also is valuable for those who plan to work in private industry.

Beginning statisticians generally are supervised by an experienced statistician. With experience, they may advance to positions with more technical responsibility and, in some cases, supervisory duties. However, opportunities for promotion are greater for persons with advanced degrees. Master's and Ph.D. degree holders usually enjoy independence in their work and may become qualified to engage in research; develop statistical methods; or, after a number of years of experience in a particular area, become statistical consultants.

Employment

Statisticians held about 19,000 jobs in 2004. Twenty percent of these jobs were in the federal government, where statisticians were concentrated in the Departments of Commerce, Agriculture, and Health and Human Services. Another 20 percent were found in state and local governments, including state colleges and universities. Most of the remaining jobs were in private industry, especially in scientific research and development services, insurance carriers, and pharmaceutical and medicine manufacturing. In addition, many professionals with a background in statistics were among the 53,000 postsecondary mathematical science teachers. (See the description of teachers—postsecondary elsewhere in this book.)

Job Outlook

Employment of statisticians is projected to grow more slowly than the average for all occupations over the 2004–2014 period because many jobs that require a degree in statistics will not carry the title "statistician." However, job opportunities should remain favorable for individuals with a degree in statistics. For example, many jobs involve the analysis and interpretation of data from economics, biological science, psychology, computer software engineering, and other disciplines. Despite the limited number of jobs resulting from growth, a number of openings will become available as statisticians transfer to other occupations or retire or leave the workforce for other reasons.

The use of statistics is widespread and growing. Among graduates with a master's degree in statistics, those with a strong background in an allied field, such as finance, biology, engineering, or computer science, should have the best prospects of finding jobs related to their field of study. Federal agencies will hire statisticians in many fields, including demography, agriculture, consumer and producer surveys, Social Security, health care, and environmental quality. Because the federal government is one of the few employers that considers a bachelor's degree an adequate entry-level qualification, competition for entry-level positions in the federal government is expected to be strong for persons just meeting the minimum qualifications for statisticians. Those who meet state certification requirements may become high school statistics teachers.

Manufacturing firms will hire statisticians with master's and doctoral degrees for quality control of various products, including pharmaceuticals, motor vehicles, aircraft, chemicals, and food. For example, pharmaceutical firms will employ statisticians to assess the effectiveness and safety of new drugs, to decide whether to market them, and to make sure they comply with federal standards. To address global product competition, motor vehicle manufacturers will need statisticians to improve the quality of automobiles, trucks, and their components by developing and testing new designs. Statisticians with knowledge of engineering and the physical sciences will find jobs in research and development, working with teams of scientists and engineers to help improve design and production processes to ensure consistent quality of newly developed products. Many statisticians also will find opportunities developing statistical software for computer software manufacturing firms.

Firms will rely heavily on workers with a background in statistics to forecast sales, analyze business conditions, and help to solve management problems to maximize profits. In addition, consulting firms increasingly will offer sophisticated statistical services to other businesses. Because of the widespread use of computers in this field and the growing number of widely used software packages, statisticians in all industries should have good computer programming skills and knowledge of statistical software.

Earnings

Median annual earnings of statisticians were $58,620 in May 2004. The middle 50 percent earned between $42,770 and $80,690. The lowest 10 percent earned less than $32,870, while the highest 10 percent earned more than $100,500.

The average annual salary for statisticians in the federal government in nonsupervisory, supervisory, and managerial positions was $81,262 in 2005, while mathematical statisticians averaged $91,446. According to a 2005 survey by the National Association of Colleges and Employers, starting salary offers for mathematics/statistics graduates with a bachelor's degree averaged $43,448 a year.

Related Occupations

People in a wide range of occupations work with statistics. Among these are actuaries, mathematicians, operations research analysts, computer scientists and database administrators, computer systems analysts, computer programmers, computer software engineers, engineers, economists, market and survey researchers, and financial analysts and personal financial advisors. Some statisticians also work as secondary or postsecondary teachers.

Sources of Additional Information

For information about career opportunities in statistics, contact

▸ American Statistical Association, 1429 Duke St., Alexandria, VA 22314-3415. Internet: http://www.amstat.org

For more information on doctoral-level careers and training in mathematics, a field closely related to statistics, contact

▸ American Mathematical Society, 201 Charles St., Providence, RI 02904-2213. Internet: http://www.ams.org

Information on obtaining positions as statisticians with the federal government is available from the Office of Personnel Management through USAJOBS, the federal government's official employment information system. This resource for locating and applying for job opportunities can be accessed through the Internet at http://www.usajobs.opm.gov or through an interactive voice response telephone system at (703) 724-1850 or TDD (978) 461-8404. These numbers are not toll free, and charges may result.

Teachers—Postsecondary

(O*NET 25-1011.00, 25-1021.00, 25-1022.00, 25-1031.00,
25-1032.00, 25-1041.00, 25-1042.00, 25-1043.00, 25-1051.00,
25-1052.00, 25-1053.00, 25-1054.00, 25-1061.00, 25-1062.00,
25-1063.00, 25-1064.00, 25-1065.00, 25-1066.00, 25-1067.00,
25-1069.99, 25-1071.00, 25-1072.00, 25-1081.00, 25-1082.00,
25-1111.00, 25-1112.00, 25-1113.00, 25-1121.00, 25-1122.00,
25-1123.00, 25-1124.00, 25-1125.00, 25-1126.00, 25-1191.00,
25-1192.00, 25-1193.00, 25-1194.00, and 25-1199.99)

Significant Points

■ Opportunities for postsecondary teaching jobs are expected to be good, but many new openings will be for part-time or non-tenure-track positions.

■ Prospects for teaching jobs will be better and earnings higher in academic fields in which many qualified teachers opt for nonacademic careers, such as health specialties, business, and computer science, for example.

■ Educational qualifications for postsecondary teacher jobs range from expertise in a particular field to a Ph.D., depending on the subject being taught and the type of educational institution.

Nature of the Work

Postsecondary teachers instruct students in a wide variety of academic and vocational subjects beyond the high school level that may lead to a degree or to improvement in one's knowledge or career skills. These teachers include college and university faculty, postsecondary career and technical education teachers, and graduate teaching assistants.

College and university faculty make up the majority of postsecondary teachers. They teach and advise more than 16 million full- and part-time college students and perform a significant part of our nation's research. Faculty also keep up with new developments in their field and may consult with government, business, nonprofit, and community organizations.

Faculty usually are organized into departments or divisions, based on academic subject or field. They usually teach several different related courses in their subject—algebra, calculus, and statistics, for example. They may instruct undergraduate or graduate students or both. College and university faculty may give lectures to several hundred students in large halls, lead small seminars, or supervise students in laboratories. They prepare lectures, exercises, and laboratory experiments; grade exams and papers; and advise and work with students individually. In universities, they also supervise graduate students' teaching and research. College faculty work with an increasingly varied student population made up of growing shares of part-time, older, and culturally and racially diverse students.

Faculty keep abreast of developments in their field by reading current literature, talking with colleagues, and participating in professional conferences. They may also do their own research to expand knowledge in their field. They may perform experiments; collect and analyze data; and examine original documents, literature, and other source material. From this process, they arrive at conclusions and publish their findings in scholarly journals, books, and electronic media.

Most college and university faculty extensively use computer technology, including the Internet; e-mail; CD-ROMs; and software programs, such as statistical packages. They may use computers in the classroom as teaching aids and may post course content, class notes, class schedules, and other information on the Internet. The use of e-mail, chat rooms, and other techniques has greatly improved communications between students and teachers and among students.

Some faculty use the Internet to teach courses to students at remote sites. These so-called "distance learning" courses are an increasingly popular option for non-traditional students such as working adults. While the courses are more convenient for students, faculty who teach these courses must be able to adapt existing courses to make them successful online or design a new course that takes advantage of the format.

Most faculty members serve on academic or administrative committees that deal with the policies of their institution, departmental matters, academic issues, curricula, budgets, equipment purchases, and hiring. Some work with student and community organizations. Department chairpersons are faculty members who usually teach some courses but have heavier administrative responsibilities.

The proportion of time spent on research, teaching, administrative, and other duties varies by individual circumstance and type of institution. Faculty members at universities normally spend a significant part of their time doing research; those in 4-year colleges, somewhat less; and those in 2-year colleges, relatively little. The teaching load, however, often is heavier in 2-year colleges and somewhat lighter at 4-year institutions. Full professors at all types of institutions usually spend a larger portion of their time conducting research than do assistant professors, instructors, and lecturers.

In addition to traditional 2- and 4-year institutions, an increasing number of faculty work in alternative schools or in programs that are aimed at providing career-related education for working adults. Courses are usually offered online or on nights and weekends. Faculty at these programs generally work part time and are only responsible for teaching, with little to no administrative and research responsibilities.

Postsecondary vocational education teachers, also known as *postsecondary career and technical education teachers,* provide instruction for occupations that require specialized training but may not require a 4-year degree, such as welder, dental hygienist, X-ray technician, auto mechanic, and cosmetologist. Classes often are taught in an industrial or laboratory setting where students are provided hands-on experience. For example, welding instructors show students various welding techniques and essential safety practices, watch them use tools and equipment, and have them repeat procedures until they meet the specific standards required by the trade. Increasingly, career and technical education teachers are integrating academic and vocational curriculums so that students obtain a variety of skills that can be applied to the "real world."

Career and technical education teachers have many of the same responsibilities that other college and university faculty have. They must prepare lessons, grade papers, attend faculty meetings, and keep abreast of developments in their field. Career and technical education teachers at community colleges and career and technical schools also often play a key role in students' transition from school to work by helping to establish internship programs for students and by facilitating contact between students and prospective employers.

Graduate teaching assistants, often referred to as *graduate TAs*, assist faculty, department chairs, or other professional staff at colleges and universities by performing teaching or teaching-related duties. In addition to their work responsibilities, assistants have their own school commitments, as they are also students who are working towards earning a graduate degree, such as a Ph.D. Some teaching assistants have full responsibility for teaching a course—usually one that is introductory in nature—which can include preparation of lectures and exams and assigning final grades to students. Others provide assistance to faculty members, which may consist of a variety of tasks such as grading papers, monitoring exams, holding office hours or help-sessions for students, conducting laboratory sessions, or administering quizzes to the class. Teaching assistants generally meet initially with the faculty member whom they are going to assist in order to determine exactly what is expected of them, as each faculty member may have his or her own needs. For example, some faculty members prefer assistants to sit in on classes, while others assign them other tasks to do during class time. Graduate teaching assistants may work one-on-one with a faculty member or, for large classes, they may be one of several assistants.

Working Conditions

Postsecondary teachers who work full time usually have flexible schedules. They must be present for classes, usually 12 to 16 hours per week, and for faculty and committee meetings. Most establish regular office hours for student consultations, usually 3 to 6 hours per week. Otherwise, teachers are free to decide when and where they will work and how much time to devote to course preparation, grading, study, research, graduate student supervision, and other activities.

Some teach night and weekend classes. This is particularly true for teachers at 2-year community colleges or institutions with large enrollments of older students who have full-time jobs or family responsibilities. Most colleges and universities require teachers to work 9 months of the year, which allows them the time to teach additional courses, do research, travel, or pursue nonacademic interests during the summer and school holidays. Colleges and universities usually have funds to support research or other professional development needs of full-time faculty, including travel to conferences and research sites.

About 3 out of 10 college and university faculty worked part time in 2004. Some part-timers, known as "adjunct faculty," have primary jobs outside of academia—in government, private industry, or nonprofit research—and teach "on the side." Others prefer to work part-time hours or seek full-time jobs but are unable to obtain them due to intense competition for available openings. Some work part time in more than one institution. Some adjunct faculty are not qualified for tenure-track positions because they lack a doctoral degree.

University faculty may experience a conflict between their responsibilities to teach students and the pressure to do research and publish their findings. This may be a particular problem for young faculty seeking advancement in 4-year research universities. Also,

recent cutbacks in support workers and the hiring of more part-time faculty have put a greater administrative burden on full-time faculty. Requirements to teach online classes also have added greatly to the workloads of postsecondary teachers. Many find that developing the courses to put online, plus learning how to operate the technology and answering large amounts of e-mail, is very time-consuming.

Graduate TAs usually have flexibility in their work schedules like college and university faculty, but they also must spend a considerable amount of time pursuing their own academic coursework and studies. The number of hours that TAs work varies, depending on their assignments. Work may be stressful, particularly when assistants are given full responsibility for teaching a class; however, these types of positions allow graduate students the opportunity to gain valuable teaching experience. This experience is especially helpful for those graduate teaching assistants who seek to become faculty members at colleges and universities after completing their degree.

Training, Other Qualifications, and Advancement

The education and training required of postsecondary teachers varies widely, depending on the subject taught and educational institution employing them. Educational requirements for teachers are generally the highest at 4-year research universities while experience and expertise in a related occupation is the principal qualification at career and technical institutes.

Postsecondary teachers should communicate and relate well with students, enjoy working with them, and be able to motivate them. They should have inquiring and analytical minds and a strong desire to pursue and disseminate knowledge. Additionally, they must be self-motivated and able to work in an environment in which they receive little direct supervision.

Training requirements for postsecondary career and technical education teachers vary by state and by subject. In general, teachers need a bachelor's or higher degree plus at least 3 years of work experience in their field. In some fields, a license or certificate that demonstrates one's qualifications may be all that is required. Teachers update their skills through continuing education in order to maintain certification. They must also maintain ongoing dialogue with businesses to determine the most current skills needed in the workplace.

Four-year colleges and universities usually consider doctoral degree holders for full-time, tenure-track positions, but may hire master's degree holders or doctoral candidates for certain disciplines, such as the arts, or for part-time and temporary jobs. Most college and university faculty are in four academic ranks—professor, associate professor, assistant professor, and instructor. These positions usually are considered to be tenure-track positions. Most faculty members are hired as instructors or assistant professors. A smaller number of additional faculty members, called lecturers, are usually employed on contracts for a single academic term and are not on the tenure track.

In 2-year colleges, master's degree holders fill most full-time positions. However, in certain fields where there may be more applicants than available jobs, institutions can be more selective in their hiring practices. In these fields, master's degree holders may be passed over in favor of candidates holding Ph.D.s. Many 2-year institutions increasingly prefer job applicants to have some teaching experience or experience with distance learning. Preference also may be given to those holding dual master's degrees, especially at smaller institutions, because they can teach more subjects.

Schools and programs that provide education and training for working adults generally hire people who are experienced in the field to teach part time. A master's degree is also usually required.

Doctoral programs take an average of 6 years of full-time study beyond the bachelor's degree, including time spent completing a master's degree and a dissertation. Some programs, such as those in the humanities, may take longer to complete; others, such as those in engineering, usually are shorter. Candidates specialize in a subfield of a discipline—for example, organic chemistry, counseling psychology, or European history—but also take courses covering the entire discipline. Programs typically include 20 or more increasingly specialized courses and seminars plus comprehensive examinations on all major areas of the field. Candidates also must complete a dissertation—a written report on original research in the candidate's major field of study. The dissertation sets forth an original hypothesis or proposes a model and tests it. Students in the natural sciences and engineering usually do laboratory work; in the humanities, they study original documents and other published material. The dissertation is done under the guidance of one or more faculty advisors and usually takes 1 or 2 years of full-time work.

Some students, particularly those who studied in the natural sciences, spend additional years after earning their degree on postdoctoral research and study before taking a faculty position. Some Ph.D.s are able to extend postdoctoral appointments, or take new ones, if they are unable to find a faculty job. Most of these appointments offer a nominal salary.

Obtaining a position as a graduate teaching assistant is a good way to gain college teaching experience. To qualify, candidates must be enrolled in a graduate school program. In addition, some colleges and universities require teaching assistants to attend classes or take some training prior to being given responsibility for a course.

Although graduate teaching assistants usually work at the institution and in the department where they are earning their degree, teaching or internship positions for graduate students at institutions that do not grant a graduate degree have become more common in recent years. For example, a program called Preparing Future Faculty, administered by the Association of American Colleges and Universities and the Council of Graduate Schools, has led to the creation of many now-independent programs that offer graduate students at research universities the opportunity to work as teaching assistants at other types of institutions, such as liberal arts or community colleges. Working with a mentor, the graduate students teach classes and learn how to improve their teaching techniques. They may attend faculty and committee meetings; develop a curriculum; and learn how to balance the teaching, research, and administrative roles that faculty play. These programs provide valuable learning opportunities for graduate students interested in teaching at the postsecondary level and also help to make these students aware of the differences among the various types of institutions at which they may someday work.

For faculty, a major step in the traditional academic career is attaining tenure. New tenure-track faculty usually are hired as instructors or assistant professors and must serve a period—usually 7 years—under term contracts. At the end of the period, their record of teaching, research, and overall contribution to the institution is reviewed; tenure is granted if the review is favorable. Those denied tenure usually must leave the institution. Tenured professors cannot be fired without just cause and due process. Tenure protects the faculty's academic freedom—the ability to teach and conduct research without fear of being fired for advocating controversial or unpopular ideas. It also gives both faculty and institutions the stability needed for effective research and teaching and provides financial security for faculty. Some institutions have adopted post-tenure review policies to encourage ongoing evaluation of tenured faculty.

The number of tenure-track positions is declining as institutions seek flexibility in dealing with financial matters and changing student interests. Institutions rely more heavily on limited term contracts and part-time, or adjunct, faculty, thus shrinking the total pool of tenured faculty. Limited-term contracts—typically 2 to 5 years, may be terminated or extended when they expire, but generally do not lead to the granting of tenure. In addition, some institutions have limited the percentage of faculty who can be tenured.

For most postsecondary teachers, advancement involves a move into administrative and managerial positions, such as departmental chairperson, dean, and president. At 4-year institutions, such advancement requires a doctoral degree. At 2-year colleges, a doctorate is helpful but not usually required, except for advancement to some top administrative positions.

Employment

Postsecondary teachers held nearly 1.6 million jobs in 2004. Most were employed in public and private 4-year colleges and universities and in 2-year community colleges. Other postsecondary teachers are employed by schools and institutes that specialize in training people in a specific field, such as technology centers or culinary schools, or work for businesses that provide professional development courses to employees of companies. Some career and technical education teachers work for state and local governments and job training facilities. The following tabulation shows postsecondary teaching jobs in specialties having 20,000 or more jobs in 2004:

Health specialties teachers 150,000
Graduate teaching assistants 143,000
Vocational education teachers 127,000
Business teachers 85,000
Art, drama, and music teachers 78,000
Biological science teachers 76,000
English language and literature teachers...............69,000
Education teachers 60,000
Mathematical science teachers...........................53,000
Computer science teachers 45,000
Engineering teachers 42,000
Nursing instructors and teachers 41,000
Psychology teachers...37,000
Foreign language and literature teachers...............27,000

Communications teachers 26,000

History teachers 24,000

Chemistry teachers 23,000

Philosophy and religion teachers 23,000

Job Outlook

Overall, employment of postsecondary teachers is expected to grow much faster than the average for all occupations through 2014. A significant proportion of these new jobs will be part-time positions. Job opportunities are generally expected to be very good—although they will vary somewhat from field to field—as numerous openings for all types of postsecondary teachers result from retirements of current postsecondary teachers and continued increases in student enrollments.

Projected growth in college and university enrollment over the next decade stems mainly from the expected increase in the population of 18- to 24-year-olds, who constitute the majority of students at postsecondary institutions, and from the increasing number of high school graduates who choose to attend these institutions. Adults returning to college to enhance their career prospects or to update their skills also will continue to create new opportunities for postsecondary teachers, particularly at community colleges and for-profit institutions that cater to working adults. However, many postsecondary educational institutions receive a significant portion of their funding from state and local governments, so expansion of public higher education will be limited by state and local budgets. Nevertheless, in addition to growth in enrollments, the need to replace the large numbers of postsecondary teachers who are likely to retire over the next decade will also create a significant number of openings. Many postsecondary teachers were hired in the late 1960s and the 1970s to teach members of the baby boom generation, and they are expected to retire in growing numbers in the years ahead.

Ph.D. recipients seeking jobs as postsecondary teachers will experience favorable job prospects over the next decade. While competition will remain tight for tenure-track positions at 4-year colleges and universities, there will be a considerable number of part-time or renewable term appointments at these institutions and positions at community colleges available to them. Opportunities for master's degree holders are also expected to be favorable, as community colleges and other institutions that employ them, such as professional career education programs, are expected to experience considerable growth.

Opportunities for graduate teaching assistants are expected to be very good due to prospects for much higher undergraduate enrollments coupled with more modest graduate enrollment increases. Constituting almost 9 percent of all postsecondary teachers, graduate teaching assistants play an integral role in the postsecondary education system, and they are expected to continue to do so in the future.

One of the main reasons why students attend postsecondary institutions is to prepare themselves for careers, so the best job prospects for postsecondary teachers are likely to be in fields where job growth is expected to be strong over the next decade. These will include fields such as business, health specialties, nursing, and biological sciences. Community colleges and other institutions offering career and technical education have been among the most rapidly growing, and these institutions are expected to offer some of the best opportunities for postsecondary teachers.

Earnings

Median annual earnings of all postsecondary teachers in May 2004 were $51,800. The middle 50 percent earned between $36,590 and $72,490. The lowest 10 percent earned less than $25,460, and the highest 10 percent earned more than $99,980.

Earnings for college faculty vary according to rank and type of institution, geographic area, and field. According to a 2004–2005 survey by the American Association of University Professors, salaries for full-time faculty averaged $68,505. By rank, the average was $91,548 for professors, $65,113 for associate professors, $54,571 for assistant professors, $39,899 for instructors, and $45,647 for lecturers. Faculty in 4-year institutions earn higher salaries, on average, than do those in 2-year schools. In 2004–2005, faculty salaries averaged $79,342 in private independent institutions, $66,851 in public institutions, and $61,103 in religiously affiliated private colleges and universities. In fields with high-paying nonacademic alternatives—medicine, law, engineering, and business, among others—earnings exceed these averages. In other fields—such as the humanities and education—they are lower.

Many faculty members have significant earnings in addition to their base salary from consulting, teaching additional courses, research, writing for publication, or other employment. In addition, many college and university faculty enjoy some unique benefits, including access to campus facilities, tuition waivers for dependents, housing and travel allowances, and paid sabbatical leaves. Part-time faculty usually have fewer benefits than full-time faculty.

Earnings for postsecondary career and technical education teachers vary widely by subject, academic credentials, experience, and region of the country. Part-time instructors usually receive few benefits.

Related Occupations

Postsecondary teaching requires the ability to communicate ideas well, motivate students, and be creative. Workers in other occupations that require these skills are teachers—preschool, kindergarten, elementary, middle, and secondary; education administrators; librarians; counselors; writers and editors; public relations specialists; and management analysts. Faculty research activities often are similar to those of scientists, as well as to those of managers and administrators in industry, government, and nonprofit research organizations.

Sources of Additional Information

Professional societies related to a field of study often provide information on academic and nonacademic employment opportunities. Names and addresses of many of these societies appear in job descriptions elsewhere in this book.

Special publications on higher education, such as *The Chronicle of Higher Education*, list specific employment opportunities for faculty. These publications are available in libraries.

For information on the Preparing Future Faculty program, contact

▸ Council of Graduate Schools, One Dupont Circle NW, Suite 430, Washington, DC 20036-1173. Internet: http://www.preparing-faculty.org

For information on postsecondary career and technical education teaching positions, contact state departments of career and technical education. General information on adult and career and technical education is available from

▸ Association for Career and Technical Education, 1410 King St., Alexandria, VA 22314. Internet: http://www.acteonline.org

Urban and Regional Planners

(O*NET 19-3051.00)

Significant Points

■ Local governments employ 7 out of 10 urban and regional planners.

■ Most entry-level jobs require a master's degree; bachelor's-degree holders may find some entry-level positions, but advancement opportunities are limited.

■ Most new jobs will be in affluent, rapidly growing urban and suburban communities.

Nature of the Work

Planners develop long- and short-term plans to use land for the growth and revitalization of urban, suburban, and rural communities while helping local officials make decisions concerning social, economic, and environmental problems. Because local governments employ the majority of urban and regional planners, they often are referred to as *community, regional,* or *city planners.*

Planners promote the best use of a community's land and resources for residential, commercial, institutional, and recreational purposes. Planners may be involved in various other activities, including making decisions relating to establishing alternative public transportation systems, developing resources, and protecting ecologically sensitive regions. Urban and regional planners address issues such as traffic congestion, air pollution, and the effects of growth and change on a community. They may formulate plans relating to the construction of new school buildings, public housing, or other kinds of infrastructure. Some planners are involved in environmental issues ranging from pollution control to wetland preservation, forest conservation, and the location of new landfills. Planners also may be involved in drafting legislation on environmental, social, and economic issues, such as sheltering the homeless, planning a new park, or meeting the demand for new correctional facilities.

Planners examine proposed community facilities, such as schools, to be sure that these facilities will meet the changing demands placed upon them over time. They keep abreast of economic and legal issues involved in zoning codes, building codes, and environmental regulations. They ensure that builders and developers follow these codes and regulations. Planners also deal with land-use issues created by population movements. For example, as suburban growth and economic development create more new jobs outside cities, the need for public transportation that enables workers to get to those jobs increases. In response, planners develop transportation models and explain their details to planning boards and the general public.

Before preparing plans for community development, planners report on the current use of land for residential, business, and community purposes. Their reports include information on the location and capacity of streets, highways, airports, water and sewer lines, schools, libraries, and cultural and recreational sites. They also provide data on the types of industries in the community, the characteristics of the population, and employment and economic trends. Using this information, along with input from citizens' advisory committees, planners design the layout of land uses for buildings and other facilities, such as subway lines and stations. Planners prepare reports showing how their programs can be carried out and what they will cost.

Planners use computers to record and analyze information and to prepare reports and recommendations for government executives and others. Computer databases, spreadsheets, and analytical techniques are utilized to project program costs and forecast future trends in employment, housing, transportation, or population. Computerized geographic information systems enable planners to map land areas, to overlay maps with geographic variables such as population density, and to combine or manipulate geographic information to produce alternative plans for land use or development.

Urban and regional planners often confer with land developers, civic leaders, and public officials and may function as mediators in community disputes, presenting alternatives that are acceptable to opposing parties. Planners may prepare material for community relations programs, speak at civic meetings, and appear before legislative committees and elected officials to explain and defend their proposals.

In large organizations, planners usually specialize in a single area, such as transportation, demography, housing, historic preservation, urban design, environmental and regulatory issues, or economic development. In small organizations, planners do various kinds of planning.

Working Conditions

Urban and regional planners often travel to inspect the features of land under consideration for development or regulation, including its current use and the types of structures on it. Some local government planners involved in site development inspections spend most of their time in the field. Although most planners have a scheduled 40-hour workweek, they frequently attend evening or weekend meetings or public hearings with citizens' groups. Planners may experience the pressure of deadlines and tight work schedules, as well as political pressure generated by interest groups affected by proposals related to urban development and land use.

Training, Other Qualifications, and Advancement

For jobs as urban and regional planners, employers prefer workers who have advanced training. Most entry-level jobs in federal, state, and local government agencies require a master's degree from an accredited program in urban or regional planning or a master's degree in a related field, such as urban design or geography. A bachelor's degree from an accredited planning program, coupled with a master's degree in architecture, landscape architecture, or civil engineering, is good preparation for entry-level planning jobs in various areas, including urban design, transportation, and the environment. A master's degree from an accredited planning program provides the best training for a wide range of planning fields. Although graduates from one of the limited number of accredited bachelor's degree programs qualify for some entry-level positions, their advancement opportunities often are limited unless they acquire an advanced degree.

Courses in related disciplines, such as architecture, law, earth sciences, demography, economics, finance, health administration, geographic information systems, and management, are highly recommended. Because familiarity with computer models and statistical techniques is important, courses in statistics and computer science also are recommended.

In 2005, 68 colleges and universities offered an accredited master's degree program, and 15 offered an accredited bachelor's degree program, in urban or regional planning. Accreditation for these programs is from the Planning Accreditation Board, which consists of representatives of the American Institute of Certified Planners, the American Planning Association, and the Association of Collegiate Schools of Planning. Most graduate programs in planning require a minimum of 2 years of study.

Specializations most commonly offered by planning schools are environmental planning, land use and comprehensive planning, economic development, housing, historic preservation, and social planning. Other popular offerings include community development, transportation, and urban design. Graduate students spend considerable time in studios, workshops, and laboratory courses learning to analyze and solve planning problems. They often are required to work in a planning office part time or during the summer. Local government planning offices frequently offer students internships, providing experience that proves invaluable in obtaining a full-time planning position after graduation.

The American Institute of Certified Planners, a professional institute within the American Planning Association, grants certification to individuals who have the appropriate combination of education and professional experience and who pass an examination. Certification may be helpful for promotion.

Planners must be able to think in terms of spatial relationships and visualize the effects of their plans and designs. They should be flexible and be able to reconcile different viewpoints and make constructive policy recommendations. The ability to communicate effectively, both orally and in writing, is necessary for anyone interested in this field.

After a few years of experience, planners may advance to assignments requiring a high degree of independent judgment, such as designing the physical layout of a large development or recommending policy and budget options. Some public-sector planners are promoted to community planning director and spend a great deal of time meeting with officials, speaking to civic groups, and supervising a staff. Further advancement occurs through a transfer to a larger jurisdiction with more complex problems and greater responsibilities or into related occupations, such as director of community or economic development.

Employment

Urban and regional planners held about 32,000 jobs in 2004. About 7 out of 10 were employed by local governments. Companies involved with architectural, engineering, and related services, as well as management, scientific, and technical consulting services, employ an increasing proportion of planners in the private sector. Others are employed in state government agencies dealing with housing, transportation, or environmental protection, and a small number work for the federal government.

Job Outlook

Employment of urban and regional planners is expected to grow about as fast as average for all occupations through 2014. Employment growth will be driven by the need for state and local governments to provide public services such as regulation of commercial development, the environment, transportation, housing, and land use and development for an expanding population. Nongovernmental initiatives dealing with historic preservation and redevelopment will provide additional openings. Some job openings also will arise from the need to replace experienced planners who transfer to other occupations, retire, or leave the labor force for other reasons. Graduates with a master's degree from an accredited program should have an advantage in the job market.

Most new jobs for urban and regional planners will be in local government, as planners will be needed to address an array of problems associated with population growth, especially in affluent, rapidly expanding communities. For example, new housing developments require roads, sewer systems, fire stations, schools, libraries, and recreation facilities that must be planned for in the midst of a consideration of budgetary constraints. Small-town chambers of commerce, economic development authorities, and tourism bureaus may hire planners, preferably with some background in marketing and public relations.

The fastest job growth for urban and regional planners will occur in the private sector, primarily in professional, scientific, and technical services. For example, planners may be employed by these firms to help design security measures for a building that meet a desired security level but that also are subtle and blend in with the surrounding area. However, because the private sector employs fewer than 2 out of 10 urban and regional planners, not as many new jobs will be created in the private sector as in government.

Earnings

Median annual earnings of urban and regional planners were $53,450 in May 2004. The middle 50 percent earned between $41,950 and $67,530. The lowest 10 percent earned less than $33,840, and the highest 10 percent earned more than $82,610. Median annual earnings in local government, the industry employing the largest number of urban and regional planners, were $52,520.

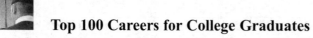

Related Occupations

Urban and regional planners develop plans for the growth of urban, suburban, and rural communities. Others whose work is similar include architects, civil engineers, environmental engineers, landscape architects, and geographers.

Sources of Additional Information

Information on careers, salaries, and certification in urban and regional planning is available from

▸ American Planning Association, 1776 Massachusetts Ave. NW, Washington, DC 20036-1904. Internet: http://www.planning.org

Information on accredited urban and regional planning programs is available from

▸ Association of Collegiate Schools of Planning, 6311 Mallard Trace, Tallahassee, FL 32312. Internet: http://www.acsp.org

Jobs Typically Requiring a Bachelor's Degree Plus Work Experience

Actuaries

Administrative Services Managers

Advertising, Marketing, Promotions, Public Relations, and Sales Managers

Computer and Information Systems Managers

Education Administrators

Engineering and Natural Sciences Managers

Financial Managers

Judges, Magistrates, and Other Judicial Workers

Management Analysts

Medical and Health Services Managers

Top Executives

Actuaries

(O*NET 15-2011.00)

Significant Points

- A strong background in mathematics is essential; actuaries must pass a series of examinations to gain full professional status.

- About 6 out of 10 actuaries are employed in the insurance industry.

- Employment opportunities should remain good for those who qualify because the stringent qualifying examination system restricts the number of candidates.

Nature of the Work

One of the main functions of *actuaries* is to help businesses assess the risk of certain events occurring and to formulate policies that minimize the cost of that risk. For this reason, actuaries are essential to the insurance industry. Actuaries assemble and analyze data to estimate the probability and likely cost of the occurrence of an event such as death, sickness, injury, disability, or loss of property. Actuaries also address financial questions, including those involving the level of pension contributions required to produce a certain retirement income and the way in which a company should invest resources to maximize its return on investments in light of potential risk. Using their broad knowledge of statistics, finance, and business, actuaries help design insurance policies, pension plans, and other financial strategies in a manner that will help ensure that the plans are maintained on a sound financial basis.

Most actuaries are employed in the insurance industry, specializing in life and health insurance or property and casualty insurance. They produce probability tables that determine the likelihood that a potential future event will generate a claim. From these tables, they estimate the amount a company can expect to pay in claims. For example, property and casualty actuaries calculate the expected amount payable in claims resulting from automobile accidents, an amount that varies with the insured person's age, sex, driving history, type of car, and other factors. Actuaries ensure that the price, or premium, charged for such insurance will enable the company to cover claims and other expenses. The premium must be profitable yet competitive with other insurance companies. Within the life and health insurance fields, actuaries are helping to develop long-term-care insurance and annuity policies, the latter a growing investment tool for many individuals.

Actuaries in other financial services industries manage credit and price corporate security offerings. They also devise new investment tools to help their firms compete with other financial services companies. Pension actuaries working under the provisions of the Employee Retirement Income Security Act (ERISA) of 1974 evaluate pension plans covered by that act and report on the plans' financial soundness to participants, sponsors, and federal regulators. Actuaries working in government help manage social programs such as Social Security and Medicare.

Actuaries may play a role in determining company policy and may need to explain complex technical matters to company executives, government officials, shareholders, policyholders, or the public in general. They may testify before public agencies on proposed legislation affecting their businesses or explain changes in contract provisions to customers. They also may help companies develop plans to enter new lines of business or new geographic markets with existing lines of business by forecasting demand in competitive settings.

Both staff actuaries employed by businesses and consulting actuaries provide advice to clients on a contract basis. The duties of most consulting actuaries are similar to those of other actuaries. For example, some may evaluate company pension plans by calculating the future value of employee and employer contributions and determining whether the amounts are sufficient to meet the future needs of retirees. Others help companies reduce their insurance costs by lowering the level of risk the companies assume. For instance, they may provide advice on how to lessen the risk of injury on the job, which will lower worker's compensation costs. Consulting actuaries sometimes testify in court regarding the value of the potential lifetime earnings of a person who is disabled or killed in an accident, the current value of future pension benefits (in divorce cases), or other values arrived at by complex calculations. Many consulting actuaries work in reinsurance, a field in which one insurance company arranges to share a large prospective liability policy with another insurance company in exchange for a percentage of the premium.

Working Conditions

Actuaries have desk jobs, and their offices usually are comfortable and pleasant. They often work at least 40 hours a week. Some actuaries—particularly consulting actuaries—may travel to meet with clients. Consulting actuaries also may experience more erratic employment and be expected to work more than 40 hours per week.

Training, Other Qualifications, and Advancement

Actuaries need a strong background in mathematics. Applicants for beginning actuarial jobs usually have a bachelor's degree in mathematics; actuarial science; statistics; or a business-related discipline such as economics, finance, or accounting. About 100 colleges and universities offer an actuarial science program, and most offer a degree in mathematics, statistics, economics, or finance. Some companies hire applicants without specifying a major, provided that the applicant has a working knowledge of mathematics, including calculus, probability, and statistics, and has demonstrated this knowledge by passing one or two actuarial exams required for professional designation. Courses in economics, accounting, finance, and insurance also are useful. Companies increasingly prefer well-rounded individuals who, in addition to having acquired a strong technical background, have some training in liberal arts and business and possess strong communication skills.

In addition to knowledge of mathematics, computer skills are becoming increasingly important. Actuaries should be able to develop and use spreadsheets and databases as well as standard statistical analysis software. Knowledge of computer programming languages, such as Visual Basic, also is useful.

Two professional societies sponsor programs leading to full professional status in their specialty. The Society of Actuaries (SOA) administers a series of actuarial examinations in the life insurance, health benefits systems, retirement systems, and finance and investment fields. The Casualty Actuarial Society (CAS) gives a series of examinations in the property and casualty field, which includes fire, accident, medical malpractice, worker's compensation, and personal injury liability.

The first four exams in the SOA and CAS examination series are jointly sponsored by the two societies and cover the same material. For this reason, students do not need to commit themselves to a specialty until they have taken the initial examinations, which test an individual's competence in probability, calculus, statistics, and other branches of mathematics. The first few examinations help students evaluate their potential as actuaries. Many prospective actuaries begin taking the exams in college with the help of self-study guides and courses. Those who pass one or more examinations have better opportunities for employment at higher starting salaries than those who do not.

After graduating from college, most prospective actuaries gain on-the-job experience at an insurance company or consulting firm while at the same time working to complete the examination process. Actuaries are encouraged to finish the entire series of examinations as soon as possible, advancing first to the Associate level (with an ASA or ACAS designation) and then to the Fellowship level (FSA or FCAS designation). Advanced topics in the casualty field include investment and assets, dynamic financial analysis, and valuation of insurance. Candidates in the SOA examination series must choose a specialty—group and health benefits, individual life and annuities, pensions, investments, or finance. Examinations are given twice a year, in the spring and the fall. Although many companies allot time to their employees for study, home study is required to pass the examinations, and many actuaries study for months to prepare for each examination. It is likewise common for employers to pay the hundreds of dollars for examination fees and study materials. Most actuaries reach the Associate level within 4 to 6 years and the Fellowship level a few years later.

Specific requirements apply to pension actuaries, who verify the financial status of defined benefit pension plans for the federal government. These actuaries must be enrolled by the Joint Board of the U.S. Treasury Department and the U.S. Department of Labor for the Enrollment of Actuaries. To qualify for enrollment, applicants must meet certain experience and examination requirements, as stipulated by the Board.

To perform their duties effectively, actuaries must keep up with current economic and social trends and legislation, as well as with health, business, finance, and economic developments that could affect insurance or investment practices. Good communication and interpersonal skills also are important, particularly for prospective consulting actuaries.

Beginning actuaries often rotate among different jobs in an organization to learn various actuarial operations and phases of insurance work, such as marketing, underwriting, and product development. At first, they prepare data for actuarial projects or perform other simple tasks. As they gain experience, actuaries may supervise clerks, prepare correspondence, draft reports, and conduct research. They may move from one company to another early in their careers as they advance to higher positions.

Advancement depends largely on job performance and the number of actuarial examinations passed. Actuaries with a broad knowledge of the insurance, pension, investment, or employee benefits fields can rise to administrative and executive positions in their companies. Actuaries with supervisory ability may advance to management positions in other areas, such as underwriting, accounting, data processing, marketing, and advertising. Some actuaries assume college and university faculty positions. (See the description of teachers—postsecondary elsewhere in this book.)

Employment

Actuaries held about 18,000 jobs in 2004, with 6 out of 10 employed in the insurance industry. A growing number of actuaries work for firms providing a variety of corporate services, especially management and public relations, or for firms offering consulting services. A relatively small number of actuaries are employed by security and commodity brokers or by government agencies.

Job Outlook

Employment of actuaries is expected to grow faster than average for all occupations through 2014. Employment opportunities should remain good for those who qualify because the stringent qualifying examination system restricts the number of candidates. Employment growth in the insurance industry is expected to continue at a stable pace, while more significant job growth is likely in some other industries. In addition, a small number of jobs will open up each year to replace actuaries who leave the occupation to retire or who find new jobs.

Steady demand by the insurance industry—the largest employer of actuaries—should ensure the creation of new actuary jobs in this key industry over the projection period. Actuaries will continue to be needed to develop, price, and evaluate a variety of insurance products and calculate the costs of new risks. Although employment of actuaries in life insurance had begun to decline recently, the growing popularity of annuities, a financial product offered primarily by life insurance companies, has resulted in some job growth in this specialty. Also, new actuarial positions have been created in property-casualty insurance to analyze evolving risks, such as terrorism.

Some new employment opportunities for actuaries should also become available in the health care field as health care issues and Medicare reform continue to receive growing attention. Increased regulation of managed health care companies and the desire to contain health care costs will continue to provide job opportunities for actuaries, who will also be needed to evaluate the risks associated with new medical issues, such as genetic testing and the impact of new diseases. Others in this field are involved in drafting health care legislation.

A significant proportion of new actuaries will find employment with consulting firms. Companies that may not find it cost-effective to hire their own actuaries are increasingly hiring consulting actuaries to analyze various risks. Other areas with notable growth prospects are information services and accounting services. Also, because actuarial skills are increasingly seen as useful to other industries that deal with risk, such as the airline and the banking industries, additional job openings may be created in these industries.

The best job prospects for entry-level positions will be for those candidates who have passed at least one or two of the initial actuarial exams. Candidates with additional knowledge or experience, such as those who possess computer programming skills, will be particularly attractive to employers. Most jobs in this occupation are located in urban areas, but opportunities vary by geographic location. States in which actuary jobs are concentrated include Illinois, New Jersey, New York, and Connecticut.

Earnings

Median annual earnings of actuaries were $76,340 in May 2004. The middle 50 percent earned between $54,770 and $107,650. According to the National Association of Colleges and Employers, annual starting salaries for graduates with a bachelor's degree in actuarial science averaged $52,741 in 2005. Insurance companies and consulting firms give merit increases to actuaries as they gain experience and pass examinations. Some companies also offer cash bonuses for each professional designation achieved.

Related Occupations

Actuaries need a strong background in mathematics, statistics, and related fields. Other workers whose jobs involve related skills include accountants and auditors, budget analysts, economists, market and survey researchers, financial analysts and personal financial advisors, insurance underwriters, mathematicians, and statisticians.

Sources of Additional Information

Career information on actuaries specializing in pensions is available from

▸ American Society of Pension Actuaries, 4245 N. Fairfax Dr., Suite 750, Arlington, VA 22203. Internet: http://www.aspa.org

For information about actuarial careers in life and health insurance, employee benefits and pensions, and finance and investments, contact

▸ Society of Actuaries (SOA), 475 N. Martingale Rd., Suite 600, Schaumburg, IL 60173-2226. Internet: http://www.soa.org

For information about actuarial careers in property and casualty insurance, contact

▸ Casualty Actuarial Society (CAS), 1100 N. Glebe Rd., Suite 600, Arlington, VA 22201-0425. Internet: http://www.casact.org

The SOA and CAS jointly sponsor a Web site for those interested in pursuing an actuarial career. Internet: http://www.BeAnActuary.org

For general information on a career as an actuary, contact

▸ American Academy of Actuaries, 1100 17th St. NW, 7th Floor, Washington, DC 20036. Internet: http://www.actuary.org

Administrative Services Managers

(O*NET 11-3011.00)

Significant Points

■ Applicants will face keen competition because of the substantial supply of competent, experienced workers seeking managerial jobs.

■ Administrative services managers work throughout private industry and government and have a wide range of responsibilities, experience, earnings, and education.

■ Administrative services managers should be analytical, detail-oriented, flexible, and decisive and have good communication skills.

Nature of the Work

Administrative services managers perform a broad range of duties in virtually every sector of the economy. They coordinate and direct support services to organizations as diverse as insurance companies, computer manufacturers, and government offices. These workers manage the many services that allow organizations to operate efficiently, such as secretarial and reception; administration; payroll; conference planning and travel; information and data processing; mail; materials scheduling and distribution; printing and reproduction; records management; telecommunications management; security; parking; and personal property procurement, supply, and disposal.

Specific duties for these managers vary by degree of responsibility and authority. First-line administrative services managers directly supervise a staff that performs various support services. Mid-level managers, on the other hand, develop departmental plans, set goals and deadlines, implement procedures to improve productivity and customer service, and define the responsibilities of supervisory-level managers. Some mid-level administrative services managers oversee first-line supervisors from various departments, including the clerical staff. Mid-level managers also may be involved in the hiring and dismissal of employees, but they generally have no role in the formulation of personnel policy. Some of these managers advance to upper-level positions, such as vice president of administrative services, which are discussed in the description of top executives elsewhere in this book.

In small organizations, a single administrative services manager may oversee all support services. In larger ones, however, first-line administrative services managers often report to mid-level managers who, in turn, report to owners or top-level managers. As the size of the firm increases, administrative services managers are more likely to specialize in specific support activities. For example, some administrative services managers work primarily as office managers, contract administrators, or unclaimed property officers. In many cases, the duties of these administrative services managers are similar to those of other managers and supervisors, some of which are discussed in other job descriptions in this book.

The nature of managerial jobs varies as significantly as the range of administrative services required by organizations. For example, administrative services managers who work as contract administrators oversee the preparation, analysis, negotiation, and review of contracts related to the purchase or sale of equipment, materials, supplies, products, or services. In addition, some administrative services managers acquire, distribute, and store supplies, while others dispose of surplus property or oversee the disposal of unclaimed property.

Administrative services managers who work as facility managers plan, design, and manage buildings and grounds in addition to people. This task requires integrating the principles of business administration, architecture, and behavioral and engineering science. Although the specific tasks assigned to facility managers vary substantially depending on the organization, the duties fall into several categories relating to operations and maintenance, real estate, project planning and management, communication, finance, quality assessment, facility function, technology integration, and management of human and environmental factors. Tasks within these broad categories may include space and workplace planning, budgeting, purchase and sale of real estate, lease management, renovations, or architectural planning and design. Facility managers may suggest and oversee renovation projects for a variety of reasons ranging from improving efficiency to ensuring that facilities meet government regulations and environmental, health, and security standards. Additionally, facility managers continually monitor the facility to ensure that it remains safe, secure, and well-maintained. Often, the facility manager is responsible for directing staff, including maintenance, grounds, and custodial workers.

Working Conditions

Administrative services managers generally work in comfortable offices. Managers involved in contract administration and personal property procurement, use, and disposal may travel between their home office, branch offices, vendors' offices, and property sales sites. Also, facility managers who are responsible for the design of workspaces may spend time at construction sites and may travel between different facilities while monitoring the work of maintenance, grounds, and custodial staffs. However, new technology has increased the number of managers who telecommute from home or other offices, and teleconferencing has reduced the need for travel.

Most administrative services managers work a standard 40-hour week. However, uncompensated overtime frequently is required to resolve problems and meet deadlines. Facility managers often are "on call" to address a variety of problems that can arise in a facility during nonwork hours.

Training, Other Qualifications, and Advancement

Educational requirements for these managers vary widely, depending on the size and complexity of the organization. In small organizations, experience may be the only requirement needed to enter a position as office manager. When an opening in administrative

services management occurs, the office manager may be promoted to the position based on past performance. In large organizations, however, administrative services managers normally are hired from outside and each position has formal education and experience requirements. Some administrative services managers have advanced degrees.

Specific requirements vary by job responsibility. For first-line administrative services managers of secretarial, mailroom, and related support activities, many employers prefer an associate degree in business or management, although a high school diploma may suffice when combined with appropriate experience. For managers of audiovisual, graphics, and other technical activities, postsecondary technical school training is preferred. Managers of highly complex services, such as contract administration, generally need at least a bachelor's degree in business, human resources, or finance. Regardless of major, the curriculum should include courses in office technology, accounting, business mathematics, computer applications, human resources, and business law. Most facility managers have an undergraduate or graduate degree in engineering, architecture, construction management, business administration, or facility management. Many have a background in real estate, construction, or interior design in addition to managerial experience.

Whatever the manager's educational background, it must be accompanied by related work experience reflecting demonstrated ability. For this reason, many administrative services managers have advanced through the ranks of their organization, acquiring work experience in various administrative positions before assuming first-line supervisory duties. All managers who oversee departmental supervisors should be familiar with office procedures and equipment. Managers of personal property acquisition and disposal need experience in purchasing and sales and knowledge of a variety of supplies, machinery, and equipment. Managers concerned with supply, inventory, and distribution should be experienced in receiving, warehousing, packaging, shipping, transportation, and related operations. Contract administrators may have worked as contract specialists, cost analysts, or procurement specialists. Managers of unclaimed property often have experience in insurance claims analysis and records management.

Persons interested in becoming administrative services managers should have good communication skills and be able to establish effective working relationships with many different people, ranging from managers, supervisors, and professionals to clerks and blue-collar workers. They should be analytical, detail-oriented, flexible, and decisive. They must be able to coordinate several activities at once, quickly analyze and resolve specific problems, and cope with deadlines.

Most administrative services managers in small organizations advance by moving to other management positions or to a larger organization. Advancement is easier in large firms that employ several levels of administrative services managers. Attainment of the Certified Manager (CM) designation offered by the Institute of Certified Professional Managers (ICPM), through education, work experience, and successful completion of examinations, can enhance a manager's advancement potential. In addition, a master's degree in business administration or a related field enhances a first-level manager's opportunities to advance to a mid-level management position, such as director of administrative services, and eventually to a top-level management position, such as executive vice president for administrative services. Those with enough money and experience can establish their own management consulting firm.

Advancement of facility managers is based on the practices and size of individual companies. Some facility managers transfer from other departments within the organization or work their way up from technical positions. Others advance through a progression of facility management positions that offer additional responsibilities. Completion of the competency-based professional certification program offered by the International Facility Management Association can give prospective candidates an advantage. In order to qualify for this Certified Facility Manager (CFM) designation, applicants must meet certain educational and experience requirements. People entering the profession also may obtain the Facility Management Professional (FMP) credential, a stepping-stone to the CFM.

Employment

Administrative services managers held about 268,000 jobs in 2004. About 80 percent worked in service-providing industries, including federal, state, and local government; health care; financial services; professional, scientific, and technical services; administrative and support services; and education. Most of the remaining managers worked in wholesale and retail trade, in management of companies and enterprises, or in manufacturing.

Job Outlook

Employment of administrative services managers is projected to grow about as fast as the average for all occupations through 2014. Like persons seeking other managerial positions, applicants will face keen competition because there will be more competent, experienced workers seeking jobs than there will be positions available. However, demand should be strong for facility managers because businesses increasingly are realizing the importance of maintaining, securing, and efficiently operating their facilities, which are very large investments for most organizations. Administrative services managers employed in management services and management consulting also should be in demand as public and private organizations continue to streamline and, in some cases, contract out administrative services functions in an effort to cut costs.

At the same time, continuing corporate restructuring and increasing utilization of office technology should result in a flatter organizational structure with fewer levels of management, reducing the need for some middle management positions. This should adversely affect administrative services managers who oversee first-line managers. However, the effects of these changes on employment should be less severe for administrative services managers, who have a wide range of responsibilities, than for other middle managers who specialize in certain functions. In addition to new administrative services management jobs created over the 2004–2014 projection period, many job openings will stem from the need to replace workers who transfer to other jobs, retire, or leave the occupation for other reasons.

Earnings

Earnings of administrative services managers vary greatly depending on the employer, the specialty, and the geographic area. In general, however, median annual earnings of administrative services managers in May 2004 were $60,290. The middle 50 percent earned between $42,680 and $83,510. The lowest 10 percent earned less than $31,120, and the highest 10 percent earned more than $110,270. Median annual earnings in the industries employing the largest numbers of these managers in May 2004 were

Management of companies and enterprises	$71,870
Elementary and secondary schools	65,850
Colleges, universities, and professional schools	61,020
Local government	59,380
State government	55,500

In the federal government, industrial specialists in nonsupervisory, supervisory, and managerial positions averaged $69,802 a year in 2005. Corresponding averages were $69,211 for facility operations services managers, $67,185 for industrial property managers, $63,614 for property disposal specialists, $67,855 for administrative officers, and $60,370 for support services administrators.

Related Occupations

Administrative services managers direct and coordinate support services and oversee the purchase, use, and disposal of personal property. Occupations with similar functions include office and administrative support worker supervisors and managers; cost estimators; property, real estate, and community association managers; purchasing managers, buyers, and purchasing agents; and top executives.

Sources of Additional Information

For information about careers and education and degree programs in facility management, as well as the Certified Facility Manager designation, contact

▸ International Facility Management Association, 1 East Greenway Plaza, Suite 1100, Houston, TX 77046-0194. Internet: http://www.ifma.org

General information regarding facility management and a list of facility management education and degree programs may be obtained from

▸ Association of Higher Education Facilities Officers, 1643 Prince St., Alexandria, VA 22314-2818. Internet: http://www.appa.org

For information about the Certified Manager (CM) designation, contact

▸ Institute of Certified Professional Managers, James Madison University, MSC 5504, Harrisonburg, VA 22807.

Advertising, Marketing, Promotions, Public Relations, and Sales Managers

(O*NET 11-2011.00, 11-2021.00, 11-2022.00, and 11-2031.00)

Significant Points

- Keen competition for jobs is expected.
- College graduates with related experience, a high level of creativity, strong communication skills, and computer skills should have the best job opportunities.
- High earnings, substantial travel, and long hours, including evenings and weekends, are common.

Nature of the Work

The objective of any firm is to market and sell its products or services profitably. In small firms, the owner or chief executive officer might assume all advertising, promotions, marketing, sales, and public relations responsibilities. In large firms, which may offer numerous products and services nationally or even worldwide, an executive vice president directs overall advertising, promotions, marketing, sales, and public relations policies. (Executive vice presidents are included in the job description of top executives elsewhere in this book.) Advertising, marketing, promotions, public relations, and sales managers coordinate the market research, marketing strategy, sales, advertising, promotion, pricing, product development, and public relations activities.

Advertising managers oversee advertising and promotion staffs, which usually are small, except in the largest firms. In a small firm, managers may serve as liaisons between the firm and the advertising or promotion agency to which many advertising or promotional functions are contracted out. In larger firms, advertising managers oversee in-house account, creative, and media services departments. The *account executive* manages the account services department, assesses the need for advertising, and, in advertising agencies, maintains the accounts of clients. The creative services department develops the subject matter and presentation of advertising. The *creative director* oversees the copy chief, art director, and associated staff. The *media director* oversees planning groups that select the communication media—for example, radio, television, newspapers, magazines, the Internet, or outdoor signs—to disseminate the advertising.

Promotions managers supervise staffs of promotion specialists. These managers direct promotion programs that combine advertising with purchase incentives to increase sales. In an effort to establish closer contact with purchasers—dealers, distributors, or consumers—promotion programs may use direct mail, telemarketing, television or radio advertising, catalogs, exhibits, inserts in newspapers, Internet advertisements or Web sites, in-store displays or product endorsements, and special events. Purchasing incentives may include discounts, samples, gifts, rebates, coupons, sweepstakes, and contests.

Marketing managers develop the firm's marketing strategy in detail. With the help of subordinates, including *product development managers* and *market research managers*, they estimate the demand for products and services offered by the firm and its competitors. In addition, they identify potential markets—for example, business firms, wholesalers, retailers, government, or the general public. Marketing managers develop pricing strategy to help firms maximize profits and market share while ensuring that the firm's customers are satisfied. In collaboration with sales, product development, and other managers, they monitor trends that indicate the need for new products and services and they oversee product development. Marketing managers work with advertising and promotion managers to promote the firm's products and services and to attract potential users.

Public relations managers supervise public relations specialists. (See the description of public relations specialists elsewhere in this book.) These managers direct publicity programs to a targeted audience. They often specialize in a specific area, such as crisis management, or in a specific industry, such as health care. They use every available communication medium to maintain the support of the specific group upon whom their organization's success depends, such as consumers, stockholders, or the general public. For example, public relations managers may clarify or justify the firm's point of view on health or environmental issues to community or special-interest groups.

Public relations managers also evaluate advertising and promotion programs for compatibility with public relations efforts and serve as the eyes and ears of top management. They observe social, economic, and political trends that might ultimately affect the firm, and they make recommendations to enhance the firm's image on the basis of those trends.

Public relations managers may confer with labor relations managers to produce internal company communications—such as newsletters about employee–management relations—and with financial managers to produce company reports. They assist company executives in drafting speeches, arranging interviews, and maintaining other forms of public contact; oversee company archives; and respond to requests for information. In addition, some of these managers handle special events, such as the sponsorship of races, parties introducing new products, or other activities that the firm supports in order to gain public attention through the press without advertising directly.

Sales managers direct the firm's sales program. They assign sales territories, set goals, and establish training programs for the sales representatives. (See the description of sales representatives, wholesale and manufacturing, elsewhere in this book.) Sales managers advise the sales representatives on ways to improve their sales performance. In large, multiproduct firms, they oversee regional and local sales managers and their staffs. Sales managers maintain contact with dealers and distributors. They analyze sales statistics gathered by their staffs to determine sales potential and inventory requirements and to monitor customers' preferences. Such information is vital in the development of products and the maximization of profits.

Working Conditions

Advertising, marketing, promotions, public relations, and sales managers work in offices close to those of top managers. Long hours, including evenings and weekends, are common. In 2004, about two-thirds of advertising, marketing, and public relations managers worked more than 40 hours a week. Working under pressure is unavoidable when schedules change and problems arise, but deadlines and goals must still be met.

Substantial travel may be involved. For example, attendance at meetings sponsored by associations or industries often is mandatory. Sales managers travel to national, regional, and local offices and to the offices of various dealers and distributors. Advertising and promotions managers may travel to meet with clients or representatives of communications media. At times, public relations managers travel to meet with special-interest groups or government officials. Job transfers between headquarters and regional offices are common, particularly among sales managers.

Training, Other Qualifications, and Advancement

A wide range of educational backgrounds is suitable for entry into advertising, marketing, promotions, public relations, and sales managerial jobs, but many employers prefer those with experience in related occupations plus a broad liberal arts background. A bachelor's degree in sociology, psychology, literature, journalism, or philosophy, among other subjects, is acceptable. However, requirements vary, depending upon the particular job.

For marketing, sales, and promotions management positions, some employers prefer a bachelor's or master's degree in business administration with an emphasis on marketing. Courses in business law, economics, accounting, finance, mathematics, and statistics are advantageous. In highly technical industries, such as computer and electronics manufacturing, a bachelor's degree in engineering or science, combined with a master's degree in business administration, is preferred.

For advertising management positions, some employers prefer a bachelor's degree in advertising or journalism. A course of study should include marketing, consumer behavior, market research, sales, communication methods and technology, and visual arts—for example, art history and photography.

For public relations management positions, some employers prefer a bachelor's or master's degree in public relations or journalism. The applicant's curriculum should include courses in advertising, business administration, public affairs, public speaking, political science, and creative and technical writing.

For all these specialties, courses in management and the completion of an internship while the candidate is in school are highly recommended. Familiarity with word-processing and database applications also is important for many positions. Computer skills are vital because marketing, product promotion, and advertising on the Internet are increasingly common. Also, the ability to communicate in a foreign language may open up employment opportunities in many rapidly growing areas around the country, especially cities with large Spanish-speaking populations.

Most advertising, marketing, promotions, public relations, and sales management positions are filled by promoting experienced staff or related professional personnel. For example, many managers are former sales representatives; purchasing agents; buyers; or product, advertising, promotions, or public relations specialists. In small firms, where the number of positions is limited, advancement to a management position usually comes slowly. In large firms, promotion may occur more quickly.

Although experience, ability, and leadership are emphasized for promotion, advancement can be accelerated by participation in management training programs conducted by larger firms. Many firms also provide their employees with continuing education opportunities—either in-house or at local colleges and universities—and encourage employee participation in seminars and conferences, often held by professional societies. In collaboration with colleges and universities, numerous marketing and related associations sponsor national or local management training programs. Course subjects include brand and product management, international marketing, sales management evaluation, telemarketing and direct sales, interactive marketing, promotion, marketing communication, market research, organizational communication, and data-processing systems procedures and management. Many firms pay all or part of the cost for employees who successfully complete courses.

Some associations offer certification programs for these managers. Certification—an indication of competence and achievement—is particularly important in a competitive job market. While relatively few advertising, marketing, promotions, public relations, and sales managers currently are certified, the number of managers who seek certification is expected to grow. Today, there are numerous management certification programs based on education and job performance. In addition, The Public Relations Society of America offers a certification program for public relations practitioners based on years of experience and performance on an examination.

Persons interested in becoming advertising, marketing, promotions, public relations, and sales managers should be mature, creative, highly motivated, resistant to stress, flexible, and decisive. The ability to communicate persuasively, both orally and in writing, with other managers, staff, and the public is vital. These managers also need tact, good judgment, and exceptional ability to establish and maintain effective personal relationships with supervisory and professional staff members and client firms.

Because of the importance and high visibility of their jobs, advertising, marketing, promotions, public relations, and sales managers often are prime candidates for advancement to the highest ranks. Well-trained, experienced, and successful managers may be promoted to higher positions in their own or another firm; some become top executives. Managers with extensive experience and sufficient capital may open their own businesses.

Employment

Advertising, marketing, promotions, public relations, and sales managers held about 646,000 jobs in 2004. The following tabulation shows the distribution of jobs by occupational specialty:

Sales managers 337,000

Marketing managers 188,000

Advertising and promotions managers....................64,000

Public relations managers 58,000

These managers were found in virtually every industry. Sales managers held almost half of the jobs; most were employed in wholesale and retail trade and finance and insurance industries. Marketing managers held more than one-fourth of the jobs; the professional, scientific, and technical services industries employed almost one-third of marketing managers. About one-fourth of advertising and promotions managers worked in the professional, scientific, and technical services industries and the information industries, including advertising and related services and publishing industries. Most public relations managers were employed in service-providing industries, such as professional, scientific, and technical services; finance and insurance; health care and social assistance; and educational services.

Job Outlook

Advertising, marketing, promotions, public relations, and sales manager jobs are highly coveted and will be sought by other managers or highly experienced professionals, resulting in keen competition. College graduates with related experience, a high level of creativity, and strong communication skills should have the best job opportunities. In particular, employers will seek those who have the computer skills to conduct advertising, marketing, promotions, public relations, and sales activities on the Internet.

Employment of advertising, marketing, promotions, public relations, and sales managers is expected to increase faster than the average for all occupations through 2014, spurred by intense domestic and global competition in products and services offered to consumers. However, projected employment growth varies by industry. For example, employment is projected to grow much faster than average in scientific, professional, and related services, such as computer systems design and related services, and in advertising and related services as businesses increasingly hire contractors for these services instead of additional full-time staff. By contrast, a decline in employment is expected in many manufacturing industries.

Earnings

Median annual earnings in May 2004 were $63,610 for advertising and promotions managers, $87,640 for marketing managers, $84,220 for sales managers, and $70,000 for public relations managers.

Median annual earnings of advertising and promotions managers in May 2004 in the advertising and related services industry were $89,570.

Median annual earnings in the industries employing the largest numbers of marketing managers in May 2004 were as follows:

Computer systems design and related

services $107,030

Management of companies and enterprises 98,700

Insurance carriers 86,810

Architectural, engineering, and related services 83,610

Depository credit intermediation 76,450

Median annual earnings in the industries employing the largest numbers of sales managers in May 2004 were as follows:

Computer systems design and related

services $119,140

Wholesale electronic markets and agents

and brokers 101,930

Automobile dealers 97,460

Management of companies and enterprises 95,410

Machinery, equipment, and supplies merchant

wholesalers 84,680

According to a National Association of Colleges and Employers survey, starting salaries for marketing majors graduating in 2005 averaged $33,873; starting salaries for advertising majors averaged $31,340.

Salary levels vary substantially, depending upon the level of managerial responsibility, length of service, education, size of firm, location, and industry. For example, manufacturing firms usually pay these managers higher salaries than do nonmanufacturing firms. For sales managers, the size of their sales territory is another important determinant of salary. Many managers earn bonuses equal to 10 percent or more of their salaries.

Related Occupations

Advertising, marketing, promotions, public relations, and sales managers direct the sale of products and services offered by their firms and the communication of information about their firms' activities. Other workers involved with advertising, marketing, promotions, public relations, and sales include actors, producers, and directors; advertising sales agents; artists and related workers; demonstrators, product promoters, and models; market and survey researchers; public relations specialists; sales representatives, wholesale and manufacturing; and writers and editors.

Sources of Additional Information

For information about careers in advertising management, contact

▶ American Association of Advertising Agencies, 405 Lexington Ave., New York, NY 10174-1801. Internet: http://www.aaaa.org

Information about careers and professional certification in public relations management is available from

▶ Public Relations Society of America, 33 Maiden Lane, New York, NY 10038-5150. Internet: http://www.prsa.org

Computer and Information Systems Managers

(O*NET 11-3021.00)

Significant Points

■ Employment of computer and information systems managers is expected to grow faster than the average for all occupations through the year 2014.

- Many managers possess advanced technical knowledge gained from working in a computer occupation.

- Job opportunities will be best for applicants with computer-related work experience, a master's degree in business administration (MBA) with technology as a core component, or a management information systems degree and strong communication and administrative skills.

Nature of the Work

How and when companies and organizations use technology are critical to remaining competitive. *Computer and information systems managers* play a vital role in the technological direction of their organizations. They do everything from constructing the business plan to overseeing network security to directing Internet operations.

Computer and information systems managers plan, coordinate, and direct research and facilitate the computer-related activities of firms. They help determine both technical and business goals in consultation with top management and make detailed plans for the accomplishment of these goals. For example, working with their staff, they may develop the overall concepts and requirements of a new product or service or may identify how an organization's computing capabilities can effectively aid project management.

Computer and information systems managers direct the work of systems analysts, computer programmers, support specialists, and other computer-related workers. These managers plan and coordinate activities such as installation and upgrading of hardware and software, programming and systems design, development of computer networks, and implementation of Internet and intranet sites. They are increasingly involved with the upkeep, maintenance, and security of networks. They analyze the computer and information needs of their organizations from an operational and strategic perspective and determine immediate and long-range personnel and equipment requirements. They assign and review the work of their subordinates and stay abreast of the latest technology to ensure that the organization does not lag behind competitors.

The duties of computer and information systems managers vary with their specific titles. *Chief technology officers*, for example, evaluate the newest and most innovative technologies and determine how these can help their organizations. The chief technology officer, who often reports to the organization's chief information officer, manages and plans technical standards and tends to the daily information technology issues of the firm. (Chief information officers are covered in the description of top executives elsewhere in this book.) Because of the rapid pace of technological change, chief technology officers must constantly be on the lookout for developments that could benefit their organizations. They are responsible for demonstrating to a company how information technology can be used as a competitive tool that not only cuts costs, but also increases revenue and maintains or increases competitive advantage.

Management information systems (*MIS*) *directors* manage information systems and computing resources for their organizations. They also may work under the chief information officer and plan and direct the work of subordinate information technology employees. These managers oversee a variety of user services such as an organization's help desk, which employees can call with questions or problems. MIS directors also may make hardware and software upgrade recommendations based on their experience with an organization's technology. Helping ensure the availability, continuity, and security of data and information technology services is the primary responsibility of these workers.

Project managers develop requirements, budgets, and schedules for their firms' information technology projects. They coordinate such projects from development through implementation, working with internal and external clients, vendors, consultants, and computer specialists. These managers are increasingly involved in projects that upgrade the information security of an organization.

LAN/WAN (local area network/wide area network) *managers* provide a variety of services, from design to administration of the local area network, which connects staff within an organization. These managers direct the network and its computing environment, including hardware, systems software, applications software, and all other computer-related configurations.

Computer and information systems managers need strong communication skills. They coordinate the activities of their unit with those of other units or organizations. They confer with top executives; financial, production, marketing, and other managers; and contractors and equipment and materials suppliers.

Working Conditions

Computer and information systems managers spend most of their time in an office. Most work at least 40 hours a week and may have to work evenings and weekends to meet deadlines or solve unexpected problems. Some computer and information systems managers may experience considerable pressure in meeting technical goals within short timeframes or tight budgets. As networks continue to expand and more work is done remotely, computer and information systems managers have to communicate with and oversee offsite employees using modems, laptops, e-mail, and the Internet.

Like other workers who sit continuously in front of a keyboard, computer and information systems managers are susceptible to eyestrain, back discomfort, and hand and wrist problems such as carpal tunnel syndrome.

Training, Other Qualifications, and Advancement

Advanced technical knowledge is essential for computer and information systems managers, who must understand and guide the work of their subordinates yet also explain the work in nontechnical terms to senior managers and potential customers. Therefore, many computer and information systems managers have experience in a computer occupation such as systems analyst; other managers may have worked as a computer support specialist, programmer, or other information technology professional.

A bachelor's degree usually is required for management positions, although employers often prefer a graduate degree, especially an MBA with technology as a core component. This degree differs from a traditional MBA in that there is a heavy emphasis on information technology in addition to the standard business curriculum.

This preparation is becoming important because more computer and information systems managers are making important technology decisions as well as business decisions for their organizations. Some universities specialize in offering degrees in management information systems, which blend technical core subjects with business, accounting, and communications courses. A few computer and information systems managers attain their positions with only an associate degree, but they must have sufficient experience and must have acquired additional skills on the job. To aid their professional advancement, though, many managers with an associate degree eventually earn a bachelor's or master's degree while working.

Computer and information systems managers need a broad range of skills. Employers want managers who have experience with the specific software or technology used on the job as well as a background in either consulting or business management. The expansion of electronic commerce has elevated the importance of business insight; many computer and information systems managers are called on to make important business decisions. Managers need a keen understanding of people, management processes, and customers' needs.

Computer and information systems managers must possess strong interpersonal, communication, and leadership skills because they are required to interact not only with their staff, but also with other people inside and outside their organizations. They also must possess team skills to work on group projects and other collaborative efforts. Computer and information systems managers increasingly interact with persons outside their organizations, reflecting their emerging role as vital parts of their firms' executive teams.

Computer and information systems managers may advance to progressively higher leadership positions in their field. Some may become managers in nontechnical areas such as marketing, human resources, or sales. In high-technology firms, managers in nontechnical areas often must possess the same specialized knowledge as do managers in technical areas.

Employment

Computer and information systems managers held about 280,000 jobs in 2004. About 9 in 10 computer managers worked in service-providing industries, mainly in computer systems design and related services. This industry provides services related to the commercial use of computers on a contract basis, including custom computer programming services; computer systems integration design services; computer facilities management services, including computer systems or data-processing facilities support services; and other computer-related services, such as disaster recovery services and software installation. Other large employers include insurance and financial firms, government agencies, and manufacturers.

Job Outlook

Employment of computer and information systems managers is expected to grow faster than the average for all occupations through the year 2014. Technological advancements will boost the employment of computer-related workers; as a result, the demand for managers to direct these workers also will increase. In addition, job openings will result from the need to replace managers who retire or move into other occupations. Opportunities for obtaining a management position will be best for those with computer-related work

experience; an MBA with technology as a core component or a management information systems degree; and strong communication and administrative skills.

Despite the downturn in the technology sector in the early part of the decade, the outlook for computer and information systems managers remains strong. To remain competitive, firms will continue to install sophisticated computer networks and set up more complex Internet and intranet sites. Keeping a computer network running smoothly is essential to almost every organization. Firms will be more willing to hire managers who can accomplish that.

Similarly, the security of computer networks will continue to increase in importance as more business is conducted over the Internet. The security of the nation's entire electronic infrastructure has come under renewed scrutiny in light of recent threats. Organizations need to understand how their systems are vulnerable and how to protect their infrastructure and Internet sites from hackers, viruses, and other acts of cyberterrorism. The emergence of cyber-security as a key issue facing most organizations should lead to strong growth for computer managers. Firms will increasingly hire cybersecurity experts to fill key leadership roles in their information technology departments because the integrity of their computing environments is of utmost concern. As a result, there will be a high demand for managers proficient in computer security issues.

With the explosive growth of electronic commerce and the capacity of the Internet to create new relationships with customers, the role of computer and information systems managers will continue to evolve. Persons in these jobs will become increasingly vital to their companies. The expansion of the wireless Internet will spur the need for computer and information systems managers with both business savvy and technical proficiency.

Opportunities for those who wish to become computer and information systems managers should be closely related to the growth of the occupations they supervise and the industries in which they are found. (See the descriptions of computer programmers, computer software engineers, computer support specialists and systems administrators, computer systems analysts, and computer scientists and database administrators elsewhere in this book.)

Earnings

Earnings for computer and information systems managers vary by specialty and level of responsibility. Median annual earnings of these managers in May 2004 were $92,570. The middle 50 percent earned between $71,650 and $118,330. Median annual earnings in the industries employing the largest numbers of computer and information systems managers in May 2004 were as follows:

Software publishers	$107,870
Computer systems design and related services	103,850
Management of companies and enterprises	99,880
Insurance carriers	97,900
Depository credit intermediation	86,450

According to Robert Half International, a professional staffing and consulting services firm, average starting salaries in 2005 for high-level information technology managers ranged from $80,250 to $112,250. According to a 2005 survey by the National Association of Colleges and Employers, starting salary offers for those with an

MBA, a technical undergraduate degree, and 1 year or less of experience averaged $52,300; for those with a master's degree in management information systems/business data processing, the starting salary averaged $56,909.

In addition, computer and information systems managers, especially those at higher levels, often receive more employment-related benefits—such as expense accounts, stock option plans, and bonuses—than do nonmanagerial workers in their organizations.

Related Occupations

The work of computer and information systems managers is closely related to that of computer programmers, computer software engineers, computer systems analysts, computer scientists and database administrators, and computer support specialists and systems administrators. Computer and information systems managers also have some high-level responsibilities similar to those of top executives.

Sources of Additional Information

For information about a career as a computer and information systems manager, contact the sources of additional information for the various computer occupations discussed elsewhere in this book.

Education Administrators

(O*NET 11-9031.00, 11-9032.00, 11-9033.00, and 11-9039.99)

Significant Points

- Many jobs require a master's or doctoral degree and experience in a related occupation, such as teacher or admissions counselor.

- Strong interpersonal and communication skills are essential because much of an administrator's job involves working and collaborating with others.

- Excellent opportunities are expected since a large proportion of education administrators is expected to retire over the next 10 years.

Nature of the Work

Smooth operation of an educational institution requires competent administrators. *Education administrators* provide instructional leadership as well as manage the day-to-day activities in schools, preschools, daycare centers, and colleges and universities. They also direct the educational programs of businesses, correctional institutions, museums, and job training and community service organizations. (College presidents and school superintendents are covered in the job description of top executives elsewhere in this book.) Education administrators set educational standards and goals and establish the policies and procedures to carry them out. They also supervise managers, support staff, teachers, counselors, librarians, coaches, and others. They develop academic programs; monitor students' educational progress; train and motivate teachers and other

staff; manage career counseling and other student services; administer recordkeeping; prepare budgets; handle relations with parents, prospective and current students, employers, and the community; and perform many other duties. In an organization such as a small daycare center, one administrator may handle all these functions. In universities or large school systems, responsibilities are divided among many administrators, each with a specific function.

Educational administrators who manage elementary, middle, and secondary schools are called *principals*. They set the academic tone and hire, evaluate, and help improve the skills of teachers and other staff. Principals confer with staff to advise, explain, or answer procedural questions. They visit classrooms, observe teaching methods, review instructional objectives, and examine learning materials. They actively work with teachers to develop and maintain high curriculum standards, develop mission statements, and set performance goals and objectives. Principals must use clear, objective guidelines for teacher appraisals because pay often is based on performance ratings.

Principals also meet and interact with other administrators, students, parents, and representatives of community organizations. Decision-making authority has increasingly shifted from school district central offices to individual schools. School principals have greater flexibility in setting school policies and goals, but when making administrative decisions they must pay attention to the concerns of parents, teachers, and other members of the community.

Principals prepare budgets and reports on various subjects, including finances and attendance, and oversee the requisition and allocation of supplies. As school budgets become tighter, many principals have become more involved in public relations and fundraising to secure financial support for their schools from local businesses and the community.

Principals must take an active role to ensure that students meet national, state, and local academic standards. Many principals develop school/business partnerships and school-to-work transition programs for students. Increasingly, principals must be sensitive to the needs of the rising number of non-English-speaking and culturally diverse students. In some areas growing enrollments also are a cause for concern because they are leading to overcrowding at many schools. When addressing problems of inadequate resources, administrators serve as advocates for the building of new schools or the repair of existing ones. During summer months, principals are responsible for planning for the upcoming year, overseeing summer school, participating in workshops for teachers and administrators, supervising building repairs and improvements, and working to be sure the school has adequate staff for the school year.

Schools continue to be involved with students' emotional welfare as well as their academic achievement. As a result, principals face responsibilities outside the academic realm. For example, in response to the growing numbers of dual-income and single-parent families and teenage parents, schools have established before- and after-school childcare programs or family resource centers, which also may offer parenting classes and social service referrals. With the help of community organizations, some principals have established programs to combat increases in crime, drug and alcohol abuse, and sexually transmitted diseases among students.

Assistant principals aid the principal in the overall administration of the school. Some assistant principals hold this position for several years to prepare for advancement to principal jobs; others are career assistant principals. They are primarily responsible for scheduling student classes; ordering textbooks and supplies; and coordinating transportation, custodial, cafeteria, and other support services. They usually handle student discipline and attendance problems, social and recreational programs, and health and safety matters. They also may counsel students on personal, educational, or vocational matters. With the advent of site-based management, assistant principals are playing a greater role in ensuring the academic success of students by helping to develop new curriculums, evaluating teachers, and dealing with school-community relations—responsibilities previously assumed solely by the principal. The number of assistant principals that a school employs may vary, depending on the number of students.

Administrators in school district central offices oversee public schools under their jurisdiction. This group includes those who direct subject-area programs such as English, music, vocational education, special education, and mathematics. They supervise instructional coordinators and curriculum specialists and work with them to evaluate curriculums and teaching techniques and improve them. (Instructional coordinators are covered elsewhere in this book.) Administrators also may oversee career counseling programs and testing that measures students' abilities and helps to place them in appropriate classes. Others may also direct programs such as school psychology, athletics, curriculum and instruction, and professional development. With site-based management, administrators have transferred primary responsibility for many of these programs to the principals, assistant principals, teachers, instructional coordinators, and other staff in the schools.

In preschools and childcare centers, education administrators are the director or supervisor of the school or center. Their job is similar to that of other school administrators in that they oversee daily activities and operation of the schools, hire and develop staff, and make sure that the school meets required regulations.

In colleges and universities, *provosts,* also known as *chief academic officers,* assist presidents, make faculty appointments and tenure decisions, develop budgets, and establish academic policies and programs. With the assistance of *academic deans* and *deans of faculty,* they also direct and coordinate the activities of deans of individual colleges and chairpersons of academic departments. Fundraising is the chief responsibility of the *director of development* and also is becoming an essential part of the job for all administrators.

College or university department heads or *chairpersons* are in charge of departments that specialize in particular fields of study, such as English, biological science, or mathematics. In addition to teaching, they coordinate schedules of classes and teaching assignments; propose budgets; recruit, interview, and hire applicants for teaching positions; evaluate faculty members; encourage faculty development; serve on committees; and perform other administrative duties. In overseeing their departments, chairpersons must consider and balance the concerns of faculty, administrators, and students.

Higher-education administrators also direct and coordinate the provision of student services. *Vice presidents of student affairs* or *student life, deans of students,* and *directors of student services* may

direct and coordinate admissions, foreign student services, health and counseling services, career services, financial aid, and housing and residential life, as well as social, recreational, and related programs. In small colleges, they may counsel students. In larger colleges and universities, separate administrators may handle each of these services. *Registrars* are custodians of students' records. They register students, record grades, prepare student transcripts, evaluate academic records, assess and collect tuition and fees, plan and implement commencement, oversee the preparation of college catalogs and schedules of classes, and analyze enrollment and demographic statistics. *Directors of admissions* manage the process of recruiting, evaluating, and admitting students and work closely with *financial aid directors,* who oversee scholarship, fellowship, and loan programs. Registrars and admissions officers at most institutions need computer skills because they use electronic student information systems. For example, for those whose institutions present college catalogs, schedules, and other information on the Internet, knowledge of online resources, imaging, and other computer skills is important. *Athletic directors* plan and direct intramural and intercollegiate athletic activities, seeing to publicity for athletic events, preparation of budgets, and supervision of coaches. Other increasingly important administrators direct public relations, distance learning, and technology.

Working Conditions

Education administrators hold leadership positions with significant responsibility. Most find working with students extremely rewarding, but as the responsibilities of administrators have increased in recent years, so has the stress. Coordinating and interacting with faculty, parents, students, community members, business leaders, and state and local policymakers can be fast-paced and stimulating, but also stressful and demanding. Principals and assistant principals, whose varied duties include discipline, may find working with difficult students to be challenging. They are also increasingly being held accountable for ensuring that their schools meet recently imposed state and federal guidelines for student performance and teacher qualifications.

Many education administrators work more than 40 hours a week, often including school activities at night and on weekends. Most administrators work 11 or 12 months out of the year. Some jobs include travel.

Training, Other Qualifications, and Advancement

Most education administrators begin their careers in related occupations, often as teachers, and prepare for advancement into education administration by completing a master's or doctoral degree. Because of the diversity of duties and levels of responsibility, their educational backgrounds and experience vary considerably. Principals, assistant principals, central office administrators, academic deans, and preschool directors usually have held teaching positions before moving into administration. Some teachers move directly into principal positions; others first become assistant principals or gain experience in other administrative jobs at either the school or district level in positions such as department head, curriculum specialist, or subject matter advisor. In some cases, administrators move up from related staff jobs such as recruiter, school counselor, librarian, residence hall director, or financial aid or admissions counselor.

To be considered for education administrator positions, workers must first prove themselves in their current jobs. In evaluating candidates, supervisors look for leadership, determination, confidence, innovativeness, and motivation. The ability to make sound decisions and to organize and coordinate work efficiently is essential. Because much of an administrator's job involves interacting with others—such as students, parents, teachers, and the community—a person in such a position must have strong interpersonal skills and be an effective communicator and motivator. Knowledge of leadership principles and practices, gained through work experience and formal education, is important. A familiarity with computer technology is a necessity for principals, who are required to gather information and coordinate technical resources for their students, teachers, and classrooms.

In most public schools, principals, assistant principals, and school district administrators need a master's degree in education administration or educational leadership. Some principals and central office administrators have a doctorate or specialized degree in education administration. Most states require principals to be licensed as school administrators. License requirements vary by state, but nearly all states require either a master's degree or some other graduate-level training. Some states also require candidates for licensure to pass a test. Increasingly, on-the-job training, often with a mentor, is required or recommended for new school leaders. Some states require administrators to take continuing education courses to keep their license, thus ensuring that administrators have the most up-to-date skills. The number and types of courses required to maintain licensure vary by state. In private schools, which are not subject to state licensure requirements, some principals and assistant principals hold only a bachelor's degree, but the majority have a master's or doctoral degree.

Educational requirements for administrators of preschools and childcare centers vary depending on the setting of the program and the state of employment. Administrators who oversee preschool programs in public schools are often required to have at least a bachelor's degree. Child care directors are generally not required to have a degree; however, most states require a general preschool education credential, such as the Child Development Associate credential (CDA) sponsored by the Council for Professional Recognition, or a credential specifically designed for administrators. The National Child Care Association offers a National Administration Credential, which some recent college graduates voluntarily earn to better qualify for positions as childcare center directors.

Academic deans and chairpersons usually have a doctorate in their specialty. Most have held a professorship in their department before advancing. Admissions, student affairs, and financial aid directors and registrars sometimes start in related staff jobs with bachelor's degrees—any field usually is acceptable—and obtain advanced degrees in college student affairs, counseling, or higher education administration. A Ph.D. or Ed.D. usually is necessary for top student affairs positions. Computer literacy and a background in accounting or statistics may be assets in admissions, records, and financial work.

Advanced degrees in higher education administration, educational leadership, and college student affairs are offered in many colleges and universities. Education administration degree programs include courses in school leadership, school law, school finance and budgeting, curriculum development and evaluation, research design and data analysis, community relations, politics in education, and counseling. The National Council for Accreditation of Teacher Education and the Educational Leadership Constituent Council accredit programs designed for elementary and secondary school administrators. While completion of an accredited program is not required, it may assist in fulfilling licensure requirements.

Education administrators advance through promotion to more responsible administrative positions or by transferring to more responsible positions at larger schools or systems. They also may become superintendents of school systems or presidents of educational institutions.

Employment

Education administrators held about 442,000 jobs in 2004. Of these, 58,000 were preschool or child care administrators, 225,000 were elementary or secondary school administrators, and 132,000 were postsecondary administrators. About 2 in 10 worked for private education institutions, and 6 in 10 worked for state and local governments, mainly in schools, colleges and universities, and departments of education. Less than 4 percent were self-employed. The rest worked in child daycare centers, religious organizations, job training centers, and businesses and other organizations that provided training for their employees.

Job Outlook

Employment of education administrators is projected to grow as fast as the average for all occupations through 2014. As education and training take on greater importance in everyone's lives, the need for people to administer education programs will grow. Job opportunities for many of these positions should also be excellent because a large proportion of education administrators are expected to retire over the next 10 years.

Enrollments of school-age children are the primary factor determining the demand for education administrators. Enrollment of students in elementary and secondary schools is expected to grow slowly over the next decade, which will limit the growth of principals and other administrators in these schools. However, preschool and childcare center administrators are expected to experience substantial growth as enrollments in formal child care programs continue to expand as fewer private households care for young children. Additionally, as more states begin implementing public preschool programs, more preschool directors will be needed. The number of postsecondary school students is projected to grow more rapidly than other student populations, creating significant demand for administrators at that level. Opportunities may vary by geographical area, as enrollments are expected to increase the fastest in the West and South, where the population is growing, and to decline or remain stable in the Northeast and the Midwest. School administrators also are in greater demand in rural and urban areas, where pay is generally lower than in the suburbs.

Principals and assistant principals should have very favorable job prospects. A sharp increase in responsibilities in recent years has made the job more stressful and has discouraged some teachers from taking positions in administration. Principals are now being held more accountable for the performance of students and teachers, while at the same time they are required to adhere to a growing number of government regulations. In addition, overcrowded classrooms, safety issues, budgetary concerns, and teacher shortages in some areas all are creating additional stress for administrators. Many teachers feel the higher pay of administrators is not high enough to compensate for the greater responsibilities.

Job prospects also are expected to be favorable for college and university administrators, particularly those seeking nonacademic positions. Public colleges and universities may be subject to funding shortfalls during economic downturns, but increasing enrollments over the projection period will require that institutions replace the large numbers of administrators who retire and even hire additional administrators. In addition, a significant portion of growth will stem from growth in the private and for-profit segments of higher education. Many of these schools cater to working adults who might not ordinarily participate in postsecondary education. These schools allow students to earn a degree; receive job-specific training; or update their skills in a convenient manner, such as through part-time programs or distance learning. As the number of these schools continues to grow, more administrators will be needed to oversee them.

While competition among faculty for prestigious positions as academic deans and department heads is likely to remain keen, fewer applicants are expected for nonacademic administrative jobs, such as director of admissions or student affairs. Furthermore, many people are discouraged from seeking administrator jobs by the requirement that they have a master's or doctoral degree in education administration—as well as by the opportunity to earn higher salaries in other occupations.

Earnings

In May 2004, elementary and secondary school administrators had median annual earnings of $74,190; postsecondary school administrators had median annual earnings of $68,340, while preschool and childcare center administrators earned a median of $35,730 per year. Salaries of education administrators depend on several factors, including the location and enrollment level in the school or school district. According to a survey of public schools, conducted by the Educational Research Service, average salaries for principals and assistant principals in the 2004–2005 school year were as follows:

Principals:

Senior high school	$82,225
Jr. high/middle school	78,160
Elementary school	74,062

Assistant principals:

Senior high school	$68,945
Jr. high/middle school	66,319
Elementary school	63,398

According to the College and University Professional Association for Human Resources, median annual salaries for selected administrators in higher education in 2004–2005 were as follows:

Chief academic officer	$127,066

Academic deans:

Business	$120,460
Arts and sciences	110,412
Graduate programs	109,309
Education	107,660
Nursing	100,314
Health-related professions	100,185
Continuing education	91,800
Occupational or vocational education	79,845

Other administrators:

Chief development officer	$114,400
Dean of students	75,245
Director, student financial aid	63,130
Registrar	61,953
Director, student activities	45,636

Benefits for education administrators are generally very good. Many get 4 or 5 weeks of vacation every year and have generous health and pension packages. Many colleges and universities offer free tuition to employees and their families.

Related Occupations

Education administrators apply organizational and leadership skills to provide services to individuals. Workers in related occupations include administrative services managers; office and administrative support worker supervisors and managers; and human resource, training, and labor relations managers and specialists. Education administrators also work with students and have backgrounds similar to those of counselors; librarians; instructional coordinators; teachers—preschool, kindergarten, elementary, middle, and secondary; and teachers—postsecondary.

Sources of Additional Information

For information on principals, contact

▸ The National Association of Elementary School Principals, 1615 Duke St., Alexandria, VA 22314-3483. Internet: http://www.naesp.org

▸ The National Association of Secondary School Principals, 1904 Association Drive, Reston, VA 20191-1537. Internet: http://www.nassp.org

For a list of nationally recognized programs in elementary and secondary educational administration, contact

▸ The Educational Leadership Constituent Council, 1904 Association Drive, Reston, VA 20191. Internet: http://www.npbea.org/ELCC/index.html

For information on collegiate registrars and admissions officers, contact

▸ American Association of Collegiate Registrars and Admissions Officers, One Dupont Circle NW, Suite 520, Washington, DC 20036-1171. Internet: http://www.aacrao.org

For information on professional development and graduate programs for college student affairs administrators, contact

▸ NASPA, Student Affairs Administrators in Higher Education, 1875 Connecticut Ave. NW, Suite 418, Washington, DC 20009. Internet: http://www.naspa.org

Engineering and Natural Sciences Managers

(O*NET 11-9041.00 and 11-9121.00)

Significant Points

■ Most engineering and natural sciences managers have previous experience as engineers, scientists, or mathematicians.

■ Projected employment growth for engineering and natural sciences managers should be closely related to growth in employment of the engineers and scientists they supervise and of the industries in which they are found.

■ Opportunities will be best for workers with strong communication and business management skills.

Nature of the Work

Engineering and natural sciences managers plan, coordinate, and direct research, design, and production activities. They may supervise engineers, scientists, and technicians, along with support personnel. These managers use their knowledge of engineering and natural sciences to oversee a variety of activities. They determine scientific and technical goals within broad outlines provided by top executives. These goals may include improving manufacturing processes, advancing scientific research, or developing new products. Managers make detailed plans to accomplish these goals. For example, they may develop the overall concepts of a new product or identify technical problems preventing the completion of a project.

To perform effectively, they also must acquire knowledge of administrative procedures, such as budgeting, hiring, and supervision. These managers propose budgets for projects and programs and determine staff, training, and equipment needs. They hire and assign scientists, engineers, and support personnel to carry out specific parts of each project. They also supervise the work of these employees, review their output, and establish administrative procedures and policies—including environmental standards, for example.

In addition, these managers use communication skills extensively. They spend a great deal of time coordinating the activities of their unit with those of other units or organizations. They confer with higher levels of management; with financial, production, marketing, and other managers; and with contractors and equipment and materials suppliers.

Engineering managers may supervise people who design and develop machinery, products, systems, and processes, or they may direct and coordinate production, operations, quality assurance, testing, or maintenance in industrial plants. Many are plant engineers, who direct and coordinate the design, installation, operation, and maintenance of equipment and machinery in industrial plants. Others manage research and development teams that produce new products and processes or improve existing ones.

Natural sciences managers oversee the work of life and physical scientists (including agricultural scientists, chemists, biologists, geoscientists, medical scientists, and physicists). These managers direct research and development projects and coordinate activities such as testing, quality control, and production. They may work on basic research projects or on commercial activities. Science managers sometimes conduct their own research in addition to managing the work of others.

Working Conditions

Engineering and natural sciences managers spend most of their time in an office. Some managers, however, also may work in laboratories, where they may be exposed to the same conditions as research scientists, or in industrial plants, where they may be exposed to the same conditions as production workers. Most managers work at least 40 hours a week and may work much longer on occasion to meet project deadlines. Some may experience considerable pressure to meet technical or scientific goals on a short deadline or within a tight budget.

Training, Other Qualifications, and Advancement

Strong technical knowledge is essential for engineering and natural sciences managers, who must understand and guide the work of their subordinates and explain the work in nontechnical terms to senior management and potential customers. Therefore, these management positions usually require work experience and formal education as an engineer, scientist, or mathematician.

Most engineering managers begin their careers as engineers after completing a bachelor's degree in the field. To advance to higher-level positions, engineers generally must assume management responsibility. To fill management positions, employers seek engineers who possess administrative and communication skills in addition to technical knowledge in their specialty. Many engineers gain these skills by obtaining a master's degree in engineering management or a master's degree in business administration (MBA). Employers often pay for such training. In large firms, some courses required in these degree programs may be offered onsite. Typically, engineers who prefer to manage in technical areas pursue a master's degree in engineering management, while those interested in nontechnical management earn an MBA.

Many science managers begin their careers as scientists, such as chemists, biologists, geologists, or mathematicians. Most scientists or mathematicians engaged in basic research have a Ph.D.; some in applied research and other activities may have a bachelor's or master's degree. Science managers must be specialists in the work they supervise. In addition, employers prefer managers with good communication and administrative skills. Graduate programs allow scientists to augment their undergraduate training with instruction in other fields, such as management or computer technology. Given the rapid pace of scientific developments, science managers must continuously upgrade their knowledge.

Engineering and natural sciences managers may advance to progressively higher leadership positions within their discipline. Some may become managers in nontechnical areas such as marketing, human resources, or sales. In high technology firms, managers in nontechnical areas often must possess the same specialized knowledge as do managers in technical areas. For example, employers in an engineering firm may prefer to hire experienced engineers as sales workers because the complex services offered by the firm can be marketed only by someone with specialized engineering knowledge. Such sales workers could eventually advance to jobs as sales managers.

Employment

Engineering and natural sciences managers held about 233,000 jobs in 2004. About 27 percent worked in professional, scientific, and technical services industries, primarily for firms providing architectural, engineering, and related services; computer systems design and related services; and scientific research and development services. Manufacturing industries employed 37 percent of engineering and natural sciences managers. Manufacturing industries with the largest employment include those producing computer and electronic equipment; transportation equipment, including aerospace products and parts; chemicals, including pharmaceuticals; and machinery manufacturing. Other large employers include government agencies and telecommunications and utilities companies.

Job Outlook

Employment of engineering and natural sciences managers is expected to grow about as fast as the average for all occupations through the year 2014—in line with projected employment growth in engineering and most sciences. However, many additional jobs will result from the need to replace managers who retire or move into other occupations. Opportunities for obtaining a management position will be best for workers with advanced technical knowledge and strong communication skills. Because engineering and natural sciences managers are involved in their firms' financial, production, and marketing activities, business management skills are also important.

Projected employment growth for engineering and natural sciences managers should be closely related to the growth of the occupations they supervise and of the industries in which they are found. For example, opportunities for managers should be better in rapidly growing areas of engineering—such as environmental and biomedical engineering—than in more slowly growing areas, such as nuclear and aerospace engineering. (See the description of engineers elsewhere in this book.) In addition, many employers are finding it more efficient to contract engineering and science management services to outside companies and consultants, creating good opportunities for managers in management services and management, scientific, and technical consulting firms.

Earnings

Earnings for engineering and natural sciences managers vary by specialty and by level of responsibility. Median annual earnings of engineering managers were $97,630 in May 2004. The middle 50 percent earned between $78,820 and $121,090. Median annual earnings in the industries employing the largest numbers of engineering managers in May 2004 are shown here:

Semiconductor and other electronic component
  manufacturing $116,400
Navigational, measuring, electromedical, and
  control instruments manufacturing....................107,160
Aerospace product and parts manufacturing..........103,570
Federal government 97,000
Architectural, engineering, and related services 96,020

Median annual earnings of natural sciences managers were $88,660 in May 2004. The middle 50 percent earned between $64,550 and $118,210. Median annual earnings in the industries employing the largest numbers of natural sciences managers in May 2004 are shown here:

Scientific research and development services $106,530
Federal government 81,460

A survey of manufacturing firms, conducted by Abbot, Langer, and Associates, found that engineering department managers and superintendents earned a median annual income of $89,232 in 2004, while research and development managers earned $90,377.

In addition, engineering and natural sciences managers, especially those at higher levels, often receive more benefits—such as expense accounts, stock option plans, and bonuses—than do nonmanagerial workers in their organizations.

Related Occupations

The work of engineering and natural sciences managers is closely related to that of engineers; mathematicians; and physical and life scientists, including agricultural and food scientists, atmospheric scientists, biological scientists, conservation scientists and foresters, chemists and materials scientists, environmental scientists and hydrologists, geoscientists, medical scientists, and physicists and astronomers. It also is related to the work of other managers, especially top executives.

Sources of Additional Information

For information about a career as an engineering and natural sciences manager, contact the sources of additional information for engineers that are listed at the end of the engineers job description elsewhere in this book.

Financial Managers

(O*NET 11-3031.01 and 11-3031.02)

Significant Points

■ About 3 out of 10 work in finance and insurance industries.

■ A bachelor's degree in finance, accounting, or a related field is the minimum academic preparation, but many employers increasingly seek graduates with a master's degree in business administration, economics, finance, or risk management.

- Experience may be more important than formal education for some financial manager positions—most notably, branch managers in banks.

- Jobseekers are likely to face competition.

Nature of the Work

Almost every firm, government agency, and other type of organization has one or more *financial managers* who oversee the preparation of financial reports, direct investment activities, and implement cash management strategies. Because computers are increasingly used to record and organize data, many financial managers are spending more time developing strategies and implementing the long-term goals of their organization.

The duties of financial managers vary with their specific titles, which include controller, treasurer or finance officer, credit manager, cash manager, and risk and insurance manager. *Controllers* direct the preparation of financial reports that summarize and forecast the organization's financial position, such as income statements, balance sheets, and analyses of future earnings or expenses. Controllers also are in charge of preparing special reports required by regulatory authorities. Often, controllers oversee the accounting, audit, and budget departments. *Treasurers* and *finance officers* direct the organization's financial goals, objectives, and budgets. They oversee the investment of funds, manage associated risks, supervise cash management activities, execute capital-raising strategies to support a firm's expansion, and deal with mergers and acquisitions. *Credit managers* oversee the firm's issuance of credit, establishing credit-rating criteria, determining credit ceilings, and monitoring the collections of past-due accounts. Managers specializing in international finance develop financial and accounting systems for the banking transactions of multinational organizations.

Cash managers monitor and control the flow of cash receipts and disbursements to meet the business and investment needs of the firm. For example, cash flow projections are needed to determine whether loans must be obtained to meet cash requirements or whether surplus cash should be invested in interest-bearing instruments. *Risk* and *insurance managers* oversee programs to minimize risks and losses that might arise from financial transactions and business operations undertaken by the institution. They also manage the organization's insurance budget.

Financial institutions, such as commercial banks, savings and loan associations, credit unions, and mortgage and finance companies, employ additional financial managers who oversee various functions, such as lending, trusts, mortgages, and investments, or programs, including sales, operations, or electronic financial services. These managers may be required to solicit business, authorize loans, and direct the investment of funds, always adhering to federal and state laws and regulations. (Chief financial officers and other executives are included with the description of top executives elsewhere in this book.)

Branch managers of financial institutions administer and manage all of the functions of a branch office, which may include hiring personnel, approving loans and lines of credit, establishing a rapport with the community to attract business, and assisting customers with account problems. The trend is for branch managers to become more oriented toward sales and marketing. It is important that they have substantial knowledge about all types of products that the bank sells. Financial managers who work for financial institutions must keep abreast of the rapidly growing array of financial services and products.

In addition to carrying out the preceding general duties, all financial managers perform tasks unique to their organization or industry. For example, government financial managers must be experts on the government appropriations and budgeting processes, whereas health care financial managers must be knowledgeable about issues surrounding health care financing. Moreover, financial managers must be aware of special tax laws and regulations that affect their industry.

Financial managers play an increasingly important role in mergers and consolidations and in global expansion and related financing. These areas require extensive specialized knowledge on the part of the financial manager to reduce risks and maximize profit. Financial managers increasingly are hired on a temporary basis to advise senior managers on these and other matters. In fact, some small firms contract out all their accounting and financial functions to companies that provide such services.

The role of the financial manager, particularly in business, is changing in response to technological advances that have significantly reduced the amount of time it takes to produce financial reports. Financial managers now perform more data analysis and use it to offer senior managers ideas on how to maximize profits. They often work on teams, acting as business advisors to top management. Financial managers need to keep abreast of the latest computer technology in order to increase the efficiency of their firm's financial operations.

Working Conditions

Working in comfortable offices, often close to top managers and to departments that develop the financial data those managers need, financial managers typically have direct access to state-of-the-art computer systems and information services. They commonly work long hours, often up to 50 or 60 per week. Financial managers generally are required to attend meetings of financial and economic associations and may travel to visit subsidiary firms or to meet customers.

Training, Other Qualifications, and Advancement

A bachelor's degree in finance, accounting, economics, or business administration is the minimum academic preparation for financial managers. However, many employers now seek graduates with a master's degree, preferably in business administration, economics, finance, or risk management. These academic programs develop analytical skills and provide knowledge of the latest financial analysis methods and technology.

Experience may be more important than formal education for some financial manager positions—most notably, branch managers in banks. Banks typically fill branch manager positions by promoting experienced loan officers and other professionals who excel at their jobs. Other financial managers may enter the profession through formal management training programs offered by the company. The American Institute of Banking, which is affiliated with the American Bankers Association, sponsors educational and training programs for bank officers through a wide range of banking schools and educational conferences.

Continuing education is vital to financial managers, who must cope with the growing complexity of global trade, changes in federal and state laws and regulations, and the proliferation of new and complex financial instruments. Firms often provide opportunities for workers to broaden their knowledge and skills by encouraging them to take graduate courses at colleges and universities or attend conferences related to their specialty. Financial management, banking, and credit union associations, often in cooperation with colleges and universities, sponsor numerous national and local training programs. Persons enrolled prepare extensively at home and then attend sessions on subjects such as accounting management, budget management, corporate cash management, financial analysis, international banking, and information systems. Many firms pay all or part of the costs for employees who successfully complete courses. Although experience, ability, and leadership are emphasized for promotion, advancement may be accelerated by this type of special study.

In some cases, financial managers also may broaden their skills and exhibit their competency by attaining professional certification. Many different associations offer professional certification programs. For example, the CFA Institute confers the Chartered Financial Analyst designation on investment professionals who have a bachelor's degree, pass three sequential examinations, and meet work experience requirements. The Association for Financial Professionals (AFP) confers the Certified Cash Manager credential to those who pass a computer-based exam and have a minimum of 2 years of relevant experience. The Institute of Management Accountants offers a Certified in Financial Management designation to members with a bachelor's degree and at least 2 years of work experience who pass the institute's four-part examination and fulfill continuing education requirements. Also, financial managers who specialize in accounting may earn the Certified Public Accountant (CPA) or Certified Management Accountant (CMA) designation. (See accountants and auditors elsewhere in this book.)

Candidates for financial management positions need a broad range of skills. Interpersonal skills are important because these jobs involve managing people and working as part of a team to solve problems. Financial managers must have excellent communication skills to explain complex financial data. Because financial managers work extensively with various departments in their firm, a broad overview of the business is essential.

Financial managers should be creative thinkers and problem-solvers, applying their analytical skills to business. They must be comfortable with the latest computer technology. Financial operations are increasingly being affected by the global economy, so financial managers must have knowledge of international finance. Proficiency in a foreign language also may be important.

Because financial management is critical to efficient business operations, well-trained, experienced financial managers who display a strong grasp of the operations of various departments within their organization are prime candidates for promotion to top management positions. Some financial managers transfer to closely related positions in other industries. Those with extensive experience and access to sufficient capital may start their own consulting firms.

Employment

Financial managers held about 528,000 jobs in 2004. Although they can be found in every industry, approximately 3 out of 10 are employed by finance and insurance establishments, such as banks, savings institutions, finance companies, credit unions, insurance carriers, and securities dealers. About 1 in 10 works for federal, state, or local government.

Job Outlook

Employment of financial managers is expected to grow about as fast as average for all occupations through 2014. The increasing need for financial expertise as a result of regulatory reforms and the expansion of the economy will drive job growth over the next decade. As the economy expands, both the growth of established companies and the creation of new businesses will spur demand for financial managers. However, mergers, acquisitions, and corporate downsizing are likely to restrict the employment growth to some extent.

As in other managerial occupations, jobseekers are likely to face competition because the number of job openings is expected to be less than the number of applicants. Candidates with expertise in accounting and finance—particularly those with a master's degree—should enjoy the best job prospects. Strong computer skills and knowledge of international finance are important; so are excellent communication skills, because financial management jobs involve working on strategic planning teams. In addition, a good knowledge of compliance procedures is essential because of the many regulatory changes instituted in recent years.

Over the short term, employment growth in this occupation may slow or even reverse due to economic downturns, during which companies are more likely to close departments or even go out of business—decreasing the need for financial managers.

The banking industry will continue to consolidate, although at a slower rate than in previous years. In spite of this trend, employment of bank branch managers is expected to increase because banks are refocusing on the importance of their existing branches and are creating new branches to serve a growing population. As banks expand the range of products and services they offer to include insurance and investment products, branch managers with knowledge in these areas will be needed. As a result, candidates who are licensed to sell insurance or securities will have the most favorable prospects. (See the descriptions of insurance sales agents and securities, commodities, and financial services sales agents elsewhere in this book.)

The long-run prospects for financial managers in the securities and commodities industry should be favorable because more people will be needed to handle increasingly complex financial transactions and manage a growing amount of investments. Financial managers also will be needed to handle mergers and acquisitions, raise capital, and assess global financial transactions. Risk managers, who assess risks for insurance and investment purposes, also will be in demand.

Some companies may hire financial managers on a temporary basis to see the organization through a short-term crisis or to offer suggestions for boosting profits. Other companies may contract out all accounting and financial operations. Even in these cases, however, financial managers may be needed to oversee the contracts.

Computer technology has reduced the amount of time and the staff required to produce financial reports. As a result, forecasting earnings, profits, and costs and generating ideas and creative ways to increase profitability will become a major role of corporate financial managers over the next decade. Financial managers who are familiar with computer software that can assist them in this role will be needed.

Earnings

Median annual earnings of financial managers were $81,880 in May 2004. The middle 50 percent earned between $59,490 and $112,320. Median annual earnings in the industries employing the largest numbers of financial managers in 2004 were as follows:

Securities and commodity contracts intermediation and brokerage	$129,770
Management of companies and enterprises	97,730
Nondepository credit intermediation	88,870
Local government	67,260
Depository credit intermediation	64,530

According to a 2005 survey by Robert Half International, a staffing services firm specializing in accounting and finance professionals, directors of finance earned between $78,500 and $178,250 and corporate controllers earned between $61,250 and $147,250.

A 2004 survey of manufacturing firms conducted by Abbot, Langer, and Associates, Inc., a human resources management consulting firm, reported the following median annual incomes: chief corporate financial officers, $130,000; corporate controllers, $86,150; cost accounting managers, $67,161; and general accounting managers, $64,100.

Large organizations often pay more than small ones, and salary levels also can depend on the type of industry and location. Many financial managers in both public and private industry receive additional compensation in the form of bonuses, which, like salaries, vary substantially by size of firm. Deferred compensation in the form of stock options is becoming more common, especially for senior-level executives.

Related Occupations

Financial managers combine formal education with experience in one or more areas of finance, such as asset management, lending, credit operations, securities investment, or insurance risk and loss control. Workers in other occupations requiring similar training and skills include accountants and auditors; budget analysts; financial analysts and personal financial advisors; insurance sales agents; insurance underwriters; loan officers; securities, commodities, and financial services sales agents; and real estate brokers and sales agents.

Sources of Additional Information

For information about careers and certification in financial management, contact

▸ Financial Management Association International, College of Business Administration, University of South Florida, Tampa, FL 33620-5500. Internet: http://www.fma.org

For information about careers in financial and treasury management and the Certified Cash Manager program, contact

▸ Association for Financial Professionals, 7315 Wisconsin Ave., Suite 600 West, Bethesda, MD 20814. Internet: http://www.afponline.org

For information about the Chartered Financial Analyst program, contact

▸ CFA Institute, P.O. Box 3668, 560 Ray Hunt Dr., Charlottesville, VA 22903-0668. Internet: http://www.cfainstitute.org

For information on the Financial Risk Manager program, contact

▸ Global Association of Risk Professionals, 100 Pavonia Ave., Suite 405, Jersey City, NJ 07310.

For information about the Certified in Financial Management designation, contact

▸ Institute of Management Accountants, 10 Paragon Dr., Montvale, NJ 07645-1718. Internet: http://www.imanet.org

Judges, Magistrates, and Other Judicial Workers

(O*NET 23-1021.00, 23-1022.00, and 23-1023.00)

Significant Points

■ A bachelor's degree and work experience are the minimum requirements for a judgeship or magistrate position, but most workers filling these positions also have law degrees.

■ Overall employment is projected to grow about as fast as the average, but varies by occupational specialty.

■ Judges and magistrates are expected to encounter competition for jobs because of the prestige associated with serving on the bench.

Nature of the Work

Judges, magistrates, and other judicial workers apply the law and oversee the legal process in courts according to local, state, and federal statutes. They preside over cases concerning every aspect of society, from traffic offenses to disputes over the management of professional sports to issues concerning the rights of huge corporations. All judicial workers must ensure that trials and hearings are conducted fairly and that the court safeguards the legal rights of all parties involved.

The most visible responsibility of *judges* is presiding over trials or hearings and listening as attorneys represent the parties present. Judges rule on the admissibility of evidence and the methods of conducting testimony, and they may be called on to settle disputes between opposing attorneys. Also, they ensure that rules and procedures are followed, and, if unusual circumstances arise for which standard procedures have not been established, judges interpret the law to determine the manner in which the trial will proceed.

Judges often hold pretrial hearings for cases. They listen to allegations and determine whether the evidence presented merits a trial. In criminal cases, judges may decide that persons charged with crimes should be held in jail pending trial, or they may set conditions for their release. In civil cases, they occasionally impose restrictions on the parties until a trial is held.

In many trials, juries are selected to decide guilt or innocence in criminal cases or liability and compensation in civil cases. Judges instruct juries on applicable laws, direct them to deduce the facts from the evidence presented, and hear their verdict. When the law does not require a jury trial or when the parties waive their right to a jury, judges decide cases. In such instances, the judge determines guilt in criminal cases and imposes sentences; in civil cases, the judge awards relief—such as compensation for damages—to the parties to the lawsuit, called litigants. Judges also work outside the courtroom in their chambers or private offices. There, judges read documents on pleadings and motions, research legal issues, write opinions, and oversee the court's operations. In some jurisdictions, judges also manage the courts' administrative and clerical staff.

Judges' duties vary according to the extent of their jurisdictions and powers. *General trial court judges* of the federal and state court systems have jurisdiction over any case in their system. They usually try civil cases transcending the jurisdiction of lower courts and all cases involving felony offenses. Federal and state *appellate court judges*, although few in number, have the power to overrule decisions made by *trial court* or *administrative law judges*; appellate court judges exercise their power if they determine that legal errors were made in a case or if legal precedent does not support the judgment of the lower court. Appellate court judges rule on a small number of cases and rarely have direct contact with litigants. Instead, they usually base their decisions on lower court records and on lawyers' written and oral arguments.

Many state court judges preside in courts whose jurisdiction is limited by law to certain types of cases. A variety of titles are assigned to these judges; among the most common are *municipal court judge, county court judge, magistrate,* and *justice of the peace.* Traffic violations, misdemeanors, small-claims cases, and pretrial hearings constitute the bulk of the work of state court judges, but some states allow these judges to handle cases involving domestic relations, probate, contracts, and other selected areas of the law.

Administrative law judges, sometimes called *hearing officers* or *adjudicators,* are employed by government agencies to make determinations for administrative agencies. These judges make decisions, for example, on a person's eligibility for various Social Security or workers' compensation benefits, on protection of the environment, on the enforcement of health and safety regulations, on employment discrimination, and on compliance with economic regulatory requirements.

Arbitration, mediation, and conciliation—collectively called appropriate dispute resolution (ADR)—are alternative processes that can be used to settle disputes between parties. All ADR hearings are private and confidential, and the processes are less formal than a court trial. If no settlement is reached through ADR, no statements made during the proceedings are admissible as evidence in any subsequent litigation.

There are two types of arbitration—compulsory and voluntary. During compulsory arbitration, opposing parties submit their dispute to one or more impartial persons, called *arbitrators,* for a final and nonbinding decision. Either party may reject the ruling and request a trial in court. Voluntary arbitration is a process in which opposing parties choose one or more arbitrators to hear their dispute and submit a final, binding decision. Arbitrators usually are attorneys or business persons with expertise in a particular field. The parties identify, in advance, the issues to be resolved by arbitration, the scope of the relief to be awarded, and many of the procedural aspects of the process.

Mediation, or neutral evaluation, involves an attempt by the parties to resolve their dispute with the aid of a neutral third party. This process generally is used when the parties wish to preserve their relationship. A *mediator* may offer suggestions, but resolution of the dispute rests with the parties themselves. Mediation proceedings also are confidential and private. If the parties are unable to reach a settlement, they are free to pursue other options. The parties usually decide in advance how they will contribute to the cost of mediation. However, many mediators volunteer their services, or they may be court staff. Courts ask that voluntary mediators provide their services at the lowest possible rate and that parties split the cost. Depending on the type of case, court-referred community mediation centers may charge a small fee to the parties involved in mediation.

Conciliation, or facilitation, is similar to mediation. The *conciliator's* role is to guide the parties to a settlement. The parties must decide in advance whether they will be bound by the conciliator's recommendations; they generally share equally in the cost of the conciliation.

Working Conditions

Judges, magistrates, and other judicial workers do most of their work in offices, law libraries, and courtrooms. Work in these occupations presents few hazards, although sitting in the same position in the courtroom for long periods can be tiring. Most judges wear robes when they are in a courtroom. Judges typically work a standard 40-hour week, but many work more than 50 hours per week. Some judges with limited jurisdiction are employed part time and divide their time between their judicial responsibilities and other careers.

Arbitrators, mediators, and conciliators usually work in private offices or meeting rooms; no public record is made of the proceedings.

Training, Other Qualifications, and Advancement

A bachelor's degree and work experience usually constitute the minimum requirements for a judgeship or magistrate position. A number of lawyers become judges, and most judges have first been lawyers. In fact, federal and state judges usually are required to be lawyers. About 40 states allow non-lawyers to hold limited-jurisdiction judgeships, but opportunities are better for those with law experience. Federal administrative law judges must be lawyers and pass a competitive examination administered by the U.S. Office of

Personnel Management. Some state administrative law judges and other hearing officials are not required to be lawyers.

Federal administrative law judges are appointed by various federal agencies, with virtually lifetime tenure. Federal magistrate judges are appointed by district judges—the life-tenured federal judges of district courts—to serve in a U.S. district court for 8 years. A part-time federal magistrate judge's term of office is 4 years. Some state judges are appointed, but the remainder are elected in partisan or nonpartisan state elections. Many state and local judges serve fixed renewable terms ranging from 4 or 6 years for some trial court judgeships to as long as 14 years or even life for other trial or appellate court judgeships. Judicial nominating commissions, composed of members of the bar and the public, are used to screen candidates for judgeships in many states and for some federal judgeships.

All states have some type of orientation for newly elected or appointed judges. The Federal Judicial Center, American Bar Association, National Judicial College, and National Center for State Courts provide judicial education and training for judges and other judicial-branch personnel. General and continuing education courses usually last from a few days to 3 weeks in length. More than half of all states, as well as Puerto Rico, require judges to enroll in continuing education courses while serving on the bench.

Training and education requirements for arbitrators, mediators, and conciliators differ from those for judges. Mediators who practice in state-funded or court-funded mediation programs usually must meet specific training or experience standards, which vary by state and court. In most states, individuals who offer private mediation services do not need a license, certification, or specific coursework; however, many private mediators and most of those affiliated with mediation organizations and programs have completed mediation training and agreed to comply with certain ethical standards. For example, the American Arbitration Association (AAA) requires mediators listed on its mediation panel to complete an AAA training course, receive recommendations from the trainers, and complete an apprenticeship.

Training for arbitrators, mediators, and conciliators is available through independent mediation programs, national and local mediation membership organizations, and postsecondary schools. In 2004, 16 colleges or universities in the United States offered master's degrees in dispute resolution or conflict management, and 2 offered doctoral degrees. Many more schools offer conflict-management specializations within other degree programs. Degrees in public policy, law, and related fields also provide good background for prospective arbitrators, mediators, and conciliators.

Employment

Judges, magistrates, and other judicial workers held 47,000 jobs in 2004. Judges, magistrates, and magistrate judges held 27,000 jobs, all in state and local governments. Administrative law judges, adjudicators, and hearing officers held about 16,000 jobs; 52 percent were in state governments, 29 percent in federal government, and 20 percent in local governments. Arbitrators, mediators, and conciliators held another 5,200 jobs. Approximately 40 percent worked for state and local governments. The remainder worked for labor organizations, law offices, insurance carriers, and other private companies and for organizations that specialize in providing dispute resolution services.

Job Outlook

Overall employment of judges, magistrates, and other judicial workers is projected to grow about as fast as average for all occupations through 2014. Budgetary pressures at all levels of government will hold down the hiring of judges, despite rising caseloads, particularly in federal courts. Most job openings will arise as judges retire. However, additional openings will occur when new judgeships are authorized by law or when judges are elevated to higher judicial offices.

Public concerns about crime and safety, as well as a public willingness to go to court to settle disputes, should spur demand for judges. Both the quantity and the complexity of judges' work have increased because of developments in information technology, medical science, electronic commerce, and globalization. The prestige associated with serving on the bench will ensure continued competition for judge and magistrate positions. However, a growing number of judges and candidates for judgeships are choosing to forgo the bench and work in the private sector, where pay is significantly higher. This movement may lessen the competition somewhat. Becoming a judge often is difficult because judicial candidates must compete with other qualified people and because they frequently must gain political support to be elected or appointed, and getting that support can be expensive.

Employment of arbitrators, mediators, and conciliators is expected to grow about as fast as the average for all occupations through 2014. Many individuals and businesses try to avoid litigation, which can involve lengthy delays, high costs, unwanted publicity, and ill will. Arbitration and other alternatives to litigation usually are faster, less expensive, and more conclusive, spurring demand for the services of arbitrators, mediators, and conciliators. Administrative law judges also are expected to experience average growth in employment.

Earnings

Judges, magistrate judges, and magistrates had median annual earnings of $93,070 in May 2004. The middle 50 percent earned between $54,140 and $124,400. The top 10 percent earned more than $141,750, while the bottom 10 percent earned less than $29,920. Median annual earnings in the industries employing the largest numbers of judges, magistrate judges, and magistrates in May 2004 were $111,810 in state government and $65,800 in local government. Administrative law judges, adjudicators, and hearing officers earned a median of $68,930, and arbitrators, mediators, and conciliators earned a median of $54,760.

In the federal court system, the Chief Justice of the U.S. Supreme Court earned $208,100 in 2005, and the Associate Justices earned $199,200. Federal court of appeals judges earned $171,800 a year, while district court judges had salaries of $162,100, as did judges in the Court of Federal Claims and the Court of International Trade. Federal judges with limited jurisdiction, such as magistrates and bankruptcy court judges, had salaries of $149,132.

According to a 2004 survey by the National Center for State Courts, salaries of chief justices of state high courts averaged $130,461 and ranged from $95,000 to $191,483. Annual salaries of associate justices of the state highest courts averaged $126,159 and ranged from $95,000 to $175,575. Salaries of state intermediate appellate court judges averaged $122,682 and ranged from $94,212 to $164,604. Salaries of state judges of general jurisdiction trial courts averaged $113,504 and ranged from $88,164 to $158,100.

Most salaried judges are provided health, life, and dental insurance; pension plans; judicial immunity protection; expense accounts; vacation, holiday, and sick leave; and contributions to retirement plans made on their behalf. In many states, judicial compensation committees, which make recommendations on the amount of salary increases, determine judicial salaries. States without commissions have statutes that regulate judicial salaries, link judicial salaries to the increases in pay for federal judges, or adjust annual pay according to the change in the Consumer Price Index, calculated by the U.S. Bureau of Labor Statistics.

Related Occupations

Legal training and mediation skills are useful to those in many other occupations, including counselors; lawyers; paralegals and legal assistants; title examiners, abstractors, and searchers; law clerks; and private detectives and investigators.

Sources of Additional Information

Information on judges, magistrates, and other judicial workers may be obtained from

▶ National Center for State Courts, 300 Newport Ave., Williamsburg, VA 23185-4147. Internet: http://www.ncsconline.org

Information on arbitrators, mediators, and conciliators may be obtained from

▶ American Arbitration Association, 335 Madison Ave., Floor 10, New York, NY 10017-4605. Internet: http://www.adr.org

Management Analysts

(O*NET 13-1111.00)

Significant Points

■ Despite fast employment growth, keen competition is expected for jobs; opportunities should be best for those with a graduate degree, specific industry expertise, and a talent for salesmanship and public relations.

■ About 29 percent, more than 3 times the average for all occupations, are self-employed.

■ Most positions in private industry require a master's degree and additional years of specialized experience; a bachelor's degree is sufficient for entry-level government jobs.

Nature of the Work

As business becomes more complex, the nation's firms are continually faced with new challenges. Firms increasingly rely on management analysts to help them remain competitive amidst these changes. *Management analysts,* often referred to as *management consultants* in private industry, analyze and propose ways to improve an organization's structure, efficiency, or profits. For example, a small but rapidly growing company that needs help improving the system of control over inventories and expenses may decide to employ a consultant who is an expert in just-in-time inventory management. In another case, a large company that has recently acquired a new division may hire management analysts to help reorganize the corporate structure and eliminate duplicate or nonessential jobs. In recent years, information technology and electronic commerce have provided new opportunities for management analysts. Companies hire consultants to develop strategies for entering and remaining competitive in the new electronic marketplace. (For information on computer specialists working in consulting, see the following job descriptions elsewhere in this book: computer software engineers, computer scientists and database administrators, and computer programmers.)

Firms providing management analysis range in size from a single practitioner to large international organizations employing thousands of consultants. Some analysts and consultants specialize in a specific industry, such as health care or telecommunications, while others specialize by type of business function, such as human resources, marketing, logistics, or information systems. In government, management analysts tend to specialize by type of agency. The work of management analysts and consultants varies with each client or employer and from project to project. Some projects require a team of consultants, each specializing in one area. In other projects, consultants work independently with the organization's managers. In all cases, analysts and consultants collect, review, and analyze information in order to make recommendations to managers.

Both public and private organizations use consultants for a variety of reasons. Some lack the internal resources needed to handle a project, while others need a consultant's expertise to determine what resources will be required and what problems may be encountered if they pursue a particular opportunity. To retain a consultant, a company first solicits proposals from a number of consulting firms specializing in the area in which it needs assistance. These proposals include the estimated cost and scope of the project, staffing requirements, references from a number of previous clients, and a completion deadline. The company then selects the proposal that best suits its needs.

After obtaining an assignment or contract, management analysts first define the nature and extent of the problem. During this phase, they analyze relevant data—which may include annual revenues, employment, or expenditures—and interview managers and employees while observing their operations. The analyst or consultant then develops solutions to the problem. While preparing their recommendations, they take into account the nature of the organization, the relationship it has with others in the industry, and its internal organization and culture. Insight into the problem often is gained by building and solving mathematical models.

Once they have decided on a course of action, consultants report their findings and recommendations to the client. These suggestions usually are submitted in writing, but oral presentations regarding findings also are common. For some projects, management analysts are retained to help implement the suggestions they have made.

Like their private-sector colleagues, management analysts in government agencies try to increase efficiency and worker productivity and to control costs. For example, if an agency is planning to purchase personal computers, it must first determine which type to buy, given its budget and data-processing needs. In this case, management analysts would assess the prices and characteristics of various machines and determine which ones best meet the agency's needs. Analysts may manage contracts for a wide range of goods and services to ensure quality performance and to prevent cost overruns.

Working Conditions

Management analysts usually divide their time between their offices and the client's site. In either situation, much of an analyst's time is spent indoors in clean, well-lit offices. Because they must spend a significant portion of their time with clients, analysts travel frequently.

Analysts and consultants generally work at least 40 hours a week. Uncompensated overtime is common, especially when project deadlines are approaching. Analysts may experience a great deal of stress as a result of trying to meet a client's demands, often on a tight schedule.

Self-employed consultants can set their workload and hours and work at home. On the other hand, their livelihood depends on their ability to maintain and expand their client base. Salaried consultants also must impress potential clients to get and keep clients for their company.

Training, Other Qualifications, and Advancement

Educational requirements for entry-level jobs in this field vary widely between private industry and government. Most employers in private industry generally seek individuals with a master's degree in business administration or a related discipline. Some employers also require additional years of experience in the field or industry in which the worker plans to consult in addition to a master's degree. Some will hire workers with a bachelor's degree as a research analyst or associate. Research analysts usually need to pursue a master's degree in order to advance to a consulting position. Most government agencies hire people with a bachelor's degree and no pertinent work experience for entry-level management analyst positions.

Few universities or colleges offer formal programs of study in management consulting; however, many fields of study provide a suitable educational background for this occupation because of the wide range of areas addressed by management analysts. Common educational backgrounds include most academic programs in business and management, such as accounting and marketing, as well as economics, computer and information sciences, and engineering. In addition to the appropriate formal education, most entrants to this occupation have years of experience in management, human resources, information technology, or other specialties. Analysts also routinely attend conferences to keep abreast of current developments in their field.

Management analysts often work with minimal supervision, so they need to be self-motivated and disciplined. Analytical skills, the ability to get along with a wide range of people, strong oral and written communication skills, good judgment, time management skills, and creativity are other desirable qualities. The ability to work in teams also is an important attribute as consulting teams become more common.

As consultants gain experience, they often become solely responsible for a specific project, taking on more responsibility and managing their own hours. At the senior level, consultants may supervise teams working on more complex projects and become more involved in seeking out new business. Those with exceptional skills may eventually become a partner in the firm. Others with entrepreneurial ambition may open their own firm.

A high percentage of management consultants are self-employed, partly because business startup costs are low. Self-employed consultants also can share office space, administrative help, and other resources with other self-employed consultants or small consulting firms, thus reducing overhead costs. Since many small consulting firms fail each year because of lack of managerial expertise and clients, persons interested in opening their own firm must have good organizational and marketing skills and several years of consulting experience.

The Institute of Management Consultants USA, Inc. (IMC USA), offers a wide range of professional development programs and resources, such as meetings and workshops, which can be helpful for management consultants. The IMC USA also offers the Certified Management Consultant (CMC) designation to those who meet minimum levels of education and experience, submit client reviews, and pass an interview and exam covering the IMC USA's Code of Ethics. Management consultants with a CMC designation must be recertified every 3 years. Certification is not mandatory for management consultants, but it may give a jobseeker a competitive advantage.

Employment

Management analysts held about 605,000 jobs in 2004. About 29 percent of these workers, more than 3 times the average for all occupations, were self-employed. Management analysts are found throughout the country, but employment is concentrated in large metropolitan areas. Management analyst jobs are found in a wide range of industries, including management, scientific, and technical consulting firms; computer systems design and related services firms; and federal, state, and local governments. The majority of those working for the federal government are in the U.S. Department of Defense.

Job Outlook

Despite projected rapid employment growth, keen competition is expected for jobs as management analysts. The pool of applicants from which employers can draw is quite large because analysts can come from very diverse educational backgrounds. Furthermore, the independent and challenging nature of the work, combined with high earnings potential, makes this occupation attractive to many. Job opportunities are expected to be best for those with a graduate degree, specific industry expertise, and a talent for salesmanship and public relations.

Employment of management analysts is expected to grow faster than the average for all occupations through 2014 as industry and government increasingly rely on outside expertise to improve the performance of their organizations. Job growth is projected in very large consulting firms with international expertise and in smaller consulting firms that specialize in specific areas, such as biotechnology, health care, information technology, human resources, engineering, and marketing. Growth in the number of individual practitioners may be hindered by increasing use of consulting teams that can expedite solutions to a variety of different issues and problems within an organization.

Employment growth of management analysts has been driven by a number of changes in the business environment that have forced firms to take a closer look at their operations. These changes include developments in information technology and the growth of electronic commerce. Traditional companies hire analysts to help design intranets or company Web sites or to establish online businesses. New Internet startup companies hire analysts not only to design Web sites but also to advise them in more traditional business practices, such as pricing strategies, marketing, and inventory and human resource management. In order to offer clients better quality and a wider variety of services, consulting firms are partnering with traditional computer software and technology firms. Also, many computer firms are developing consulting practices of their own in order to take advantage of this expanding market. Although information technology consulting should remain one of the fastest-growing consulting areas, the volatility of the computer services industry necessitates that the most successful management analysts have knowledge of traditional business practices in addition to computer applications, systems integration, Web design, and management skills.

The growth of international business also has contributed to an increase in demand for management analysts. As U.S. firms expand their business abroad, many will hire management analysts to help them form the right strategy for entering the market; to advise them on legal matters pertaining to specific countries; or to help them with organizational, administrative, and other issues, especially if the U.S. company is involved in a partnership or merger with a local firm. These trends provide management analysts with more opportunities to travel or work abroad but also require them to have a more comprehensive knowledge of international business and foreign cultures and languages.

Furthermore, as international and domestic markets have become more competitive, firms have needed to use resources more efficiently. Management analysts increasingly are sought to help reduce costs, streamline operations, and develop marketing strategies. As this process continues and businesses downsize, even more opportunities will be created for analysts to perform duties that previously were handled internally. Finally, more management analysts also will be needed in the public sector as federal, state, and local government agencies seek ways to become more efficient.

Though management consultants are continually expanding their services, employment growth could be hampered by increasing competition for clients from occupations that do not traditionally perform consulting work, such as accountants, financial analysts, lawyers, and computer systems analysts. Furthermore, economic downturns also can have adverse effects on employment for some management consultants. In these times, businesses look to cut costs, and consultants may be considered an excess expense. On the other hand, some consultants might experience an increase in work during recessions because they advise businesses on how to cut costs and remain profitable.

Earnings

Salaries for management analysts vary widely by years of experience and education, geographic location, sector of expertise, and size of employer. Generally, management analysts employed in large firms or in metropolitan areas have the highest salaries. Median annual wage and salary earnings of management analysts in May 2004 were $63,450. The middle 50 percent earned between $48,340 and $86,650. The lowest 10 percent earned less than $37,680, and the highest 10 percent earned more than $120,220. Median annual earnings in the industries employing the largest numbers of management analysts in May 2004 were

Management, scientific, and technical consulting services	$72,480
Federal government	72,440
Computer systems design and related services	69,800
Management of companies and enterprises	59,420
State government	48,070

According to a the Association of Management Consulting Firms, typical earnings in 2004—including bonuses and profit sharing—averaged $52,482 for research associates in member firms, $65,066 for entry-level consultants, $89,116 for management consultants, $123,305 for senior consultants, $191,664 for junior partners, and $317,339 for senior partners. Only the most experienced workers in highly successful management consulting firms earn these top salaries.

Salaried management analysts usually receive common benefits, such as health and life insurance, a retirement plan, vacation, and sick leave, as well as less-common benefits, such as profit sharing and bonuses for outstanding work. In addition, all travel expenses usually are reimbursed by the employer. Self-employed consultants have to maintain their own office and provide their own benefits.

Related Occupations

Management analysts collect, review, and analyze data; make recommendations; and implement their ideas. Occupations with similar duties include accountants and auditors; budget analysts; cost estimators; financial analysts and personal financial advisors; operations research analysts; economists; and market and survey researchers. Some management analysts specialize in information technology and work with computers, as do computer systems analysts and computer scientists and database administrators. Most management analysts also have managerial experience similar to that of administrative services managers; advertising, marketing, promotions, public relations, and sales managers; financial

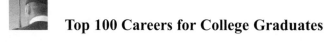

managers; human resources, training, and labor relations managers and specialists; and top executives.

Sources of Additional Information

Information about career opportunities in management consulting is available from

▸ Association of Management Consulting Firms, 380 Lexington Ave., Suite 1700, New York, NY 10168. Internet: http://www.amcf.org

Information about the Certified Management Consultant designation can be obtained from

▸ Institute of Management Consultants USA, Inc., 2025 M St. NW, Suite 800, Washington, DC 20036. Internet: http://www.imcusa.org

Information on obtaining a management analyst position with the federal government is available from the Office of Personnel Management (OPM) through USAJOBS, the federal government's official employment information system. This resource for locating and applying for job opportunities can be accessed through the Internet at http://www.usajobs.opm.gov or through an interactive voice response telephone system at (703) 724-1850 or TDD (978) 461-8404. These numbers are not toll free, and charges may result.

Medical and Health Services Managers

(O*NET 11-9111.00)

Significant Points

■ Rapid employment growth is projected; job opportunities will be especially good in offices of health practitioners, general medical and surgical hospitals, home health care services, and outpatient care centers.

■ Applicants with work experience in health care and strong business and management skills likely will have the best opportunities.

■ Earnings are high, but long work hours are common.

■ A master's degree is the standard credential for most positions, although a bachelor's degree is adequate for some entry-level positions in smaller facilities and in health information management.

Nature of the Work

Health care is a business and, like every other business, it needs good management to keep it running smoothly. *Medical and health services managers,* also referred to as *health care executives* or *health care administrators*, plan, direct, coordinate, and supervise the delivery of health care. Medical and health services managers include specialists and generalists. Specialists are in charge of specific clinical departments or services, while generalists manage or help manage an entire facility or system.

The structure and financing of health care are changing rapidly. Future medical and health services managers must be prepared to deal with evolving integrated health care delivery systems, technological innovations, an increasingly complex regulatory environment, restructuring of work, and an increased focus on preventive care. They will be called on to improve efficiency in health care facilities and the quality of the health care provided. Increasingly, medical and health services managers will work in organizations in which they must optimize efficiency of a variety of related services—for example, those ranging from inpatient care to outpatient followup care.

Large facilities usually have several assistant administrators to aid the top administrator and to handle daily decisions. Assistant administrators may direct activities in clinical areas such as nursing, surgery, therapy, medical records, or health information. (Managers in nonhealth areas, such as administrative services, computer and information systems, finance, and human resources, are not included in this statement. For information about them, see the descriptions of other management occupations elsewhere in this book.)

In smaller facilities, top administrators handle more of the details of daily operations. For example, many nursing home administrators manage personnel, finances, facility operations, and admissions and also have a larger role in resident care.

Clinical managers have training or experience in a specific clinical area and, accordingly, have more specific responsibilities than do generalists. For example, directors of physical therapy are experienced physical therapists, and most health information and medical record administrators have a bachelor's degree in health information or medical record administration. Clinical managers establish and implement policies, objectives, and procedures for their departments; evaluate personnel and work; develop reports and budgets; and coordinate activities with other managers.

Health information managers are responsible for the maintenance and security of all patient records. Recent regulations enacted by the federal government require that all health care providers maintain electronic patient records and that these records be secure. As a result, health information managers must keep up with current computer and software technology and with legislative requirements and developments. In addition, as patient data become more frequently used for quality management and in medical research, health information managers ensure that databases are complete, accurate, and available only to authorized personnel.

In group medical practices, managers work closely with physicians. Whereas an office manager might handle business affairs in small medical groups, leaving policy decisions to the physicians themselves, larger groups usually employ a full-time administrator to help formulate business strategies and coordinate day-to-day business.

A small group of 10 to 15 physicians might employ 1 administrator to oversee personnel matters, billing and collection, budgeting, planning, equipment outlays, and patient flow. A large practice of 40 to 50 physicians might have a chief administrator and several assistants, each responsible for different areas.

Medical and health services managers in managed care settings perform functions similar to those of their counterparts in large group practices except that they could have larger staffs to manage. In addition, they might do more community outreach and preventive care than do managers of a group practice.

Some medical and health services managers oversee the activities of a number of facilities in health systems. Such systems might contain both inpatient and outpatient facilities and offer a wide range of patient services.

Working Conditions

Most medical and health services managers work long hours. Facilities such as nursing care facilities and hospitals operate around the clock, and administrators and managers may be called at all hours to deal with problems. They also may travel to attend meetings or inspect satellite facilities.

Some managers work in comfortable, private offices; others share space with other managers or staff. They may spend considerable time walking to consult with co-workers.

Training, Other Qualifications, and Advancement

Medical and health services managers must be familiar with management principles and practices. A master's degree in health services administration, long-term care administration, health sciences, public health, public administration, or business administration is the standard credential for most generalist positions in this field. However, a bachelor's degree is adequate for some entry-level positions in smaller facilities, at the departmental level within health care organizations, and in health information management. Physicians' offices and some other facilities may substitute on-the-job experience for formal education.

Bachelor's, master's, and doctoral degree programs in health administration are offered by colleges; universities; and schools of public health, medicine, allied health, public administration, and business administration. In 2005, 70 schools had accredited programs leading to the master's degree in health services administration, according to the Commission on Accreditation of Healthcare Management Education.

For persons seeking to become heads of clinical departments, a degree in the appropriate field and work experience may be sufficient early in their career. However, a master's degree in health services administration or a related field might be required to advance. For example, nursing service administrators usually are chosen from among supervisory registered nurses with administrative abilities and graduate degrees in nursing or health services administration.

Health information managers require a bachelor's degree from an accredited program and a Registered Health Information Administrator (RHIA) certification from the American Health Information Management Association. In 2005, there were 45 accredited bachelor's programs in health information management, according to the Commission on Accreditation for Health Informatics and Information Management Education.

Some graduate programs seek students with undergraduate degrees in business or health administration; however, many graduate programs prefer students with a liberal arts or health profession background. Candidates with previous work experience in health care also may have an advantage. Competition for entry into these programs is keen, and applicants need above-average grades to gain admission. Graduate programs usually last between 2 and 3 years. They may include up to 1 year of supervised administrative experience and coursework in areas such as hospital organization and management, marketing, accounting and budgeting, human resources administration, strategic planning, law and ethics, biostatistics or epidemiology, health economics, and health information systems. Some programs allow students to specialize in one type of facility—hospitals, nursing care facilities, mental health facilities, or medical groups. Other programs encourage a generalist approach to health administration education.

New graduates with master's degrees in health services administration may start as department managers or as staff. The level of the starting position varies with the experience of the applicant and the size of the organization. Hospitals and other health facilities offer postgraduate residencies and fellowships, which usually are staff positions. Graduates from master's degree programs also take jobs in large medical group practices, clinics, mental health facilities, nursing care corporations, and consulting firms.

Graduates with bachelor's degrees in health administration usually begin as administrative assistants or assistant department heads in larger hospitals. They also may begin as department heads or assistant administrators in small hospitals or nursing care facilities.

All states and the District of Columbia require nursing care facility administrators to have a bachelor's degree, pass a licensing examination, complete a state-approved training program, and pursue continuing education. Some states also require licenses for administrators in assisted living facilities. A license is not required in other areas of medical and health services management.

Medical and health services managers often are responsible for millions of dollars' worth of facilities and equipment and hundreds of employees. To make effective decisions, they need to be open to different opinions and good at analyzing contradictory information. They must understand finance and information systems and be able to interpret data. Motivating others to implement their decisions requires strong leadership abilities. Tact, diplomacy, flexibility, and communication skills are essential because medical and health services managers spend most of their time interacting with others.

Medical and health services managers advance by moving into more responsible and higher-paying positions, such as assistant or associate administrator, department head, or CEO, or by moving to larger facilities. Some experienced managers also may become consultants or professors of health care management.

Employment

Medical and health services managers held about 248,000 jobs in 2004. About 30 percent worked in private hospitals, and another 16 percent worked in offices of physicians or in nursing care facilities. The remainder worked mostly in home health care services, federal government health care facilities, ambulatory facilities run by state and local governments, outpatient care centers, insurance carriers, and community care facilities for the elderly.

Job Outlook

Employment of medical and health services managers is expected to grow faster than average for all occupations through 2014 as the health care industry continues to expand and diversify. Job opportunities will be especially good in offices of health practitioners, general medical and surgical hospitals, home health care services, and outpatient care centers. Applicants with work experience in the health care field and strong business and management skills should have the best opportunities. Competition for jobs at the highest management levels will be keen because of the high pay and prestige.

Managers in all settings will be needed to improve quality and efficiency of health care while controlling costs as insurance companies and Medicare demand higher levels of accountability. Managers also will be needed to computerize patient records and to ensure their security as required by law. Additional demand for managers will stem from the need to recruit workers and increase employee retention, to comply with changing regulations, to implement new technology, and to help improve the health of their communities by emphasizing preventive care.

Hospitals will continue to employ the most medical and health services managers over the 2004–2014 projection period. However, the number of new jobs created is expected to increase at a slower rate in hospitals than in many other industries because of the growing utilization of clinics and other outpatient care sites. Despite relatively slow employment growth, a large number of new jobs will be created because of the industry's large size. Medical and health services managers with experience in large facilities will enjoy the best job opportunities as hospitals become larger and more complex.

Employment will grow fastest in practitioners' offices and in home health care agencies. Many services previously provided in hospitals will continue to shift to these sectors, especially as medical technologies improve. Demand in medical group practice management will grow as medical group practices become larger and more complex. Managers with specialized experience in a particular field, such as reimbursement, should have good opportunities.

Medical and health services managers also will be employed by health care management companies that provide management services to hospitals and other organizations as well as to specific departments such as emergency, information management systems, managed care contract negotiations, and physician recruiting.

Earnings

Median annual earnings of medical and health services managers were $67,430 in May 2004. The middle 50 percent earned between $52,530 and $88,210. The lowest 10 percent earned less than $41,450, and the highest 10 percent earned more than $117,990. Median annual earnings in the industries employing the largest numbers of medical and health services managers in May 2004 were as follows:

Federal government	$87,200
General medical and surgical hospitals	71,280
Offices of physicians	61,320
Nursing care facilities	60,940
Home health care services	60,320

Earnings of medical and health services managers vary by type and size of the facility as well as by level of responsibility. For example, the Medical Group Management Association reported that, in 2004, median salaries for administrators were $72,875 in practices with 6 or fewer physicians, $95,766 in practices with 7 to 25 physicians, and $132,955 in practices with 26 or more physicians.

According to a survey by *Modern Healthcare* magazine, median annual compensation in 2004 for hospital administrators of selected clinical departments was $76,800 in respiratory care, $81,100 in physical therapy, $87,700 in home health care, $88,800 in laboratory services, $90,200 in long-term care, $93,500 in medical imaging/diagnostic radiology, $94,400 in rehabilitation services, $95,200 in cancer treatment facilities, $96,200 in cardiology, $102,800 in nursing services, and $113,200 in pharmacies. Salaries also varied according to size of facility and geographic region.

According to a survey by the Professional Association of Health Care Office Management, total 2004 median compensation for office managers in specialty physicians' practices was $72,047 in gastroenterology, $66,946 in dermatology, $66,207 in cardiology, $64,543 in ophthalmology, $63,801 in obstetrics and gynecology, $62,545 in orthopedics, $58,595 in pediatrics, $52,211 in internal medicine, $50,924 in psychiatry, and $50,049 in family practice.

Related Occupations

Medical and health services managers have training or experience in both health and management. Other occupations requiring knowledge of both fields are insurance underwriters and social and community service managers.

Sources of Additional Information

Information about undergraduate and graduate academic programs in this field is available from

▸ Association of University Programs in Health Administration, 2000 North 14th St., Suite 780, Arlington, VA 22201. Internet: http://www.aupha.org

For a list of accredited graduate programs in medical and health services administration, contact

▸ Commission on Accreditation of Healthcare Management Education, 2000 North 14th St., Suite 780, Arlington, VA 22201. Internet: http://www.cahmeweb.org

For information about career opportunities in health care management, contact

▸ American College of Healthcare Executives, One N. Franklin St., Suite 1700, Chicago, IL 60606-4425. Internet: http://www.healthmanagementcareers.org

For information about career opportunities in long-term care administration, contact

▸ American College of Health Care Administrators, 300 N. Lee St., Suite 301, Alexandria, VA 22314. Internet: http://www.achca.org

For information about career opportunities in medical group practices and ambulatory care management, contact

▸ Medical Group Management Association, 104 Inverness Terrace East, Englewood, CO 80112-5306. Internet: http://www.mgma.org

For information about medical and health care office managers, contact

▶ Professional Association of Health Care Office Management, 461 East Ten Mile Rd., Pensacola, FL 32534-9712.

For information about career opportunities in health information management, contact

▶ American Health Information Management Association, 233 N. Michigan Ave., Suite 2150, Chicago, IL 60601-5800. Internet: http://www.ahima.org

Top Executives

(O*NET 11-1011.01, 11-1011.02, and 11-1021.00)

Significant Points

■ Keen competition is expected because the prestige and high pay attract a large number of qualified applicants.

■ Top executives are among the highest-paid workers; however, long hours, considerable travel, and intense pressure to succeed are common.

■ The formal education and experience of top executives vary as widely as the nature of their responsibilities.

Nature of the Work

All organizations have specific goals and objectives that they strive to meet. *Top executives* devise strategies and formulate policies to ensure that these objectives are met. Although they have a wide range of titles—such as chief executive officer, chief operating officer, board chair, president, vice president, school superintendent, county administrator, or tax commissioner—all formulate policies and direct the operations of businesses and corporations, public-sector organizations, nonprofit institutions, and other organizations.

A corporation's goals and policies are established by the *chief executive officer* in collaboration with other top executives, who are overseen by a board of directors. In a large corporation, the chief executive officer meets frequently with subordinate executives to ensure that operations are conducted in accordance with these policies. The chief executive officer of a corporation retains overall accountability; however, a *chief operating officer* may be delegated several responsibilities, including the authority to oversee executives who direct the activities of various departments and implement the organization's policies on a day-to-day basis. In publicly held and nonprofit corporations, the board of directors ultimately is accountable for the success or failure of the enterprise, and the chief executive officer reports to the board.

The nature of other high-level executives' responsibilities depends on the size of the organization. In large organizations, the duties of such executives are highly specialized. Some managers, for instance, are responsible for the overall performance of one aspect of the organization, such as manufacturing, marketing, sales, purchasing, finance, personnel, training, administrative services, computer and information systems, property management, transportation, or legal services. (Some of these and other management occupations are discussed elsewhere in this book.)

In smaller organizations, such as independent retail stores or small manufacturers, a partner, owner, or general manager often is responsible for purchasing, hiring, training, quality control, and day-to-day supervisory duties.

Chief financial officers direct the organization's financial goals, objectives, and budgets. They oversee the investment of funds and manage associated risks, supervise cash management activities, execute capital-raising strategies to support a firm's expansion, and deal with mergers and acquisitions.

Chief information officers are responsible for the overall technological direction of their organizations. They are increasingly involved in the strategic business plan of a firm as part of the executive team. To perform effectively, they also need knowledge of administrative procedures, such as budgeting, hiring, and supervision. These managers propose budgets for projects and programs and make decisions on staff training and equipment purchases. They hire and assign computer specialists, information technology workers, and support personnel to carry out specific parts of the projects. They supervise the work of these employees, review their output, and establish administrative procedures and policies. Chief information officers also provide organizations with the vision to master information technology as a competitive tool.

Chief executives have overall responsibility for the operation of their organizations. Working with executive staff, they set goals and arrange programs to attain these goals. Executives also appoint department heads, who manage the employees who carry out programs. Chief executives also oversee budgets and ensure that resources are used properly and that programs are carried out as planned.

Chief executive officers carry out a number of other important functions, such as meeting with staff and board members to determine the level of support for proposed programs. In addition, they often nominate citizens to boards and commissions, encourage business investment, and promote economic development in their communities. To do all of these varied tasks effectively, chief executives rely on a staff of highly skilled personnel. Executives who control small companies, however, often do this work by themselves.

General and operations managers plan, direct, or coordinate the operations of companies or public- and private-sector organizations. Their duties include formulating policies, managing daily operations, and planning the use of materials and human resources, but are too diverse and general in nature to be classified in any one area of management or administration, such as personnel, purchasing, or administrative services. In some organizations, the duties of general and operations managers may overlap the duties of chief executive officers.

In addition to being responsible for the operational success of a company, top executives also are increasingly being held accountable for the accuracy of their financial reporting, particularly among publicly traded companies. For example, recently enacted legislation contains provisions for corporate governance, internal control, and financial reporting.

Working Conditions

Top executives typically have spacious offices and numerous support staff. General managers in large firms or nonprofit organizations usually have comfortable offices close to those of the top executives to whom they report. Long hours, including evenings and weekends, are standard for most top executives and general managers, although their schedules may be flexible.

Substantial travel between international, national, regional, and local offices to monitor operations and meet with customers, staff, and other executives often is required of managers and executives. Many managers and executives also attend meetings and conferences sponsored by various associations. The conferences provide an opportunity to meet with prospective donors, customers, contractors, or government officials and allow managers and executives to keep abreast of technological and managerial innovations.

In large organizations, job transfers between local offices or subsidiaries are common for persons on the executive career track. Top executives are under intense pressure to succeed; depending on the organization, this may mean earning higher profits, providing better service, or attaining fundraising and charitable goals. Executives in charge of poorly performing organizations or departments usually find their jobs in jeopardy.

Training, Other Qualifications, and Advancement

The formal education and experience of top executives vary as widely as the nature of their responsibilities. Many top executives have a bachelor's or higher degree in business administration or liberal arts. College presidents typically have a doctorate in the field in which they originally taught, and school superintendents often have a master's degree in education administration. (For information on lower-level managers in educational services, see the job description of education administrators elsewhere in this book.) A brokerage office manager needs a strong background in securities and finance, and department store executives generally have extensive experience in retail trade.

Some top executives in the public sector have a background in public administration or liberal arts. Others might have a background related to their jobs. For example, a health commissioner might have a graduate degree in health services administration or business administration. (For information on lower-level managers in health services, see the job description of medical and health services managers elsewhere in this book.)

Many top executive positions are filled from within the organization by promoting experienced lower-level managers when an opening occurs. In industries such as retail trade or transportation, for instance, it is possible for individuals without a college degree to work their way up within the company and become managers. However, many companies prefer that their top executives have specialized backgrounds and, therefore, hire individuals who have been managers in other organizations.

Top executives must have highly developed personal skills. An analytical mind able to quickly assess large amounts of information and data is very important, as is the ability to consider and evaluate the relationships between numerous factors. Top executives also must be able to communicate clearly and persuasively. Other qualities critical for managerial success include leadership, self-confidence, motivation, decisiveness, flexibility, sound business judgment, and determination.

Advancement may be accelerated by participation in company training programs that impart a broader knowledge of company policy and operations. Managers also can help their careers by becoming familiar with the latest developments in management techniques at national or local training programs sponsored by various industry and trade associations. Managers who have experience in a particular field, such as accounting or engineering, may attend executive development programs to facilitate their promotion to an even higher level. Participation in conferences and seminars can expand knowledge of national and international issues influencing the organization and can help the participants develop a network of useful contacts.

General managers may advance to a top executive position, such as executive vice president, in their own firm or they may take a corresponding position in another firm. They may even advance to peak corporate positions such as chief operating officer or chief executive officer. Chief executive officers often become members of the board of directors of one or more firms, typically as a director of their own firm and often as chair of its board of directors. Some top executives establish their own firms or become independent consultants.

Employment

Top executives held about 2.3 million jobs in 2004. Employment by detailed occupation was distributed as follows:

General and operations managers 1,807,000
Chief executives 444,000
Legislators 66,000

Top executives are found in every industry, but service-providing industries, including government, employ 8 out of 10.

Job Outlook

Keen competition is expected for top executive positions because the prestige and high pay attract a large number of qualified applicants. Because this is a large occupation, numerous openings will occur each year as executives transfer to other positions, start their own businesses, or retire. However, many executives who leave their jobs transfer to other executive positions, a pattern that tends to limit the number of job openings for new entrants.

Experienced managers whose accomplishments reflect strong leadership qualities and the ability to improve the efficiency or competitive position of an organization will have the best opportunities. In an increasingly global economy, experience in international economics, marketing, and information systems and knowledge of several languages also may be beneficial.

Employment of top executives—including chief executives and general and operations managers—is expected to grow about as fast as average for all occupations through 2014. Because top managers are essential to the success of any organization, their jobs are unlikely to be automated or to be eliminated through corporate restructuring—trends that are expected to adversely affect employment of lower-level managers. Projected employment growth of top executives over the 2004–2014 period varies by industry. For example, employment growth is expected to be much faster than average in professional, scientific, and technical services and in administrative and support services. However, employment is projected to decline in some manufacturing industries.

Earnings

Top executives are among the highest-paid workers in the U.S. economy. However, salary levels vary substantially depending on the level of managerial responsibility; length of service; and type, size, and location of the firm. For example, a top manager in a very large corporation can earn significantly more than a counterpart in a small firm.

Median annual earnings of general and operations managers in May 2004 were $77,420. The middle 50 percent earned between $52,420 and $118,310. Because the specific responsibilities of general and operations managers vary significantly within industries, earnings also tend to vary considerably. Median annual earnings in the industries employing the largest numbers of general and operations managers in May 2004 were

Computer systems design and related
  services $117,730
Management of companies and enterprises 99,670
Building equipment contractors............................83,080
Depository credit intermediation 76,060
Local government 68,590

Median annual earnings of chief executives in May 2004 were $140,350, although chief executives in some industries earned considerably more.

Salaries vary substantially by type and level of responsibilities and by industry. According to a 2005 survey by Abbott, Langer, and Associates, the median income of chief executive officers in the nonprofit sector was $88,006 in 2005, but some of the highest-paid made more than $700,000.

In addition to salaries, total compensation often includes stock options, dividends, and other performance bonuses. The use of executive dining rooms and company aircraft and cars, expense allowances, and company-paid insurance premiums and physical examinations also are among benefits commonly enjoyed by top executives in private industry. A number of chief executive officers also are provided with company-paid club memberships and other amenities.

Related Occupations

Top executives plan, organize, direct, control, and coordinate the operations of an organization and its major departments or programs. The members of the board of directors and lower-level managers also are involved in these activities. Many other management occupations have similar responsibilities; however, they are concentrated in specific industries or are responsible for a specific department within an organization. A few examples are administrative services managers; education administrators; financial managers; food service managers; and advertising, marketing, promotions, public relations, and sales managers. Legislators oversee their staffs and help set public policies in federal, state, and local governments.

Sources of Additional Information

For a variety of information on top executives, including educational programs, certification programs, and job listings, contact

▸ American Management Association, 1601 Broadway, 6th Floor, New York, NY 10019. Internet: http://www.amanet.org

▸ International Public Management Association for Human Resources, 1617 Duke St., Alexandria, VA 22314. Internet: http://www.ipma-hr.org

▸ National Management Association, 2210 Arbor Blvd., Dayton, OH 45439. Internet: http://www.nma1.org

For information on executive financial management careers and certification, contact

▸ Financial Executives International, 200 Campus Dr., P.O. Box 674, Florham Park, NJ 07932-0674. Internet: http://www.fei.org

▸ Financial Management Association International, College of Business Administration, University of South Florida, 4202 East Fowler Ave., BSN 3331, Tampa, FL 33620-5500. Internet: http://www.fma.org

Jobs Typically Requiring a Bachelor's Degree

Accountants and Auditors

Agricultural and Food Scientists

Architects, Except Landscape and Naval

Athletic Trainers

Atmospheric Scientists

Budget Analysts

Chemists and Materials Scientists

Commercial and Industrial Designers

Computer Programmers

Computer Scientists and Database Administrators

Computer Software Engineers

Computer Systems Analysts

Conservation Scientists and Foresters

Construction Managers

Dietitians and Nutritionists

Engineers

Fashion Designers

Financial Analysts and Personal Financial Advisors

Graphic Designers

Human Resources, Training, and Labor Relations Managers and Specialists

Insurance Sales Agents

Insurance Underwriters

Interior Designers

Landscape Architects

Loan Officers

Meeting and Convention Planners

News Analysts, Reporters, and Correspondents

Occupational Therapists

Physician Assistants

Probation Officers and Correctional Treatment Specialists

Property, Real Estate, and Community Association Managers

Public Relations Specialists

Recreation Workers

Recreational Therapists

Sales Engineers

Securities, Commodities, and Financial Services Sales Agents

Tax Examiners, Collectors, and Revenue Agents

Teachers—Adult Literacy and Remedial Education

Teachers—Preschool, Kindergarten, Elementary, Middle, and Secondary

Teachers—Special Education

Accountants and Auditors

(O*NET 13-2011.01 and 13-2011.02)

Significant Points

■ Most jobs require at least a bachelor's degree in accounting or a related field.

■ Overall job opportunities should be favorable; jobseekers who obtain professional recognition through certification or licensure, a master's degree, proficiency in accounting and auditing computer software, or specialized expertise will have the best opportunities.

■ An increase in the number of businesses, changing financial laws and regulations, and greater scrutiny of company finances will drive faster-than-average growth of accountants and auditors.

Nature of the Work

Accountants and auditors help to ensure that the nation's firms are run efficiently, its public records kept accurately, and its taxes paid properly and on time. They perform these vital functions by offering an increasingly wide array of business and accounting services, including public, management, and government accounting, as well as internal auditing, to their clients. Beyond carrying out the fundamental tasks of the occupation—preparing, analyzing, and verifying financial documents in order to provide information to clients—many accountants now are required to possess a wide range of knowledge and skills. Accountants and auditors are broadening the services they offer to include budget analysis, financial and investment planning, information technology consulting, and limited legal services.

Specific job duties vary widely among the four major fields of accounting: public, management, and government accounting and internal auditing.

Public accountants perform a broad range of accounting, auditing, tax, and consulting activities for their clients, which may be corporations, governments, nonprofit organizations, or individuals. For example, some public accountants concentrate on tax matters, such as advising companies about the tax advantages and disadvantages of certain business decisions and preparing individual income tax returns. Others offer advice in areas such as compensation or employee health care benefits, the design of accounting and data-processing systems, and the selection of controls to safeguard assets. Still others audit clients' financial statements and inform investors and authorities that the statements have been correctly prepared and reported. Public accountants, many of whom are Certified Public Accountants (CPAs), generally have their own businesses or work for public accounting firms.

Some public accountants specialize in forensic accounting—investigating and interpreting white-collar crimes such as securities fraud and embezzlement; bankruptcies and contract disputes; and other complex and possibly criminal financial transactions, including money laundering by organized criminals. Forensic accountants combine their knowledge of accounting and finance with law and investigative techniques in order to determine whether an activity is illegal. Many forensic accountants work closely with law enforcement personnel and lawyers during investigations and often appear as expert witnesses during trials.

In response to recent accounting scandals, new federal legislation restricts the nonauditing services that public accountants can provide to clients. If an accounting firm audits a client's financial statements, that same firm cannot provide advice on human resources, technology, investment banking, or legal matters, although accountants may still advise on tax issues, such as establishing a tax shelter. Accountants may still advise other clients in these areas or may provide advice within their own firm.

Management accountants—also called *cost, managerial, industrial, corporate,* or *private accountants*—record and analyze the financial information of the companies for which they work. Among their other responsibilities are budgeting, performance evaluation, cost management, and asset management. Usually, management accountants are part of executive teams involved in strategic planning or the development of new products. They analyze and interpret the financial information that corporate executives need in order to make sound business decisions. They also prepare financial reports for other groups, including stockholders, creditors, regulatory agencies, and tax authorities. Within accounting departments, management accountants may work in various areas, including financial analysis, planning and budgeting, and cost accounting.

Government accountants and auditors work in the public sector, maintaining and examining the records of government agencies and auditing private businesses and individuals whose activities are subject to government regulations or taxation. Accountants employed by federal, state, and local governments guarantee that revenues are received and expenditures are made in accordance with laws and regulations. Those employed by the federal government may work as Internal Revenue Service agents or in financial management, financial institution examination, or budget analysis and administration.

Internal auditors verify the accuracy of their organization's internal records and check for mismanagement, waste, or fraud. Internal auditing is an increasingly important area of accounting and auditing. Internal auditors examine and evaluate their firms' financial and information systems, management procedures, and internal controls to ensure that records are accurate and controls are adequate to protect against fraud and waste. They also review company operations, evaluating their efficiency; effectiveness; and compliance with corporate policies and procedures, laws, and government regulations. There are many types of highly specialized auditors, such as electronic data-processing, environmental, engineering, legal, insurance premium, bank, and health care auditors. As computer systems make information timelier, internal auditors help managers to base their decisions on actual data rather than personal observation. Internal auditors also may recommend controls for their organization's computer system to ensure the reliability of the system and the integrity of the data.

Computers are rapidly changing the nature of the work of most accountants and auditors. With the aid of special software packages, accountants summarize transactions in standard formats used by financial records and organize data in special formats employed in financial analysis. These accounting packages greatly reduce the amount of tedious manual work associated with data management and recordkeeping. Computers enable accountants and auditors to be more mobile and to use their clients' computer systems to extract information from databases and the Internet. As a result, a growing number of accountants and auditors with extensive computer skills are specializing in correcting problems with software or in developing software to meet unique data management and analytical needs. Accountants also are beginning to perform more technical duties, such as implementing, controlling, and auditing systems and networks, developing technology plans, and analyzing and devising budgets.

Increasingly, accountants also are assuming the role of a personal financial advisor. They not only provide clients with accounting and tax help, but also help them develop personal budgets, manage assets and investments, plan for retirement, and recognize and reduce their exposure to risks. This role is a response to clients' demands for a single trustworthy individual or firm to meet all of their financial needs. However, accountants are restricted from providing these services to clients whose financial statements they also prepare. (See the description of financial analysts and personal financial advisors elsewhere in this book.)

Working Conditions

Most accountants and auditors work in a typical office setting. Self-employed accountants may be able to do part of their work at home. Accountants and auditors employed by public accounting firms and government agencies may travel frequently to perform audits at branches of their firm, clients' places of business, or government facilities.

Most accountants and auditors generally work a standard 40-hour week, but many work longer hours, particularly if they are self-employed and have numerous clients. Tax specialists often work long hours during the tax season.

Training, Other Qualifications, and Advancement

Most accountant and auditor positions require at least a bachelor's degree in accounting or a related field. Beginning accounting and auditing positions in the federal government, for example, usually require 4 years of college (including 24 semester hours in accounting or auditing) or an equivalent combination of education and experience. Some employers prefer applicants with a master's degree in accounting or with a master's degree in business administration with a concentration in accounting.

Previous experience in accounting or auditing can help an applicant get a job. Many colleges offer students an opportunity to gain experience through summer or part-time internship programs conducted by public accounting or business firms. In addition, practical knowledge of computers and their applications in accounting and internal auditing is a great asset for jobseekers in the accounting field.

Professional recognition through certification or licensure provides a distinct advantage in the job market. CPAs are licensed by a state board of accountancy. The vast majority of states require CPA can-

didates to be college graduates, but a few states substitute a number of years of public accounting experience for a college degree.

As of early 2005, on the basis of recommendations made by the American Institute of Certified Public Accountants (AICPA), 42 states and the District of Columbia required CPA candidates to complete 150 semester hours of college coursework—an additional 30 hours beyond the usual 4-year bachelor's degree. Another five states have adopted similar legislation that will become effective between 2006 and 2009. Colorado, Delaware, New Hampshire, and Vermont are the only states that do not require 150 semester hours. In response to this trend, many schools have altered their curricula accordingly, with most programs offering master's degrees as part of the 150 hours, so prospective accounting majors should carefully research accounting curricula and the requirements of any states in which they hope to become licensed.

All states use the four part Uniform CPA Examination prepared by the AICPA. The 2-day CPA examination is rigorous, and only about one-quarter of those who take it each year pass every part they attempt. Candidates are not required to pass all four parts at once, but most states require candidates to pass at least two parts for partial credit and to complete all four sections within a certain period. The CPA exam is now computerized and is offered quarterly at various testing centers throughout the United States. Most states also require applicants for a CPA certificate to have some accounting experience.

The AICPA also offers members with valid CPA certificates the option to receive any or all of the Accredited in Business Valuation (ABV), Certified Information Technology Professional (CITP), or Personal Financial Specialist (PFS) designations. CPAs with these designations may claim a certain level of expertise in the nontraditional areas in which accountants are practicing ever more frequently. The ABV designation requires a written exam as well as the completion of a minimum of 10 business valuation projects that demonstrate a candidate's experience and competence. The CITP requires payment of a fee, a written statement of intent, and the achievement of a set number of points awarded for business experience and education. Those who do not meet the required number of points may substitute a written exam. Candidates for the PFS designation also must achieve a certain level of points, based on experience and education, and must pass a written exam and submit references.

Nearly all states require CPAs and other public accountants to complete a certain number of hours of continuing professional education before their licenses can be renewed. The professional associations representing accountants sponsor numerous courses, seminars, group study programs, and other forms of continuing education.

Accountants and auditors also can seek to obtain other forms of credentials from professional societies on a voluntary basis. Voluntary certification can attest to professional competence in a specialized field of accounting and auditing. It also can certify that a recognized level of professional competence has been achieved by accountants and auditors who have acquired some skills on the job without the formal education or public accounting work experience needed to meet the rigorous standards required to take the CPA examination.

The Institute of Management Accountants (IMA) confers the Certified Management Accountant (CMA) designation upon applicants who complete a bachelor's degree or who attain a minimum score or higher on specified graduate school entrance exams. Applicants, who must have worked at least 2 years in management accounting, also must pass a four-part examination, agree to meet continuing education requirements, and comply with standards of professional conduct. The CMA exam provides an in-depth measure of competence in areas such as financial statement analysis, working-capital policy, capital structure, valuation issues, and risk management. The CMA program is administered by the Institute of Certified Management Accountants, an affiliate of the IMA.

Graduates from accredited colleges and universities who have worked for 2 years as internal auditors and have passed a four-part examination may earn the Certified Internal Auditor (CIA) designation from the Institute of Internal Auditors (IIA). The IIA recently implemented three new specialty designations: Certification in Control Self-Assessment (CCSA), Certified Government Auditing Professional (CGAP), and Certified Financial Services Auditor (CFSA). Requirements are similar to those of the CIA. The Information Systems Audit and Control Association confers the Certified Information Systems Auditor (CISA) designation upon candidates who pass an examination and have 5 years of experience auditing information systems. Auditing or data-processing experience and a college education may be substituted for up to 2 years of work experience in this program. Accountants and auditors may hold multiple designations. For instance, an internal auditor might be a CPA, CIA, and CISA.

The Accreditation Council for Accountancy and Taxation, a satellite organization of the National Society of Public Accountants, confers four designations—Accredited Business Accountant (ABA), Accredited Tax Advisor (ATA), Accredited Tax Preparer (ATP), and Elder Care Specialist (ECS)—on accountants specializing in tax preparation for small and medium-sized businesses. Candidates for the ABA must pass an exam; candidates for the ATA, ATP, and ECS must complete the required coursework and pass an exam. Often, a practitioner will hold multiple licenses and designations.

The Association of Government Accountants grants the Certified Government Financial Manager (CGFM) designation for accountants, auditors, and other government financial personnel at the federal, state, and local levels. Candidates must have a minimum of a bachelor's degree, 24 hours of study in financial management, and 2 years' experience in government and must pass a series of three exams. The exams cover topics in governmental environment; governmental accounting, financial reporting, and budgeting; and financial management and control.

Persons planning a career in accounting should have an aptitude for mathematics and be able to analyze, compare, and interpret facts and figures quickly. They must be able to clearly communicate the results of their work to clients and managers both verbally and in writing. Accountants and auditors must be good at working with people as well as with business systems and computers. At a minimum, accountants should be familiar with basic accounting software packages. Because financial decisions are made on the basis of their statements and services, accountants and auditors should have high standards of integrity.

Capable accountants and auditors may advance rapidly; those having inadequate academic preparation may be assigned routine jobs and find promotion difficult. Many graduates of junior colleges or business or correspondence schools, as well as bookkeepers and accounting clerks who meet the education and experience requirements set by their employers, can obtain junior accounting positions and advance to positions with more responsibilities by demonstrating their accounting skills on the job.

Beginning public accountants usually start by assisting with work for several clients. They may advance to positions with more responsibility in 1 or 2 years and to senior positions within another few years. Those who excel may become supervisors, managers, or partners; open their own public accounting firm; or transfer to executive positions in management accounting or internal auditing in private firms.

Management accountants often start as cost accountants, junior internal auditors, or trainees for other accounting positions. As they rise through the organization, they may advance to accounting manager, chief cost accountant, budget director, or manager of internal auditing. Some become controllers, treasurers, financial vice presidents, chief financial officers, or corporation presidents. Many senior corporation executives have a background in accounting, internal auditing, or finance.

In general, public accountants, management accountants, and internal auditors have much occupational mobility. Practitioners often shift into management accounting or internal auditing from public accounting or between internal auditing and management accounting. It is less common for accountants and auditors to move from either management accounting or internal auditing into public accounting.

Employment

Accountants and auditors held about 1.2 million jobs in 2004. They worked throughout private industry and government, but 1 out of 4 wage and salary accountants worked for accounting, tax preparation, bookkeeping, and payroll services firms. Approximately 1 out of 10 accountants or auditors were self-employed.

Many accountants and auditors are unlicensed management accountants, internal auditors, or government accountants and auditors; however, a large number are licensed CPAs. Most accountants and auditors work in urban areas, where public accounting firms and central or regional offices of businesses are concentrated.

Some individuals with backgrounds in accounting and auditing are full-time college and university faculty; others teach part time while working as self-employed accountants or as accountants for private industry or government. (See teachers—postsecondary elsewhere in this book.)

Job Outlook

Employment of accountants and auditors is expected to grow faster than the average for all occupations through the year 2014. An increase in the number of businesses, changing financial laws and regulations, and increased scrutiny of company finances will drive growth. In addition to openings resulting from growth, the need to replace accountants and auditors who retire or transfer to other occupations will produce numerous job openings in this large occupation.

As the economy grows, the number of business establishments will increase, requiring more accountants and auditors to set up books, prepare taxes, and provide management advice. As these businesses grow, the volume and complexity of information developed by accountants and auditors regarding costs, expenditures, and taxes will increase as well. An increased need for accountants and auditors will arise from changes in legislation related to taxes, financial reporting standards, business investments, mergers, and other financial events. The growth of international business also has led to more demand for accounting expertise and services related to international trade and accounting rules as well as to international mergers and acquisitions. These trends should create more jobs for accountants and auditors.

As a result of accounting scandals at several large corporate companies, Congress passed legislation in an effort to curb corporate accounting fraud. This legislation requires public companies to maintain well-functioning internal controls to ensure the accuracy and reliability of their financial reporting. It also holds the company's chief executive personally responsible for falsely reporting financial information.

These changes should lead to increased scrutiny of company finances and accounting procedures and should create opportunities for accountants and auditors, particularly CPAs, to audit financial records more thoroughly. In order to ensure that finances comply with the law before public accountants conduct audits, management accountants and internal auditors increasingly will be needed to discover and eliminate fraud. Also, in an effort to make government agencies more efficient and accountable, demand for government accountants should increase.

Increased awareness of financial crimes such as embezzlement, bribery, and securities fraud will increase the demand for forensic accountants to detect illegal financial activity by individuals, companies, and organized crime rings. Computer technology has made these crimes easier to commit, and they are on the rise. At the same time, the development of new computer software and electronic surveillance technology has made tracking down financial criminals easier, thus increasing the ease with which, and likelihood that, forensic accountants will discover their crimes. As success rates of investigations grow, demand also will grow for forensic accountants.

The changing role of accountants and auditors also will spur job growth, although this growth will be limited as a result of financial scandals. In response to demand, some accountants were offering more financial management and consulting services as they assumed a greater advisory role and developed more sophisticated accounting systems. Because federal legislation now prohibits accountants from providing nontraditional services to clients whose books they audit, opportunities for accountants to offer such services could be limited. However, accountants will still be able to advise on other financial matters for clients that are not publicly traded companies and for nonaudit clients, but growth in these areas will be slower than in the past. Also, due to the increasing popularity of tax preparation firms and computer software, accountants will shift away from tax preparation. As computer programs continue to simplify some accounting-related tasks, clerical staff will increasingly handle many routine calculations.

Overall, job opportunities for accountants and auditors should be favorable. After most states instituted the 150-hour rule for CPAs, enrollment in accounting programs declined; however, enrollment is slowly beginning to grow again as more students become attracted to the profession because of the attention from the accounting scandals. Those who earn a CPA should have excellent job prospects. However, many accounting graduates are instead pursuing other certifications, such as the CMA and CIA, so job prospects may not be as favorable in management accounting and internal auditing as in public accounting. Regardless of specialty, accountants and auditors who have earned professional recognition through certification or licensure should have the best job prospects. Applicants with a master's degree in accounting, or a master's degree in business administration with a concentration in accounting, also will have an advantage. In the aftermath of the accounting scandals, professional certification is even more important in order to ensure that accountants' credentials and ethics are sound.

Proficiency in accounting and auditing computer software or expertise in specialized areas such as international business, specific industries, or current legislation may be helpful in landing certain accounting and auditing jobs. In addition, employers increasingly are seeking applicants with strong interpersonal and communication skills. Because many accountants work on teams with others from different backgrounds, they must be able to communicate accounting and financial information clearly and concisely. Regardless of one's qualifications, however, competition will remain keen for the most prestigious jobs in major accounting and business firms.

Earnings

Median annual wage and salary earnings of accountants and auditors were $50,770 in May 2004. The middle half of the occupation earned between $39,890 and $66,900. The top 10 percent of accountants and auditors earned more than $88,610, and the bottom 10 percent earned less than $32,320. In May 2004, median annual earnings in the industries employing the largest numbers of accountants and auditors were as follows:

Federal executive branch and United States Postal Service	$56,900
Accounting, tax preparation, bookkeeping, and payroll services	53,870
Management of companies and enterprises	52,260
Local government	47,440
State government	43,400

According to a salary survey conducted by the National Association of Colleges and Employers, bachelor's degree candidates in accounting received starting offers averaging $43,269 a year in 2005; master's degree candidates in accounting were offered $46,251 initially.

According to a 2005 salary survey conducted by Robert Half International, a staffing services firm specializing in accounting and finance, accountants and auditors with up to 1 year of experience earned between $28,250 and $45,000 a year. Those with 1 to 3 years of experience earned between $33,000 and $52,000. Senior accountants and auditors earned between $40,750 and $69,750, managers between $48,000 and $90,000, and directors of accounting and auditing between $64,750 and $200,750. The variation in salaries reflects differences in size of firm, location, level of education, and professional credentials.

In the federal government, the starting annual salary for junior accountants and auditors was $24,677 in 2005. Candidates who had a superior academic record might start at $30,567, while applicants with a master's degree or 2 years of professional experience usually began at $37,390. Beginning salaries were slightly higher in selected areas where the prevailing local pay level was higher. Accountants employed by the federal government in nonsupervisory, supervisory, and managerial positions averaged $74,907 a year in 2005; auditors averaged $78,890.

Related Occupations

Accountants and auditors design internal control systems and analyze financial data. Others for whom training in accounting is valuable include budget analysts; cost estimators; loan officers; financial analysts and personal financial advisors; tax examiners, collectors, and revenue agents; bill and account collectors; and bookkeeping, accounting, and auditing clerks. Recently, accountants have assumed the role of management analysts and are involved in the design, implementation, and maintenance of accounting software systems. Others who perform similar work include computer programmers, computer software engineers, and computer support specialists and systems administrators.

Sources of Additional Information

Information on accredited accounting programs can be obtained from

▸ AACSB International—Association to Advance Collegiate Schools of Business, 777 South Harbour Island Blvd., Suite 750, Tampa FL 33602-5730. Internet: http://www.aacsb.edu/accreditation/AccreditedMembers.asp

Information about careers in certified public accounting and CPA standards and examinations may be obtained from

▸ American Institute of Certified Public Accountants, 1211 Avenue of the Americas, New York, NY 10036. Internet: http://www.aicpa.org

Information on CPA licensure requirements by state may be obtained from

▸ National Association of State Boards of Accountancy, 150 Fourth Ave. North, Suite 700, Nashville, TN 37219-2417. Internet: http://www.nasba.org

Information on careers in management accounting and the CMA designation may be obtained from

▸ Institute of Management Accountants, 10 Paragon Dr., Montvale, NJ 07645-1718. Internet: http://www.imanet.org

Information on the Accredited in Accountancy, Accredited Business Accountant, Accredited Tax Advisor, or Accredited Tax Preparer designation may be obtained from

▸ Accreditation Council for Accountancy and Taxation, 1010 North Fairfax St., Alexandria, VA 22314-1574 Internet: http://www.acatcredentials.org

Information on careers in internal auditing and the CIA designation may be obtained from

▸ The Institute of Internal Auditors, 247 Maitland Ave., Altamonte Springs, FL 32701-4201. Internet: http://www.theiia.org

Information on careers in information systems auditing and the CISA designation may be obtained from

▸ Information Systems Audit and Control Association, 3701 Algonquin Rd., Suite 1010, Rolling Meadows, IL 60008. Internet: http://www.isaca.org

Information on careers in government accounting and the CGFM designation may be obtained from

▸ Association of Government Accountants, 2208 Mount Vernon Ave., Alexandria, VA 22301. Internet: http://www.agacgfm.org

Information on obtaining positions as an accountant or auditor with the federal government is available from the Office of Personnel Management through USAJOBS, the federal government's official employment information system. This resource for locating and applying for job opportunities can be accessed through the Internet at http://www.usajobs.opm.gov or through an interactive voice response telephone system at (703) 724-1850 or TDD (978) 461-8404. These numbers are not toll free, and charges may result.

Agricultural and Food Scientists

(O*NET 19-1011.00, 19-1012.00, 19-1013.01, and 19-1013.02)

Significant Points

■ About 1 in 4 agricultural and food scientists work for federal, state, or local governments.

■ A bachelor's degree in agricultural science is sufficient for some jobs in applied research; a master's or Ph.D. degree is required for basic research or teaching.

■ Over 1 in 3 agricultural and food scientists are self-employed.

Nature of the Work

The work of agricultural and food scientists plays an important part in maintaining the nation's food supply by ensuring agricultural productivity and the safety of the food supply. Agricultural scientists study farm crops and animals and develop ways of improving their quantity and quality. They look for ways to improve crop yield with less labor, control pests and weeds more safely and effectively, and conserve soil and water. They research methods of converting raw agricultural commodities into attractive and healthy food products for consumers.

Agricultural science is closely related to biological science, and agricultural scientists use the principles of biology, chemistry, physics, mathematics, and other sciences to solve problems in agriculture. They often work with biological scientists on basic biological research and on applying to agriculture the advances in knowledge brought about by biotechnology.

In the past two decades, rapid advances in basic biological knowledge related to genetics spurred growth in the field of biotechnology. Some agricultural and food scientists use this technology to manipulate the genetic material of plants and crops, attempting to make organisms more productive or resistant to disease. These advances in biotechnology have opened up research opportunities in many areas of agricultural and food science, including commercial applications in agriculture, environmental remediation, and the food industry. Another emerging technology expected to affect agriculture is nanotechnology—a future molecular manufacturing technology which promises to revolutionize methods of manufacturing and distribution in many industries.

Many agricultural scientists work in basic or applied research and development. Others manage or administer research and development programs or manage marketing or production operations in companies that produce food products or agricultural chemicals, supplies, and machinery. Some agricultural scientists are consultants to business firms, private clients, or government.

Depending on the agricultural or food scientist's area of specialization, the nature of the work performed varies.

Food science. Food scientists and technologists usually work in the food processing industry, universities, or the federal government and help to meet consumer demand for food products that are healthful, safe, palatable, and convenient. To do this, they use their knowledge of chemistry, physics, engineering, microbiology, biotechnology, and other sciences to develop new or better ways of preserving, processing, packaging, storing, and delivering foods. Some food scientists engage in basic research, discovering new food sources; analyzing food content to determine levels of vitamins, fat, sugar, or protein; or searching for substitutes for harmful or undesirable additives, such as nitrites. They also develop ways to process, preserve, package, or store food according to industry and government regulations. Traditional food processing research into functions involving baking, blanching, canning, drying, evaporation, and pasteurization will continue to be conducted and will find new applications. Other food scientists enforce government regulations, inspecting food processing areas and ensuring that sanitation, safety, quality, and waste management standards are met. Food technologists generally work in product development, applying the findings from food science research to the selection, preservation, processing, packaging, distribution, and use of safe, nutritious, and wholesome food.

Plant science. Agronomy, crop science, entomology, and plant breeding are included in plant science. Scientists in these disciplines study plants and their growth in soils, helping producers of food, feed, and fiber crops to continue to feed a growing population while conserving natural resources and maintaining the environment. Agronomists and crop scientists not only help increase productivity, but also study ways to improve the nutritional value of crops and the quality of seed, often through biotechnology. Some crop scientists study the breeding, physiology, and management of crops and use genetic engineering to develop crops resistant to pests and drought. Entomologists conduct research to develop new technologies to control or eliminate pests in infested areas and to prevent the spread of harmful pests to new areas, as well as technologies that are compatible with the environment. They also conduct research or engage in oversight activities aimed at halting the spread of insect-borne disease.

Soil science. Soil scientists study the chemical, physical, biological, and mineralogical composition of soils as they relate to plant or crop growth. They also study the responses of various soil types to fertilizers, tillage practices, and crop rotation. Many soil scientists who work for the federal government conduct soil surveys, classifying and mapping soils. They provide information and recommendations to farmers and other landowners regarding the best use of land, plant growth, and methods to avoid or correct problems such as erosion. They may also consult with engineers and other technical personnel working on construction projects about the effects of, and solutions to, soil problems. Because soil science is closely related to environmental science, persons trained in soil science also apply their knowledge to ensure environmental quality and effective land use.

Animal science. Animal scientists work to develop better, more efficient ways of producing and processing meat, poultry, eggs, and milk. Dairy scientists, poultry scientists, animal breeders, and other scientists in related fields study the genetics, nutrition, reproduction, growth, and development of domestic farm animals. Some animal scientists inspect and grade livestock food products, purchase livestock, or work in technical sales or marketing. As extension agents or consultants, animal scientists advise agricultural producers on how to upgrade animal housing facilities properly, lower mortality rates, handle waste matter, or increase production of animal products such as milk or eggs.

Working Conditions

Agricultural scientists involved in management or basic research tend to work regular hours in offices and laboratories. The work environment for those engaged in applied research or product development varies, depending on the discipline of agricultural science and on the type of employer. For example, food scientists in private industry may work in test kitchens while investigating new processing techniques. Animal scientists working for federal, state, or university research stations may spend part of their time at dairies, farrowing houses, feedlots, or farm animal facilities or outdoors conducting research associated with livestock. Soil and crop scientists also spend time outdoors conducting research on farms and agricultural research stations. Entomologists work in laboratories, insectories, or agricultural research stations and also may spend time outdoors studying or collecting insects in their natural habitat.

Training, Other Qualifications, and Advancement

Training requirements for agricultural scientists depend on their specialty and on the type of work they perform. A bachelor's degree in agricultural science is sufficient for some jobs in applied research or for assisting in basic research, but a master's or doctoral degree is required for basic research. A Ph.D. in agricultural science usually is needed for college teaching and for advancement to administrative research positions. Degrees in related sciences such as biology, chemistry, or physics or in related engineering specialties also may qualify persons for some agricultural science jobs.

All states have a land-grant college that offers agricultural science degrees. Many other colleges and universities also offer agricultural science degrees or some agricultural science courses. However, not every school offers all specialties. A typical undergraduate agricultural science curriculum includes communications, mathematics, economics, business, and physical and life sciences courses in addition to a wide variety of technical agricultural science courses. For prospective animal scientists, these technical agricultural science courses might include animal breeding, reproductive physiology,

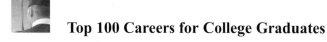

nutrition, and meats and muscle biology. Graduate students typically specialize in a subfield of agricultural science, such as animal breeding and genetics, crop science, or horticulture science, depending on their interest and the kind of work they wish to do. For example, those interested in doing genetic and biotechnological research in the food industry need to develop a strong background in life and physical sciences, such as cell and molecular biology, microbiology, and inorganic and organic chemistry. However, students normally need not specialize at the undergraduate level. In fact, undergraduates who are broadly trained have greater flexibility when changing jobs than if they had narrowly defined their interests.

Students preparing as food scientists take courses such as food chemistry, food analysis, food microbiology, food engineering, and food processing operations. Those preparing as crop or soil scientists take courses in plant pathology, soil chemistry, entomology, plant physiology, and biochemistry, among others. Advanced degree programs include classroom and fieldwork, laboratory research, and a thesis or dissertation based on independent research.

Agricultural and food scientists should be able to work independently or as part of a team and be able to communicate clearly and concisely, both orally and in writing. Most of these scientists also need an understanding of basic business principles and the ability to apply basic statistical techniques. Employers increasingly prefer job applicants who are able to apply computer skills to determine solutions to problems, to collect and analyze data, and to control various processes.

The American Society of Agronomy offers certification programs in crop science, agronomy, crop advising, soil science, plant pathology, and weed science. To become certified, applicants must pass designated examinations and have at least 2 years of experience with at least a bachelor's degree in agriculture or 4 years of experience with no degree. To become a certified crop advisor, however, candidates do not need a degree.

Agricultural scientists who have advanced degrees usually begin in research or teaching. With experience, they may advance to jobs such as supervisors of research programs or managers of other agriculture-related activities.

Employment

Agricultural and food scientists held about 30,000 jobs in 2004. In addition, several thousand persons held agricultural science faculty positions in colleges and universities. (See the description of teachers—postsecondary elsewhere in this book.)

About 1 in 4 salaried agricultural and food scientists worked for federal, state, or local governments. One out of 7 worked for state governments at state agricultural colleges or agricultural research stations. Another 1 out of 10 worked for the federal government in 2004, mostly in the U.S. Department of Agriculture. Some worked for agricultural service companies; others worked for commercial research and development laboratories, seed companies, pharmaceutical companies, wholesale distributors, and food products companies. About 10,000 agricultural scientists were self-employed in 2004, mainly as consultants.

Job Outlook

Employment of agricultural and food scientists is expected to grow about as fast as average for all occupations through 2014. Past agricultural research has resulted in the development of higher-yielding crops, crops with better resistance to pests and plant pathogens, and chemically based fertilizers and pesticides. Research is still necessary, particularly as insects and diseases continue to adapt to pesticides and as soil fertility and water quality continue to need improvement, resulting in job opportunities in biotechnology. Agricultural scientists are using new avenues of research in biotechnology to develop plants and food crops that require less fertilizer, fewer pesticides and herbicides, and even less water for growth. Emerging biotechnologies and nanotechnologies will play an increasingly larger role in creating more plentiful global food supplies.

Biotechnological research will continue to offer possibilities for the development of new food products. This research will allow agricultural and food scientists to develop techniques to detect and control food pathogens and should lead to better understanding of other infectious agents in foods.

Agricultural scientists will be needed to balance increased agricultural output with protection and preservation of soil, water, and ecosystems. They will increasingly encourage the practice of "sustainable agriculture" by developing and implementing plans to manage pests, crops, soil fertility and erosion, and animal waste in ways that reduce the use of harmful chemicals and do little damage to farms and the natural environment.

Further studies at scientific research and development services firms will result in more job opportunities for food scientists and technologists. This research will be stimulated by a heightened public focus on diet, health, changes in food safety, and biosecurity—preventing the introduction of infectious agents such as foot-and-mouth disease into a herd of animals. Increasing demand for these workers also will stem from issues such as a growing world population; availability and cost of usable water; shrinking natural resources, including the loss of arable land; and deforestation, environmental pollution, and climate change.

Graduates with a bachelor's degree should find work in a variety of fields, mostly in the private sector, although many of the positions may be related to agricultural or food science rather than as an agricultural or food scientist. A bachelor's degree in agricultural science is useful for managerial jobs in businesses that deal with ranchers and farmers, such as feed, fertilizer, seed, and farm equipment manufacturers; retailers or wholesalers; and farm credit institutions. In some cases, persons with a 4-year degree can provide consulting services or work in sales and marketing—promoting high-demand products such as organic foods. Bachelor's degree holders also can work in some applied research and product development positions under the guidance of a Ph.D. scientist, but usually only in certain subfields, such as food science and technology. The federal government hires bachelor's degree holders to work as soil scientists. Four-year degrees also may help persons enter occupations such as farmer or farm or ranch manager, cooperative extension service agent, agricultural products inspector, or purchasing or sales agent for agricultural commodity or farm supply companies.

Opportunities may be better for those with a master's degree, particularly for graduates seeking applied research positions in a laboratory. Master's degree candidates also can seek to become a certified crop advisor, helping farmers better manage their crops. Those with a Ph.D. in agricultural and food science will experience the best opportunities, especially in basic research and teaching positions at colleges and universities as retirements of faculty are expected to accelerate during the projection period.

Fewer opportunities for agricultural and food scientists are expected in the federal government, mostly because of budgetary cutbacks at the U.S. Department of Agriculture.

Employment of agricultural and food scientists is relatively stable during periods of economic recession. Layoffs are less likely among agricultural and food scientists than in some other occupations because food is a staple item and its demand fluctuates very little with economic activity.

Earnings

Median annual earnings of food scientists and technologists were $50,840 in May 2004. The middle 50 percent earned between $36,450 and $72,510. The lowest 10 percent earned less than $28,410, and the highest 10 percent earned more than $91,300. Median annual earnings of soil and plant scientists were $51,200 in May 2004. The middle 50 percent earned between $37,890 and $69,120. The lowest 10 percent earned less than $30,660, and the highest 10 percent earned more than $88,840. In May 2004, median annual earnings of animal scientists were $49,920.

The average federal salary for employees in nonsupervisory, supervisory, and managerial positions in 2005 was $87,025 in animal science and $73,573 in agronomy.

According to the National Association of Colleges and Employers, beginning salary offers in 2005 for graduates with a bachelor's degree in animal sciences averaged $30,614 a year; plant sciences, $31,649 a year; and in other agricultural sciences, $36,189 a year.

Related Occupations

The work of agricultural scientists is closely related to that of other scientists, including biological scientists, chemists, and conservation scientists and foresters. It also is related to the work of managers of agricultural production, such as farmers, ranchers, and agricultural managers. Certain specialties of agricultural science also are related to other occupations. For example, the work of animal scientists is related to the work of veterinarians, and horticulturists perform duties similar to duties of landscape architects.

Sources of Additional Information

Agricultural career brochures are available from

▸ American Society of Agronomy, Crop Science Society of America, Soil Science Society of America, 677 S. Segoe Rd., Madison, WI 53711-1086. Internet: http://www.agronomy.org

Information on careers in agricultural science is available from

▸ Food and Agricultural Careers for Tomorrow, Purdue University, 1140 Agricultural Administration Bldg., West Lafayette, IN 47907-1140.

Information on acquiring a job as an agricultural scientist with the federal government is available from the Office of Personnel Management through USAJOBS, the federal government's official employment information system. This resource for locating and applying for job opportunities can be accessed through the Internet at http://www.usajobs.opm.gov or through an interactive voice response telephone system at (703) 724-1850 or TDD (978) 461-8404. These numbers are not toll free, and charges may result.

Architects, Except Landscape and Naval

(O*NET 17-1011.00)

Significant Points

■ About 1 in 4 architects are self-employed—more than three times the proportion for all professional and related occupations.

■ Licensing requirements include a professional degree in architecture, 3 years of practical work training, and passing all divisions of the Architect Registration Examination.

■ Architecture graduates may face competition, especially for jobs in the most prestigious firms; opportunities will be best for those with experience working for a firm while still in school and for those with knowledge of computer-aided design and drafting technology.

Nature of the Work

People need places in which to live, work, play, learn, worship, meet, govern, shop, and eat. These places may be private or public; indoors or outdoors; or rooms, buildings, or complexes, and together, they make up neighborhoods, towns, suburbs, and cities. *Architects*—licensed professionals trained in the art and science of building design—transform these needs into concepts and then develop the concepts into images and plans of buildings that can be constructed by others.

Architects design the overall aesthetic and look of buildings and other structures, but the design of a building involves far more than its appearance. Buildings also must be functional, safe, and economical and must suit the needs of the people who use them. Architects consider all these factors when they design buildings and other structures.

Architects provide professional services to individuals and organizations planning a construction project. They may be involved in all phases of development, from the initial discussion with the client through the entire construction process. Their duties require specific skills—designing, engineering, managing, supervising, and communicating with clients and builders. Architects spend a great deal of time explaining their ideas to clients, construction contractors, and others. Successful architects must be able to communicate their unique vision persuasively.

The architect and client discuss the objectives, requirements, and budget of a project. In some cases, architects provide various predesign services—conducting feasibility and environmental impact studies, selecting a site, or specifying the requirements the design must meet. For example, they may determine space requirements by researching the numbers and types of potential users of a building. The architect then prepares drawings and a report presenting ideas for the client to review.

After discussing and agreeing on the initial proposal, architects develop final construction plans that show the building's appearance and details for its construction. Accompanying these plans are drawings of the structural system; air-conditioning, heating, and ventilating systems; electrical systems; communications systems; plumbing; and, possibly, site and landscape plans. The plans also specify the building materials and, in some cases, the interior furnishings. In developing designs, architects follow building codes; zoning laws; fire regulations; and other ordinances, such as those requiring easy access by disabled persons. Throughout the planning stage, they make necessary changes. Computer-aided design and drafting (CADD) technology has replaced traditional paper and pencil as the most common method for creating design and construction drawings. Continual revision of plans on the basis of client needs and budget constraints is often necessary.

Architects may also assist clients in obtaining construction bids, selecting contractors, and negotiating construction contracts. As construction proceeds, they may visit building sites to make sure that contractors follow the design, adhere to the schedule, use the specified materials, and meet work quality standards. The job is not complete until all construction is finished, required tests are conducted, and construction costs are paid. Sometimes, architects also provide postconstruction services, such as facilities management. They advise on energy efficiency measures, evaluate how well the building design adapts to the needs of occupants, and make necessary improvements.

Architects design a wide variety of buildings, such as office and apartment buildings, schools, churches, factories, hospitals, houses, and airport terminals. They also design complexes such as urban centers, college campuses, industrial parks, and entire communities. In addition, they may advise on the selection of building sites, prepare cost analysis and land-use studies, and do long-range planning for land development.

Architects sometimes specialize in one phase of work. Some specialize in the design of one type of building—for example, hospitals, schools, or housing. Others focus on planning and predesign services or construction management and do minimal design work. They often work with engineers, urban planners, interior designers, landscape architects, and other professionals. In fact, architects spend a great deal of their time coordinating information from, and the work of, others engaged in the same project. Many architects—particularly at larger firms—use the Internet and e-mail to update designs and communicate changes efficiently. Architects also use the Internet to research product specifications and government regulations.

Working Conditions

Architects usually work in a comfortable environment. Most of their time is spent in offices consulting with clients, developing reports and drawings, and working with other architects and engineers. However, they often visit construction sites to review the progress of projects. Although most architects work approximately 40 hours per week, they often have to work nights and weekends to meet deadlines.

Training, Other Qualifications, and Advancement

All states and the District of Columbia require individuals to be licensed (registered) before they may call themselves architects and contract to provide architectural services. During this time between graduation and becoming licensed, architecture school graduates generally work in the field under supervision of a licensed architect who takes legal responsibility for all work. Licensing requirements include a professional degree in architecture, a period of practical training or internship, and a passing score on all divisions of the Architect Registration Examination (ARE).

In most states, the professional degree in architecture must be from one of the 113 schools of architecture that have degree programs accredited by the National Architectural Accrediting Board (NAAB). However, state architectural registration boards set their own standards, so graduation from a non-NAAB-accredited program may meet the educational requirement for licensing in a few states. Three types of professional degrees in architecture are available through colleges and universities. The majority of all architectural degrees are from 5-year Bachelor of Architecture programs, intended for students entering university-level studies from high school or with no previous architectural training. In addition, a number of schools offer a 2-year Master of Architecture program for students with a preprofessional undergraduate degree in architecture or a related area or a 3- or 4-year Master of Architecture program for students with a degree in another discipline.

The choice of degree depends upon each individual's preference and educational background. Prospective architecture students should consider the available options before committing to a program. For example, although the 5-year Bachelor of Architecture program offers the fastest route to the professional degree, courses are specialized, and if the student does not complete the program, transferring to a program offered by another discipline may be difficult. A typical program includes courses in architectural history and theory, building design, structures, technology, construction methods, professional practice, math, physical sciences, and liberal arts. Central to most architectural programs is the design studio, where students put into practice the skills and concepts learned in the classroom. During the final semester of many programs, students devote their studio time to creating an architectural project from beginning to end, culminating in a three-dimensional model of their design.

Many schools of architecture also offer postprofessional degrees for those who already have a bachelor's or master's degree in architecture or other areas. Although graduate education beyond the professional degree is not required for practicing architects, it may be for research, teaching, and certain specialties.

Architects must be able to communicate their ideas visually to their clients. Artistic and drawing ability is helpful, but not essential, to such communication. More important are a visual orientation and the ability to conceptualize and understand spatial relationships. Good communication skills, the ability to work independently or as part of a team, and creativity are important qualities for anyone interested in becoming an architect. Computer literacy also is required for writing specifications, for two- and three-dimensional drafting, and for financial management. Knowledge of CADD is essential and has become a critical tool for architects. Most schools now teach students CADD programs and methods that adhere to the National CAD Standards.

All state architectural registration boards require architecture graduates to complete a training period—usually 3 years—before they may sit for the ARE, the third and final requirement for becoming licensed. Every state, with the exception of Arizona, has adopted the training standards established by the Intern Development Program, a branch of the American Institute of Architects and the National Council of Architectural Registration Boards (NCARB). These standards stipulate broad and diversified training under the supervision of a licensed architect over a 3-year period. Most new graduates complete their training period by working as interns at architectural firms. Some states allow a portion of the training to occur in the offices of related professionals, such as engineers or general contractors. Architecture students who complete internships in architectural firms while still in school can count some of that time toward the required 3-year training period.

Interns in architectural firms may assist in the design of one part of a project, help prepare architectural documents or drawings, build models, or prepare construction drawings on CADD. Interns also may research building codes and materials or write specifications for building materials, installation criteria, the quality of finishes, and other related details.

After completing their on-the-job training period, interns are eligible to sit for the ARE. The examination tests a candidate's knowledge, skills, and ability to provide the various services required in the design and construction of buildings. The test is broken down into 9 divisions consisting of either multiple-choice or graphical questions; states give candidates an eligibility period for completion of all divisions of the exam that varies by state. Candidates who pass the ARE and meet all standards established by their state board become licensed to practice in that state.

Most states require some form of continuing education to maintain a license, and many others are expected to adopt mandatory continuing education. Requirements vary by state, but usually involve the completion of a certain number of credits annually or biennially through workshops, formal university classes, conferences, self-study courses, or other sources.

A growing number of architects voluntarily seek certification by the NCARB, which can facilitate an individual's becoming licensed to practice in additional states. This practice is known as "reciprocity." Certification is awarded after independent verification of the candidate's educational transcripts, employment record, and professional references. Certification is the primary requirement for reciprocity of licensing among state boards that are NCARB members. In 2004, approximately one-third of all licensed architects had NCARB certification.

After becoming licensed and gaining experience, architects take on increasingly responsible duties, eventually managing entire projects. In large firms, architects may advance to supervisory or managerial positions. Some architects become partners in established firms, while others set up their own practices. Graduates with degrees in architecture also enter related fields, such as graphic, interior, or industrial design; urban planning; real estate development; civil engineering; and construction management.

Employment

Architects held about 129,000 jobs in 2004. Approximately 3 out of 5 jobs were in the architectural, engineering, and related services industry—mostly in architectural firms with fewer than five workers. A small number worked for residential and nonresidential building construction firms and for government agencies responsible for housing, community planning, or construction of government buildings, such as the U.S. Departments of Defense and Interior and the General Services Administration. About 1 in 4 architects were self-employed.

Job Outlook

Employment of architects is expected to grow about as fast as the average for all occupations through 2014. Besides employment growth, additional job openings will arise from the need to replace the many architects who are nearing retirement and others who transfer to other occupations or stop working for other reasons. Internship opportunities for new architectural students are expected to be good over the next decade, but more students are graduating with architectural degrees and some competition for entry-level jobs can be anticipated. Competition will be especially keen for jobs at the most prestigious architectural firms as prospective architects try to build their reputation. Prospective architects who have had internships while in school will have an advantage in obtaining intern positions after graduation.

Employment of architects is strongly tied to the activity of the construction industry. Strong growth is expected to come from nonresidential construction as demand for commercial space increases. Residential construction, buoyed by low interest rates, is also expected to grow as more and more people become homeowners. If interest rates rise significantly, this sector may see a falloff in home building.

Current demographic trends also support an increase in demand for architects. As the population of Sunbelt states continues to grow, the people living there will need new places to live and work. As the population continues to live longer and baby boomers begin to retire, there will be a need for more health care facilities, nursing homes, and retirement communities. In education, buildings at all levels are getting older and class sizes are getting larger. This will require many school districts and universities to build new facilities and renovate existing ones.

Some types of construction are sensitive to cyclical changes in the economy. Architects seeking design projects for office and retail construction will face especially strong competition for jobs or clients during recessions, and layoffs may ensue in less successful firms. Those involved in the design of institutional buildings, such as schools, hospitals, nursing homes, and correctional facilities, will be less affected by fluctuations in the economy. Residential construction makes up a small portion of work for architects, so major changes in the housing market would not be as significant as fluctuations in the nonresidential market.

Despite good overall job opportunities, some architects may not fare as well as others. The profession is geographically sensitive, and some parts of the nation may have fewer new building projects than others. Also, many firms specialize in specific buildings, such as hospitals or office towers, and demand for these buildings may vary by region. Architects may find it increasingly necessary to gain reciprocity in order to compete for the best jobs and projects in other states.

In recent years, some architecture firms have outsourced to architecture firms overseas the drafting of construction documents for large-scale commercial and residential projects. This trend is expected to continue and may have a negative impact on employment growth for lower-level architects and interns who would normally gain experience by producing these drawings. However, most firms will keep design services in-house, and opportunities will be best for those architects that are able to distinguish themselves from others with their creativity.

Earnings

Median annual earnings of wage and salary architects were $60,300 in May 2004. The middle 50 percent earned between $46,690 and $79,230. The lowest 10 percent earned less than $38,060, and the highest 10 percent earned more than $99,800. Those just starting their internships can expect to earn considerably less.

Earnings of partners in established architectural firms may fluctuate because of changing business conditions. Some architects may have difficulty establishing their own practices and may go through a period when their expenses are greater than their income, requiring substantial financial resources.

Related Occupations

Architects design buildings and related structures. Construction managers, like architects, also plan and coordinate activities concerned with the construction and maintenance of buildings and facilities. Others who engage in similar work are landscape architects; civil engineers; urban and regional planners; and designers, including interior designers, commercial and industrial designers, and graphic designers.

Sources of Additional Information

Information about education and careers in architecture can be obtained from

▸ The American Institute of Architects, 1735 New York Ave. NW, Washington, DC 20006. Internet: http://www.aia.org

▸ Intern Development Program, National Council of Architectural Registration Boards, Suite 1100K, 1801 K Street NW, Washington, D.C. 20006-1310. Internet: http://www.ncarb.org

Athletic Trainers

(O*NET 29-9091.00)

Significant Points

■ Job prospects should be good in the health care industry; however, competition is expected for positions with sports teams.

■ Long hours, sometimes including nights and weekends, are common.

■ About one-third of athletic trainers work in health care.

■ About 7 out of 10 athletic trainers have a master's or higher degree.

Nature of the Work

Athletic trainers help prevent and treat injuries for people of all ages. Their clients include everyone from professional athletes to industrial workers. Recognized by the American Medical Association as allied health professionals, athletic trainers specialize in the prevention, assessment, treatment, and rehabilitation of musculoskeletal injuries. Athletic trainers are often one of the first heath care providers on the scene when injuries occur and therefore must be able to recognize, evaluate, and assess injuries and provide immediate care when needed. They also are heavily involved in the rehabilitation and reconditioning of injuries.

Athletic trainers often help prevent injuries by advising on the proper use of equipment and applying protective or injury-preventive devices such as tape, bandages, and braces. Injury prevention also often includes educating people on what they should do to avoid putting themselves at risk for injuries. Athletic trainers should not be confused with fitness trainers or personal trainers, who are not health care workers but rather train people to become physically fit.

Athletic trainers work under the supervision of a licensed physician and in cooperation with other health care providers. The level of medical supervision varies depending upon the setting. Some athletic trainers meet with the team physician or consulting physician once or twice a week; others interact with a physician every day. The extent of the supervision ranges from discussing specific injuries and treatment options with a physician to performing evaluations and treatments as directed by a physician.

Athletic trainers also may have administrative responsibilities. These may include regular meetings with an athletic director or other administrative officer to deal with budgets, purchasing, policy implementation, and other business-related issues.

Working Conditions

The work of athletic trainers requires frequent interaction with others. This includes consulting with physicians as well as frequent contact with athletes and patients to discuss and administer treatments, rehabilitation programs, injury-preventive practices, and other health-related issues. Many athletic trainers work indoors most of the time; others, especially those in some sports-related jobs, spend much of their time working outdoors. The job also might require standing for long periods; working with medical equipment or machinery; and being able to walk, run, kneel, crouch, stoop, or crawl. Some travel may be required.

Schedules vary by work setting. Athletic trainers in nonsports settings generally have an established schedule with nights and weekends off; the number of hours differs by employer, but usually are about 40 to 50 hours per week. Trainers working in hospitals and clinics spend part of their time working at other locations on an outreach basis. Most commonly, those outreach programs include secondary schools, colleges, and commercial business locations. Athletic trainers in sports settings, however, deal with schedules that are longer and more variable. These trainers must be present for team practices and games, which often are on evenings and weekends, and their schedules can change on short notice when games and practices have to be rescheduled. As a result, athletic trainers in sports settings regularly may have to work 6 or 7 days per week, including late hours.

In high schools, athletic trainers who also teach may work at least 60 to 70 hours a week. In NCAA Division I colleges and universities, athletic trainers generally work with one team; when that team's sport is in season, working at least 50 to 60 hours a week is common. Athletic trainers in smaller colleges and universities often work with several teams and have teaching responsibilities. During the off-season, a 40-hour to 50-hour work week may be normal in most settings. Athletic trainers for professional sports teams generally work the most hours per week. During training camps, practices, and competitions, they may be required to work up to 12 hours a day.

There is some stress involved with being an athletic trainer, as there is with most health-related occupations. Athletic trainers are responsible for their clients' health and sometimes have to make quick decisions that could affect the health or career of their clients. Athletic trainers also can be affected by the pressure to win that is typical of competitive sports teams.

Training, Other Qualifications, and Advancement

A bachelor's degree from an accredited college or university is required for almost all jobs as an athletic trainer. In 2004, there were more than 300 accredited programs nationwide. Students in these programs are educated both in the classroom and in clinical settings. Formal education includes many science and health-related courses, such as human anatomy, physiology, nutrition, and biomechanics.

A bachelor's degree with a major in athletic training from an accredited program is part of the requirement for becoming certified by the Board of Certification (BOC). In addition, a successful candidate for board certification must pass an examination that includes written questions and practical applications. To retain certification, credential holders must continue taking medical-related courses and adhere to standards of practice. In the 43 states with athletic trainer licensure or registration or both in 2004, BOC certification was required.

According to the National Athletic Trainers Association, 70 percent of athletic trainers have a master's or doctoral degree. Athletic trainers

may need a master's or higher degree to be eligible for some positions, especially those in colleges and universities, and to increase their advancement opportunities. Because some positions in high schools involve teaching along with athletic trainer responsibilities, a teaching certificate or license could be required.

There are a number of ways in which athletic trainers can advance or move into related positions. Assistant athletic trainers may become head athletic trainers and, eventually, athletic directors. Athletic trainers might also enter a physician group practice and assume a management role. Some athletic trainers move into sales and marketing positions, using their athletic trainer expertise to sell medical and athletic equipment.

Because all athletic trainers deal directly with a variety of people, they need good social and communication skills. They should be able to manage difficult situations and the stress associated with them—for example, when disagreements arise with coaches, clients, or parents regarding suggested treatment. Athletic trainers also should be organized, be able to manage time wisely, be inquisitive, and have a strong desire to help people.

Employment

Athletic trainers held about 15,000 jobs in 2004 and are found in every part of the country. Most athletic trainer jobs are related to sports, although many also work in nonsports settings. About one-third of athletic trainers worked in health care, including jobs in hospitals, offices of physicians, and offices of other health practitioners. Another one-third were found in public and private educational services, primarily in colleges, universities, and high schools. About 20 percent worked in fitness and recreational sports centers.

Job Outlook

Employment of athletic trainers is expected to grow much faster than the average for all occupations through 2014. Job growth will be concentrated in health care industry settings, such as ambulatory heath care services and hospitals. Growth in sports-related positions will be somewhat slower, as most professional sports clubs and colleges, universities, and professional schools already have complete athletic training staffs. Job prospects should be good for people looking for a position in the health care industry. Athletic trainers looking for a position with a sports team, however, may face competition.

The demand for health care should grow dramatically as the result of advances in technology, increasing emphasis on preventive care, and an increasing number of older people who are more likely to need medical care. Athletic trainers will benefit from this expansion because they provide a cost-effective way to increase the number of health professionals in an office or other setting. Also, employers increasingly emphasize sports medicine, in which an immediate responder, such as an athletic trainer, is on site to help prevent injuries and provide immediate treatment for any injuries that do occur. Athletic trainers' increased licensure requirements and regulation has led to a greater acceptance of their role as qualified health care providers. As a result, third-party reimbursement is expected to continue to grow for athletic training services. As athletic trainers continue to expand their services, more employers are expected to use these workers to realize the cost savings that can be achieved by providing health care in-house. Settings outside the sports world, especially those that focus on health care, are expected to experience fast employment growth among athletic trainers over the next decade. Continuing efforts to have an athletic trainer in every high school reflect concern for student-athletes' health as well as efforts to provide more funding for schools and may lead to growth in the number of athletic trainers employed in high schools.

Turnover among athletic trainers is limited. When dealing with sports teams, there is a tendency to want to continue to work with the same coaches, administrators, and players when a good working relationship already exists. Because of relatively low worker turnover, the settings with the best job prospects will be the ones that are expected to grow most quickly, primarily positions in heath care settings. There will also be opportunities in elementary and secondary schools as more positions are created. Some of these positions also will require teaching responsibilities. There will be more competition for positions within colleges, universities, and professional schools as well as professional sports clubs. The occupation is expected to continue to change over the next decade, including more administrative responsibilities, adapting to new technology, and working with larger populations, and job seekers must be able to adapt to these changes.

Earnings

Most athletic trainers work in full-time positions and typically receive benefits. The salary of an athletic trainer depends on experience and job responsibilities and varies by job setting. Median annual earnings of athletic trainers were $33,940 in May 2004. The middle 50 percent earned between $27,140 and $42,380. The lowest 10 percent earned less than $20,770, while the top 10 percent earned more than $53,760. Also, many employers pay for some of the continuing education required of ATCs, although the amount covered varies from employer to employer.

Related Occupations

The American Medical Association recognizes athletic trainers as allied health professionals. They work under the direction of physicians and provide immediate care for injuries. Also, they provide education and advice on the prevention of injuries and work closely with injured patients to rehabilitate and recondition injuries, often through therapy. Other occupations that may require similar responsibilities include emergency medical technicians and paramedics, physical therapists, physician assistants, registered nurses, licensed practical and licensed vocational nurses, recreational therapists, occupational therapists, and respiratory therapists.

There also are opportunities for athletic trainers to join the military, although they would not be classified as an athletic trainer. Enlisted soldiers and officers who are athletic trainers are usually placed in another program in which their skills are useful, such as health educator or training specialist. (For information on military careers, see the description of job opportunities in the Armed Forces elsewhere in this book.)

Sources of Additional Information

For further information on careers in athletic training, contact

▸ National Athletic Trainers' Association, 2952 Stemmons Freeway, Dallas, TX 75247. Internet: http://www.nata.org

For further information on certification, contact

▸ Board of Certification, Inc., 4223 South 143rd Circle, Omaha, NE 68137. Internet: http://www.bocatc.org

Atmospheric Scientists

(O*NET 19-2021.00)

Significant Points

■ 4 in 10 atmospheric scientists work for the federal government, the largest employer of these workers.

■ A bachelor's degree in meteorology, or in a closely related field with courses in meteorology, is the minimum educational requirement; a master's degree is necessary for some positions, and a doctoral degree (Ph.D.) is required for most basic research positions.

■ Job opportunities are expected to be better in private industry than in the federal government; opportunities in broadcasting, however, are rare and highly competitive.

Nature of the Work

Atmospheric science is the study of the atmosphere—the blanket of air covering the Earth. *Atmospheric scientists*, commonly called *meteorologists*, study the atmosphere's physical characteristics, motions, and processes and the way in which these factors affect the rest of our environment. The best-known application of this knowledge is forecasting the weather. In addition to predicting the weather, atmospheric scientists attempt to identify and interpret climate trends, understand past weather, and analyze today's weather. Weather information and meteorological research are also applied in air-pollution control; agriculture; forestry; air and sea transportation; defense; and the study of possible trends in the Earth's climate, such as global warming, droughts, and ozone depletion.

Atmospheric scientists who forecast the weather, known professionally as *operational meteorologists*, are the largest group of specialists. They study information on air pressure, temperature, humidity, and wind velocity and they apply physical and mathematical relationships to make short-range and long-range weather forecasts. Their data come from weather satellites, radars, sensors, and stations in many parts of the world. Meteorologists use sophisticated computer models of the world's atmosphere to make long-term, short-term, and local-area forecasts. More accurate instruments for measuring and observing weather conditions, as well as high-speed computers to process and analyze weather data, have revolutionized weather forecasting. Using satellite data, climate theory, and sophisticated computer models of the world's atmosphere, meteorologists can more effectively interpret the results of these models to make local-area weather predictions. These forecasts inform not only the general public, but also those who need accurate weather information for both economic and safety reasons, such as the shipping, air transportation, agriculture, fishing, forestry, and utilities industries.

The use of weather balloons, launched a few times a day to measure wind, temperature, and humidity in the upper atmosphere, is currently supplemented by sophisticated atmospheric monitoring equipment that transmits data as frequently as every few minutes. Doppler radar, for example, can detect airflow patterns in violent storm systems—allowing forecasters to better predict thunderstorms, flash floods, tornadoes, and other hazardous winds and to monitor the direction and intensity of storms.

Some atmospheric scientists work in research. *Physical meteorologists*, for example, study the atmosphere's chemical and physical properties; the transmission of light, sound, and radio waves; and the transfer of energy in the atmosphere. They also study factors affecting the formation of clouds, rain, and snow; the dispersal of air pollutants over urban areas; and other weather phenomena, such as the mechanics of severe storms. *Synoptic meteorologists* develop new tools for weather forecasting, using computers and sophisticated mathematical models of atmospheric activity. *Climatologists* study climactic variations spanning hundreds or even millions of years. They also may collect, analyze, and interpret past records of wind, rainfall, sunshine, and temperature in specific areas or regions. Their studies are used to design buildings, plan heating and cooling systems, and aid in effective land use and agricultural production. Environmental problems, such as pollution and shortages of fresh water, have widened the scope of the meteorological profession. *Environmental meteorologists* study these problems and may evaluate and report on air quality for environmental impact statements. Other research meteorologists examine the most effective ways to control or diminish air pollution.

Working Conditions

Most weather stations operate around the clock, 7 days a week. Jobs in such facilities usually involve night, weekend, and holiday work, often with rotating shifts. During weather emergencies, such as hurricanes, operational meteorologists may work overtime. Operational meteorologists also are often under pressure to meet forecast deadlines. Weather stations are found everywhere—at airports, in or near cities, and in isolated and remote areas. Some atmospheric scientists also spend time observing weather conditions and collecting data from aircraft. Weather forecasters who work for radio or television stations broadcast their reports from station studios and may work evenings and weekends. Meteorologists in smaller weather offices often work alone; in larger ones, they work as part of a team. Meteorologists who are not involved in forecasting tasks work regular hours, usually in offices. Those who work for private consulting firms or for companies analyzing and monitoring emissions to improve air quality usually work with other scientists or engineers; fieldwork and travel may be common for these workers.

Training, Other Qualifications, and Advancement

A bachelor's degree in meteorology or atmospheric science, or in a closely related field with courses in meteorology, usually is the minimum educational requirement for an entry-level position as an atmospheric scientist.

The preferred educational requirement for entry-level meteorologists in the federal government is a bachelor's degree—not necessarily in meteorology—with at least 24 semester hours of meteorology courses, including 6 hours in the analysis and prediction of weather systems, 6 hours of atmospheric dynamics and thermodynamics, 3 hours of physical meteorology, and 2 hours of remote sensing of the atmosphere or instrumentation. Other required courses include 3 semester hours of ordinary differential equations, 6 hours of college physics, and at least 9 hours of courses appropriate for a physical science major—such as statistics, chemistry, physical oceanography, physical climatology, physical hydrology, radiative transfer, aeronomy, advanced thermodynamics, advanced electricity and magnetism, light and optics, and computer science. Sometimes, a combination of education and appropriate experience may be substituted for a degree.

Although positions in operational meteorology are available for those with only a bachelor's degree, obtaining a second bachelor's degree or a master's degree enhances employment opportunities, pay, and advancement potential. A master's degree usually is necessary for conducting applied research and development, and a Ph.D. is required for most basic research positions. Students planning on a career in research and development do not necessarily need to major in atmospheric science or meteorology as an undergraduate. In fact, a bachelor's degree in mathematics, physics, or engineering provides excellent preparation for graduate study in atmospheric science.

Because atmospheric science is a small field, relatively few colleges and universities offer degrees in meteorology or atmospheric science, although many departments of physics, earth science, geography, and geophysics offer atmospheric science and related courses. In 2005, the American Meteorological Society (AMS) approved approximately 100 undergraduate and graduate atmospheric science programs. Many of these programs combine the study of meteorology with another field, such as agriculture, hydrology, oceanography, engineering, or physics. For example, hydrometeorology is the blending of hydrology (the science of Earth's water) and meteorology and is the field concerned with the effect of precipitation on the hydrologic cycle and the environment.

Prospective students should make certain that courses required by the National Weather Service and other employers are offered at the college they are considering. Computer science courses, additional meteorology courses, a strong background in mathematics and physics, and good communication skills are important to prospective employers.

Students should also take courses in subjects that are most relevant to their desired area of specialization. For example, those who wish to become broadcast meteorologists for radio or television stations should develop excellent communication skills through courses in speech, journalism, and related fields. Students interested in air quality work should take courses in chemistry and supplement their technical training with coursework in policy or government affairs. Prospective meteorologists seeking opportunities at weather consulting firms should possess knowledge of business, statistics, and economics, as an increasing emphasis is being placed on long-range seasonal forecasting to assist businesses.

Beginning atmospheric scientists often do routine data collection, computation, or analysis and some basic forecasting. Entry-level operational meteorologists in the federal government usually are placed in intern positions for training and experience. During this period, they learn about the Weather Service's forecasting equipment and procedures and rotate to different offices to learn about various weather systems. After completing the training period, they are assigned to a permanent duty station. Experienced meteorologists may advance to supervisory or administrative jobs or may handle more complex forecasting jobs. After several years of experience, some meteorologists establish their own weather consulting services.

AMS offers professional certification of consulting meteorologists administered by a Board of Certified Consulting Meteorologists. Applicants must meet formal education requirements (but not necessarily have a college degree), pass an examination to demonstrate thorough meteorological knowledge, have a minimum of 5 years of experience or a combination of experience plus an advanced degree, and provide character references from fellow professionals. In addition, AMS also offers professional certification for broadcast meteorologists.

Employment

Atmospheric scientists held about 7,400 jobs in 2004. The federal government was the largest single employer of civilian meteorologists, accounting for about 2,900. The National Oceanic and Atmospheric Administration (NOAA) employed most federal meteorologists in National Weather Service stations throughout the nation; the remainder of NOAA's meteorologists worked mainly in research and development or management. The U.S. Department of Defense employed several hundred civilian meteorologists. Others worked for professional, scientific, and technical services firms, including private weather consulting services, radio and television broadcasting, air carriers, and state government.

Although several hundred people teach atmospheric science and related courses in college and university departments of meteorology or atmospheric science, physics, earth science, or geophysics, these individuals are classified as college or university faculty rather than atmospheric scientists. (See the description of teachers—postsecondary elsewhere in this book.)

In addition to civilian meteorologists, hundreds of Armed Forces members are involved in forecasting and other meteorological work. (See the description of job opportunities in the Armed Forces elsewhere in this book.)

Job Outlook

Employment of atmospheric scientists is projected to increase about as fast as average for all occupations through 2014. The National Weather Service has completed an extensive modernization of its weather forecasting equipment and finished all hiring of meteorologists needed to staff the upgraded stations, however. The Service has no plans to increase the number of weather stations or the number of meteorologists in existing stations. Employment of meteorologists in other federal agencies is expected to remain stable.

In private industry, on the other hand, job opportunities for atmospheric scientists are expected to be better than in the federal government over the 2004–2014 period. As research leads to continuing

improvements in weather forecasting, demand should grow for private weather consulting firms to provide more detailed information than has formerly been available, especially to climate-sensitive industries. Farmers; commodity investors; radio and television stations; and utilities, transportation, and construction firms can greatly benefit from additional weather information more closely targeted to their needs than the general information provided by the National Weather Service. Additionally, research on seasonal and other long-range forecasting is yielding positive results, which should spur demand for more atmospheric scientists to interpret these forecasts and advise climate-sensitive industries. However, because many customers for private weather services are in industries sensitive to fluctuations in the economy, the sales and growth of private weather services depend on the health of the economy.

There will continue to be demand for atmospheric scientists to analyze and monitor the dispersion of pollutants into the air to ensure compliance with federal environmental regulations, but related employment increases are expected to be small. Efforts toward making and improving global weather observations also could have a positive impact on employment. Opportunities in broadcasting are rare and highly competitive, however, making for very few job openings in this industry. Prospects for academic positions may improve. While a competitive job market will continue to exist for independent research positions in universities and for college and university faculty, opportunities are expected to be better than in the past as an increasing number of faculty are expected to retire through the projection period.

Earnings

Median annual earnings of atmospheric scientists in May 2004 were $70,100. The middle 50 percent earned between $48,880 and $86,610. The lowest 10 percent earned less than $34,590, and the highest 10 percent earned more than $106,020.

The average salary for meteorologists in nonsupervisory, supervisory, and managerial positions employed by the federal government was about $80,499 in 2005. Meteorologists in the federal government with a bachelor's degree and no experience received a starting salary of $27,955 or $34,544, depending on their college grades. Those with a master's degree could start at $42,090 or $54,393, and those with a Ph.D. could begin at $70,280. Beginning salaries for all degree levels are slightly higher in areas of the country where the prevailing local pay level is higher.

Related Occupations

Workers in other occupations concerned with the physical environment include environmental scientists and geoscientists; physicists and astronomers; mathematicians; and civil, chemical, and environmental engineers.

Sources of Additional Information

Information about careers in meteorology and a listing of colleges and universities offering meteorology programs is provided by the American Meteorological Society on the Internet at http://www.ametsoc.org/AMS.

Information on obtaining a position as a meteorologists with the federal government is available from the Office of Personnel Management through USAJOBS, the federal government's official employment information system. This resource for locating and applying for job opportunities can be accessed through the Internet at http://www.usajobs.opm.gov or through an interactive voice response telephone system at (703) 724-1850 or TDD (978) 461-8404. These numbers are not toll free, and charges may result.

Budget Analysts

(O*NET 13-2031.00)

Significant Points

■ Competition for jobs is expected.

■ Although a bachelor's degree generally is the minimum educational requirement, many employers prefer or require a master's degree.

■ About 52 percent of all budget analysts work in federal, state, and local governments.

Nature of the Work

Deciding how to efficiently distribute limited financial resources is an important challenge in all organizations. In most large and complex organizations, this task would be nearly impossible without budget analysts. These workers play the primary role in the development, analysis, and execution of budgets, which are used to allocate current resources and estimate future financial requirements. Without effective budget analysis and feedback about budgetary problems, many private and public organizations could become bankrupt.

Budget analysts can be found in private industry, nonprofit organizations, and the public sector. In private-sector firms, a budget analyst examines budgets and seeks new ways to improve efficiency and increase profits. Although analysts working in nonprofit and governmental organizations usually are not concerned with profits, they still try to find the most efficient distribution of funds and other resources among various departments and programs.

Budget analysts have many responsibilities in these organizations, but their primary task is providing advice and technical assistance in the preparation of annual budgets. At the beginning of each budget cycle, managers and department heads submit proposed operational and financial plans to budget analysts for review. These plans outline prospective programs, including proposed funding increases and new initiatives, estimated costs and expenses, and capital expenditures needed to finance these programs.

Analysts examine the budget estimates or proposals for completeness; accuracy; and conformance with established procedures, regulations, and organizational objectives. Sometimes they employ cost-benefit analysis to review financial requests, assess program tradeoffs, and explore alternative funding methods. They also examine past and current budgets and research economic and financial developments that affect the organization's spending. This process

enables analysts to evaluate proposals in terms of the organization's priorities and financial resources.

After the initial review process, budget analysts consolidate individual departmental budgets into operating and capital budget summaries. These summaries contain comments and statements that support or argue against funding requests. Budget summaries then are submitted to senior management or, as is often the case in local and state governments, to appointed or elected officials. Budget analysts then help the chief operating officer, agency head, or other top managers analyze the proposed plan and devise possible alternatives if the projected results are unsatisfactory. The final decision to approve the budget, however, usually is made by the organization head in a private firm or by elected officials in government, such as the state legislature.

Throughout the remainder of the year, analysts periodically monitor the budget by reviewing reports and accounting records to determine if allocated funds have been spent as specified. If deviations appear between the approved budget and actual performance, budget analysts may write a report providing reasons for the variations along with recommendations for new or revised budget procedures. To avoid or alleviate deficits, budget analysts may recommend program cuts or reallocation of excess funds. They also inform program managers and others within their organization of the status and availability of funds in different budget accounts. Before any changes are made to an existing program, or before a new one is implemented, a budget analyst must assess the program's efficiency and effectiveness. Analysts also may be involved in long-range planning activities such as projecting future budget needs.

The amount of data and information that budget analysts are able to analyze has greatly increased through the use of computerized financial software programs. The analysts also make extensive use of spreadsheet, database, and word-processing software.

Budget analysts have seen their role broadened as limited funding has led to downsizing and restructuring throughout private industry and government. Not only do they develop guidelines and policies governing the formulation and maintenance of the budget, but they also measure organizational performance, assess the effects of various programs and policies on the budget, and help draft budget-related legislation. In addition, budget analysts sometimes conduct training sessions for company or government agency personnel regarding new budget procedures.

Working Conditions

Budget analysts usually work in a comfortable office setting. Long hours are common among these workers, especially during the initial development and midyear and final reviews of budgets. The pressures of deadlines and tight work schedules during these periods can be stressful, and analysts usually are required to work more than the routine 40 hours a week.

Budget analysts spend the majority of their time working independently, compiling and analyzing data and preparing budget proposals. Nevertheless, their schedules sometimes are interrupted by special budget requests, meetings, and training sessions. Some budget analysts travel to obtain budget details and explanations of various programs from co-workers or to personally verify funding allocation.

Training, Other Qualifications, and Advancement

Private firms and government agencies generally require candidates for budget analyst positions to have at least a bachelor's degree, but many prefer or require a master's degree. Within the federal government, a bachelor's degree in any field is sufficient for an entry-level budget analyst position, but, again, master's degrees are preferred. State and local governments have varying requirements, but a bachelor's degree in one of many areas—accounting, finance, business, public administration, economics, statistics, political science, or sociology—may qualify one for employment. Many states, especially larger, more urban states, require a master's degree. Sometimes a degree in a field closely related to that of the employing industry or organization, such as engineering, may be preferred. Some firms prefer candidates with a degree in business because business courses emphasize quantitative and analytical skills. Many government employers prefer candidates with strong analytic and policy analysis backgrounds that may be obtained through such majors as political science, economics, public administration, or public finance. Occasionally, budget-related or finance-related work experience can be substituted for formal education.

Because developing a budget involves manipulating numbers and requires strong analytical skills, courses in statistics or accounting are helpful, regardless of the prospective budget analyst's major field of study. Financial analysis is automated in almost every organization and, therefore, familiarity with word-processing programs and with financial software packages used in budget analysis often is required. Software packages commonly used by budget analysts include electronic spreadsheet, database, and graphics programs. Employers usually prefer candidates who already possess these computer skills.

Those seeking a career as a budget analyst also must be able to work under strict time constraints. Strong oral and written communication skills are essential for analysts because they must prepare, present, and defend budget proposals to decision makers.

In addition, budget analysts, along with all other financial officers, must abide by strict ethical standards. Integrity, objectivity, and confidentiality are all important to budget analysis, and budget analysts must avoid any personal conflicts of interest.

Entry-level budget analysts may receive some formal training when they begin their jobs, but most employers feel that the best training is obtained by working through one complete budget cycle. During the cycle, which typically is 1 year, analysts become familiar with the various steps involved in the budgeting process. The federal government, on the other hand, offers extensive on-the-job and classroom training for entry-level trainees. In addition to on-the-job training, budget analysts are encouraged to participate in various professional development classes throughout their careers.

Some government budget analysts employed at the federal, state, or local level may earn the Certified Government Financial Manager (CGFM) designation granted by the Association of Government Accountants. Other government financial officers also may earn this designation. To do so, candidates must have a minimum of a bachelor's degree, 24 hours of study in financial management, and 2 years of government work experience in financial management. They also must pass a series of three exams that cover topics on the organization and structure of government; governmental accounting, financial reporting, and budgeting; and financial management and control. To maintain the CGFM designation, individuals must complete 80 hours of continuing professional education every 2 years.

Budget analysts start their careers with limited responsibilities. In the federal government, for example, beginning budget analysts compare projected costs with prior expenditures, consolidate and enter data prepared by others, and assist higher-grade analysts by doing research. As analysts progress in their careers, they begin to develop and formulate budget estimates and justification statements, perform detailed analyses of budget requests, write statements supporting funding requests, advise program managers and others on the status and availability of funds for various budget activities, and present and defend budget proposals to senior managers.

Beginning analysts usually work under close supervision. Capable entry-level analysts can be promoted to intermediate-level positions within 1 to 2 years and then to senior positions within a few more years. Progressing to higher levels means added budgetary responsibility and can lead to a supervisory role. Because of the importance and high visibility of their jobs, senior budget analysts are prime candidates for promotion to management positions in various parts of their organizations or with other organizations with which they have worked.

Employment

Budget analysts held 58,000 jobs throughout private industry and government in 2004. Federal, state, and local governments are major employers, accounting for 52 percent of budget analyst jobs. About 23 percent worked for the federal government. Many other budget analysts worked in manufacturing, financial services, or management services. Other employers include schools and hospitals.

Job Outlook

Competition for budget analyst jobs is expected over the 2004–2014 projection period. Candidates with a master's degree should have the best job opportunities. Familiarity with computer financial software packages also should enhance a jobseeker's employment prospects.

Employment of budget analysts is expected to grow about as fast as the average for all occupations through 2014. Employment growth will be driven by the continuing demand for sound financial analysis in both the public and the private sectors. In addition to employment growth, many job openings will result from the need to replace experienced budget analysts who transfer to other occupations or leave the labor force.

The increasing efficiency of computer applications used in budget analysis has increased worker productivity by enabling analysts to process more data in less time. However, because budget analysts now have much more data available to them, their jobs are becoming more complicated. In addition, as businesses and other organizations become more complex and specialized, budget planning and financial control will demand greater attention. These factors should offset any adverse effects of computer applications on employment of budget analysts.

In coming years, all types of organizations will continue to rely heavily on budget analysts to develop and analyze budgets. Because of the importance of financial analysis performed by budget analysts, employment of these workers should remain relatively unaffected by any downsizing in the nation's workplaces. In addition, budget analysts usually are less subject to layoffs than are many other workers during economic downturns because financial and budget reports must be completed during periods of both economic growth and slowdowns.

Earnings

Salaries of budget analysts vary widely by experience, education, and employer. Median annual earnings of budget analysts in May 2004 were $56,040. The middle 50 percent earned between $45,170 and $70,530. The lowest 10 percent earned less than $36,850, and the highest 10 percent earned more than $87,380. Median annual earnings in the industries employing the largest numbers of budget analysts in May 2004 were

Federal government $61,640

Local government 52,520

State government 51,870

According to a 2005 survey conducted by Robert Half International—a staffing services firm specializing in accounting and finance—starting salaries of financial, budget, treasury, and cost analysts in small companies ranged from $29,750 to $36,250. In large companies, starting salaries ranged from $33,500 to $40,000.

In the federal government, budget analysts usually started as trainees earning $24,677 or $30,567 a year in 2005. Candidates with a master's degree began at $37,390. Beginning salaries were slightly higher in areas where the prevailing local pay level was higher. The average annual salary in 2005 for budget analysts employed by the federal government in nonsupervisory, supervisory, and managerial positions was $67,767.

Related Occupations

Budget analysts analyze and interpret financial data, make recommendations for the future, and assist in the implementation of new ideas and financial strategies. Other workers who have similar duties include accountants and auditors, cost estimators, economists, financial analysts and personal financial advisors, financial managers, loan counselors and officers, and management analysts.

Sources of Additional Information

Information about career opportunities as a budget analyst may be available from your state or local employment service.

Information on careers in government financial management and the CGFM designation may be obtained from

▸ Association of Government Accountants, 2208 Mount Vernon Ave., Alexandria, VA 22301. Internet: http://www.agacgfm.org

Information on careers in budget analysis at the state government level may be obtained from

▸ National Association of State Budget Officers, Hall of the States Building, Suite 642, 444 North Capitol St. NW, Washington, DC 20001-1511. Internet: http://www.nasbo.org

Information on obtaining positions as occupational health and safety specialists and technicians with the federal government is available from the Office of Personnel Management through USAJOBS, the federal government's official employment information system. This resource for locating and applying for job opportunities can be accessed through the Internet at http://www.usajobs.opm.gov or through an interactive voice response telephone system at (703) 724-1850 or TDD (978) 461-8404. These numbers are not toll free, and charges may result.

Chemists and Materials Scientists

(O*NET 19-2031.00 and 19-2032.00)

Significant Points

■ A bachelor's degree in chemistry or a related discipline is the minimum educational requirement; however, many research jobs require a master's degree or, more often, a Ph.D.

■ Slower-than-average growth in employment is projected.

■ Job growth will be concentrated in pharmaceutical and medicine manufacturing companies and in professional, scientific, and technical services firms.

■ Graduates with a bachelor's degree will have opportunities at smaller research organizations; those with a master's degree, and particularly those with a Ph.D., will enjoy better opportunities at larger pharmaceutical and biotechnology firms.

Nature of the Work

Everything in the environment, whether naturally occurring or of human design, is composed of chemicals. Chemists and materials scientists search for and use new knowledge about chemicals. Chemical research has led to the discovery and development of new and improved synthetic fibers, paints, adhesives, drugs, cosmetics, electronic components, lubricants, and thousands of other products. Chemists and materials scientists also develop processes such as improved oil refining and petrochemical processing that save energy and reduce pollution. Research on the chemistry of living things spurs advances in medicine, agriculture, food processing, and other fields.

Materials scientists study the structures and chemical properties of various materials to develop new products or enhance existing ones. They also determine ways to strengthen or combine materials or develop new materials for use in a variety of products. Materials science encompasses the natural and synthetic materials used in a wide range of products and structures, from airplanes, cars, and bridges to clothing and household goods. Companies whose products are made of metals, ceramics, and rubber employ most materials scientists. Other applications of materials science include studies of superconducting materials, graphite materials, integrated-circuit chips, and fuel cells. Materials scientists, applying chemistry and physics, study all aspects of these materials. Chemistry plays an increasingly dominant role in materials science because it provides information about the structure and composition of materials. Materials scientists often specialize in specific areas such as ceramics or metals.

Many chemists and materials scientists work in research and development (R&D). In basic research, they investigate properties, composition, and structure of matter and the laws that govern the combination of elements and reactions of substances. In applied R&D, they create new products and processes or improve existing ones, often using knowledge gained from basic research. For example, synthetic rubber and plastics resulted from research on small molecules uniting to form large ones, a process called polymerization. R&D chemists and materials scientists use computers and a wide variety of sophisticated laboratory instrumentation for modeling and simulation in their work.

The use of computers to analyze complex data has allowed chemists and materials scientists to practice combinatorial chemistry. This technique makes and tests large quantities of chemical compounds simultaneously to find those with certain desired properties. Combinatorial chemistry has allowed chemists to produce thousands of compounds more quickly and inexpensively than was formerly possible and assisted in the completion of the sequencing of human genes. Today, specialty chemists, such as medicinal and organic chemists, are working with life scientists to translate this knowledge into new drugs.

Chemists also work in production and quality control in chemical manufacturing plants. They prepare instructions for plant workers that specify ingredients, mixing times, and temperatures for each stage in the process. They also monitor automated processes to ensure proper product yield and test samples of raw materials or finished products to ensure that they meet industry and government standards, including regulations governing pollution. Chemists report and document test results and analyze those results in hopes of improving existing theories or developing new test methods.

Chemists often specialize. *Analytical chemists* determine the structure, composition, and nature of substances by examining and identifying their various elements or compounds. These chemists are absolutely crucial to the pharmaceutical industry because pharmaceutical companies need to know the identity of compounds that they hope to turn into drugs. Furthermore, analytical chemists study the relations and interactions of the parts of compounds and develop analytical techniques. They also identify the presence and concentration of chemical pollutants in air, water, and soil. *Organic chemists* study the chemistry of the vast number of carbon compounds that make up all living things. Organic chemists who synthesize elements or simple compounds to create new compounds or substances that have different properties and applications have developed many commercial products, such as drugs, plastics, and elastomers (elastic substances similar to rubber). *Inorganic chemists* study compounds consisting mainly of elements other than carbon, such as those in electronic components. *Physical* and *theoretical chemists* study the physical characteristics of atoms and molecules and the theoretical properties of matter and investigate how chemical reactions work. Their research may result in new and better energy sources. *Macromolecular chemists* study the behavior of atoms and molecules. *Medicinal chemists* study the structural properties of compounds intended for applications to human medicine. *Materials chemists* study and develop new materials to improve existing products or make new ones. In fact, virtually all chemists are involved in this quest in one way or another. Developments in the field of chemistry that involve life sciences will expand, resulting in more interaction among biologists, engineers, computer specialists, and chemists. (*Biochemists*, whose work encompasses both biology and chemistry, are discussed in this book's description of biological scientists.)

Working Conditions

Chemists and materials scientists usually work regular hours in offices and laboratories. R&D chemists and materials scientists spend much time in laboratories but also work in offices when they do theoretical research or plan, record, and report on their lab research. Although some laboratories are small, others are large enough to incorporate prototype chemical manufacturing facilities as well as advanced equipment for chemists. In addition to working in a laboratory, materials scientists also work with engineers and processing specialists in industrial manufacturing facilities. After a material is sold, materials scientists often help customers tailor the material to suit their needs. Chemists do some of their work in a chemical plant or outdoors—while gathering water samples to test for pollutants, for example. Some chemists are exposed to health or safety hazards when handling certain chemicals, but there is little risk if proper procedures are followed.

Training, Other Qualifications, and Advancement

A bachelor's degree in chemistry or a related discipline usually is the minimum educational requirement for entry-level chemist jobs. However, many research jobs require a master's degree, or more often a Ph.D. While some materials scientists hold a degree in materials science, a bachelor's degree in chemistry, physics, or electrical engineering also is accepted. Many R&D jobs require a Ph.D. in materials science or a related science.

Many colleges and universities offer degree programs in chemistry. In 2005, the American Chemical Society (ACS) approved 631 bachelor's, 308 master's, and 192 doctoral degree programs. In addition to these schools, several hundred colleges and universities also offer advanced degree programs in chemistry. The number of colleges that offer a degree program in materials science is small but gradually increasing.

Students planning careers as chemists and materials scientists should take courses in science and mathematics, should like working with their hands building scientific apparatus and performing laboratory experiments, and should like computer modeling. Perseverance, curiosity, and the ability to concentrate on detail and to work independently are essential. Interaction among specialists in this field is increasing, especially for specialty chemists in drug development. One type of chemist often relies on the findings of another type of chemist. For example, an organic chemist must understand findings on the identity of compounds prepared by an analytical chemist.

In addition to required courses in analytical, inorganic, organic, and physical chemistry, undergraduate chemistry majors usually study biological sciences; mathematics; physics; and increasingly, computer science. Computer courses are essential because employers prefer job applicants who are able to apply computer skills to modeling and simulation tasks and operate computerized laboratory equipment. This is increasingly important as combinatorial chemistry and high-throughput screening (HTS)—the ability to enhance processing capacity—techniques are more widely applied. Those interested in the environmental field also should take courses in environmental studies and become familiar with current legislation and regulations. Specific courses should include atmospheric chemistry, water chemistry, soil chemistry, and energy. Courses in statistics are useful because both chemists and materials scientists need the ability to apply basic statistical techniques.

Because R&D chemists and materials scientists are increasingly expected to work on interdisciplinary teams, some understanding of other disciplines, including business and marketing or economics, is desirable, along with leadership ability and good oral and written communication skills. Experience, either in academic laboratories or through internships, fellowships, or work-study programs in industry, also is useful. Some employers of research chemists, particularly in the pharmaceutical industry, prefer to hire individuals with several years of postdoctoral experience.

Graduate students typically specialize in a subfield of chemistry, such as analytical chemistry or polymer chemistry, depending on their interests and the kind of work they wish to do. For example, those interested in doing drug research in the pharmaceutical industry usually develop a strong background in medicinal or synthetic organic chemistry. However, students normally need not specialize at the undergraduate level. In fact, undergraduates who are broadly trained have more flexibility when job hunting or changing jobs than if they have narrowly defined their interests. Most employers provide new graduates additional training or education.

In government or industry, beginning chemists with a bachelor's degree work in quality control, perform analytical testing, or assist senior chemists in R&D laboratories. Many employers prefer chemists and materials scientists with a Ph.D., or at least a master's degree, to lead basic and applied research. Chemists who hold a Ph.D. and have previous industrial experience may be particularly attractive to employers because such people are more likely to understand the complex regulations that apply to the pharmaceutical industry. Within materials science, a broad background in various sciences is preferred. This broad base may be obtained through degrees in physics, engineering, or chemistry. While many companies prefer hiring Ph.D.s, some may employ materials scientists with bachelor's and master's degrees.

Employment

Chemists and materials scientists held about 90,000 jobs in 2004. About 43 percent of all chemists and material scientists are employed in manufacturing firms—mostly in the chemical manufacturing industry, which includes firms that produce plastics and synthetic materials, drugs, soaps and cleaners, pesticides and fertilizers, paint, industrial organic chemicals, and other chemical products. About 15 percent of chemists and material scientists

work in scientific research and development services; 12 percent work in architectural, engineering, and related services. In addition, thousands of people with a background in chemistry and materials science hold teaching positions in high schools and in colleges and universities. (See the descriptions of teachers—postsecondary elsewhere in this book.)

Chemists and materials scientists are employed in all parts of the country, but they are mainly concentrated in large industrial areas.

Job Outlook

Employment of chemists is expected to grow more slowly than the average rate for all occupations through 2014. Job growth will be concentrated in pharmaceutical and medicine manufacturing and in professional, scientific, and technical services firms. Employment in the nonpharmaceutical segments of the chemical industry, a major employer of chemists, is expected to decline over the projection period. Consequently, new chemists at all levels may experience competition for jobs in these segments, including basic chemical manufacturing and synthetic materials. Graduates with a bachelor's degree may find science-related jobs in sales, marketing, and middle management. Some become chemical technicians or technologists or high school chemistry teachers. In addition, bachelor's degree holders are increasingly finding assistant research positions at smaller research organizations. Graduates with a master's degree, and particularly those with a Ph.D., will enjoy better opportunities at larger pharmaceutical and biotechnology firms. Furthermore, those with an advanced degree will continue to fill most senior research and upper management positions, although applicants are likely to experience competition for these jobs.

Within the chemical industry, job opportunities are expected to be most plentiful in pharmaceutical and biotechnology firms. Biotechnological research, including studies of human genes, continues to offer possibilities for the development of new drugs and products to combat illnesses and diseases that have previously been unresponsive to treatments derived by traditional chemical processes. Stronger competition among drug companies and an aging population are contributing to the need for new drugs.

Employment in the remaining segments of the chemical industry is expected to decline as companies downsize. To control costs, most chemical companies, including many large pharmaceutical and biotechnology companies, will increasingly turn to scientific R&D services firms to perform specialized research and other work formerly done by in-house chemists. As a result, these firms will experience healthy growth. Despite downsizing, some job openings will result from the need to replace chemists who retire or otherwise leave the labor force, although not all positions will be filled. Quality control will continue to be an important issue in chemical manufacturing and other industries that use chemicals in their manufacturing processes.

Chemists also will be needed to develop and improve the technologies and processes used to produce chemicals for all purposes and to monitor and measure air and water pollutants to ensure compliance with local, state, and federal environmental regulations. Environmental research will offer many new opportunities for chemists and materials scientists. To satisfy public concerns and to comply with government regulations, the chemical industry will continue to invest billions of dollars each year in technology that reduces pollution and cleans up existing waste sites. Chemists also are needed to find ways to use less energy and to discover alternative sources of energy.

During periods of economic recession, layoffs of chemists may occur—especially in the industrial chemicals industry. Layoffs are less likely in the pharmaceutical industry, where long development cycles generally overshadow short-term economic effects. The traditional chemical industry, however, provides many raw materials to the auto manufacturing and construction industries, both of which are vulnerable to temporary slowdowns during recessions.

Earnings

Median annual earnings of chemists in May 2004 were $56,060. The middle 50 percent earned between $41,900 and $76,080. The lowest 10 percent earned less than $33,170, and the highest 10 percent earned more than $98,010. Median annual earnings of materials scientists in May 2004 were $72,390. The middle 50 percent earned between $53,350 and $92,340. The lowest 10 percent earned less than $40,030, and the highest 10 percent earned more than $113,460. Median annual earnings in the industries employing the largest numbers of chemists in May 2004 are shown here:

Federal government $80,550

Scientific research and development services 62,460

Pharmaceutical and medicine manufacturing 57,050

Architectural, engineering, and related services 42,370

The ACS reports that in 2004 the median salary of all of its members with a bachelor's degree was $62,000; for those with a master's degree, it was $72,300; and for those with a Ph.D., it was $91,600. The median salary was highest for those working in private industry and lowest for those in academia. According to an ACS survey of recent graduates, inexperienced chemistry graduates with a bachelor's degree earned a median starting salary of $32,500 in October 2004; those with a master's degree earned a median salary of $43,600; and those with a Ph.D. had median earnings of $65,000. Among bachelor's degree graduates, those who had completed internships or had other work experience while in school commanded the highest starting salaries.

In 2005, chemists in nonsupervisory, supervisory, and managerial positions in the federal government averaged $83,777 a year.

Related Occupations

The research and analysis conducted by chemists and materials scientists is closely related to work done by agricultural and food scientists, biological scientists, medical scientists, chemical engineers, materials engineers, physicists, and science technicians.

Sources of Additional Information

General information on career opportunities and earnings for chemists is available from

▸ American Chemical Society, Education Division, 1155 16th St. NW, Washington, DC 20036. Internet: http://www.acs.org

Information on obtaining a position as a chemist with the federal government is available from the Office of Personnel Management through USAJOBS, the federal government's official employment information system. This resource for locating and applying for job opportunities can be accessed through the Internet at http://www.usajobs.opm.gov or through an interactive voice response telephone system at (703) 724-1850 or TDD (978) 461-8404. These numbers are not toll free, and charges may result.

Commercial and Industrial Designers

(O*NET 27-1021.00)

Significant Points

■ Commercial and industrial designers usually work closely with engineers, materials scientists, marketing and corporate strategy staff, cost estimators, and accountants.

■ About 1 out of 3 are self-employed.

■ A bachelor's degree in industrial design, architecture, or engineering is required for entry-level positions; however, many commercial and industrial designers choose to pursue a master's degree in either industrial design or business administration.

■ Keen competition is expected for most jobs because many qualified individuals are attracted to careers in this field; those with strong backgrounds in engineering and computer-aided design, as well as extensive business expertise, will have the best prospects.

Nature of the Work

Commercial and industrial designers combine the fields of art, business, and engineering to design the products used every day by businesses and consumers. These designers are responsible for the style, function, quality, and safety of most manufactured goods. Usually these designers will specialize in one particular product category. Some specialties include automobiles and other transportation vehicles, appliances, technology goods, medical equipment, furniture, toys, tools and construction equipment, and housewares.

The first steps in developing a new design, or altering an existing one, are to determine the requirements of the client, the ultimate function for which the design is intended, and its appeal to customers or users. When creating a new design, designers often begin by researching the product user or the context in which the product will be used and desired product characteristics, such as size, shape, weight, color, materials used, cost, ease of use, fit, and safety. Designers gather this information by meeting with clients; conducting market research; reading design and consumer publications; attending trade shows; and visiting potential users, suppliers, and manufacturers.

Designers then prepare conceptual sketches or diagrams—by hand or with the aid of a computer—to illustrate the vision for the design. After conducting research and consulting with a creative director or other members of the product development team, designers then create detailed sketches or renderings. Many designers use computer-aided design (CAD) tools to create and better visualize the final product. Computer models allow ease and flexibility in exploring a greater number of design alternatives, thus reducing design costs and cutting the time it takes to deliver a product to market. Industrial designers who work for manufacturing firms also use computer-aided industrial design (CAID) tools to create designs and machine-readable instructions that communicate with automated production tools. Often, designers will create physical models out of clay, wood, and other materials to give clients a better idea of what the finished product will look like.

Designers then present the designs and prototypes to their client or managers and incorporate any changes and suggestions. Designers also will work with engineers, accountants, and cost estimators to determine if the product could be made safer, easier to assemble or use, or cheaper to manufacture. Designers also may participate in usability and safety tests with prototypes in order to make further adjustments to the design before it goes to manufacturing.

Commercial and industrial designers also work with marketing staff to develop plans to best market the new product or design to consumers. Increasingly, designers are working with corporate strategy staff to ensure that their designs fit into the company's business plan and strategic vision. This involves designing new products that accurately reflect the company's image and values. It also involves identifying and designing products that best fit consumers' needs before a competitor markets a similar product. Increasingly, designers must focus on creating innovative products in addition to considering the style and technical aspects of the product.

Working Conditions

Working conditions and places of employment vary. Designers employed by manufacturing establishments, large corporations, or design firms generally work regular hours in well-lighted and comfortable settings. Designers in smaller design consulting firms, or those who freelance, may work on a contract, or job, basis. They frequently adjust their workday to suit their clients' schedules and deadlines, meeting with the clients during evening or weekend hours when necessary. Consultants and self-employed designers tend to work longer hours and in smaller, more congested environments. Additional hours may be required in order to meet deadlines.

Designers may transact business in their own offices or studios or in clients' homes or offices. They also may travel to other locations, such as testing facilities, design centers, clients' exhibit sites, users' homes or workplaces, and manufacturing facilities. With the increased speed and sophistication of computers and advanced communications networks, designers may form international design teams, serve a geographically more dispersed clientele, research design alternatives by using information on the Internet, and purchase supplies electronically.

Training, Other Qualifications, and Advancement

A bachelor's degree in industrial design, architecture, or engineering is required for most entry-level commercial and industrial design positions. Many candidates in industrial design also pursue a master's degree in order to increase their employment opportunities. Creativity and technical knowledge are crucial in this occupation. People in this field also must have a strong sense of the esthetic—an eye for color and detail and a sense of balance and proportion. Designers must understand the technical aspects of how the product functions. Despite the advancement of computer-aided design, sketching ability remains an important advantage. A good portfolio—a collection of examples of a person's best work—often is the deciding factor in getting a job.

Bachelor's of fine arts or bachelor's of science degrees in industrial design are granted at many colleges and universities and in private art and design schools. Baccalaureate curriculum includes principles of design; sketching; computer-aided design; industrial materials and processes; manufacturing methods; and some coursework in engineering, physical science, mathematics, psychology, and anthropology. Many programs also include internships in design or manufacturing firms.

Commercial and industrial designers also may pursue a master's degree in industrial design. With the growing emphasis on strategic design and how products fit into the overall business plan, an increasing number of designers are pursing a master's degree in business administration in order to gain valuable business skills. Also, a growing number of professionals in other industries, such as marketing and information technology, are entering the industrial design field by pursuing advanced degrees in design.

The National Association of Schools of Art and Design accredits about 250 postsecondary institutions with programs in art and design. Approximately 45 of these schools award a degree in industrial design. Many schools require the successful completion of 1 year of basic art and design courses before formal entry into a bachelor's degree program. Applicants also may be required to submit sketches and other examples of their artistic ability.

Employers increasingly expect new designers to be familiar with computer-aided design software as a design tool. Designers must also be creative, imaginative, and persistent and must be able to communicate their ideas in writing, visually, and verbally. Because tastes in style can change quickly, designers need to be well read, open to new ideas and influences, and quick to react to changing trends. Problem-solving skills and the ability to work independently and under pressure also are important traits. People in this field need self-discipline to start projects on their own, to budget their time, and to meet deadlines and production schedules.

As strategic design becomes more important, employers will seek designers with project management skills and knowledge of accounting, marketing, quality assurance, purchasing, and strategic planning. Good business sense and sales ability also are important, especially for those who freelance or run their own business.

Beginning commercial and industrial designers usually receive on-the-job training and normally need 1 to 3 years of training before they can advance to higher-level positions. Experienced designers in large firms may advance to chief designer, design department head, or other supervisory positions. Some designers leave the occupation to become teachers in design schools or in colleges and universities. Many faculty members continue to consult privately or operate small design studios to complement their classroom activities. Some experienced designers open their own design firms.

Employment

Commercial and industrial designers held about 49,000 jobs in 2004. About 1 out of 3 were self-employed. About 13 percent of designers were employed in either engineering or specialized design services firms. Manufacturing companies employed the rest of commercial and industrial designers, with the largest number employed in aerospace products and parts manufacturing.

Job Outlook

Employment of commercial and industrial designers is expected to grow about as fast as average for all occupations through 2014. Employment growth will arise from an expanding economy and from an increase in consumer and business demand for new or upgraded products. However, competition for jobs will be keen because many talented individuals are attracted to the design field. The best job opportunities will be in specialized design firms which are used by manufacturers to design products or parts of products. Designers with strong backgrounds in engineering and computer-aided design, as well as extensive business expertise, may have the best prospects.

Increasing demand for commercial and industrial designers will stem from the continued emphasis on the quality and safety of products, the increasing demand for new products that are easy and comfortable to use, and the development of high-technology products in consumer electronics, medicine, transportation, and other fields. However, employment can be affected by fluctuations in the economy. For example, during periods of economic downturns, companies may cut research and development spending, including new product development.

Increasingly, manufacturers have been outsourcing design work to design services firms in order to cut costs and to find the most qualified design talent. Additionally, some companies use design firms located overseas, especially for design of high-technology products. These overseas design firms are located closer to their suppliers, which reduces the time it takes to design and sell a product—an important consideration when technology is changing quickly. Off-shoring of design work, particularly for high-technology products, could continue to have a negative impact on domestic employment of commercial and industrial designers.

Despite the increase in design work performed overseas, most design jobs—particularly jobs not related to high-technology product design—will still remain in the U.S. because design is essential to a firm's success and firms will want to retain control over the design process. As the demand for design work becomes more consumer-driven, designers also will need to closely monitor, and react to, changing customer demands. Designers will increasingly have to come up with innovative new products in order to stay competitive. Domestic designers also will be required to work with marketing and strategic planning staffs to design products that will be more usable and appealing to consumers and that accurately define a company's image and brand.

Earnings

Median annual earnings for commercial and industrial designers were $52,310 in May 2004. The middle 50 percent earned between $39,130 and $68,980. The lowest 10 percent earned less than $29,080, and the highest 10 percent earned more than $86,250.

Related Occupations

Workers in other art and design occupations include artists and related workers, fashion designers, floral designers, graphic designers, and interior designers. Some other occupations that require computer-aided design skills are architects, except landscape and naval; computer software engineers; desktop publishers; drafters; and engineers.

Sources of Additional Information

For general career information on commercial and industrial design, contact

▸ Industrial Designers Society of America, 45195 Business Court, Suite 250, Dulles, VA 20166-6717. Internet: http://www.idsa.org

For general information about art and design and a list of accredited college-level programs, contact

▸ National Association of Schools of Art and Design, 11250 Roger Bacon Dr., Suite 21, Reston, VA 20190-5248. Internet: http://nasad.arts-accredit.org

Computer Programmers

(O*NET 15-1021.00)

Significant Points

■ Sixty-seven percent of computer programmers hold a college or higher degree; nearly half hold a bachelor's degree, and about 1 in 5 hold a graduate degree.

■ Employment is expected to grow much more slowly than that for other computer specialists.

■ Prospects likely will be best for college graduates with knowledge of a variety of programming languages and tools; those with less formal education or its equivalent in work experience are apt to face strong competition for programming jobs.

Nature of the Work

Computer programmers write, test, and maintain the detailed instructions, called programs, that computers must follow to perform their functions. Programmers also conceive, design, and test logical structures for solving problems by computer. Many technical innovations in programming—advanced computing technologies and sophisticated new languages and programming tools—have redefined the role of a programmer and elevated much of the programming work done today. Job titles and descriptions may vary, depending on the organization. In this occupational description, *computer programmers* are individuals whose main job function is programming; this group has a wide range of responsibilities and educational backgrounds.

Computer programs tell the computer what to do—which information to identify and access, how to process it, and what equipment to use. Programs vary widely depending on the type of information to be accessed or generated. For example, the instructions involved in updating financial records are very different from those required to duplicate conditions on an aircraft for pilots training in a flight simulator. Although simple programs can be written in a few hours, programs that use complex mathematical formulas whose solutions can only be approximated or that draw data from many existing systems may require more than a year of work. In most cases, several programmers work together as a team under a senior programmer's supervision.

Programmers write programs according to the specifications determined primarily by computer software engineers and systems analysts. (Separate descriptions of computer software engineers and of computer systems analysts appear elsewhere in this book.) After the design process is complete, it is the job of the programmer to convert that design into a logical series of instructions that the computer can follow. The programmer codes these instructions in a conventional programming language such as COBOL; an artificial intelligence language such as Prolog; or one of the most advanced object-oriented languages, such as Java, C++, or ACTOR. Different programming languages are used depending on the purpose of the program. COBOL, for example, is commonly used for business applications, whereas Fortran (short for "formula translation") is used in science and engineering. C++ is widely used for both scientific and business applications. Extensible Markup Language (XML) has become a popular programming tool for Web programmers, along with J2EE (Java 2 Platform). Programmers generally know more than one programming language and, because many languages are similar, they often can learn new languages relatively easily. In practice, programmers often are referred to by the language they know, such as Java programmers, or by the type of function they perform or environment in which they work—for example, database programmers, mainframe programmers, or Web programmers.

Many programmers update, repair, modify, and expand existing programs. When making changes to a section of code, called a routine, programmers need to make other users aware of the task that the routine is to perform. They do this by inserting comments in the coded instructions so that others can understand the program. Many programmers use computer-assisted software engineering (CASE) tools to automate much of the coding process. These tools enable a programmer to concentrate on writing the unique parts of the program because the tools automate various pieces of the program being built. CASE tools generate whole sections of code automatically rather than line by line. Programmers also use libraries of basic code that can be modified or customized for a specific application. This approach yields more reliable and consistent programs and increases programmers' productivity by eliminating some routine steps.

Programmers test a program by running it to ensure that the instructions are correct and that the program produces the desired outcome. If errors do occur, the programmer must make the appropriate change and recheck the program until it produces the correct results. This process is called testing and debugging. Programmers may continue to fix these problems throughout the life of a program. Programmers working in a mainframe environment, which involves a large centralized computer, may prepare instructions for a computer operator who will run the program. Programmers also may contribute to a manual for persons who will be using the program.

Computer programmers often are grouped into two broad types—applications programmers and systems programmers. *Applications programmers* write programs to handle a specific job, such as a program to track inventory within an organization. They also may revise existing packaged software or customize generic applications that are frequently purchased from vendors. *Systems programmers*, in contrast, write programs to maintain and control computer systems software, such as operating systems, networked systems, and database systems. These workers make changes in the instructions that determine how the network, workstations, and central processing unit of the system handle the various jobs they have been given and how they communicate with peripheral equipment such as terminals, printers, and disk drives. Because of their knowledge of the entire computer system, systems programmers often help applications programmers determine the source of problems that may occur with their programs.

Programmers in software development companies may work directly with experts from various fields to create software—either programs designed for specific clients or packaged software for general use—ranging from games and educational software to programs for desktop publishing and financial planning. Programming of packaged software constitutes one of the most rapidly growing segments of the computer services industry.

In some organizations, particularly small ones, workers commonly known as *programmer-analysts* are responsible for both the systems analysis and the actual programming work. (A more detailed description of the work of programmer-analysts is presented in the description of computer systems analysts elsewhere in this book.) Advanced programming languages and new object-oriented programming capabilities are increasing the efficiency and productivity of both programmers and users. The transition from a mainframe environment to one that is based primarily on personal computers (PCs) has blurred the once-rigid distinction between the programmer and the user. Increasingly, adept end users are taking over many of the tasks previously performed by programmers. For example, the growing use of packaged software, such as spreadsheet and database management software packages, allows users to write simple programs to access data and perform calculations.

Working Conditions

Programmers generally work in offices in comfortable surroundings. Many programmers may work long hours or weekends to meet deadlines or fix critical problems that occur during off hours. Telecommuting is becoming common for a wide range of computer professionals, including computer programmers. As computer networks expand, more programmers are able to make corrections or fix problems remotely by using modems, e-mail, and the Internet to connect to a customer's computer.

Like other workers who spend long periods in front of a computer terminal typing at a keyboard, programmers are susceptible to eyestrain, back discomfort, and hand and wrist problems such as carpal tunnel syndrome.

Training, Other Qualifications, and Advancement

Although there are many training paths available for programmers, mainly because employers' needs are so varied, the level of education and experience employers seek has been rising due to the growing number of qualified applicants and the specialization involved with most programming tasks. Bachelor's degrees are commonly required, although some programmers may qualify for certain jobs with 2-year degrees or certificates. The associate degree is a widely used entry-level credential for prospective computer programmers. Most community colleges and many independent technical institutes and proprietary schools offer an associate degree in computer science or a related information technology field.

Employers primarily are interested in programming knowledge, and computer programmers can become certified in a programming language such as C++ or Java. College graduates who are interested in changing careers or developing an area of expertise also may return to a 2-year community college or technical school for additional training. In the absence of a degree, substantial specialized experience or expertise may be needed. Even when hiring programmers with a degree, employers appear to place more emphasis on previous experience.

Some computer programmers hold a college degree in computer science, mathematics, or information systems, whereas others have taken special courses in computer programming to supplement their degree in a field such as accounting, inventory control, or another area of business. As the level of education and training required by employers continues to rise, the proportion of programmers with a college degree should increase in the future. As indicated by the following tabulation, more than two-thirds of computer programmers had a bachelor's or higher degree in 2004.

High school graduate or less	8.3%
Some college, no degree	14.1
Associate degree	10.2
Bachelor's degree	49.1
Graduate degree	18.3

Required skills vary from job to job, but the demand for various skills generally is driven by changes in technology. Employers using computers for scientific or engineering applications usually prefer college graduates who have degrees in computer or information science, mathematics, engineering, or the physical sciences. Graduate degrees in related fields are required for some jobs. Employers who use computers for business applications prefer to hire people who have had college courses in management information systems and business and who possess strong programming skills. Although knowledge of traditional languages still is important, employers are placing increasing emphasis on newer, object-oriented programming languages and tools such as C++ and Java. Additionally, employers are seeking persons familiar with fourth-generation and fifth-generation languages that involve graphic user interface and systems programming. Employers also prefer applicants who have general business skills and experience related to the operations of the firm. Students can improve their employment prospects by participating in a college work-study program or by undertaking an internship.

Most systems programmers hold a 4-year degree in computer science. Extensive knowledge of a variety of operating systems is essential for such workers. This includes being able to configure an operating system to work with different types of hardware and having the skills needed to adapt the operating system to best meet the needs of a particular organization. Systems programmers also must be able to work with database systems, such as DB2, Oracle, or Sybase.

When hiring programmers, employers look for people with the necessary programming skills who can think logically and pay close attention to detail. The job calls for patience, persistence, and the ability to work on exacting analytical work, especially under pressure. Ingenuity and creativity are particularly important when programmers design solutions and test their work for potential failures. The ability to work with abstract concepts and to do technical analysis is especially important for systems programmers because they work with the software that controls the computer's operation. Because programmers are expected to work in teams and interact directly with users, employers want programmers who are able to communicate with nontechnical personnel.

Entry-level or junior programmers may work alone on simple assignments after some initial instruction, or they may be assigned to work on a team with more experienced programmers. Either way, beginning programmers generally must work under close supervision. Because technology changes so rapidly, programmers must continuously update their knowledge and skills by taking courses sponsored by their employer or by software vendors or offered through local community colleges and universities.

For skilled workers who keep up to date with the latest technology, the prospects for advancement are good. In large organizations, programmers may be promoted to lead programmer and be given supervisory responsibilities. Some applications programmers may move into systems programming after they gain experience and take courses in systems software. With general business experience, programmers may become programmer-analysts or systems analysts or be promoted to managerial positions. Other programmers, with specialized knowledge and experience with a language or operating system, may work in research and development for multimedia or Internet technology and may even become computer software engineers. As employers increasingly contract with outside firms to do programming jobs, more opportunities should arise for experienced programmers with expertise in a specific area to work as consultants.

Certification is a way to demonstrate a level of competence and may provide a jobseeker with a competitive advantage. In addition to language-specific certificates that a programmer can obtain, product vendors or software firms also offer certification and may require professionals who work with their products to be certified. Voluntary certification also is available through various other organizations.

Employment

Computer programmers held about 455,000 jobs in 2004. Programmers are employed in almost every industry, but the largest concentration is in computer systems design and related services. Large numbers of programmers also work for telecommunications companies, software publishers, financial institutions, insurance carriers, educational institutions, and government agencies.

Many computer programmers are employed on a temporary or contract basis or work as independent consultants, providing companies expertise with new programming languages or specialized areas of application. Rather than hiring programmers as permanent employees and then laying them off after a job is completed, employers can contract with temporary help agencies, with consulting firms, or with programmers themselves. A marketing firm, for example, may require programming services only to write and debug the software necessary to get a new customer database running. Bringing in an independent contractor or consultant with experience in a new or advanced programming language enables the firm to complete the job without having to retrain existing workers. Such jobs may last anywhere from several weeks to a year or longer. There were 25,000 self-employed computer programmers in 2004.

Job Outlook

As programming tasks become increasingly sophisticated and additional levels of skill and experience are demanded by employers, graduates of 2-year programs and people with less than a 2-year degree or its equivalent in work experience will face strong competition for programming jobs. Competition for entry-level positions, however, also can affect applicants with a bachelor's degree. Prospects should be best for college graduates with knowledge of, and experience working with, a variety of programming languages and tools—including C++ and other object-oriented languages such as Java as well as newer, domain-specific languages that apply to computer networking, database management, and Internet application development. Obtaining vendor-specific or language-specific certification also can provide a competitive edge. Because demand fluctuates with employers' needs, jobseekers should keep up to date with the latest skills and technologies. Individuals who want to become programmers can enhance their prospects by combining the appropriate formal training with practical work experience.

Employment of programmers is expected to grow more slowly than the average for all occupations through the year 2014. Sophisticated computer software now has the capability to write basic code, eliminating the need for many programmers to do this routine work. The consolidation and centralization of systems and applications; developments in packaged software; advances in programming languages and tools; and the growing ability of users to design, write, and implement more of their own programs mean that more of the programming functions can be transferred from programmers to other types of information workers, such as computer software engineers.

Another factor limiting growth in employment is the outsourcing of these jobs to other countries. Computer programmers can perform their job function from anywhere in the world and can digitally transmit their programs to any location via e-mail. Programmers are at a much higher risk of having their jobs outsourced abroad than are workers involved in more complex and sophisticated information technology functions, such as software engineering, because computer programming has become an international language requiring little localized or specialized knowledge. Additionally, the work of

computer programmers can be routinized once knowledge of a particular programming language is mastered.

Nevertheless, employers will continue to need programmers who have strong technical skills and who understand an employer's business and its programming requirements. This means that programmers will have to keep abreast of changing programming languages and techniques. Given the importance of networking and the expansion of client/server, Web-based, and wireless environments, organizations will look for programmers who can support data communications and help implement electronic commerce and intranet strategies. Demand for programmers with strong object-oriented programming capabilities and technical specialization in areas such as client/server programming, wireless applications, multimedia technology, and graphic user interface likely will stem from the expansion of intranets, extranets, and Internet applications. Programmers also will be needed to create and maintain expert systems and embed these technologies in more products. Finally, a growing emphasis on cybersecurity will lead to increased demand for programmers who are familiar with digital security issues and skilled in using appropriate security technology.

Jobs for both systems and applications programmers should be most plentiful in data-processing service firms, software houses, and computer consulting businesses. These types of establishments are part of computer systems design and related services and software publishers, which are projected to be among the fastest-growing industries in the economy over the 2004–2014 period. As organizations attempt to control costs and keep up with changing technology, they will need programmers to assist in conversions to new computer languages and systems. In addition, numerous job openings will result from the need to replace programmers who leave the labor force or transfer to other occupations such as manager or systems analyst.

Earnings

Median annual earnings of computer programmers were $62,890 in May 2004. The middle 50 percent earned between $47,580 and $81,280 a year. The lowest 10 percent earned less than $36,470; the highest 10 percent earned more than $99,610. Median annual earnings in the industries employing the largest numbers of computer programmers in May 2004 are shown here:

Software publishers	$73,060
Computer systems design and related services	67,600
Data-processing, hosting, and related services	64,540
Insurance carriers	62,990
Management of companies and enterprises	62,160

According to the National Association of Colleges and Employers, starting salary offers for graduates with a bachelor's degree in computer science averaged $50,820 a year in 2005.

According to Robert Half International, a firm providing specialized staffing services, average annual starting salaries in 2005 ranged from $52,500 to $83,250 for applications development programmers/analysts and from $55,000 to $88,250 for software developers. Average starting salaries for mainframe systems programmers ranged from $50,250 to $67,500 in 2005.

Related Occupations

Other professional workers who deal extensively with data include computer software engineers, computer scientists and database administrators, computer systems analysts, statisticians, mathematicians, engineers, and operations research analysts.

Sources of Additional Information

State employment service offices can provide information about job openings for computer programmers. Municipal chambers of commerce are an additional source of information on an area's largest employers.

Further information about computer careers is available from

▸ Association for Computing Machinery, 1515 Broadway, New York, NY 10036. Internet: http://www.acm.org

▸ Institute of Electrical and Electronics Engineers Computer Society, Headquarters Office, 1730 Massachusetts Ave. NW, Washington, DC 20036-1992. Internet: http://www.computer.org

▸ National Workforce Center for Emerging Technologies, 3000 Landerholm Circle SE, Bellevue, WA 98007. Internet: http://www.nwcet.org

Computer Scientists and Database Administrators

(O*NET 15-1011.00, 15-1061.00, and 15-1099.99)

Significant Points

■ Education requirements range from an associate degree to a doctoral degree.

■ Employment is expected to increase much faster than the average as organizations continue to adopt increasingly sophisticated technologies.

■ Job prospects are favorable.

Nature of the Work

The rapid spread of computers and information technology has generated a need for highly trained workers proficient in various job functions. These workers—computer scientists, database administrators, and network systems and data communication analysts—include a wide range of computer specialists. Job tasks and occupational titles used to describe these workers evolve rapidly, reflecting new areas of specialization or changes in technology as well as the preferences and practices of employers.

Computer scientists work as theorists, researchers, or inventors. Their jobs are distinguished by the higher level of theoretical expertise and innovation they apply to complex problems and the creation or application of new technology. Those employed by academic institutions work in areas ranging from complexity theory to hardware to programming-language design. Some work on multidisciplinary projects, such as developing and advancing uses of virtual reality, extending human-computer interaction, or designing robots. Their counterparts in private industry work in areas such as

applying theory; developing specialized languages or information technologies; or designing programming tools, knowledge-based systems, or even computer games.

With the Internet and electronic business generating large volumes of data, there is a growing need to be able to store, manage, and extract data effectively. *Database administrators* work with database management systems software and determine ways to organize and store data. They identify user requirements, set up computer databases, and test and coordinate modifications to the computer database systems. An organization's database administrator ensures the performance of the system, understands the platform on which the database runs, and adds new users to the system. Because they also may design and implement system security, database administrators often plan and coordinate security measures. With the volume of sensitive data generated every second growing rapidly, data integrity, backup systems, and database security have become increasingly important aspects of the job of database administrators.

Because networks are configured in many ways, *network systems and data communications analysts* are needed to design, test, and evaluate systems such as local area networks (LANs), wide area networks (WANs), the Internet, intranets, and other data communications systems. Systems can range from a connection between two offices in the same building to globally distributed networks, voice mail, and e-mail systems of a multinational organization. Network systems and data communications analysts perform network modeling, analysis, and planning; they also may research related products and make necessary hardware and software recommendations. *Telecommunications specialists* focus on the interaction between computer and communications equipment. These workers design voice and data communication systems, supervise the installation of the systems, and provide maintenance and other services to clients after the systems are installed.

The growth of the Internet and the expansion of the World Wide Web (the graphical portion of the Internet) have generated a variety of occupations related to the design, development, and maintenance of Web sites and their servers. For example, *Webmasters* are responsible for all technical aspects of a Web site, including performance issues such as speed of access, and for approving the content of the site. *Internet developers* or *Web developers*, also called *Web designers*, are responsible for day-to-day site creation and design.

Working Conditions

Computer scientists and database administrators normally work in offices or laboratories in comfortable surroundings. They usually work about 40 hours a week—the same as many other professional or office workers do. However, evening or weekend work may be necessary to meet deadlines or solve specific problems. With the technology available today, telecommuting is common for computer professionals. As networks expand, more work can be done from remote locations through modems, laptops, electronic mail, and the Internet.

Like other workers who spend long periods in front of a computer terminal typing on a keyboard, computer scientists and database administrators are susceptible to eyestrain, back discomfort, and hand and wrist problems such as carpal tunnel syndrome or cumulative trauma disorder.

Training, Other Qualifications, and Advancement

Rapidly changing technology requires an increasing level of skill and education on the part of employees. Companies look for professionals with an ever-broader background and range of skills including not only technical knowledge, but also communication and other interpersonal skills. While there is no universally accepted way to prepare for a job as a network systems analyst, computer scientist, or database administrator, most employers place a premium on some formal college education. A bachelor's degree is a prerequisite for many jobs; however, some jobs may require only a 2-year degree. Relevant work experience also is very important. For more technically complex jobs, persons with graduate degrees are preferred.

For database administrator positions, many employers seek applicants who have a bachelor's degree in computer science, information science, or management information systems (MIS). MIS programs usually are part of the business school or college and differ considerably from computer science programs, emphasizing business and management-oriented coursework and business computing courses. Employers increasingly seek individuals with a master's degree in business administration (MBA), with a concentration in information systems, as more firms move their business to the Internet. For some network systems and data communication analysts, such as Webmasters, an associate degree or certificate is sufficient, although more advanced positions might require a computer-related bachelor's degree. For computer and information scientists, a doctoral degree generally is required because of the highly technical nature of their work.

Despite employers' preference for those with technical degrees, persons with degrees in a variety of majors find employment in these occupations. The level of education and the type of training that employers require depend on their needs. One factor affecting these needs is changes in technology. Employers often scramble to find workers capable of implementing new technologies. Workers with formal education or experience in information security, for example, are in demand because of the growing need for their skills and services. Employers also look for workers skilled in wireless technologies as wireless networks and applications have spread into many firms and organizations.

Most community colleges and many independent technical institutes and proprietary schools offer an associate's degree in computer science or a related information technology field. Many of these programs may be geared more toward meeting the needs of local businesses and are more occupation-specific than are 4-year degree programs. Some jobs may be better suited to the level of training that such programs offer. Employers usually look for people who have broad knowledge and experience related to computer systems and technologies, strong problem-solving and analytical skills, and good interpersonal skills. Courses in computer science or systems design offer good preparation for a job in these computer occupations. For jobs in a business environment, employers usually want systems analysts to have business management or closely related skills, while a background in the physical sciences, applied mathematics, or engineering is preferred for work in scientifically oriented organizations. Art or graphic design skills may be desirable for Webmasters or Web developers.

Jobseekers can enhance their employment opportunities by participating in internship or co-op programs offered through their schools. Because many people develop advanced computer skills in a non-computer occupation and then transfer those skills to a computer occupation, a background in the industry in which the person's job is located, such as financial services, banking, or accounting, can be important. Others have taken computer science courses to supplement their study in fields such as accounting, inventory control, or other business areas.

Computer scientists and database administrators must be able to think logically and have good communication skills. Because they often deal with a number of tasks simultaneously, the ability to concentrate and pay close attention to detail is important. Although these computer specialists sometimes work independently, they frequently work in teams on large projects. They must be able to communicate effectively with computer personnel, such as programmers and managers, as well as with users or other staff who may have no technical computer background.

Computer scientists employed in private industry may advance into managerial or project leadership positions. Those employed in academic institutions can become heads of research departments or published authorities in their field. Database administrators may advance into managerial positions, such as chief technology officer, on the basis of their experience managing data and enforcing security. Computer specialists with work experience and considerable expertise in a particular subject or a certain application may find lucrative opportunities as independent consultants or may choose to start their own computer consulting firms.

Technological advances come so rapidly in the computer field that continuous study is necessary to keep one's skills up to date. Employers, hardware and software vendors, colleges and universities, and private training institutions offer continuing education. Additional training may come from professional development seminars offered by professional computing societies.

Certification is a way to demonstrate a level of competence in a particular field. Some product vendors or software firms offer certification and require professionals who work with their products to be certified. Many employers regard these certifications as the industry standard. For example, one method of acquiring enough knowledge to get a job as a database administrator is to become certified in a specific type of database management. Voluntary certification also is available through various organizations associated with computer specialists. Professional certification may afford a jobseeker a competitive advantage.

Employment

Computer scientists and database administrators held about 507,000 jobs in 2004, including about 66,000 who were self-employed. Employment was distributed among the detailed occupations as follows:

Network systems and data communication analysts	231,000
Database administrators	104,000
Computer and information scientists, research	22,000
Computer specialists, all other	149,000

Although they are increasingly employed in every sector of the economy, the greatest concentration of these workers is in the computer systems design and related services industry. Firms in this industry provide services related to the commercial use of computers on a contract basis, including custom computer programming services; computer systems integration design services; computer facilities management services, including computer systems or data-processing facilities support services for clients; and other computer-related services, such as disaster recovery services and software installation. Many computer scientists and database administrators are employed by Internet service providers; Web search portals; and data-processing, hosting, and related services firms. Others work for government, manufacturers of computer and electronic products, insurance companies, financial institutions, and universities.

A growing number of computer specialists, such as network and data communications analysts, are employed on a temporary or contract basis; many of these individuals are self-employed, working independently as contractors or consultants. For example, a company installing a new computer system may need the services of several network systems and data communication analysts just to get the system running. Because not all of the analysts would be needed once the system is functioning, the company might contract for such employees with a temporary help agency or a consulting firm or with the network systems analysts themselves. Such jobs may last from several months to 2 years or more. This growing practice enables companies to bring in people with the exact skills they need to complete a particular project instead of having to spend time or money training or retraining existing workers. Often, experienced consultants then train a company's in-house staff as a project develops.

Job Outlook

Computer scientists and database administrators should continue to enjoy favorable job prospects. As technology becomes more sophisticated and complex, however, employers demand a higher level of skill and expertise from their employees. Individuals with an advanced degree in computer science or computer engineering or with an MBA with a concentration in information systems should enjoy favorable employment prospects. College graduates with a bachelor's degree in computer science, computer engineering, information science, or MIS also should enjoy favorable prospects, particularly if they have supplemented their formal education with practical experience. Because employers continue to seek computer specialists who can combine strong technical skills with good interpersonal and business skills, graduates with degrees in fields other than computer science who have had courses in computer programming, systems analysis, and other information technology areas also should continue to find jobs in these computer fields. In fact, individuals with the right experience and training can work in these computer occupations regardless of their college major or level of formal education.

Computer scientists and database administrators are expected to be among the fastest-growing occupations through 2014. Employment of these computer specialists is expected to grow much faster than the average for all occupations as organizations continue to adopt and integrate increasingly sophisticated technologies. Job increases will be driven by very rapid growth in computer systems design and related services, which is projected to be one of the fastest-growing industries in the U.S. economy. Job growth will not be as rapid as during the previous decade, however, as the information technology sector begins to mature and as routine work is increasingly outsourced overseas. In addition to growth, many job openings will arise annually from the need to replace workers who move into managerial positions or other occupations or who leave the labor force.

The demand for networking to facilitate the sharing of information, the expansion of client-server environments, and the need for computer specialists to use their knowledge and skills in a problem-solving capacity will be major factors in the rising demand for computer scientists and database administrators. Moreover, falling prices of computer hardware and software should continue to induce more businesses to expand their computerized operations and integrate new technologies into them. To maintain a competitive edge and operate more efficiently, firms will keep demanding computer specialists who are knowledgeable about the latest technologies and are able to apply them to meet the needs of businesses.

Increasingly, more sophisticated and complex technology is being implemented across all organizations, fueling demand for computer scientists and database administrators. There is growing demand for network systems and data communication analysts to help firms maximize their efficiency with available technology. Expansion of electronic commerce—doing business on the Internet—and the continuing need to build and maintain databases that store critical information on customers, inventory, and projects are fueling demand for database administrators familiar with the latest technology. Also, the increasing importance placed on cybersecurity—the protection of electronic information—will result in a need for workers skilled in information security.

The development of new technologies usually leads to demand for various kinds of workers. The expanding integration of Internet technologies into businesses, for example, has resulted in a growing need for specialists who can develop and support Internet and intranet applications. The growth of electronic commerce means that more establishments use the Internet to conduct their business online. The introduction of the wireless Internet, known as WiFi, creates new systems to be analyzed and new data to be administered. The spread of such new technologies translates into a need for information technology professionals who can help organizations use technology to communicate with employees, clients, and consumers. Explosive growth in these areas also is expected to fuel demand for specialists who are knowledgeable about network, data, and communications security.

Earnings

Median annual earnings of computer and information scientists, research, were $85,190 in May 2004. The middle 50 percent earned between $64,860 and $108,440. The lowest 10 percent earned less than $48,930, and the highest 10 percent earned more than $132,700. Median annual earnings of computer and information scientists employed in computer systems design and related services in May 2004 were $85,530.

Median annual earnings of database administrators were $60,650 in May 2004. The middle 50 percent earned between $44,490 and $81,140. The lowest 10 percent earned less than $33,380, and the highest 10 percent earned more than $97,450. In May 2004, median annual earnings of database administrators employed in computer systems design and related services were $70,530, and for those in management of companies and enterprises, earnings were $65,990.

Median annual earnings of network systems and data communication analysts were $60,600 in May 2004. The middle 50 percent earned between $46,480 and $78,060. The lowest 10 percent earned less than $36,260, and the highest 10 percent earned more than $95,040. Median annual earnings in the industries employing the largest numbers of network systems and data communications analysts in May 2004 are shown here:

Wired telecommunications carriers	$65,130
Insurance carriers	64,660
Management of companies and enterprises	64,170
Computer systems design and related services	63,910
Local government	52,300

Median annual earnings of all other computer specialists were $59,480 in May 2004. Median annual earnings of all other computer specialists employed in computer systems design and related services were $57,430, and, for those in management of companies and enterprises, earnings were $68,590 in May 2004.

According to the National Association of Colleges and Employers, starting offers for graduates with a doctoral degree in computer science averaged $93,050 in 2005. Starting offers averaged $50,820 for graduates with a bachelor's degree in computer science; $46,189 for those with a degree in computer systems analysis; $44,417 for those with a degree in management information systems; and $44,775 for those with a degree in information sciences and systems.

According to Robert Half International, a firm providing specialized staffing services, starting salaries in 2005 ranged from $67,750 to $95,500 for database administrators. Salaries for networking and Internet-related occupations ranged from $47,000 to $68,500 for LAN administrators and from $51,750 to $74,520 for Web developers. Starting salaries for information security professionals ranged from $63,750 to $93,000 in 2005.

Related Occupations

Others who work with large amounts of data are computer programmers, computer software engineers, computer and information systems managers, engineers, mathematicians, and statisticians.

Sources of Additional Information

Further information about computer careers is available from:

▶ Association for Computing Machinery (ACM), 1515 Broadway, New York, NY 10036. Internet: http://www.acm.org

▶ Institute of Electrical and Electronics Engineers Computer Society, Headquarters Office, 1730 Massachusetts Ave. NW, Washington, DC 20036-1992. Internet: http://www.computer.org

▶ National Workforce Center for Emerging Technologies, 3000 Landerholm Circle SE, Bellevue, WA 98007. Internet: http://www.nwcet.org

Computer Software Engineers

(O*NET 15-1031.00 and 15-1032.00)

Significant Points

■ Computer software engineers are projected to be one of the fastest-growing occupations over the 2004–2014 period.

■ Very good opportunities are expected for college graduates with at least a bachelor's degree in computer engineering or computer science and with practical work experience.

■ Computer software engineers must continually strive to acquire new skills in conjunction with the rapid changes that are occurring in computer technology.

Nature of the Work

The explosive impact of computers and information technology on our everyday lives has generated a need to design and develop new computer software systems and to incorporate new technologies into a rapidly growing range of applications. The tasks performed by workers known as computer software engineers evolve quickly, reflecting new areas of specialization or changes in technology as well as the preferences and practices of employers. Computer software engineers apply the principles and techniques of computer science, engineering, and mathematical analysis to the design, development, testing, and evaluation of the software and systems that enable computers to perform their many applications. (A separate description of engineers appears elsewhere in this book.)

Software engineers working in applications or systems development analyze users' needs and design, construct, test, and maintain computer applications software or systems. Software engineers can be involved in the design and development of many types of software, including software for operating systems and network distribution and compilers, which convert programs for execution on a computer. In programming, or coding, software engineers instruct a computer, line by line, how to perform a function. They also solve technical problems that arise. Software engineers must possess strong programming skills but are more concerned with developing algorithms and analyzing and solving programming problems than with actually writing code. (A separate description of computer programmers appears elsewhere in this book.)

Computer applications software engineers analyze users' needs and design, construct, and maintain general computer applications software or specialized utility programs. These workers use different programming languages, depending on the purpose of the program. The programming languages most often used are C, C++, and Java, with Fortran and COBOL used less commonly. Some software engineers develop both packaged systems and systems software or create customized applications.

Computer systems software engineers coordinate the construction and maintenance of a company's computer systems and plan their future growth. Working with the company, they coordinate each department's computer needs—ordering, inventory, billing, and payroll recordkeeping, for example—and make suggestions about its technical direction. They also might set up the company's intranets—networks that link computers within the organization and ease communication among the various departments.

Systems software engineers work for companies that configure, implement, and install complete computer systems. These workers may be members of the marketing or sales staff, serving as the primary technical resource for sales workers and customers. They also may be involved in product sales and in providing their customers with continuing technical support. Since the selling of complex computer systems often requires substantial customization for the purchaser's organization, software engineers help to explain the requirements necessary for installing and operating the new system in the purchaser's computing environment. In addition, systems software engineers are responsible for ensuring security across the systems they are configuring.

Computer software engineers often work as part of a team that designs new hardware, software, and systems. A core team may comprise engineering, marketing, manufacturing, and design people, who work together until the product is released.

Working Conditions

Computer software engineers normally work in well-lighted and comfortable offices or laboratories in which computer equipment is located. Most software engineers work at least 40 hours a week; however, due to the project-oriented nature of the work, they also may have to work evenings or weekends to meet deadlines or solve unexpected technical problems. Like other workers who sit for hours at a computer, typing on a keyboard, software engineers are susceptible to eyestrain, back discomfort, and hand and wrist problems such as carpal tunnel syndrome.

As they strive to improve software for users, many computer software engineers interact with customers and co-workers. Computer software engineers who are employed by software vendors and consulting firms, for example, spend much of their time away from their offices, frequently traveling overnight to meet with customers. They call on customers in businesses ranging from manufacturing plants to financial institutions.

As networks expand, software engineers may be able to use modems, laptops, e-mail, and the Internet to provide more technical support and other services from their main office, connecting to a customer's computer remotely to identify and correct developing problems.

Training, Other Qualifications, and Advancement

Most employers prefer to hire persons who have at least a bachelor's degree and broad knowledge of, and experience with, a variety of computer systems and technologies. The usual degree concentration for applications software engineers is computer science or software engineering; for systems software engineers, it is computer science or computer information systems. Graduate degrees are preferred for some of the more complex jobs.

Academic programs in software engineering emphasize software and may be offered as a degree option or in conjunction with computer science degrees. Increasing emphasis on computer security

suggests that software engineers with advanced degrees that include mathematics and systems design will be sought after by software developers, government agencies, and consulting firms specializing in information assurance and security. Students seeking software engineering jobs enhance their employment opportunities by participating in internship or co-op programs offered through their schools. These experiences provide the students with broad knowledge and experience, making them more attractive candidates to employers. Inexperienced college graduates may be hired by large computer and consulting firms that train new employees in intensive company-based programs. In many firms, new hires are mentored, and their mentors have an input into the performance evaluations of these new employees.

For systems software engineering jobs that require workers to have a college degree, a bachelor's degree in computer science or computer information systems is typical. For systems engineering jobs that place less emphasis on workers having a computer-related degree, computer training programs leading to certification are offered by systems software vendors. Nonetheless, most training authorities feel that program certification alone is not sufficient for the majority of software engineering jobs.

Persons interested in jobs as computer software engineers must have strong problem-solving and analytical skills. They also must be able to communicate effectively with team members, other staff, and the customers they meet. Because they often deal with a number of tasks simultaneously, they must be able to concentrate and pay close attention to detail.

As is the case with most occupations, advancement opportunities for computer software engineers increase with experience. Entry-level computer software engineers are likely to test and verify ongoing designs. As they become more experienced, they may become involved in designing and developing software. Eventually, they may advance to become a project manager, manager of information systems, or chief information officer. Some computer software engineers with several years of experience or expertise find lucrative opportunities working as systems designers or independent consultants or starting their own computer consulting firms.

As technological advances in the computer field continue, employers demand new skills. Computer software engineers must continually strive to acquire such skills if they wish to remain in this extremely dynamic field. For example, computer software engineers interested in working for a bank should have some expertise in finance as they integrate new technologies into the computer system of the bank. To help them keep up with the changing technology, continuing education and professional development seminars are offered by employers, software vendors, colleges and universities, private training institutions, and professional computing societies.

Employment

Computer software engineers held about 800,000 jobs in 2004. Approximately 460,000 were computer applications software engineers, and around 340,000 were computer systems software engineers. Although they are employed in most industries, the largest concentration of computer software engineers—almost 30 percent—are in computer systems design and related services. Many computer software engineers also work for establishments in other industries, such as software publishers, government agencies, manufacturers of computers and related electronic equipment, and management of companies and enterprises.

Employers of computer software engineers range from startup companies to established industry leaders. The proliferation of Internet, e-mail, and other communications systems is expanding electronics to engineering firms that are traditionally associated with unrelated disciplines. Engineering firms specializing in building bridges and power plants, for example, hire computer software engineers to design and develop new geographic data systems and automated drafting systems. Communications firms need computer software engineers to tap into growth in the personal communications market. Major communications companies have many job openings for both computer software applications engineers and computer systems engineers.

An increasing number of computer software engineers are employed on a temporary or contract basis, with many being self-employed, working independently as consultants. Some consultants work for firms that specialize in developing and maintaining client companies' Web sites and intranets. About 23,000 computer software engineers were self-employed in 2004.

Job Outlook

Computer software engineers are projected to be one of the fastest-growing occupations from 2004 to 2014. Rapid employment growth in the computer systems design and related services industry, which employs the greatest number of computer software engineers, should result in very good opportunities for those college graduates with at least a bachelor's degree in computer engineering or computer science and practical experience working with computers. Employers will continue to seek computer professionals with strong programming, systems analysis, interpersonal, and business skills. With the software industry beginning to mature, however, and with routine software engineering work being increasingly outsourced overseas, job growth will not be as rapid as during the previous decade.

Employment of computer software engineers is expected to increase much faster than the average for all occupations as businesses and other organizations adopt and integrate new technologies and seek to maximize the efficiency of their computer systems. Competition among businesses will continue to create an incentive for increasingly sophisticated technological innovations, and organizations will need more computer software engineers to implement these changes. In addition to jobs created through employment growth, many job openings will result annually from the need to replace workers who move into managerial positions, transfer to other occupations, or leave the labor force.

Demand for computer software engineers will increase as computer networking continues to grow. For example, the expanding integration of Internet technologies and the explosive growth in electronic commerce—doing business on the Internet—have resulted in rising demand for computer software engineers who can develop Internet, intranet, and World Wide Web applications. Likewise, expanding electronic data-processing systems in business, telecommunications, government, and other settings continue to become more sophisticated and complex. Growing numbers of systems software engineers

will be needed to implement, safeguard, and update systems and resolve problems. Consulting opportunities for computer software engineers also should continue to grow as businesses seek help to manage, upgrade, and customize their increasingly complicated computer systems.

New growth areas will continue to arise from rapidly evolving technologies. The increasing uses of the Internet, the proliferation of Web sites, and mobile technology such as the wireless Internet have created a demand for a wide variety of new products. As individuals and businesses rely more on hand-held computers and wireless networks, it will be necessary to integrate current computer systems with this new, more mobile technology. Also, information security concerns have given rise to new software needs. Concerns over "cyber security" should result in businesses and government continuing to invest heavily in software that protects their networks and vital electronic infrastructure from attack. The expansion of this technology in the next 10 years will lead to an increased need for computer engineers to design and develop the software and systems to run these new applications and integrate them into older systems.

As with other information technology jobs, employment growth of computer software engineers may be tempered somewhat as more software development is contracted out abroad. Firms may look to cut costs by shifting operations to lower-wage foreign countries with highly educated workers who have strong technical skills. At the same time, jobs in software engineering are less prone to being sent abroad compared with jobs in other computer specialties because the occupation requires innovation and intense research and development.

Earnings

Median annual earnings of computer applications software engineers who worked full time in May 2004 were about $74,980. The middle 50 percent earned between $59,130 and $92,130. The lowest 10 percent earned less than $46,520, and the highest 10 percent earned more than $113,830. Median annual earnings in the industries employing the largest numbers of computer applications software engineers in May 2004 were as follows:

Software publishers	$79,930
Management, scientific, and technical consulting services	78,460
Computer systems design and related services	76,910
Management of companies and enterprises	70,520
Insurance carriers	68,440

Median annual earnings of computer systems software engineers who worked full time in May 2004 were about $79,740. The middle 50 percent earned between $63,150 and $98,220. The lowest 10 percent earned less than $50,420, and the highest 10 percent earned more than $118,350. Median annual earnings in the industries employing the largest numbers of computer systems software engineers in May 2004 are as follows:

Scientific research and development services	$91,390
Computer and peripheral equipment manufacturing	87,800
Software publishers	83,670

Computer systems design and related services 79,950

Wired telecommunications carriers 74,370

According to the National Association of Colleges and Employers, starting salary offers for graduates with a bachelor's degree in computer engineering averaged $52,464 in 2005; offers for those with a master's degree averaged $60,354. Starting salary offers for graduates with a bachelor's degree in computer science averaged $50,820.

According to Robert Half International, starting salaries for software engineers in software development ranged from $63,250 to $92,750 in 2005. For network engineers, starting salaries in 2005 ranged from $61,250 to $88,250.

Related Occupations

Other workers who use mathematics and logic extensively include computer systems analysts, computer scientists and database administrators, computer programmers, computer hardware engineers, computer support specialists and systems administrators, engineers, statisticians, mathematicians, and actuaries.

Sources of Additional Information

Additional information on a career in computer software engineering is available from the following organizations:

▶ Association for Computing Machinery (ACM), 1515 Broadway, New York, NY 10036. Internet: http://www.acm.org

▶ Institute of Electronics and Electrical Engineers Computer Society, Headquarters Office, 1730 Massachusetts Ave. NW, Washington, DC 20036-1992. Internet: http://www.computer.org

▶ National Workforce Center for Emerging Technologies, 3000 Landerholm Circle SE, Bellevue, WA 98007. Internet: http://www.nwcet.org

Computer Systems Analysts

(O*NET 15-1051.00)

Significant Points

■ Employers generally prefer applicants who have at least a bachelor's degree in computer science, information science, or management information systems (MIS).

■ Employment is expected to increase much faster than the average as organizations continue to adopt increasingly sophisticated technologies.

■ Job prospects are favorable.

Nature of the Work

All organizations rely on computer and information technology to conduct business and operate more efficiently. The rapid spread of technology across all industries has generated a need for highly trained workers to help organizations incorporate new technologies. The tasks performed by workers known as *computer systems analysts* evolve rapidly, reflecting new areas of specialization or changes in technology as well as the preferences and practices of employers.

Computer systems analysts solve computer problems and apply computer technology to meet the individual needs of an organization. They help an organization to realize the maximum benefit from its investment in equipment, personnel, and business processes. Systems analysts may plan and develop new computer systems or devise ways to apply existing systems' resources to additional operations. They may design new systems, including both hardware and software, or add a new software application to harness more of the computer's power. Most systems analysts work with specific types of systems—for example, business, accounting, or financial systems or scientific and engineering systems—that vary with the kind of organization. Some systems analysts also are known as *systems developers* or *systems architects*.

Systems analysts begin an assignment by discussing the systems problem with managers and users to determine its exact nature. Defining the goals of the system and dividing the solutions into individual steps and separate procedures, systems analysts use techniques such as structured analysis, data modeling, information engineering, mathematical model building, sampling, and cost accounting to plan the system. They specify the inputs to be accessed by the system, design the processing steps, and format the output to meet users' needs. They also may prepare cost-benefit and return-on-investment analyses to help management decide whether implementing the proposed technology will be financially feasible.

When a system is accepted, systems analysts determine what computer hardware and software will be needed to set the system up. They coordinate tests and observe the initial use of the system to ensure that it performs as planned. They prepare specifications, flow charts, and process diagrams for computer programmers to follow; then, they work with programmers to "debug," or eliminate, errors from the system. Systems analysts who do more in-depth testing of products may be referred to as *software quality assurance analysts*. In addition to running tests, these individuals diagnose problems, recommend solutions, and determine whether program requirements have been met.

In some organizations, *programmer-analysts* design and update the software that runs a computer. Because they are responsible for both programming and systems analysis, these workers must be proficient in both areas. (A separate description of computer programmers appears elsewhere in this book.) As this dual proficiency becomes more commonplace, these analysts are increasingly working with databases and object-oriented programming languages as well as client-server applications development and multimedia and Internet technology.

One obstacle associated with expanding computer use is the need for different computer systems to communicate with each other. Because of the importance of maintaining up-to-date information—accounting records, sales figures, or budget projections, for example—systems analysts work on making the computer systems within an organization, or among organizations, compatible so that information can be shared among them. Many systems analysts are involved with "networking," connecting all the computers internally—in an individual office, department, or establishment—or externally because many organizations rely on e-mail or the Internet. A primary goal of networking is to allow users to retrieve data from a mainframe computer or a server and use it on their desktop computer. Systems analysts must design the hardware and software to allow the free exchange of data, custom applications, and the computer power to process it all. For example, analysts are called upon to ensure the compatibility of computing systems between and among businesses to facilitate electronic commerce.

Working Conditions

Computer systems analysts work in offices or laboratories in comfortable surroundings. They usually work about 40 hours a week—the same as many other professional or office workers do. However, evening or weekend work may be necessary to meet deadlines or solve specific problems. Given the technology available today, telecommuting is common for computer professionals. As networks expand, more work can be done from remote locations through modems, laptops, electronic mail, and the Internet.

Like other workers who spend long periods in front of a computer terminal typing on a keyboard, computer systems analysts are susceptible to eyestrain, back discomfort, and hand and wrist problems such as carpal tunnel syndrome or cumulative trauma disorder.

Training, Other Qualifications, and Advancement

Rapidly changing technology requires an increasing level of skill and education on the part of employees. Companies increasingly look for professionals with a broad background and range of skills, including not only technical knowledge but also communication and other interpersonal skills. This shift from requiring workers to possess solely sound technical knowledge emphasizes workers who can handle various responsibilities. While there is no universally accepted way to prepare for a job as a systems analyst, most employers place a premium on some formal college education. Relevant work experience also is very important. For more technically complex jobs, persons with graduate degrees are preferred.

Many employers seek applicants who have at least a bachelor's degree in computer science, information science, or management information systems (MIS). MIS programs usually are part of the business school or college and differ considerably from computer science programs, emphasizing business and management-oriented coursework and business computing courses. Employers are increasingly seeking individuals with a master's degree in business administration (MBA), with a concentration in information systems, as more firms move their business to the Internet.

Despite employers' preference for those with technical degrees, persons with degrees in a variety of majors find employment as system analysts. The level of education and type of training that employers require depend on their needs. One factor affecting these needs is changes in technology. Employers often scramble to find workers capable of implementing "hot" new technologies such as wireless Internet. Those workers with formal education or experience in information security, for example, are in demand because of the growing need for their skills and services. Another factor driving employers' needs is the timeframe during which a project must be completed.

Employers usually look for people who have broad knowledge and experience related to computer systems and technologies, strong problem-solving and analytical skills, and good interpersonal skills.

Courses in computer science or systems design offer good preparation for a job in these computer occupations. For jobs in a business environment, employers usually want systems analysts to have business management or closely related skills, while a background in the physical sciences, applied mathematics, or engineering is preferred for work in scientifically oriented organizations.

Job seekers can enhance their employment opportunities by participating in internship or co-op programs offered through their schools. Because many people develop advanced computer skills in a non-computer-related occupation and then transfer those skills to a computer occupation, a background in the industry in which the person's job is located, such as financial services, banking, or accounting, can be important. Others have taken computer science courses to supplement their study in fields such as accounting, inventory control, or other business areas.

Computer systems analysts must be able to think logically and have good communication skills. Because they often deal with a number of tasks simultaneously, the ability to concentrate and pay close attention to detail is important. Although these workers sometimes work independently, they frequently work in teams on large projects. They must be able to communicate effectively with computer personnel, such as programmers and managers, as well as with users or other staff who may have no technical computer background.

Systems analysts may be promoted to senior or lead systems analyst. Those who show leadership ability also can become project managers or advance into management positions such as manager of information systems or chief information officer. Workers with work experience and considerable expertise in a particular subject or a certain application may find lucrative opportunities as independent consultants or may choose to start their own computer consulting firms.

Technological advances come so rapidly in the computer field that continuous study is necessary to keep one's skills up to date. Employers, hardware and software vendors, colleges and universities, and private training institutions offer continuing education. Additional training may come from professional development seminars offered by professional computing societies.

Employment

Computer systems analysts held about 487,000 jobs in 2004; about 28,000 were self-employed.

Although they are increasingly employed in every sector of the economy, the greatest concentration of these workers is in the computer systems design and related services industry. Firms in this industry provide services related to the commercial use of computers on a contract basis, including custom computer programming services; computer systems integration design services; computer facilities management services, including computer systems or data-processing facilities; support services for clients; and other computer services, such as disaster recovery services and software installation. Computer systems analysts are also employed by governments, insurance companies, financial institutions, Internet service providers, data-processing services firms, and universities.

A growing number of systems analysts are employed on a temporary or contract basis; many of these individuals are self-employed, working independently as contractors or consultants. For example, a company installing a new computer system may need the services of several systems analysts just to get the system running. Because not all of the analysts would be needed once the system is functioning, the company might contract for such employees with a temporary help agency or a consulting firm or with the systems analysts themselves. Such jobs may last from several months up to 2 years or more. This growing practice enables companies to bring in people with the exact skills the firm needs to complete a particular project instead of having to spend time or money training or retraining existing workers. Often, experienced consultants then train a company's in-house staff as a project develops.

Job Outlook

Employment of computer systems analysts is expected to grow much faster than the average for all occupations through the year 2014 as organizations continue to adopt and integrate increasingly sophisticated technologies. Job increases will be driven by very rapid growth in computer system design and related services, which is projected to be among the fastest-growing industries in the U.S. economy. In addition, many job openings will arise annually from the need to replace workers who move into managerial positions or other occupations or who leave the labor force. Job growth will not be as rapid as during the previous decade, however, as the information technology sector begins to mature and as routine work is increasingly outsourced to lower-wage foreign countries.

Workers in the occupation should enjoy favorable job prospects. The demand for networking to facilitate the sharing of information, the expansion of client-server environments, and the need for computer specialists to use their knowledge and skills in a problem-solving capacity will be major factors in the rising demand for computer systems analysts. Moreover, falling prices of computer hardware and software should continue to induce more businesses to expand their computerized operations and integrate new technologies into them. In order to maintain a competitive edge and operate more efficiently, firms will keep demanding system analysts who are knowledgeable about the latest technologies and are able to apply them to meet the needs of businesses.

Increasingly, more sophisticated and complex technology is being implemented across all organizations, which should fuel the demand for these computer occupations. There is a growing demand for system analysts to help firms maximize their efficiency with available technology. Expansion of electronic commerce—doing business on the Internet—and the continuing need to build and maintain databases that store critical information on customers, inventory, and projects are fueling demand for database administrators familiar with the latest technology. Also, the increasing importance being placed on "cybersecurity"—the protection of electronic information—will result in a need for workers skilled in information security.

The development of new technologies usually leads to demand for various kinds of workers. The expanding integration of Internet technologies into businesses, for example, has resulted in a growing need for specialists who can develop and support Internet and intranet applications. The growth of electronic commerce means that more establishments use the Internet to conduct their business online. The introduction of wireless Internet, known as WiFi, creates new systems to be analyzed. The spread of such new technologies translates into a need for information technology professionals who can help organizations use technology to communicate with employees, clients, and consumers. Explosive growth in these areas also is expected to fuel demand for analysts who are knowledgeable about network, data, and communications security.

As technology becomes more sophisticated and complex, employers demand a higher level of skill and expertise from their employees. Individuals with an advanced degree in computer science or computer engineering, or with an MBA with a concentration in information systems, should enjoy favorable employment prospects. College graduates with a bachelor's degree in computer science, computer engineering, information science, or MIS also should enjoy favorable prospects for employment, particularly if they have supplemented their formal education with practical experience. Because employers continue to seek computer specialists who can combine strong technical skills with good interpersonal and business skills, graduates with non–computer science degrees who have had courses in computer programming, systems analysis, and other information technology subjects also should continue to find jobs in computer fields. In fact, individuals with the right experience and training can work in computer occupations regardless of their college major or level of formal education.

Earnings

Median annual earnings of computer systems analysts were $66,460 in May 2004. The middle 50 percent earned between $52,400 and $82,980 a year. The lowest 10 percent earned less than $41,730, and the highest 10 percent earned more than $99,180. Median annual earnings in the industries employing the largest numbers of computer systems analysts in May 2004 were

Federal government $71,770

Computer systems design and related services 69,560

Management of companies and enterprises 67,230

Insurance carriers 66,840

State government 57,040

According to the National Association of Colleges and Employers, starting offers for graduates with a master's degree in computer science averaged $62,727 in 2005. Starting offers averaged $50,820 for graduates with a bachelor's degree in computer science, $46,189 for those with a degree in computer systems analysis, $44,417 for those with a degree in management information systems, and $44,775 for those with a degree in information sciences and systems.

According to Robert Half International, starting salaries for systems analysts ranged from $61,500 to $82,500 in 2005.

Related Occupations

Other workers who use computers extensively and who use logic and creativity to solve business and technical problems include computer programmers, computer software engineers, computer and information systems managers, engineers, mathematicians, statisticians, operations research analysts, management analysts, and actuaries.

Sources of Additional Information

Further information about computer careers is available from

▶ Association for Computing Machinery (ACM), 1515 Broadway, New York, NY 10036. Internet: http://www.acm.org

▶ Institute of Electrical and Electronics Engineers Computer Society, Headquarters Office, 1730 Massachusetts Ave. NW, Washington, DC 20036-1992. Internet: http://www.computer.org

▶ National Workforce Center for Emerging Technologies, 3000 Landerholm Circle SE, Bellevue, WA 98007. Internet: http://www.nwcet.org

Conservation Scientists and Foresters

(O*NET 19-1031.01, 19-1031.02, 19-1031.03, and 19-1032.00)

Significant Points

■ About two thirds of salaried conservation scientists and foresters work for federal, state, or local governments.

■ A bachelor's degree in forestry, range management, or a related discipline is the minimum educational requirement.

■ Slower-than-average job growth is projected; most new jobs will be in state and local governments and in private-sector forestry and conservation consulting.

Nature of the Work

Forests and rangelands supply wood products, livestock forage, minerals, and water; serve as sites for recreational activities; and provide habitats for wildlife.

Conservation scientists and foresters manage their use and development and help to protect these and other natural resources, and for this reason, they are becoming known as natural resource managers.

Foresters manage forested lands for a variety of purposes. Those working in private industry may manage company-owned forest land or procure timber from private landowners. Company forests usually are managed to produce a sustainable supply of wood for company mills. *Procurement foresters* contact local forest owners and gain permission to take inventory of the type, amount, and location of all standing timber on the property, a process known as timber cruising. These foresters then appraise the timber's worth, negotiate its purchase, and draw up a contract for procurement. Next, they subcontract with loggers or pulpwood cutters for tree removal and aid in laying out roads to access the timber. Throughout the process, foresters maintain close contact with the subcontractor's workers and the landowner to ensure that the work meets the landowner's requirements, as well as federal, state, and local environmental specifications. Forestry consultants often act as agents for forest owners, monitoring the growth of the timber on the owners' property and negotiating timber sales with industrial procurement foresters.

Foresters, referred to as *land management foresters,* work for both government and private industry and manage and protect the forests and supervise harvests. These foresters supervise the planting and growing of new trees, called regeneration. They choose and direct the preparation of the site, using controlled burning, bulldozers, or herbicides to clear weeds, brush, and logging debris. They advise on the type, number, and placement of trees to be planted. Foresters then monitor the seedlings to ensure healthy growth and to determine the best time for harvesting. If they detect signs of disease or harmful insects, they consult with specialists in forest pest management to decide on the best course of treatment. They may also design campgrounds and recreation areas on public lands.

Throughout the forest management and procurement processes, foresters consider the economics as well as the environmental impact on natural resources. To do this, they determine how to conserve wildlife habitats, creek beds, water quality, and soil stability and how best to comply with environmental regulations. Foresters must balance the desire to conserve forested ecosystems for future generations with the need to use forest resources for recreational or economic purposes.

Foresters use a number of tools to perform their jobs. Clinometers measure the height of trees, diameter tapes measure the diameter, and increment borers and bark gauges measure the growth of trees so that timber volumes can be computed and growth rates estimated. Remote sensing (aerial photographs and other imagery taken from airplanes and satellites) and Geographic Information Systems (GIS) data often are used for mapping large forest areas and for detecting widespread trends of forest and land use. Once the map is generated, the data are digitized to create a computerized inventory of information required to manage the forest land and its resources. Moreover, hand-held computers, Global Positioning Systems (GPS), and World Wide Web–based applications are used extensively.

Conservation scientists manage, improve, and protect the country's natural resources. They work with the landowners and federal, state, and local governments to devise ways to use and improve the land without damaging the environment. Although conservation scientists mainly advise farmers, farm managers, and ranchers on ways they can improve their land for agricultural purposes and to control erosion, a growing number are advising landowners and governments on recreational uses for the land.

Two of the more common conservation scientists are range managers and soil conservationists. *Range managers*, also called *range conservationists*, *range ecologists*, or *range scientists*, study, manage, improve, and protect rangelands to maximize their use without damaging the environment. Rangelands cover hundreds of millions of acres of the United States, mostly in western states and Alaska. They contain many natural resources, including grass and shrubs for animal grazing, wildlife habitats, water from vast watersheds, recreation facilities, and valuable mineral and energy resources. Range managers may inventory soils, plants, and animals; develop resource management plans; help to restore degraded ecosystems; or assist in managing a ranch. For example, they may help ranchers attain optimum livestock production by determining the number and kind of animals to graze, the grazing system to use, and the best season for grazing. At the same time, however, range managers maintain soil stability and vegetation for other uses such as wildlife habitats and outdoor recreation. They also plan and implement revegetation of disturbed sites.

Soil and water conservationists provide technical assistance to farmers, ranchers, forest managers, state and local agencies, and others concerned with the conservation of soil, water, and related natural resources. They develop programs for private landowners designed to make the most productive use of land without damaging it. Soil conservationists also assist landowners by visiting areas with erosion problems, finding the source of the problem, and helping landowners and managers develop management practices to combat it. Water conservationists also assist private landowners and federal, state, and local governments by advising on a broad range of natural resource topics—specifically, issues of water quality, preserving water supplies, groundwater contamination, and management and conservation of water resources.

Conservation scientists and foresters often specialize in one area, such as wildlife management, urban forestry, pest management, native species, or forest economics.

Working Conditions

Working conditions vary considerably. Although some of the work is solitary, foresters and conservation scientists also deal regularly with landowners, loggers, forestry technicians and aides, farmers, ranchers, government officials, special interest groups, and the public in general. Some foresters and conservation scientists work regular hours in offices or labs. Others may split their time between fieldwork and office work, while independent consultants and especially new, less experienced workers spend the majority of their time outdoors overseeing or participating in hands-on work.

The work can be physically demanding. Some conservation scientists and foresters work outdoors in all types of weather, sometimes in isolated areas, and consequently may need to walk long distances through densely wooded land to carry out their work. Foresters also may work long hours fighting fires. Conservation scientists often are called to prevent erosion after a forest fire, and they provide emergency help after floods, mudslides, and tropical storms.

Training, Other Qualifications, and Advancement

A bachelor's degree in forestry, biology, natural resource management, environmental sciences, or a related discipline is the minimum educational requirement for careers in forestry or conservation science. In the federal government, a combination of experience and appropriate education occasionally may substitute for a 4-year forestry degree, but job competition makes this difficult. Foresters who wish to perform specialized research or teach should have an advanced degree, preferably a Ph.D.

Seventeen states have mandatory licensing and/or voluntary registration requirements that a forester must meet in order to acquire the title "professional forester" and practice forestry in the state. Of those 17 states, 9 have mandatory licensing; 8 have mandatory registration. Both licensing and registration requirements usually entail completing a 4-year degree in forestry and several years of forestry

work experience. Candidates pursuing licensing also may be required to pass a comprehensive written exam.

Most land-grant colleges and universities offer a bachelor's or higher degree in forestry. The Society of American Foresters accredits about 48 such programs throughout the country. Curriculums stress four components: forest ecology and biology, measurement of forest resources, management of forest resources, and public policy. Students should balance general science courses such as ecology, biology, tree physiology, taxonomy, and soil formation with technical forestry courses, such as forest inventory or wildlife habitat assessment, remote sensing, land surveying, GPS technology, integrated forest resource management, silviculture, and forest protection. In addition, mathematics, statistics, and computer science courses also are recommended. Many forestry curriculums include advanced computer applications such as GIS and resource assessment programs. Courses in resource policy and administration, specifically forest economics and business administration, supplement the student's scientific and technical knowledge. Forestry curriculums increasingly include courses on best management practices, wetlands analysis, and sustainability and regulatory issues in response to the growing focus on protecting forested lands during timber harvesting operations. Prospective foresters should have a strong grasp of federal, state, and local policy issues and of increasingly numerous and complex environmental regulations that affect many forestry-related activities. Many colleges require students to complete a field session either in a camp operated by the college or in a cooperative work-study program with a federal or state agency or with private industry. All schools encourage students to take summer jobs that provide experience in forestry or conservation work.

Conservation scientists generally hold a minimum of a bachelor's degree in fields such as ecology, natural resource management, agriculture, biology, environmental science, or a related field. A master's or Ph.D. degree is usually required for teaching and research positions.

Range managers usually have a degree in range management or range science. Nine colleges and universities offer degrees in range management that are accredited by the Society of Range Management. More than forty other schools offer course work in range science or in a closely related discipline offering a range management or range science option. Specialized range management courses combine plant, animal, and soil sciences with principles of ecology and resource management. Desirable electives include economics, statistics, forestry, hydrology, agronomy, wildlife, animal husbandry, computer science, and recreation. Selection of a minor in range management, such as wildlife ecology, watershed management, animal science, or agricultural economics, can often enhance qualifications for certain types of employment.

The Society for Range Management offers two types of certification: one as a certified professional in rangeland management (CPRM) and another as a certified range management consultant. Candidates seeking certification must have at least a bachelor's degree in range science or a closely related field, have a minimum of 6 years of full-time work experience, and pass a comprehensive written exam.

The Society of American Foresters has a Certified Forester Program. To become certified through this program, a candidate must graduate with at least a bachelor's degree from a forestry program accredited by the Society or from a forestry program that, though not accredited by the Society, is substantially equivalent. In addition, the candidate must have five years of qualifying professional experience and pass an examination.

Additionally, a graduate with the proper coursework in college can seek certification as a wetland scientist through the Society of Wetland Scientists and certification as a professional wildlife biologist through the Wildlife Society.

Very few colleges and universities offer degrees in soil conservation. Most soil conservationists have degrees in environmental studies, agronomy, general agriculture, hydrology, or crop or soil science; a few have degrees in related fields such as wildlife biology, forestry, and range management. Programs of study usually include 30 semester hours in natural resources or agriculture, including at least 3 hours in soil science.

In addition to meeting the demands of forestry and conservation research and analysis, foresters and conservation scientists generally must enjoy working outdoors, be able to tolerate extensive walking and other types of physical exertion, and be willing to move to where the jobs are. They also must work well with people and have good communication skills.

Recent forestry and conservation scientist graduates usually work under the supervision of experienced foresters or scientists. After gaining experience, they may advance to more responsible positions. In the federal government, most entry-level foresters work in forest resource management. An experienced federal forester may supervise a ranger district and may advance to forest supervisor, to regional forester, or to a top administrative position in the national headquarters. In private industry, foresters start by learning the practical and administrative aspects of the business and acquiring comprehensive technical training. They are then introduced to contract writing, timber harvesting, and decisionmaking. Some foresters work their way up to top managerial positions within their companies. Foresters in management usually leave the fieldwork behind, spending more of their time in an office, working with teams to develop management plans and supervising others. After gaining several years of experience, some foresters may become consulting foresters, working alone or with one or several partners. They contract with state or local governments, private landowners, private industry, or other forestry consulting groups.

Soil conservationists usually begin working within one county or conservation district and, with experience, may advance to the area, state, regional, or national level. Also, soil conservationists can transfer to related occupations, such as farm or ranch management advisor or land appraiser.

Employment

Conservation scientists and foresters held about 32,000 jobs in 2004. More than 1 in 3 workers were employed by the federal government, mostly in the U.S. Departments of Agriculture (USDA) and Interior. Foresters were concentrated in the USDA's Forest Service; soil conservationists were employed primarily in the USDA's Natural Resource Conservation Service. Most range managers worked in the U.S. Department of the Interior's Bureau of Land Management, the Natural Resource Conservation Service, or the Forest Service. Another 21 percent of conservation scientists and foresters worked

for state governments, and about 11 percent worked for local governments. The remainder worked in private industry, mainly in support activities for agriculture and forestry or in wood product manufacturing. Some were self-employed as consultants for private landowners, federal and state governments, and forestry-related businesses.

Although conservation scientists and foresters work in every state, employment of foresters is concentrated in the western and southeastern states, where many national and private forests and parks, and most of the lumber and pulpwood-producing forests, are located. Range managers work almost entirely in the western states, where most of the rangeland is located. Soil conservationists, on the other hand, are employed in almost every county in the country. Besides the jobs described here, some foresters and conservation scientists held faculty positions in colleges and universities. (See the description of teachers—postsecondary elsewhere in this book.)

Job Outlook

Employment of conservation scientists and foresters is expected to increase more slowly than the average for all occupations through 2014. Growth should be strongest in private-sector consulting firms. Demand will be spurred by a continuing emphasis on environmental protection, responsible land management, and water-related issues. Growing interest in developing private lands and forests for recreational purposes will generate additional jobs for foresters and conservation scientists. Fire prevention is another area of growth for these two occupations.

Job opportunities for conservation scientists will arise because government regulations, such as those regarding the management of storm water and coastlines, have created demand for persons knowledgeable about runoff and erosion on farms and in cities and suburbs. Soil and water quality experts will be needed as states design initiatives to improve water resources by preventing pollution by agricultural producers and industrial plants.

Overall employment of conservation scientists and foresters is expected to decline slightly in the federal government, mostly because of budgetary constraints and the trend among all levels of government toward contracting these functions out to private consulting firms. Also, federal land management agencies, such as the USDA Forest Service, have de-emphasized their timber programs and increasingly focused on wildlife, recreation, and sustaining ecosystems, thereby spurring demand for other life and social scientists rather than for foresters. However, departures of foresters who retire or leave the government for other reasons will result in many job openings. Additionally, state governments are expected to increase their hiring of conservation scientists and foresters as their budgetary situations improve. A small number of new jobs will result from the need for range and soil conservationists to provide technical assistance to owners of grazing land through the Natural Resource Conservation Service.

Foresters involved with timber harvesting will find good opportunities in the Southeast, where much forested land is privately owned. However, the recent opening of public lands, especially in the West, to commercial activity will also help the outlook for foresters. Salaried foresters working for private industry—such as paper companies, sawmills, and pulpwood mills—and consulting foresters will be needed to provide technical assistance and management plans to landowners.

Scientific research and development services have increased their hiring of conservation scientists and foresters in recent years in response to demand for professionals to prepare environmental impact statements and erosion and sediment control plans; monitor water quality near logging sites; and advise on tree harvesting practices required by federal, state, or local regulations. Hiring in these firms should continue during the 2004–2014 period.

Earnings

Median annual earnings of conservation scientists in May 2004 were $52,480. The middle 50 percent earned between $39,660 and $65,550. The lowest 10 percent earned less than $30,740, and the highest 10 percent earned more than $78,470.

Median annual earnings of foresters in 2004 were $48,230. The middle 50 percent earned between $37,260 and $60,500. The lowest 10 percent earned less than $29,770, and the highest 10 percent earned more than $72,050.

In 2005, most bachelor's degree graduates entering the federal government as foresters, range managers, or soil conservationists started at $24,677 or $30,567, depending on academic achievement. Those with a master's degree could start at $37,390 or $45,239. Holders of doctorates could start at $54,221. Beginning salaries were slightly higher in selected areas where the prevailing local pay level was higher. In 2005, the average federal salary for foresters in nonsupervisory, supervisory, and managerial positions was $63,492; for soil conservationists, $60,671; and for rangeland managers, $58,162.

According to the National Association of Colleges and Employers, graduates with a bachelor's degree in conservation and renewable natural resources received an average starting salary offer of $27,950 in 2005.

In private industry, starting salaries for students with a bachelor's degree were comparable with starting salaries in the federal government, but starting salaries in state and local governments were usually lower.

Conservation scientists and foresters who work for federal, state, and local governments and large private firms generally receive more generous benefits than do those working for smaller firms.

Related Occupations

Conservation scientists and foresters manage, develop, and protect natural resources. Other workers with similar responsibilities include environmental engineers; agricultural and food scientists; biological scientists; environmental scientists and geoscientists; and farmers, ranchers, and agricultural managers.

Sources of Additional Information

For information about the forestry profession and lists of schools offering education in forestry, send a self-addressed, stamped business envelope to

▶ Society of American Foresters, 5400 Grosvenor Lane, Bethesda, MD 20814-2198. Internet: http://www.safnet.org

Information about a career as a range manager, as well as a list of schools offering training, is available from

▶ Society for Range Management, 445 Union Blvd., Suite 230, Lakewood, CO 80228-1259. Internet: http://www.rangelands.org

For information on certification as a professional wildlife biologist, contact

▶ The Wildlife Society, 5410 Grosvenor Lane, Suite 200, Bethesda, MD 20814-2197. Internet: http://www.wildlife.org/certification/index.cfm

Information on obtaining a position as a conservation scientist or forester with the federal government is available from the Office of Personnel Management (OPM) through USAJOBS, the federal government's official employment information system. This resource for locating and applying for job opportunities can be accessed through the Internet at http://www.usajobs.opm.gov or through an interactive voice response telephone system at (703) 724-1850 or TDD (978)461-8404. These numbers are not toll free, and charges may result.

Construction Managers

(O*NET 11-9021.00)

Significant Points

■ Construction managers must be available—often 24 hours a day—to deal with delays, bad weather, or emergencies at the jobsite.

■ Employers prefer individuals who combine construction industry work experience with a bachelor's degree in construction science, construction management, or civil engineering.

■ Excellent employment opportunities are expected as the increasing complexity of many construction projects requires more managers to oversee them.

Nature of the Work

Construction managers plan, direct, and coordinate a wide variety of construction projects, including the building of all types of residential, commercial, and industrial structures; roads; bridges; wastewater treatment plants; and schools and hospitals. Construction managers may oversee an entire project or just part of a project and, although they usually play no direct role in the actual construction of a structure, they typically schedule and coordinate all design and construction processes, including the selection, hiring, and oversight of specialty trade contractors.

Construction managers are salaried or self-employed managers who oversee construction supervisors and workers. They often go by the job titles program manager, constructor, construction superintendent, project engineer, project manager, construction supervisor, general contractor, or similar designations. Construction managers may be owners or salaried employees of a construction management or contracting firm or may work under contract or as a salaried employee of the property owner, developer, or contracting firm overseeing the construction project.

Construction managers coordinate and supervise the construction process from the conceptual development stage through final construction, making sure that the project gets done on time and within budget. They often work with owners, engineers, architects, and others who are involved in the construction process. Given the designs for buildings, roads, bridges, or other projects, construction managers oversee the planning, scheduling, and implementation of the project to execute those designs.

Large construction projects, such as an office building or industrial complex, are often too complicated for one person to manage. Therefore, these projects are divided into many segments: site preparation, including land clearing and earth moving; sewage systems; landscaping and road construction; building construction, including excavation and laying of foundations and erection of the structural framework, floors, walls, and roofs; and building systems, including fire-protection, electrical, plumbing, air-conditioning, and heating. Construction managers may be in charge of one or more of these activities.

Construction managers evaluate and help determine appropriate construction delivery systems and the most cost-effective plan and schedule for completing the project. They divide all required construction site activities into logical steps, budgeting the time required to meet established deadlines. This may require sophisticated estimating and scheduling techniques and use of computers with specialized software.

Construction managers oversee the selection of general contractors and trade contractors to complete specific pieces of the project—which could include everything from structural metalworking and plumbing to painting and carpet installation. Construction managers determine the labor requirements and, in some cases, supervise or monitor the hiring and dismissal of workers. They oversee the performance of all trade contractors and are responsible for ensuring that all work is completed on schedule.

Construction managers direct and monitor the progress of construction activities, sometimes through construction supervisors or other construction managers. They oversee the delivery and use of materials, tools, and equipment and the quality of construction, worker productivity, and safety. They are responsible for obtaining all necessary permits and licenses and, depending upon the contractual arrangements, direct or monitor compliance with building and safety codes and other regulations. Also, they continually track and control construction costs to avoid cost overruns. They may direct the work of several subordinates, such as assistant managers or superintendents, field engineers, or crew supervisors.

Working Conditions

Construction managers work out of a main office from which the overall construction project is monitored or out of a field office at the construction site. Advances in telecommunications and Internet access allow construction managers to be onsite without being out of contact with the main office. Management decisions regarding daily construction activities generally are made at the jobsite. Managers may travel extensively when the construction site is not close

to their main office or when they are responsible for activities at two or more sites. Management of overseas construction projects usually entails temporary residence in another country.

Construction managers may be "on call"—often 24 hours a day—to deal with delays, the effects of bad weather, or emergencies at the site. Most work more than a standard 40-hour week because construction may proceed around the clock. They may have to work this type of schedule for days, even weeks, to meet special project deadlines, especially if there are delays.

Although the work usually is not considered inherently dangerous, construction managers must be careful while performing onsite services.

Training, Other Qualifications, and Advancement

Persons interested in becoming a construction manager need a solid background in building science, business, and management, as well as related work experience within the construction industry. They need to understand contracts, plans, and specifications and to be knowledgeable about construction methods, materials, and regulations. Familiarity with computers and software programs for job costing, online collaboration, scheduling, and estimating also is important. The ability to converse fluently in Spanish is also an asset because Spanish is the first language of many workers in the construction industry.

Construction managers should be flexible and work effectively in a fast-paced environment. They should be decisive and work well under pressure, particularly when faced with unexpected occurrences or delays. The ability to coordinate several major activities at once, while analyzing and resolving specific problems, is essential, as is an understanding of engineering, architectural, and other construction drawings. Good oral and written communication skills also are important, as are leadership skills. Managers must be able to establish a good working relationship with many different people, including owners, other managers, designers, supervisors, and craftworkers.

For construction manager jobs, employers increasingly prefer to hire individuals with a bachelor's degree in construction science, construction management, or civil engineering, as well as industry work experience. Practical industry experience is very important, whether it is acquired through an internship, a cooperative education program, or work experience in a trade or another job in the industry. Traditionally, persons advanced to construction management positions after having substantial experience as construction craftworkers—carpenters, masons, plumbers, or electricians, for example—or after having worked as construction supervisors or as owners of independent specialty contracting firms, overseeing workers in one or more construction trades. However, as construction processes become increasingly complex, employers are placing a growing importance on postsecondary education.

Many colleges and universities offer 4-year degree programs in construction management, construction science, and construction engineering. These programs include courses in project control and development, site planning, design, construction methods, construction materials, value analysis, cost estimating, scheduling, contract administration, accounting, business and financial management, safety, building codes and standards, inspection procedures, engineering and architectural sciences, mathematics, statistics, and information technology. Graduates from 4-year degree programs usually are hired as assistants to project managers, field engineers, schedulers, or cost estimators. An increasing number of graduates in related fields—engineering or architecture, for example—also enter construction management, often after acquiring substantial experience on construction projects or after completing graduate studies in construction management or building science.

Several colleges and universities offer a master's degree program in construction management or construction science. Master's degree recipients, especially those with work experience in construction, typically become construction managers in very large construction or construction management companies. Often, individuals who hold a bachelor's degree in an unrelated field seek a master's degree in construction management or construction science in order to work in the construction industry. Some construction managers obtain a master's degree in business administration or finance to further their career prospects. Doctoral degree recipients usually become college professors or conduct research.

Many individuals also attend training and educational programs sponsored by industry associations, often in collaboration with post-secondary institutions. A number of 2-year colleges throughout the country offer construction management or construction technology programs.

There is a growing movement towards certification of construction managers to ensure that a construction manager has a certain body of knowledge, abilities, and experience. Although certification is not required to work in the construction industry, voluntary certification can be valuable because it provides evidence of competence and experience. Both the American Institute of Constructors (AIC) and the Construction Management Association of America (CMAA) have established voluntary certification programs for construction managers. Requirements combine written examinations with verification of education and professional experience. AIC awards the Associate Constructor (AC) and Certified Professional Constructor (CPC) designations to candidates who meet its requirements and pass the appropriate construction examinations. CMAA awards the Certified Construction Manager (CCM) designation to practitioners who meet its requirements through work performed in a construction management organization and by passing a technical examination. Applicants for the CMAA certification also must complete a self-study course that covers a broad range of topics central to construction management, including the professional role of a construction manager, legal issues, and allocation of risk.

Advancement opportunities for construction managers vary depending upon an individual's performance and the size and type of company for which they work. Within large firms, managers may eventually become top-level managers or executives. Highly experienced individuals may become independent consultants; some serve as expert witnesses in court or as arbitrators in disputes. Those with the required capital may establish their own construction management services, specialty contracting, or general contracting firm.

Employment

Construction managers held 431,000 jobs in 2004. Over half were self-employed, many as owners of general or specialty trade construction firms. Most of the rest were employed in the construction industry, 13 percent by specialty trade contractors—for example, plumbing, heating and air-conditioning and electrical contractors—and 18 percent by general building contractors. Others were employed by architectural, engineering, and related services firms and by local governments.

Job Outlook

Excellent employment opportunities for construction managers are expected through 2014 because the number of job openings will exceed the number of qualified individuals seeking to enter the occupation. This situation is expected to continue even as college construction management programs expand to meet the current high demand for graduates. The construction industry often does not attract sufficient numbers of qualified job seekers because it is often seen as having poor working conditions.

Employment of construction managers is projected to increase about as fast as average for all occupations through 2014. In addition to job openings arising from employment growth, many additional openings should result annually from the need to replace workers who transfer to other occupations or who retire or leave the labor force for other reasons. More construction managers will be needed as the level of construction activity continues to grow. In addition, opportunities will increase for construction managers to start their own firms. However, employment of construction managers can be sensitive to the short-term nature of many projects and to cyclical fluctuations in construction activity.

The increasing complexity of construction projects is boosting the demand for management-level personnel within the construction industry. Sophisticated technology and the proliferation of laws setting standards for buildings and construction materials, worker safety, energy efficiency, and environmental protection have further complicated the construction process. Advances in building materials and construction methods, the need to replace portions of the nation's infrastructure, and the growing number of multipurpose buildings and energy-efficient structures will further add to the demand for more construction managers. More opportunities for construction managers also will result from the need for greater cost control and financial management of projects and to oversee the numerous subcontractors being employed.

Prospects for individuals seeking construction manager jobs in construction management, architectural and engineering services, and construction contracting firms should be best for persons who have a bachelor's or higher degree in construction science, construction management, or civil engineering—but also practical experience working in construction. Employers will increasingly prefer applicants with college degrees; previous construction work experience, including internships; and a strong background in building technology.

Earnings

Earnings of salaried construction managers and self-employed independent construction contractors vary depending upon the size and nature of the construction project, its geographic location, and economic conditions. In addition to typical benefits, many salaried construction managers receive benefits such as bonuses and use of company motor vehicles.

Median annual earnings of construction managers in May 2004 were $69,870. The middle 50 percent earned between $53,430 and $92,350. The lowest-paid 10 percent earned less than $42,120, and the highest-paid 10 percent earned more than $126,330. Median annual earnings in the industries employing the largest numbers of construction managers in 2004 were as follows:

Building equipment contractors	$72,560
Nonresidential building construction	71,700
Other specialty trade contractors	68,110
Residential building construction	67,190
Foundation, structure, and building exterior contractors	64,250

According to a July 2005 salary survey by the National Association of Colleges and Employers, candidates with a bachelor's degree in construction science/management received job offers averaging $42,923 a year.

Related Occupations

Construction managers participate in the conceptual development of a construction project and oversee its organization, scheduling, and implementation. Other workers who perform similar functions include architects, except landscape and naval; civil engineers; cost estimators; landscape architects; and engineering and natural sciences managers.

Sources of Additional Information

For information about constructor certification, contact

▸ American Institute of Constructors, 717 Princess St., Alexandria, VA 22314. Internet: http://www.constructorcertification.org or http://www.aicnet.org

For information about construction management and construction manager certification, contact

▸ Construction Management Association of America, 7918 Jones Branch Dr., Suite 540, McLean, VA 22102-3307. Internet: http://www.cmaanet.org

Information on accredited construction science and management educational programs and accreditation requirements is available from

▸ American Council for Construction Education, 1717 North Loop 1604 E, Ste 320, San Antonio, TX 78232 Internet: http://www.acce-hq.org

▸ National Center for Construction Education and Research, P.O. Box 141104, Gainesville, FL 32614. Internet: http://www.nccer.org

Dietitians and Nutritionists

(O*NET 29-1031.00)

Significant Points

■ Most jobs are in hospitals, nursing care facilities, and offices of physicians or other health practitioners.

■ Dietitians and nutritionists need at least a bachelor's degree in dietetics, foods and nutrition, food service systems management, or a related area.

■ Faster-than-average employment growth is expected; however, growth may be constrained if employers substitute other workers for dietitians and if limitations are placed on insurance reimbursement for dietetic services.

■ Those who have specialized training in renal or diabetic diets or have a master's degree should experience good employment opportunities.

Nature of the Work

Dietitians and nutritionists plan food and nutrition programs and supervise the preparation and serving of meals. They help to prevent and treat illnesses by promoting healthy eating habits and recommending dietary modifications, such as the use of less salt for those with high blood pressure or the reduction of fat and sugar intake for those who are overweight.

Dietitians manage food service systems for institutions such as hospitals and schools, promote sound eating habits through education, and conduct research. Major areas of practice include clinical, community, management, and consultant dietetics.

Clinical dietitians provide nutritional services for patients in institutions such as hospitals and nursing care facilities. They assess patients' nutritional needs, develop and implement nutrition programs, and evaluate and report the results. They also confer with doctors and other health care professionals to coordinate medical and nutritional needs. Some clinical dietitians specialize in the management of overweight patients or in the care of critically ill or renal (kidney) and diabetic patients. In addition, clinical dietitians in nursing care facilities, small hospitals, or correctional facilities may manage the food service department.

Community dietitians counsel individuals and groups on nutritional practices designed to prevent disease and promote health. Working in places such as public health clinics, home health agencies, and health maintenance organizations, community dietitians evaluate individual needs, develop nutritional care plans, and instruct individuals and their families. Dietitians working in home health agencies provide instruction on grocery shopping and food preparation to the elderly, individuals with special needs, and children.

Increased public interest in nutrition has led to job opportunities in food manufacturing, advertising, and marketing. In these areas, dietitians analyze foods; prepare literature for distribution; or report on issues such as the nutritional content of recipes, dietary fiber, or vitamin supplements.

Management dietitians oversee large-scale meal planning and preparation in health care facilities, company cafeterias, prisons, and schools. They hire, train, and direct other dietitians and food service workers; budget for and purchase food, equipment, and supplies; enforce sanitary and safety regulations; and prepare records and reports.

Consultant dietitians work under contract with health care facilities or in their own private practice. They perform nutrition screenings for their clients and offer advice on diet-related concerns such as weight loss and cholesterol reduction. Some work for wellness programs, sports teams, supermarkets, and other nutrition-related businesses. They may consult with food service managers, providing expertise in sanitation, safety procedures, menu development, budgeting, and planning.

Working Conditions

Most full-time dietitians and nutritionists work a regular 40-hour week, although some work weekends. About 1 in 4 worked part time in 2004.

Dietitians and nutritionists usually work in clean, well-lighted, and well-ventilated areas. However, some dietitians work in warm, congested kitchens. Many dietitians and nutritionists are on their feet for much of the workday.

Training, Other Qualifications, and Advancement

High school students interested in becoming a dietitian or nutritionist should take courses in biology, chemistry, mathematics, health, and communications. Dietitians and nutritionists need at least a bachelor's degree in dietetics, foods and nutrition, food service systems management, or a related area. College students in these majors take courses in foods, nutrition, institution management, chemistry, biochemistry, biology, microbiology, and physiology. Other suggested courses include business, mathematics, statistics, computer science, psychology, sociology, and economics.

Of the 46 states and jurisdictions with laws governing dietetics, 31 require licensure, 14 require certification, and 1 requires registration. Requirements vary by state. As a result, interested candidates should determine the requirements of the state in which they want to work before sitting for any exam. Although not required, the Commission on Dietetic Registration of the American Dietetic Association (ADA) awards the Registered Dietitian credential to those who pass an exam after completing their academic coursework and supervised experience.

As of 2004, there were about 227 bachelor's and master's degree programs approved by the ADA's Commission on Accreditation for Dietetics Education (CADE).

Supervised practice experience can be acquired in two ways. The first requires the completion of a CADE-accredited program. As of 2004, there were more than 50 accredited programs, which combined academic and supervised practice experience and generally lasted 4 to 5 years. The second option requires the completion of 900 hours of supervised practice experience in any of the 265 CADE-accredited internships. These internships may be full-time programs lasting 6 to 12 months or part-time programs lasting 2 years. To maintain a registered dietitian status, at least 75 credit hours in approved continuing education classes are required every 5 years.

Students interested in research, advanced clinical positions, or public health may need an advanced degree.

Experienced dietitians may advance to management positions, such as assistant director, associate director, or director of a dietetic department, or may become self-employed. Some dietitians specialize in areas such as renal, diabetic, cardiovascular, or pediatric dietetics. Others may leave the occupation to become sales representatives for equipment, pharmaceutical, or food manufacturers.

Employment

Dietitians and nutritionists held about 50,000 jobs in 2004. More than half of all jobs were in hospitals, nursing care facilities, outpatient care centers, or offices of physicians and other health practitioners. State and local government agencies provided about 1 job in 5—mostly in correctional facilities, health departments, and other public-health-related areas. Some dietitians and nutritionists were employed in special food services, an industry made up of firms providing food services on contract to facilities such as colleges and universities, airlines, correctional facilities, and company cafeterias. Other jobs were in public and private educational services, community care facilities for the elderly (which includes assisted-living facilities), individual and family services, home health care services, and the federal government—mostly in the U.S. Department of Veterans Affairs.

Some dietitians were self-employed, working as consultants to facilities such as hospitals and nursing care facilities or providing dietary counseling to individuals.

Job Outlook

Employment of dietitians is expected to grow faster than the average for all occupations through 2014 as a result of increasing emphasis on disease prevention through improved dietary habits. A growing and aging population will boost the demand for meals and nutritional counseling in hospitals, residential care facilities, schools, prisons, community health programs, and home health care agencies. Public interest in nutrition and increased emphasis on health education and prudent lifestyles also will spur demand, especially in management. In addition to employment growth, job openings will result from the need to replace experienced workers who leave the occupation.

The number of dietitian positions in nursing care facilities and in state government hospitals is expected to decline as these establishments continue to contract with outside agencies for food services. However, employment is expected to grow rapidly in contract providers of food services, in outpatient care centers, and in offices of physicians and other health practitioners. With increased public awareness of obesity and diabetes, Medicare coverage may be expanded to include medical nutrition therapy for renal and diabetic patients. As a result, dietitians that have specialized training in renal or diabetic diets or have a master's degree should experience good employment opportunities.

Employment growth for dietitians and nutritionists may be constrained if some employers substitute other workers, such as health educators, food service managers, and dietetic technicians. Growth also may be curbed by limitations on insurance reimbursement for dietetic services.

Earnings

Median annual earnings of dietitians and nutritionists were $43,630 in May 2004. The middle 50 percent earned between $35,940 and $53,370. The lowest 10 percent earned less than $27,500, and the highest 10 percent earned more than $63,760. In May 2004, median annual earnings in general medical and surgical hospitals, the industry employing the largest number of dietitians and nutritionists, were $44,050.

According to the American Dietetic Association, median annualized wages for registered dietitians in 2005 varied by practice area as follows: $53,800 in consultation and business; $60,000 in food and nutrition management; $60,200 in education and research; $48,800 in clinical nutrition/ambulatory care; $50,000 in clinical nutrition/long-term care; $44,800 in community nutrition; and $45,000 in clinical nutrition/acute care. Salaries also vary by years in practice, education level, geographic region, and size of the community.

Related Occupations

Workers in other occupations who may apply the principles of dietetics include food service managers, health educators, dietetic technicians, and registered nurses.

Sources of Additional Information

For a list of academic programs, scholarships, and other information about dietetics, contact

▶ The American Dietetic Association, 120 South Riverside Plaza, Suite 2000, Chicago, IL 60606-6995. Internet: http://www.eatright.org

Engineers

(O*NET 17-2011.00, 17-2021.00, 17-2031.00, 17-2041.00, 17-2051.00, 17-2061.00, 17-2071.00, 17-2072.00, 17-2081.00, 17-2111.01, 17-2111.02, 17-2111.03, 17-2112.00, 17-2121.01, 17-2121.02, 17-2131.00, 17-2141.00, 17-2151.00, 17-2161.00, 17-2171.00, and 17-2199.99)

Significant Points

■ Overall job opportunities in engineering are expected to be good, but will vary by specialty.

■ A bachelor's degree is required for most entry-level jobs.

■ Starting salaries are significantly higher than those of college graduates in other fields.

■ Continuing education is critical for engineers wishing to enhance their value to employers as technology evolves.

Nature of the Work

Engineers apply the principles of science and mathematics to develop economical solutions to technical problems. Their work is the link between perceived social needs and commercial applications.

Engineers consider many factors when developing a new product. For example, in developing an industrial robot, engineers precisely specify the functional requirements; design and test the robot's components; integrate the components to produce the final design; and evaluate the design's overall effectiveness, cost, reliability, and safety. This process applies to the development of many different products, such as chemicals, computers, gas turbines, helicopters, and toys.

In addition to design and development, many engineers work in testing, production, or maintenance. These engineers supervise production in factories, determine the causes of component failure, and test manufactured products to maintain quality. They also estimate the time and cost to complete projects. Some move into engineering management or into sales. In sales, an engineering background enables them to discuss technical aspects and assist in product planning, installation, and use. Supervisory engineers are responsible for major components or entire projects. (See the descriptions of sales engineers and engineering and natural sciences managers elsewhere in this book.)

Engineers use computers extensively to produce and analyze designs; to simulate and test how a machine, structure, or system operates; and to generate specifications for parts. Many engineers also use computers to monitor product quality and control process efficiency. The field of nanotechnology, which involves the creation of high-performance materials and components by integrating atoms and molecules, also is introducing entirely new principles to the design process.

Most engineers specialize. This section provides details on the 17 engineering specialties covered in the federal government's Standard Occupational Classification system and on engineering in general. Numerous specialties are recognized by professional societies, and the major branches of engineering have numerous subdivisions. Some examples include structural and transportation engineering, which are subdivisions of civil engineering, and ceramic, metallurgical, and polymer engineering, which are subdivisions of materials engineering. Engineers also may specialize in one industry, such as motor vehicles, or in one type of technology, such as turbines or semiconductor materials.

■ **Aerospace engineers** design, develop, and test aircraft, spacecraft, and missiles and supervise the manufacture of these products. Those who work with aircraft are called *aeronautical engineers*, and those working specifically with spacecraft are *astronautical engineers*. Aerospace engineers develop new technologies for use in aviation, defense systems, and space exploration, often specializing in areas such as structural design, guidance, navigation and control, instrumentation and communication, or production methods. They also may specialize in a particular type of aerospace product, such as commercial aircraft, military fighter jets, helicopters, spacecraft, or missiles and rockets, and may become experts in aerodynamics, thermodynamics, celestial mechanics, propulsion, acoustics, or guidance and control systems.

■ **Agricultural engineers** apply knowledge of engineering technology and science to agriculture and the efficient use of biological resources. (See the descriptions of biological scientists and agricultural and food scientists elsewhere in this book.)

They design agricultural machinery and equipment and agricultural structures. Some specialize in areas such as power systems and machinery design, structures and environment engineering, and food and bioprocess engineering. They develop ways to conserve soil and water and to improve the processing of agricultural products. Agricultural engineers often work in research and development, production, sales, or management.

■ **Biomedical engineers** develop devices and procedures that solve medical and health-related problems by combining their knowledge of biology and medicine with engineering principles and practices. Many do research, along with life scientists, chemists, and medical scientists, to develop and evaluate systems and products such as artificial organs, prostheses (artificial devices that replace missing body parts), instrumentation, medical information systems, and health management and care delivery systems. (See biological scientists, medical scientists, and chemists and materials scientists elsewhere in this book.) Biomedical engineers may also design devices used in various medical procedures, imaging systems such as magnetic resonance imaging (MRI), and devices for automating insulin injections or controlling body functions. Most engineers in this specialty need a sound background in another engineering specialty, such as mechanical or electronics engineering, in addition to specialized biomedical training. Some specialties within biomedical engineering include biomaterials, biomechanics, medical imaging, rehabilitation engineering, and orthopedic engineering.

■ **Chemical engineers** apply the principles of chemistry to solve problems involving the production or use of chemicals and biochemicals. They design equipment and processes for large-scale chemical manufacturing, plan and test methods of manufacturing products and treating byproducts, and supervise production. Chemical engineers also work in a variety of manufacturing industries other than chemical manufacturing, such as those producing energy, electronics, food, clothing, and paper. They also work in health care, biotechnology, and business services. Chemical engineers apply principles of chemistry, physics, mathematics, and mechanical and electrical engineering. (See chemists and materials scientists, physicists and astronomers, and mathematicians elsewhere in this book.) Some may specialize in a particular chemical process, such as oxidation or polymerization. Others specialize in a particular field, such as materials science, or in the development of specific products. They must be aware of all aspects of chemicals manufacturing and how the manufacturing process affects the environment and the safety of workers and consumers.

■ **Civil engineers** design and supervise the construction of roads, buildings, airports, tunnels, dams, bridges, and water supply and sewage systems. They must consider many factors in the design process, from the construction costs and expected lifetime of a project to government regulations and potential environmental hazards such as earthquakes. Civil engineering, considered one of the oldest engineering disciplines, encompasses many specialties. The major specialties are structural, water resources, construction, environmental, transportation, and geotechnical engineering. Many civil engineers hold supervisory or administrative positions, from supervisor of a construction site to city engineer. Others may work in design, construction, research, and teaching.

■ **Computer hardware engineers** research, design, develop, test, and oversee the installation of computer hardware and supervise its manufacture and installation. Hardware refers to computer chips; circuit boards; computer systems; and related equipment such as keyboards, modems, and printers. (Computer software engineers—often simply called computer engineers—design and develop the software systems that control computers. These workers are covered elsewhere in this book.) The work of computer hardware engineers is very similar to that of electronics engineers, but, unlike electronics engineers, computer hardware engineers work exclusively with computers and computer-related equipment. The rapid advances in computer technology are largely a result of the research, development, and design efforts of computer hardware engineers.

■ **Electrical engineers** design, develop, test, and supervise the manufacture of electrical equipment. Some of this equipment includes electric motors; machinery controls, lighting, and wiring in buildings; automobiles; aircraft; radar and navigation systems; and power-generating, -controlling, and -transmission devices used by electric utilities. Although the terms "electrical" and "electronics" engineering often are used interchangeably in academia and industry, electrical engineers have traditionally focused on the generation and supply of power, whereas electronics engineers have worked on applications of electricity to control systems or signal processing. Electrical engineers specialize in areas such as power systems engineering or electrical equipment manufacturing.

■ **Electronics engineers, except computer,** are responsible for a wide range of technologies, from portable music players to the global positioning system (GPS), which can continuously provide the location of a vehicle. Electronics engineers design, develop, test, and supervise the manufacture of electronic equipment such as broadcast and communications systems. Many electronics engineers also work in areas closely related to computers. However, engineers whose work is related exclusively to computer hardware are considered computer hardware engineers. Electronics engineers specialize in areas such as communications, signal processing, and control systems or have a specialty within one of these areas—industrial robot control systems or aviation electronics, for example.

■ **Environmental engineers** develop solutions to environmental problems using the principles of biology and chemistry. They are involved in water and air pollution control, recycling, waste disposal, and public health issues. Environmental engineers conduct hazardous-waste management studies in which they evaluate the significance of the hazard, advise on treatment and containment, and develop regulations to prevent mishaps. They design municipal water supply and industrial wastewater treatment systems. They conduct research on the environmental impact of proposed construction projects, analyze scientific data, and perform quality-control checks. Environmental engineers are concerned with local and worldwide environmental issues. They study and attempt to minimize the effects of acid rain, global warming, automobile emissions, and ozone depletion. They may also be involved in the protection of wildlife. Many environmental engineers work as consultants, helping their clients to comply with regulations and to clean up hazardous sites.

- **Health and safety engineers, except mining safety engineers and inspectors,** promote worksite or product safety by applying knowledge of industrial processes and mechanical, chemical, and human performance principles. Using this specialized knowledge, they identify and measure potential hazards to people or property, such as the risk of fires or the dangers involved in the handling of toxic chemicals. Health and safety engineers develop procedures and designs to reduce the risk of injury or damage. Some work in manufacturing industries to ensure that the designs of new products do not create unnecessary hazards. They must be able to anticipate, recognize, and evaluate hazardous conditions, as well as develop hazard control methods.

- **Industrial engineers** determine the most effective ways to use the basic factors of production—people, machines, materials, information, and energy—to make a product or to provide a service. They are mostly concerned with increasing productivity through the management of people, methods of business organization, and technology. To solve organizational, production, and related problems efficiently, industrial engineers carefully study the product requirements, use mathematical methods to meet those requirements, and design manufacturing and information systems. They develop management control systems to aid in financial planning and cost analysis and design production planning and control systems to coordinate activities and ensure product quality. They also design or improve systems for the physical distribution of goods and services as well as determine the most efficient plant locations. Industrial engineers develop wage and salary administration systems and job evaluation programs. Many industrial engineers move into management positions because the work is closely related to the work of managers.

- **Marine engineers and naval architects** are involved in the design, construction, and maintenance of ships, boats, and related equipment. They design and supervise the construction of everything from aircraft carriers to submarines and from sailboats to tankers. Naval architects work on the basic design of ships, including hull form and stability. Marine engineers work on the propulsion, steering, and other systems of ships. Marine engineers and naval architects apply knowledge from a range of fields to the entire design and production process of all water vehicles. Workers who operate or supervise the operation of marine machinery on ships and other vessels also may be called marine engineers or, more frequently, ship engineers.

- **Materials engineers** are involved in the development, processing, and testing of the materials used to create a range of products, from computer chips and television screens to golf clubs and snow skis. They work with metals, ceramics, plastics, semiconductors, and composites to create new materials that meet certain mechanical, electrical, and chemical requirements. They also are involved in selecting materials for new applications. Materials engineers have developed the ability to create and then study materials at an atomic level, using advanced processes to replicate the characteristics of materials and their

components with computers. Most materials engineers specialize in a particular material. For example, metallurgical engineers specialize in metals such as steel, and ceramic engineers develop ceramic materials and the processes for making ceramic materials into useful products such as glassware or fiber-optic communication lines.

- **Mechanical engineers** research, develop, design, manufacture, and test tools, engines, machines, and other mechanical devices. They work on power-producing machines such as electric generators, internal combustion engines, and steam and gas turbines, as well as power-using machines such as refrigeration and air-conditioning equipment, machine tools, material handling systems, elevators and escalators, industrial production equipment, and robots used in manufacturing. Mechanical engineers also design tools that other engineers need for their work. Mechanical engineering is one of the broadest engineering disciplines. Mechanical engineers may work in production operations in manufacturing or agriculture, maintenance, or technical sales; many are administrators or managers.

- **Mining and geological engineers, including mining safety engineers,** find, extract, and prepare coal, metals, and minerals for use by manufacturing industries and utilities. They design open-pit and underground mines, supervise the construction of mine shafts and tunnels in underground operations, and devise methods for transporting minerals to processing plants. Mining engineers are responsible for the safe, economical, and environmentally sound operation of mines. Some mining engineers work with geologists and metallurgical engineers to locate and appraise new ore deposits. Others develop new mining equipment or direct mineral-processing operations that separate minerals from the dirt, rock, and other materials with which they are mixed. Mining engineers frequently specialize in the mining of one mineral or metal, such as coal or gold. With increased emphasis on protecting the environment, many mining engineers work to solve problems related to land reclamation and water and air pollution. Mining safety engineers use their knowledge of mine design and practices to ensure the safety of workers and to comply with state and federal safety regulations. They inspect walls and roof surfaces, monitor air quality, and examine mining equipment for compliance with safety practices.

- **Nuclear engineers** research and develop the processes, instruments, and systems used to derive benefits from nuclear energy and radiation. They design, develop, monitor, and operate nuclear plants to generate power. They may work on the nuclear fuel cycle—the production, handling, and use of nuclear fuel and the safe disposal of waste produced by the generation of nuclear energy—or on the development of fusion energy. Some specialize in the development of nuclear power sources for spacecraft; others find industrial and medical uses for radioactive materials, as in equipment used to diagnose and treat medical problems.

- **Petroleum engineers** search the world for reservoirs containing oil or natural gas. Once these resources are discovered, petroleum engineers work with geologists and other specialists to understand the geologic formation and properties of the rock containing the reservoir, determine the drilling methods to be used, and monitor drilling and production operations. They design equipment and processes to achieve the maximum profitable recovery of oil and gas. Because only a small proportion of oil and gas in a reservoir flows out under natural forces, petroleum engineers develop and use various enhanced recovery methods. These include injecting water, chemicals, gases, or steam into an oil reservoir to force out more of the oil and doing computer-controlled drilling or fracturing to connect a larger area of a reservoir to a single well. Because even the best techniques in use today recover only a portion of the oil and gas in a reservoir, petroleum engineers research and develop technology and methods to increase recovery and lower the cost of drilling and production operations.

Working Conditions

Most engineers work in office buildings, laboratories, or industrial plants. Others may spend time outdoors at construction sites and oil and gas exploration and production sites, where they monitor or direct operations or solve onsite problems. Some engineers travel extensively to plants or worksites.

Many engineers work a standard 40-hour week. At times, deadlines or design standards may bring extra pressure to a job, requiring engineers to work longer hours.

Training, Other Qualifications, and Advancement

A bachelor's degree in engineering is required for almost all entry-level engineering jobs. College graduates with a degree in a physical science or mathematics occasionally may qualify for some engineering jobs, especially in specialties in high demand. Most engineering degrees are granted in electrical, electronics, mechanical, or civil engineering. However, engineers trained in one branch may work in related branches. For example, many aerospace engineers have training in mechanical engineering. This flexibility allows employers to meet staffing needs in new technologies and specialties in which engineers may be in short supply. It also allows engineers to shift to fields with better employment prospects or to those that more closely match their interests.

Most engineering programs involve a concentration of study in an engineering specialty along with courses in both mathematics and the physical and life sciences. General courses not directly related to engineering, such as those in the social sciences or humanities, are often a required component of programs. Many programs also include courses in general engineering. A design course, sometimes accompanied by a computer or laboratory class or both, is part of the curriculum of most programs.

In addition to the standard engineering degree, many colleges offer 2- or 4-year degree programs in engineering technology. These programs, which usually include various hands-on laboratory classes that focus on current issues in the application of engineering principles, prepare students for practical design and production work rather than for jobs that require more theoretical and scientific knowledge. Graduates of 4-year technology programs may get jobs similar to those obtained by graduates with a bachelor's degree in engineering. Engineering technology graduates, however, are not qualified to register as professional engineers under the same terms as graduates with degrees in engineering. Some employers regard technology program graduates as having skills between those of a technician and an engineer.

Graduate training is essential for engineering faculty positions and many research and development programs, but is not required for the majority of entry-level engineering jobs. Many engineers obtain graduate degrees in engineering or business administration to learn new technology and broaden their education. Many high-level executives in government and industry began their careers as engineers.

About 360 colleges and universities offer bachelor's degree programs in engineering that are accredited by the Accreditation Board for Engineering and Technology, Inc. (ABET), and about 230 colleges offer accredited programs in engineering technology. ABET accreditation is based on an examination of an engineering program's student achievement, program improvement, faculty, curriculum, facilities, and institutional commitment to certain principles of quality and ethics. Although most institutions offer programs in the major branches of engineering, only a few offer programs in the smaller specialties. Also, programs of the same title may vary in content. For example, some programs emphasize industrial practices, preparing students for a job in industry, whereas others are more theoretical and are designed to prepare students for graduate work. Therefore, students should investigate curriculums and check accreditations carefully before selecting a college.

Admissions requirements for undergraduate engineering schools include a solid background in mathematics (algebra, geometry, trigonometry, and calculus) and science (biology, chemistry, and physics), with courses in English, social studies, and humanities. Bachelor's degree programs in engineering typically are designed to last 4 years, but many students find that it takes between 4 and 5 years to complete their studies. In a typical 4-year college curriculum, the first 2 years are spent studying mathematics, basic sciences, introductory engineering, humanities, and social sciences. In the last 2 years, most courses are in engineering, usually with a concentration in one specialty. Some programs offer a general engineering curriculum; students then specialize on the job or in graduate school.

Some engineering schools and 2-year colleges have agreements whereby the 2-year college provides the initial engineering education and the engineering school automatically admits students for their last 2 years. In addition, a few engineering schools have arrangements that allow students who spend 3 years in a liberal arts college studying pre-engineering subjects and 2 years in an engineering school studying core subjects to receive a bachelor's degree from each school. Some colleges and universities offer 5-year master's degree programs. Some 5-year or even 6-year cooperative plans combine classroom study and practical work, permitting students to gain valuable experience and to finance part of their education.

All 50 states and the District of Columbia require licensure for engineers who offer their services directly to the public. Engineers who are licensed are called professional engineers (PE). This licensure generally requires a degree from an ABET-accredited engineering program, 4 years of relevant work experience, and successful completion of a state examination. Recent graduates can start the licensing process by taking the examination in two stages. The initial Fundamentals of Engineering (FE) examination can be taken upon graduation. Engineers who pass this examination commonly are called engineers in training (EIT) or engineer interns (EI). After acquiring suitable work experience, EITs can take the second examination, the Principles and Practice of Engineering exam. Several states have imposed mandatory continuing education requirements for relicensure. Most states recognize licensure from other states, provided that the manner in which the initial license was obtained meets or exceeds their own licensure requirements. Many civil, electrical, mechanical, and chemical engineers are licensed PEs. Independent of licensure, various certification programs are offered by professional organizations to demonstrate competency in specific fields of engineering.

Engineers should be creative, inquisitive, analytical, and detail oriented. They should be able to work as part of a team and to communicate well, both orally and in writing. Communication abilities are important because engineers often interact with specialists in a wide range of fields outside engineering.

Beginning engineering graduates usually work under the supervision of experienced engineers and, in large companies, also may receive formal classroom or seminar-type training. As new engineers gain knowledge and experience, they are assigned more difficult projects with greater independence to develop designs, solve problems, and make decisions. Engineers may advance to become technical specialists or to supervise a staff or team of engineers and technicians. Some may eventually become engineering managers or enter other managerial or sales jobs.

Employment

In 2004, engineers held 1.4 million jobs. The distribution of employment by engineering specialty is as follows:

Total, all engineers	1,449,000	100%
Civil	237,000	16.4
Mechanical	226,000	15.6
Industrial	177,000	12.2
Electrical	156,000	10.8
Electronics, except computer	143,000	9.9
Computer hardware	77,000	5.3
Aerospace	76,000	5.2
Environmental	49,000	3.4
Chemical	31,000	2.1
Health and safety, except mining safety	27,000	1.8
Materials	21,000	1.5
Nuclear	17,000	1.2
Petroleum	16,000	1.1
Biomedical	9,700	0.7
Marine engineers and naval architects	6,800	0.5
Mining and geological, including mining safety	5,200	0.4
Agricultural	3,400	0.2
All other engineers	172,000	11.8

About 555,000 engineering jobs were found in manufacturing industries, and another 378,000 wage and salary jobs were in the professional, scientific, and technical services sector, primarily in architectural, engineering, and related services and in scientific research and development services. Many engineers also worked in the construction and transportation, telecommunications, and utilities industries.

Federal, state, and local governments employed about 194,000 engineers in 2004. About 91,000 of these were in the federal government, mainly in the U.S. Departments of Defense, Transportation, Agriculture, Interior, and Energy and in the National Aeronautics and Space Administration. Most engineers in state and local government agencies worked in highway and public works departments. In 2004, about 41,000 engineers were self-employed, many as consultants.

Engineers are employed in every state, in small and large cities and in rural areas. Some branches of engineering are concentrated in particular industries and geographic areas—for example, petroleum engineering jobs tend to be located in areas with sizable petroleum deposits, such as Texas, Louisiana, Oklahoma, Alaska, and California. Others, such as civil engineering, are widely dispersed, and engineers in these fields often move from place to place to work on different projects.

Engineers are employed in every major industry. The industries employing the most engineers in each specialty are given in the table below, along with the percent of occupational employment in the industry.

Table 1. Percent concentration of engineering specialty employment in key industries, 2004

Specialty/Industry	Percent
Aerospace	
Aerospace product and parts manufacturing	59.6
Agricultural	
State and local government	22.6
Biomedical	
Scientific research and development services	18.7
Pharmaceutical and medicine manufacturing	15.6
Chemical	
Chemical manufacturing	27.8
Architectural, engineering, and related services	16.3
Civil	
Architectural, engineering, and related services	46.0
Computer hardware	
Computer and electronic product manufacturing	43.2
Computer systems design and related services	15.0
Electrical	
Architectural, engineering, and related services	19.6
Navigational, measuring, electromedical, and control instruments manufacturing	10.8
Electronics, except computer	
Telecommunications	17.5
Federal government	14.4
Environmental	
Architectural, engineering, and related services	28.9
State and local government	19.6

(continued)

(continued)

Specialty/Industry	Percent
Health and safety, except mining safety	
State and local government	12.4
Industrial	
Machinery manufacturing	7.8
Motor vehicle parts manufacturing	7.1
Marine engineers and naval architects	
Architectural, engineering, and related services	34.5
Materials	
Computer and electronic product manufacturing	14.3
Mechanical	
Architectural, engineering, and related services	18.1
Machinery manufacturing	13.4
Mining and geological, including mining safety	
Mining	49.9
Nuclear	
Electric power generation, transmission and distribution	36.1
Petroleum	
Oil and gas extraction	47.4

Job Outlook

Overall engineering employment is expected to grow about as fast as the average for all occupations over the 2004–2014 period. Engineers have traditionally been concentrated in slow-growing manufacturing industries, in which they will continue to be needed to design, build, test, and improve manufactured products. However, increasing employment of engineers in faster-growing service industries should generate most of the employment growth. Overall job opportunities in engineering are expected to be favorable because the number of engineering graduates should be in rough balance with the number of job openings over this period. However, job outlook varies by specialty, as discussed later in this section.

Competitive pressures and advancing technology will force companies to improve and update product designs and optimize their manufacturing processes. Employers will rely on engineers to further increase productivity as investments in plant and equipment increase to expand output of goods and services. New technologies continue to improve the design process, enabling engineers to produce and analyze various product designs much more rapidly than in the past. Unlike in other fields, however, technological advances are not expected to limit employment opportunities substantially, because they will permit the development of new products and processes.

There are many well-trained, often English-speaking engineers available around the world willing to work at much lower salaries than are U.S. engineers. The rise of the Internet has made it relatively easy for much of the engineering work previously done by engineers in this country to be done by engineers in other countries, a factor that will tend to hold down employment growth. Even so, the need for onsite engineers to interact with other employees and with clients will remain.

Compared with most other workers, a smaller proportion of engineers leave their jobs each year. Nevertheless, many job openings will arise from replacement needs, reflecting the large size of this profession. Numerous job openings will be created by engineers who transfer to management, sales, or other professional occupations; additional openings will arise as engineers retire or leave the labor force for other reasons.

Many engineers work on long-term research and development projects or in other activities that continue even during economic slowdowns. In industries such as electronics and aerospace, however, large cutbacks in defense expenditures and in government funding for research and development have resulted in significant layoffs of engineers in the past. The trend toward contracting for engineering work with engineering services firms, both domestic and foreign, has had the same result.

It is important for engineers, as it is for those working in other technical and scientific occupations, to continue their education throughout their careers because much of their value to their employer depends on their knowledge of the latest technology. Engineers in high-technology areas, such as advanced electronics or information technology, may find that technical knowledge can become outdated rapidly. By keeping current in their field, engineers are able to deliver the best solutions and greatest value to their employers. Engineers who have not kept current in their field may find themselves passed over for promotions or vulnerable to layoffs.

The following section discusses job outlook by engineering specialty.

- **Aerospace engineers** are expected to have slower-than-average growth in employment over the projection period. Although increases in the number and scope of military aerospace projects likely will generate new jobs, increased efficiency will limit the number of new jobs in the design and production of commercial aircraft. Even with slow growth, the employment outlook for aerospace engineers through 2014 appears favorable: The number of degrees granted in aerospace engineering declined for many years because of a perceived lack of opportunities in this field, and, although this trend is reversing, new graduates continue to be needed to replace aerospace engineers who retire or leave the occupation for other reasons.

- **Agricultural engineers** are expected to have employment growth about as fast as the average for all occupations through 2014. The growing interest in worldwide standardization of agricultural equipment should result in increased employment of agricultural engineers. Job opportunities also should result from the need to feed a growing population, develop more efficient agricultural production, and conserve resources.

- **Biomedical engineers** are expected to have employment growth that is much faster than the average for all occupations through 2014. The aging of the population and the focus on health issues will drive demand for better medical devices and equipment designed by biomedical engineers. Along with the demand for more sophisticated medical equipment and procedures, an increased concern for cost-effectiveness will boost demand for biomedical engineers, particularly in pharmaceutical manufacturing and related industries. However, because of the growing interest in this field, the number of degrees granted in biomedical engineering has increased greatly. Biomedical engineers, particularly those with only a bachelor's degree, may face competition for jobs. Unlike the case for many other engineering specialties, a graduate degree is recommended or required for many entry-level jobs.

- **Chemical engineers** are expected to have employment growth about as fast as the average for all occupations though 2014. Although overall employment in the chemical manufacturing industry is expected to decline, chemical companies will continue to research and develop new chemicals and more efficient processes to increase output of existing chemicals. Among manufacturing industries, pharmaceuticals may provide the best opportunities for jobseekers. However, most employment growth for chemical engineers will be in service industries such as scientific research and development services, particularly in energy and the developing fields of biotechnology and nanotechnology.

- **Civil engineers** are expected to see average employment growth through 2014. Spurred by general population growth and an increased emphasis on infrastructure security, more civil engineers will be needed to design and construct safe and higher-capacity transportation, water supply, and pollution control systems, as well as large buildings and building complexes. They also will be needed to repair or replace existing roads, bridges, and other public structures. Because construction and related industries—including those providing design services—employ many civil engineers, employment opportunities will vary by geographic area and may decrease during economic slowdowns, when construction often is curtailed.

- **Computer hardware engineers** are expected to have average employment growth through 2014. Although the use of information technology continues to expand rapidly, the manufacture of computer hardware is expected to be adversely affected by intense foreign competition. As computer and semiconductor manufacturing contract out more of their engineering needs, much of the growth in employment should occur in the computer systems design and related services industry. However, use of foreign computer hardware engineering services also will serve to limit job growth. Computer engineers should still have favorable employment opportunities, as the number of new entrants is expected to be in balance with demand.

- **Electrical engineers** should have favorable employment opportunities. The number of job openings resulting from employment growth and from the need to replace electrical engineers who transfer to other occupations or leave the labor force is expected to be in rough balance with the supply of graduates. Employment of electrical engineers is expected to increase about as fast as the average for all occupations through 2014. Although international competition and the use of engineering services performed in other countries may limit employment growth, strong demand for electrical devices such as giant electric power generators or wireless phone transmitters should boost growth. Prospects should be particularly good for electrical engineers working in engineering services firms providing technical expertise to other companies on specific projects.

- **Electronics engineers, except computer,** should have good job opportunities, and employment is expected to increase about as fast as the average for all occupations through 2014. Although rising demand for electronic goods—including

advanced communications equipment, defense-related electronic equipment, medical electronics, and consumer products—should continue to increase employment, foreign competition in electronic products development and the use of engineering services performed in other countries will act to limit employment growth. Job growth is expected to be fastest in service-providing industries—particularly consulting firms that provide expertise in electronics engineering.

- **Environmental engineers** should have favorable job opportunities. Employment of environmental engineers is expected to increase much faster than the average for all occupations through 2014. More environmental engineers will be needed to comply with environmental regulations and to develop methods of cleaning up existing hazards. A shift in emphasis toward preventing problems rather than controlling those that already exist, as well as increasing public health concerns, also will spur demand for environmental engineers. Even though employment of environmental engineers should be less affected by economic conditions than that of most other types of engineers, a significant economic downturn could reduce the emphasis on environmental protection, reducing environmental engineers' job opportunities.

- **Health and safety engineers, except mining safety engineers and inspectors,** are projected to experience average employment growth through 2014. Because the main function of health and safety engineers is to make products and production processes as safe as possible, their services should be in demand as concern for health and safety within work environments increases. As new technologies for production or processing are developed, health and safety engineers will be needed to ensure their safety.

- **Industrial engineers** are expected to have employment growth about as fast as the average for all occupations through 2014. As firms seek to reduce costs and increase productivity, they increasingly will turn to industrial engineers to develop more efficient processes to reduce costs, delays, and waste. Because their work is similar to that done in management occupations, many industrial engineers leave the occupation to become managers. Many openings will be created by the need to replace industrial engineers who transfer to other occupations or leave the labor force.

- **Marine engineers and naval architects** likely will experience employment growth that is slower than the average for all occupations. Strong demand for naval vessels and for yachts and other small craft should more than offset the long-term decline in the domestic design and construction of large ocean-going vessels. There should be good prospects for marine engineers and naval architects because of growth in employment, the need to replace workers who retire or take other jobs, and the limited number of students pursuing careers in this occupation.

- **Materials engineers, including mining safety engineers,** are expected to have employment growth about as fast as the average for all occupations through 2014. Although many of the manufacturing industries in which materials engineers are concentrated are expected to experience declining employment, materials engineers still will be needed to develop new materials for electronics, biotechnology, and plastics products. Growth should be particularly strong for materials engineers working on nanomaterials and biomaterials. As manufacturing firms contract for their materials engineering needs, employment growth is expected in professional, scientific, and technical services industries.

- **Mechanical engineers** are projected to have an average rate of employment growth through 2014. Although total employment in manufacturing industries—in which employment of mechanical engineers is concentrated—is expected to decline, employment of mechanical engineers in manufacturing should increase as the demand for improved machinery and machine tools grows and as industrial machinery and processes become increasingly complex. Also, emerging technologies in biotechnology, materials science, and nanotechnology will create new job opportunities for mechanical engineers. Additional opportunities for mechanical engineers will arise because the skills acquired through earning a degree in mechanical engineering often can be applied in other engineering specialties.

- **Mining and geological engineers, including mining safety engineers**, are expected to have good employment opportunities, despite a projected decline in employment. Many mining engineers currently employed are approaching retirement age, a factor that should create some job openings over the 2004–2014 period. In addition, relatively few schools offer mining engineering programs, and the small number of yearly graduates is not expected to increase substantially. Favorable job opportunities also may be available worldwide as mining operations around the world recruit graduates of U.S. mining engineering programs. As a result, some graduates may travel frequently or even live abroad. Employment of mining and geological engineers, including mining safety engineers, is projected to decline through 2014, primarily because most of the industries in which mining engineers are concentrated—such as coal, metal, and copper mining—are expected to experience declines in employment.

- **Nuclear engineers** are expected to have good opportunities because the small number of nuclear engineering graduates is likely to be in rough balance with the number of job openings. Employment of nuclear engineers is expected to grow more slowly than the average for all occupations through 2014. Most openings will result from the need to replace nuclear engineers who transfer to other occupations or leave the labor force. Although no commercial nuclear power plants have been built in the United States for many years, nuclear engineers will be needed to operate existing plants. In addition, nuclear engineers may be needed to research and develop future nuclear power sources. They also will be needed to work in defense-related areas, to develop nuclear medical technology, and to improve and enforce waste management and safety standards.

- **Petroleum engineers** are expected to have a decline in employment through 2014 because most of the potential petroleum-producing areas in the United States already have been explored. Even so, favorable opportunities are expected for petroleum engineers because the number of job openings is likely to exceed the relatively small number of graduates. All job openings should result from the need to replace petroleum

engineers who transfer to other occupations or leave the labor force. Petroleum engineers work around the world and, in fact, the best employment opportunities may be in other countries. Many foreign employers seek U.S.-trained petroleum engineers, and many U.S. employers maintain overseas branches.

Earnings

Earnings for engineers vary significantly by specialty, industry, and education. Even so, as a group, engineers earn some of the highest average starting salaries among those holding bachelor's degrees. The following tabulation shows average starting salary offers for engineers, according to a 2005 survey by the National Association of Colleges and Employers.

Curriculum	Bachelor's	Master's	Ph.D.
Aerospace/aeronautical/ astronautical	$50,993	$62,930	$72,529
Agricultural	46,172	53,022	
Bioengineering & biomedical	48,503	59,667	
Chemical	53,813	57,260	79,591
Civil	43,679	48,050	59,625
Computer	52,464	60,354	69,625
Electrical/electronics & communications	51,888	64,416	80,206
Environmental/ environmental health	47,384		
Industrial/manufacturing	49,567	56,561	85,000
Materials	50,982		
Mechanical	50,236	59,880	68,299
Mining & mineral	48,643		
Nuclear	51,182	58,814	
Petroleum	61,516	58,000	

Variation in median earnings and in the earnings distributions for engineers in the various branches of engineering also is significant. For engineers in specialties covered in this job description, earnings distributions by percentile in May 2004 are shown in the following tabulation.

Specialty	10%	25%	50%	75%	90%
Aerospace	$52,820	$64,380	$79,100	$94,900	$113,520
Agricultural	37,680	43,270	56,520	77,740	90,410
Biomedical	41,260	51,620	67,690	86,400	107,530
Chemical	49,030	60,920	76,770	94,740	115,180
Civil	42,610	51,430	64,230	79,920	94,660
Computer hardware	50,490	63,730	81,150	102,100	123,560
Electrical	47,310	57,540	71,610	88,400	108,070
Electronics, except computer	49,120	60,280	75,770	92,870	112,200
Environmental	40,620	50,740	66,480	83,690	100,050

Specialty	10%	25%	50%	75%	90%
Health and safety, except mining safety	39,930	49,900	63,730	79,500	92,870
Industrial	42,450	52,210	65,020	79,830	93,950
Marine engineers and naval architects	43,790	54,530	72,040	89,900	109,190
Materials	44,130	53,510	67,110	83,830	101,120
Mechanical	43,900	53,070	66,320	82,380	97,850
Mining and geological, including mining safety	39,700	50,500	64,690	83,050	103,790
Nuclear	61,790	73,340	84,880	100,220	118,870
Petroleum	48,260	65,350	88,500	113,180	140,800

In the federal government, mean annual salaries for engineers ranged from $100,059 in ceramic engineering to $70,086 in agricultural engineering in 2005.

Related Occupations

Engineers apply the principles of physical science and mathematics in their work. Other workers who use scientific and mathematical principles include architects, except landscape and naval; engineering and natural sciences managers; computer and information systems managers; computer programmers; computer software engineers; mathematicians; drafters; engineering technicians; sales engineers; science technicians; and physical and life scientists, including agricultural and food scientists, biological scientists, conservation scientists and foresters, atmospheric scientists, chemists and materials scientists, environmental scientists and hydrologists, geoscientists, and physicists and astronomers.

Sources of Additional Information

Information about careers in engineering is available from

▸ JETS, 1420 King St., Suite 405, Alexandria, VA 22314-2794. Internet: http://www.jets.org

Information on ABET-accredited engineering programs is available from

▸ Accreditation Board for Engineering and Technology, Inc., 111 Market Place, Suite 1050, Baltimore, MD 21202-4012. Internet: http://www.abet.org

Those interested in information on the Professional Engineer licensure should contact

▸ National Society of Professional Engineers, 1420 King St., Alexandria, VA 22314-2794. Internet: http://www.nspe.org

▸ National Council of Examiners for Engineering and Surveying, P.O. Box 1686, Clemson, SC 29633-1686. Internet: http://www.ncees.org

Information on general engineering education and career resources is available from

▸ American Society for Engineering Education, 1818 N St. NW, Suite 600, Washington, DC 20036-2479. Internet: http://www.asee.org

Information on obtaining positions as engineers with the federal government is available from the Office of Personnel Management through USAJOBS, the federal government's official employment information system. This resource for locating and applying for job opportunities can be accessed through the Internet at http://www.usajobs.opm.gov or through an interactive voice response telephone system at (703) 724-1850 or TDD (978) 461-8404. These numbers are not toll free, and charges may result.

For more detailed information on an engineering specialty, contact societies representing the individual branches of engineering. Each can provide information about careers in the particular branch.

Aerospace engineers

▸ Aerospace Industries Association, 1000 Wilson Blvd., Suite 1700, Arlington, VA 22209-3901. Internet: http://www.aia-aerospace.org

▸ American Institute of Aeronautics and Astronautics, Inc., 1801 Alexander Bell Dr., Suite 500, Reston, VA 20191-4344. Internet: http://www.aiaa.org

Agricultural engineers

▸ American Society of Agricultural and Biological Engineers, 2950 Niles Rd., St. Joseph, MI 49085-9659. Internet: http://www.asabe.org

Biomedical engineers

▸ Biomedical Engineering Society, 8401 Corporate Dr., Suite 225, Landover, MD 20785-2224. Internet: http://www.bmes.org

Chemical engineers

▸ American Institute of Chemical Engineers, 3 Park Ave., New York, NY 10016-5991. Internet: http://www.aiche.org

▸ American Chemical Society, Department of Career Services, 1155 16th St. NW, Washington, DC 20036. Internet: http://www.chemistry.org/portal/Chemistry

Civil engineers

▸ American Society of Civil Engineers, 1801 Alexander Bell Dr., Reston, VA 20191-4400. Internet: http://www.asce.org

Computer hardware engineers

▸ IEEE Computer Society, 1730 Massachusetts Ave. NW, Washington, DC 20036-1992. Internet: http://www.computer.org

Electrical and electronics engineers

▸ Institute of Electrical and Electronics Engineers—USA, 1828 L St. NW, Suite 1202, Washington, DC 20036. Internet: http://www.ieeeusa.org

Environmental engineers

▸ American Academy of Environmental Engineers, 130 Holiday Court, Suite 100, Annapolis, MD 21401. Internet: http://www.aaee.net

Health and safety engineers

▸ American Society of Safety Engineers, 1800 E Oakton St., Des Plaines, IL 60018. Internet: http://www.asse.org

▸ Board of Certified Safety Professionals, 208 Burwash Ave., Savoy, IL 61874. Internet: http://www.bcsp.org

Industrial engineers

▸ Institute of Industrial Engineers, 3577 Parkway Lane, Suite 200, Norcross, GA 30092. Internet: http://www.iienet.org

Materials engineers

▸ The Minerals, Metals, & Materials Society, 184 Thorn Hill Rd., Warrendale, PA 15086-7514. Internet: http://www.tms.org

▶ ASM International, 9639 Kinsman Rd., Materials Park, OH 44073-0002. Internet: http://www.asminternational.org

Mechanical engineers

▶ The American Society of Mechanical Engineers, 3 Park Ave., New York, NY 10016-5990. Internet: http://www.asme.org

▶ American Society of Heating, Refrigerating, and Air-Conditioning Engineers, Inc., 1791 Tullie Circle NE, Atlanta, GA 30329. Internet: http://www.ashrae.org

▶ Society of Automotive Engineers, 400 Commonwealth Dr., Warrendale, PA 15096-0001. Internet: http://www.sae.org

Marine engineers and naval architects

▶ Society of Naval Architects and Marine Engineers, 601 Pavonia Ave., Jersey City, NJ 07306. Internet: http://www.sname.org

Mining and geological engineers, including mining safety engineers

▶ The Society for Mining, Metallurgy, and Exploration, Inc., 8307 Shaffer Parkway, Littleton, CO 80127-4102. Internet: http://www.smenet.org

Nuclear engineers

▶ American Nuclear Society, 555 North Kensington Ave., LaGrange Park, IL 60526. Internet: http://www.ans.org

Petroleum engineers

▶ Society of Petroleum Engineers, P.O. Box 833836, Richardson, TX 75083-3836. Internet: http://www.spe.org

Fashion Designers

(O*NET 27-1022.00)

Significant Points

■ In 2004, two-thirds of salaried fashion designers were employed in either New York or California.

■ Employers seek designers with a 2- or 4-year degree who are knowledgeable about textiles, fabrics, ornamentation, and fashion trends.

■ Job competition is expected to be keen as many designers are attracted to the creativity and glamour associated with the occupation, while relatively few job openings arise.

■ More than 1 out of 4 are self-employed.

Nature of the Work

Fashion designers help create the billions of clothing articles, shoes, and accessories purchased every year by consumers. Designers study fashion trends, sketch designs of clothing and accessories, select colors and fabrics, and oversee the final production of their designs. Clothing designers create and help produce men's, women's, and children's apparel, including casual wear, suits, sportswear, formalwear, outerwear, maternity wear, and intimate apparel. *Footwear designers* help create and produce different styles of shoes and boots. *Accessory designers* help create and produce items that add the finishing touches to an outfit, such as handbags, belts, scarves, hats, hosiery, and eyewear. Some fashion designers specialize in clothing, footwear, or accessory design, while others create designs in all three fashion categories.

The design process from initial design inception to final production takes between 18 and 24 months. The first step in creating a design is researching fashion trends and making predictions of future trends. Some designers conduct their own research, while others rely on trend reports published by fashion industry trade groups. Trend reports indicate what styles, colors, and fabrics will be popular for a particular season in the future. Textile manufacturers use these trend reports to begin designing fabrics and patterns while fashion designers begin to sketch preliminary designs. Designers will then visit manufacturers or trade shows to procure samples of fabrics and decide which fabrics to use with which designs.

Once designs and fabrics are chosen, a prototype of the article using cheaper materials is created and then worn by a model to see what adjustments to the design need to be made. During this time, designers usually will narrow down their choices of which designs to offer for sale. After the final adjustments and selections have been made, samples of the article using the actual materials are sewn and then marketed to clothing retailers. Many designs are shown at fashion and trade shows a few times a year. Retailers will then place orders for certain items, which are then manufactured and distributed to stores.

Computer-aided design (CAD) is increasingly being used in the fashion design industry. While most designers initially sketch designs by hand, a growing number also translate these hand sketches to the computer. CAD allows designers to view designs of clothing on virtual models and in various colors and shapes, thus saving time by requiring fewer adjustments of prototypes and samples later.

Depending on the size of the design firm and level of experience, fashion designers may have varying levels of involvement in different aspects of design and production. In large design firms, fashion designers often are the lead designers who are responsible for creating the designs, choosing the colors and fabrics, and overseeing technical designers who turn the designs into a final product. They are responsible for creating the prototypes and patterns and work with the manufacturers and suppliers during the production stages. Large design houses also employ their own patternmakers, tailors, and sewers who create the master patterns for the design and sew the prototypes and samples. Designers working in small firms, or those new to the job, usually perform most of the technical, patternmaking, and sewing tasks in addition to designing the clothing.

Fashion designers working for apparel wholesalers or manufacturers create designs for the mass market. These designs are manufactured in various sizes and colors. A small number of high-fashion (haute couture) designers are self-employed and create custom designs for individual clients, usually at very high prices. Other high-fashion designers sell their designs in their own retail stores or cater to specialty stores or high-fashion department stores. These designers create a mixture of original garments and those that follow established fashion trends.

Some fashion designers specialize in costume design for performing arts, motion picture, and television productions. The work of costume designers is similar to other fashion designers. Costume designers perform extensive research into the styles worn during the period in which the performance takes place or work with directors to select appropriate attire for performances. They make sketches of designs, select fabric and other materials, and oversee the production of the costumes. They also must stay within the costume budget for the particular production.

Working Conditions

Fashion designers employed by manufacturing establishments, wholesalers, or design firms generally work regular hours in well-lighted and comfortable settings. Designers who freelance generally work on a contract, or job, basis. They frequently adjust their work-day to suit their clients' schedules and deadlines, meeting with the clients during evening or weekend hours when necessary. Freelance designers tend to work longer hours and in smaller, more congested, environments and are under pressure to please clients and to find new ones in order to maintain a steady income. Regardless of their work setting, all fashion designers occasionally work long hours to meet production deadlines or prepare for fashion shows.

The global nature of the fashion business requires constant communication with suppliers, manufacturers, and customers all over the United States and the world. Most fashion designers travel several times a year to trade and fashion shows in order to learn about the latest fashion trends. Designers also may travel frequently to meet with fabric and materials suppliers and with manufacturers who produce the final apparel products.

Training, Other Qualifications, and Advancement

In fashion design, employers seek individuals with a 2-year or 4-year degree who are knowledgeable about textiles, fabrics, ornamentation, and fashion trends. Designers must have a strong sense of the esthetic—an eye for color and detail, a sense of balance and proportion, and an appreciation for beauty. Fashion designers also need excellent communication and problem-solving skills. Despite the advancement of computer-aided design, sketching ability remains an important advantage in fashion design. A good portfolio—a collection of examples of a person's best work—often is the deciding factor in getting a job.

Bachelor's of fine arts and associate degree programs in fashion design are offered at many colleges, universities, and private art and design schools. Some fashion designers also combine a fashion design degree with a business, marketing, or fashion merchandising degree, especially those who want to run their own business or retail store. Basic coursework includes color, textiles, sewing and tailoring, pattern making, fashion history, CAD, and design of different types of clothing such as menswear or footwear. Coursework in human anatomy, mathematics, and psychology also is useful.

The National Association of Schools of Art and Design accredits approximately 250 postsecondary institutions with programs in art and design. Most of these schools award degrees in fashion design. Many schools do not allow formal entry into a program until a student has successfully completed basic art and design courses. Applicants usually have to submit sketches and other examples of their artistic ability.

In addition to creativity and sketching ability, fashion designers also need to have sewing and patternmaking skills, even if they do not perform these tasks themselves. Designers need to be able to understand these skills so they can give proper instructions as to how the garment should be constructed. Fashion designers also need strong sales and presentation skills in order to persuade clients to purchase their designs. Good teamwork and communication skills also are necessary because of the increasingly international nature of the business that requires constant contact with suppliers, manufacturers, and buyers around the world.

Aspiring fashion designers can learn these necessary skills through internships with design or manufacturing firms. Some designers also gain valuable experience working in retail stores, as personal stylists, or as custom tailors. Such experience can help designers gain sales and marketing skills while learning what styles and fabrics look good on different people. Designers also can gain exposure to potential employers by entering their designs in student or amateur contests. Because of the global nature of the fashion industry, experience in one of the international fashion centers, such as Milan or Paris, can be useful.

Beginning fashion designers usually start out as pattern makers or sketching assistants for more experienced designers before they can advance to higher-level positions. Experienced designers may advance to chief designer, design department head, or other supervisory position. Some designers may start their own design company or sell their designs in their own retail stores. A few of the most successful designers can work for high-fashion design houses that offer personalized design services to wealthy clients.

Employment

Fashion designers held about 17,000 jobs in 2004. More than 1 out of 4 were self-employed. About 25 percent of fashion designers worked for apparel and piece goods merchant wholesalers. Another 15 percent worked in cut and sew apparel manufacturing. The remainder worked for corporate offices involved in the management of companies and enterprises, clothing stores, performing arts companies, specialized design services firms, textile and textile product mills, and footwear and accessories manufacturers.

Employment of fashion designers tends to be concentrated in regional fashion centers. In 2004, two-thirds of salaried fashion designers were employed in either New York or California.

Job Outlook

Job competition is expected be keen as many designers are attracted to the creativity and glamour associated with the occupation, while relatively few job openings arise because of low job turnover and a small number of new openings created every year. Employment of fashion designers is projected to grow more slowly than average for all occupations through 2014. Employment declines in cut and sew apparel manufacturing are projected to offset increases in apparel wholesalers.

Employment growth for fashion designers will stem from a growing population demanding more clothing, footwear, and accessories. Demand is increasing for stylish clothing that is affordable, especially among middle-income consumers. The best job opportunities will be in design firms that design mass market clothing sold in department stores and retail chain stores, such as apparel wholesale firms. Few employment opportunities are expected in design firms that cater to high-end department stores and specialty boutiques as demand for expensive, high-fashion design declines relative to other luxury goods and services.

Job opportunities in cut and sew manufacturing will continue to decline as apparel is increasingly manufactured overseas. However, employment of fashion designers in this industry will not decline as fast as other occupations because firms are more likely to keep design work in-house.

Earnings

Median annual earnings for fashion designers were $55,840 in May 2004. The middle 50 percent earned between $38,800 and $77,580. The lowest 10 percent earned less than $27,970, and the highest 10 percent earned more than $112,840.

Earnings in fashion design can vary widely based on the employer and years of experience. Starting salaries in fashion design tend to be very low until designers are established in the industry. Salaried fashion designers usually earn higher and more stable incomes than self-employed or freelance designers. However, a few of the most successful self-employed fashion designers may earn many times the salary of the highest-paid salaried designers. Self-employed fashion designers must provide their own benefits and retirement.

Related Occupations

Workers in other art and design occupations include artists and related workers, commercial and industrial designers, floral designers, graphic designers, and interior designers. Jewelers and precious stone and metal workers also design wearable accessories. Other common occupations in the fashion industry include demonstrators, product promoters, and models; photographers; purchasing managers, buyers, and purchasing agents; retail salespersons; and textile, apparel, and furnishings occupations.

Sources of Additional Information

For general information about art and design and a list of accredited college-level programs, contact

▸ National Association of Schools of Art and Design, 11250 Roger Bacon Dr., Suite 21, Reston, VA 20190-5248. Internet: http://nasad.arts-accredit.org

For general information about careers in fashion design, contact

▸ Fashion Group International, 8 West 40th St., 7th Floor, New York, NY 10018. Internet: http://www.fgi.org

Financial Analysts and Personal Financial Advisors

(O*NET 13-2051.00 and 13-2052.00)

Significant Points

■ A college degree and good interpersonal skills are among the most important qualifications for these workers.

■ Although both occupations will benefit from an increase in investing by individuals, personal financial advisors will benefit more.

■ Financial analysts and personal financial advisors who have earned a professional designation are expected to have the best opportunities; competition is anticipated to be keen for highly lucrative positions in investment banking.

■ About 4 out of 10 personal financial advisors are self-employed.

Nature of the Work

Financial analysts and personal financial advisors provide analysis and guidance to businesses and individuals to help them with their investment decisions. Both types of specialists gather financial information, analyze it, and make recommendations to their clients. However, their job duties differ because of the type of investment information they provide and the clients for whom they work. *Financial analysts* assess the economic performance of companies and industries for firms and institutions with money to invest. *Personal financial advisors* generally assess the financial needs of individuals, offering them a wide range of options.

Financial analysts, also called *securities analysts* and *investment analysts*, work for banks, insurance companies, mutual and pension funds, securities firms, and other businesses, helping these companies or their clients make investment decisions. Financial analysts read company financial statements and analyze commodity prices, sales, costs, expenses, and tax rates in order to determine a company's value and to project its future earnings. They often meet with company officials to gain a better insight into the firm's prospects and to determine its managerial effectiveness. Usually, financial analysts study an entire industry, assessing current trends in business practices, products, and industry competition. They must keep abreast of new regulations or policies that may affect the industry as well as monitor the economy to determine its effect on earnings.

Financial analysts use spreadsheet and statistical software packages to analyze financial data, spot trends, and develop forecasts. On the basis of their results, they write reports and make presentations, usually making recommendations to buy or sell a particular investment or security. Senior analysts may even be the ones who decide to buy or sell if they are responsible for managing the company's or client's assets. Other analysts use the data they find to measure the financial risks associated with making a particular investment decision.

Financial analysts in investment banking departments of securities or banking firms often work in teams, analyzing the future prospects of companies that want to sell shares to the public for the first time. They also ensure that the forms and written materials necessary for compliance with Securities and Exchange Commission regulations are accurate and complete. They may make presentations to prospective investors about the merits of investing in the new company. Financial analysts also work in mergers and acquisitions departments, preparing analyses on the costs and benefits of a proposed merger or takeover.

Some financial analysts, called *ratings analysts*, evaluate the ability of companies or governments that issue bonds to repay their debts. On the basis of their evaluation, a management team assigns a rating to a company's or government's bonds. Other financial analysts perform budget, cost, and credit analysis as part of their responsibilities.

Personal financial advisors, also called *financial planners* or *financial consultants*, use their knowledge of investments, tax laws, and insurance to recommend financial options to individuals in accordance with the individual's short-term and long-term goals. Some of the issues that planners address are retirement and estate planning, funding for college, and general investment options. While most planners offer advice on a wide range of topics, some specialize in areas such as retirement and estate planning or risk management.

An advisor's work begins with a consultation with the client, from whom the advisor obtains information on the client's finances and financial goals. The advisor then develops a comprehensive financial plan that identifies problem areas, makes recommendations for improvement, and selects appropriate investments compatible with the client's goals, attitude toward risk, and expectation or need for a return on the investment. Sometimes this plan is written, but more often it is in the form of verbal advice. Financial advisors usually meet with established clients at least once a year to update them on potential investments and to determine whether the clients have been through any life changes—such as marriage, disability, or retirement—that might affect their financial goals. Financial advisors also answer questions from clients regarding changes in benefit plans or the consequences of a change in their jobs or careers. A large part of the success of financial planners depends on their ability to educate their clients about risks and various possible scenarios so that the clients don't harbor unrealistic expectations.

Some advisors buy and sell financial products, such as mutual funds or insurance, or refer clients to other companies for products and services—for example, the preparation of taxes or wills. A number of advisors take on the responsibility of managing the clients' investments for them.

Finding clients and building a customer base are two of the most important parts of a financial advisor's job because referrals from satisfied clients are an important source of new business. Many advisors also contact potential clients by giving seminars or lectures or meet clients through business and social contacts.

Working Conditions

Financial analysts and personal financial advisors usually work indoors in safe, comfortable offices or their own homes. Many of these workers enjoy the challenge of helping firms or people make financial decisions. However, financial analysts may face long hours, frequent travel to visit companies and talk to potential investors, and the pressure of deadlines. Much of their research must be done after office hours because their day is filled with telephone calls and meetings. Personal financial advisors usually work standard business hours, but they also schedule meetings with clients in the evenings or on weekends. Many teach evening classes or hold seminars in order to bring in more clients.

Training, Other Qualifications, and Advancement

A college education is required for financial analysts and is strongly preferred for personal financial advisors. Most companies require financial analysts to have at least a bachelor's degree in business administration, accounting, statistics, or finance. Coursework in statistics, economics, and business is required, and knowledge of accounting policies and procedures, corporate budgeting, and financial analysis methods is recommended. A master's degree in business administration is desirable. Advanced courses in options pricing or bond valuation and knowledge of risk management also are suggested.

Employers usually do not require a specific field of study for personal financial advisors, but a bachelor's degree in accounting, finance, economics, business, mathematics, or law provides good preparation for the occupation. Courses in investments, taxes, estate planning, and risk management also are helpful. Programs in financial planning are becoming more widely available in colleges and universities. Working for a broker-dealer is a good way to gain experience that can help individuals pass the security license exams needed to practice financial planning. Individuals who start out as independent financial planners may find it more difficult to build their client base, and they often start by servicing their family members and friends. However, many financial planners enter the field after working in a related occupation, such as accountant; auditor; insurance sales agent; lawyer; or securities, commodities, and financial services sales agent.

Mathematical, computer, analytical, and problem-solving skills are essential qualifications for financial analysts and personal financial advisors. Good communication skills also are necessary because these workers must present complex financial concepts and strategies in easy-to-understand language to clients and other professionals. Self-confidence, maturity, and the ability to work independently are important as well. Financial analysts must be detail oriented; motivated to seek out obscure information; and familiar with the workings of the economy, tax laws, and money markets. Strong interpersonal skills and sales ability are crucial to the success of both financial analysts and personal financial advisors.

Although not required for financial analysts or personal financial advisors to practice, certification can enhance one's professional standing and is strongly recommended by many employers. Financial analysts may receive the Chartered Financial Analyst (CFA) designation, sponsored by the CFA Institute. To qualify for this designation, applicants need a bachelor's degree and 3 years of work experience in a related field and must pass a series of three examinations. These essay exams, administered once a year for 3 years, cover subjects such as accounting, economics, securities analysis, financial markets and instruments, corporate finance, asset valuation, and portfolio management. Personal financial advisors may obtain the Certified Financial Planner credential, often referred to as CFP (R), demonstrating extensive training and competency in financial planning. This certification, issued by the Certified Financial Planner Board of Standards, requires relevant experience, the completion of education requirements, passing a comprehensive examination, and adherence to an enforceable code of ethics. The CFP (R) exams test the candidate's knowledge of the financial planning process, insurance and risk management, employee benefits planning, taxes and retirement planning, and investment and estate planning. The exam has been revised in recent years. Candidates are now required to have a working knowledge of debt management, planning liability, emergency fund reserves, and statistical modeling. It may take from 2 to 3 years of study to complete these programs.

Personal financial advisors also may obtain the Chartered Financial Consultant (ChFC) designation, issued by the American College in Bryn Mawr, Pennsylvania, which requires experience and the completion of an eight-course program of study. The ChFC designation and other professional designations have continuing education requirements.

A license is not required to work as a personal financial advisor, but advisors who sell stocks, bonds, mutual funds, insurance, or real estate may need licenses to perform these additional services. Also, if legal advice is provided, a license to practice law may be required. Financial advisors who do not offer these additional services often refer clients to those who are qualified to provide them.

Financial analysts may advance by becoming portfolio managers or financial managers, directing the investment portfolios of their companies or of clients. Personal financial advisors who work in firms also may move into managerial positions, but most advisors advance by accumulating clients and managing more assets.

Employment

Financial analysts and personal financial advisors held 355,000 jobs in 2004, of which financial analysts held 197,000. Many financial analysts work at the headquarters of large financial companies, several of which are based in New York City. More than 4 out of 10 financial analysts work for finance and insurance industries, including securities and commodity brokers, banks and credit institutions, and insurance carriers. Others worked throughout private industry and government.

Personal financial advisors held 158,000 jobs in 2004. Much like financial analysts, more than half work for finance and insurance industries, including securities and commodity brokers, banks, insurance carriers, and financial investment firms. However, 4 out of 10 personal financial advisors are self-employed, operating small investment advisory firms, usually in urban areas.

Job Outlook

Overall employment of financial analysts and personal financial advisors is expected to increase faster than average for all occupations through 2014, resulting from increased investment by businesses and individuals. Personal financial advisors will benefit even more than financial analysts as baby boomers save for retirement and as a generally better-educated and wealthier population requires investment advice. In addition, people are living longer and must plan to finance more years of retirement. The globalization of the securities markets also will increase the need for analysts and advisors to help investors make financial choices. Financial analysts and personal financial advisors who have earned a professional designation are expected to have the best opportunities.

Deregulation of the financial services industry is expected to spur demand for financial analysts and personal financial advisors. In recent years, banks, insurance companies, and brokerage firms have been allowed to broaden their financial services. Many firms are adding investment advice to their list of services and are expected to increase their hiring of personal financial advisors. Many banks are entering the securities brokerage and investment banking fields and will increasingly need the skills of financial analysts.

Employment of personal financial advisors is projected to grow faster than the average for all occupations. The rapid expansion of self-directed retirement plans, such as 401(k) plans, is expected to continue. As the number and complexity of investments rises, more individuals will look to financial advisors to help manage their money.

Employment of financial analysts is expected to grow about as fast as the average for all occupations. As the number of mutual funds and the amount of assets invested in the funds increase, mutual fund companies will need increased numbers of financial analysts to recommend which financial products the funds should buy or sell.

Financial analysts also will be needed in the investment banking field, where they help companies raise money and work on corporate mergers and acquisitions. However, growth in demand for financial analysts to do company research has been, and will continue to be, constrained by regulations that require investment firms to separate research from investment banking. As a result, firms have eliminated research jobs in an effort to contain the costs of implementing these regulations.

Demand for financial analysts in investment banking fluctuates because investment banking is sensitive to changes in the stock market. In addition, further consolidation in the finance industries may eliminate some financial analyst positions, dampening overall employment growth somewhat. Competition is expected to be keen for these highly lucrative positions, with many more applicants than jobs.

Earnings

Median annual earnings of financial analysts were $61,910 in May 2004. The middle 50 percent earned between $47,410 and $82,730. The lowest 10 percent earned less than $37,580, and the highest 10 percent earned more than $113,490. Median annual earnings in the industries employing the largest numbers of financial analysts in 2004 were as follows:

Other financial investment activities	$74,580
Securities and commodity contracts intermediation and brokerage	67,730
Management of companies and enterprises	62,890
Insurance carriers	58,120
Depository credit intermediation	56,860

Median annual earnings of personal financial advisors were $62,700 in May 2004. The middle 50 percent earned between $41,860 and $108,280. Median annual earnings in the industries employing the largest number of personal financial advisors in 2004 were as follows:

Other financial investment activities	$78,350
Securities and commodity contracts intermediation and brokerage	63,310
Depository credit intermediation	57,180
Agencies, brokerages, and other insurance-related activities	56,950

Many financial analysts receive a bonus in addition to their salary, and the bonus can add substantially to their earnings. Usually, the bonus is based on how well their predictions compare to the actual performance of a benchmark investment. Personal financial advisors who work for financial services firms are generally paid a salary plus bonus. Advisors who work for financial investment or planning firms or who are self-employed either charge hourly fees for their services or charge one set fee for a comprehensive plan, based on its complexity. Advisors who manage a client's assets may charge a percentage of those assets. Advisors generally receive commissions for financial products they sell in addition to charging a fee.

Related Occupations

Other jobs requiring expertise in finance and investment or in the sale of financial products include accountants and auditors; financial managers; insurance sales agents; real estate brokers and sales agents; and securities, commodities, and financial services sales agents.

Sources of Additional Information

For information on a career in financial planning, contact

▶ The Financial Planning Association, 4100 E. Mississippi Ave., Suite 400, Denver, CO 80246-3053. Internet: http://www.fpanet.org

For information about the Certified Financial Planner (CFP) (R) certification, contact

▶ Certified Financial Planner Board of Standards, Inc., 1670 Broadway, Suite 600, Denver, CO 80202-4809. Internet: http://www.cfp.net/become

For information about the Chartered Financial Consultant (ChFC) designation, contact

▶ The American College, 270 South Bryn Mawr Ave., Bryn Mawr, PA 19010. Internet: http://www.theamericancollege.edu

For information on a career as a financial analyst, contact either of the following organizations:

▶ American Academy of Financial Management, 2 Canal St., Suite 2317, New Orleans, LA 70130. Internet: http://www.financialanalyst.org

▶ CFA Institute, P.O. Box 3668, 560 Ray C. Hunt Dr., Charlottesville, VA 22903. Internet: http://www.cfainstitute.org

Graphic Designers

(O*NET 27-1024.00)

Significant Points

■ Among the five design occupations, graphic designers are expected to have the most new jobs through 2014; however, job seekers are expected to face keen competition for available positions.

■ Graphic designers with Web site design and animation experience will have the best opportunities.

■ A bachelor's degree is required for most entry-level positions; however, an associate degree may be sufficient for technical positions.

■ About 3 out of 10 designers are self-employed; many do free-lance work in addition to holding a salaried job in design or in another occupation.

Nature of the Work

Graphic designers—or *graphic artists*—plan, analyze, and create visual solutions to communications problems. They decide the most effective way of getting a message across in print, electronic, and film media using a variety of methods such as color, type, illustration, photography, animation, and various print and layout techniques. Graphic designers develop the overall layout and production design of magazines, newspapers, journals, corporate reports, and other publications. They also produce promotional displays, packaging, and marketing brochures for products and services; design distinctive logos for products and businesses; and develop signs and signage systems—called environmental graphics—for business and government. An increasing number of graphic designers also are developing material for Internet Web pages, interactive media, and multimedia projects. Graphic designers also may produce the credits that appear before and after television programs and movies.

The first step in developing a new graphic design is to determine the needs of the client, the message the design should portray, and its appeal to customers or users. Graphic designers consider cognitive, cultural, physical, and social factors in planning and executing designs for the target audience. Designers gather relevant information by meeting with clients and creative or art directors and by performing their own research. Identifying the needs of consumers is becoming increasingly important for graphic designers as the scope of their work continues to focus on creating corporate communication strategies in addition to technical design and layout work.

Graphic designers prepare sketches or layouts—by hand or with the aid of a computer—to illustrate the vision for the design. They select colors, sound, artwork, photography, animation, style of type, and other visual elements for the design. Designers also select the size and arrangement of the different elements on the page or screen. They also may create graphs and charts from data for use in publications, and they often consult with copywriters on any text that may accompany the visual part of the design. Designers then present the completed design to their clients or art or creative director for approval. In printing and publishing firms, graphic designers also may assist the printers by selecting the type of paper and ink for the publication and reviewing the mock-up design for errors before final publication.

Graphic designers use a variety of graphics and layout computer software to assist in their designs. Designers creating Web pages or other interactive media designs also will use computer animation and programming packages. Computer software programs allow ease and flexibility in exploring a greater number of design alternatives, thus reducing design costs and cutting the time it takes to deliver a product to market.

Graphic designers sometimes supervise assistants who carry out their creations. Designers who run their own businesses also may devote a considerable amount of time to developing new business contacts, examining equipment and space needs, and performing administrative tasks such as reviewing catalogues and ordering samples. The need for up-to-date computer and communications equipment is an ongoing consideration for graphic designers.

Working Conditions

Working conditions and places of employment vary. Graphic designers employed by large advertising, publishing, or design firms generally work regular hours in well-lighted and comfortable settings. Designers in smaller design consulting firms, or those who freelance, generally work on a contract, or job, basis. They frequently adjust their workday to suit their clients' schedules and deadlines. Consultants and self-employed designers tend to work longer hours and in smaller, more congested environments.

Designers may transact business in their own offices or studios or in clients' offices. Designers who are paid by the assignment are under pressure to please clients and to find new ones in order to maintain a steady income. All designers sometimes face frustration when their designs are rejected or when their work is not as creative as they wish. Graphic designers may work evenings or weekends to meet production schedules, especially in the printing and publishing industries where deadlines are shorter and more frequent.

Training, Other Qualifications, and Advancement

A bachelor's degree is required for most entry-level and advanced graphic design positions, although some entry-level technical positions may only require an associate degree. In addition to postsecondary training in graphic design, creativity and communication and problem-solving skills are crucial. Graphic designers also need to be familiar with computer graphics and design software. A good portfolio—a collection of examples of a person's best work—often is the deciding factor in getting a job.

Bachelor's of fine arts degree programs in graphic design are offered at many colleges, universities, and private design schools. The curriculum includes studio art, principles of design, computerized design, commercial graphics production, printing techniques, and Web site design. In addition to design courses, a liberal arts education or a program that includes courses in art history, writing, psychology, sociology, foreign languages and cultural studies, marketing, and business are useful in helping designers work effectively with the content of their work. Graphic designers must effectively communicate complex subjects to a variety of audiences. Increasingly, clients rely on graphic designers to develop the content and the context of the message in addition to performing technical layout work.

Associate degrees and certificates in graphic design also are available from 2- and 3-year professional schools. These programs usually focus on the technical aspects of graphic design and include very few liberal arts courses. Graduates of 2-year programs normally qualify as assistants to graphic designers or for positions requiring technical skills only. Individuals who wish to pursue a career in graphic design—and who already possess a bachelor's

degree in another field—can complete a 2-year or 3-year program in graphic design to learn the technical requirements.

The National Association of Schools of Art and Design accredits about 250 postsecondary institutions with programs in art and design. Most of these schools award a degree in graphic design. Many schools do not allow formal entry into a bachelor's degree program until a student has successfully finished a year of basic art and design courses. Applicants may be required to submit sketches and other examples of their artistic ability.

Increasingly, employers expect new graphic designers to be familiar with computer graphics and design software. Graphic designers must continually keep up to date with the development of new and updated software, usually either on their own or through software training programs.

Graphic designers also must be creative and able to communicate their ideas in writing, visually, and verbally. Because consumer tastes can change quickly, designers need to be well read, open to new ideas and influences, and quick to react to changing trends. Problem-solving skills, paying attention to detail, and the ability to work independently and under pressure also are important traits. People in this field need self-discipline to start projects on their own, to budget their time, and to meet deadlines and production schedules. Good business sense and sales ability also are important, especially for those who freelance or run their own business.

Beginning graphic designers usually receive on-the-job training and normally need 1 to 3 years of training before they can advance to higher-level positions. Experienced graphic designers in large firms may advance to chief designer, art or creative director, or other supervisory positions. Some designers leave the occupation to become teachers in design schools or in colleges and universities. Many faculty members continue to consult privately or operate small design studios to complement their classroom activities. Some experienced designers open their own firms or choose to specialize in one area of graphic design.

Employment

Graphic designers held about 228,000 jobs in 2004. About 7 out of 10 were wage and salary designers. Most worked in specialized design services; advertising and related services; printing and related support activities; or newspaper, periodical, book, and directory publishers. Other graphic designers produced computer graphics for computer systems design firms or motion picture production firms. A small number of designers also worked in engineering services or for management, scientific, and technical consulting firms.

About 3 out of 10 designers were self-employed. Many did freelance work—full time or part time—in addition to holding a salaried job in design or in another occupation.

Job Outlook

Employment of graphic designers is expected to grow about as fast as average for all occupations through the year 2014 as demand for graphic design continues to increase from advertisers, publishers, and computer design firms. Among the five different design occupations, graphic designers will have the most new jobs. However, graphic designers are expected to face keen competition for available positions. Many talented individuals are attracted to careers as graphic designers. Individuals with a bachelor's degree and knowledge of computer design software, particularly those with Web site design and animation experience, will have the best opportunities.

Demand for graphic designers should increase because of the rapidly expanding market for Web-based information and expansion of the video entertainment market, including television, movies, video, and made-for-Internet outlets. Graphic designers with Web site design and animation experience will especially be needed as demand for design projects increase for interactive media—Web sites, video games, cellular telephones, personal digital assistants (PDAs), and other technology. Demand for graphic designers also will increase as advertising firms create print and Web marketing and promotional materials for a growing number of products and services.

In recent years, some computer, printing, and publishing firms have outsourced basic layout and design work to design firms overseas. This trend is expected to continue and may have a negative impact on employment growth for lower-level technical graphic design workers. However, most higher-level graphic design jobs will remain in the U.S. and will focus on developing communication strategies, called strategic design, for clients and firms in order for them to gain competitive advantages in the market. Strategic design work requires close proximity to the consumer in order to identify and target their needs and interests. Graphic designers with a broad liberal arts education and experience in marketing and business management will be best suited for these positions.

Earnings

Median annual earnings for graphic designers were $38,030 in May 2004. The middle 50 percent earned between $29,360 and $50,840. The lowest 10 percent earned less than $23,220, and the highest 10 percent earned more than $65,940. Median annual earnings in the industries employing the largest numbers of graphic designers were

Architectural, engineering, and related services	$42,740
Specialized design services	41,620
Advertising and related services	40,010
Printing and related support activities	32,830
Newspaper, periodical, book, and directory publishers	32,390

The American Institute of Graphic Arts reported 2005 median annual total cash compensation for graphic designers according to level of responsibility. Entry-level designers earned a median salary of $32,000 in 2005, while staff-level graphic designers earned $42,500. Senior designers, who may supervise junior staff or have some decision-making authority that reflects their knowledge of graphic design, earned $56,000. Solo designers, who freelanced or worked under contract to another company, reported median

earnings of $60,000. Design directors, the creative heads of design firms or in-house corporate design departments, earned $90,000. Graphic designers with ownership or partnership interests in a firm or who were principals of the firm in some other capacity earned $100,000.

Related Occupations

Workers in other occupations in the art and design field include artists and related workers, commercial and industrial designers, fashion designers, floral designers, and interior designers. Other occupations that require computer-aided design skills include computer software engineers, drafters, and desktop publishers. Other occupations involved in the design, layout, and copy of publications include advertising, marketing, promotions, public relations, and sales managers; photographers; writers and editors; and prepress technicians and workers.

Sources of Additional Information

For general information about art and design and a list of accredited college-level programs, contact

▸ National Association of Schools of Art and Design, 11250 Roger Bacon Dr., Suite 21, Reston, VA 20190-5248. Internet: http://nasad.arts-accredit.org

For information about graphic, communication, or interaction design careers, contact

▸ American Institute of Graphic Arts, 164 Fifth Ave., New York, NY 10010. Internet: http://www.aiga.org

For information on workshops, scholarships, internships, and competitions for graphic design students interested in advertising careers, contact

▸ Art Directors Club, 106 West 29th St., New York, NY 10001. Internet: http://www.adcglobal.org

Human Resources, Training, and Labor Relations Managers and Specialists

(O*NET 11-3040.00, 11-3041.00, 11-3042.00, 11-3049.99, 13-1071.01, 13-1071.02, 13-1072.00, 13-1073.00, and 13-1079.99)

Significant Points

- In filling entry-level jobs, many employers seek college graduates who have majored in human resources, human resources administration, or industrial and labor relations; other employers look for college graduates with a technical or business background or a well-rounded liberal arts education.

- For many specialized jobs, previous experience is an asset; for more advanced positions, including those of managers, arbitrators, and mediators, it is essential.

- Keen competition for jobs is expected because of the plentiful supply of qualified college graduates and experienced workers.

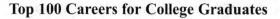

Nature of the Work

Attracting the most-qualified employees and matching them to the jobs for which they are best suited is significant for the success of any organization. However, many enterprises are too large to permit close contact between top management and employees. Human resources, training, and labor relations managers and specialists provide this connection. In the past, these workers have been associated with performing the administrative function of an organization, such as handling employee benefits questions or recruiting, interviewing, and hiring new staff in accordance with policies and requirements that have been established in conjunction with top management. Today's human resources workers manage these tasks and, increasingly, consult top executives regarding strategic planning. They have moved from behind-the-scenes staff work to leading the company in suggesting and changing policies. Senior management is recognizing the significance of the human resources department to their financial success.

In an effort to enhance morale and productivity, limit job turnover, and help organizations increase performance and improve business results, they also help their firms effectively use employee skills, provide training and development opportunities to improve those skills, and increase employees' satisfaction with their jobs and working conditions. Although some jobs in the human resources field require only limited contact with people outside the office, dealing with people is an important part of the job.

In a small organization, a *human resources generalist* may handle all aspects of human resources work and thus require an extensive range of knowledge. The responsibilities of human resources generalists can vary widely, depending on their employer's needs. In a large corporation, the top human resources executive usually develops and manages human resources programs and policies. (Executives are included in the description of top executives elsewhere in this book.) These policies usually are implemented by a director or manager of human resources and, in some cases, a director of industrial relations.

The *director of human resources* may supervise several departments, each headed by an experienced manager who most likely specializes in one human resources activity, such as employment, compensation, benefits, training and development, or employee relations.

Employment and placement managers supervise the hiring and separation of employees and supervise various workers, including equal employment opportunity specialists and recruitment specialists. *Employment, recruitment,* and *placement specialists* recruit and place workers.

Recruiters maintain contacts within the community and may travel considerably, often to college campuses, to search for promising job applicants. Recruiters screen, interview, and occasionally test applicants. They also may check references and extend job offers. These workers must be thoroughly familiar with the organization and its human resources policies in order to discuss wages, working conditions, and promotional opportunities with prospective employees. They also must keep informed about equal employment opportunity (EEO) and affirmative action guidelines and laws, such as the Americans with Disabilities Act.

EEO officers, representatives, or *affirmative action coordinators* handle EEO matters in large organizations. They investigate and resolve EEO grievances, examine corporate practices for possible violations, and compile and submit EEO statistical reports.

Employer relations representatives, who usually work in government agencies, maintain working relationships with local employers and promote the use of public employment programs and services. Similarly, *employment interviewers*—whose many job titles include *human resources consultants, human resources development specialists,* and *human resources coordinators*—help to match employers with qualified jobseekers.

Compensation, benefits, and job analysis specialists conduct programs for employers and may specialize in specific areas such as position classifications or pensions. *Job analysts,* occasionally called *position classifiers,* collect and examine detailed information about job duties in order to prepare job descriptions. These descriptions explain the duties, training, and skills that each job requires. Whenever a large organization introduces a new job or reviews existing jobs, it calls upon the expert knowledge of the job analyst.

Occupational analysts conduct research, usually in large firms. They are concerned with occupational classification systems and study the effects of industry and occupational trends upon worker relationships. They may serve as technical liaison between the firm and other firms, government, and labor unions.

Establishing and maintaining a firm's pay system is the principal job of the *compensation manager.* Assisted by staff specialists, compensation managers devise ways to ensure fair and equitable pay rates. They may conduct surveys to see how their firm's rates compare with others and to see that the firm's pay scale complies with changing laws and regulations. In addition, compensation managers often manage their firm's performance evaluation system, and they may design reward systems such as pay-for-performance plans.

Employee benefits managers and specialists manage the company's employee benefits program, notably its health insurance and pension plans. Expertise in designing and administering benefits programs continues to take on importance as employer-provided benefits account for a growing proportion of overall compensation costs and as benefit plans increase in number and complexity. For example, pension benefits might include savings and thrift, profit-sharing, and stock ownership plans; health benefits might include long-term catastrophic illness insurance and dental insurance. Familiarity with health benefits is a top priority for employee benefits managers and specialists as more firms struggle to cope with the rising cost of health care for employees and retirees. In addition to health insurance and pension coverage, some firms offer employees life and accidental death and dismemberment insurance, disability insurance, and relatively new benefits designed to meet the needs of a changing workforce, such as parental leave, child and elder care, long-term nursing home care insurance, employee assistance and wellness programs, and flexible benefits plans. Benefits managers must keep abreast of changing federal and state regulations and legislation that may affect employee benefits.

Employee assistance plan managers, also called *employee welfare managers,* are responsible for a wide array of programs covering occupational safety and health standards and practices; health promotion and physical fitness, medical examinations, and minor health treatment, such as first aid; plant security; publications; food service and recreation activities; carpooling and transportation programs, such as transit subsidies; employee suggestion systems; child care and elder care; and counseling services. Child care and elder care are increasingly significant because of growth in the number of dual-income households and the elderly population. Counseling may help employees deal with emotional disorders; alcoholism; or marital, family, consumer, legal, and financial problems. Some employers offer career counseling as well. In large firms, certain programs, such as those dealing with security and safety, may be in separate departments headed by other managers.

Training and development managers and specialists conduct and supervise training and development programs for employees. Increasingly, management recognizes that training offers a way of developing skills, enhancing productivity and quality of work, building worker loyalty to the firm, and, most importantly, increasing individual and organizational performance to achieve business results. While training is widely accepted as an employee benefit and a method of improving employee morale, enhancing employee skills has become a business imperative. Increasingly, managers and leaders realize that the key to business growth and success is through developing the skills and knowledge of its workforce.

Other factors involved in determining whether training is needed include the complexity of the work environment, the rapid pace of organizational and technological change, and the growing number of jobs in fields that constantly generate new knowledge and thus require new skills. In addition, advances in learning theory have provided insights into how adults learn and how training can be organized most effectively for them.

Training managers provide worker training either in the classroom or onsite. This includes setting up teaching materials prior to the class, involving the class, and issuing completion certificates at the end of the class. They have the responsibility for the entire learning process, and its environment, to ensure that the course meets its objectives and is measured and evaluated to understand how learning impacts business results.

Training specialists plan, organize, and direct a wide range of training activities. Trainers respond to corporate and worker service requests. They consult with onsite supervisors regarding available performance improvement services and conduct orientation sessions and arrange on-the-job training for new employees. They help all employees maintain and improve their job skills and possibly prepare for jobs requiring greater skill. They help supervisors improve their interpersonal skills in order to deal effectively with employees. They may set up individualized training plans to strengthen an employee's existing skills or teach new ones. Training specialists in some companies set up leadership or executive development programs among employees in lower-level positions. These programs are designed to develop leaders to replace those leaving the organization and as part of a succession plan. Trainers also lead programs to assist employees with job transitions as a result of mergers and acquisitions as well as technological changes. In government-supported training programs, training specialists function as case managers. They first assess the training needs of clients and then guide them through the most appropriate training method. After training, clients may either be referred to employer relations representatives or receive job placement assistance.

Planning and program development is an essential part of the training specialist's job. In order to identify and assess training needs within the firm, trainers may confer with managers and supervisors or conduct surveys. They also evaluate training effectiveness to ensure that the training employees receive helps the organization meet its strategic business goals and achieve results.

Depending on the size, goals, and nature of the organization, trainers may differ considerably in their responsibilities and in the methods they use. Training methods include on-the-job training; operating schools that duplicate shop conditions for trainees prior to putting them on the shop floor; apprenticeship training; classroom training; and electronic learning, which may involve interactive Internet-based training, multimedia programs, distance learning, satellite training, other computer-aided instructional technologies, videos, simulators, conferences, and workshops.

An organization's *director of industrial relations* forms labor policy, oversees industrial labor relations, negotiates collective bargaining agreements, and coordinates grievance procedures to handle complaints resulting from management disputes with unionized employees. The director of industrial relations also advises and collaborates with the director of human resources, other managers, and members of their staff because all aspects of human resources policy—such as wages, benefits, pensions, and work practices—may be involved in drawing up a new or revised union contract.

Labor relations managers and their staffs implement industrial labor relations programs. Labor relations specialists prepare information for management to use during collective bargaining agreement negotiations, a process that requires the specialist to be familiar with economic and wage data and to have extensive knowledge of labor law and collective bargaining trends. The labor relations staff interprets and administers the contract with respect to grievances, wages and salaries, employee welfare, health care, pensions, union and management practices, and other contractual stipulations. As union membership continues to decline in most industries, industrial relations personnel are working more often with employees who are not members of a labor union.

Dispute resolution—attaining tacit or contractual agreements—has become increasingly significant as parties to a dispute attempt to avoid costly litigation, strikes, or other disruptions. Dispute resolution also has become more complex, involving employees, management, unions, other firms, and government agencies. Specialists involved in dispute resolution must be highly knowledgeable and experienced and often report to the director of industrial relations. *Conciliators*, or *mediators*, advise and counsel labor and management to prevent and, when necessary, resolve disputes over labor agreements or other labor relations issues. *Arbitrators*, occasionally called umpires or referees, decide disputes that bind both labor and management to specific terms and conditions of labor contracts. Labor relations specialists who work for unions perform many of the same functions on behalf of the union and its members.

Other emerging specialties include *international human resources managers*, who handle human resources issues related to a company's foreign operations, and *human resources information system specialists*, who develop and apply computer programs to process human resources information, match job seekers with job openings, and handle other human resources matters.

Working Conditions

Human resources work usually takes place in clean, pleasant, and comfortable office settings. Arbitrators and mediators may work out of their homes. Many human resources, training, and labor relations managers and specialists work a standard 35- to 40-hour week. However, longer hours might be necessary for some workers—for example, labor relations managers and specialists, arbitrators, and mediators—when contract agreements are being prepared and negotiated.

Although most human resources, training, and labor relations managers and specialists work in the office, some travel extensively. For example, recruiters regularly attend professional meetings and visit college campuses to interview prospective employees; arbitrators and mediators often must travel to the site chosen for negotiations.

Training, Other Qualifications, and Advancement

The educational backgrounds of human resources, training, and labor relations managers and specialists vary considerably because of the diversity of duties and levels of responsibility. In filling entry-level jobs, many employers seek college graduates who have majored in human resources, human resources administration, or industrial and labor relations. Other employers look for college graduates with a technical or business background or a well-rounded liberal arts education.

Many colleges and universities have programs leading to a degree in personnel, human resources, or labor relations. Some offer degree programs in human resources administration or human resources management, training and development, or compensation and benefits. Depending on the school, courses leading to a career in human resources management may be found in departments of business administration, education, instructional technology, organizational development, human services, communication, or public administration or within a separate human resources institution or department.

Because an interdisciplinary background is appropriate in this field, a combination of courses in the social sciences, business, and behavioral sciences is useful. Some jobs may require a more technical or specialized background in engineering, science, finance, or law, for example. Most prospective human resources specialists should take courses in compensation, recruitment, training and development, and performance appraisal as well as courses in principles of management, organizational structure, and industrial psychology. Other relevant courses include business administration, public administration, psychology, sociology, political science, economics, and statistics. Courses in labor law, collective bargaining, labor economics, labor history, and industrial psychology also provide a valuable background for the prospective labor relations specialist. As in many other fields, knowledge of computers and information systems also is useful.

An advanced degree is increasingly important for some jobs. Many labor relations jobs require graduate study in industrial or labor relations. A strong background in industrial relations and law is highly desirable for contract negotiators, mediators, and arbitrators; in fact, many people in these specialties are lawyers. A background in law

also is desirable for employee benefits managers and others who must interpret the growing number of laws and regulations. A master's degree in human resources, labor relations, or business administration with a concentration in human resources management is highly recommended for those seeking general and top management positions.

For many specialized jobs in the human resources field, previous experience is an asset; for more advanced positions, including those of managers as well as arbitrators and mediators, it is essential. Many employers prefer entry-level workers who have gained some experience through an internship or work-study program while in school. Human resources administration and human resources development require the ability to work with individuals as well as a commitment to organizational goals. This field also demands other skills that people may develop elsewhere—using computers, selling, teaching, supervising, and volunteering, among others. The field offers clerical workers opportunities for advancement to professional positions. Responsible positions occasionally are filled by experienced individuals from other fields, including business, government, education, social services administration, and the military.

The human resources field demands a range of personal qualities and skills. Human resources, training, and labor relations managers and specialists must speak and write effectively. The growing diversity of the workforce requires that they work with or supervise people with various cultural backgrounds, levels of education, and experience. They must be able to cope with conflicting points of view; function under pressure; and demonstrate discretion, integrity, fair-mindedness, and a persuasive and congenial personality.

The duties given to entry-level workers will vary, depending on whether the new workers have a degree in human resource management, have completed an internship, or have some other type of human resources-related experience. Entry-level employees commonly learn the profession by performing administrative duties—helping to enter data into computer systems, compiling employee handbooks, researching information for a supervisor, or answering the phone and handling routine questions. Entry-level workers often enter formal or on-the-job training programs in which they learn how to classify jobs, interview applicants, or administer employee benefits. They then are assigned to specific areas in the human resources department to gain experience. Later, they may advance to a managerial position, supervising a major element of the human resources program—compensation or training, for example.

Exceptional human resources workers may be promoted to director of human resources or industrial relations, which can eventually lead to a top managerial or executive position. Others may join a consulting firm or open their own business. A Ph.D. is an asset for teaching, writing, or consulting work.

Most organizations specializing in human resources offer classes intended to enhance the marketable skills of their members. Some organizations offer certification programs, which are signs of competence and can enhance one's advancement opportunities. For example, the International Foundation of Employee Benefit Plans confers a designation to persons who complete a series of college-level courses and pass exams covering employee benefit plans. The American Society for Training & Development Certification Institute offers certification; it requires passing a knowledge-based exam and successful work product. The Society for Human Resource

Management has two levels of certification; both require experience and a passing score on a comprehensive exam.

Employment

Human resources, training, and labor relations managers and specialists held about 820,000 jobs in 2004. The following tabulation shows the distribution of jobs by occupational specialty:

Training and development specialists 216,000

Employment, recruitment, and
placement specialists 182,000

Human resources, training, and labor relations
specialists, all other 166,000

Human resources managers 157,000

Compensation, benefits, and job analysis
specialists 99,000

Human resources, training, and labor relations managers and specialists were employed in virtually every industry. About 21,000 specialists were self-employed, working as consultants to public and private employers.

The private sector accounted for more than 8 out of 10 salaried jobs, including 11 percent in administrative and support services; 9 percent in professional, scientific, and technical services; 9 percent in manufacturing; 9 percent in health care and social assistance; and 9 percent in finance and insurance firms.

Government employed 17 percent of human resources managers and specialists. They handled the recruitment, interviewing, job classification, training, salary administration, benefits, employee relations, and other matters related to the nation's public employees.

Job Outlook

The abundant supply of qualified college graduates and experienced workers should create keen competition for jobs. Overall employment of human resources, training, and labor relations managers and specialists is expected to grow faster than the average for all occupations through 2014. In addition to openings due to growth, many job openings will arise from the need to replace workers who transfer to other occupations or leave the labor force.

Legislation and court rulings setting standards in various areas—occupational safety and health, equal employment opportunity, wages, health care, pensions, and family leave, among others—will increase demand for human resources, training, and labor relations experts. Rising health care costs should continue to spur demand for specialists to develop creative compensation and benefits packages that firms can offer prospective employees. Employment of labor relations staff, including arbitrators and mediators, should grow as firms become more involved in labor relations and attempt to resolve potentially costly labor-management disputes out of court. Additional job growth may stem from increasing demand for specialists in international human resources management and human resources information systems.

Demand may be particularly strong for certain specialists. For example, employers are expected to devote greater resources to job-specific training programs in response to the increasing complexity of many jobs, the aging of the workforce, and technological advances that can leave employees with obsolete skills. This should result in strong demand for training and development specialists. In addition, increasing efforts throughout industry to recruit and retain quality employees should create many jobs for employment, recruitment, and placement specialists.

Among industries, firms involved in management, consulting, and employment services should offer many job opportunities as businesses increasingly contract out human resources functions or hire human resources specialists on a temporary basis in order to deal with the increasing cost and complexity of training and development programs. Demand also should increase in firms that develop and administer complex employee benefits and compensation packages for other organizations.

Demand for human resources, training, and labor relations managers and specialists also is governed by the staffing needs of the firms for which they work. A rapidly expanding business is likely to hire additional human resources workers—either as permanent employees or consultants—while a business that has experienced a merger or a reduction in its workforce will require fewer human resources workers. Also, as human resources management becomes increasingly important to the success of an organization, some small and medium-size businesses that do not have a human resources department may assign employees various human resources duties together with other unrelated responsibilities. In any particular firm, the size and the job duties of the human resources staff are determined by the firm's organizational philosophy and goals, skills of its workforce, pace of technological change, government regulations, collective bargaining agreements, standards of professional practice, and labor market conditions.

Job growth could be limited by the widespread use of computerized human resources information systems that make workers more productive. Like that of other workers, employment of human resources, training, and labor relations managers and specialists, particularly in larger firms, may be adversely affected by corporate downsizing, restructuring, and mergers.

Earnings

Annual salary rates for human resources workers vary according to occupation, level of experience, training, location, and size of the firm and whether they are union members.

Median annual earnings of compensation and benefits managers were $66,530 in May 2004. The middle 50 percent earned between $49,970 and $89,340. The lowest 10 percent earned less than $39,250, and the highest 10 percent earned more than $118,880. In May 2004, median annual earnings were $81,080 in the management of companies and enterprises industry.

Median annual earnings of training and development managers were $67,460 in May 2004. The middle 50 percent earned between $49,060 and $91,020. The lowest 10 percent earned less than $36,430, and the highest 10 percent earned more than $119,580.

Median annual earnings of human resources managers, all other were $81,810 in May 2004. The middle 50 percent earned between $62,080 and $106,440. The lowest 10 percent earned less than $48,060, and the highest 10 percent earned more than $136,600. In May 2004, median annual earnings were $92,590 in the management of companies and enterprises industry.

Median annual earnings of employment, recruitment, and placement specialists were $41,190 in May 2004. The middle 50 percent earned between $31,820 and $55,540. The lowest 10 percent earned less than $25,690, and the highest 10 percent earned more than $76,230. In May 2004, median annual earnings in the industries employing the largest numbers of employment, recruitment, and placement specialists were

Management, scientific, and technical consulting services	$52,800
Management of companies and enterprises	46,780
Local government	40,540
Employment services	37,780
State government	35,390

Median annual earnings of compensation, benefits, and job analysis specialists were $47,490 in May 2004. The middle 50 percent earned between $37,050 and $59,860. The lowest 10 percent earned less than $30,030, and the highest 10 percent earned more than $74,650. In May 2004, median annual earnings in the industries employing the largest numbers of compensation, benefits, and job analysis specialists were

Local government	$51,430
Management of companies and enterprises	50,970
State government	39,150

Median annual earnings of training and development specialists were $44,570 in May 2004. The middle 50 percent earned between $33,530 and $58,750. The lowest 10 percent earned less than $25,800, and the highest 10 percent earned more than $74,650. In May 2004, median annual earnings in the industries employing the largest numbers of training and development specialists were

Management of companies and enterprises	$49,540
Insurance carriers	47,300
Local government	45,320
State government	41,770
Federal government	38,930

According to a 2005 salary survey conducted by the National Association of Colleges and Employers, bachelor's degree candidates majoring in human resources, including labor relations, received starting offers averaging $36,967 a year.

The average salary for human resources managers employed by the federal government was $71,232 in 2005; for employee relations specialists, $84,847; for labor relations specialists, $93,895; and for employee development specialists, $80,958. Salaries were slightly higher in areas where the prevailing local pay level was higher. There are no formal entry-level requirements for managerial positions. Applicants must possess a suitable combination of educational attainment, experience, and record of accomplishment.

Related Occupations

All human resources occupations are closely related. Other workers with skills and expertise in interpersonal relations include counselors, education administrators, public relations specialists, lawyers, psychologists, social and human service assistants, and social workers.

Sources of Additional Information

For information about human resource management careers and certification, contact

▸ Society for Human Resource Management, 1800 Duke St., Alexandria, VA 22314. Internet: http://www.shrm.org

For information about careers in employee training and development and certification, contact

▸ American Society for Training & Development, 1640 King St., Box 1443, Alexandria, VA 22313-2043. Internet: http://www.astd.org

For information about careers and certification in employee compensation and benefits, contact

▸ International Foundation of Employee Benefit Plans, 18700 W. Bluemound Rd., P.O. Box 69, Brookfield, WI 53008-0069. Internet: http://www.ifebp.org

▸ World at Work, 14040 N. Northsight Blvd., Scottsdale, AZ 85260. Internet: http://www.worldatwork.org

For information about academic programs in labor and employment relations, write to

▸ Labor and Employment Relations Association, University of Illinois at Urbana-Champaign, 121 Labor and Industrial Relations Bldg., 504 E. Armory Ave., Champaign, IL 61820. Internet: http://www.lera.uiuc.edu

Information about human resources careers in the health care industry is available from

▸ American Society for Healthcare Human Resources Administration, One North Franklin, 31st Floor, Chicago, IL 60606. Internet: http://www.ashhra.org

Insurance Sales Agents

(O*NET 41-3021.00)

Significant Points

■ Agents increasingly offer comprehensive financial planning services, including retirement and estate planning; as a result, in addition to offering insurance policies, agents sell mutual funds, annuities, and securities.

■ Agents must obtain a license in the states where they plan to do their selling.

■ Despite slower-than-average growth, job opportunities should be good for college graduates who have sales ability, excellent interpersonal skills, and expertise in a wide range of insurance and financial services.

■ Successful agents often have high earnings, but many beginning agents fail to earn enough from commissions to meet their income goals and eventually transfer to other careers.

Nature of the Work

Most people have their first contact with an insurance company through an *insurance sales agent*. These workers help individuals, families, and businesses select insurance policies that provide the best protection for their lives, health, and property. Insurance sales agents who work exclusively for one insurance company are referred to as captive agents. Independent insurance agents, or brokers, represent several companies and place insurance policies for their clients with the company that offers the best rate and coverage. In either case, agents prepare reports, maintain records, seek out new clients, and, in the event of a loss, help policyholders settle their insurance claims. Increasingly, some are also offering their clients financial analysis or advice on ways the clients can minimize risk.

Insurance sales agents, commonly referred to as "producers" in the insurance industry, sell one or more types of insurance, such as property and casualty, life, health, disability, and long-term care. Property and casualty insurance agents sell policies that protect individuals and businesses from financial loss resulting from automobile accidents, fire, theft, storms, and other events that can damage property. For businesses, property and casualty insurance can also cover injured workers' compensation, product liability claims, or medical malpractice claims.

Life insurance agents specialize in selling policies that pay beneficiaries when a policyholder dies. Depending on the policyholder's circumstances, a cash-value policy can be designed to provide retirement income, funds for the education of children, or other benefits. Life insurance agents also sell annuities that promise a retirement income. Health insurance agents sell health insurance policies that cover the costs of medical care and loss of income due to illness or injury. They also may sell dental insurance and short-term and long-term-disability insurance policies.

An increasing number of insurance sales agents are offering comprehensive financial planning services to their clients, such as retirement planning, estate planning, or assistance in setting up pension plans for businesses. As a result, many insurance agents are involved in "cross-selling" or "total account development." Besides offering insurance, these agents may become licensed to sell mutual funds, variable annuities, and other securities. This practice is most common with life insurance agents who already sell annuities; however, property and casualty agents also sell financial products. (See the description of securities, commodities, and financial services sales agents elsewhere in this book.)

Technology has greatly affected the insurance agency, making it much more efficient and giving the agent the ability to take on more clients. Agents' computers are now linked directly to the insurance carriers via the Internet, making the tasks of obtaining price quotes and processing applications and service requests faster and easier. Computers also allow agents to be better informed about new products that the insurance carriers may be offering.

The growth of the Internet in the insurance industry is gradually altering the relationship between agent and client. In the past, agents devoted much of their time to marketing and selling products to new clients, a practice that is now changing. Increasingly, clients are obtaining insurance quotes from a company's Web site and then contacting the company directly to purchase policies. This interaction gives the client a more active role in selecting a policy at the best price while reducing the amount of time agents spend actively seeking new clients. Because insurance sales agents also obtain many new accounts through referrals, it is important that they maintain regular contact with their clients to ensure that the clients' financial needs are being met. Developing a satisfied clientele that will recommend an agent's services to other potential customers is a key to success in this field.

Increasing competition in the insurance industry has spurred carriers and agents to find new ways to keep their clients satisfied. One solution is to increase the use of call centers, which usually are accessible to clients 24 hours a day, 7 days a week. Insurance carriers and sales agents also are hiring customer service representatives to handle routine tasks such as answering questions, making changes in policies, processing claims, and selling more products to clients. The opportunity to cross-sell new products to clients will help agents' businesses grow. The use of call centers also allows agents to concentrate their efforts on seeking out new clients and maintaining relationships with old ones.

Working Conditions

Most insurance sales agents are based in small offices, from which they contact clients and provide information on the policies they sell. However, much of their time may be spent outside their offices, traveling locally to meet with clients, close sales, or investigate claims. Agents usually determine their own hours of work and often schedule evening and weekend appointments for the convenience of clients. Although most agents work a 40-hour week, some work 60 hours a week or longer. Commercial sales agents, in particular, may meet with clients during business hours and then spend evenings doing paperwork and preparing presentations to prospective clients.

Training, Other Qualifications, and Advancement

For insurance sales agent jobs, most companies and independent agencies prefer to hire college graduates—especially those who have majored in business or economics. High school graduates are occasionally hired if they have proven sales ability or have been successful in other types of work. In fact, many entrants to insurance sales agent jobs transfer from other occupations. In selling commercial insurance, technical experience in a particular field can help sell policies to those in the same profession. As a result, new agents tend to be older than entrants in many other occupations.

College training may help agents grasp the technical aspects of insurance policies and the fundamentals and procedures of selling insurance. Many colleges and universities offer courses in insurance, and a few schools offer a bachelor's degree in the field. College courses in finance, mathematics, accounting, economics, business law, marketing, and business administration enable insurance sales agents to understand how social and economic conditions relate to the insurance industry. Courses in psychology, sociology, and public speaking can prove useful in improving sales techniques. In addition, because computers provide instantaneous information on a wide variety of financial products and greatly improve agents' efficiency, familiarity with computers and popular software packages has become very important.

Insurance sales agents must obtain a license in the states where they plan to do their selling. Separate licenses are required for agents to sell life and health insurance and property and casualty insurance. In most states, licenses are issued only to applicants who complete specified prelicensing courses and who pass state examinations covering insurance fundamentals and state insurance laws. The insurance industry is increasingly moving toward uniform state licensing standards and reciprocal licensing, allowing agents who earn a license in one state to become licensed in other states upon passing the appropriate courses and examination.

A number of organizations offer professional designation programs that certify one's expertise in specialties such as life, health, and property and casualty insurance, as well as financial consulting. For example, The National Alliance for Education and Research offers a wide variety of courses in health, life and property, and casualty insurance for independent insurance agents. Although voluntary, such programs assure clients and employers that an agent has a thorough understanding of the relevant specialty. Agents are usually required to complete a specified number of hours of continuing education to retain their designation.

Employers also are placing greater emphasis on continuing professional education as the diversity of financial products sold by insurance agents increases. It is important for insurance agents to keep up to date on issues concerning clients. Changes in tax laws, government benefits programs, and other state and federal regulations can affect the insurance needs of clients and the way in which agents conduct business. Agents can enhance their selling skills and broaden their knowledge of insurance and other financial services by taking courses at colleges and universities and by attending institutes, conferences, and seminars sponsored by insurance organizations. Most state licensing authorities also have mandatory continuing education requirements focusing on insurance laws, consumer protection, and the technical details of various insurance policies.

As the demand for financial products and financial planning increases, many insurance agents are choosing to gain the proper licensing and certification to sell securities and other financial products. Doing so, however, requires substantial study and passing an additional examination—either the Series 6 or Series 7 licensing exam, both of which are administered by the National Association of Securities Dealers (NASD). The Series 6 exam is for individuals who wish to sell only mutual funds and variable annuities, whereas the Series 7 exam is the main NASD series license that qualifies agents as general securities sales representatives. In addition, to further demonstrate competency in the area of financial planning, many agents find it worthwhile to earn the certified financial planner or chartered financial consultant designation. The Certified Financial Planner credential, issued by the Certified Financial Planner Board of Standards, requires relevant experience, completion of education requirements, passing a comprehensive examination, and adherence to an enforceable code of ethics. The CFP exams test the candidate's knowledge of the financial planning process, insurance and risk management, employee benefits planning, taxes and retirement planning, and investment and estate planning. The Chartered Financial Consultant (ChFC) designation, issued by the American College in Bryn Mawr, Pennsylvania, requires experience and the completion of an eight-course program of study. The CFP and ChFC designation and other professional designations have continuing education requirements.

Insurance sales agents should be flexible, enthusiastic, confident, disciplined, hard working, and willing to solve problems. They should communicate effectively and inspire customer confidence. Because they usually work without supervision, sales agents must be able to plan their time well and have the initiative to locate new clients.

An insurance sales agent who shows ability and leadership may become a sales manager in a local office. A few advance to agency superintendent or executive positions. However, many who have built up a good clientele prefer to remain in sales work. Some—particularly in the property and casualty field—establish their own independent agencies or brokerage firms.

Employment

Insurance sales agents held about 400,000 jobs in 2004. Most insurance sales agents employed in wage and salary positions work for insurance agencies and brokerages. A decreasing number work directly for insurance carriers. Although most insurance agents specialize in life and health insurance or property and casualty insurance, a growing number of "multiline" agents sell all lines of insurance. A small number of agents work for banks and securities brokerages as a result of the increasing integration of finance and insurance industries. Approximately 1 out of 4 insurance sales agents are self-employed.

Insurance sales agents are employed throughout the country, but most work in or near large urban centers. Some are employed in the headquarters of insurance companies, but the majority work out of local offices or independent agencies.

Job Outlook

Although employment of insurance sales agents is expected to grow more slowly than average for all occupations through 2014, opportunities will be favorable for college graduates who have sales ability, excellent interpersonal skills, and expertise in a wide range of insurance and financial services. Multilingual agents also should be in high demand because they can serve a wider range of customers. Insurance language tends to be quite technical, so it is important for insurance sales agents to have a firm understanding of relevant technical and legal terms. Many beginning agents fail to earn enough from commissions to meet their income goals and eventually transfer to other careers. Most job openings are likely to result from the need to replace agents who leave the occupation or retire. A large number of agents are expected to retire over the next decade.

Future demand for insurance sales agents depends largely on the volume of sales of insurance and other financial products. Sales of health insurance and long-term-care insurance are expected to rise sharply as the population ages. In addition, a growing population will increase demand for insurance for automobiles, homes, and high-priced valuables and equipment. As new businesses emerge and existing firms expand their insurance coverage, sales of commercial insurance also should increase, including coverage such as product liability, workers' compensation, employee benefits, and pollution liability insurance.

Employment of agents will not keep up with the rising level of insurance sales, however. Many insurance carriers are trying to contain costs. As a result, many are shedding their captive agents—those agents working directly for insurance carriers—and are relying more on independent agents or direct marketing through the mail, by phone, or on the Internet.

Agents who incorporate new technology into their existing businesses will remain competitive. Agents who use the Internet to market their products will reach a broader client base and expand their businesses, but because most clients value their relationship with their agent, the Internet should not threaten jobs, given that many individuals still prefer discussing their policies directly with their agents, rather than through a computer. Also, the automation of policy and claims processing is allowing insurance agents to take on more clients.

Agents may face increased competition from traditional securities brokers and bankers as they begin to sell insurance policies. Because of increasing consolidation among insurance companies, banks, and brokerage firms, and due to increasing demands from clients for more comprehensive financial planning, insurance sales agents will need to expand the products and services they offer.

Agents who offer better customer service also will remain competitive. Call centers are another important way carriers and agents are offering better service to customers because such centers provide greater access to their policies and more prompt services.

Insurance and investments are becoming more complex, and many people and businesses lack the time and expertise to buy insurance without the advice of an agent. Moreover, most individuals and businesses consider insurance a necessity, regardless of economic conditions. Therefore, agents are not likely to face unemployment because of a recession.

Earnings

The median annual earnings of wage and salary insurance sales agents were $41,720 in May 2004. The middle 50 percent earned between $29,980 and $66,160. The lowest 10 percent had earnings of $23,170 or less, while the highest 10 percent earned more than $108,800. Median annual earnings in May 2004 in the two industries employing the largest number of insurance sales agents were $42,010 for insurance carriers and $41,840 for agencies, brokerages, and other insurance-related activities.

Many independent agents are paid by commission only, whereas sales workers who are employees of an agency or an insurance carrier may be paid in one of three ways—salary only, salary plus commission, or salary plus bonus. In general, commissions are the most common form of compensation, especially for experienced agents. The amount of the commission depends on the type and amount of insurance sold and on whether the transaction is a new policy or a renewal. Bonuses usually are awarded when agents meet their sales goals or when an agency meets its profit goals. Some agents involved with financial planning receive a fee for their services rather than a commission.

Company-paid benefits to insurance sales agents usually include continuing education, training to qualify for licensing, group insur-

ance plans, office space, and clerical support services. Some companies also may pay for automobile and transportation expenses, attendance at conventions and meetings, promotion and marketing expenses, and retirement plans. Independent agents working for insurance agencies receive fewer benefits, but their commissions may be higher to help them pay for marketing and other expenses.

Related Occupations

Other workers who provide or sell financial products or services include real estate sales agents and brokers; securities, commodities, and financial services sales agents; financial analysts and personal financial advisors; and financial managers. Other occupations in the insurance industry include insurance underwriters and claims adjusters, examiners, and investigators.

Sources of Additional Information

Occupational information about insurance sales agents is available from the home office of many insurance companies.

Information on state licensing requirements may be obtained from the department of insurance at any state capital.

For information about insurance sales careers and training, contact

▸ Independent Insurance Agents of America, 127 S. Peyton St., Alexandria, VA 22314. Internet: http://www.iiaa.org

▸ Insurance Vocational Education Student Training (InVEST), 127 S. Peyton St., Alexandria, VA 22314. Internet: http://www.investprogram.org

For information about health insurance sales careers, contact

▸ National Association of Health Underwriters, 2000 N. 14th St., Suite 450, Arlington, VA 22201. Internet: http://www.nahu.org

For general information on the property and casualty field, contact

▸ Insurance Information Institute, 110 William St., New York, NY 10038. Internet: http://www.iii.org

For information about professional designation programs, contact

▸ The American Institute for Chartered Property and Casualty Underwriters/Insurance Institute of America, 720 Providence Rd., P.O. Box 3016, Malvern, PA 19355-0716. Internet: http://www.aicpcu.org

▸ The American College, 270 Bryn Mawr Ave., Bryn Mawr, PA 19010-2195. Internet: http://www.theamericancollege.edu

Insurance Underwriters

(O*NET 13-2053.00)

Significant Points

■ Most large insurance companies prefer college graduates who have a degree in business administration or finance with courses in accounting; however, a bachelor's degree in any field—plus courses in business law and accounting—may be sufficient to qualify.

■ Continuing education is necessary for advancement.

- Employment is expected to grow more slowly than average as the continuing spread of underwriting software increases worker productivity.

- Job opportunities should be best for those with a background in finance and strong computer and communication skills.

Nature of the Work

Insurance companies protect individuals and organizations from financial loss by assuming billions of dollars in risk each year. *Underwriters* are needed to identify and calculate the risk of loss from policyholders, establish appropriate premium rates, and write policies that cover this risk. An insurance company may lose business to competitors if the underwriter appraises risks too conservatively, or it may have to pay excessive claims if the underwriting actions are too liberal.

With the aid of computers, underwriters analyze information in insurance applications to determine whether a risk is acceptable and will not result in a loss. Applications often are supplemented with reports from loss-control consultants, medical reports, reports from data vendors, and actuarial studies. Underwriters then must decide whether to issue the policy and, if so, the appropriate premium to charge. In making this determination, underwriters serve as the main link between the insurance carrier and the insurance agent. On occasion, they accompany sales agents to make presentations to prospective clients.

Technology plays an important role in an underwriter's job. Underwriters use computer applications called "smart systems" to manage risks more efficiently and accurately. These systems automatically analyze and rate insurance applications, recommend acceptance or denial of the risk, and adjust the premium rate in accordance with the risk. With these systems, underwriters are better equipped to make sound decisions and avoid excessive losses.

The Internet also has affected the work of underwriters. Many insurance carriers' computer systems are now linked to different databases on the Internet that allow immediate access to information—such as driving records—necessary in determining a potential client's risk. This kind of access reduces the amount of time and paperwork necessary for an underwriter to complete a risk assessment.

Most underwriters specialize in one of three major categories of insurance: life, health, and property and casualty. *Life and health insurance underwriters* may further specialize in group or individual policies.

Property and casualty underwriters usually specialize in either commercial or personal insurance and then by type of risk insured, as in fire, homeowners', automobile, marine, or liability insurance or workers' compensation. In cases where casualty companies provide insurance through a single "package" policy covering various types of risks, the underwriter must be familiar with different lines of insurance. For business insurance, the underwriter often must be able to evaluate the firm's entire operation in appraising its application for insurance.

An increasing proportion of insurance sales, particularly in life and health insurance, is being made through group contracts. A standard group policy insures everyone in a specified group through a single contract at a standard premium rate. The group underwriter analyzes the overall composition of the group to ensure that the total risk is not excessive. Another type of group policy provides members of a group—a labor union, for example—with individual policies reflecting their needs. These usually are casualty policies, such as those covering automobiles. The casualty underwriter analyzes the application of each group member and makes individual appraisals. Some group underwriters meet with union or employer representatives to discuss the types of policies available to their group.

Working Conditions

Underwriters have desk jobs that require no unusual physical activity. Their offices usually are comfortable and pleasant. Although underwriters typically work a standard 40-hour week, more are working longer hours due to the downsizing of many insurance companies. Most underwriters are based in a home or regional branch office, but they occasionally attend meetings away from home for several days. Construction and marine underwriters frequently travel to inspect worksites and assess risks.

Training, Other Qualifications, and Advancement

For entry-level underwriting jobs, most large insurance companies prefer college graduates who have a degree in business administration or finance with courses or experience in accounting. However, a bachelor's degree in almost any field—plus courses in business law and accounting—provides a good general background and may be sufficient to qualify an individual. Because computers are an integral part of most underwriters' jobs, computer skills are essential.

New employees usually start as underwriter trainees or assistant underwriters. They may help collect information on applicants and evaluate routine applications under the supervision of an experienced risk analyst. Property and casualty trainees study claims files to become familiar with factors associated with certain types of losses. Many larger insurers offer work-study training programs lasting from a few months to a year. As trainees gain experience, they are assigned policy applications that are more complex and cover greater risks. Analyzing and processing these applications efficiently requires the use of computers.

Underwriting can be a satisfying career for people who enjoy analyzing information and paying attention to detail. In addition, underwriters must possess good judgment in order to make sound decisions. Excellent communication and interpersonal skills also are essential, as much of the underwriter's work involves dealing with agents and other insurance professionals.

Continuing education is necessary for advancement. Insurance companies usually pay tuition for underwriting courses that their trainees complete; some also offer salary incentives. Independent-study programs for experienced property and casualty underwriters are available as well. The Insurance Institute of America offers both a program called "Introduction to Underwriting" for beginning underwriters and the specialty designation of Associate in Commercial Underwriting (ACU), a formal step in developing a career in underwriting business insurance policies. Those interested in developing a career underwriting personal insurance policies may earn the

Associate in Personal Insurance (API) designation. To earn either the ACU or API designation, underwriters complete a series of courses and examinations that generally last 1 to 2 years.

The American Institute for Chartered Property Casualty Underwriters (AICPCU) awards the Chartered Property and Casualty Underwriter (CPCU) designation, the final stage of development for an underwriter. Earning the CPCU designation requires passing 10 exams, meeting a requirement of at least 3 years of insurance experience, and abiding by the AICPCU's code of professional ethics. Exams cover risk management, insurance operations and regulations, business and insurance law, and financial management and financial institutions. In conjunction with the Insurance Institute of America, the AICPCU offers 22 insurance-related educational programs, including associate designation programs in claims underwriting, risk management, and reinsurance. The American College offers the Chartered Life Underwriter (CLU) designation and the Registered Health Underwriter (RHU) designation for all life and health insurance professionals.

Experienced underwriters who complete courses of study may advance to senior underwriter or underwriting manager positions. Some underwriting managers are promoted to senior managerial jobs. Some employers require a master's degree to achieve this level. Other underwriters are attracted to the earnings potential of sales and, therefore, obtain state licenses to sell insurance and related financial products as agents or brokers.

Employment

Insurance underwriters held about 101,000 jobs in 2004. Approximately 2 out of 3 underwriters work for insurance carriers. Most of the remaining underwriters work in insurance agencies or for organizations that offer insurance services to insurance companies and policyholders. A small number of underwriters work in agencies owned and operated by banks, mortgage companies, and real estate firms.

Most underwriters are based in the insurance company's home office, but some, mainly in the property and casualty area, work out of regional branch offices of the insurance company. These underwriters usually have the authority to underwrite most risks and determine an appropriate rating without consulting the home office.

Job Outlook

Employment of underwriters is expected to grow more slowly than average for all occupations through 2014. Underwriting software will continue to make workers more productive; however, because computer software does not do away with the need for human skills, employment will increase as economic and population growth result in increased insurance needs by businesses and individuals. Job opportunities should be best for those with a background in finance and strong computer and communication skills. In addition to openings arising from some job growth, openings will be created by the need to replace underwriters who transfer to another job or leave the occupation.

Insurance carriers always are assessing new risks and offering policies to meet changing circumstances. Underwriters are needed particularly in the area of product development, where they assess risks and set the premiums for new lines of insurance. One new line of

insurance being offered by life insurance carriers that may provide job opportunities for underwriters is long-term care insurance.

Demand for underwriters also is expected to improve as insurance carriers try to restore profitability to make up for an unusually large number of underwriting losses in recent years. As the carriers' returns on their investments have declined, insurers are placing more emphasis on underwriting to generate revenues. This renewed interest in underwriting should result in job opportunities for underwriters.

Because insurance is considered a necessity for people and businesses, there will always be a need for underwriters—a profession that is less subject to recession and layoffs than other fields.

Earnings

Median annual earnings of insurance underwriters were $48,550 in May 2004. The middle 50 percent earned between $37,490 and $65,450 a year. The lowest 10 percent earned less than $30,410, while the highest 10 percent earned more than $86,110. Median annual earnings of underwriters working with insurance carriers were $49,280, while earnings of these in agencies, brokerages, and other insurance-related activities were $46,750.

Insurance companies usually provide better-than-average benefits, including retirement plans and employer-financed group life and health insurance.

Related Occupations

Underwriters make decisions on the basis of financial and statistical data. Other workers with the same type of responsibility include accountants and auditors, actuaries, budget analysts, cost estimators, financial analysts and personal financial advisors, financial managers, loan officers, and credit analysts. Other related jobs in the insurance industry include insurance sales agents and claims adjusters, appraisers, examiners, and investigators.

Sources of Additional Information

Information about a career as an insurance underwriter is available from the home offices of many insurance companies.

Information about the property-casualty insurance field can be obtained by contacting

▸ Insurance Information Institute, 110 William St., New York, NY 10038. Internet: http://www.iii.org

Information on careers in the life insurance field can be obtained from

▸ LIMRA International, P.O. Box 203, Hartford, CT 06141.

Information on the underwriting function and the CPCU and AU designations can be obtained from

▸ American Institute for Chartered Property and Casualty Underwriters and Insurance Institute of America, 720 Providence Rd., P.O. Box 3016, Malvern, PA 19355-0716. Internet: http://www.aicpcu.org

Information on the CLU and RHU designations can be obtained from

▸ American College, 270 South Bryn Mawr Ave., Bryn Mawr, PA 19010-2196. Internet: http://www.theamericancollege.edu

Interior Designers

(O*NET 27-1025.00)

Significant Points

■ Keen competition is expected for jobs in interior design because many talented individuals are attracted to careers as interior designers.

■ Individuals with little or no formal training in interior design, as well as those lacking creativity and perseverance, will find it very difficult to establish and maintain a career in this occupation.

■ About 3 out of 10 are self-employed.

■ Postsecondary education—especially a bachelor's degree—is recommended for entry-level positions in interior design; licensure is required in 23 states, the District of Columbia, and Puerto Rico.

Nature of the Work

Interior designers draw upon many disciplines to enhance the function, safety, and aesthetics of interior spaces. Interior designers are concerned with how different colors, textures, furniture, lighting, and space work together to meet the needs of a building's occupants. Designers are involved in planning the interior spaces of almost all buildings—offices, airport terminals, theaters, shopping malls, restaurants, hotels, schools, hospitals, and private residences. Designers help to improve these spaces in order to boost office productivity, increase sales, attract a more affluent clientele, provide a more relaxing hospital stay, or increase the building's market value.

Traditionally, most interior designers focused on decorating: choosing a style and color palette and then selecting appropriate furniture, floor and window coverings, artwork, and lighting. However, an increasing number of designers are becoming more involved in designing architectural detailing, such as crown molding and built-in bookshelves, or planning layouts of buildings undergoing renovation, including helping to determine the location of windows, stairways, escalators, and walkways. Interior designers must be able to read blueprints, understand building and fire codes, and know how to make the space accessible to the disabled. Designers frequently collaborate with architects, electricians, and building contractors to ensure that their designs are safe and meet construction requirements.

Despite the varied building spaces interior designers work with, almost all projects follow the same design process. The first step in developing a new design is to determine the needs of the client, known as programming. The designer usually will meet face-to-face with the client in order to find out how the space will be used and to get an idea of the client's design preferences and budget. For example, the designer might inquire about a family's cooking habits if the family is remodeling a kitchen or ask about a store or restaurant's target customer in order to pick an appropriate design. The designer also will visit the space and take inventory of the existing furniture and equipment as well as identify the any potential design problems and the positive attributes of the space.

Following the initial meeting with the client, the designer will formulate a design plan and estimate the costs on the basis of the client's goals and budget. Today, designs often are created with the use of computer-aided design (CAD), which provides a more detailed layout and also allows for easier corrections than sketches made by hand. Once the designer has completed the proposed design, he or she will present it to the client and make revisions on the basis of the client's input.

When a design concept has been finalized, the designer will begin specifying the materials, finishes, and furnishings required, such as furniture, lighting, flooring, wall covering, and artwork. In addition, depending on the complexity of the project, the designer will need to prepare drawings and submit them for architectural review and approval by a construction inspector to ensure that the design meets all applicable building codes. If a project requires any structural work, the designer will need to work with an architect or engineer for that part of the project. Most designs also will require the hiring of contractors to do such technical work as lighting, plumbing, or electrical wiring. When necessary, the designer will choose qualified contractors and write up work contracts.

Finally, the designer will develop a timeline for the project and ensure that it is completed on time, including coordinating the work schedules of contractors if necessary. The designer will oversee the installation of the design elements, and after the project is complete, the designer, together with the client, will pay follow-up visits to the building site to ensure that the client is satisfied with the final product. If the client is not satisfied, the designer will make all necessary corrections.

Designers who work as in-store designers for furniture or home and garden stores offer their design services in addition to selling the store's merchandise. In-store designers provide services similar to those offered by other interior designers, such as selecting a style and color scheme that fits the client's needs or finding suitable accessories and lighting. However, in-store designers rarely visit their clients' spaces and are limited in using only a particular store's products.

Interior designers sometimes supervise assistants who carry out their creations and perform administrative tasks, such as reviewing catalogues and ordering samples. Designers who run their own businesses also may devote a considerable amount of time meeting with clients and contractors, developing new business contacts, examining equipment and space needs, and attending to business matters.

Although most interior designers do many kinds of projects, some specialize in one area of interior design. Some specialize in the type of building space—usually residential or commercial—while others specialize in a certain design element or type of client, such as health care facilities. The most common specialties of this kind are lighting, kitchen and bath, and closet designs. However, designers can specialize in almost any area of design, including acoustics and noise abatement, security, electronics and home theaters, home spas, and indoor gardens.

Three areas of design that are becoming increasingly popular are ergonomic design, elder design, and environmental—or green—design. Ergonomic design involves designing work spaces and furniture that emphasize good posture and minimize muscle strain on the body. Elder design involves planning interior space to aid in the movement of the elderly and disabled, such as widening passageways to accommodate wheelchairs. Green design involves selecting furniture and carpets that are free of chemicals and hypoallergenic and selecting construction materials that are energy efficient or are made from renewable resources.

Working Conditions

Working conditions and places of employment vary. Interior designers employed by large corporations or design firms generally work regular hours in well-lighted and comfortable settings. Designers in smaller design consulting firms or those who freelance generally work on a contract, or job, basis. They frequently adjust their workday to suit their clients' schedules and deadlines, meeting with the clients during evening or weekend hours when necessary. Consultants and self-employed designers tend to work longer hours and in smaller, more congested environments.

Interior designers may work under stress to meet deadlines, stay on budget, and please clients. Self-employed designers also are under pressure to find new clients in order to maintain a steady income.

Designers may transact business in their own offices or studios or in clients' homes or offices. They also may travel to other locations, such as showrooms, design centers, clients' exhibit sites, and manufacturing facilities. With the increased speed and sophistication of computers and advanced communications networks, designers may form international design teams, serve a geographically more dispersed clientele, research design alternatives by using information on the Internet, and purchase supplies electronically, all with the aid of a computer in their workplace or studio.

Training, Other Qualifications, and Advancement

Postsecondary education—especially a bachelor's degree—is recommended for entry-level positions in interior design. In addition, 24 states, the District of Columbia, and Puerto Rico register or license interior designers. Following formal training, graduates usually enter a 1-year to 3-year apprenticeship to gain experience before taking a national licensing exam or joining a professional association. Designers in states that do not require the exam may opt to take it as proof of their qualifications. The National Council administers the licensing exam for Interior Design Qualification (NCIDQ). To be eligible to take the exam, applicants must have at least 6 years of combined education and experience in interior design, of which at least 2 years constitute postsecondary education in design. Once candidates have passed the qualifying exam, they are granted the title of Certified, Registered, or Licensed Interior Designer, depending on the state. Continuing education is required in order to maintain one's licensure.

Training programs are available from professional design schools or from colleges and universities and usually take 2 to 4 years to complete. Graduates of 2-year and 3-year programs are awarded certificates or associate's degrees in interior design and normally qualify as assistants to interior designers upon graduation. Graduates with bachelor's degrees usually qualify for entry into a formal design apprenticeship program. Basic coursework includes computer-aided design (CAD), drawing, perspective, spatial planning, color and fabrics, furniture design, architecture, ergonomics, ethics, and psychology.

The National Association of Schools of Art and Design accredits approximately 250 postsecondary institutions with programs in art and design. Most of these schools award a degree in interior design. Applicants may be required to submit sketches and other examples of their artistic ability.

The Foundation for Interior Design Education Research also accredits interior design programs that lead to a bachelor's degree. In 2005, there were 137 accredited bachelor's degree programs in interior design in the United States, located primarily in schools of art, architecture, and home economics.

After the completion of formal training, interior designers will enter a 1-year to 3-year apprenticeship to gain experience before taking a licensing exam. Most apprentices work in design or architecture firms under the strict supervision of an experienced designer. Apprentices also may choose to gain experience working as an in-store designer in furniture stores. The NCIDQ offers the Interior Design Experience Program (IDEP), which helps entry-level interior designers gain valuable work experience by supervising work experience and offering mentoring services and workshops to new designers.

Following the apprenticeship, designers will take the national licensing exam or choose to become members of a professional association. Because registration or licensure is not mandatory in all states, membership in a professional association is an indication of an interior designer's qualifications and professional standing. The American Society of Interior Designers (ASID) is the largest professional association for interior designers in the United States. Interior designers can qualify for membership with at least a 2-year or higher degree and work experience.

In addition to national licensure and membership in a professional association, optional certifications in kitchen and bath design are available from the National Kitchen and Bath Association. The association offers three different levels of certification for kitchen and bath designers, each completed through training seminars that culminate in certification exams.

Employers increasingly prefer interior designers who are familiar with CAD software. Interior designers also increasingly need to know the basics of architecture and engineering in order to ensure that their designs meet building safety codes.

In addition to possessing technical knowledge, interior designers must be creative, imaginative, and persistent and must be able to communicate their ideas in writing, visually, and verbally. Because tastes in style can change quickly, designers need to be well read, open to new ideas and influences, and quick to react to changing trends. Problem-solving skills and the ability to work independently and under pressure are important traits. People in this field need self-discipline to start projects on their own, to budget their time, and to meet deadlines and production schedules. Good business sense and sales ability also are important, especially for those who freelance or run their own business.

Beginning interior designers receive on-the-job training and normally need 1 to 3 years of training before they can advance to higher-level positions. Experienced designers in large firms may advance to chief designer, design department head, or some other supervisory position. Some experienced designers open their own firms or decide to specialize in one aspect of interior design. Other designers leave the occupation to become teachers in schools of design or in colleges and universities. Many faculty members continue to consult privately or operate small design studios to complement their classroom activities.

Employment

Interior designers held about 65,000 jobs in 2004. Approximately 3 out of 10 were self-employed. About 2 out of 10 wage and salary interior designers worked in specialized design services. Another 1 out of 10 worked in architectural and landscape architectural services. The remaining of interior designers provided design services in furniture and home-furnishing stores, building material and supplies dealers, and residential building construction companies. Many interior designers also performed freelance work in addition to holding a salaried job in interior design or another occupation.

Job Outlook

Employment of interior designers is expected to grow about as fast as the average for all occupations through 2014. Economic expansion, growing homeowner wealth, and an increased interest in interior design will increase demand for designers. However, interior designers are expected to face keen competition for available positions because many talented individuals are attracted to this profession. Individuals with little or no formal training in interior design, as well as those lacking creativity and perseverance, will find it very difficult to establish and maintain a career in this occupation.

As the economy grows, more private businesses and consumers will request the services of interior designers. However, design services are considered a luxury expense and may be subject to fluctuations in the economy. For example, decreases in consumer and business income and spending caused by a slow economy can have a detrimental effect on employment of interior designers. Nevertheless, demand from the health care industry is expected to be especially high because of an anticipated increase in demand for facilities that will accommodate the aging population. Designers will be needed to make these facilities as comfortable and homelike as possible for patients. Demand from businesses in the hospitality industry— hotels, resorts, and restaurants—also is expected to be high because of an expected increase in tourism.

Recent increases in homeowner wealth and the growing popularity of home improvement television programs have increased demand for residential design services. Homeowners increasingly have been using the equity in their homes to finance new additions, remodel aging kitchens and bathrooms, and update the general décor of the home. Many homeowners also have requested design help in adding year-round outdoor living spaces.

Growth in home improvement television programs and discount furniture stores has spurred a trend in do-it-yourself design, which could hamper employment growth of designers. However, some clients will still hire designers for a few initial consultations, but then will purchase and install the design elements themselves.

Some interior designers are choosing to specialize in one design element in order to create a niche for themselves in an increasingly competitive market. The demand for kitchen and bath design is growing in response to the increasing demand for home remodeling. Designs utilizing the latest technology, such as home theaters, state-of-the-art conference facilities, and security systems, are expected to be especially popular. In addition, demand for home spas, indoor gardens, and outdoor living spaces is expected to continue to increase.

Extensive knowledge of ergonomics and green design are expected to be in demand. Ergonomic design has gained in popularity with the growth in the elderly population and workplace safety requirements. The public's growing awareness of environmental quality and the growing number of individuals with allergies and asthma are expected to increase the demand for green design.

Earnings

Median annual earnings for interior designers were $40,670 in May 2004. The middle 50 percent earned between $30,890 and $53,790. The lowest 10 percent earned less than $23,440, and the highest 10 percent earned more than $71,220. Median annual earnings in the industries employing the largest numbers of interior designers in May 2004 were as follows:

Architectural, engineering, and related services	$44,740
Specialized design services	42,000
Furniture stores	37,750

Interior design salaries vary widely with the specialty, type of employer, number of years of experience, and reputation of the individuals. Among salaried interior designers, those in large specialized design and architectural firms tend to earn higher and more stable salaries. Interior designers working in retail stores usually earn a commission, which can be irregular.

For residential design projects, self-employed interior designers and those working in smaller firms usually earn a per-hour consulting fee plus a percentage of the total cost of furniture, lighting, artwork, and other design elements. For commercial projects, they might charge a per-hour consulting fee, charge by the square footage, or charge a flat fee for the whole project. Also, designers who use specialty contractors usually earn a percentage of the contractor's earnings on the project in return for hiring the contractor. Self-employed designers must provide their own benefits.

Related Occupations

Workers in other occupations who design or arrange objects to enhance their appearance and function include architects, except landscape and naval; artists and related workers; commercial and industrial designers; fashion designers; floral designers; graphic designers; and landscape architects.

Sources of Additional Information

For information on degrees, continuing education, and licensure programs in interior design and interior design research, contact

▶ American Society of Interior Designers, 608 Massachusetts Ave. NE, Washington, DC 20002-6006. Internet: http://www.asid.org

For a list of schools with accredited bachelor's degree programs in interior design, contact

▶ Foundation for Interior Design Education Research, 146 Monroe Center NW, Suite 1318, Grand Rapids, MI 49503-2822. Internet: http://www.fider.org

For general information about art and design and a list of accredited college-level programs, contact

▶ National Association of Schools of Art and Design, 11250 Roger Bacon Dr., Suite 21, Reston, VA 20190-5248. Internet: http://nasad.arts-accredit.org

For information on state licensing requirements and exams and the Interior Design Experience Program, contact

▶ National Council for Interior Design Qualification, 1200 18th St. NW, Suite 1001, Washington, DC 20036-2506. Internet: http://www.ncidq.org

For information on careers, continuing education, and certification programs in the interior design specialty of residential kitchen and bath design, contact

▶ National Kitchen and Bath Association, 687 Willow Grove St., Hackettstown, NJ 07840. Internet: http://www.nkba.org/student

Landscape Architects

(O*NET 17-1012.00)

Significant Points

■ More than 26 percent of all landscape architects are self-employed—more than 3 times the proportion for all professionals.

■ A bachelor's degree in landscape architecture is the minimum requirement for entry-level jobs; many employers prefer to hire landscape architects who also have completed at least one internship.

■ Landscape architect jobs are expected to increase due to a growing demand for incorporating natural elements into man-made environments, along with the need to meet a wide array of environmental restrictions.

Nature of the Work

Everyone enjoys attractively designed residential areas, public parks and playgrounds, college campuses, shopping centers, golf courses, parkways, and industrial parks. *Landscape architects* design these areas so that they are not only functional, but also beautiful, and compatible with the natural environment. They plan the location of buildings, roads, and walkways and the arrangement of flowers, shrubs, and trees.

Landscape architects work for many types of organizations—from real estate development firms starting new projects to municipalities constructing airports or parks—and they often are involved with the development of a site from its conception. Working with architects, surveyors, and engineers, landscape architects help determine the

best arrangement of roads and buildings. They also collaborate with environmental scientists, foresters, and other professionals to find the best way to conserve or restore natural resources. Once these decisions are made, landscape architects create detailed plans indicating new topography; vegetation; walkways; and other landscaping details, such as fountains and decorative features.

In planning a site, landscape architects first consider the nature and purpose of the project and the funds available. They analyze the natural elements of the site, such as the climate, soil, slope of the land, drainage, and vegetation; observe where sunlight falls on the site at different times of the day and examine the site from various angles; and assess the effect of existing buildings, roads, walkways, and utilities on the project.

After studying and analyzing the site, landscape architects prepare a preliminary design. To account for the needs of the client as well as the conditions at the site, they frequently make changes before a final design is approved. They also take into account any local, state, or federal regulations, such as those protecting wetlands or historic resources. In preparing designs, computer-aided design (CAD) has become an essential tool for most landscape architects. Many landscape architects also use video simulation to help clients envision the proposed ideas and plans. For larger-scale site planning, landscape architects also use geographic information systems technology, a computer mapping system.

Throughout all phases of the planning and design, landscape architects consult with other professionals, such as civil engineers, hydrologists, or architects, involved in the project. Once the design is complete, they prepare a proposal for the client. They produce detailed plans of the site, including written reports, sketches, models, photographs, land-use studies, and cost estimates, and submit them for approval by the client and by regulatory agencies. When the plans are approved, landscape architects prepare working drawings showing all existing and proposed features. They also outline in detail the methods of construction and draw up a list of necessary materials. Landscape architects then mainly monitor the implementation of their design, with general contractors or landscape contractors usually directing the actual construction of the site and installation of plantings.

Some landscape architects work on a variety of projects. Others specialize in a particular area, such as residential development, street and highway beautification, waterfront improvement projects, parks and playgrounds, or shopping centers. Still others work in regional planning and resource management; feasibility, environmental impact, and cost studies; or site construction. Increasingly, landscape architects are becoming involved with projects in environmental remediation, such as preservation and restoration of wetlands or abatement of stormwater runoff in new developments. Historic landscape preservation and restoration is another important area where landscape architects are increasingly playing an important role.

Most landscape architects do at least some residential work, but relatively few limit their practice to individual homeowners. Residential landscape design projects usually are too small to provide suitable income compared with larger commercial or multi-unit residential projects. Some nurseries offer residential landscape design services, but these services often are performed by design professionals with fewer formal credentials, such as landscape designers, or by others with training and experience in related areas.

Landscape architects who work for government agencies do site and landscape design for government buildings, parks, and other public lands, as well as park and recreation planning in national parks and forests. In addition, they prepare environmental impact statements and studies on environmental issues such as public land-use planning. Some restore degraded land, such as mines or landfills. Other landscape architects use their skills in traffic-calming, the "art" of slowing traffic down through use of traffic design, enhancement of the physical environment, and greater attention to aesthetics.

Working Conditions

Landscape architects spend most of their time in offices creating plans and designs, preparing models and cost estimates, doing research, or attending meetings with clients and other professionals involved in a design or planning project. The remainder of their time is spent at the site. During the design and planning stage, landscape architects visit and analyze the site to verify that the design can be incorporated into the landscape. After the plans and specifications are completed, they may spend additional time at the site observing or supervising the construction. Those who work in large national or regional firms may spend considerably more time out of the office traveling to sites away from the local area.

Salaried employees in both government and landscape architectural firms usually work regular hours; however, they may work overtime to meet a project deadline. Hours of self-employed landscape architects vary depending on the demands of the projects on which they are working.

Training, Other Qualifications, and Advancement

A bachelor's or master's degree in landscape architecture usually is necessary for entry into the profession. A bachelor's degree in landscape architecture takes 4 or 5 years to complete. There also are two types of accredited master's degree programs. The most common type of master's degree is a 3-year first professional degree program designed for students with an undergraduate degree in another discipline. The second type of master's degree is a 2-year second professional degree program for students who have a bachelor's degree in landscape architecture and who wish to teach or specialize in some aspect of landscape architecture, such as regional planning or golf course design.

In 2004, 59 colleges and universities offered 77 undergraduate and graduate programs in landscape architecture that were accredited by the Landscape Architecture Accreditation Board of the American Society of Landscape Architects. College courses required in these programs usually include technical subjects such as surveying, landscape design and construction, landscape ecology, site design, and urban and regional planning. Other courses include history of landscape architecture, plant and soil science, geology, professional practice, and general management. The design studio is another important aspect of many landscape architecture curriculums.

Whenever possible, students are assigned real projects, providing them with valuable hands-on experience. While working on these projects, students become more proficient in the use of computer-aided design, geographic information systems, and video simulation.

In 2004, 47 states required landscape architects to be licensed or registered. Licensing is based on the Landscape Architect Registration Examination (L.A.R.E.), sponsored by the Council of Landscape Architectural Registration Boards and administered in two portions, graphic and multiple choice. Each portion of the testing is conducted over two days. Admission to the exam usually requires a degree from an accredited school plus 1 to 4 years of work experience under the supervision of a registered landscape architect, although standards vary from state to state. Currently, 14 states require that a state examination be passed in addition to the L.A.R.E. to satisfy registration requirements. State examinations, which usually are 1 hour in length and completed at the end of the L.A.R.E., focus on laws, environmental regulations, plants, soils, climate, and any other characteristics unique to the state.

Because state requirements for licensure are not uniform, landscape architects may not find it easy to transfer their registration from one state to another. However, those who meet the national standards of graduating from an accredited program, serving 3 years of internship under the supervision of a registered landscape architect, and passing the L.A.R.E. can satisfy requirements in most states. Through this means, a landscape architect can obtain certification from the Council of Landscape Architectural Registration Boards and so gain reciprocity (the right to work) in other states.

In the federal government, candidates for entry positions should have a bachelor's or master's degree in landscape architecture. The federal government does not require its landscape architects to be licensed.

Persons planning a career in landscape architecture should appreciate nature, enjoy working with their hands, and possess strong analytical skills. Creative vision and artistic talent also are desirable qualities. Good oral communication skills are essential; landscape architects must be able to convey their ideas to other professionals and clients and to make presentations before large groups. Strong writing skills also are valuable, as is knowledge of computer applications of all kinds, including word processing, desktop publishing, and spreadsheets. Landscape architects use these tools to develop presentations, proposals, reports, and land impact studies for clients, colleagues, and superiors. The ability to draft and design using CAD software is essential. Many employers recommend that prospective landscape architects complete at least one summer internship with a landscape architecture firm in order to gain an understanding of the day-to-day operations of a small business, including how to win clients, generate fees, and work within a budget.

In states where licensure is required, new hires may be called "apprentices" or "intern landscape architects" until they become licensed. Their duties vary depending on the type and size of the employing firm. They may do project research or prepare working drawings, construction documents, or base maps of the area to be landscaped. Some are allowed to participate in the actual design of a project. However, interns must perform all work under the supervision of a licensed landscape architect. Additionally, all drawings and specifications must be signed and sealed by the licensed landscape architect, who takes legal responsibility for the work. After gaining experience and becoming licensed, landscape architects usually can carry a design through all stages of development. After several years, they may become project managers, taking on the responsibility for meeting schedules and budgets in addition to overseeing the project design. Later, they may become associates or partners of a firm, with a proprietary interest in the business.

Many landscape architects are self-employed because start-up costs, after an initial investment in CAD software, are relatively low. Self-discipline, business acumen, and good marketing skills are important qualities for those who choose to open their own business. Even with these qualities, however, some may struggle while building a client base.

Those with landscape architecture training also qualify for jobs closely related to landscape architecture, and may, after gaining some experience, become construction supervisors, land or environmental planners, or landscape consultants.

Employment

Landscape architects held about 25,000 jobs in 2004. Almost 6 out of 10 workers were employed in firms that provide architectural, landscape architectural, engineering, and landscaping services. State and local governments were the next largest employers. About 1 out of 4 landscape architects were self-employed.

Employment of landscape architects is concentrated in urban and suburban areas throughout the country; some landscape architects work in rural areas, particularly those employed by the federal government to plan and design parks and recreation areas.

Job Outlook

Employment of landscape architects is expected to increase faster than the average for all occupations through the year 2014. In addition to growth, the need to replace landscape architects who retire or leave the labor force will produce some additional job openings. Employment will grow because the expertise of landscape architects will be highly sought after in the planning and development of new residential, commercial, and other types of construction to meet the needs of a growing population. With land costs rising and the public desiring more beautiful spaces, the importance of good site planning and landscape design is growing. In addition, new demands to manage stormwater runoff in both existing and new landscapes, combined with the growing need to manage water resources in the western states, should cause increased demand for this occupation's services.

New construction also is increasingly contingent upon compliance with environmental regulations, zoning laws, and water restrictions, which will spur demand for landscape architects to help plan sites that meet these requirements and integrate new structures with the natural environment in the least disruptive way. Landscape architects also will be increasingly involved in preserving and restoring wetlands and other environmentally sensitive sites.

Continuation of the Transportation Equity Act for the Twenty-First Century also is expected to spur employment for landscape architects, particularly through state and local governments. This Act, known as TEA-21, provides funds for surface transportation and transit programs, such as interstate highway construction and maintenance and environment-friendly pedestrian and bicycle trails.

In addition to the work related to new development and construction, landscape architects are expected to be involved in historic preservation, land reclamation, and refurbishment of existing sites. They are also doing more residential design work as households spend more on landscaping than in the past. Because landscape architects can work on many different types of projects, they may have an easier time than other design professionals finding employment when traditional construction slows down. Opportunities will vary from year to year and by geographic region, depending on local economic conditions. During a recession, when real estate sales and construction slow down, landscape architects may face greater competition for jobs and sometimes layoffs.

New graduates can expect to face competition for jobs in the largest and most prestigious landscape architecture firms, but should face good job opportunities overall as demand increases while the number of graduates of landscape architecture holds steady or only goes up slightly. Opportunities will be best for landscape architects who develop strong technical skills—such as computer design—and communication skills, as well as knowledge of environmental codes and regulations. Those with additional training or experience in urban planning increase their opportunities for employment in landscape architecture firms that specialize in site planning as well as landscape design. Many employers prefer to hire entry-level landscape architects who have internship experience, which significantly reduces the amount of on-the-job training required.

Earnings

In May 2004, median annual earnings for landscape architects were $53,120. The middle 50 percent earned between $40,930 and $70,400. The lowest 10 percent earned less than $32,390 and the highest 10 percent earned over $90,850. Architectural, engineering, and related services employed more landscape architects than any other group of industries, and there the median annual earnings were $51,670 in May 2004.

In 2005, the average annual salary for all landscape architects in the federal government in nonsupervisory, supervisory, and managerial positions was $74,508.

Because many landscape architects work for small firms or are self-employed, benefits tend to be less generous than those provided to workers in large organizations.

Related Occupations

Landscape architects use their knowledge of design, construction, land-use planning, and environmental issues to develop a landscape project. Others whose work requires similar skills are architects, except landscape and naval; surveyors, cartographers, photogrammetrists, and surveying technicians; civil engineers; and urban and regional planners. Landscape architects also must know how to grow and use plants in the landscape. Some conservation scientists and foresters and biological scientists study plants in general and do related work, while environmental scientists and geoscientists work in the area of environmental remediation.

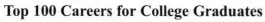

Sources of Additional Information

Additional information, including a list of colleges and universities offering accredited programs in landscape architecture, is available from

▸ American Society of Landscape Architects, Career Information, 636 Eye St. NW, Washington, DC 20001-3736. Internet: http://www.asla.org

General information on registration or licensing requirements is available from

▸ Council of Landscape Architectural Registration Boards, 144 Church Street NW, Suite 201, Vienna, VA 22180-4550. Internet: http://www.clarb.org

Loan Officers

(O*NET 13-2072.00)

Significant Points

■ About 9 out of 10 loan officers work for commercial banks, savings institutions, credit unions, and related financial institutions.

■ Loan officer positions generally require a bachelor's degree in finance, economics, or a related field; training or experience in banking, lending, or sales is advantageous.

■ Slower-than-average employment growth is expected despite rising demand for loans because technology is making for simpler and faster processing and approval of loans.

■ Earnings often fluctuate with the number of loans generated, rising substantially when the economy is good and interest rates are low.

Nature of the Work

For many individuals, taking out a loan may be the only way to afford a house, car, or college education. For businesses, loans likewise are essential to start many companies, purchase inventory, or invest in capital equipment. *Loan officers* facilitate this lending by finding potential clients and assisting them in applying for loans. Loan officers also gather personal information about clients and businesses to ensure that an informed decision is made regarding the creditworthiness of the borrower and the probability of repayment. Loan officers may provide guidance to prospective loan applicants who have problems qualifying for traditional loans. The guidance may include determining the most appropriate type of loan for a particular customer and explaining specific requirements and restrictions associated with the loan.

Loan officers usually specialize in commercial, consumer, or mortgage loans. Commercial or business loans help companies pay for new equipment or expand operations; consumer loans include home equity, automobile, and personal loans; mortgage loans are made to purchase real estate or to refinance an existing mortgage. As banks and other financial institutions begin to offer new types of loans and a growing variety of financial services, loan officers will have to

keep abreast of these new product lines so that they can meet their customers' needs.

In many instances, loan officers act as salespeople. Commercial loan officers, for example, contact firms to determine their needs for loans. If a firm is seeking new funds, the loan officer will try to persuade the company to obtain the loan from his or her institution. Similarly, mortgage loan officers develop relationships with commercial and residential real estate agencies so that, when an individual or firm buys a property, the real estate agent might recommend contacting a specific loan officer for financing.

Once the initial contact has been made, loan officers guide clients through the process of applying for a loan. The process begins with a formal meeting or telephone call with a prospective client, during which the loan officer obtains basic information about the purpose of the loan and explains the different types of loans and credit terms that are available to the applicant. Loan officers answer questions about the process and sometimes assist clients in filling out the application.

After a client completes the application, the loan officer begins the process of analyzing and verifying the information on the application to determine the client's creditworthiness. Often, loan officers can quickly access the client's credit history by computer and obtain a credit "score," representing a software program's assessment of the client's creditworthiness. In cases where a credit history is not available or in which unusual financial circumstances are present, the loan officer may request additional financial information from the client or, in the case of commercial loans, copies of the company's financial statements. With this information, loan officers who specialize in evaluating a client's creditworthiness—often called loan underwriters—may conduct a financial analysis or other risk assessment. Loan officers include such information and their written comments in a loan file, which is used to analyze whether the prospective loan meets the lending institution's requirements. Loan officers then decide, in consultation with their managers, whether to grant the loan. If the loan is approved, a repayment schedule is arranged with the client.

A loan may be approved that would otherwise be denied if the customer can provide the lender with appropriate collateral—property pledged as security for the repayment of the loan. For example, when lending money for a college education, a bank may insist that borrowers offer their home as collateral. If the borrowers should ever default on the loan, the home would be seized under court order and sold to raise the necessary money.

Some loan officers, referred to as *loan collection officers*, contact borrowers with delinquent loan accounts to help them find a method of repayment in order to avoid their defaulting on the loan. If a repayment plan cannot be developed, the loan collection officer initiates collateral liquidation, in which the lender seizes the collateral used to secure the loan—a home or car, for example—and sells it to repay the loan.

Working Conditions

Working as a loan officer usually involves considerable travel. For example, commercial and mortgage loan officers frequently work away from their offices and rely on laptop computers, cellular telephones, and pagers to keep in contact with their employers and clients. Mortgage loan officers often work out of their home or car, visiting offices or homes of clients to complete loan applications. Commercial loan officers sometimes travel to other cities to prepare complex loan agreements. Consumer loan officers, however, are likely to spend most of their time in an office.

Most loan officers work a standard 40-hour week, but many work longer, depending on the number of clients and the demand for loans. Mortgage loan officers can work especially long hours because they are free to take on as many customers as they choose. Loan officers usually carry a heavy caseload and sometimes cannot accept new clients until they complete current cases. They are especially busy when interest rates are low, a condition that triggers a surge in loan applications.

Training, Other Qualifications, and Advancement

Loan officer positions generally require a bachelor's degree in finance, economics, or a related field. Banking, lending, or sales experience is highly valued by employers. Most employers also prefer applicants who are familiar with computers and their applications in banking. Loan officers without college degrees usually advance to their positions from other jobs in an organization after acquiring several years of work experience in various other occupations, such as teller or customer service representative. Personal qualities such as sales ability, good interpersonal and communication skills, and a strong desire to succeed also are important qualities for loan officers.

There are currently no specific licensing requirements for loan officers working in banks or credit unions. Training and licensing requirements for loan officers who work in mortgage banks or brokerages vary by state.

Various banking-related associations and private schools offer courses and programs for students interested in lending as well as for experienced loan officers who want to keep their skills current. For example, the Bank Administration Institute, an affiliate of the American Banker's Association, offers the Loan Review Certificate Program for persons who review and approve loans. This program enhances the quality of reviews and improves the early detection of deteriorating loans, thereby contributing to the safety and soundness of the loan portfolio. The Certified Mortgage Banker (CMB) designation demonstrates the holder's superior knowledge, understanding, and competency in real estate finance. The Mortgage Banking Association offers three CMB designations: residential, commerce, and master's. To obtain the CMB, the candidate must have 3 years of experience, earn educational credits, and pass an exam. Completion of these courses and programs generally enhances one's employment and advancement opportunities.

Persons planning a career as a loan officer should be capable of developing effective working relationships with others, confident in their abilities, and highly motivated. For public relations purposes, loan officers must be willing to attend community events as representatives of their employer.

Capable loan officers may advance to larger branches of the firm or to managerial positions, while less capable workers—and those having weak academic preparation—could be assigned to smaller branches and might find promotion difficult without obtaining training to upgrade their skills. Advancement beyond a loan officer position usually includes supervising other loan officers and clerical staff.

Employment

Loan officers held about 291,000 jobs in 2004. About 9 out of 10 loan officers were employed by commercial banks, savings institutions, credit unions, and related financial institutions. Loan officers are employed throughout the nation, but most work in urban and suburban areas. At some banks, particularly in rural areas, the branch or assistant manager often handles the loan application process.

Job Outlook

Employment of loan officers is projected to increase more slowly than average for all occupations through 2014. College graduates and those with banking, lending, or sales experience should have the best job prospects. Employment growth stemming from economic expansion and population increases—factors that generate demand for loans—will be partially offset by increased automation that speeds lending processes and by the growing use of the Internet to apply for and obtain loans. Job opportunities for loan officers are influenced by the volume of applications, which is determined largely interest rates and by the overall level of economic activity. However, besides openings arising from growth, additional job openings will result from the need to replace workers who retire or otherwise leave the occupation permanently.

The use of credit scoring has made the loan evaluation process much simpler than in the past and even unnecessary in some cases. Credit scoring allows loan officers—particularly loan underwriters—to evaluate many more loans in much less time, thus increasing the loan officer's efficiency. In addition, the mortgage application process has become highly automated and standardized, a simplification that has enabled online mortgage loan vendors to offer their services over the Internet. Online vendors accept loan applications from customers over the Internet and determine which lenders have the best interest rates for particular loans. With this knowledge, customers can go directly to the lending institution, thereby bypassing mortgage loan brokers. Shopping for loans on the Internet is expected to become more common in the future, especially for mortgages, thereby reducing demand for loan officers.

Although loans remain a major source of revenue for banks, demand for new loans fluctuates and affects the income and employment opportunities of loan officers. An upswing in the economy or a decline in interest rates often results in a surge in real estate buying and mortgage refinancing, requiring loan officers to work long hours processing applications and inducing lenders to hire additional loan officers, who often are paid by commission on the value of the loans they place. When the real estate market slows, loan officers often suffer a decline in earnings and may even be subject to layoffs. The same applies to commercial loan officers, whose workloads increase during good economic times as companies seek to invest more in their businesses. In difficult economic conditions, an increase in the number of delinquent loans results in more demand for loan collection officers.

Earnings

Median annual earnings of loan officers were $48,830 in May 2004. The middle 50 percent earned between $35,360 and $69,160. The lowest 10 percent earned less than $27,580, while the top 10 percent earned more than $98,280. Median annual earnings in the industries employing the largest numbers of loan officers in 2004 were as follows:

Federal executive branch and United States
  Postal Service $56,900

Accounting, tax preparation, bookkeeping,
  and payroll services...53,870

Management of companies and enterprises 52,260

Local government 47,440

State government 43,400

The form of compensation for loan officers varies. Most are paid a commission that is based on the number of loans they originate. In this way, commissions are used to motivate loan officers to bring in more loans. Some institutions pay only salaries, while others pay their loan officers a salary plus a commission or bonus based on the number of loans originated. Banks and other lenders sometimes offer their loan officers free checking privileges and somewhat lower interest rates on personal loans.

According to a salary survey conducted by Robert Half International, a staffing services firm specializing in accounting and finance, mortgage loan officers earned between $30,000 and $100,000 in 2005, consumer loan officers with 1 to 3 years of experience earned between $30,000 and $35,000, and commercial loan officers with 1 to 3 years of experience made between $45,500 and $70,000. Commercial loan officers with more than 3 years of experience made between $61,750 and $100,000, and consumer loan officers earned between $25,500 and $50,000. Earnings of loan officers with graduate degrees or professional certifications are higher. Loan officers who are paid on a commission basis usually earn more than those on salary only, and those who work for smaller banks generally earn less than those employed by larger institutions.

Related Occupations

Loan officers help people manage financial assets and secure loans. Occupations that involve similar functions include those of securities, commodities, and financial services sales agents; financial analysts and personal financial advisors; real estate brokers and sales agents; insurance underwriters; insurance sales agents; and loan counselors.

Sources of Additional Information

Information about a career as a mortgage loan officer can be obtained from

▸ Mortgage Bankers Association of America, 1919 Pennsylvania Ave. NW, Washington, DC 20006-3438. Internet: http://www.mbaa.org

State bankers' associations can furnish specific information about job opportunities in their state. Also, individual banks can supply information about job openings and the activities, responsibilities, and preferred qualifications of their loan officers.

Meeting and Convention Planners

(O*NET 13-1121.00)

Significant Points

■ Planners often work long hours in the period prior to and during a meeting or convention, and extensive travel may be required.

■ Employment is expected to grow faster than average.

■ Opportunities will be best for individuals with a bachelor's degree and some meeting planning experience.

Nature of the Work

Meetings and conventions bring people together for a common purpose, and *meeting and convention planners* work to ensure that this purpose is achieved seamlessly. Meeting planners coordinate every detail of meetings and conventions, from the speakers and meeting location to arranging for printed materials and audiovisual equipment. Meeting and convention planners work for nonprofit organizations, professional and similar associations, hotels, corporations, and government. Some organizations have internal meeting planning staffs, and others hire independent meeting and convention planning firms to organize their events.

The first step in planning a meeting or convention is determining the purpose, message, or impression that the sponsoring organization wants to communicate. Planners increasingly focus on how meetings impact the goals of their organizations; for example, they may survey prospective attendees to find out what motivates them and how they learn best. Planners then choose speakers, entertainment, and content and arrange the program to present the organization's information in the most effective way.

Meeting and convention planners search for prospective meeting sites, which may be hotels, convention centers, or conference centers. They issue requests for proposals—documents that state the meeting dates and outline their needs for the meeting or convention, including meeting and exhibit space, lodging, food and beverages, telecommunications, audiovisual requirements, transportation, and any other necessities—to all the sites in which they are interested. The establishments respond with proposals describing what space and services they can supply and at what prices. Meeting and convention planners review these proposals and either make recommendations to top management or choose the site themselves.

Once the location is selected, meeting and convention planners arrange support services, coordinate needs with the facility, prepare the site staff for the meeting, and set up all forms of electronic communication needed for the meeting or convention, such as e-mail, voice mail, video, and online communication.

Meeting logistics, the management of the details of meetings and conventions, such as labor and materials, is another major component of the job. Planners register attendees and issue name badges, coordinate lodging reservations, and arrange transportation. They make sure that all necessary supplies are ordered and transported to the meeting site on time, that meeting rooms are equipped with sufficient seating and audiovisual equipment, that all exhibits and booths are set up properly, and that all materials are printed. They also make sure that the meeting adheres to fire and labor regulations and oversee food and beverage distribution.

There also is a financial management component of the work. Planners negotiate contracts with facilities and suppliers. These contracts, which have become increasingly complex, are often drawn up more than a year in advance of the meeting or convention. Contracts may include clauses requiring the planner to book a certain number of rooms for meeting attendees and imposing penalties if the rooms are not filled. Therefore, it is important that the planner is able to closely estimate how many people will attend the meeting, based on previous meeting attendance and current circumstances. Planners must also oversee the finances of meetings and conventions. They are given overall budgets by their organizations and must create a detailed budget, forecasting what each aspect of the event will cost. Additionally, some planners oversee meetings that contribute significantly to their organization's operating budget and must ensure the meeting meets income goals.

An increasingly important part of the work is measuring how well the meeting's purpose was achieved, and planners begin this measurement as they outline the meeting's goals. Planners set their own specific goals after learning an organization's goals for a meeting or convention. They choose objectives for which success is measurable and define what will constitute achievement of each goal. The most obvious way to gauge their success is to have attendees fill out surveys about their experiences at the event. Planners can ask specific questions about what the attendees learned, how well-organized the meeting or convention appeared, and how they felt about the overall experience. If the purpose of a meeting or convention is publicity, a good measure of success would be how much press coverage the event received. A more precise measurement of meeting success, and one that is gaining importance, is return on investment (ROI). Planners compare the costs and benefits of an event and show whether it was worthwhile to the organization. For example, if a company holds a meeting to motivate its employees and improve company morale, the planner might track employee turnover before and after the meeting.

An important part of all these different functions of meeting professionals is establishing and maintaining relationships. Meeting and convention planners interact with a variety of people and must communicate effectively. They must understand their organization's goals for the meeting or convention, be able to communicate their needs clearly to meeting site staff and other suppliers, maintain contact with many different people, and inform people about changes as they occur.

Some aspects of the work vary by the type of organization for which planners work. Those who work for associations must market their meetings to association members, convincing members that attending the meeting is worth their time and expense. Marketing is usually less important for corporate meeting planners because employees are generally required to attend company meetings. Corporate planners usually have shorter time frames in which to prepare

their meetings. Planners who work in federal, state, and local governments must learn how to operate within established government procedures, such as procedures and rules for procuring materials and booking lodging for government employees.

Convention service managers, meeting professionals who work in hotels, convention centers, and similar establishments, act as liaisons between the meeting facility and association, corporate, or government planners. They present food service options to outside planners, coordinate special requests, suggest hotel services based on the planners' budgets, and otherwise help outside planners present effective meetings and conventions in their facilities.

Meeting planners in small organizations perform a wider range of duties, with perhaps one person coordinating an entire meeting. These planners usually need to multi-task even more than planners in larger organizations.

In large organizations or those that sponsor large meetings or conventions, meeting professionals are more likely to specialize in a particular aspect of meeting planning. Some specialties are conference coordinators, who handle most of the meeting logistics; registrars, who handle advance registration and payment, name badges, and the set-up of on-site registration; and education planners, who coordinate the meeting content, including speakers and topics. In organizations that hold very large or complex meetings, there may be several senior positions, such as manager of registration, education seminar coordinator, or conference services director, with the entire meeting planning department headed by a department director.

Working Conditions

The work of meeting and convention planners may be considered either stressful or energizing, but there is no question that it is fast-paced and demanding. Planners oversee multiple operations at one time, face numerous deadlines, and orchestrate the activities of several different groups of people. Meeting and convention planners spend the majority of their time in offices, but during meetings, they work on-site at the hotel, convention center, or other meeting location. They travel regularly to attend meetings and to visit prospective meeting sites. The extent of travel depends upon the type of organization for which the planner works. Local and regional organizations require mostly regional travel, while national and international organizations require travel to more distant locales, including travel abroad. Working hours can be long and irregular, with planners working more than 40 hours per week in the time leading up to a meeting and fewer hours after finishing a large meeting. During meetings or conventions, planners may work very long days, possibly starting as early as 5:00 a.m. and working until midnight. They are sometimes required to work on weekends.

Some physical activity is required, including long hours of standing and walking and some lifting and carrying of boxes of materials, exhibits, or supplies. Planners work with the public and with workers from diverse backgrounds. They may get to travel to beautiful hotels and interesting places and meet speakers and meeting attendees from around the world, and they usually enjoy a high level of autonomy.

Training, Other Qualifications, and Advancement

Meeting and convention planners can qualify for their jobs through a variety of methods. Many migrate into the occupation from other occupations when they are given meeting planning duties in addition to their other duties. For example, an administrative assistant may begin planning small meetings and gradually move into a full-time position as a meeting and convention planner. Others with a variety of educational or work backgrounds may seek out meeting and convention planning positions. Although there are some certification programs and college and university courses in meeting and convention planning available, a large proportion of the skills needed is learned on the job and through experience.

Many employers prefer a person with a bachelor's degree, but this is not always required. The proportion with a bachelor's degree is increasing because the work and responsibilities are becoming more complex, causing employers to prefer workers with more formal education. Planners have backgrounds in a variety of disciplines, but some useful undergraduate majors are marketing, public relations, communications, business, and hotel or hospitality management. A few schools offer courses or degree programs in meeting and event management. Individuals who have studied hospitality management may start out with greater responsibilities than those with other academic backgrounds. Because formal education is increasingly important, those who enter the occupation may enhance their professional standing by enrolling in meeting planning courses offered by professional meeting and convention planning organizations, colleges, or universities.

Others enter the occupation after working in hotel sales or as marketing or catering coordinators. These are effective ways to learn about meeting and convention planning because these hotel personnel work with numerous meeting planners, participate in negotiations for hotel services, and witness many different meetings. Workers who enter the occupation in these ways often start at a higher level than those with bachelor's degrees and no experience.

Meeting and convention planners must have excellent written and verbal communications skills and interpersonal skills. They must be detail-oriented with excellent organizational skills, and they must be able to multi-task, meet tight deadlines, and maintain composure under pressure in a fast-paced environment. Quantitative and analytic skills are needed to formulate and follow budgets and to understand and negotiate contracts. The ability to speak multiple languages is a plus, since some planners must communicate with meeting attendees and speakers from around the world. They also need computer skills, such as the ability to use financial and registration software and the Internet. In the course of their careers, planners may work in a number of different, unrelated industries, and they must be able to learn independently about each new industry so they can coordinate programs that address the industry's important issues.

Entry-level planners, depending upon their education, generally begin by performing small tasks under the supervision of senior meeting professionals. For example, they may issue requests for proposals and discuss the resulting proposals with higher-level planners. They also may assist in registration; review of contracts; or the creation of meeting timelines, schedules, or objectives. They may

start by planning small meetings, such as committee meetings. Those who start at small organizations have the opportunity to learn more quickly, since they will be required to take on a larger number of tasks.

To advance in this occupation, planners must volunteer to take on more responsibility and find new and better ways of doing things in their organizations. The most important factors are demonstrated skill on the job, determination, and gaining the respect of others within the organization. Advancement based solely on education is uncommon. On the other hand, education may improve work performance and therefore may be an important factor in career development.

As meeting and convention planners prove themselves, they are given greater responsibilities. This may mean taking on a wider range of duties or moving to another planning specialty to gain experience in that area before moving to a higher level. For example, a planner may be promoted from conference coordinator, with responsibility for meeting logistics, to program coordinator, with responsibility for booking speakers and formatting the meeting's program. The next step up may be meeting manager, who supervises all parts of the meeting, and then director of meetings, and then possibly department director of meetings and education. Another path for promotion is to move from a small organization to a larger one, taking on responsibility for larger meetings and conventions.

At least two universities offer bachelor's degrees with majors in meetings management. Additionally, meeting and convention planning continuing education programs are offered by a few universities and colleges. These programs are designed for career development of meeting professionals as well as for people wishing to enter the occupation. Some programs may require 40 to more than 100 classroom hours during a period of one semester to two years for a certificate of completion.

The Convention Industry Council offers the Certified Meeting Professional (CMP) credential, a voluntary certification for meeting and convention planners. Although the CMP is not required, it is widely recognized in the industry and may help in career advancement. In order to qualify, candidates must have a minimum of three years of meeting management experience, full-time employment in a meeting management capacity, and proof of accountability for successfully completed meetings. Those who qualify must then pass an examination that covers topics such as adult learning, financial management, facilities and services, logistics, and meeting programs.

With significant experience, meeting planners may become independent meeting consultants, advance to vice presidents or executive directors of associations, or start their own meeting planning firms.

Employment

Meeting and convention planners held about 43,000 jobs in 2004. About 30 percent worked for religious, grantmaking, civic, professional, and similar organizations; 17 percent worked for hotels and other accommodation establishments; 9 percent worked for public and private schools, colleges, universities, and training centers; 6 percent worked for governments; and 6 percent were self-employed. The rest were employed by convention and trade show organizing firms and in other industries as corporate meeting and convention planners.

Job Outlook

Employment of meeting and convention planners is expected to grow faster than the average for all occupations over the 2004–2014 period due to growth of business, the increasing globalization of the economy, and increasing use of electronic forms of communication to bring people together. There will also be some job openings that arise due to the need to replace workers who leave the workforce or transfer to other occupations. Opportunities will be best for individuals with a bachelor's degree and some meeting planning experience.

As businesses and organizations become increasingly international, meetings and conventions become even more important. In organizations that span the country or the globe, the periodic meeting is increasingly the only time the organization can bring all of its members together. Despite the proliferation of alternative forms of communication, such as e-mail, videoconferencing, and the Web, face-to-face interaction is still a necessity. In fact, new forms of communication foster interaction and connect individuals and groups that previously would not have collaborated. By increasing the number of human connections, electronic forms of communication actually increase the demand for meetings, which may offer the only opportunity for these people to interact in person.

Industries that are experiencing high growth tend to experience corresponding growth in meetings and conferences. For example, the medical and pharmaceutical sectors in particular, because of their high growth and their knowledge-intensive natures, will experience large increases in meeting activity. However, these increases will spur employment growth of meeting professionals in medical and pharmaceutical associations rather than in the industries directly. Professional associations hold conferences and conventions that offer the continuing education, training, and opportunities to exchange ideas that are vital to medical and pharmaceutical professionals. Unlike workers in some occupations, meeting and convention planners can often change industries relatively easily, so they often are able to move to different industries in response to the growth or declines in particular sectors of the economy.

Partly because of bioterrorism and homeland security issues, government agencies are now holding more meetings than ever. Private security and insurance companies also have increased their meeting activity. Because the government increasingly outsources its non-core functions, this increased activity may spur demand for independent meeting consultants or workers in private meeting planning firms rather than increasing employment of government meeting planners.

Demand for corporate meeting planners is highly susceptible to business cycle fluctuations since meetings are usually among the first expenses to be cut when budgets are tight. For associations, fluctuations are less pronounced because meetings are generally a source of revenue rather than an expense. However, since fewer people are able to attend association meetings during recessions, associations often reduce their meeting staffs as well. Associations for industries such as health care, in which meeting attendance is required for professionals to maintain their licensure, are the least likely to experience cutbacks during downturns in the economy.

Earnings

Median annual earnings of meeting and convention planners in May 2004 were $39,620. The middle 50 percent earned between $31,180 and $50,790. The lowest 10 percent earned less than $24,660, and the highest 10 percent earned more than $65,060. In May 2004, median annual earnings in the industries employing the largest numbers of meeting and convention planners were as follows:

Business, professional, labor, political,
and similar organizations $43,100
Traveler accommodation 36,440

Related Occupations

Meeting and convention planners work to communicate a particular message or impression about an organization, as do public relations specialists. They coordinate the activities of several operations to create a service for large numbers of people, using organizational, logistical, communication, budgeting, and interpersonal skills. Food service managers use the same skills for similar purposes. Like meeting and convention planners, producers and directors coordinate a range of activities to produce a television show or movie, negotiate contracts, and communicate with a wide variety of people. Travel agents also use similar skills, such as interacting with many people and coordinating travel arrangements, including hotel accommodations, transportation, and advice on destinations.

Sources of Additional Information

For information about meeting planner certification, contact

▶ Convention Industry Council, 8201 Greensboro Dr., Suite 300, McLean, VA 22102. Internet: http://www.conventionindustry.org

For information about internships and on-campus student meeting planning organizations, contact

▶ Professional Convention Management Association, 2301 S. Lake Shore Dr., Suite 1001, Chicago, IL 60616-1419. Internet: http://www.pcma.org

For information about meeting planning education, entering the profession, and career paths, contact

▶ Meeting Professionals International, 3030 LBJ Fwy., Suite 1700, Dallas, TX 75244-5903. Internet: http://www.mpiweb.org

News Analysts, Reporters, and Correspondents

(O*NET 27-3021.00 and 27-3022.00)

Significant Points

■ Competition will be keen for jobs at large metropolitan and national newspapers, broadcast stations, and magazines; most entry-level openings arise at small broadcast stations and publications.

- Most employers prefer individuals with a bachelor's degree in journalism or mass communications and experience gained at school newspapers or broadcasting stations or through internships with news organizations.

- Jobs often involve irregular hours, night and weekend work, and pressure to meet deadlines.

- Little or no employment growth is expected.

Nature of the Work

News analysts, reporters, and correspondents gather information, prepare stories, and make broadcasts that inform us about local, state, national, and international events; present points of view on current issues; and report on the actions of public officials, corporate executives, interest groups, and others who exercise power.

News analysts—also called *newscasters* or *news anchors*—examine, interpret, and broadcast news received from various sources. News anchors present news stories and introduce videotaped news or live transmissions from on-the-scene reporters. Newscasters at large stations and networks usually specialize in a particular type of news, such as sports or weather. *Weathercasters*, also called *weather reporters,* report current and forecasted weather conditions. They gather information from national satellite weather services, wire services, and local and regional weather bureaus. Some weathercasters are trained meteorologists and can develop their own weather forecasts. (See the description of atmospheric scientists elsewhere in this book.) *Sportscasters* select, write, and deliver sports news. This may include interviews with sports personalities and coverage of games and other sporting events. *News correspondents* report on news occurring in the large U.S. and foreign cities where they are stationed.

In covering a story, *reporters* investigate leads and news tips, look at documents, observe events at the scene, and interview people. Reporters take notes and also may take photographs or shoot videos. At their office, they organize the material, determine the focus or emphasis, write their stories, and edit accompanying video material. Many reporters enter information or write stories using laptop computers and electronically submit the material to their offices from remote locations. In some cases, *newswriters* write a story from information collected and submitted by reporters. Radio and television reporters often compose stories and report "live" from the scene. At times, they later tape an introduction to or commentary on their story in the studio. Some journalists also interpret the news or offer opinions to readers, viewers, or listeners. In this role, they are called *commentators* or *columnists*.

General-assignment reporters write about newsworthy occurrences—such as accidents, political rallies, visits of celebrities, or business closings—as assigned. Large newspapers and radio and television stations assign reporters to gather news about specific topics, such as crime or education. Some reporters specialize in fields such as health, politics, foreign affairs, sports, theater, consumer affairs, social events, science, business, or religion. *Investigative reporters* cover stories that may take many days or weeks of information gathering. Some publications use teams of reporters instead of assigning each reporter one specific topic, allowing reporters to

cover a greater variety of stories. News teams may include reporters, editors, graphic artists, and photographers working together to complete a story. Reporters on small publications cover all aspects of the news. They take photographs, write headlines, lay out pages, edit wire-service stories, and write editorials. Some also solicit advertisements, sell subscriptions, and perform general office work.

Working Conditions

The work of news analysts, reporters, and correspondents is usually hectic. They are under great pressure to meet deadlines. Broadcasts sometimes are aired with little or no time for preparation. Some news analysts, reporters, and correspondents work in comfortable, private offices; others work in large rooms filled with the sound of keyboards and computer printers, as well as the voices of other reporters. Curious onlookers, police, or other emergency workers can distract those reporting from the scene for radio and television. Covering wars, political uprisings, fires, floods, and similar events is often dangerous.

Working hours vary. Reporters on morning papers often work from late afternoon until midnight. Radio and television reporters usually are assigned to a day or evening shift. Magazine reporters usually work during the day.

Reporters sometimes have to change their work hours to meet a deadline or to follow late-breaking developments. Their work demands long hours, irregular schedules, and some travel. Because many stations and networks are on the air 24 hours a day, newscasters can expect to work unusual hours.

Training, Other Qualifications, and Advancement

Most employers prefer individuals with a bachelor's degree in journalism or mass communications, but some hire graduates with other majors. They look for experience at school newspapers or broadcasting stations and internships with news organizations. Large-city newspapers and stations also may prefer candidates with a degree in a subject-matter specialty such as economics, political science, or business. Some large newspapers and broadcasters may hire only experienced reporters.

More than 1,200 institutions offer programs in communications, journalism, and related programs. In 2004, 104 of these were accredited by the Accrediting Council on Education in Journalism and Mass Communications. About three-fourths of the courses in a typical curriculum are in liberal arts; the remaining courses are in journalism. Examples of journalism courses are introductory mass media, basic reporting and copy editing, history of journalism, and press law and ethics. Students planning a career in broadcasting take courses in radio and television news and production. Those planning newspaper or magazine careers usually specialize in news-editorial journalism. To create stories for online media, they need to learn to use computer software to combine online story text with audio and video elements and graphics.

Some schools also offer a master's or Ph.D. degree in journalism. Some graduate programs are intended primarily as preparation for news careers, while others prepare journalism teachers, researchers and theorists, and advertising and public relations workers. A graduate degree may help those looking to advance.

High school courses in English, journalism, and social studies provide a good foundation for college programs. Useful college liberal arts courses include English with an emphasis on writing, sociology, political science, economics, history, and psychology. Courses in computer science, business, and speech are useful as well. Fluency in a foreign language is necessary in some jobs.

Reporters typically need more than good word-processing skills. Computer graphics and desktop-publishing skills also are useful. Computer-assisted reporting involves the use of computers to analyze data in search of a story. This technique and the interpretation of the results require computer skills and familiarity with databases. Knowledge of news photography also is valuable for entry-level positions, which sometimes combine the responsibilities of a reporter with those of a camera operator or photographer.

Employers report that practical experience is the most important part of education and training. Upon graduation, many students already have gained much practical experience through part-time or summer jobs or through internships with news organizations. Most newspapers, magazines, and broadcast news organizations offer reporting and editing internships. Work on high school and college newspapers, at broadcasting stations, or on community papers or U.S. Armed Forces publications also provides practical training. In addition, journalism scholarships, fellowships, and assistantships awarded to college journalism students by universities, newspapers, foundations, and professional organizations are helpful. Experience as a stringer or freelancer—a part-time reporter who is paid only for stories printed—is advantageous.

Reporters should be dedicated to providing accurate and impartial news. Accuracy is important, both to serve the public and because untrue or libelous statements can lead to lawsuits. A nose for news, persistence, initiative, poise, resourcefulness, a good memory, and physical stamina are important, as is the emotional stability to deal with pressing deadlines, irregular hours, and dangerous assignments. Broadcast reporters and news analysts must be comfortable on camera. All reporters must be at ease in unfamiliar places and with a variety of people. Positions involving on-air work require a pleasant voice and appearance.

Most reporters start at small publications or broadcast stations as general assignment reporters or copy editors. They are usually assigned to cover court proceedings and civic and club meetings, summarize speeches, and write obituaries. With experience, they report more difficult assignments or specialize in a particular field. Large publications and stations hire few recent graduates; as a rule, they require new reporters to have several years of experience.

Some news analysts and reporters can advance by moving to larger newspapers or stations. A few experienced reporters become columnists, correspondents, writers, announcers, or public relations specialists. Others become editors in print journalism or program managers in broadcast journalism who supervise reporters. Some eventually become broadcasting or publishing industry managers.

Employment

News analysts, reporters, and correspondents held about 64,000 jobs in 2004. About 61 percent worked for newspaper, periodical, book, and directory publishers. Another 25 percent worked in radio and television broadcasting. About 7 percent of news analysts, reporters, and correspondents were self-employed.

Job Outlook

Competition will continue to be keen for jobs on large metropolitan and national newspapers, broadcast stations and networks, and magazines. Most job opportunities will be with small-town and suburban newspapers and radio and television stations. Talented writers who can handle highly specialized scientific or technical subjects have an advantage. Also, newspapers increasingly are hiring stringers and freelancers.

Journalism graduates have the background for work in closely related fields such as advertising and public relations, and many take jobs in these fields. Other graduates accept sales, managerial, or other nonmedia positions.

Employment of news analysts, reporters, and correspondents is expected to grow more slowly than the average for all occupations through the year 2014. Many factors will contribute to the limited job growth in this occupation. Consolidation and convergence should continue in the publishing and broadcasting industries. As a result, companies will be better able to allocate their news analysts, reporters, and correspondents to cover news stories. Constantly improving technology also is allowing workers to do their jobs more efficiently, another factor that will limit the number of workers needed to cover a story or certain type of news. However, the continued demand for news will create some job opportunities. For example, some job growth likely will occur in newer media areas, such as online newspapers and magazines. Job openings also will result from the need to replace workers who leave their occupations permanently; some news analysts, reporters, and correspondents find the work too stressful and hectic or do not like the lifestyle and transfer to other occupations.

The number of job openings in the newspaper and broadcasting industries—in which news analysts, reporters, and correspondents are employed—is sensitive to economic ups and downs because these industries depend on advertising revenue.

Earnings

Salaries for news analysts, reporters, and correspondents vary widely. Median annual earnings of reporters and correspondents were $31,320 in May 2004. The middle 50 percent earned between $22,900 and $47,860. The lowest 10 percent earned less than $18,470, and the highest 10 percent earned more than $68,250. Median annual earnings of reporters and correspondents were $30,070 in newspaper, periodical, book, and directory publishers and $34,050 in radio and television broadcasting.

Median annual earnings of broadcast news analysts were $36,980 in May 2004. The middle 50 percent earned between $25,560 and $68,440. The lowest 10 percent earned less than $19,040, and the highest 10 percent earned more than $122,800. Median annual earnings of broadcast news analysts were $37,840 in radio and television broadcasting.

Related Occupations

News analysts, reporters, and correspondents must write clearly and effectively to succeed in their profession. Others for whom good writing ability is essential include writers and editors and public relations specialists. Many news analysts, reporters, and correspondents also must communicate information orally. Others for whom oral communication skills are important are announcers, interpreters and translators, those in sales and related occupations, and teachers.

Sources of Additional Information

For information on broadcasting education and scholarship resources, contact

▶ National Association of Broadcasters, 1771 N St. NW, Washington, DC 20036. Internet: http://www.nab.org

Information on careers in journalism, colleges and universities offering degree programs in journalism or communications, and journalism scholarships and internships may be obtained from

▶ Dow Jones Newspaper Fund, Inc., P.O. Box 300, Princeton, NJ 08543-0300.

Information on union wage rates for newspaper and magazine reporters is available from

▶ Newspaper Guild, Research and Information Department, 501 Third St. NW, Suite 250, Washington, DC 20001.

For a list of schools with accredited programs in journalism and mass communications, send a stamped, self-addressed envelope to

▶ Accrediting Council on Education in Journalism and Mass Communications, University of Kansas School of Journalism and Mass Communications, Stauffer-Flint Hall, 1435 Jayhawk Blvd., Lawrence, KS 66045. Internet: http://www.ku.edu/~acejmc/STUDENT/STUDENT.SHTML

Names and locations of newspapers and a list of schools and departments of journalism are published in the *Editor and Publisher International Year Book*, available in most public libraries and newspaper offices.

Occupational Therapists

(O*NET 29-1122.00)

Significant Points

■ Employment is projected to increase much faster than the average as rapid growth in the number of middle-aged and elderly individuals increases the demand for therapeutic services.

■ Beginning in 2007, a master's degree or higher in occupational therapy will be the minimum educational requirement.

■ Occupational therapists are increasingly taking on supervisory roles, allowing assistants and aides to work more closely with clients under the guidance of a therapist, in an effort to reduce the cost of therapy.

■ More than a quarter of occupational therapists work part time.

Nature of the Work

Occupational therapists (OTs) help people improve their ability to perform tasks in their daily living and working environments. They work with individuals who have conditions that are mentally, physically, developmentally, or emotionally disabling. They also help them to develop, recover, or maintain daily living and work skills. Occupational therapists help clients not only to improve their basic motor functions and reasoning abilities, but also to compensate for permanent loss of function. Their goal is to help clients have independent, productive, and satisfying lives.

Occupational therapists assist clients in performing activities of all types, ranging from using a computer to caring for daily needs such as dressing, cooking, and eating. Physical exercises may be used to increase strength and dexterity, while other activities may be chosen to improve visual acuity and the ability to discern patterns. For example, a client with short-term memory loss might be encouraged to make lists to aid recall, and a person with coordination problems might be assigned exercises to improve hand-eye coordination. Occupational therapists also use computer programs to help clients improve decisionmaking, abstract-reasoning, problem-solving, and perceptual skills, as well as memory, sequencing, and coordination—all of which are important for independent living.

Therapists instruct those with permanent disabilities, such as spinal cord injuries, cerebral palsy, or muscular dystrophy, in the use of adaptive equipment, including wheelchairs, orthotics, and aids for eating and dressing. They also design or make special equipment needed at home or at work. Therapists develop computer-aided adaptive equipment and teach clients with severe limitations how to use that equipment in order to communicate better and control various aspects of their environment.

Some occupational therapists treat individuals whose ability to function in a work environment has been impaired. These practitioners arrange employment, evaluate the work environment, plan work activities, and assess the client's progress. Therapists also may collaborate with the client and the employer to modify the work environment so that the work can be successfully completed.

Occupational therapists may work exclusively with individuals in a particular age group or with particular disabilities. In schools, for example, they evaluate children's abilities, recommend and provide therapy, modify classroom equipment, and help children participate as fully as possible in school programs and activities. A therapist may work with children individually, lead small groups in the classroom, consult with a teacher, or serve on a curriculum or other administrative committee. Early intervention therapy services are provided to infants and toddlers who have, or are at risk of having, developmental delays. Specific therapies may include facilitating the use of the hands, promoting skills for listening and following directions, fostering social play skills, or teaching dressing and grooming skills.

Occupational therapy also is beneficial to the elderly population. Therapists help the elderly lead more productive, active, and independent lives through a variety of methods, including the use of adaptive equipment. Therapists with specialized training in driver rehabilitation assess an individual's ability to drive, using both clinical and on-the-road tests. The evaluations allow the therapist to make recommendations for adaptive equipment, training to prolong driving independence, and alternative transportation options. Occupational therapists also work with the client to asses the home for hazards and to identify environmental factors that contribute to falls.

Occupational therapists in mental health settings treat individuals who are mentally ill, mentally retarded, or emotionally disturbed. To treat these problems, therapists choose activities that help people learn to engage in and cope with daily life. Activities include time management skills, budgeting, shopping, homemaking, and the use of public transportation. Occupational therapists also may work with individuals who are dealing with alcoholism, drug abuse, depression, eating disorders, or stress-related disorders.

Assessing and recording a client's activities and progress is an important part of an occupational therapist's job. Accurate records are essential for evaluating clients, for billing, and for reporting to physicians and other health care providers.

Working Conditions

Occupational therapists in hospitals and other health care and community settings usually work a 40-hour week. Those in schools may participate in meetings and other activities during and after the school day. In 2004, more than a quarter of occupational therapists worked part time.

In large rehabilitation centers, therapists may work in spacious rooms equipped with machines, tools, and other devices generating noise. The work can be tiring because therapists are on their feet much of the time. Those providing home health care services may spend time driving from appointment to appointment. Therapists also face hazards such as back strain from lifting and moving clients and equipment.

Therapists increasingly are taking on supervisory roles. Because of rising health care costs, third-party payers are beginning to encourage occupational therapist assistants and aides to take more hands-on responsibility. By having assistants and aides work more closely with clients under the guidance of a therapist, the cost of therapy should decline.

Training, Other Qualifications, and Advancement

Currently, a bachelor's degree in occupational therapy is the minimum requirement for entry into the field. Beginning in 2007, however, a master's degree or higher will be the minimum educational requirement. As a result, students in bachelor's-level programs must complete their coursework and fieldwork before 2007. All states, Puerto Rico, Guam, and the District of Columbia regulate the practice of occupational therapy. To obtain a license, applicants must graduate from an accredited educational program and pass a national certification examination. Those who pass the exam are awarded the title "Occupational Therapist Registered (OTR)." Some states have additional requirements for therapists who work in schools or early intervention programs. These requirements may include education-related classes, an education practice certificate, or early intervention certification requirements.

In 2005, 122 master's degree programs offered entry-level education, 65 programs offered a combined bachelor's and master's

degree, and 5 offered an entry-level doctoral degree. Most schools have full-time programs, although a growing number are offering weekend or part-time programs as well. Bachelor's degree programs in occupational therapy are no longer offered because of the requirement for a master's degree or higher beginning in 2007. In addition, post-baccalaureate certificate programs for students with a degree other than occupational therapy are no longer offered.

Occupational therapy coursework includes the physical, biological, and behavioral sciences and the application of occupational therapy theory and skills. The completion of 6 months of supervised fieldwork also is required.

Persons considering this profession should take high school courses in biology, chemistry, physics, health, art, and the social sciences. College admissions offices also look favorably at paid or volunteer experience in the health care field. Relevant undergraduate majors include biology, psychology, sociology, anthropology, liberal arts, and anatomy.

Occupational therapists need patience and strong interpersonal skills to inspire trust and respect in their clients. Patience is necessary because many clients may not show rapid improvement. Ingenuity and imagination in adapting activities to individual needs are assets. Those working in home health care services must be able to adapt to a variety of settings.

Employment

Occupational therapists held about 92,000 jobs in 2004. About 1 in 10 occupational therapists held more than one job. The largest number of jobs were in hospitals. Other major employers were offices of other health practitioners (including offices of occupational therapists), public and private educational services, and nursing care facilities. Some occupational therapists were employed by home health care services, outpatient care centers, offices of physicians, individual and family services, community care facilities for the elderly, and government agencies.

A small number of occupational therapists were self-employed in private practice. These practitioners saw clients referred by physicians or other health professionals or provided contract or consulting services to nursing care facilities, schools, adult day care programs, and home health care agencies.

Job Outlook

Employment of occupational therapists is expected to increase much faster than the average for all occupations through 2014. The impact of proposed federal legislation imposing limits on reimbursement for therapy services may adversely affect the job market for occupational therapists in the short run. However, over the long run, the demand for occupational therapists should continue to rise as a result of growth in the number of individuals with disabilities or limited function who require therapy services. The baby-boom generation's movement into middle age, a period when the incidence of heart attack and stroke increases, will spur demand for therapeutic services. Growth in the population 75 years and older—an age group that suffers from high incidences of disabling conditions—also will increase demand for therapeutic services. Driver rehabilitation and fall-prevention training for the elderly are emerging practice areas for occupational therapy. In addition, medical advances now enable more patients with critical problems to survive—patients who ultimately may need extensive therapy.

Hospitals will continue to employ a large number of occupational therapists to provide therapy services to acutely ill inpatients. Hospitals also will need occupational therapists to staff their outpatient rehabilitation programs.

Employment growth in schools will result from the expansion of the school-age population, the extension of services for disabled students, and an increasing prevalence of sensory disorders in children. Therapists will be needed to help children with disabilities prepare to enter special education programs.

Earnings

Median annual earnings of occupational therapists were $54,660 in May 2004. The middle 50 percent earned between $45,690 and $67,010. The lowest 10 percent earned less than $37,430, and the highest 10 percent earned more than $81,600. Median annual earnings in the industries employing the largest numbers of occupational therapists in May 2004 were

Home health care services	$58,720
Offices of other health practitioners	56,620
Nursing care facilities	56,570
General medical and surgical hospitals	55,710
Elementary and secondary schools	48,580

Related Occupations

Occupational therapists use specialized knowledge to help individuals perform daily living skills and achieve maximum independence. Other workers performing similar duties include audiologists, chiropractors, physical therapists, recreational therapists, rehabilitation counselors, respiratory therapists, and speech-language pathologists.

Sources of Additional Information

For more information on occupational therapy as a career, contact

▶ American Occupational Therapy Association, 4720 Montgomery Lane, Bethesda, MD 20824-1220. Internet: http://www.aota.org

For information regarding the requirements to practice as an occupational therapist in schools, contact the appropriate occupational therapy regulatory agency for your state.

Physician Assistants

(O*NET 29-1071.00)

Significant Points

■ Physician assistant programs usually last at least 2 years; admission requirements vary by program, but many require at least 2 years of college and some health care experience.

■ All states require physician assistants to complete an accredited education program and to pass a national exam in order to obtain a license.

■ Physician assistants rank among the fastest-growing occupations as physicians and health care institutions increasingly utilize physician assistants in order to contain costs.

■ Job opportunities should be good, particularly in rural and inner-city clinics.

Nature of the Work

Physician assistants (PAs) practice medicine under the supervision of physicians and surgeons. They should not be confused with medical assistants, who perform routine clinical and clerical tasks. PAs are formally trained to provide diagnostic, therapeutic, and preventive health care services, as delegated by a physician. Working as members of the health care team, they take medical histories, examine and treat patients, order and interpret laboratory tests and X rays, and make diagnoses. They also treat minor injuries by suturing, splinting, and casting. PAs record progress notes, instruct and counsel patients, and order or carry out therapy. In 48 states and the District of Columbia, physician assistants may prescribe medications. PAs also may have managerial duties. Some order medical supplies or equipment and supervise technicians and assistants.

Physician assistants work under the supervision of a physician. However, PAs may be the principal care providers in rural or inner-city clinics, where a physician is present for only 1 or 2 days each week. In such cases, the PA confers with the supervising physician and other medical professionals as needed and as required by law. PAs also may make house calls or go to hospitals and nursing care facilities to check on patients, after which they report back to the physician.

The duties of physician assistants are determined by the supervising physician and by state law. Aspiring PAs should investigate the laws and regulations in the states in which they wish to practice.

Many PAs work in primary care specialties, such as general internal medicine, pediatrics, and family medicine. Other specialty areas include general and thoracic surgery, emergency medicine, orthopedics, and geriatrics. PAs specializing in surgery provide preoperative and postoperative care and may work as first or second assistants during major surgery.

Working Conditions

Although PAs usually work in a comfortable, well-lighted environment, those in surgery often stand for long periods, and others do considerable walking. Schedules vary according to the practice setting and often depend on the hours of the supervising physician. The workweek of hospital-based PAs may include weekends, nights, or early morning hospital rounds to visit patients. These workers also may be on call. PAs in clinics usually work a 40-hour week.

Training, Other Qualifications, and Advancement

All states require that PAs complete an accredited, formal education program and pass a national exam to obtain a license. PA programs usually last at least 2 years and are full time. Most programs are in schools of allied health, academic health centers, medical schools, or 4-year colleges; a few are in community colleges, the military, or hospitals. Many accredited PA programs have clinical teaching affiliations with medical schools.

In 2005, more than 135 education programs for physician assistants were accredited or provisionally accredited by the American Academy of Physician Assistants. More than 90 of these programs offered the option of a master's degree, and the rest offered either a bachelor's degree or an associate degree. Most applicants to PA educational programs already have a bachelor's degree.

Admission requirements vary, but many programs require 2 years of college and some work experience in the health care field. Students should take courses in biology, English, chemistry, mathematics, psychology, and the social sciences. Many PAs have prior experience as registered nurses, while others come from varied backgrounds, including military corpsman/medics and allied health occupations such as respiratory therapists, physical therapists, and emergency medical technicians and paramedics.

PA education includes classroom instruction in biochemistry, pathology, human anatomy, physiology, microbiology, clinical pharmacology, clinical medicine, geriatric and home health care, disease prevention, and medical ethics. Students obtain supervised clinical training in several areas, including family medicine, internal medicine, surgery, prenatal care and gynecology, geriatrics, emergency medicine, psychiatry, and pediatrics. Sometimes, PA students serve one or more of these "rotations" under the supervision of a physician who is seeking to hire a PA. The rotations often lead to permanent employment.

All states and the District of Columbia have legislation governing the qualifications or practice of physician assistants. All jurisdictions require physician assistants to pass the Physician Assistant National Certifying Examination, administered by the National Commission on Certification of Physician Assistants (NCCPA) and open only to graduates of accredited PA education programs. Only those successfully completing the examination may use the credential "Physician Assistant-Certified." In order to remain certified, PAs must complete 100 hours of continuing medical education every 2 years. Every 6 years, they must pass a recertification examination or complete an alternative program combining learning experiences and a take-home examination.

Some PAs pursue additional education in a specialty such as surgery, neonatology, or emergency medicine. PA postgraduate educational programs are available in areas such as internal medicine, rural primary care, emergency medicine, surgery, pediatrics, neonatology, and occupational medicine. Candidates must be graduates of an accredited program and be certified by the NCCPA.

Physician assistants need leadership skills, self-confidence, and emotional stability. They must be willing to continue studying throughout their career to keep up with medical advances.

As they attain greater clinical knowledge and experience, PAs can advance to added responsibilities and higher earnings. However, by the very nature of the profession, clinically practicing PAs always are supervised by physicians.

Employment

Physician assistants held about 62,000 jobs in 2004. The number of jobs is greater than the number of practicing PAs because some hold two or more jobs. For example, some PAs work with a supervising physician, but also work in another practice, clinic, or hospital. According to the American Academy of Physician Assistants, about 15 percent of actively practicing PAs worked in more than one clinical job concurrently in 2004.

More than half of jobs for PAs were in the offices of physicians. About a quarter were in hospitals, public or private. The rest were mostly in outpatient care centers, including health maintenance organizations; the federal government; and public or private colleges, universities, and professional schools. A few were self-employed.

Job Outlook

Employment of PAs is expected to grow much faster than the average for all occupations through the year 2014, ranking among the fastest-growing occupations, due to anticipated expansion of the health care industry and an emphasis on cost containment, resulting in increasing utilization of PAs by physicians and health care institutions.

Physicians and institutions are expected to employ more PAs to provide primary care and to assist with medical and surgical procedures because PAs are cost-effective and productive members of the health care team. Physician assistants can relieve physicians of routine duties and procedures. Telemedicine—using technology to facilitate interactive consultations between physicians and physician assistants—also will expand the use of physician assistants. Job opportunities for PAs should be good, particularly in rural and inner-city clinics, because those settings have difficulty attracting physicians.

Besides the traditional office-based setting, PAs should find a growing number of jobs in institutional settings such as hospitals, academic medical centers, public clinics, and prisons. Additional PAs may be needed to augment medical staffing in inpatient teaching hospital settings as the number of hours physician residents are permitted to work is reduced, encouraging hospitals to use PAs to supply some physician resident services. Opportunities will be best in states that allow PAs a wider scope of practice.

Earnings

Median annual earnings of physician assistants were $69,410 in May 2004. The middle 50 percent earned between $57,110 and $83,560. The lowest 10 percent earned less than $37,320, and the highest 10 percent earned more than $94,880. Median annual earnings of physician assistants in 2004 were $70,310 in general medical and surgical hospitals and $69,210 in offices of physicians.

According to the American Academy of Physician Assistants, median income for physician assistants in full-time clinical practice in 2004 was $74,264; median income for first-year graduates was $64,536. Income varies by specialty, practice setting, geographical location, and years of experience. Employers often pay for their employees' liability insurance, registration fees with the Drug Enforcement Administration, state licensing fees, and credentialing fees.

Related Occupations

Other health care workers who provide direct patient care that requires a similar level of skill and training include audiologists, occupational therapists, physical therapists, registered nurses, and speech-language pathologists.

Sources of Additional Information

For information on a career as a physician assistant, including a list of accredited programs, contact

▶ American Academy of Physician Assistants Information Center, 950 North Washington St., Alexandria, VA 22314-1552. Internet: http://www.aapa.org

For eligibility requirements and a description of the Physician Assistant National Certifying Examination, contact

▶ National Commission on Certification of Physician Assistants, Inc., 12000 Findley Rd., Suite 200, Duluth, GA 30097. Internet: http://www.nccpa.net

Probation Officers and Correctional Treatment Specialists

(O*NET 21-1092.00)

Significant Points

■ State and local governments employ most workers.

■ A bachelor's degree in social work, criminal justice, or a related field usually is required.

■ Employment growth, which is projected to be about as fast as average, depends on government funding.

Nature of the Work

Many people who are convicted of crimes are placed on probation instead of being sent to prison. During probation, offenders must stay out of trouble and meet various other requirements. *Probation officers*, who are called community supervision officers in some states, supervise people who have been placed on probation. *Correctional treatment specialists*, who may also be known as case managers, counsel and create rehabilitation plans for offenders to follow when they are no longer in prison or on parole.

Parole officers and *pretrial services officers* perform many of the same duties that probation officers perform. The difference is that parole officers supervise offenders who have been released from prison, whereas probation officers work with those who are sentenced to probation instead of prison. In some states, the jobs of parole and probation officers are combined. Pretrial services officers conduct pretrial investigations, the findings of which help determine whether suspects should be released before their trial. When suspects are released before their trial, pretrial services officers supervise them to make sure they adhere to the terms of their release and that they show up for trial. Occasionally, in the federal courts system, probation officers perform the functions of pretrial services officers.

Probation officers supervise offenders on probation or parole through personal contact with the offenders and their families. Instead of requiring offenders to meet officers in their offices, many officers meet offenders in their homes and at their places of employment or therapy. Probation and parole agencies also seek the assistance of community organizations, such as religious institutions, neighborhood groups, and local residents, to monitor the behavior of many offenders. Some offenders are required to wear an electronic device so that probation officers can monitor their location and movements. Probation officers may arrange for offenders to get substance abuse rehabilitation or job training. Probation officers usually work with either adults or juveniles exclusively. Only in small, usually rural, jurisdictions do probation officers counsel both adults and juveniles.

Probation officers also spend much of their time working for the courts. They investigate the backgrounds of the accused, write presentence reports, and recommend sentences. They review sentencing recommendations with offenders and their families before submitting them to the court. Probation officers may be required to testify in court as to their findings and recommendations. They also attend hearings to update the court on offenders' efforts at rehabilitation and compliance with the terms of their sentences.

Correctional treatment specialists work in jails, prisons, or parole or probation agencies. In jails and prisons, they evaluate the progress of inmates. They also work with inmates, probation officers, and other agencies to develop parole and release plans. Their case reports are provided to the appropriate parole board when their clients are eligible for release. In addition, they plan education and training programs to improve offenders' job skills and provide them with coping, anger management, and drug and sexual abuse counseling either individually or in groups. They usually write treatment plans and summaries for each client. Correctional treatment specialists working in parole and probation agencies perform many of the same duties as their counterparts who work in correctional institutions.

The number of cases a probation officer or correctional treatment specialist handles at one time depends on the needs of offenders and the risks they pose. Higher-risk offenders and those who need more counseling usually command more of the officer's time and resources. Caseload size also varies by agency jurisdiction. Consequently, officers may handle from 20 to more than 100 active cases at a time.

Computers, telephones, and fax machines enable the officers to handle the caseload. Probation officers may telecommute from their homes. Other technological advancements, such as electronic monitoring devices and drug screening, also have assisted probation officers and correctional treatment specialists in supervising and counseling offenders.

Working Conditions

Probation officers and correctional treatment specialists work with criminal offenders, some of whom may be dangerous. In the course of supervising offenders, they usually interact with many other individuals, such as family members and friends of their clients, who may be angry, upset, or difficult to work with. Workers may be assigned to fieldwork in high-crime areas or in institutions where there is a risk of violence or communicable disease. Probation officers and correctional treatment specialists are required to meet many court-imposed deadlines, which contribute to heavy workloads.

In addition, extensive travel and fieldwork may be required to meet with offenders who are on probation or parole. Workers may be required to carry a firearm or other weapon for protection. They generally work a 40-hour week, but some may work longer. They may be on call 24 hours a day to supervise and assist offenders at any time. They also may be required to collect and transport urine samples of offenders for drug testing. All of these factors make for a stressful work environment. Although the high stress levels can make these jobs very difficult at times, this work also can be very rewarding. Many workers obtain personal satisfaction from counseling members of their community and helping them become productive citizens.

Training, Other Qualifications, and Advancement

Background qualifications for probation officers and correctional treatment specialists vary by state, but a bachelor's degree in social work, criminal justice, or a related field is usually required. Some employers require previous experience or a master's degree in criminal justice, social work, psychology, or a related field.

Applicants usually are administered written, oral, psychological, and physical examinations. Most probation officers and some correctional treatment specialists are required to complete a training program sponsored by their state government or the federal government, after which a certification test may be required.

Prospective probation officers or correctional treatment specialists should be in good physical and emotional condition. Most agencies require applicants to be at least 21 years old and, for federal employment, not older than 37. Those convicted of felonies may not be eligible for employment in this occupation. Familiarity with the use of computers often is required due to the increasing use of computer technology in probation and parole work. Candidates also should be knowledgeable about laws and regulations pertaining to corrections. Probation officers and correctional treatment specialists should have strong writing skills because they are required to prepare many reports.

Most probation officers and correctional treatment specialists work as trainees or on a probationary period for up to a year before being offered a permanent position. A typical agency has several levels of probation and parole officers and correctional treatment specialists, as well as supervisors. A graduate degree, such as a master's degree in criminal justice, social work, or psychology, may be helpful for advancement.

Employment

Probation officers and correctional treatment specialists held about 93,000 jobs in 2004. Most jobs are in state or local governments. In some states, the state government employs all probation officers and correctional treatment specialists; in other states, local governments are the only employers. In still other states, both levels of government employ these workers. Jobs are more plentiful in urban areas. Probation officers and correctional treatment specialists who work for the federal government are employed by the U.S. courts and by the U.S. Department of Justice's Bureau of Prisons.

Job Outlook

Employment of probation officers and correctional treatment specialists is projected to grow about as fast as the average for all occupations through 2014. In addition to openings due to growth, many openings will be created by replacement needs, especially openings due to the large number of these workers who are expected to retire. This occupation is not attractive to some potential entrants due to relatively low earnings, heavy workloads, and high stress.

Mandatory sentencing guidelines calling for longer sentences and reduced parole for inmates have resulted in a large increase in the prison population. However, mandatory sentencing guidelines are being reconsidered in many states because of budgetary constraints, court decisions, and doubts about the guidelines' effectiveness. Instead, there may be more emphasis in many states on rehabilitation and alternate forms of punishment, such as probation, spurring demand for probation and parole officers and correctional treatment specialists. However, the job outlook depends primarily on the amount of government funding that is allocated to corrections and especially to probation systems. Although community supervision is far less expensive than keeping offenders in prison, a change in political trends toward more imprisonment and away from community supervision could result in reduced employment opportunities.

Earnings

Median annual earnings of probation officers and correctional treatment specialists in May 2004 were $39,600. The middle 50 percent earned between $31,500 and $52,100. The lowest 10 percent earned less than $26,310, and the highest 10 percent earned more than $66,660. In May 2004, median annual earnings for probation officers and correctional treatment specialists employed in state government were $39,810; those employed in local government earned $40,560. Higher wages tend to be found in urban areas.

Related Occupations

Probation officers and correctional treatment specialists counsel criminal offenders while they are in prison or on parole. Other occupations that involve similar responsibilities include social workers, social and human service assistants, and counselors.

Probation officers and correctional treatment specialists also play a major role in maintaining public safety. Other occupations related to corrections and law enforcement include police and detectives, correctional officers, and fire fighting occupations.

Sources of Additional Information

For information about criminal justice job opportunities in your area, contact your state's department of corrections, criminal justice, or probation.

Further information about probation officers and correctional treatment specialists is available from

▶ American Probation and Parole Association, P.O. Box 11910, Lexington, KY 40578. Internet: http://www.appa-net.org

Property, Real Estate, and Community Association Managers

(O*NET 11-9141.00)

Significant Points

■ Opportunities should be best for those with college degrees in business administration, real estate, or related fields and with professional designations.

■ Good speaking, writing, computer, and financial skills, as well as an ability to tactfully deal with people, are essential.

■ More than half of property, real estate, and community association managers are self-employed.

Nature of the Work

Buildings can be homes, stores, or offices to those who use them. To businesses and investors, properly managed real estate is a source of income and profits; to homeowners, it is a way to preserve and enhance resale values. Property, real estate, and community association managers maintain and increase the value of real estate investments. *Property and real estate managers* oversee the performance of income-producing commercial or residential properties and ensure that real estate investments achieve their expected revenues. *Community association managers* manage the common property and services of condominiums, cooperatives, and planned communities through their homeowners' or community associations.

When owners of apartments, office buildings, or retail or industrial properties lack the time or expertise needed for the day-to-day management of their real estate investments or homeowners' associations, they often hire a property or real estate manager or a community association manager. The manager is employed either directly by the owner or indirectly through a contract with a property management firm.

Generally, property and real estate managers handle the financial operations of the property, ensuring that rent is collected and that mortgages, taxes, insurance premiums, payroll, and maintenance bills are paid on time. In community associations, although homeowners pay no rent and pay their own real estate taxes and mortgages, community association managers must collect association dues. Some property managers, called *asset property managers*, supervise the preparation of financial statements and periodically report to the owners on the status of the property, occupancy rates, expiration dates of leases, and other matters.

Often, property managers negotiate contracts for janitorial, security, groundskeeping, trash removal, and other services. When contracts are awarded competitively, managers solicit bids from several contractors and advise the owners on which bid to accept. They monitor the performance of contractors and investigate and resolve complaints from residents and tenants when services are not properly provided. Managers also purchase supplies and equipment for the property and make arrangements with specialists for repairs that cannot be handled by regular property maintenance staff.

In addition to fulfilling these duties, property managers must understand and comply with provisions of legislation, such as the Americans with Disabilities Act and the Federal Fair Housing Amendment Act, as well as local fair housing laws. They must ensure that their renting and advertising practices are not discriminatory and that the property itself complies with all of the local, state, and federal regulations and building codes.

Onsite property managers are responsible for the day-to-day operations of a single property, such as an office building, a shopping center, a community association, or an apartment complex. To ensure that the property is safe and properly maintained, onsite managers routinely inspect the grounds, facilities, and equipment to determine whether repairs or maintenance is needed. In handling requests for repairs or trying to resolve complaints, they meet not only with current residents but also with prospective residents or tenants to show vacant apartments or office space. Onsite managers also are responsible for enforcing the terms of rental or lease agreements, such as rent collection, parking and pet restrictions, and termination-of-lease procedures. Other important duties of onsite managers include keeping accurate, up-to-date records of income and expenditures from property operations and submitting regular expense reports to the asset property manager or owners.

Property managers who do not work onsite act as a liaison between the onsite manager and the owner. They also market vacant space to prospective tenants through the use of a leasing agent or by advertising or other means, and they establish rental rates in accordance with prevailing local economic conditions.

Some property and real estate managers, often called *real estate asset managers*, act as the property owners' agent and adviser for the property. They plan and direct the purchase, development, and disposition of real estate on behalf of the business and investors. These managers focus on long-term strategic financial planning rather than on day-to-day operations of the property.

In deciding to acquire property, real estate asset managers take several factors into consideration, such as property values, taxes, zoning, population growth, transportation, and traffic volume and patterns. Once a site is selected, they negotiate contracts for the purchase or lease of the property, securing the most beneficial terms. Real estate asset managers review their company's real estate holdings periodically and identify properties that are no longer financially profitable. They then negotiate the sale of, or terminate the lease on, such properties.

In many respects, the work of community association managers parallels that of property managers. They collect monthly assessments, prepare financial statements and budgets, negotiate with contractors, and help to resolve complaints. In other respects, however, the work of these managers differs from that of other residential property and real estate managers. Community association managers interact with homeowners and other residents on a daily basis. Hired by the volunteer board of directors of the association, they administer the daily affairs and oversee the maintenance of property and facilities that the homeowners own and use jointly through the association. They also assist the board and owners in complying with association and government rules and regulations.

Some associations encompass thousands of homes and employ their own onsite staff and managers. In addition to administering the associations' financial records and budget, managers may be responsible for the operation of community pools, golf courses, and community centers and for the maintenance of landscaping and parking areas. Community association managers also may meet with the elected boards of directors to discuss and resolve legal issues or disputes that may affect the owners as well as to review any proposed changes or improvements by homeowners to their properties to make sure that they comply with community guidelines.

Working Conditions

The offices of most property, real estate, and community association managers are clean, modern, and well lighted. However, many managers spend a major portion of their time away from their desks. Onsite managers in particular may spend a large portion of their workday away from their offices, visiting the building engineer, showing apartments, checking on the janitorial and maintenance staff, or investigating problems reported by tenants. Property and real estate managers frequently visit the properties they oversee, sometimes on a daily basis when contractors are doing major repair or renovation work. Real estate asset managers may spend time away from home while traveling to company real estate holdings or searching for properties to acquire.

Property, real estate, and community association managers often must attend evening meetings with residents, property owners, community association boards of directors, or civic groups. Not surprisingly, many managers put in long workweeks, especially before financial and tax reports are due and before board and annual meetings. Some apartment managers are required to live in the apartment complexes where they work so that they are available to handle any emergency that occurs, even when they are off duty. They usually receive compensatory time off for working nights or weekends. Many apartment managers receive time off during the week so that they are available on weekends to show apartments to prospective residents.

Training, Other Qualifications, and Advancement

Most employers prefer to hire college graduates for property management positions. Entrants with degrees in business administration, accounting, finance, real estate, public administration, or related fields are preferred, but those with degrees in the liberal arts also may qualify. Good speaking, writing, computer, and financial skills, as well as an ability to deal tactfully with people, are essential in all areas of property management.

Many people enter property management as onsite managers of apartment buildings, office complexes, or community associations or as employees of property management firms or community association management companies. As they acquire experience working under the direction of a property manager, they may advance to positions with greater responsibility at larger properties. Those who excel as onsite managers often transfer to assistant property manager positions in which they can acquire experience handling a broad range of property management responsibilities.

Previous employment as a real estate sales agent may be an asset to onsite managers because it provides experience that is useful in showing apartments or office space. In the past, those with backgrounds in building maintenance have advanced to onsite manager positions on the strength of their knowledge of building mechanical systems, but this path is becoming less common as employers place greater emphasis on administrative, financial, and communication abilities for managerial jobs.

Although many people entering jobs such as assistant property manager do so by having previously gained onsite management experience, employers increasingly are hiring inexperienced college graduates with bachelor's or master's degrees in business administration, accounting, finance, or real estate for these positions. Assistants work closely with a property manager and learn how to prepare budgets, analyze insurance coverage and risk options, market property to prospective tenants, and collect overdue rent payments. In time, many assistants advance to property manager positions.

The responsibilities and compensation of property, real estate, and community association managers increase as these workers manage more and larger properties. Most property managers, often called *portfolio managers,* are responsible for several properties at a time. As their careers advance, they gradually are entrusted with larger properties that are more complex to manage. Many specialize in the management of one type of property, such as apartments, office buildings, condominiums, cooperatives, homeowners' associations, or retail properties. Managers who excel at marketing properties to tenants might specialize in managing new properties, while those who are particularly knowledgeable about buildings and their mechanical systems might specialize in the management of older properties requiring renovation or more frequent repairs. Some experienced managers open their own property management firms.

Persons most commonly enter real estate asset manager jobs by transferring from positions as property managers or real estate brokers. Real estate asset managers must be good negotiators, adept at persuading and handling people, and good at analyzing data in order to assess the fair market value of property or its development potential. Resourcefulness and creativity in arranging financing are essential for managers who specialize in land development.

Many employers encourage attendance at short-term formal training programs conducted by various professional and trade associations that are active in the real estate field. Employers send managers to these programs to improve their management skills and expand their knowledge of specialized subjects, such as the operation and maintenance of building mechanical systems, the enhancement of property values, insurance and risk management, personnel management, business and real estate law, community association risks and liabilities, tenant relations, communications, accounting and financial concepts, and reserve funding. Managers also participate in these programs to prepare themselves for positions of greater responsibility in property management. The completion of these programs, related job experience, and a satisfactory score on a written examination leads to certification, or the formal award of a professional designation, by the sponsoring association. (Some organizations offering such programs are listed as sources of additional information at the end of this statement.) In addition to seeking these qualifications, some associations require their members to adhere to a specific code of ethics. In a few states, community association managers must be licensed.

Managers of public housing subsidized by the federal government are required to be certified, but many property, real estate, and community association managers who work with all types of property choose to earn a professional designation voluntarily because it represents formal recognition of their achievements and status in the occupation. Real estate asset managers who buy or sell property are required to be licensed by the state in which they practice.

Employment

Property, real estate, and community association managers held about 361,000 jobs in 2004. More that one-third worked for real estate agents and brokers, lessors of real estate, or property management firms. Others worked for real estate development companies, government agencies that manage public buildings, and corporations with extensive holdings of commercial properties. More than half of property, real estate, and community association managers were self-employed.

Job Outlook

Employment of property, real estate, and community association managers is projected to increase about as fast as average for all occupations through the year 2014. In addition to job growth, a number of openings are expected to occur as managers transfer to other occupations or leave the labor force. Opportunities should be best for those with a college degree in business administration, real estate, or a related field and for those who attain a professional designation.

Job growth among onsite property managers in commercial real estate is expected to accompany the projected expansion of the real estate and rental and leasing industry. An increase in the nation's stock of apartments, houses, and offices also should require more property managers. Developments of new homes increasingly are being organized with community or homeowners' associations that provide community services and oversee jointly owned common areas requiring professional management. To help properties become more profitable or to enhance the resale values of homes,

more commercial and residential property owners are expected to place their investments in the hands of professional managers.

The changing demographic composition of the population also should create more jobs for property, real estate, and community association managers. The number of older people will grow during the 2004–2014 projection period, increasing the need for various types of suitable housing, such as assisted-living facilities and retirement communities. Accordingly, demand will rise for property and real estate managers to operate these facilities—especially those individuals who have a background in the operation and administrative aspects of running a health unit.

Earnings

Median annual earnings of salaried property, real estate, and community association managers were $39,980 in May 2004. The middle 50 percent earned between $27,190 and $59,360 a year. The lowest 10 percent earned less than $18,510, and the highest 10 percent earned more than $89,840 a year. Median annual earnings of salaried property, real estate, and community association managers in the largest industries that employed them in 2004 were as follows:

Local government	$51,980
Offices of real estate agents and brokers	40,000
Activities related to real estate	38,370
Lessors of real estate	34,300

Many resident apartment managers and onsite association managers receive the use of an apartment as part of their compensation package. Managers often are reimbursed for the use of their personal vehicles, and managers employed in land development often receive a small percentage of ownership in the projects that they develop.

Related Occupations

Property, real estate, and community association managers plan, organize, staff, and manage the real estate operations of businesses. Workers who perform similar functions in other fields include administrative services managers, education administrators, food service managers, lodging managers, medical and health services managers, real estate brokers and sales agents, and urban and regional planners.

Sources of Additional Information

For information about education and careers in property management, as well as information about professional designation and certification programs in both residential and commercial property management, contact

▸ Institute of Real Estate Management, 430 N. Michigan Ave., Chicago, IL 60611. Internet: http://www.irem.org

For information on careers and certification programs in commercial property management, contact

▸ Building Owners and Managers Institute, 1521 Ritchie Hwy., Arnold, MD 21012. Internet: http://www.bomi-edu.org

For information on careers and professional designation and certification programs in residential property management and community association management, contact

▶ Community Associations Institute, 225 Reinekers Lane, Suite 300, Alexandria, VA 22314. Internet: http://www.caionline.org

▶ National Board of Certification for Community Association Managers, 225 Reinekers Lane, Suite 310, Alexandria, VA 22314. Internet: http://www.nbccam.org

Public Relations Specialists

(O*NET: 27-3031.00)

Significant Points

■ Although employment is projected to grow faster than average, keen competition is expected for entry-level jobs.

■ Opportunities should be best for college graduates who combine a degree in public relations, journalism, or another communications-related field with a public relations internship or other related work experience.

■ Creativity, initiative, and the ability to communicate effectively are essential.

Nature of the Work

An organization's reputation, profitability, and even its continued existence can depend on the degree to which its targeted "publics" support its goals and policies. *Public relations specialists*—also referred to as *communications specialists* and *media specialists*, among other titles—serve as advocates for businesses, nonprofit associations, universities, hospitals, and other organizations and build and maintain positive relationships with the public. As managers recognize the importance of good public relations to the success of their organizations, they increasingly rely on public relations specialists for advice on the strategy and policy of such programs.

Public relations specialists handle organizational functions such as media, community, consumer, industry, and governmental relations; political campaigns; interest-group representation; conflict mediation; and employee and investor relations. They do more than "tell the organization's story." They must understand the attitudes and concerns of community, consumer, employee, and public interest groups and establish and maintain cooperative relationships with them and with representatives from print and broadcast journalism.

Public relations specialists draft press releases and contact people in the media who might print or broadcast their material. Many radio or television special reports, newspaper stories, and magazine articles start at the desks of public relations specialists. Sometimes the subject is an organization and its policies toward its employees or its role in the community. Often the subject is a public issue, such as health, energy, or the environment, and what an organization does to advance that issue.

Public relations specialists also arrange and conduct programs to keep up contact between organization representatives and the public. For example, they set up speaking engagements and often prepare speeches for company officials. These media specialists represent employers at community projects; make film, slide, or other visual presentations at meetings and school assemblies; and

plan conventions. In addition, they are responsible for preparing annual reports and writing proposals for various projects.

In government, public relations specialists—who may be called *press secretaries, information officers, public affairs specialists,* or *communication specialists*—keep the public informed about the activities of agencies and officials. For example, public affairs specialists in the U.S. Department of State keep the public informed of travel advisories and of U.S. positions on foreign issues. A press secretary for a member of Congress keeps constituents aware of the representative's accomplishments.

In large organizations, the key public relations executive, who often is a vice president, may develop overall plans and policies with other executives. In addition, public relations departments employ public relations specialists to write, research, prepare materials, maintain contacts, and respond to inquiries.

People who handle publicity for an individual or who direct public relations for a small organization may deal with all aspects of the job. They contact people, plan and research, and prepare materials for distribution. They also may handle advertising or sales promotion work to support marketing efforts.

Working Conditions

Some public relations specialists work a standard 35- to 40-hour week, but unpaid overtime is common. Occasionally, they must be at the job or on call around the clock, especially if there is an emergency or crisis. Public relations offices are busy places; work schedules can be irregular and frequently interrupted. Schedules often have to be rearranged so that workers can meet deadlines, deliver speeches, attend meetings and community activities, and travel.

Training, Other Qualifications, and Advancement

There are no defined standards for entry into a public relations career. A college degree combined with public relations experience, usually gained through an internship, is considered excellent preparation for public relations work; in fact, internships are becoming vital to obtaining employment. The ability to communicate effectively is essential. Many entry-level public relations specialists have a college major in public relations, journalism, advertising, or communication. Some firms seek college graduates who have worked in electronic or print journalism. Other employers seek applicants with demonstrated communication skills and training or experience in a field related to the firm's business—information technology, health, science, engineering, sales, or finance, for example.

Many colleges and universities offer bachelor's and postsecondary degrees in public relations, usually in a journalism or communications department. In addition, many other colleges offer at least one course in this field. A common public relations sequence includes courses in public relations principles and techniques; public relations management and administration, including organizational development; writing, emphasizing news releases, proposals, annual reports, scripts, speeches, and related items; visual communications, including desktop publishing and computer graphics; and research, emphasizing social science research and survey design and implementation. Courses in advertising, journalism, business administration, finance, political science, psychology, sociology, and creative writing also are helpful. Specialties are offered in public relations for business, government, and nonprofit organizations.

Many colleges help students gain part-time internships in public relations that provide valuable experience and training. Membership in local chapters of the Public Relations Student Society of America (affiliated with the Public Relations Society of America) or in student chapters of the International Association of Business Communicators provides an opportunity for students to exchange views with public relations specialists and to make professional contacts that may help them find a job in the field. A portfolio of published articles, television or radio programs, slide presentations, and other work is an asset in finding a job. Writing for a school publication or television or radio station provides valuable experience and material for one's portfolio.

Creativity, initiative, good judgment, and the ability to communicate thoughts clearly and simply are essential in this occupation. Decision-making, problem-solving, and research skills also are important. People who choose public relations as a career need an outgoing personality, self-confidence, an understanding of human psychology, and an enthusiasm for motivating people. They should be competitive, yet able to function as part of a team and open to new ideas.

Some organizations, particularly those with large public relations staffs, have formal training programs for new employees. In smaller organizations, new employees work under the guidance of experienced staff members. Beginners often maintain files of material about company activities, scan newspapers and magazines for appropriate articles to clip, and assemble information for speeches and pamphlets. They also may answer calls from the press and the public, work on invitation lists and details for press conferences, or escort visitors and clients. After gaining experience, they write news releases, speeches, and articles for publication or plan and carry out public relations programs. Public relations specialists in smaller firms usually get all-around experience, whereas those in larger firms tend to be more specialized.

The Universal Accreditation Board accredits public relations specialists who are members of the Public Relations Society of America and who participate in the Examination for Accreditation in Public Relations process. This process includes both a readiness review and an examination, which are designed for candidates who have at least 5 years of full-time work or teaching experience in public relations and who have earned a bachelor's degree in a communications-related field. The readiness review includes a written submission by each candidate, a portfolio review, and dialogue between the candidate and a three-member panel. Candidates who successfully advance through readiness review and pass the computer-based examination earn the Accredited in Public Relations (APR) designation.

The International Association of Business Communicators (IABC) also has an accreditation program for professionals in the communications field, including public relations specialists. Those who meet all the requirements of the program earn the Accredited Business Communicator (ABC) designation. Candidates must have at least 5 years of experience and a bachelor's degree in a communications field and must pass written and oral examinations. They also must submit a portfolio of work samples demonstrating involvement in a range of communications projects and a thorough understanding of communications planning.

Employers may consider professional recognition through accreditation as a sign of competence in this field, which could be especially helpful in a competitive job market.

Promotion to supervisory jobs may come to public relations specialists who show that they can handle more demanding assignments. In public relations firms, a beginner might be hired as a research assistant or account coordinator and be promoted to account executive, senior account executive, account manager, and eventually vice president. A similar career path is followed in corporate public relations, although the titles may differ. Some experienced public relations specialists start their own consulting firms. (For more information on public relations managers, see the job description of advertising, marketing, promotions, public relations, and sales managers elsewhere in this book.)

Employment

Public relations specialists held about 188,000 jobs in 2004. Public relations specialists are concentrated in service-providing industries such as advertising and related services; health care and social assistance; educational services; and government. Others worked for communications firms, financial institutions, and government agencies.

Public relations specialists are concentrated in large cities, where press services and other communications facilities are readily available and many businesses and trade associations have their headquarters. Many public relations consulting firms, for example, are in New York, Los Angeles, San Francisco, Chicago, and Washington, DC. There is a trend, however, for public relations jobs to be dispersed throughout the nation, closer to clients.

Job Outlook

Keen competition likely will continue for entry-level public relations jobs, as the number of qualified applicants is expected to exceed the number of job openings. Many people are attracted to this profession because of the high-profile nature of the work. Opportunities should be best for college graduates who combine a degree in journalism, public relations, advertising, or another communications-related field with a public relations internship or other related work experience. Applicants without the appropriate educational background or work experience will face the toughest obstacles.

Employment of public relations specialists is expected to grow faster than average for all occupations through 2014. The need for good public relations in an increasingly competitive business environment should spur demand for public relations specialists in organizations of all types and sizes. The value of a company is measured not just by its balance sheet, but also by the strength of its relationships with those on whom it depends for its success. With the increasing demand for corporate accountability, more emphasis will be placed on improving the image of the client as well as on building public confidence.

Employment in public relations firms should grow as firms hire contractors to provide public relations services rather than support full-time staff. In addition to those arising from employment growth, job opportunities should result from the need to replace public relations specialists who leave the occupation.

Earnings

Median annual earnings for salaried public relations specialists were $43,830 in May 2004. The middle 50 percent earned between $32,970 and $59,360; the lowest 10 percent earned less than $25,750, and the top 10 percent earned more than $81,120. Median annual earnings in the industries employing the largest numbers of public relations specialists in May 2004 were

Advertising and related services	$50,450
Management of companies and enterprises	47,330
Business, professional, labor, political, and similar organizations	45,400
Local government	44,550
Colleges, universities, and professional schools	39,610

Related Occupations

Public relations specialists create favorable attitudes among various organizations, interest groups, and the public through effective communication. Other workers with similar jobs include advertising, marketing, promotions, public relations, and sales managers; demonstrators, product promoters, and models; news analysts, reporters, and correspondents; lawyers; market and survey researchers; sales representatives, wholesale and manufacturing; and police and detectives involved in community relations.

Sources of Additional Information

A comprehensive directory of schools offering degree programs, a sequence of study in public relations, a brochure on careers in public relations, and a $5 brochure entitled *Where Shall I Go to Study Advertising and Public Relations* are available from

▸ Public Relations Society of America, Inc., 33 Maiden Lane, New York, NY 10038-5150. Internet: http://www.prsa.org

For information on accreditation for public relations professionals and the IABC Student Web site, contact

▸ International Association of Business Communicators, One Hallidie Plaza, Suite 600, San Francisco, CA 94102.

Recreation Workers

(O*NET 39-9032.00)

Significant Points

■ Educational requirements for recreation workers range from a high school diploma to a graduate degree. Competition will remain keen for full-time career positions in recreation. The recreation field offers an unusually large number of part-time and seasonal job opportunities.

Nature of the Work

People spend much of their leisure time participating in a wide variety of organized recreational activities, such as arts and crafts, the performing arts, camping, and sports. *Recreation workers* plan, organize, and direct these activities in local playgrounds and recreation areas, parks, community centers, religious organizations, camps, theme parks, and tourist attractions. Increasingly, recreation workers also are being found in workplaces, where they organize and direct leisure activities for employees.

Recreation workers hold a variety of positions at different levels of responsibility. *Recreation leaders*, who are responsible for a recreation program's daily operation, primarily organize and direct participants. They may lead and give instruction in dance, drama, crafts, games, and sports; schedule the use of facilities; keep records of equipment use; and ensure that recreation facilities and equipment are used properly. Workers who provide instruction and coach groups in specialties such as art, music, drama, swimming, or tennis may be called *activity specialists*. *Recreation supervisors* oversee recreation leaders and plan, organize, and manage recreational activities to meet the needs of a variety of populations. These workers often serve as liaisons between the director of the park or recreation center and the recreation leaders. Recreation supervisors with more specialized responsibilities also may direct special activities or events or oversee a major activity, such as aquatics, gymnastics, or performing arts. *Directors of recreation and parks* develop and manage comprehensive recreation programs in parks, playgrounds, and other settings. Directors usually serve as technical advisors to state and local recreation and park commissions and may be responsible for recreation and park budgets. (Workers in a related occupation, recreational therapists, help individuals to recover from or adjust to illness, disability, or specific social problems; this occupation is described elsewhere in this book.)

Camp counselors lead and instruct children and teenagers in outdoor-oriented forms of recreation, such as swimming, hiking, horseback riding, and camping. In addition, counselors provide campers with specialized instruction in subjects such as archery, boating, music, drama, gymnastics, tennis, and computers. In resident camps, counselors also provide guidance and supervise daily living and general socialization. *Camp directors* typically supervise camp counselors, plan camp activities or programs, and perform the various administrative functions of a camp.

Working Conditions

Recreation workers may work in a variety of settings—for example, a cruise ship, a woodland recreational park, a summer camp, or a playground in the center of a large urban community. Regardless of the setting, most recreation workers spend much of their time outdoors and may work in a variety of weather conditions. Recreation directors and supervisors, however, typically spend most of their time in an office, planning programs and special events. Directors and supervisors generally engage in less physical activity than do lower-level recreation workers. Nevertheless, recreation workers at all levels risk suffering injuries during physical activities.

Many recreation workers work about 40 hours a week. People entering this field, especially camp counselors, should expect some night and weekend work and irregular hours. Many recreation jobs are seasonal.

Training, Other Qualifications, and Advancement

Educational requirements for recreation workers range from a high school diploma—or sometimes less for those seeking many summer jobs—to graduate degrees for some administrative positions in large public recreation systems. Full-time career professional positions usually require a college degree with a major in parks and recreation or leisure studies, but a bachelor's degree in any liberal arts field may be sufficient for some jobs in the private sector. In industrial recreation, or "employee services" as it is more commonly called, companies prefer to hire those with a bachelor's degree in recreation or leisure studies and a background in business administration.

Specialized training or experience in a particular field, such as art, music, drama, or athletics, is an asset for many jobs. Some jobs also require certification. For example, a lifesaving certificate is a prerequisite for teaching or coaching water-related activities. Graduates of associate's degree programs in parks and recreation, social work, and other human services disciplines also enter some career recreation positions. High school graduates occasionally enter career positions, but this is not common. Some college students work part time as recreation workers while earning degrees.

A bachelor's degree in a recreation-related discipline and experience are preferred for most recreation supervisor jobs and are required for higher-level administrative jobs. However, an increasing number of recreation workers who aspire to administrative positions are obtaining master's degrees in parks and recreation, business administration, or public administration. Certification in the recreation field may be helpful for advancement. Also, many persons in other disciplines, including social work, forestry, and resource management, pursue graduate degrees in recreation.

Programs leading to an associate's or bachelor's degree in parks and recreation, leisure studies, or related fields are offered at several hundred colleges and universities. Many also offer master's or doctoral degrees in the field. In 2004, about 100 bachelor's degree programs in parks and recreation were accredited by the National Recreation and Park Association (NRPA). Accredited programs provide broad exposure to the history, theory, and practice of park and recreation management. Courses offered include community organization; supervision and administration; recreational needs of special populations, such as the elderly or disabled; and supervised fieldwork. Students may specialize in areas such as therapeutic recreation, park management, outdoor recreation, industrial or commercial recreation, or camp management.

The NRPA certifies individuals for professional and technical jobs. Certified Park and Recreation Professionals must pass an exam; earn a bachelor's degree with a major in recreation, park resources, or leisure services from a program accredited by the NRPA and the American Association for Leisure and Recreation; or earn a bachelor's degree and have at least 5 years of relevant full-time work experience. Continuing education is necessary to remain certified.

Persons planning recreation careers should be outgoing, good at motivating people, and sensitive to the needs of others. Excellent health and physical fitness are often required due to the physical nature of some jobs. Volunteer experience, part-time work during school, or a summer job can lead to a full-time career as a recreation worker. As in many fields, managerial skills are needed to advance to supervisory or managerial positions.

Employment

Recreation workers held about 310,000 jobs in 2004, and many additional workers held summer jobs in the occupation. Of those with year-round jobs as recreation workers, about 35 percent worked for local governments, primarily in park and recreation departments. Around 11 percent of recreation workers were employed in civic and social organizations, such as the Boy Scouts or Girl Scouts or the Red Cross. Another 15 percent of recreation workers were employed by nursing and other personal care facilities.

The recreation field has an unusually large number of part-time, seasonal, and volunteer jobs, including summer camp counselors, craft specialists, and after-school and weekend recreation program leaders. In addition, many teachers and college students accept jobs as recreation workers when school is not in session. The vast majority of volunteers serve as activity leaders at local day camp programs or in youth organizations, camps, nursing homes, hospitals, senior centers, and other settings.

Job Outlook

Competition will remain keen for career positions as recreation workers because the field attracts many applicants and because the number of career positions is limited compared with the number of lower-level seasonal jobs. Opportunities for staff positions should be best for persons with formal training and experience gained in part-time or seasonal recreation jobs. Those with graduate degrees should have the best opportunities for supervisory or administrative positions. Job openings also will stem from the need to replace the large numbers of workers who leave the occupation each year.

Overall employment of recreation workers is expected to grow about as fast as the average for all occupations through 2014. People will spend more time and money on recreation, spurring growth in civic and social organizations and, to a lesser degree, state and local government. Much growth will be driven by retiring baby boomers, who, with more leisure time, high disposable income, and concern for health and fitness, are expected to increase their consumption of recreation services. Job growth also will be driven by rapidly increasing employment in nursing and residential care facilities. Employment growth may be inhibited, however, by budget constraints that local governments may face over the 2004–2014 projection period.

The large number of temporary, seasonal jobs in the recreation field typically are filled by high school or college students, generally do not have formal education requirements, and are open to anyone with the desired personal qualities. Employers compete for a share of the vacationing student labor force, and although salaries in recreation often are lower than those in other fields, the nature of the work and the opportunity to work outdoors are attractive to many.

Earnings

In May 2004, median annual earnings of recreation workers who worked full time were $19,320. The middle 50 percent earned between $15,640 and $25,380. The lowest-paid 10 percent earned less than $13,260, while the highest-paid 10 percent earned $34,280 or more. However, earnings of recreation directors and others in supervisory or managerial positions can be substantially higher. Most public and private recreation agencies provide full-time recreation workers with typical benefits; part-time workers receive few, if any, benefits. In May 2004, median annual earnings in the industries employing the largest numbers of recreation workers were as follows:

Nursing care facilities...$20,660
Local government 19,650
Individual and family services 19,260
Other amusement and recreation industries 17,060
Civic and social organizations 16,950

Related Occupations

Recreation workers must exhibit leadership and sensitivity when dealing with people. Other occupations that require similar personal qualities include counselors, probation officers and correctional treatment specialists, psychologists, recreational therapists, and social workers.

Sources of Additional Information

For information on jobs in recreation, contact employers such as local government departments of parks and recreation, nursing and personal care facilities, the Boy Scouts or Girl Scouts, or local social or religious organizations.

For information on careers, certification, and academic programs in parks and recreation, contact

▸ National Recreation and Park Association, Division of Professional Services, 22377 Belmont Ridge Rd., Ashburn, VA 20148-4501. Internet: http://www.nrpa.org

For career information about camp counselors, contact

▸ American Camping Association, 5000 State Road 67 North, Martinsville, IN 46151-7902. Internet: http://www.acacamps.org

Recreational Therapists

(O*NET 29-1125.00)

Significant Points

■ Overall employment of recreational therapists is expected to grow more slowly than the average for all occupations, but employment of therapists who work in community care facilities for the elderly and in residential mental retardation, mental health, and substance abuse facilities should grow faster than the average.

■ Opportunities should be best for persons with a bachelor's degree in therapeutic recreation or in recreation with a concentration in therapeutic recreation.

■ Recreational therapists should be comfortable working with persons who are ill or who have disabilities.

Nature of the Work

Recreational therapists, also referred to as *therapeutic recreation specialists,* provide treatment services and recreation activities to individuals with disabilities or illnesses. Using a variety of techniques, including arts and crafts, animals, sports, games, dance and movement, drama, music, and community outings, therapists treat and maintain the physical, mental, and emotional well-being of their clients. Therapists help individuals reduce depression, stress, and anxiety; recover basic motor functioning and reasoning abilities; build confidence; and socialize effectively so that they can enjoy greater independence, as well as reduce or eliminate the effects of their illness or disability. In addition, therapists help integrate people with disabilities into the community by teaching them how to use community resources and recreational activities. Recreational therapists should not be confused with recreation workers, who organize recreational activities primarily for enjoyment. (Recreation workers are discussed elsewhere in this book.)

In acute health care settings, such as hospitals and rehabilitation centers, recreational therapists treat and rehabilitate individuals with specific health conditions, usually in conjunction or collaboration with physicians, nurses, psychologists, social workers, and physical and occupational therapists. In long-term and residential care facilities, recreational therapists use leisure activities—especially structured group programs—to improve and maintain their clients' general health and well-being. They also may provide interventions to prevent the client from suffering further medical problems and complications related to illnesses and disabilities.

Recreational therapists assess clients on the basis of information the therapists learn from standardized assessments, observations, medical records, the medical staff, the clients' families, and the clients themselves. They then develop and carry out therapeutic interventions consistent with the clients' needs and interests. For example, clients who are isolated from others or who have limited social skills may be encouraged to play games with others, and right-handed persons with right-side paralysis may be instructed in how to adapt to using their unaffected left side to throw a ball or swing a racket. Recreational therapists may instruct patients in relaxation techniques to reduce stress and tension, stretching and limbering exercises, proper body mechanics for participation in recreational activities, pacing and energy conservation techniques, and individual as well as team activities. In addition, therapists observe and document a patient's participation, reactions, and progress.

Community-based recreational therapists may work in park and recreation departments, special-education programs for school districts, or programs for older adults and people with disabilities. Included in the last group are programs and facilities such as assisted-living, adult day care, and substance abuse rehabilitation centers. In these programs, therapists use interventions to develop specific skills while providing opportunities for exercise, mental stimulation, creativity, and fun. Although most therapists are employed in other areas, those who work in schools help counselors, teachers, and parents address the special needs of students, including easing disabled students' transition into adult life.

Working Conditions

Recreational therapists provide services in special activity rooms but also plan activities and prepare documentation in offices. When working with clients during community integration programs, they may travel locally to instruct the clients regarding the accessibility of public transportation and other public areas, such as parks, playgrounds, swimming pools, restaurants, and theaters.

Therapists often lift and carry equipment, as well as lead recreational activities. Recreational therapists generally work a 40-hour week that may include some evenings, weekends, and holidays.

Training, Other Qualifications, and Advancement

A bachelor's degree in therapeutic recreation, or in recreation with a concentration in therapeutic recreation, is the usual requirement for entry-level positions. Persons may qualify for paraprofessional positions with an associate degree in therapeutic recreation or a health care–related field. An associate degree in recreational therapy; training in art, drama, or music therapy; or qualifying work experience may be sufficient for activity director positions in nursing homes.

Approximately 150 programs prepare students to become recreational therapists. Most offer bachelor's degrees, although some also offer associate, master's, or doctoral degrees. Programs include courses in assessment, treatment and program planning, intervention design, and evaluation. Students also study human anatomy, physiology, abnormal psychology, medical and psychiatric terminology, characteristics of illnesses and disabilities, professional ethics, and the use of assistive devices and technology.

Although certification is usually voluntary, most employers prefer to hire candidates who are certified therapeutic recreation specialists. The National Council for Therapeutic Recreation Certification is the certificatory agency. To become certified, specialists must have a bachelor's degree, pass a written certification examination, and complete an internship of at least 480 hours. Additional requirements apply in order to maintain certification and to recertify. Some states require licensure or certification to practice recreational therapy.

Recreational therapists should be comfortable working with persons who are ill or who have disabilities. Therapists must be patient, tactful, and persuasive when working with people who have a variety of special needs. Ingenuity, a sense of humor, and imagination are needed to adapt activities to individual needs, and good physical coordination is necessary to demonstrate or participate in recreational activities.

Therapists may advance to supervisory or administrative positions. Some teach, conduct research, or consult for health or social services agencies.

Employment

Recreational therapists held about 24,000 jobs in 2004. About 6 out of 10 were in nursing care facilities and hospitals. Others worked in state and local government agencies and in community care facilities for the elderly, including assisted-living facilities. The rest worked primarily in residential mental retardation, mental health, and substance abuse facilities; individual and family services; federal government agencies; educational services; and outpatient care centers. Only a small number of therapists were self-employed, generally contracting with long-term care facilities or community agencies to develop and oversee programs.

Job Outlook

Overall employment of recreational therapists is expected to grow more slowly than the average for all occupations through the year 2014. In nursing care facilities—the largest industry employing recreational therapists—employment will grow slightly faster than the occupation as a whole as the number of older adults continues to grow. Employment is expected to decline, however, in hospitals as services shift to outpatient settings and employers emphasize cost containment. Fast employment growth is expected in the residential and outpatient settings that serve disabled persons; the elderly; or those diagnosed with mental retardation, mental illness, or substance abuse problems. Among these settings are community care facilities for the elderly (including assisted-living facilities); residential mental retardation, mental health, and substance abuse facilities; and facilities that provide individual and family services (such as day care centers for disabled persons and the elderly). Opportunities should be best for persons with a bachelor's degree in therapeutic recreation or in recreation with an option in therapeutic recreation. Opportunities also should be good for therapists who hold specialized certifications, for example, in aquatic therapy, meditation, or crisis intervention.

Health care facilities will support a growing number of jobs in adult day care and outpatient programs offering short-term mental health and alcohol or drug abuse services. Rehabilitation, home health care, and transitional programs will provide additional jobs.

The rapidly growing number of older adults is expected to spur job growth for recreational therapy professionals and paraprofessionals in assisted-living facilities, adult day care programs, and other social assistance agencies. Continued growth also is expected in community residential care facilities, as well as in day care programs for individuals with disabilities.

Earnings

Median annual earnings of recreational therapists were $32,900 in May 2004. The middle 50 percent earned between $25,520 and $42,130. The lowest 10 percent earned less than $20,130, and the highest 10 percent earned more than $51,800. In May 2004, median annual earnings for recreational therapists were $28,130 in nursing care facilities.

Related Occupations

Recreational therapists primarily design activities to help people with disabilities lead more fulfilling and independent lives. Other workers who have similar jobs are occupational therapists, physical therapists, recreation workers, and rehabilitation counselors.

Sources of Additional Information

For information on how to order materials describing careers and academic programs in recreational therapy, contact

▸ American Therapeutic Recreation Association, 1414 Prince St., Suite 204, Alexandria, VA 22314-2853. Internet: http://www.atra-tr.org

▸ National Therapeutic Recreation Society, 22377 Belmont Ridge Rd., Ashburn, VA 20148-4501. Internet: http://www.nrpa.org/content/default.aspx?documentid=530

Information on certification may be obtained from

▸ National Council for Therapeutic Recreation Certification, 7 Elmwood Dr., New City, NY 10956. Internet: http://www.nctrc.org

Sales Engineers

(O*NET 41-9031.00)

Significant Points

▪ A bachelor's degree in engineering typically is required; many sales engineers have previous work experience in an engineering specialty.

▪ Projected employment growth stems from the increasing number and technical nature of products and services to be sold.

▪ More job opportunities are expected in independent sales agencies.

▪ Earnings are based on a combination of salary and commissions.

Nature of the Work

Many products and services, especially those purchased by large companies and institutions, are highly complex. *Sales engineers*—who also may be called *manufacturers' agents, sales representatives,* or *technical sales support workers*—work with the production, engineering, or research and development departments of their companies or with independent sales firms to determine how products and services could be designed or modified to suit customers' needs. They also may advise customers on how best to use the products or services provided.

Selling, of course, is an important part of the job. Sales engineers use their technical skills to demonstrate to potential customers how and why the products or services they are selling would suit the customer better than competitors' products. Often, there may not be a directly competitive product. In these cases, the job of the sales engineer is to demonstrate to the customer the usefulness of the product or service—for example, how much money new production machinery would save.

Most sales engineers have a bachelor's degree in engineering, and many have previous work experience in an engineering specialty. Engineers apply the theories and principles of science and mathematics to technical problems. Their work is the link between scientific discoveries and commercial applications. Many sales engineers specialize in an area related to an engineering specialty. For example, sales engineers selling chemical products may have chemical engineering backgrounds, while those selling business software or information systems may have degrees in computer engineering. Information on engineers, including 17 engineering specialties, appears elsewhere in this book.

Many of the duties of sales engineers are similar to those of other salespersons. They must interest the client in purchasing their products, many of which are durable manufactured products such as turbines. Sales engineers often are teamed with other salespersons who concentrate on the marketing and sales, enabling the sales engineer to concentrate on the technical aspects of the job. By working on a sales team, each member is able to focus on his or her strengths and knowledge.

Sales engineers tend to employ selling techniques that are different from those used by most other sales workers. They generally use a "consultative" style; that is, they focus on the client's problem and show how it could be solved or mitigated with their product or service. This selling style differs from the "benefits and features" method, whereby the salesperson describes the product and leaves the customer to decide how it would be useful.

In addition to maintaining current clients and attracting new ones, sales engineers help clients solve any problems that arise when the product is installed. Afterward, they may continue to serve as a liaison between the client and their company. Increasingly, sales engineers are asked to undertake tasks related to sales, such as market research, because of their familiarity with clients' purchasing needs. Drawing on this same familiarity, sales engineers may help identify and develop new products.

Sales engineers may work directly for manufacturers or service providers, or they may work in small independent sales firms. In an independent firm, they may sell complementary products from several different suppliers and be paid entirely on commission.

Working Conditions

Many sales engineers work more than 40 hours per week to meet sales goals and their clients' needs. Selling can be stressful because sales engineers' income and job security often directly depend on their success in sales and customer service.

Some sales engineers have large territories and travel extensively. Because sales regions may cover several states, sales engineers may be away from home for several days or even weeks at a time. Others work near their home base and travel mostly by car. International travel, to secure contracts with foreign clients, is becoming more common.

Although the hours may be long and often are irregular, many sales engineers have the freedom to determine their own schedule. Consequently, they often can arrange their appointments so that they can have time off when they want it. However, most independent sales engineers do not earn any income while on vacation.

Training, Other Qualifications, and Advancement

A bachelor's degree in engineering usually is required to become a sales engineer. However, some workers with previous experience in sales combined with technical experience or training sometimes hold the title of sales engineer. Also, workers who have a degree in a science, such as chemistry, or even a degree in business with little or no previous sales experience, may be termed sales engineers.

Admissions requirements for undergraduate engineering schools include a solid background in mathematics (algebra, geometry, trigonometry, and calculus) and the physical sciences (biology, chemistry, and physics), as well as basic courses in English, social studies, humanities, and computer science. University programs vary in content, though all require the development of computer skills. For example, some programs emphasize industrial practices, preparing students for a job in industry, whereas others are more theoretical and prepare students for graduate school. Therefore, students should investigate curriculums and check accreditations carefully before making a selection. Once a university has been selected, a student must choose an area of engineering in which to specialize. Some programs offer a general engineering curriculum; students then specialize on the job or in graduate school. Most engineering degrees are granted in electrical, mechanical, or civil engineering. However, engineers trained in one branch may work in related branches.

Many sales engineers first work as engineers. For some, the engineering experience is necessary to obtain the technical background needed to sell their employers' products or services effectively. Others move into the occupation because it offers better earnings and advancement potential or because they are looking for a new challenge.

New graduates with engineering degrees may need sales experience and training before they can work directly as sales engineers. Training may involve teaming with a sales mentor who is familiar with the employer's business practices, customers, procedures, and company culture. After the training period has been completed, sales engineers may continue to partner with someone who lacks technical skills, yet excels in the art of sales.

Promotion may include a higher commission rate, larger sales territory, or elevation to the position of supervisor or marketing manager. Alternatively, sales engineers may leave their companies and form independent firms that may offer higher commissions and more freedom. Independent firms tend to be small, although relatively few sales engineers are self-employed.

It is important for sales engineers to continue their engineering and sales education throughout their careers because much of their value to their employers depends on their knowledge of the latest technology and their ability to sell that technology. Sales engineers in high-technology areas, such as information technology or advanced electronics, may find that technical knowledge rapidly becomes obsolete.

Employment

Sales engineers held about 74,000 jobs in 2004. About 35 percent were employed in wholesale trade and another 27 percent were employed in the manufacturing industries. Smaller numbers of sales engineers worked in information industries, such as software publishers and telecommunications; professional, scientific, and technical services, such as computer systems designs and related services and architectural, engineering, and related services; and other industries. Unlike workers in many other sales occupations, very few sales engineers are self-employed.

Job Outlook

Employment of sales engineers is expected to grow about as fast as the average for all occupations through the year 2014. Projected employment growth stems from the increasing variety and technical nature of goods and services to be sold. Competitive pressures and advancing technology will force companies to improve and update product designs more frequently and to optimize their manufacturing and sales processes. In addition to new positions created as companies expand their sales forces, some openings will arise each year from the need to replace sales engineers who transfer to other occupations or leave the labor force.

Manufacturers, especially foreign manufacturers that sell their products in the United States, are expected to continue outsourcing more of their sales functions to independent sales agencies in an attempt to control costs. This should result in more job opportunities for sales engineers in independent agencies.

In wholesale trade, both outsourcing to independent sales agencies and the use of information technology are expected to affect employment opportunities for sales engineers. Although outsourcing should lead to more jobs in independent agencies, employment growth for sales engineers in wholesale trade likely will be dampened by the increasing ability of businesses to find, order, and track shipments directly from wholesalers through the Internet without assistance from sales engineers. Since direct purchases from wholesalers are more likely to be of commodity products, their impact on sales engineers should remain somewhat limited.

Employment opportunities and earnings may fluctuate from year to year because sales are affected by changing economic conditions, legislative issues, and consumer preferences. Prospects will be best for those with the appropriate knowledge or technical expertise, as well as the personal traits necessary for successful sales work.

Earnings

Compensation varies significantly by the type of firm and the product sold. Most employers offer a combination of salary and commission payments or a salary plus a bonus. Commissions usually are based on the amount of sales, whereas bonuses may depend on individual performance, on the performance of all workers in the group or district, or on the company's performance. Earnings from commissions and bonuses may vary greatly from year to year, depending on sales ability, the demand for the company's products or services, and the overall economy.

Median annual earnings of sales engineers, including commissions, were $70,620 in May 2004. The middle 50 percent earned between $53,270 and $91,500 a year. The lowest 10 percent earned less than $41,430, and the highest 10 percent earned more than $117,260 a year. Median annual earnings of those employed by firms in the computer systems design and related services industry were $86,980.

In addition to their earnings, sales engineers who work for manufacturers usually are reimbursed for expenses such as transportation, meals, hotels, and customer entertainment. In addition to typical benefits, sales engineers often get personal use of a company car and frequent-flyer mileage. Some companies offer incentives such as free vacation trips or gifts for outstanding performance. Sales engineers who work in independent firms may have higher but less stable earnings and, often, relatively few benefits.

Related Occupations

Sales engineers must have sales ability and knowledge of the products and services they sell, as well as technical and analytical skills. Other occupations that require similar skills include advertising, marketing, promotions, public relations, and sales managers, engineers; insurance sales agents; purchasing managers, buyers, and purchasing agents; real estate brokers and sales agents; sales representatives, wholesale and manufacturing; and securities, commodities, and financial services sales agents.

Sources of Additional Information

Information on careers for manufacturers' representatives and agents is available from

▸ Manufacturers' Agents National Association, P.O. Box 3467, Laguna Hills, CA 92654-3467. Internet: http://www.manaonline.org

▸ Manufacturers' Representatives Educational Research Foundation, P.O. Box 247, Geneva, IL 60134. Internet: http://www.mrerf.org

Securities, Commodities, and Financial Services Sales Agents

(O*NET 41-3031.01 and 41-3031.02)

Significant Points

■ A college degree, sales ability, good interpersonal and communication skills, and a strong desire to succeed are important qualifications.

■ Securities and commodities sales agents must pass licensing exams.

■ Competition for entry-level jobs usually is keen, especially in larger firms; opportunities should be better in smaller firms.

■ Turnover is high for beginning agents, who often are unable to establish a sizable clientele; once established, securities and commodities sales agents have a very strong attachment to their occupation because of their high earnings and considerable investment in training.

Nature of the Work

Most investors, whether they are individuals with a few hundred dollars to invest or large institutions with millions, use *securities, commodities, and financial services sales agents* when buying or selling stocks, bonds, shares in mutual funds, insurance annuities, or other financial products. In addition, many clients seek out these agents for advice on investments, insurance, tax planning, estate planning, and other financial matters.

Securities and commodities sales agents—also called *brokers, stockbrokers, registered representatives, account executives,* or *financial consultants*—perform a variety of tasks, depending on their specific job duties. When an investor wishes to buy or sell a security, for example, sales agents may relay the order through their firm's computers to the floor of a securities exchange, such as the New York Stock Exchange. There, securities and commodities sales agents known as *floor brokers* negotiate the price with other floor brokers, make the sale, and forward the purchase price to the sales agents. If a security is not traded on an exchange, as in the case of bonds and over-the-counter stocks, the broker sends the order to the firm's trading department. Here, using their own funds or those of the firm, other securities sales agents, known as *dealers*, buy and sell securities directly from other dealers with the intention of reselling the security to customers at a profit. After the transaction has been completed, the broker notifies the customer of the final price.

Securities and commodities sales agents also provide many related services for their customers. They may explain stock market terms and trading practices; offer financial counseling or advice on the purchase or sale of particular securities; and design an individual client's financial portfolio, which could include securities, life insurance, corporate and municipal bonds, mutual funds, certificates of deposit, annuities, and other investments.

Not all customers have the same investment goals. Some individuals prefer long-term investments for capital growth or to provide income over a number of years; others might want to invest in speculative securities, which they hope will quickly rise in price. On the basis of each customer's objectives, securities and commodities sales agents furnish information about the advantages and disadvantages of an investment. They also supply the latest price quotes on any securities, as well as information on the activities and financial positions of the corporations issuing the securities.

Most securities and commodities sales agents serve individual investors; others specialize in institutional investors, such as banks and pension funds. In institutional investing, sales agents usually concentrate on a specific financial product, such as stocks, bonds, options, annuities, or commodity futures. At other times, they may also handle the sale of new issues, such as corporate securities issued to finance the expansion of a plant.

The most important part of a sales representative's job is finding clients and building a customer base. Thus, beginning securities and commodities sales agents spend much of their time searching for customers—relying heavily on telephone solicitation. They also may meet clients through business and social contacts. Agents often join civic organizations and other social organizations to expand their networks. Many sales agents find it useful to contact potential clients by teaching adult education investment courses or by giving lectures at libraries or social clubs. Brokerage firms may give sales agents lists of people with whom the firm has done business in the past. Some agents inherit the clients of agents who have retired. After an agent is established, referrals from satisfied clients are an important source of new business.

Financial services sales agents sell a wide variety of banking and related services. They contact potential customers to explain their services and to ascertain customers' banking and other financial needs. In doing so, they discuss services such as loans, deposit accounts, lines of credit, sales or inventory financing, certificates of deposit, cash management, mutual funds, or investment services. They also may solicit businesses to participate in consumer credit card programs. Financial services sales agents who serve all the financial needs of a single affluent individual or a business often are called private bankers or relationship managers.

With deregulation of the financial services industry, the distinctions among sales agents are becoming less clear as securities firms, banks, and insurance companies venture further into each other's products and services. The agents' jobs also are becoming more important as competition between the firms intensifies.

Working Conditions

Most securities and commodities sales agents work in offices under fairly stressful conditions. They have access to "quote boards" or computer terminals that continually provide information on the prices of securities. When sales activity increases, due perhaps to unanticipated changes in the economy, the pace can become very hectic.

Established securities and commodities sales agents usually work a standard 40-hour week. Beginners who are seeking customers usually work longer hours. New brokers spend a great deal of time learning the firm's products and services and studying for exams in order to qualify to sell other products, such as insurance and commodities. Most securities and commodities sales agents accommodate customers by meeting with them in the evenings or on weekends.

A growing number of securities sales agents, employed mostly by discount or online brokerage firms, work in call-center environments. In these centers, hundreds of agents spend much of the day on the telephone taking orders from clients or offering advice and information on different securities. Often, such call centers operate 24 hours a day, requiring agents to work in shifts.

Financial services sales agents normally work 40 hours a week in a comfortable, less stressful office environment. They may spend considerable time outside the office, meeting with current and prospective clients, attending civic functions, and participating in trade association meetings. Some financial services sales agents work exclusively inside banks, providing service to walk-in customers.

Training, Other Qualifications, and Advancement

Because securities and commodities sales agents must be knowledgeable about economic conditions and trends, a college education is important, especially in larger securities firms. In fact, the overwhelming majority of workers in this occupation are college graduates. Although employers seldom require specialized academic training, courses in business administration, economics, and finance are helpful.

Many employers consider personal qualities and skills more important than academic training. Employers seek applicants who have considerable sales ability, good interpersonal and communication skills, and a strong desire to succeed. Some employers also make sure that applicants have a good credit history and a clean record. Self-confidence and an ability to handle frequent rejections are important ingredients for success.

Because maturity and the ability to work independently are important, many employers prefer to hire those who have achieved success in other jobs. Most firms prefer candidates with sales experience, particularly those who have worked on commission in areas such as real estate or insurance. Therefore, most entrants to this occupation transfer from other jobs. Some begin working as securities and commodities sales agents following retirement from other fields.

Securities and commodities sales agents must meet state licensing requirements, which usually include passing an examination and, in some cases, furnishing a personal bond. In addition, sales agents must register as representatives of their firm with the National Association of Securities Dealers, Inc. (NASD). Before beginners can qualify as registered representatives, they must pass the General Securities Registered Representative Examination (Series 7 exam), administered by the NASD, and be an employee of a registered firm for at least 4 months.

Most states require a second examination—the Uniform Securities Agents State Law Examination. This test measures the prospective representative's knowledge of the securities business in general, customer protection requirements, and recordkeeping procedures. Many take correspondence courses in preparation for the securities examinations. Within 2 years, brokers are encouraged to take additional licensing exams in order to sell mutual funds, insurance, and commodities.

Most employers provide on-the-job training to help securities and commodities sales agents meet the registration requirements for certification. In most firms, the training period takes about 4 months. Trainees in large firms may receive classroom instruction in securities analysis, effective speaking, and the finer points of selling; may take courses offered by business schools and associations; and may undergo a period of on-the-job training lasting up to 2 years. Many firms like to rotate their trainees among various departments to give them a broad perspective of the securities business. In small firms, sales agents often receive training in outside institutions and on the job.

Securities and commodities sales agents must understand the basic characteristics of the wide variety of financial products offered by brokerage firms. Brokers periodically take training through their firms or outside institutions in order to keep abreast of new financial products and to improve their sales techniques. Computer training also is important because the securities sales business is highly automated. It is mandatory for all registered securities and commodities sales agents to attend periodic continuing education classes to maintain their licenses. Courses consist of computer-based training in regulatory matters and company training on new products and services. In addition, more sales agents are taking courses to become certified financial planners. The Certified Financial Planner credential, issued by the Certified Financial Planner Board of Standards, requires relevant experience, completion of education requirements, passing a comprehensive examination, and adherence to an enforceable code of ethics. The CFP exams test the candidate's knowledge of the financial planning process, insurance and risk management, employee benefits planning, taxes and retirement planning, and investment and estate planning.

The principal form of advancement for securities and commodities sales agents is an increase in the number and size of the accounts they handle. Although beginners usually service the accounts of individual investors, they may eventually handle very large institutional accounts, such as those of banks and pension funds. After taking a series of tests, some brokers become portfolio managers and have greater authority to make investment decisions regarding an account. Some experienced sales agents become branch office managers and supervise other sales agents while continuing to provide services for their own customers. A few agents advance to top management positions or become partners in their firms.

Banks and other credit institutions prefer to hire college graduates for financial services sales jobs. A business administration degree with a specialization in finance or a liberal arts degree that includes courses in accounting, economics, and marketing serves as excellent preparation for this job. Often, financial services sales agents learn their jobs through on-the-job training under the supervision of bank officers. However, those who wish to sell mutual funds and insurance products may need to undergo formal training and pass some of the same exams required of securities sales agents.

Employment

Securities, commodities, and financial services sales agents held about 281,000 jobs in 2004. More than half of jobs were found in securities, commodity contracts, and other financial investments and related activities. One in 5 worked in depository and nondepository credit intermediation, including commercial banks, savings institutions, and credit unions. Although securities and commodities sales agents are employed by firms in all parts of the country, many work for a small number of large securities and investment banking firms headquartered in New York City. About 1 out of 8 securities, commodities, and financial services sales agents were self-employed.

Job Outlook

Employment of securities, commodities, and financial services sales agents is expected to grow about as fast as average for all occupations through 2014. As people's incomes continue to climb, they will increasingly seek the advice and services of securities, commodities, and financial services sales agents to realize their financial goals. Growth in the volume of stocks traded over the Internet will limit job growth. Nevertheless, the overall increase in investment is expected to spur employment growth among these workers, with a majority of transactions still requiring the advice and services of securities, commodities, and financial services sales agents.

Baby boomers in their peak savings years will fuel much of this increase in investment. Saving for retirement has been made much easier by the government, which continues to offer a number of tax-favorable pension plans, such as the 401(k) and the Roth IRA. The

participation of more women in the workforce also means higher household incomes and more women qualifying for pensions. Many of these pensions are self-directed, meaning that the recipient has the responsibility for investing the money. With such large amounts of money to invest, sales agents, in their role as financial advisors, will be in great demand.

Other factors that will affect the demand for brokers are the increasing number and complexity of investment products as well as the effects of globalization. As the public and businesses become more sophisticated about investing, they are venturing into the options and futures markets. Brokers are needed to buy or sell these products, which are not traded online. Also, markets for investment are expanding with the increase in global trading of stocks and bonds. Furthermore, the New York Stock Exchange has extended its trading hours to accommodate trading in foreign stocks and compete with foreign exchanges.

Employment of sales agents is adversely affected by downturns in the stock market or the economy. Turnover is high for beginning agents, who often are unable to establish a sizable clientele even in good times. Once established, securities and commodities sales agents have a very strong attachment to their occupation because of their high earnings and considerable investment in training. Competition usually is keen, especially in larger companies with more applicants than jobs. Opportunities for beginning sales agents should be better in smaller firms.

Employment of financial services sales agents in banks will increase as banks expand their product offerings in order to compete directly with other investment firms.

Earnings

Median annual earnings of securities, commodities, and financial services sales agents were $69,200 in May 2004. The middle half earned between $40,750 and $131,290.

Median annual earnings in the industries employing the largest numbers of securities, commodities, and financial services sales agents in 2004 were

Other financial investment activities	$94,670
Securities and commodity contracts intermediation and brokerage	85,350
Management of companies and enterprises	67,690
Nondepository credit intermediation	51,820
Depository credit intermediation	44,670

Stockbrokers, who provide personalized service and more guidance with respect to a client's investments, usually are paid a commission based on the amount of stocks, bonds, mutual funds, insurance, and other products they sell. Earnings from commissions are likely to be high when there is much buying and selling and low when there is a slump in market activity. Most firms provide sales agents with a steady income by paying a "draw against commission"—a minimum salary based on commissions they can be expected to earn. Securities and commodities sales agents who can provide their clients with the most thorough financial services should enjoy the greatest income stability. Trainee brokers usually are paid a salary until they develop a client base. The salary gradually decreases in favor of commissions as the broker gains clients. A small, but increasing, number of full-service brokers are paid a percentage of the assets they oversee. This fee often covers a certain number of trades done for free.

Brokers who work for discount brokerage firms that promote the use of telephone and online trading services usually are paid a salary, sometimes boosted by bonuses that reflect the profitability of the office. Financial services sales agents usually are paid a salary also; however, bonuses or commissions from sales are starting to account for a larger share of their income.

Related Occupations

Other jobs requiring knowledge of finance and an ability to sell include insurance sales agents, real estate brokers and sales agents, and financial analysts and personal financial advisors.

Sources of Additional Information

For general information on the securities industry, contact

▸ Securities Industry Association, 120 Broadway, New York, NY 10271.

For information about job opportunities for financial services sales agents in various states, contact state bankers' associations or write directly to a particular bank.

Tax Examiners, Collectors, and Revenue Agents

(O*NET 13-2081.00)

Significant Points

■ Tax examiners, collectors, and revenue agents work for federal, state, and local governments.

■ A bachelor's degree in accounting is becoming the standard source of training; in state and local government, less formal education or work experience may be sufficient.

■ Employment is expected to grow more slowly than average.

■ Because of the relatively small number of openings, jobseekers can expect to face competition; workers with knowledge of tax laws and experience working with complex tax issues will have the best opportunities.

Nature of the Work

Taxes are one of the certainties of life, and as long as governments collect taxes, there will be jobs for tax examiners, collectors, and revenue agents. By reviewing tax returns, conducting audits, identifying taxes payable, and collecting overdue tax dollars, these workers ensure that governments obtain revenues from businesses and citizens.

Tax examiners do similar work whether they are employed at the federal, state, or local government level. They review filed tax returns for accuracy and determine whether tax credits and deductions are allowed by law. Because many states assess individual income taxes

based on the taxpayer's reported federal adjusted gross income, tax examiners working for the federal government report any adjustments or corrections they make to the states. State tax examiners then determine whether the adjustments affect the taxpayer's state tax liability. At the local level, tax examiners often have additional duties, but an integral part of the work still includes the need to determine the factual basis for claims for refunds.

Tax examiners usually deal with the simplest tax returns—those filed by individual taxpayers with few deductions or those filed by small businesses. At the entry level, many tax examiners perform clerical duties, such as reviewing tax returns and entering them into a computer system for processing. If there is a problem, tax examiners may contact the taxpayer to resolve it.

Tax examiners also review returns for accuracy, checking taxpayers' math and making sure that the amounts that they report match those reported from other sources, such as employers and banks. In addition, examiners verify that Social Security numbers match names and that taxpayers have correctly interpreted the instructions on tax forms.

Much of a tax examiner's job involves making sure that tax credits and deductions claimed by taxpayers are legitimate. Tax examiners contact taxpayers by mail or telephone to address discrepancies and request supporting documentation. They may notify taxpayers of any overpayment or underpayment and either issue a refund or request further payment. If a taxpayer owes additional taxes, tax examiners adjust the total amount by assessing fees, interest, and penalties and notify the taxpayer of the total liability. Although most tax examiners deal with uncomplicated returns, some may work in more complex tax areas, such as pensions or business net operating losses.

Revenue agents specialize in tax-related accounting work for the U.S. Internal Revenue Service (IRS) and for equivalent agencies in state and local governments. Like tax examiners, they audit returns for accuracy. However, revenue agents handle complicated income, sales, and excise tax returns of businesses and large corporations. As a result, their work differs in a number of ways from that of tax examiners.

Entry-level federal revenue agents usually audit tax returns of small businesses whose market specializations are similar. As they develop expertise in an industry, such as construction; retail sales; or finance, insurance, and real estate, revenue agents work with tax returns of larger corporations.

Many experienced revenue agents specialize; for example, they may focus exclusively on multinational businesses. But all revenue agents working for the federal government must keep abreast of the lengthy, complex, and frequently changing tax code. Computer technology has simplified the research process, allowing revenue agents Internet access to relevant legal bulletins, IRS notices, and tax-related court decisions. Revenue agents are increasingly using computers to analyze data and identify trends that help to pinpoint tax offenders.

At the state level, revenue agents have duties similar to those of their counterparts in the federal government. State revenue agents use revenue adjustment reports forwarded by the IRS to determine whether adjustments made by federal revenue agents affect a taxpayer's taxable income in the eyes of the states. In addition, state agents consider the sales and income taxes for their own states.

At the local level, revenue agents have varying titles and duties, but they still perform field audits or office audits of financial records for business firms. In some cases, local revenue agents also examine financial records of individuals. These local agents, like their state counterparts, rely on the information contained in federal tax returns. However, local agents also must be knowledgeable enough to apply local tax laws regarding income, utility fees, or school taxes.

Collectors, also called *revenue officers* in the IRS, deal with delinquent accounts. The process of collecting a delinquent account starts with the revenue agent or tax examiner sending a report to the taxpayer. If the taxpayer makes no effort to resolve the delinquent account, the case is assigned to a collector. When a collector takes a case, he or she first sends the taxpayer a notice. The collector then works with the taxpayer on how to settle the debt.

In cases in which taxpayers fail to file a tax return, federal collectors may request that the IRS prepare the return on a taxpayer's behalf. In other instances, collectors are responsible for verifying claims that delinquent taxpayers cannot pay their taxes. They investigate these claims by researching court information on the status of liens, mortgages, or financial statements; locating assets through third parties, such as neighbors or local departments of motor vehicles; and requesting legal summonses for other records. Ultimately, collectors must decide whether the IRS should take a lien—a claim on an asset such as a bank account, real estate, or an automobile—to settle a debt. Collectors also have the discretion to garnish wages—that is, take a portion of earned wages—to collect taxes owed.

A big part of a collector's job at the federal level is imposing and following up on delinquent taxpayers' payment deadlines. For each case file, collectors must maintain records, including contacts, telephone numbers, and actions taken.

Like tax examiners and revenue agents, collectors use computers to maintain files. Computer technology also gives collectors access to data to help them identify high-risk debtors—those who are unlikely to pay or are likely to flee.

Collectors at the IRS usually work independently. However, they call on experts when tax examiners or revenue agents find fraudulent returns or when the seizure of a property will involve complex legal steps.

At the state level, collectors decide whether to take action on the basis of their own states' tax returns. Collection work may be handled over the telephone or turned over to a collector who specializes in obtaining settlements. These collectors contact people directly and have the authority to issue subpoenas and request seizures of property. At the local levels, collectors have less power than their state and federal counterparts. Although they can start the processes leading to the seizure of property and garnishment of wages, they must go through the local court system.

Working Conditions

Tax examiners, collectors, and revenue agents generally work a 40-hour week, although some overtime might be needed during the tax season. State and local tax examiners, who may review sales, gasoline, and cigarette taxes instead of handling tax returns, may have a steadier workload year-round. Stress can result from the need to work under a deadline in checking returns and evaluating taxpayer claims. Collectors also must face the unpleasant task of confronting delinquent taxpayers.

Tax examiners, collectors, and revenue agents work in clean, well-lighted offices, either in cubicles or at desks. Sometimes travel is necessary. Revenue agents at both the federal and state levels spend a significant portion of their time in the offices of private firms, accessing tax-related records. Some agents may be permanently stationed in the offices of large corporations with complicated tax structures. Agents at the local level usually work in city halls or municipal buildings. Collectors travel to local courthouses, county and municipal seats of government, businesses, and taxpayers' homes to look up records, search for assets, and settle delinquent accounts.

Training, Other Qualifications, and Advancement

Tax examiners, collectors, and revenue agents work with confidential financial and personal information; therefore, trustworthiness is crucial for maintaining the confidentiality of individuals and businesses. Applicants for federal government jobs must submit to a background investigation.

A degree in accounting is becoming the standard source of training for tax examiners, collectors, and revenue agents. A bachelor's degree generally is required for employment with the federal government. In state and local governments, prospective workers may be able to enter the occupation with an associate's degree in accounting or with a combination of related tax and accounting work experience and some college-level business classes. For more advanced entry-level positions, applicants must have a bachelor's degree; demonstrate specialized experience working with tax records, tax laws and regulations, documents, financial accounts, or similar records; or have some combination of postsecondary education and specialized experience.

Tax examiners must be able to understand fundamental tax regulations and procedures, pay attention to detail, and cope well with deadlines. After they are hired, tax examiners receive some formal training. In addition, annual employer-provided updates keep tax examiners current with changes in procedures and regulations.

Revenue agents need strong analytical, organizational, and time management skills. They also must be able to work independently, because they spend so much time away from their home office, and they must keep current with changes in the tax code and laws. Newly hired revenue agents expand their accounting knowledge and remain up to date by consulting auditing manuals and other sources for detailed information about individual industries. Employers also continually offer training in new auditing techniques and tax-related issues and court decisions.

Collectors need good interpersonal and communication skills because they deal directly with the public and because their reports are scrutinized when the IRS must legally justify attempts to seize assets. They also must be able to act independently and to exercise good judgment in deciding when and how to collect a debt.

Applicants for collector jobs need experience demonstrating knowledge of business and financial practices or knowledge of credit operations and collection of delinquent accounts.

Entry-level collectors receive formal and on-the-job training under an instructor's guidance before working independently. Collectors usually complete initial training by the end of their second year of service, but may receive advanced technical instruction as they gain seniority and take on more difficult cases. Also, collectors are encouraged to continue their professional education by attending meetings to exchange information about how changes in tax laws affect collection methods.

Advancement potential within federal, state, and local agencies varies for tax examiners, revenue agents, and collectors. For related jobs outside government, experienced workers can take a licensing exam administered by the federal government to become enrolled agents—nongovernment tax professionals authorized to represent taxpayers before the IRS.

As revenue agents gain experience, they may specialize in an industry, work with larger corporations, and cover increasingly complex tax returns. Some revenue agents also specialize in assisting in criminal investigations, auditing the books of known or suspected criminals such as drug dealers or money launderers. Some agents work with grand juries to help secure indictments. Others become international agents, assessing taxes on companies with subsidiaries abroad.

Collectors who demonstrate leadership skills and a thorough knowledge of collection activities may advance to supervisory or managerial collector positions in which they oversee the activities of other collectors. It is only these higher-level supervisors and managers who may authorize the more serious actions against individuals and businesses. The more complex collection attempts, which usually are directed at larger businesses, are reserved for collectors at these higher levels.

Employment

In 2004, tax examiners, revenue agents, and collectors held about 76,000 jobs at all levels of government. About half worked for the federal government, 3 out of 10 for state governments, and the remainder in local governments. Among those employed by the IRS, tax examiners and revenue agents predominate because of the need to examine or audit tax returns. Collectors make up a smaller proportion because most disputed tax liabilities do not require enforced collection.

Job Outlook

Employment of tax examiners, collectors, and revenue agents is projected to grow more slowly than the average for all occupations during the 2004–2014 projection period. Because of the relatively small number of openings, jobseekers can expect to face competition.

Demand for tax examiners, revenue agents, and tax collectors will stem from changes in government policy toward tax enforcement and from growth in the number of businesses. The federal government is expected to increase its tax enforcement efforts. Also, new technology and information sharing among tax agencies make it easier for agencies to pinpoint potential offenders, increasing the

number of cases for audit and collection. These two factors should increase the demand for revenue agents and tax collectors. The IRS plans to streamline its tax examination and collections process, and both state and federal tax agencies are turning their enforcement focus to higher-income taxpayers and businesses, which file more complicated tax returns. Because of these shifts, workers with knowledge of tax laws and experience working with complex tax issues will have the best opportunities.

Several factors may limit the growth of these occupations. Because much of the simpler work done by tax examiners, collectors, and revenue agents is now computerized, productivity has increased, limiting the need for more workers. The work of tax examiners is especially well suited to automation, adversely affecting demand for these workers in particular. In addition, more than 40 states and many local tax agencies contract out their tax collection functions to private-sector collection agencies in order to reduce costs, and this trend is likely to continue. In 2005, the IRS received Congressional approval to begin outsourcing tax collection. IRS outsourcing will dampen growth in employment of revenue officers but is not expected to affect employment of revenue agents.

Employment at the state and local levels may fluctuate with the overall state of the economy. When the economy is contracting, state and local governments are likely to freeze hiring and lay off workers in response to budgetary constraints. Opportunities at the federal level will reflect the tightening or relaxation of budget constraints imposed on the IRS, the primary employer of these workers.

Earnings

In May 2004, median annual earnings for all tax examiners, collectors, and revenue agents were $43,490. The middle 50 percent earned between $32,520 and $62,570. The bottom 10 percent earned less than $25,120, and the top 10 percent earned more than $81,240.

However, median earnings vary considerably, depending on the level of government. At the federal level, May 2004 median annual earnings for tax examiners were $52,830; at the state level, they were $41,920; and at the local level, they were $31,310. Earnings also vary by occupational specialty. For example, in the federal government in 2005, tax examiners earned an average of $36,963, revenue agents earned $81,417, and tax specialists earned $54,364.

Related Occupations

Tax examiners, collectors, and revenue agents analyze and interpret financial data. Occupations with similar responsibilities include accountants and auditors, budget analysts, cost estimators, financial analysts and personal financial advisors, financial managers, and loan officers.

Sources of Additional Information

Information on obtaining positions as tax examiners, collectors, or revenue agents with the federal government is available from the Office of Personnel Management through USAJOBS, the federal government's official employment information system. This resource for locating and applying for job opportunities can be accessed through the Internet at http://www.usajobs.opm.gov or through an interactive voice response telephone system at

(703) 724-1850 or TDD (978) 461-8404. These numbers are not toll free, and charges may result.

State or local government personnel offices can provide information about tax examiner, collector, or revenue agent jobs at those levels of government.

For information about careers at the Internal Revenue Service, contact

▸ Internal Revenue Service, 1111 Constitution Ave. NW, Washington, DC 20224. Internet: http://www.jobs.irs.gov/index.html

Teachers—Adult Literacy and Remedial Education

(O*NET 25-3011.00)

Significant Points

■ Many adult literacy and remedial education teachers work part time and receive no benefits; unpaid volunteers also teach these subjects.

■ Most programs require teachers to have at least a bachelor's degree; a public school teaching license is required for public programs in some states.

■ Opportunities for teachers of English as a second language are expected to be very good because their classes should be in demand by the increasing number of residents with limited English skills.

Nature of the Work

Adult literacy and remedial education teachers instruct adults and out-of-school youths in reading, writing, speaking English, and performing elementary mathematical calculations—basic skills that equip them to solve problems well enough to become active participants in our society, to hold a job, and to further their education. The instruction provided by these teachers can be divided into three principle categories: *Remedial or adult basic education (ABE)* is geared toward adults whose skills are either at or below an eighth-grade level; *adult secondary education (ASE)* is geared towards students who wish to obtain their General Educational Development (GED) certificate or other high school equivalency credential; and *English literacy* instruction is for adults with limited proficiency in English. Traditionally, the students in these adult education classes have been primarily those who did not graduate high school or who passed through school without acquiring the knowledge needed to meet their educational goals or to participate fully in today's high-skill society. Increasingly, however, students in these classes are immigrants or other people whose native language is not English. Educators who work with adult English-language learners are usually called *teachers of English as a second language (ESL)* or *teachers of English to speakers of other languages (ESOL)*.

Remedial education teachers, more commonly called adult basic education teachers, teach basic academic courses in mathematics, languages, history, reading, writing, science, and other areas, using instructional methods geared toward adult learning. They teach these subjects to students 16 years of age and older who demonstrate the need to increase their skills in one or more of the subject areas mentioned. Classes are taught to appeal to a variety of learning styles and usually include large-group, small-group, and one-on-one instruction. Because the students often are at different proficiency levels for different subjects, adult basic education teachers must make individual assessments of each student's abilities beforehand. In many programs, the assessment is used to develop an individualized education plan for each student. Teachers are required to evaluate students periodically to determine their progress and potential for advancement to the next level.

Teachers in remedial or adult basic education may have to assist students in acquiring effective study skills and the self-confidence they need to reenter an academic environment. Teachers also may encounter students with a learning or physical disability that requires additional expertise. Teachers should possess an understanding of how to help these students achieve their goals, but they also may need to have the knowledge to detect challenges their students may have and provide them with access to a broader system of additional services that are required to address their challenges.

For students who wish to get a GED credential in order to get a job or qualify for postsecondary education, adult secondary education, or GED, teachers provide help in acquiring the necessary knowledge and skills to pass the test. The GED tests students in subject areas such as reading, writing, mathematics, science, and social studies while at the same time measuring students' communication, information-processing, problem-solving, and critical-thinking skills. The emphasis in class is on acquiring the knowledge needed to pass the GED test, as well as preparing students for success in further educational endeavors.

ESOL teachers help adults to speak, listen, read, and write in English, often in the context of real-life situations to promote learning. More-advanced students may concentrate on writing and conversational skills or focus on learning more academic or job-related communication skills. ESOL teachers teach adults who possess a wide range of cultures and abilities and who speak a variety of languages. Some of their students have a college degree and many advance quickly through the program owing to a variety of factors, such as their age, previous language experience, educational background, and native language. Others may need additional time due to these same factors. Because the teacher and students often do not share a common language, creativity is an important part of fostering communication in the classroom and achieving learning goals.

All adult literacy and remedial teachers must prepare lessons beforehand, do any related paperwork, and stay current in their fields. Attendance for students is mostly voluntary and course work is rarely graded. Many teachers also must learn the latest uses for computers in the classroom, as computers are increasingly being used to supplement instruction in basic skills and in teaching ESOL.

Working Conditions

A large number of adult literacy and remedial education teachers work part time. Some have several part-time teaching assignments or work full time in addition to their part-time teaching job. Classes for adults are held on days and at times that best accommodate students who may have a job or family responsibilities.

Because many of these teachers work with adult students, they do not encounter some of the behavioral or social problems sometimes found with younger students. Adults attend by choice, are highly motivated, and bring years of experience to the classroom—attributes that can make teaching these students rewarding and satisfying. However, many adult education programs are located in cramped facilities that lack modern amenities, which can be frustrating for teachers.

Training, Other Qualifications, and Advancement

Requirements for teaching adult literacy and basic and secondary education vary by state and by program. Programs that are run by state and local governments require high accountability to student achievement standards. Most states require teachers in these programs to have some form of credential; the most common are a public school teacher license, an adult education credential, or both. However, programs in states that do not have these requirements still generally require that adult education teachers have at least a bachelor's degree and, preferably, a master's degree. Teaching experience, especially with adults, also is preferred or required. Those programs run by private religious, community, or volunteer organizations generally develop standards based on their own needs and organizational goals, but generally also require paid teachers to have at least a bachelor's degree. Volunteers usually do not need a bachelor's degree, but often must attend a training program before they are allowed to work with students.

Most programs recommend that adult literacy and basic and secondary education teachers take classes or workshops on teaching adults, using technology to teach, working with learners from a variety of cultures, and teaching adults with learning disabilities. ESOL teachers also should have courses or training in second-language acquisition theory and linguistics. In addition, knowledge of the citizenship and naturalization process may be useful. Knowledge of a second language is not necessary to teach ESOL students, but can be helpful in understanding the students' perspectives. GED teachers should know what is required to pass the GED and be able to instruct students in the subject matter. Training for literacy volunteers usually consists of instruction in effective teaching practices, needs assessment, lesson planning, the selection of appropriate instructional materials, characteristics of adult learners, and cross-cultural awareness.

Adult education and literacy teachers must have the ability to work with students who come from a variety of cultural, educational, and economic backgrounds. They must be understanding and respectful of their students' circumstances and be familiar with their concerns. All teachers, both paid and volunteer, should be able to communicate well and motivate their students.

Professional development among adult education and literacy teachers varies widely. Both part-time and full-time teachers are expected to participate in ongoing professional development activities in order to keep current on new developments in the field and to enhance skills already acquired. Each state's professional development system reflects the unique needs and organizational structure

of that state. Attendance by teachers at professional development workshops and other activities is often outlined in state or local policy. Some teachers are able to access professional development activities through alternative delivery systems such as the Internet or distance learning.

Opportunities for advancement for adult education and literacy teachers again vary from state to state and program to program. Some part-time teachers are able to move into full-time teaching positions or program administrator positions, such as coordinator or director, when such vacancies occur. Others may decide to use their classroom experience to move into policy work at a nonprofit organization or with the local, state, or federal government or to perform research.

Employment

Teachers of adult literacy and remedial education held about 98,000 jobs in 2004. About 1 in 3 were self-employed. Many additional teachers worked as unpaid volunteers. Many of the jobs are federally funded, with additional funds coming from state and local governments. State and local governments employ the majority of these teachers, who work in adult learning centers, libraries, community colleges, juvenile detention centers, and corrections institutions, among other places. Others work for private educational institutions and for social service organizations, such as job-training or residential care facilities.

Job Outlook

Opportunities for jobs as adult literacy and remedial education teachers are expected to be favorable. Employment is expected to grow as fast as the average for all occupations through 2014, and a large number of job openings is expected due to the need to replace people who leave the occupation or retire.

As employers increasingly require a more literate workforce, workers' demand for adult literacy, basic education, and secondary education classes is expected to grow. Significant employment growth is anticipated especially for ESOL teachers, who will be needed by the increasing number of immigrants and other residents living in this country that need to learn or improve their English skills. In addition, greater proportions of these groups are expected to take ESOL classes. Demand for ESOL teachers will be greatest in states that have large populations of residents who have limited English skills—such as California, Florida, Texas, and New York. However, many other parts of the nation have begun to attract large numbers of immigrants, making good opportunities in this field widely available.

The demand for adult literacy and basic and secondary education often fluctuates with the economy. When the economy is good and workers are hard to find, employers relax their standards and hire workers without a degree or GED or good proficiency in English. As the economy softens, employers can be more selective, and more students may find that they need additional education to get a job. In addition, adult education classes often are subject to changes in funding levels, which can cause the number of teaching jobs to fluctuate from year to year. In particular, budget pressures may limit federal funding of adult education, which may cause programs to rely more on volunteers if other organizations and governments do not make up the difference. Other factors such as immigration policies and the relative prosperity of the United States compared with other countries also may have an impact on the number of immigrants entering this country and, consequently, on the demand for ESOL teachers.

Earnings

Median hourly earnings of adult literacy and remedial education teachers were $18.74 in May 2004. The middle 50 percent earned between $14.07 and $25.49. The lowest 10 percent earned less than $10.57, and the highest 10 percent earned more than $34.94. Part-time adult literacy and remedial education instructors are usually paid by the hour or for each class that they teach, and they receive few or no benefits. Full-time teachers are generally paid a salary and receive health insurance and other benefits if they work for a school system or government.

Related Occupations

The work of adult literacy and remedial education teachers is closely related to that of other types of teachers, especially preschool, kindergarten, elementary school, middle school, and secondary school teachers. In addition, adult literacy and basic and secondary education teachers require a wide variety of skills and aptitudes. Not only must they be able to teach and motivate students (including, at times, those with learning disabilities), but they also must often take on roles as advisers and mentors. Workers in other occupations that require these aptitudes include special-education teachers, counselors, and social workers.

Sources of Additional Information

Information on adult literacy, basic and secondary education programs, and teacher certification requirements is available from state departments of education, local school districts, and literacy resource centers. Information also may be obtained through local religious and charitable organizations.

For information on adult education and family literacy programs, contact

▶ The U.S. Department of Education, Office of Vocational and Adult Education, Potomac Center Plaza, 400 Maryland Ave. SW, Washington, DC 20202. Internet: http://www.ed.gov/about/offices/list/ovae/index.html

For information on teaching English as a second language, contact

▶ The Center for Adult English Language Acquisition, 4646 40th St. NW, Washington, DC 20016. Internet: http://www.cal.org/caela

Teachers—Preschool, Kindergarten, Elementary, Middle, and Secondary

(O*NET 25-2011.00, 25-2012.00, 25-2021.00, 25-2022.00, 25-2023.00, 25-2031.00, and 25-2032.00)

Significant Points

■ Public school teachers must have at least a bachelor's degree, complete an approved teacher education program, and be licensed.

■ Many states offer alternative licensing programs to attract people into teaching, especially for hard-to-fill positions.

■ Excellent job opportunities are expected as retirements, especially among secondary school teachers, outweigh slowing enrollment growth; opportunities will vary by geographic area and subject taught.

Nature of the Work

Teachers act as facilitators or coaches, using interactive discussions and "hands-on" approaches to help students learn and apply concepts in subjects such as science, mathematics, or English. They utilize "props" or "manipulatives" to help children understand abstract concepts, solve problems, and develop critical thought processes. For example, they teach the concepts of numbers or of addition and subtraction by playing board games. As the children get older, the teachers use more sophisticated materials, such as science apparatus, cameras, or computers.

To encourage collaboration in solving problems, students are increasingly working in groups to discuss and solve problems together. Preparing students for the future workforce is a major stimulus generating changes in education. To be prepared, students must be able to interact with others, adapt to new technology, and think through problems logically. Teachers provide the tools and the environment for their students to develop these skills.

Preschool, kindergarten, and elementary school teachers play a vital role in the development of children. What children learn and experience during their early years can shape their views of themselves and the world and can affect their later success or failure in school, work, and their personal lives. Preschool, kindergarten, and elementary school teachers introduce children to mathematics, language, science, and social studies. They use games, music, artwork, films, books, computers, and other tools to teach basic skills.

Preschool children learn mainly through play and interactive activities. *Preschool teachers* capitalize on children's play to further language and vocabulary development (using storytelling, rhyming games, and acting games), improve social skills (having the children work together to build a neighborhood in a sandbox), and introduce scientific and mathematical concepts (showing the children how to balance and count blocks when building a bridge or how to mix colors when painting). Thus, a less-structured approach, including small-group lessons; one-on-one instruction; and learning through creative activities such as art, dance, and music, is adopted to teach preschool children. Play and hands-on teaching also are used by *kindergarten teachers*, but academics begin to take priority in kindergarten classrooms. Letter recognition, phonics, numbers, and awareness of nature and science, introduced at the preschool level, are taught primarily in kindergarten.

Most *elementary school teachers* instruct one class of children in several subjects. In some schools, two or more teachers work as a team and are jointly responsible for a group of students in at least one subject. In other schools, a teacher may teach one special subject—usually music, art, reading, science, arithmetic, or physical education—to a number of classes. A small but growing number of teachers instruct multilevel classrooms, with students at several different learning levels.

Middle school teachers and *secondary school teachers* help students delve more deeply into subjects introduced in elementary school and expose them to more information about the world. Middle and secondary school teachers specialize in a specific subject, such as English, Spanish, mathematics, history, or biology. They also can teach subjects that are career oriented. *Vocational education teachers*, also referred to as career and technical or career-technology teachers, instruct and train students to work in a wide variety of fields, such as health care, business, auto repair, communications, and, increasingly, technology. They often teach courses that are in high demand by area employers, who may provide input into the curriculum and offer internships to students. Many vocational teachers play an active role in building and overseeing these partnerships. Additional responsibilities of middle and secondary school teachers may include career guidance and job placement, as well as follow-ups with students after graduation. (Special education teachers—who instruct elementary and secondary school students who have a variety of disabilities—are discussed separately in this book.)

Computers play an integral role in the education teachers provide. Resources such as educational software and the Internet expose students to a vast range of experiences and promote interactive learning. Through the Internet, students can communicate with other students anywhere in the world, allowing them to share experiences and differing viewpoints. Students also use the Internet for individual research projects and to gather information. Computers are used in other classroom activities as well, from solving math problems to learning English as a second language. Teachers also may use computers to record grades and perform other administrative and clerical duties. They must continually update their skills so that they can instruct and use the latest technology in the classroom.

Teachers often work with students from varied ethnic, racial, and religious backgrounds. With growing minority populations in most parts of the country, it is important for teachers to work effectively with a diverse student population. Accordingly, some schools offer training to help teachers enhance their awareness and understanding of different cultures. Teachers may also include multicultural programming in their lesson plans to address the needs of all students, regardless of their cultural background.

Teachers design classroom presentations to meet students' needs and abilities. They also work with students individually. Teachers plan, evaluate, and assign lessons; prepare, administer, and grade tests; listen to oral presentations; and maintain classroom discipline. They observe and evaluate a student's performance and potential and increasingly are asked to use new assessment methods. For example, teachers may examine a portfolio of a student's artwork or writing in order to judge the student's overall progress. They then can provide additional assistance in areas in which a student needs help. Teachers also grade papers, prepare report cards, and meet with parents and school staff to discuss a student's academic progress or personal problems.

In addition to conducting classroom activities, teachers oversee study halls and homerooms, supervise extracurricular activities, and accompany students on field trips. They may identify students with physical or mental problems and refer the students to the proper authorities. Secondary school teachers occasionally assist students in choosing courses, colleges, and careers. Teachers also participate in education conferences and workshops.

In recent years, site-based management, which allows teachers and parents to participate actively in management decisions regarding school operations, has gained popularity. In many schools, teachers are increasingly involved in making decisions regarding the budget, personnel, textbooks, curriculum design, and teaching methods.

Working Conditions

Seeing students develop new skills and gain an appreciation of knowledge and learning can be very rewarding. However, teaching may be frustrating when one is dealing with unmotivated or disrespectful students. Occasionally, teachers must cope with unruly behavior and violence in the schools. Teachers may experience stress in dealing with large classes, heavy workloads, or old schools that are run down and lack many modern amenities. Accountability standards also may increase stress levels, with teachers expected to produce students who are able to exhibit satisfactory performance on standardized tests in core subjects. Many teachers, particularly in public schools, are also frustrated by the lack of control they have over what they are required to teach.

Teachers in private schools generally enjoy smaller class sizes and more control over establishing the curriculum and setting standards for performance and discipline. Their students also tend to be more motivated, since private schools can be selective in their admissions processes.

Teachers are sometimes isolated from their colleagues because they work alone in a classroom of students. However, some schools allow teachers to work in teams and with mentors to enhance their professional development.

Including school duties performed outside the classroom, many teachers work more than 40 hours a week. Part-time schedules are more common among preschool and kindergarten teachers. Although some school districts have gone to all-day kindergartens, most kindergarten teachers still teach two kindergarten classes a day. Most teachers work the traditional 10-month school year with a 2-month vacation during the summer. During the vacation break, those on the 10-month schedule may teach in summer sessions, take other jobs, travel, or pursue personal interests. Many enroll in college courses or workshops to continue their education. Teachers in districts with a year-round schedule typically work 8 weeks, are on vacation for 1 week, and have a 5-week midwinter break. Preschool teachers working in day care settings often work year round.

Most states have tenure laws that prevent public school teachers from being fired without just cause and due process. Teachers may obtain tenure after they have satisfactorily completed a probationary period of teaching, normally 3 years. Tenure does not absolutely guarantee a job, but it does provide some security.

Training, Other Qualifications, and Advancement

All 50 states and the District of Columbia require public school teachers to be licensed. Licensure is not required for teachers in private schools in most states. Usually licensure is granted by the State Board of Education or a licensure advisory committee. Teachers may be licensed to teach the early childhood grades (usually preschool through grade 3); the elementary grades (grades 1 through 6 or 8); the middle grades (grades 5 through 8); a secondary-education subject area (usually grades 7 through 12); or a special subject, such as reading or music (usually grades kindergarten through 12).

Requirements for regular licenses to teach kindergarten through grade 12 vary by state. However, all states require general education teachers to have a bachelor's degree and to have completed an approved teacher training program with a prescribed number of subject and education credits, as well as supervised practice teaching. Some states also require technology training and the attainment of a minimum grade point average. A number of states require that teachers obtain a master's degree in education within a specified period after they begin teaching.

Almost all states require applicants for a teacher's license to be tested for competency in basic skills, such as reading and writing, and in teaching. Almost all also require the teacher to exhibit proficiency in his or her subject. Many school systems are presently moving toward implementing performance-based systems for licensure, which usually require a teacher to demonstrate satisfactory teaching performance over an extended period in order to obtain a provisional license, in addition to passing an examination in their subject. Most states require continuing education for renewal of the teacher's license. Many states have reciprocity agreements that make it easier for teachers licensed in one state to become licensed in another.

Many states also offer alternative licensure programs for teachers who have a bachelor's degree in the subject they will teach, but who lack the necessary education courses required for a regular license. Many of these alternative licensure programs are designed to ease shortages of teachers of certain subjects, such as mathematics and science. Other programs provide teachers for urban and rural schools that have difficulty filling positions with teachers from traditional licensure programs. Alternative licensure programs are intended to attract people into teaching who do not fulfill traditional licensing standards, including recent college graduates who did not complete education programs and those changing from another career to teaching. In some programs, individuals begin teaching quickly under provisional licensure. After working under the close supervision of experienced educators for 1 or 2 years while taking education courses outside school hours, they receive regular licensure if they have progressed satisfactorily. In other programs, college graduates who do not meet licensure requirements take only those courses that they lack and then become licensed. This approach may take 1 or 2 semesters of full-time study. States may issue emergency licenses to individuals who do not meet the requirements for a regular license when schools cannot attract enough qualified teachers to fill positions. Teachers who need to be licensed may enter programs that grant a master's degree in education as well as a license.

In many states, vocational teachers have many of the same requirements for teaching as their academic counterparts. However, because knowledge and experience in a particular field are important criteria for the job, some states will license vocational education teachers without a bachelor's degree, provided they can demonstrate expertise in their field. A minimum number of hours in education courses may also be required.

Licensing requirements for preschool teachers also vary by state. Requirements for public preschool teachers are generally more stringent than those for private preschool teachers. Some states require a bachelor's degree in early childhood education, while others require an associate's degree and still others require certification by a nationally recognized authority. The Child Development Associate (CDA) credential, the most common type of certification, requires a mix of classroom training and experience working with children, along with an independent assessment of an individual's competence.

Private schools are generally exempt from meeting state licensing standards. For secondary school teacher jobs, they prefer candidates who have a bachelor's degree in the subject they intend to teach or in childhood education for elementary school teachers. They seek candidates among recent college graduates as well as from those who have established careers in other fields. Private schools associated with religious institutions also desire candidates who share the values that are important to the institution.

In some cases, teachers of kindergarten through high school may attain professional certification in order to demonstrate competency beyond that required for a license. The National Board for Professional Teaching Standards offers a voluntary national certification. To become nationally accredited, experienced teachers must prove their aptitude by compiling a portfolio showing their work in the classroom and by passing a written assessment and evaluation of their teaching knowledge. Currently, teachers may become certified in a variety of areas on the basis of the age of the students and, in some cases, the subject taught. For example, teachers may obtain a certificate for teaching English language arts to early adolescents (aged 11 to 15), or they may become certified as early childhood generalists. All states recognize national certification, and many states and school districts provide special benefits to teachers holding such certification. Benefits typically include higher salaries and reimbursement for continuing education and certification fees. In addition, many states allow nationally certified teachers to carry a license from one state to another.

The National Council for Accreditation of Teacher Education currently accredits teacher education programs across the United States. Graduation from an accredited program is not necessary to become a teacher, but it does make it easier to fulfill licensure requirements. Generally, 4-year colleges require students to wait until their sophomore year before applying for admission to teacher education programs. Traditional education programs for kindergarten and elementary school teachers include courses—designed specifically for those preparing to teach—in mathematics, physical science, social science, music, art, and literature, as well as prescribed professional education courses, such as philosophy of education, psychology of learning, and teaching methods. Aspiring secondary school teachers most often major in the subject they plan to teach while also taking a program of study in teacher preparation.

Teacher education programs are now required to include classes in the use of computers and other technologies in order to maintain their accreditation. Most programs require students to perform a student-teaching internship.

Many states now offer professional development schools—partnerships between universities and elementary or secondary schools. Students enter these 1-year programs after completion of their bachelor's degree. Professional development schools merge theory with practice and allow the student to experience a year of teaching firsthand, under professional guidance.

In addition to being knowledgeable in their subject, teachers must have the ability to communicate, inspire trust and confidence, and motivate students, as well as understand the students' educational and emotional needs. Teachers must be able to recognize and respond to individual and cultural differences in students and employ different teaching methods that will result in higher student achievement. They should be organized, dependable, patient, and creative. Teachers also must be able to work cooperatively and communicate effectively with other teachers, support staff, parents, and members of the community.

With additional preparation, teachers may move into positions as school librarians, reading specialists, instructional coordinators, or guidance counselors. Teachers may become administrators or supervisors, although the number of these positions is limited and competition can be intense. In some systems, highly qualified, experienced teachers can become senior or mentor teachers, with higher pay and additional responsibilities. They guide and assist less experienced teachers while keeping most of their own teaching responsibilities. Preschool teachers usually work their way up from assistant teacher to teacher to lead teacher—who may be responsible for the instruction of several classes—and, finally, to director of the center. Preschool teachers with a bachelor's degree frequently are qualified to teach kindergarten through grade 3 as well. Teaching at these higher grades often results in higher pay.

Employment

Preschool, kindergarten, elementary school, middle school, and secondary school teachers, except special education, held about 3.8 million jobs in 2004. Of the teachers in those jobs, about 1.5 million are elementary school teachers, 1.1 million are secondary school teachers, 628,000 are middle school teachers, 431,000 are preschool teachers, and 171,000 are kindergarten teachers. The majority work in local government educational services. About 10 percent work for private schools. Preschool teachers, except special education, are most often employed in child daycare services (61 percent), religious organizations (12 percent), local government educational services (9 percent), and private educational services (7 percent). Employment of teachers is geographically distributed much the same as the population.

Job Outlook

Job opportunities for teachers over the next 10 years will vary from good to excellent, depending on the locality, grade level, and subject taught. Most job openings will result from the need to replace the large number of teachers who are expected to retire over the 2004–2014 period. Also, many beginning teachers decide to leave teaching after a year or two—especially those employed in poor, urban schools—creating additional job openings for teachers. Shortages of qualified teachers will likely continue, resulting in competition among some localities, with schools luring teachers from other states and districts with bonuses and higher pay.

Through 2014, overall student enrollments in elementary, middle, and secondary schools—a key factor in the demand for teachers—are expected to rise more slowly than in the past as children of the baby boom generation leave the school system. This will cause employment to grow as fast as the average for teachers from kindergarten through the secondary grades. Projected enrollments will vary by region. Fast-growing states in the West—particularly California, Idaho, Hawaii, Alaska, Utah, and New Mexico—will experience the largest enrollment increases. Enrollments in the South will increase at a more modest rate than in recent years, while those in the Northeast and Midwest are expected to hold relatively steady or decline. Teachers who are geographically mobile and who obtain licensure in more than one subject should have a distinct advantage in finding a job.

The job market for teachers also continues to vary by school location and by subject taught. Job prospects should be better in inner cities and rural areas than in suburban districts. Many inner cities—often characterized by overcrowded, ill-equipped schools and higher-than-average poverty rates—and rural areas—characterized by their remote location and relatively low salaries—have difficulty attracting and retaining enough teachers. Currently, many school districts have difficulty hiring qualified teachers in some subject areas—most often mathematics, science (especially chemistry and physics), bilingual education, and foreign languages. Increasing enrollments of minorities, coupled with a shortage of minority teachers, should cause efforts to recruit minority teachers to intensify. Also, the number of non-English-speaking students will continue to grow, creating demand for bilingual teachers and for those who teach English as a second language. Specialties that have an adequate number of qualified teachers include general elementary education, physical education, and social studies. Qualified vocational teachers also are currently in demand in a variety of fields at both the middle school and secondary school levels.

The number of teachers employed is dependent as well on state and local expenditures for education and on the enactment of legislation to increase the quality and scope of public education. At the federal level, there has been a large increase in funding for education, particularly for the hiring of qualified teachers in lower-income areas. Also, some states are instituting programs to improve early childhood education, such as offering full-day kindergarten and universal preschool. These last two programs, along with projected higher enrollment growth for preschool-age children, will create many new jobs for preschool teachers, which are expected to grow much faster than the average for all occupations.

The supply of teachers is expected to increase in response to reports of improved job prospects, better pay, more teacher involvement in school policy, and greater public interest in education. In recent years, the total number of bachelor's and master's degrees granted in education has increased steadily. Because of a shortage of teachers in certain locations, and in anticipation of the loss of a number of teachers to retirement, many states have implemented policies that will encourage more students to become teachers. In addition, more teachers may be drawn from a reserve pool of career changers, substitute teachers, and teachers completing alternative certification programs.

Earnings

Median annual earnings of kindergarten, elementary, middle, and secondary school teachers ranged from $41,400 to $45,920 in May 2004; the lowest 10 percent earned $26,730 to $31,180; the top 10 percent earned $66,240 to $71,370. Median earnings for preschool teachers were $20,980.

According to the American Federation of Teachers, beginning teachers with a bachelor's degree earned an average of $31,704 in the 2003–2004 school year. The estimated average salary of all public elementary and secondary school teachers in the 2003–2004 school year was $46,597. Private school teachers generally earn less than public school teachers, but may be given other benefits, such as free or subsidized housing.

In 2004, more than half of all elementary, middle, and secondary school teachers belonged to unions—mainly the American Federation of Teachers and the National Education Association—that bargain with school systems over wages, hours, and other terms and conditions of employment. Fewer preschool and kindergarten teachers were union members—about 17 percent in 2004.

Teachers can boost their salary in a number of ways. In some schools, teachers receive extra pay for coaching sports and working with students in extracurricular activities. Getting a master's degree or national certification often results in a raise in pay, as does acting as a mentor. Some teachers earn extra income during the summer by teaching summer school or performing other jobs in the school system.

Related Occupations

Preschool, kindergarten, elementary school, middle school, and secondary school teaching requires a variety of skills and aptitudes, including a talent for working with children; organizational, administrative, and recordkeeping abilities; research and communication skills; the power to influence, motivate, and train others; patience; and creativity. Workers in other occupations requiring some of these aptitudes include teachers—postsecondary; counselors; teacher assistants; education administrators; librarians; childcare workers; public relations specialists; social workers; and athletes, coaches, umpires, and related workers.

Sources of Additional Information

Information on licensure or certification requirements and approved teacher training institutions is available from local school systems and state departments of education.

Information on the teaching profession and on how to become a teacher can be obtained from

▸ Recruiting New Teachers, Inc., 385 Concord Ave., Suite 103, Belmont, MA 02478. Internet: http://www.recruitingteachers.org

Information on teachers' unions and education-related issues may be obtained from the following sources

▸ American Federation of Teachers, 555 New Jersey Ave. NW, Washington, DC 20001.

▸ National Education Association, 1201 16th St. NW, Washington, DC 20036.

A list of institutions with accredited teacher education programs can be obtained from

▸ National Council for Accreditation of Teacher Education, 2010 Massachusetts Ave. NW, Suite 500, Washington, DC 20036-1023. Internet: http://www.ncate.org

Information on alternative certification programs can be obtained from

▸ National Center for Alternative Certification, 1901 Pennsylvania Ave. NW, Suite 201, Washington, DC 20006. Internet: http://www.teach-now.org

For information on vocational education and vocational education teachers, contact

▸ Association for Career and Technical Education, 1410 King St., Alexandria, VA 22314. Internet: http://www.acteonline.org

For information on careers in educating children and issues affecting preschool teachers, contact either of the following organizations:

▸ National Association for the Education of Young Children, 1509 16th St. NW, Washington, DC 20036. Internet: http://www.naeyc.org

▸ Council for Professional Recognition, 2460 16th St. NW, Washington, DC 20009-3575. Internet: http://www.cdacouncil.org

Teachers—Special Education

(O*NET 25-2041.00, 25-2042.00, and 25-2043.00)

Significant Points

■ All states require teachers to be licensed; licensing requires the completion of a teacher training program and at least a bachelor's degree, though many states require a master's degree.

■ Excellent job prospects are expected due to rising enrollments of special education students and reported shortages of qualified teachers.

■ Many states offer alternative licensure programs to attract people to these jobs who do not have the qualifications to become teachers under normal procedures.

Nature of the Work

Special education teachers work with children and youths who have a variety of disabilities. A small number of special education teachers work with students with mental retardation or autism, primarily teaching them life skills and basic literacy. However, the majority of special education teachers work with children with mild to moderate disabilities, using the general education curriculum or modifying it to meet the child's individual needs. Most special education teachers instruct students at the elementary, middle, and secondary school level, although some teachers work with infants and toddlers.

The various types of disabilities that qualify individuals for special education programs include specific learning disabilities, speech or language impairments, mental retardation, emotional disturbance, multiple disabilities, hearing impairments, orthopedic impairments, visual impairments, autism, combined deafness and blindness, traumatic brain injury, and other health impairments. Students are classified under one of the categories, and special education teachers are prepared to work with specific groups. Early identification of a child with special needs is an important part of a special education teacher's job. Early intervention is essential in educating children with disabilities.

Special education teachers use various techniques to promote learning. Depending on the disability, teaching methods can include individualized instruction, problem-solving assignments, and small-group work. When students need special accommodations in order to take a test, special education teachers see that appropriate ones are provided, such as having the questions read orally or lengthening the time allowed to take the test.

Special education teachers help to develop an Individualized Education Program (IEP) for each special education student. The IEP sets personalized goals for each student and is tailored to the student's individual needs and ability. When appropriate, the program includes a transition plan outlining specific steps to prepare students with disabilities for middle school or high school or, in the case of older students, a job or postsecondary study. Teachers review the IEP with the student's parents, school administrators, and the student's general education teacher. Teachers work closely with parents to inform them of their child's progress and suggest techniques to promote learning at home.

Special education teachers design and teach appropriate curricula, assign work geared toward each student's needs and abilities, and grade papers and homework assignments. They are involved in the students' behavioral, social, and academic development, helping the students develop emotionally, feel comfortable in social situations, and be aware of socially acceptable behavior. Preparing special education students for daily life after graduation also is an important aspect of the job. Teachers provide students with career counseling or help them learn routine skills, such as balancing a checkbook.

As schools become more inclusive, special education teachers and general education teachers are increasingly working together in general education classrooms. Special education teachers help general educators adapt curriculum materials and teaching techniques to meet the needs of students with disabilities. They coordinate the work of teachers, teacher assistants, and related personnel, such as therapists and social workers, to meet the individualized needs of the student within inclusive special education programs. A large part of a special education teacher's job involves interacting with others. Special education teachers communicate frequently with parents, social workers, school psychologists, occupational and physical therapists, school administrators, and other teachers.

Special education teachers work in a variety of settings. Some have their own classrooms and teach only special education students; others work as special education resource teachers and offer individualized help to students in general education classrooms; still others teach together with general education teachers in classes composed of both general and special education students. Some teachers work with special education students for several hours a day in a resource room, separate from their general education classroom. Considerably fewer special education teachers work in residential facilities or tutor students in homebound or hospital environments.

Special education teachers who work with infants usually travel to the child's home to work with the child and his or her parents. Many of these infants have medical problems that slow or preclude normal development. Special education teachers show parents techniques and activities designed to stimulate the infant and encourage the growth and development of the child's skills. Toddlers usually receive their services at a preschool where special education teachers help them develop social, self-help, motor, language, and cognitive skills, often through the use of play.

Technology is playing an increasingly important role in special education. Teachers use specialized equipment such as computers with synthesized speech, interactive educational software programs, and audiotapes to assist children.

Working Conditions

Special education teachers enjoy the challenge of working with students with disabilities and the opportunity to establish meaningful relationships with them. Although helping these students can be highly rewarding, the work also can be emotionally and physically draining. Many special education teachers are under considerable stress due to heavy workloads and administrative tasks. They must produce a substantial amount of paperwork documenting each student's progress and work under the threat of litigation against the school or district by students' parents if correct procedures are not followed or if the parents feel that their child is not receiving an adequate education, although recent legislation that has been passed is intended to reduce the burden of paperwork and the threat of litigation. The physical and emotional demands of the job cause some special education teachers to leave the occupation.

Some schools offer year-round education for special education students, but most special education teachers work only the traditional 10-month school year.

Training, Other Qualifications, and Advancement

All 50 states and the District of Columbia require special education teachers to be licensed. The state board of education or a licensure advisory committee usually grants licenses, and licensure varies by state. In some states, special education teachers receive a general education credential to teach kindergarten through grade 12. These teachers then train in a specialty, such as learning disabilities or behavioral disorders. Many states offer general special education licenses across a variety of disability categories, while others license several different specialties within special education.

For traditional licensing, all states require a bachelor's degree and the completion of an approved teacher preparation program with a prescribed number of subject and education credits and supervised practice teaching. However, many states require a master's degree in special education, involving at least 1 year of additional course work, including a specialization, beyond the bachelor's degree. Often a prospective teacher must pass a professional assessment test as well. Some states have reciprocity agreements allowing special education teachers to transfer their licenses from one state to another, but many others still require that experienced teachers reapply and pass licensing requirements to work in the state.

Many states also offer alternative routes to licensing because there are not enough graduates from education programs to meet the needs of most schools. Alternative licensure programs are intended to attract people into teaching who do not fulfill traditional licensing standards, including recent college graduates who did not complete education programs and those changing from another career to teaching. Requirements vary by state, but generally require holding a bachelor's degree, successfully accomplishing a period of supervised preparation and induction, and passing an assessment test. In some programs, individuals begin teaching quickly under a provisional license and can obtain a regular license after teaching under the supervision of licensed teachers for a period of 1 to 2 years and completing required education courses.

Many colleges and universities across the United States offer programs in special education at the undergraduate, master's, and doctoral degree levels. Special education teachers usually undergo longer periods of training than do general education teachers. Most bachelor's degree programs are 4-year programs that include general and specialized courses in special education. However, an increasing number of institutions are requiring a 5th year or other graduate-level preparation. Among the courses offered are educational psychology, legal issues of special education, and child growth and development; programs also include courses imparting knowledge and skills needed for teaching students with disabilities. Some programs require specialization, while others offer generalized special education degrees or a course of study in several specialized areas. The last year of the program usually is spent student teaching in a classroom supervised by a certified teacher.

Special education teachers must be patient, able to motivate students, understanding of their students' special needs, and accepting of differences in others. Teachers must be creative and apply different types of teaching methods to reach students who are having difficulty learning. Communication and cooperation are essential skills because special education teachers spend a great deal of time interacting with others, including students, parents, and school faculty and administrators.

Special education teachers can advance to become supervisors or administrators. They may also earn advanced degrees and become instructors in colleges that prepare others to teach special education. In some school systems, highly experienced teachers can become mentors to less experienced ones, providing guidance to those teachers while maintaining a light teaching load.

Employment

Special education teachers held a total of about 441,000 jobs in 2004. A great majority, about 90 percent, work in public schools. Another 6 percent work at private schools. Almost half work in elementary schools. A few worked for individual and social assistance agencies or residential facilities or in homebound or hospital environments.

Job Outlook

Employment of special education teachers is expected to increase faster than the average for all occupations through 2014. Although student enrollments are expected to grow only slowly, additional positions for these workers will be created by continued increases in the number of special education students needing services, by legislation emphasizing training and employment for individuals with disabilities, and by educational reforms requiring higher standards for graduation. In addition to job openings resulting from growth, a large number of openings will result from the need to replace special education teachers who switch to teaching general education, change careers altogether, or retire. At the same time, many school districts report difficulty finding sufficient numbers of qualified teachers. As a result, special education teachers should have excellent job prospects.

The job outlook varies by geographic area and specialty. Although most areas of the country report difficulty finding qualified applicants, positions in inner cities and rural areas usually are more plentiful than job openings in suburban or wealthy urban areas. Student populations, in general, also are expected to increase more rapidly in certain parts of the country, such as the South and West, resulting in increased demand for special education teachers in those regions. In addition, job opportunities may be better in certain specialties—such as teachers who work with children with multiple disabilities or severe disabilities like autism—because of large increases in the enrollment of special education students classified under those categories. Legislation encouraging early intervention and special education for infants, toddlers, and preschoolers has created a need for early childhood special education teachers. Bilingual special education teachers and those with multicultural experience also are needed to work with an increasingly diverse student population.

The number of students requiring special education services has grown steadily in recent years as improvements in identification has allowed learning disabilities to be diagnosed at earlier ages. In addition, medical advances have resulted in more children surviving serious accidents or illnesses, but with impairments that require special accommodations. The percentage of foreign-born special education students also is expected to grow, as teachers become more adept in recognizing learning disabilities in that population. Finally, more parents are expected to seek special services for those of their children who have difficulty meeting the new, higher standards required of students.

Earnings

Median annual earnings in May 2004 of special education teachers who worked primarily in preschools, kindergartens, and elementary schools were $43,570. The middle 50 percent earned between $35,340 and $55,350. The lowest 10 percent earned less than $29,880, and the highest 10 percent earned more than $68,660.

Median annual earnings in May 2004 of middle school special education teachers were $44,160. The middle 50 percent earned between $35,650 and $57,070. The lowest 10 percent earned less than $30,230, and the highest 10 percent earned more than $74,230.

Median annual earnings in May 2004 of special education teachers who worked primarily in secondary schools were $45,700. The middle 50 percent earned between $36,920 and $59,340. The lowest 10 percent earned less than $30,860, and the highest 10 percent earned more than $73,190.

In 2004, about 62 percent of special education teachers belonged to unions—mainly the American Federation of Teachers and the National Education Association—that bargain with school systems over wages, hours, and the terms and conditions of employment.

In most schools, teachers receive extra pay for coaching sports and working with students in extracurricular activities. Some teachers earn extra income during the summer by working in the school system or in other jobs.

Related Occupations

Special education teachers work with students who have disabilities and special needs. Other occupations involved with the identification, evaluation, and development of students with disabilities include psychologists; social workers; speech-language pathologists; audiologists; counselors; teacher assistants; occupational therapists; recreational therapists; and teachers—preschool, kindergarten, elementary, middle, and secondary.

Sources of Additional Information

For information on professions related to early intervention and education for children with disabilities, listings of schools with special education training programs, information on teacher certification, and general information on related personnel issues, contact

▸ The Council for Exceptional Children, 1110 N. Glebe Rd., Suite 300, Arlington, VA 22201-5704. Internet: http://www.cec.sped.org

▸ National Center for Special Education Personnel & Related Service Providers, National Association of State Directors of Special Education, 1800 Diagonal Rd., Suite 320, Alexandria, VA 22314. Internet: http://www.personnelcenter.org

To learn more about the special education teacher certification and licensing requirements in individual states, contact the state's department of education.

Jobs That May Not Require a Bachelor's Degree But Are Often Held by College Graduates

Actors, Producers, and Directors

Aircraft Pilots and
Flight Engineers

Armed Forces

Artists and Related Workers

Computer Support Specialists and
Systems Administrators

Interpreters and Translators

Musicians, Singers, and Related
Workers

Nuclear Medicine Technologists

Occupational Health and
Safety Specialists and Technicians

Paralegals and Legal Assistants

Police and Detectives

Purchasing Managers, Buyers,
and Purchasing Agents

Radiologic Technologists
and Technicians

Real Estate Brokers
and Sales Agents

Registered Nurses

Respiratory Therapists

Sales Representatives,
Wholesale and Manufacturing

Surveyors, Cartographers,
Photogrammetrists, and
Surveying Technicians

Television, Video, and Motion
Picture Camera Operators
and Editors

Actors, Producers, and Directors

(O*NET 27-2011.00, 27-2012.01, 27-2012.02, 27-2012.03, 27-2012.04, and 27-2012.05)

Significant Points

■ Actors endure long periods of unemployment, intense competition for roles, and frequent rejections in auditions.

■ Formal training through a university or acting conservatory is typical; however, many actors, producers, and directors find work on the basis of their experience and talent alone.

■ Because earnings for actors are erratic, many supplement their incomes by holding jobs in other fields.

Nature of the Work

Actors, producers, and directors express ideas and create images in theater, film, radio, television, and other performing arts media. They interpret a writer's script to entertain, inform, or instruct an audience. Although the most famous actors, producers, and directors work in film, network television, or theater in New York or Los Angeles, far more work in local or regional television studios, theaters, or film production companies preparing advertising, public-relations, or independent small-scale movie productions.

Actors perform in stage, radio, television, video, or motion picture productions. They also work in cabarets, nightclubs, theme parks, commercials, and "industrial" films produced for training and educational purposes. Most actors struggle to find steady work; only a few ever achieve recognition as stars. Some well-known, experienced performers may be cast in supporting roles. Others work as "extras," with no lines to deliver, or make brief cameo appearances, speaking only one or two lines. Some actors do voiceover and narration work for advertisements, animated features, books on tape, and other electronic media, including computer games. They also teach in high school or university drama departments, acting conservatories, or public programs.

Producers are entrepreneurs, overseeing the business and financial decisions of a motion picture, made-for-television feature, or stage production. They select scripts, approve the development of ideas for the production, arrange financing, and determine the size and cost of the endeavor. Producers hire or approve the selection of directors, principal cast members, and key production staff members. They also negotiate contracts with artistic and design personnel in accordance with collective bargaining agreements and guarantee payment of salaries, rent, and other expenses. Television and radio producers determine which programs, episodes, or news segments get aired. They may research material, write scripts, and oversee the production of individual pieces. Producers in any medium coordinate the activities of writers, directors, managers, and agents to ensure that each project stays on schedule and within budget.

Directors are responsible for the creative decisions of a production. They interpret scripts, express concepts to set and costume designers, audition and select cast members, conduct rehearsals, and direct the work of cast and crew. They approve the design elements of a production, including the sets, costumes, choreography, and music. Assistant directors cue the performers and technicians to make entrances or to make light, sound, or set changes.

Working Conditions

Actors, producers, and directors work under constant pressure. Many face stress from the continual need to find their next job. To succeed, actors, producers, and directors need patience and commitment to their craft. Actors strive to deliver flawless performances, often while working under undesirable and unpleasant conditions. Producers and directors organize rehearsals and meet with writers, designers, financial backers, and production technicians. They experience stress not only from these activities, but also from the need to adhere to budgets, union work rules, and production schedules.

Acting assignments typically are short term—ranging from 1 day to a few months—which means that actors frequently experience long periods of unemployment between jobs. The uncertain nature of the work results in unpredictable earnings and intense competition for even the lowest-paid jobs. Often, actors, producers, and directors must hold other jobs in order to sustain a living.

When performing, actors typically work long, irregular hours. For example, stage actors may perform one show at night while rehearsing another during the day. They also might travel with a show when it tours the country. Movie actors may work on location, sometimes under adverse weather conditions, and may spend considerable time in their trailers or dressing rooms waiting to perform their scenes. Actors who perform in a television series often appear on camera with little preparation time because scripts tend to be revised frequently or even written moments before taping. Those who appear live or before a studio audience must be able to handle impromptu situations and calmly ad lib, or substitute, lines when necessary.

Evening and weekend work is a regular part of a stage actor's life. On weekends, more than one performance may be held per day. Actors and directors working on movies or television programs—especially those who shoot on location—may work in the early morning or late evening hours to film night scenes or tape scenes inside public facilities outside of normal business hours.

Actors should be in good physical condition and have the necessary stamina and coordination to move about theater stages and large movie and television studio lots. They also need to maneuver about complex technical sets while staying in character and projecting their voices audibly. Actors must be fit to endure heat from stage or studio lights and the weight of heavy costumes. Producers and directors ensure the safety of actors by conducting extra rehearsals on the set so that the actors can learn the layout of set pieces and props, by allowing time for warmups and stretching exercises to guard against physical and vocal injuries, and by providing an adequate number of breaks to prevent heat exhaustion and dehydration.

Training, Other Qualifications, and Advancement

Persons who become actors, producers, and directors follow many paths. Employers generally look for people with the creative instincts, innate talent, and intellectual capacity to perform. Actors should possess a passion for performing and enjoy entertaining others. Most aspiring actors participate in high school and college plays, work in college radio stations, or perform with local community theater groups. Local and regional theater experience and work in summer stock, on cruise lines, or in theme parks helps many young actors hone their skills and earn qualifying credits toward membership in one of the actors' unions. Union membership and work experience in smaller communities may lead to work in larger cities, notably New York or Los Angeles. In television and film, actors and directors typically start in smaller television markets or with independent movie production companies and then work their way up to larger media markets and major studio productions. Intense competition, however, can be expected at each level, because ever more applicants will be vying for increasingly fewer numbers of available positions.

Formal dramatic training, either through an acting conservatory or a university program, generally is necessary, but some people successfully enter the field without it. Most people studying for a bachelor's degree take courses in radio and television broadcasting, communications, film, theater, drama, or dramatic literature. Many continue their academic training and receive a Master of Fine Arts (MFA) degree. Advanced curricula may include courses in stage speech and movement, directing, playwriting, and design, as well as intensive acting workshops. The National Association of Schools of Theatre accredits 135 programs in theater arts. A few people go into acting following successful careers in other fields, such as broadcasting or announcing.

Actors, regardless of experience level, may pursue workshop training through acting conservatories or mentoring by a drama coach. Actors also research roles so that they can grasp concepts quickly during rehearsals and understand the story's setting and background. Sometimes actors learn a foreign language or train with a dialect coach to develop an accent to make their characters more realistic.

Actors need talent, creativity, and training that will enable them to portray different characters. Because competition for parts is fierce, versatility and a wide range of related performance skills, such as singing, dancing, skating, juggling, or miming, are especially useful. Experience in horseback riding, fencing, or stage combat also can lift some actors above the average and get them noticed by producers and directors. Actors must have poise, stage presence, the capability to affect an audience, and the ability to follow direction. Modeling experience also may be helpful. Physical appearance, such as possessing the right size, weight, or features, often is a deciding factor in being selected for particular roles.

Many professional actors rely on agents or managers to find work, negotiate contracts, and plan their careers. Agents generally earn a percentage of the pay specified in an actor's contract. Other actors rely solely on attending open auditions for parts. Trade publications list the times, dates, and locations of these auditions.

To become a movie extra, one usually must be listed by a casting agency, such as Central Casting, a no-fee agency that supplies extras to the major movie studios in Hollywood. Applicants are accepted only when the numbers of persons of a particular type on the list—for example, athletic young women, old men, or small children—falls below the foreseeable need. In recent years, only a very small proportion of applicants have succeeded in being listed.

There are no specific training requirements for producers. They come from many different backgrounds. Talent, experience, and business acumen are important determinants of success for producers. Actors, writers, film editors, and business managers commonly enter the field. Also, many people who start out as actors move into directing, while some directors might try their hand at acting. Producers often start in a theatrical management office, working for a press agent, managing director, or business manager. Some start in a performing arts union or service organization. Others work behind the scenes with successful directors, serve on boards of directors, or promote their own projects. No formal training exists for producers; however, a growing number of colleges and universities now offer degree programs in arts management and in managing nonprofits.

As the reputations and box-office draw of actors, producers, and directors grow, they might work on bigger-budget productions, on network or syndicated broadcasts, or in more prestigious theaters. Actors may advance to lead roles and receive star billing. A few actors move into acting-related jobs, such as drama coaches or directors of stage, television, radio, or motion picture productions. Some teach drama privately or in colleges and universities.

Employment

In 2004, actors, producers, and directors held about 157,000 jobs, primarily in motion picture and video, performing arts, and broadcast industries. Because many others were between jobs, the total number of actors, producers, and directors available for work was higher. Employment in the theater, and other performing arts companies, is cyclical—higher in the fall and spring seasons—and concentrated in New York and other major cities with large commercial houses for musicals and touring productions. Also, many cities support established professional regional theaters that operate on a seasonal or year-round basis. About one-fourth of actors, producers, and directors were self-employed.

Actors, producers, and directors may find work in summer festivals, on cruise lines, and in theme parks. Many smaller, nonprofit professional companies, such as repertory companies; dinner theaters; and theaters affiliated with drama schools, acting conservatories, and universities, provide employment opportunities for local amateur talent and professional entertainers. Auditions typically are held in New York for many productions across the country and for shows that go on the road.

Employment in motion pictures and in films for television is centered in New York and Hollywood. However, small studios are located throughout the country. Many films are shot on location and may employ local professional and nonprofessional actors. In television, opportunities are concentrated in the network centers of New York and Los Angeles, but cable television services and local television stations around the country also employ many actors, producers, and directors.

A growing number of actors and other entertainers appear on the payrolls of firms who do accounting and payroll work. Frequently, film production companies will hire actors through casting agencies or contract out their payroll services to accounting firms. Similarly, many actors arrange with a company in this industry to collect their pay from producers or entrepreneurs; make the appropriate deductions for taxes, union dues, and benefits payments; and pay them their net earnings for each job. The result of these increasingly more common payroll arrangements is that many actors appear to be working for accounting offices rather than for the theatrical production companies or studios where they actually perform.

Job Outlook

Employment of actors, producers, and directors is expected to grow about as fast as the average for all occupations through 2014. Although a growing number of people will aspire to enter these professions, many will leave the field early because the work—when it is available—is hard, the hours are long, and the pay is low. Competition for jobs will be stiff, in part because the large number of highly trained and talented actors auditioning for roles generally exceeds the number of parts that become available. Only performers with the most stamina and talent will find regular employment.

Expanding cable and satellite television operations; increasing production and distribution of major studio and independent films; and continued growth and development of interactive media, such as direct-for-Web movies and videos, should increase demand for actors, producers, and directors. However, greater emphasis on national, rather than local, entertainment productions may restrict employment opportunities in the broadcasting industry.

Venues for live entertainment, such as Broadway and off-Broadway theaters, touring productions, and repertory theaters in many major metropolitan areas, as well as theme parks and resorts, are expected to offer many job opportunities. However, prospects in these venues are more variable because they fluctuate with economic conditions.

Earnings

Median hourly earnings of actors were $11.28 in May 2004. The middle 50 percent earned between $7.75 and $30.76. The lowest 10 percent earned less than $6.63, and the highest 10 percent earned more than $56.48. Median annual earnings were $15.20 in performing arts companies and $9.27 in motion picture and video industries. Annual earnings data for actors were not available because of the wide variation in the number of hours worked by actors and the short-term nature of many jobs, which may last for 1 day or 1 week; it is extremely rare for actors to have guaranteed employment that exceeded 3 to 6 months.

Minimum salaries, hours of work, and other conditions of employment are covered in collective bargaining agreements between the producers and the unions representing workers. The Actors' Equity Association (Equity) represents stage actors; the Screen Actors Guild (SAG) covers actors in motion pictures, including television, commercials, and films; and the American Federation of Television and Radio Artists (AFTRA) represents television and radio studio performers. Some actors who regularly work in several media find it advantageous to join multiple unions, while SAG and AFTRA may share jurisdiction for work in additional areas, such as the production of training or educational films not slated for broadcast,

television commercial work, and interactive media. While these unions generally determine minimum salaries, any actor or director may negotiate for a salary higher than the minimum.

Under terms of a joint SAG and AFTRA contract covering all unionized workers, motion picture and television actors with speaking parts earned a minimum daily rate of $716, or $2,483 for a 5-day week, as of October 1, 2005. Actors also receive contributions to their health and pension plans and additional compensation for reruns and foreign telecasts of the productions in which they appear.

According to Equity, the minimum weekly salary for actors in Broadway productions as of June 30, 2005, was $1,422. Actors in off-Broadway theaters received minimums ranging from $493 to $857 a week as of October 23, 2005, depending on the seating capacity of the theater. Regional theaters that operate under an Equity agreement pay actors $531 to $800 per week. For touring productions, actors receive an additional $777 per week for living expenses ($819 per week in higher-cost cities). New terms were negotiated under an "experimental touring program" provision for lower-budget musicals that tour to smaller cities or that perform for fewer performances at each stop. In an effort to increase the number of paid workweeks while on tour, actors may be paid less than the full production rate for touring shows in exchange for higher per diems and profit participation.

Some well-known actors—stars—earn well above the minimum; their salaries are many times the figures cited, creating the false impression that all actors are highly paid. For example, of the nearly 100,000 SAG members, only about 50 might be considered stars. The average income that SAG members earn from acting—less than $5,000 a year—is low because employment is sporadic. Therefore, most actors must supplement their incomes by holding jobs in other occupations.

Many actors who work more than a qualifying number of days or weeks per year or earn over a set minimum pay are covered by a union health, welfare, and pension fund, which includes hospitalization insurance to which employers contribute. Under some employment conditions, Equity and AFTRA members receive paid vacations and sick leave.

Median annual earnings of salaried producers and directors were $52,840 in May 2004. The middle 50 percent earned between $35,550 and $87,980. Median annual earnings were $75,200 in motion picture and video industries and $43,890 in radio and television broadcasting.

Many stage directors belong to the Society of Stage Directors and Choreographers (SSDC), and film and television directors belong to the Directors Guild of America. Earnings of stage directors vary greatly. According to the SSDC, summer theaters offer compensation, including "royalties" (based on the number of performances), usually ranging from $2,500 to $8,000 for a 3- to 4-week run. Directing a production at a dinner theater generally will pay less than directing one at a summer theater, but has more potential for generating income from royalties. Regional theaters may hire directors for longer periods, increasing compensation accordingly. The highest-paid directors work on Broadway and commonly earn $50,000 per show. However, they also receive payment in the form of royalties—a negotiated percentage of gross box office receipts—that can exceed their contract fee for long-running box office successes.

Stage producers seldom get a set fee; instead, they get a percentage of a show's earnings or ticket sales.

Related Occupations

People who work in performing arts occupations that may require acting skills include announcers; dancers and choreographers; and musicians, singers, and related workers. Others working in film- and theater-related occupations are makeup artists, theatrical and performance; fashion designers; set and exhibit designers; and writers and authors. Producers share many responsibilities with those who work as top executives.

Sources of Additional Information

For general information about theater arts and a list of accredited college-level programs, contact

▸ National Association of Schools of Theater, 11250 Roger Bacon Dr., Suite 21, Reston, VA 20190. Internet: http://nast.arts-accredit.org

For general information on actors, producers, and directors, contact any of the following organizations:

▸ Actors Equity Association, 165 West 46th St., New York, NY 10036. Internet: http://www.actorsequity.org

▸ Screen Actors Guild, 5757 Wilshire Blvd., Los Angeles, CA 90036-3600. Internet: http://www.sag.org

▸ American Federation of Television and Radio Artists—Screen Actors Guild, 4340 East-West Hwy., Suite 204, Bethesda, MD 20814-4411. Internet: http://www.aftra.org or http://www.sag.org

Aircraft Pilots and Flight Engineers

(O*NET 53-2011.00 and 53-2012.00)

Significant Points

■ Regional and low-fare airlines offer the best opportunities; pilots attempting to get jobs at the major airlines will face strong competition.

■ Pilots usually start with smaller commuter and regional airlines to acquire the experience needed to qualify for higher-paying jobs with national or major airlines.

■ Many pilots have learned to fly in the military, but growing numbers have college degrees with flight training from civilian flying schools that are certified by the Federal Aviation Administration (FAA).

■ Earnings of airline pilots are among the highest in the nation.

Nature of the Work

Pilots are highly trained professionals who either fly airplanes or helicopters to carry out a wide variety of tasks. Most are *airline pilots*, *copilots*, and *flight engineers* who transport passengers and cargo, but 1 out of 5 pilots is a *commercial pilot* involved in tasks such as dusting crops, spreading seed for reforestation, testing aircraft, flying passengers and cargo to areas not served by regular

airlines, directing fire fighting efforts, tracking criminals, monitoring traffic, and rescuing and evacuating injured persons.

Except on small aircraft, two pilots usually make up the cockpit crew. Generally, the most experienced pilot, the *captain*, is in command and supervises all other crew members. The pilot and the copilot, often called the *first officer*, share flying and other duties, such as communicating with air traffic controllers and monitoring the instruments. Some large aircraft have a third pilot, the *flight engineer*, who assists the other pilots by monitoring and operating many of the instruments and systems, making minor in-flight repairs, and watching for other aircraft. The flight engineer also assists the pilots with the company, air traffic control, and cabin crew communications. New technology can perform many flight tasks, however, and virtually all new aircraft now fly with only two pilots, who rely more heavily on computerized controls.

Before departure, pilots plan their flights carefully. They thoroughly check their aircraft to make sure that the engines, controls, instruments, and other systems are functioning properly. They also make sure that baggage or cargo has been loaded correctly. They confer with flight dispatchers and aviation weather forecasters to find out about weather conditions en route and at their destination. Based on this information, they choose a route, altitude, and speed that will provide the safest, most economical, and smoothest flight. When flying under instrument flight rules—procedures governing the operation of the aircraft when there is poor visibility—the pilot in command, or the company dispatcher, normally files an instrument flight plan with air traffic control so that the flight can be coordinated with other air traffic.

Takeoff and landing are the most difficult parts of the flight and require close coordination between the pilot and first officer. For example, as the plane accelerates for takeoff, the pilot concentrates on the runway while the first officer scans the instrument panel. To calculate the speed they must attain to become airborne, pilots consider the altitude of the airport, outside temperature, weight of the plane, and speed and direction of the wind. The moment the plane reaches takeoff speed, the first officer informs the pilot, who then pulls back on the controls to raise the nose of the plane. Pilots and first officers usually alternate flying each leg from takeoff to landing.

Unless the weather is bad, the flight itself is relatively routine. Airplane pilots, with the assistance of autopilot and the flight management computer, steer the plane along their planned route and are monitored by the air traffic control stations they pass along the way. They regularly scan the instrument panel to check their fuel supply; the condition of their engines; and the air-conditioning, hydraulic, and other systems. Pilots may request a change in altitude or route if circumstances dictate. For example, if the ride is rougher than expected, pilots may ask air traffic control if pilots flying at other altitudes have reported better conditions; if so, they may request an altitude change. This procedure also may be used to find a stronger tailwind or a weaker headwind to save fuel and increase speed. In contrast, because helicopters are used for short trips at relatively low altitude, helicopter pilots must be constantly on the lookout for trees, bridges, power lines, transmission towers, and other dangerous obstacles. Regardless of the type of aircraft, all pilots must monitor warning devices designed to help detect sudden shifts in wind conditions that can cause crashes.

Pilots must rely completely on their instruments when visibility is poor. On the basis of altimeter readings, they know how high above ground they are and whether they can fly safely over mountains and other obstacles. Special navigation radios give pilots precise information that, with the help of special maps, tells them their exact position. Other very sophisticated equipment provides directions to a point just above the end of a runway and enables pilots to land completely without an outside visual reference. Once on the ground, pilots must complete records on their flight and the aircraft maintenance status for their company and the FAA.

The number of nonflying duties that pilots have depends on the employment setting. Airline pilots have the services of large support staffs and, consequently, perform few nonflying duties. However, because of the large numbers of passengers, airline pilots may be called upon to coordinate handling of disgruntled or disruptive passengers. Pilots employed by other organizations, such as charter operators or businesses, have many other duties. They may load the aircraft, handle all passenger luggage to ensure a balanced load, and supervise refueling; other nonflying responsibilities include keeping records, scheduling flights, arranging for major maintenance, and performing minor aircraft maintenance and repairs.

Some pilots are flight instructors. They teach their students in ground-school classes, in simulators, and in dual-controlled planes and helicopters. A few specially trained pilots are examiners or check pilots. They periodically fly with other pilots or pilot's license applicants to make sure that they are proficient.

Working Conditions

Because of FAA regulations, airline pilots flying large aircraft cannot fly more than 100 hours a month or more than 1,000 hours a year. Most airline pilots fly an average of 75 hours a month and work an additional 75 hours a month performing nonflying duties. Most pilots have a variable work schedule, working several days on, then several days off. Most spend a considerable amount of time away from home because the majority of flights involve overnight layovers. When pilots are away from home, the airlines provide hotel accommodations, transportation between the hotel and airport, and an allowance for meals and other expenses. Airlines operate flights at all hours of the day and night, so work schedules often are irregular. Flight assignments are based on seniority. An airline seniority number is normally assigned to a pilot on completion of training. The sooner pilots are hired, the lower their seniority number and the stronger their bidding power.

Commercial pilots also may have irregular schedules, flying 30 hours one month and 90 hours the next. Because these pilots frequently have many nonflying responsibilities, they have much less free time than do airline pilots. Except for corporate flight department pilots, most commercial pilots do not remain away from home overnight, but they may work odd hours. However, if the company owns a fleet of planes, pilots may fly a regular schedule. Flight instructors may have irregular and seasonal work schedules, depending on their students' available time and the weather. Instructors frequently work in the evening or on weekends.

Airline pilots, especially those on international routes, often experience jet lag—fatigue caused by many hours of flying through different time zones. To guard against pilot fatigue, which could result in unsafe flying conditions, the FAA requires airlines to allow pilots at least 8 hours of uninterrupted rest in the 24 hours before finishing their flight duty.

Commercial pilots face other types of job hazards. The work of test pilots, who check the flight performance of new and experimental planes, may be dangerous. Pilots who are crop-dusters may be exposed to toxic chemicals and seldom have the benefit of a regular landing strip. Helicopter pilots involved in rescue and police work may be subject to personal injury.

Although flying does not involve much physical effort, the mental stress of being responsible for a safe flight, regardless of the weather, can be tiring. Pilots must be alert and quick to react if something goes wrong, particularly during takeoff and landing.

Training, Other Qualifications, and Advancement

All pilots who are paid to transport passengers or cargo must have a commercial pilot's license with an instrument rating issued by the FAA. Helicopter pilots must hold a commercial pilot's certificate with a helicopter rating. To qualify for these licenses, applicants must be at least 18 years old and have at least 250 hours of flight experience. The experience required can be reduced through participation in certain flight school curricula approved by the FAA. Applicants also must pass a strict physical examination to make sure that they are in good health and have 20/20 vision with or without glasses, good hearing, and no physical handicaps that could impair their performance. They must pass a written test that includes questions on the principles of safe flight, navigation techniques, and FAA regulations, and they must demonstrate their flying ability to FAA or designated examiners.

To fly during periods of low visibility, pilots must be rated by the FAA to fly by instruments. Pilots may qualify for this rating by having the required hours of flight experience, including 40 hours of experience in flying by instruments; they also must pass a written examination on procedures and FAA regulations covering instrument flying and demonstrate to an examiner their ability to fly by instruments. Requirements for the instrument rating vary depending on the certification level of flight school.

Airline pilots must fulfill additional requirements. Pilots must have an airline transport pilot's license. Applicants for this license must be at least 23 years old and have a minimum of 1,500 hours of flying experience, including night and instrument flying, and must pass FAA written and flight examinations. Usually, they also have one or more advanced ratings depending on the requirements of their particular job. Because pilots must be able to make quick decisions and accurate judgments under pressure, many airline companies reject applicants who do not pass required psychological and aptitude tests. All licenses are valid so long as a pilot can pass the periodic physical and eye examinations and tests of flying skills required by the FAA and company regulations.

The U.S. Armed Forces have always been an important source of trained pilots for civilian jobs. Military pilots gain valuable experience on jet aircraft and helicopters, and persons with this experience—because of the extensive flying time military pilots receive—usually are preferred for civilian pilot jobs. Those without Armed Forces training may become pilots by attending flight schools or by taking lessons from FAA-certified flight instructors. The FAA has certified about 600 civilian flying schools, including some colleges and universities that offer degree credit for pilot training. Until 2014, trained pilots leaving the military are not expected to increase very much in number as the need for pilots grows in civilian aviation. As a result, FAA-certified schools will train a larger share of pilots than in the past.

Although some small airlines hire high school graduates, most airlines require at least 2 years of college and prefer to hire college graduates. In fact, most entrants to this occupation have a college degree. Because the number of college-educated applicants continues to increase, many employers are making a college degree an educational requirement.

Depending on the type of aircraft, new airline pilots start as first officers or flight engineers. Although some airlines favor applicants who already have a flight engineer's license, they may provide flight engineer training for those who have only the commercial license. Many pilots begin with smaller regional or commuter airlines, where they obtain experience flying passengers on scheduled flights into busy airports in all weather conditions. These jobs often lead to higher-paying jobs with bigger, national, or major airlines.

Initial training for airline pilots includes a week of company indoctrination; 3 to 6 weeks of ground school and simulator training; and 25 hours of initial operating experience, including a check-ride with an FAA aviation safety inspector. Once trained, pilots are required to attend recurrent training and simulator checks once or twice a year throughout their career.

Companies other than airlines usually require less flying experience. However, a commercial pilot's license is a minimum requirement, and employers prefer applicants who have experience in the type of craft they will be flying. New employees usually start as first officers or fly less-sophisticated equipment. Test pilots often are required to have an engineering degree.

Advancement for all pilots usually is limited to other flying jobs. Many pilots start as flight instructors, building up their flying hours while they earn money teaching. As they become more experienced, these pilots occasionally fly charter planes or perhaps get jobs with small air transportation firms, such as air-taxi companies. Some advance to flying corporate planes. A small number get flight engineer jobs with the airlines.

In the airlines, advancement usually depends on seniority provisions of union contracts. After 1 to 5 years, flight engineers advance according to seniority to first officer and, after 5 to 15 years, to captain. Seniority also determines which pilots get the more desirable routes. In a nonairline job, a first officer may advance to pilot and, in large companies, to chief pilot or director of aviation in charge of aircraft scheduling, maintenance, and flight procedures.

Employment

Civilian aircraft pilots and flight engineers held about 106,000 jobs in 2004. About 84,000 worked as airline pilots, copilots, and flight engineers. The remainder were commercial pilots who worked as flight instructors at local airports or for large businesses that fly company cargo and executives in their own airplanes or helicopters.

Some commercial pilots flew small planes for air-taxi companies, usually to or from lightly traveled airports not served by major airlines. Others worked for a variety of businesses, performing tasks such as dusting crops, inspecting pipelines, or conducting sightseeing trips. Federal, state, and local governments also employed pilots. A few pilots were self-employed.

Pilots are located across the country, but airline pilots usually are based near major metropolitan airports or airports operating as hubs for the major airlines.

Job Outlook

The passenger airline industry is undergoing many changes, with some airlines posting increases in passenger traffic and adding routes while others are cutting back. Overall, the employment of aircraft pilots is projected to increase about as fast as the average for all occupations through 2014. In the long run, demand for air travel is expected to grow along with the population and the economy. In the short run, however, employment of pilots is generally sensitive to cyclical swings in the economy. During recessions, when a decline in the demand for air travel forces airlines to curtail the number of flights, airlines may temporarily furlough some pilots.

After September 11, 2001, air travel was severely depressed. A number of the major airlines were forced to reduce schedules, lay off pilots, and even declare bankruptcy. At the same time, hiring continued at regional and low-fare airlines. Job opportunities are expected to continue to be better with the regional airlines and low-fare carriers, which are growing faster than the more well-known major airlines. Opportunities with air cargo carriers also should arise because of increasing security requirements for shipping freight on passenger airlines and growth in electronic commerce. Business and corporate travel also should provide some new jobs for pilots.

Pilots attempting to get jobs at the major airlines will face strong competition, as those firms tend to attract many more applicants than they have jobs. They also will have to compete with laid-off pilots for any available jobs. Pilots who have logged the greatest number of flying hours using sophisticated equipment typically have the best prospects. For this reason, military pilots often have an advantage over other applicants. However, prior to September 11, 2001, some airlines reported a shortage of qualified pilots to operate the most sophisticated aircraft. Thus, when hiring improves, jobseekers with the most FAA licenses will have a competitive advantage.

Fewer flight engineers will be needed as new planes requiring only two pilots replace older planes that required flight engineers. Pilots also will experience some productivity improvements as airlines switch to larger planes and adopt the low-fare carrier model that emphasizes faster turnaround times for flights, keeping more pilots in the air rather than waiting on the ground.

Earnings

Earnings of aircraft pilots and flight engineers vary greatly depending whether they work as airline or commercial pilots. Earnings of airline pilots are among the highest in the nation and depend on factors such as the type, size, and maximum speed of the plane and the number of hours and miles flown. For example, pilots who fly jet aircraft usually earn higher salaries than do pilots who fly turboprops. Airline pilots and flight engineers may earn extra pay for night and international flights. In May 2004, median annual earnings of airline pilots, copilots, and flight engineers were $129,250.

Median annual earnings of commercial pilots were $53,870 in May 2004. The middle 50 percent earned between $37,170 and $79,390. The lowest 10 percent earned less than $26,300, and the highest 10 percent earned more than $110,070.

Airline pilots usually are eligible for life and health insurance plans. They also receive retirement benefits and, if they fail the FAA physical examination at some point in their careers, they get disability payments. In addition, pilots receive an expense allowance, or "per diem," for every hour they are away from home. Some airlines also provide allowances to pilots for purchasing and cleaning their uniforms. As an additional benefit, pilots and their immediate families usually are entitled to free or reduced-fare transportation on their own and other airlines.

More than half of all aircraft pilots are members of unions. Most of the pilots who fly for the major airlines are members of the Airline Pilots Association, International, but those employed by one major airline are members of the Allied Pilots Association. Some flight engineers are members of the Flight Engineers' International Association.

Related Occupations

Although they are not in the cockpit, air traffic controllers and airfield operation specialists also play an important role in making sure flights are safe and on schedule and participate in many of the decisions that pilots must make.

Sources of Additional Information

Information about job opportunities, salaries for a particular airline, and qualifications required may be obtained by writing to the personnel manager of the airline.

For information on airline pilots, contact

‣ Air Line Pilots Association, International, 1625 Massachusetts Ave. NW, Washington, DC 20036.

‣ Air Transport Association of America, Inc., 1301 Pennsylvania Ave. NW, Suite 1100, Washington, DC 20004.

‣ Federal Aviation Administration, 800 Independence Ave. SW, Washington, DC 20591. Internet: http://www.faa.gov

For information on helicopter pilots, contact

‣ Helicopter Association International, 1635 Prince St., Alexandria, VA 22314.

For information about job opportunities in companies other than airlines, consult the classified section of aviation trade magazines and apply to companies that operate aircraft at local airports.

Armed Forces

(O*NET 55-1011.00, 55-1012.00, 55-1013.00, 55-1014.00, 55-1015.00, 55-1016.00, 55-1017.00, 55-1019.99, 55-2011.00, 55-2012.00, 55-2013.00, 55-3011.00, 55-3012.00, 55-3013.00, 55-3014.00, 55-3015.00, 55-3016.00, 55-3017.00, 55-3018.00, and 55-3019.99)

Significant Points

■ Some training and duty assignments are hazardous, even in peacetime; hours and working conditions can be arduous and vary substantially.

■ Enlisted personnel need at least a high school diploma or its equivalent, while officers need a bachelor's or an advanced degree.

■ Opportunities should be good in all branches of the Armed Forces for applicants who meet designated standards.

Nature of the Work

Maintaining a strong national defense encompasses such diverse activities as running a hospital, commanding a tank, programming computers, operating a nuclear reactor, or repairing and maintaining a helicopter. The military provides training and work experience in these and many other fields for more than 2.6 million people. More than 1.4 million people serve in the active Army, Navy, Marine Corps, and Air Force, and more than 1.2 million serve in their Reserve components and the Air and Army National Guard. The Coast Guard, which is also discussed in this description, is now part of the U.S. Department of Homeland Security.

The military distinguishes between enlisted and officer careers. Enlisted personnel, who make up about 85 percent of the Armed Forces, carry out the fundamental operations of the military in areas such as combat, administration, construction, engineering, health care, and human services. Officers, who make up the remaining 15 percent of the Armed Forces, are the leaders of the military, supervising and managing activities in every occupational specialty of the Armed Forces.

The sections that follow discuss the major occupational groups for enlisted personnel and officers.

Enlisted occupational groups

Administrative careers include a wide variety of positions. The military must keep accurate information for planning and managing its operations. Both paper and electronic records are kept on personnel and on equipment, funds, supplies, and all other aspects of the military. Administrative personnel record information, type reports, maintain files, and review information to assist military officers. Personnel may work in a specialized area such as finance, accounting, legal affairs, maintenance, supply, or transportation.

Combat specialty occupations refer to enlisted specialties, such as infantry, artillery, and special forces, whose members operate weapons or execute special missions during combat. Persons in these occupations normally specialize by the type of weapon system or combat operation. These personnel maneuver against enemy forces and position and fire artillery, guns, and missiles to destroy enemy positions. They also may operate tanks and amphibious assault vehicles in combat or scouting missions. When the military has difficult and dangerous missions to perform, they call upon special forces teams. These elite combat forces maintain a constant state of readiness to strike anywhere in the world on a moment's notice. Team members from the special forces conduct offensive raids, demolitions, intelligence, search-and-rescue missions, and other operations from aboard aircraft, helicopters, ships, or submarines.

Construction occupations in the military include personnel who build or repair buildings, airfields, bridges, foundations, dams, bunkers, and the electrical and plumbing components of these structures. Personnel in construction occupations operate bulldozers, cranes, graders, and other heavy equipment. Construction specialists also may work with engineers and other building specialists as part of military construction teams. Some personnel specialize in areas such as plumbing or electrical wiring. Plumbers and pipefitters install and repair the plumbing and pipe systems needed in buildings and on aircraft and ships. Building electricians install and repair electrical-wiring systems in offices, airplane hangars, and other buildings on military bases.

Electronic and electrical equipment repair personnel repair and maintain electronic and electrical equipment used in the military. Repairers normally specialize by type of equipment, such as avionics, computer, optical, communications, or weapons systems. For example, electronic instrument repairers install, test, maintain, and repair a wide variety of electronic systems, including navigational controls and biomedical instruments. Weapons maintenance technicians maintain and repair weapons used by combat forces; most of these weapons have electronic components and systems that assist in locating targets and in aiming and firing the weapon.

Engineering, science, and technical personnel in the military require specific knowledge to operate technical equipment, solve complex problems, or provide and interpret information. Personnel normally specialize in one area, such as space operations, information technology, environmental health and safety, or intelligence. Space operations specialists use and repair ground-control command equipment having to do with spacecraft, including electronic systems that track the location and operation of a craft. Information technology specialists develop software programs and operate computer systems. Environmental health and safety specialists inspect military facilities and food supplies for the presence of disease, germs, or other conditions hazardous to health and the environment. Intelligence specialists gather and study information by means of aerial photographs and various types of radar and surveillance systems.

Health care personnel assist medical professionals in treating and providing services for men and women in the military. They may work as part of a patient-service team in close contact with doctors, dentists, nurses, and physical therapists to provide the necessary support functions within a hospital or clinic. Health care specialists normally specialize in a particular area—emergency medical treatment, the operation of diagnostic tools such as X-ray and ultrasound equipment, laboratory testing of tissue and blood samples, or maintaining pharmacy supplies or patients' records, among others.

Dental and optical laboratory technicians construct and repair dental equipment and eyeglasses for military personnel.

Human resources development specialists recruit and place qualified personnel and provide the training programs necessary to help people perform their jobs effectively. Personnel in this career area normally specialize by activity. For example, recruiting specialists provide information about military careers to young people, parents, schools, and local communities and explain the Armed Service's employment and training opportunities, pay and benefits, and service life. Personnel specialists collect and store information about the people in the military, including information on their previous and current training, job assignments, promotions, and health. Training specialists and instructors teach classes and give demonstrations to provide military personnel with the knowledge they need to perform their jobs.

Machine operator and production personnel operate industrial equipment, machinery, and tools to fabricate and repair parts for a variety of items and structures. They may operate engines, turbines, nuclear reactors, and water pumps. Often, they specialize by type of work performed. Welders and metalworkers, for instance, work with various types of metals to repair or form the structural parts of ships, submarines, buildings, or other equipment. Survival equipment specialists inspect, maintain, and repair survival equipment such as parachutes and aircraft life support equipment.

Media and public affairs personnel deal with the public presentation and interpretation of military information and events. They take and develop photographs; film, record, and edit audio and video programs; present news and music programs; and produce graphic artwork, drawings, and other visual displays. Other public affairs specialists act as interpreters and translators to convert written or spoken foreign languages into English or other languages.

Protective service personnel include those who enforce military laws and regulations and provide emergency response to natural and human-made disasters. These personnel normally specialize by function. For example, military police control traffic, prevent crime, and respond to emergencies. Other law enforcement and security specialists investigate crimes committed on military property and guard inmates in military correctional facilities. Fire fighters put out, control, and help prevent fires in buildings, on aircraft, and aboard ships.

Support service personnel provide subsistence services and support the morale and well-being of military personnel and their families. Food service specialists prepare all types of food in dining halls, hospitals, and ships. Counselors help military personnel and their families deal with personal issues. They work as part of a team that may include social workers, psychologists, medical officers, chaplains, personnel specialists, and commanders. Religious program specialists assist chaplains with religious services, religious education programs, and related administrative duties.

Transportation and material handling specialists ensure the safe transport of people and cargo. Most personnel within this occupational group are classified according to mode of transportation, such as aircraft, motor vehicle, or ship. Aircrew members operate equipment on board aircraft during operations. Vehicle drivers operate all types of heavy military vehicles, including fuel or water tank trucks,

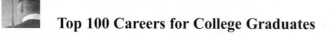

semi-trailers, heavy troop transports, and passenger buses. Quartermasters and boat operators navigate and pilot many types of small watercraft, including tugboats, gunboats, and barges. Cargo specialists load and unload military supplies, using equipment such as forklifts and cranes.

Vehicle and machinery mechanics conduct preventive and corrective maintenance on aircraft, automotive and heavy equipment, heating and cooling systems, marine engines, and powerhouse station equipment. These workers typically specialize by the type of equipment that they maintain. For example, aircraft mechanics inspect, service, and repair helicopters and airplanes. Automotive and heavy equipment mechanics maintain and repair vehicles such as humvees, trucks, tanks, self-propelled missile launchers, and other combat vehicles. They also repair bulldozers, power shovels, and other construction equipment. Heating and cooling mechanics install and repair air-conditioning, refrigeration, and heating equipment. Marine engine mechanics repair and maintain gasoline and diesel engines on ships, boats, and other watercraft. They also repair shipboard mechanical and electrical equipment. Powerhouse mechanics install, maintain, and repair electrical and mechanical equipment in power-generating stations.

Officer occupational groups

Combat specialty officers plan and direct military operations, oversee combat activities, and serve as combat leaders. This category includes officers in charge of tanks and other armored assault vehicles, artillery systems, special forces, and infantry. Combat specialty officers normally specialize by the type of unit that they lead. Within the unit, they may specialize by the type of weapon system. Artillery and missile system officers, for example, direct personnel as they target, launch, test, and maintain various types of missiles and artillery. Special-operations officers lead their units in offensive raids, demolitions, intelligence gathering, and search-and-rescue missions.

Engineering, science, and technical officers have a wide range of responsibilities based on their area of expertise. They lead or perform activities in areas such as space operations, environmental health and safety, and engineering. These officers may direct the operations of communications centers or the development of complex computer systems. Environmental health and safety officers study the air, ground, and water to identify and analyze sources of pollution and its effects. They also direct programs to control safety and health hazards in the workplace. Other personnel work as aerospace engineers to design and direct the development of military aircraft, missiles, and spacecraft.

Executive, administrative, and managerial officers oversee and direct military activities in key functional areas such as finance, accounting, health administration, international relations, and supply. Health services administrators, for instance, are responsible for the overall quality of care provided at the hospitals and clinics they operate. They must ensure that each department works together to provide the highest quality of care. As another example, purchasing and contracting managers negotiate and monitor contracts for the purchase of the billions of dollars worth of equipment, supplies, and services that the military buys from private industry each year.

Health care officers provide health services at military facilities on the basis of their area of specialization. Officers who examine, diagnose, and treat patients with illness, injury, or disease include physicians, registered nurses, and dentists. Other health care officers provide therapy, rehabilitative treatment, and additional services for patients. Physical and occupational therapists plan and administer therapy to help patients adjust to disabilities, regain independence, and return to work. Speech therapists evaluate and treat patients with hearing and speech problems. Dietitians manage food service facilities and plan meals for hospital patients and for outpatients who need special diets. Pharmacists manage the purchase, storage, and dispensation of drugs and medicines. Physicians and surgeons in this occupational group provide the majority of medical services to the military and their families. Dentists treat diseases and disorders of the mouth. Optometrists treat vision problems by prescribing eyeglasses or contact lenses. psychologists provide mental health care and also conduct research on behavior and emotions.

Human resource development officers manage recruitment, placement, and training strategies and programs in the military. They normally specialize by activity. Recruiting managers direct recruiting efforts and provide information about military careers to young people, parents, schools, and local communities. Personnel managers direct military personnel functions such as job assignment, staff promotion, and career counseling. Training and education directors identify training needs and develop and manage educational programs designed to keep military personnel current in the skills they need to perform their jobs.

Media and public affairs officers oversee the development, production, and presentation of information or events for the public. These officers may produce and direct motion pictures, videotapes, and television and radio broadcasts that are used for training, news, and entertainment. Some plan, develop, and direct the activities of military bands. Public information officers respond to inquiries about military activities and prepare news releases and reports to keep the public informed.

Protective service officers are responsible for the safety and protection of individuals and property on military bases and vessels. Emergency management officers plan and prepare for all types of natural and human-made disasters. They develop warning, control, and evacuation plans to be used in the event of a disaster. Law enforcement and security officers enforce all applicable laws on military bases and investigate crimes when the law has been broken.

Support services officers manage food service activities and perform services in support of the morale and well-being of military personnel and their families. Food services managers oversee the preparation and delivery of food services within dining facilities located on military installations and vessels. Social workers focus on improving conditions that cause social problems such as drug and alcohol abuse, racism, and sexism. Chaplains conduct worship services for military personnel and perform other spiritual duties covering the beliefs and practices of all religious faiths.

Transportation officers manage and perform activities related to the safe transport of military personnel and material by air and water. These officers normally specialize by mode of transportation or area of expertise because, in many cases, they must meet licensing and certification requirements. Pilots in the military fly various types of specialized airplanes and helicopters to carry troops and equipment and to execute combat missions. Navigators use radar, radio, and other navigation equipment to determine their position and plan their route of travel. Officers on ships and submarines work as a team to manage the various departments aboard their vessels. Ship engineers direct engineering departments aboard ships and submarines, including engine operations, maintenance, repair, heating, and power generation.

Training, Other Qualifications, and Advancement

Enlisted personnel. In order to join the services, enlisted personnel must sign a legal agreement called an enlistment contract, which usually involves a commitment to 8 years of service. Depending on the terms of the contract, 2 to 6 years are spent on active duty, and the balance is spent in the National Guard or Reserves. The enlistment contract obligates the service to provide the agreed-upon job, rating, pay, cash bonuses for enlistment in certain occupations, medical and other benefits, occupational training, and continuing education. In return, enlisted personnel must serve satisfactorily for the period specified.

Requirements for each service vary, but certain qualifications for enlistment are common to all branches. In order to enlist, one must be between 17 and 35 years old for active service, be a U.S. citizen or an alien holding permanent resident status, not have a felony record, and possess a birth certificate. Applicants who are aged 17 must have the consent of a parent or legal guardian before entering the service. Coast Guard enlisted personnel must enter active duty before their 28th birthday, whereas Marine Corps enlisted personnel must not be over the age of 29. Applicants must both pass a written examination—the Armed Services Vocational Aptitude Battery—and meet certain minimum physical standards, such as height, weight, vision, and overall health. All branches of the Armed Forces require high school graduation or its equivalent. In 2004, more than 9 out of 10 recruits were high school graduates.

People thinking about enlisting in the military should learn as much as they can about military life before making a decision. Doing so is especially important if you are thinking about making the military a career. Speaking to friends and relatives with military experience is a good idea. Find out what the military can offer you and what it will expect in return. Then, talk to a recruiter, who can determine whether you qualify for enlistment, explain the various enlistment options, and tell you which military occupational specialties currently have openings. Bear in mind that the recruiter's job is to recruit promising applicants into his or her branch of military service, so the information that the recruiter gives you is likely to stress the positive aspects of military life in the branch in which he or she serves.

Ask the recruiter for the branch you have chosen to assess your chances of being accepted for training in the occupation of your choice, or, better still, take the aptitude exam to see how well you score. The military uses this exam as a placement exam, and test scores largely determine an individual's chances of being accepted into a particular training program. Selection for a particular type of training depends on the needs of the service, your general and technical aptitudes, and your personal preference. Because all prospective recruits are required to take the exam, those who do so before committing themselves to enlist have the advantage of knowing in advance whether they stand a good chance of being accepted for

training in a particular specialty. The recruiter can schedule you for the Armed Services Vocational Aptitude Battery without any obligation. Many high schools offer the exam as an easy way for students to explore the possibility of a military career, and the test also affords an insight into career areas in which the student has demonstrated aptitudes and interests.

If you decide to join the military, the next step is to pass the physical examination and sign an enlistment contract. Negotiating the contract involves choosing, qualifying for, and agreeing on a number of enlistment options, such as the length of active-duty time, which may vary according to the option. Most active-duty programs have first-term enlistments of 4 years, although there are some 2-, 3-, and 6-year programs. The contract also will state the date of enlistment and other options—for example, bonuses and the types of training to be received. If the service is unable to fulfill any of its obligations under the contract, such as providing a certain kind of training, the contract may become null and void.

All branches of the Armed Services offer a delayed entry program (DEP) by which an individual can delay entry into active duty for up to 1 year after enlisting. High school students can enlist during their senior year and enter a service after graduation. Others choose this program because the job training they desire is not currently available, but will be within the coming year, or because they need time to arrange their personal affairs.

Women are eligible to enter most military specialties; for example, they may become mechanics, missile maintenance technicians, heavy-equipment operators, and fighter pilots, or they may enter into medical care, administrative support, and intelligence specialties. Generally, only occupations involving direct exposure to combat are excluded.

People planning to apply the skills gained through military training to a civilian career should first determine how good the prospects are for civilian employment in jobs related to the military specialty that interests them. Second, they should know the prerequisites for the related civilian job. Because many civilian occupations require a license, certification, or minimum level of education, it is important to determine whether military training is sufficient for a person to enter the civilian equivalent or, if not, what additional training will be required. Other descriptions in this book discuss the job outlook, training requirements, and other aspects of civilian occupations for which military training and experience are helpful. Additional information often can be obtained from school counselors.

Following enlistment, new members of the Armed Forces undergo initial-entry training, better known as "basic training" or "boot camp." Through courses in military skills and protocol recruit training provides a 6-week to 13-week introduction to military life. Days and nights are carefully structured and include rigorous physical exercise designed to improve strength and endurance and build each unit's cohesion.

Following basic training, most recruits take additional training at technical schools that prepare them for a particular military occupational specialty. The formal training period generally lasts from 10 to 20 weeks, although training for certain occupations—nuclear power plant operator, for example—may take as long as a year. Recruits not assigned to classroom instruction receive on-the-job training at their first duty assignment.

Many service people get college credit for the technical training they receive on duty, which, combined with off-duty courses, can lead to an associate degree through programs in community colleges such as the Community College of the Air Force. In addition to on-duty training, military personnel may choose from a variety of educational programs. Most military installations have tuition assistance programs for people wishing to take courses during off-duty hours. The courses may be correspondence courses or courses in degree programs offered by local colleges or universities. Tuition assistance pays up to 100 percent of college costs up to a credit-hour and annual limit. Each branch of the service provides opportunities for full-time study to a limited number of exceptional applicants. Military personnel accepted into these highly competitive programs—in law or medicine, for example—receive full pay, allowances, tuition, and related fees. In return, they must agree to serve an additional amount of time in the service. Other highly selective programs enable enlisted personnel to qualify as commissioned officers through additional military training.

Warrant officers. Warrant officers are technical and tactical leaders who specialize in a specific technical area; for example, Army aviators make up one group of warrant officers. The Army Warrant Officer Corps constitutes less than 5 percent of the total Army. Although the Corps is small in size, its level of responsibility is high. Its members receive extended career opportunities, worldwide leadership assignments, and increased pay and retirement benefits. Selection to attend the Warrant Officer Candidate School is highly competitive and restricted to those who meet rank and length-of-service requirements. The only exception is the Army aviator warrant officer, which has no prior military service requirements (table 1).

Officers. Officer training in the Armed Forces is provided through the federal service academies (Military, Naval, Air Force, and Coast Guard); the Reserve Officers Training Corps (ROTC) program offered at many colleges and universities; Officer Candidate School (OCS) or Officer Training School (OTS); the National Guard (State Officer Candidate School programs); the Uniformed Services University of Health Sciences; and other programs. All are highly selective and are good options for those wishing to make the military a career. Persons interested in obtaining training through the federal service academies must be single to enter and graduate, while those seeking training through OCS, OTS, or ROTC need not be single. Single parents with one or more minor dependents are not eligible to become commissioned officers.

Federal service academies provide a 4-year college program leading to a Bachelor of Science degree. Midshipmen or cadets are provided free room and board, tuition, medical and dental care, and a monthly allowance. Graduates receive regular or reserve commissions and have a 5-year active-duty obligation, or more if they are entering flight training.

To become a candidate for appointment as a cadet or midshipman in one of the service academies, applicants are required to obtain a nomination from an authorized source, usually a member of Congress. Candidates do not need to know a member of Congress personally to request a nomination. Nominees must have an academic record of the requisite quality, college aptitude test scores above an established minimum, and recommendations from teachers or school officials; they also must pass a medical examination. Appointments are made from the list of eligible nominees. Appointments to the Coast Guard Academy, however, are based strictly on merit and do not require a nomination.

ROTC programs train students in about 575 Army, 130 Navy and Marine Corps, and 300 Air Force units at participating colleges and universities. Trainees take 3 to 5 hours of military instruction a week in addition to regular college courses. After graduation, they may serve as officers on active duty for a stipulated period. Some may serve their obligation in the Reserves or National Guard. In the last 2 years of a ROTC program, students typically receive a monthly allowance while attending school, as well as additional pay for summer training. ROTC scholarships for 2, 3, and 4 years are available on a competitive basis. All scholarships pay for tuition and have allowances for textbooks, supplies, and other costs.

College graduates can earn a commission in the Armed Forces through OCS or OTS programs in the Army, Navy, Air Force, Marine Corps, Coast Guard, and National Guard. These officers generally must serve their obligation on active duty. Those with training in certain health professions may qualify for direct appointment as officers. In the case of persons studying for the health professions, financial assistance and internship opportunities are available from the military in return for specified periods of military service. Prospective medical students can apply to the Uniformed Services University of Health Sciences, which offers a salary and free tuition in a program leading to a Doctor of Medicine (M.D.) degree. In return, graduates must serve for 7 years in either the military or the U.S. Public Health Service. Direct appointments also are available for those qualified to serve in other specialty areas, such as the judge advocate general (legal) or chaplain corps. Flight training is available to commissioned officers in each branch of the Armed Forces. In addition, the Army has a direct enlistment option to become a warrant officer aviator.

Each service has different criteria for promoting personnel. Generally, the first few promotions for both enlisted and officer personnel come easily; subsequent promotions are much more competitive. Criteria for promotion may include time in service and in grade, job performance, a fitness report (supervisor's recommendation), and passing scores on written examinations. Table 1 shows the officer, warrant officer, and enlisted ranks by service.

Employment

In 2005, more than 2.6 million people served in the Armed Forces. More than 1.4 million were on active duty in the Armed Forces—about 487,000 in the Army, 350,000 in the Navy, 356,000 in the Air Force, and 185,000 in the Marine Corps. In addition, more than 1.2 million people served in their Reserve components, and the Air and Army National Guard. In addition, 33,000 individuals served in the Coast Guard, which is now part of the U.S. Department of Homeland Security. Table 2 shows the occupational composition of the 1.2 million active-duty enlisted personnel in February 2005; table 3 presents similar information for the 216,000 active-duty officers.

Military personnel are stationed throughout the United states and in many countries around the world. About half of all military jobs in the U.S. are located in California, Texas, North Carolina, Virginia, Florida, and Georgia. Approximately 169,000 service members were deployed to Operation Iraqi Freedom either in or around Iraq in June 2005. An additional 278,000 individuals were stationed outside the United States, including 21,000 assigned to ships at sea. About 106,000 were stationed in Europe, mainly in Germany, and another 81,000 were assigned to East Asia and the Pacific area, mostly in Japan and the Republic of Korea.

Table 1. Military rank and employment for active duty personnel, January 2005

Grade	Army	Navy	Air Force	Marine Corps	Employment Total
Commissioned officers:					
O-10	General	Admiral	General	General	34
O-9	Lieutenant General	Vice Admiral	Lieutenant General	Lieutenant General	125
O-8	Major General	Rear Admiral Upper	Major General	Major General	276
O-7	Brigadier General	Rear Admiral Lower	Brigadier General	Brigadier General	439
O-6	Colonel	Captain	Colonel	Colonel	11,483
O-5	Lieutenant Colonel	Commander	Lieutenant Colonel	Lieutenant Colonel	28,378
O-4	Major	Lieutenant Commander	Major	Major	43,846
O-3	Captain	Lieutenant	Captain	Captain	70,500
O-2	1st Lieutenant	Lieutenant (JG)	1st Lieutenant	1st Lieutenant	30,853
O-1	2nd Lieutenant	Ensign	2nd Lieutenant	2nd Lieutenant	24,948
Warrant officers:					
W-5	Chief Warrant Officer	Chief Warrant Officer	—	Chief Warrant Officer	540
W-4	Chief Warrant Officer	Chief Warrant Officer	—	Chief Warrant Officer	2,180
W-3	Chief Warrant Officer	Chief Warrant Officer	—	Chief Warrant Officer	4,618
W-2	Chief Warrant Officer	Chief Warrant Officer	—	Chief Warrant Officer	6,227
W-1	Warrant Officer	Warrant Officer	—	Warrant Officer	2,193
Enlisted personnel:					
E-9	Sergeant Major	Master Chief Petty Officer	Chief Master Sergeant	Sergeant Major/Master Gunnery Sergeant	10,704
E-8	1st Sergeant/ Master Sergeant	Senior Chief Petty Officer	Senior Master Sergeant	1st Sergeant/ Master Sergeant	27,229
E-7	Sergeant First Class	Chief Petty Officer	Master Sergeant	Gunnery Sergeant	100,458
E-6	Staff Sergeant	Petty Officer 1st Class	Technical Sergeant	Staff Sergeant	174,467
E-5	Sergeant	Petty Officer 2nd Class	Staff Sergeant	Sergeant	249,816
E-4	Corporal	Petty Officer 3rd Class	Senior Airman	Corporal	260,631
E-3	Private First Class	Seaman	Airman 1st Class	Lance Corporal	216,321
E-2	Private	Seaman Apprentice	Airman	Private 1st Class	82,008
E-1	Private	Seaman Recruit	Airman Basic	Private	48,818

SOURCE: U.S. Department of Defense

Table 2. Military enlisted personnel by broad occupational category and branch of military service, February 2005

Occupational Group - Enlisted	Army	Air Force	Coast Guard	Marine Corps	Navy	Total, all services
Administrative occupations	14,016	25,008	2,241	9,612	25,923	76,800
Combat specialty occupations	113,689	398	851	52,256	6,264	173,458
Construction occupations	15,544	6,407	—	5,147	5,085	32,183
Electronic and electrical repair occupations	39,601	40,083	3,045	15,586	58,992	157,307
Engineering, science, and technical occupations	35,482	50,732	986	23,656	41,951	152,807
Health care occupations	27,031	17,924	682	—	26,614	72,251
Human resource development occupations	15,908	12,468	—	6,803	4,822	40,001

(continued)

(continued)

Occupational Group - Enlisted	Army	Air Force	Coast Guard	Marine Corps	Navy	Total, all services
Machine operator and precision work occupations	4,103	7,409	1,548	2,439	12,274	27,773
Media and public affairs occupations	4,867	6,453	121	2,258	5,047	18,746
Protective service occupations	23,270	31,716	2,695	5,733	12,215	75,629
Support services occupations	13,438	1,667	1,146	2,264	10,699	29,214
Transportation and material handling occupations	53,349	34,588	10,549	22,825	42,860	164,171
Vehicle machinery mechanic occupations	48,577	50,532	5,538	18,076	50,020	172,743
Total, by service	408,875	285,385	29,402	166,655	302,766	1,193,083

SOURCE: U.S. Department of Defense, Defense Manpower Data Center

Table 3. Military officer personnel by broad occupational category and branch of service, February 2005

Occupational Group - Officer	Army	Air Force	Coast Guard	Marine Corps	Navy	Total, all services
Combat specialty occupations	18,835	6,007	—	4,662	5,463	34,967
Engineering, science, and technical occupations	19,137	17,503	1,576	3,576	9,778	51,087
Executive, administrative, and managerial occupations	11,262	10,395	282	2,582	7,450	31,971
Health care occupations	9,792	9,413	43	—	6,983	26,231
Human resource development occupations	2,128	2,418	213	299	3,258	8,316
Media and public affairs occupations	224	500	20	44	282	1,070
Protective service occupations	2,237	1,410	104	309	890	4,950
Support services occupations	1,525	830	—	38	1,003	3,396
Transportation occupations	13,216	19,729	2,250	7,082	11,975	54,252
Total, by service	78,356	68,205	4,005	18,592	47,082	216,240

SOURCE: U.S. Department of Defense, Defense Manpower Data Center

Job Outlook

Opportunities should be good for qualified individuals in all branches of the Armed Forces through 2014. Many military personnel retire with a pension after 20 years of service, while they still are young enough to start a new career. About 170,000 personnel must be recruited each year to replace those who complete their commitment or retire. Since the end of the draft in 1973, the military has met its personnel requirements with volunteers. When the economy is good and civilian employment opportunities generally are more favorable, it is more difficult for all the services to meet their recruitment quotas. It is also more difficult to meet these goals during times of war, when recruitment goals typically rise.

America's strategic position is stronger than it has been in decades. Despite reductions in personnel due to the elimination of the threats of the Cold War, the number of active-duty personnel is expected to remain roughly constant through 2014. However, recent conflicts and the resulting strain on the Armed Forces may lead to an increasing number of active-duty personnel. The Armed Forces' current goal is to maintain a sufficient force to fight and win two major regional conflicts at the same time. Political events, however, could lead to a significant restructuring with or without an increase in size.

Educational requirements will continue to rise as military jobs become more technical and complex. High school graduates and applicants with a college background will be sought to fill the ranks of enlisted personnel, while virtually all officers will need at least a bachelor's degree and, in some cases, an advanced degree as well.

Earnings

The earnings structure for military personnel is shown in table 4. Most enlisted personnel started as recruits at Grade E-1 in 2004; however, those with special skills or above-average education started as high as Grade E-4. Most warrant officers had started at Grade W-1 or W-2, depending upon their occupational and academic qualifications and the branch of service of which they were a member, but warrant officer typically is not an entry-level occupation and, consequently, most of these individuals had previous military service. Most commissioned officers started at Grade O-1; some with advanced education started at Grade O-2, and some highly trained officers—for example, physicians and dentists—started as high as Grade O-3. Pay varies by total years of service as well as rank. Because it usually takes many years to reach the higher ranks, most personnel in higher ranks receive the higher pay rates awarded to those with many years of service.

In addition to receiving their basic pay, military personnel are provided with free room and board (or a tax-free housing and subsistence allowance), free medical and dental care, a military clothing allowance, military supermarket and department store shopping privileges, 30 days of paid vacation a year (referred to as leave), and travel opportunities. In many duty stations, military personnel may receive a housing allowance that can be used for off-base housing. This allowance can be substantial, but varies greatly by rank and duty station. For example, in fiscal year 2005, the average housing allowance for an E-4 with dependents was $958 per month; for a comparable individual without dependents, it was $752. The allowance for an O-4 with dependents was $1,645 per month; for a comparable individual without dependents, it was $1,428. Other allowances are paid for foreign duty, hazardous duty, submarine and flight duty, and employment as a medical officer. Athletic and other facilities—such as gymnasiums, tennis courts, golf courses, bowling centers, libraries, and movie theaters—are available on many military installations. Military personnel are eligible for retirement benefits after 20 years of service.

The Veterans Administration (VA) provides numerous benefits to those who have served at least 24 months of continuous active duty in the Armed Forces. Veterans are eligible for free care in VA hospitals for all service-related disabilities, regardless of time served; those with other medical problems are eligible for free VA care if they are unable to pay the cost of hospitalization elsewhere.

Admission to a VA medical center depends on the availability of beds, however. Veterans also are eligible for certain loans, including loans to purchase a home. Veterans, regardless of health, can convert a military life insurance policy to an individual policy with any participating company upon separation from the military. In addition, job counseling, testing, and placement services are available.

Veterans who participate in the Montgomery GI Bill Program receive education benefits. Under this program, Armed Forces personnel may elect to deduct up to $100 a month from their pay during the first 12 months of active duty, putting the money toward their future education. In fiscal year 2005, veterans who served on active duty for 3 or more years or who spent 2 years in active duty plus 4 years in the Selected Reserve received $1,004 a month in basic benefits for 36 months of full-time institutional training. Those who enlisted and serve less than 3 years received $816 a month for 36 months for the same. In addition, each service provides its own contributions to the enlistee's future education. The sum of the amounts from all these sources becomes the service member's educational fund. Upon separation from active duty, the fund can be used to finance educational costs at any VA-approved institution. Among those institutions which are approved by the VA are many vocational, correspondence, certification, business, technical, and flight-training schools; community and junior colleges; and colleges and universities.

Table 4. Military basic monthly pay by grade for active duty personnel, January 2005

	Years of service					
Grade	Less than 2	Over 4	Over 8	Over 12	Over 16	Over 20
O-10	—	—	—	—	—	$12,963.00
O-9	—	—	—	—	—	11,337.90
O-8	$8,022.30	$8,508.30	$9,089.40	$9,519.00	$9,915.30	10,742.40
O-7	6,666.00	6,233.00	7,642.50	8,113.50	9,089.40	9,714.60
O-6	4,940.70	5,784.00	6,054.90	6,087.90	7,045.50	7,763.40
O-5	4,118.70	5,021.40	5,341.80	5,799.00	6,431.10	6,793.20
O-4	3,553.80	4,449.60	4,977.60	5,582.70	5,872.20	5,933.70
O-3	3,124.50	4,168.20	4,586.70	4,962.00	5,083.20	5,083.20
O-2	2,699.40	3,660.90	3,736.20	3,736.20	3,736.20	3,736.20
O-1	2,343.60	2,948.10	2,948.10	2,948.10	2,948.10	2,948.10
W-5	—	—	—	—	—	5,548.20
W-4	3,228.60	3,671.40	4,007.10	4,341.00	4,779.00	5,117.40
W-3	2,948.40	3,238.80	3,522.30	3,918.90	4,285.50	4,509.30
W-2	2,593.50	2,965.50	3,268.20	3,564.00	3,771.30	3,977.40
W-1	2,290.20	2,684.40	3,030.90	3,275.40	3,438.30	3,659.70
E-9	—	—	—	3,989.70	4,232.40	4,575.90
E-8	—	—	3,193.50	3,442.10	3,640.50	3,949.20
E-7	2,220.00	2,638.80	2,899.50	3,084.60	3,332.40	3,458.70
E-6	1,920.30	2,296.50	2,604.30	2,779.20	2,888.70	2,908.20
E-5	1,759.50	2,060.70	2,329.80	2,450.70	2,450.70	2,450.70
E-4	1,612.80	1,877.70	1,957.80	1,957.80	1,957.80	1,957.80

(continued)

(continued)

			Years of service			
Grade	Less than 2	Over 4	Over 8	Over 12	Over 16	Over 20
E-3	1,456.20	1,641.00	1,641.00	1,641.00	1,641.00	1,641.00
E-2	1,384.50	1,384.50	1,384.50	1,384.50	1,384.50	1,384.50
E-1 4mos+	1,235.10	1,235.10	1,235.10	1,235.10	1,235.10	1,235.10
E-1 <4mos	1,142.70	—	—	—	—	—

SOURCE: U.S. Department of Defense, Defense Finance and Accounting Service

Sources of Additional Information

Each of the military services publishes handbooks, fact sheets, and pamphlets describing entrance requirements, training and advancement opportunities, and other aspects of military careers. These publications are widely available at all recruiting stations, at most state employment service offices, and in high schools, colleges, and public libraries. Information on educational and other veterans' benefits is available from VA offices located throughout the country.

In addition, the Defense Manpower Data Center, an agency of the U.S. Department of Defense, publishes *Military Career Guide Online*, a compendium of military occupational, training, and career information designed for use by students and jobseekers. This information is available on the Internet: http://www.todaysmilitary.com

Artists and Related Workers

(O*NET 27-1011.00, 27-1012.00, 27-1013.01, 27-1013.02, 27-1013.03, 27-1013.04, and 27-1014.00)

Significant Points

- About 63 percent of artists and related workers are self-employed.

- Keen competition is expected for both salaried jobs and freelance work; the number of qualified workers exceeds the number of available openings because the arts attract many talented people with creative ability.

- Artists usually develop their skills through a bachelor's degree program or other postsecondary training in art or design.

- Earnings for self-employed artists vary widely; some well-established artists earn more than salaried artists, while others find it difficult to rely solely on income earned from selling art.

Nature of the Work

Artists create art to communicate ideas, thoughts, or feelings. They use a variety of methods—painting, sculpting, or illustration—and an assortment of materials, including oils, watercolors, acrylics, pastels, pencils, pen and ink, plaster, clay, and computers. Artists' works may be realistic, stylized, or abstract and may depict objects, people, nature, or events.

Artists generally fall into one of four categories. *Art directors* formulate design concepts and presentation approaches for visual communications media. *Craft artists* create or reproduce handmade objects for sale or exhibition. *Fine artists, including painters, sculptors, and illustrators,* create original artwork, using a variety of media and techniques. *Multi-media artists and animators* create special effects, animation, or other visual images on film, on video, or with computers or other electronic media.

Art directors develop design concepts and review material that is to appear in periodicals, newspapers, and other printed or digital media. They decide how best to present the information visually so that it is eye catching, appealing, and organized. Art directors decide which photographs or artwork to use and oversee the layout design and production of the printed material. They may direct workers engaged in artwork, layout design, and copywriting.

Craft artists hand-make a wide variety of objects that are sold either in their own studios, in retail outlets, or at arts-and-crafts shows. Some craft artists may display their works in galleries and museums. Craft artists work with many different materials—ceramics, glass, textiles, wood, metal, and paper—to create unique pieces of art, such as pottery, stained glass, quilts, tapestries, lace, candles, and clothing. Many craft artists also use fine-art techniques—for example, painting, sketching, and printing—to add finishing touches to their art.

Fine artists typically display their work in museums, commercial art galleries, corporate collections, and private homes. Some of their artwork may be commissioned (done on request from clients), but most is sold by the artist or through private art galleries or dealers. The gallery and the artist predetermine how much each will earn from the sale. Only the most successful fine artists are able to support themselves solely through the sale of their works. Most fine artists have at least one other job to support their art careers. Some work in museums or art galleries as fine-arts directors or as curators, planning and setting up art exhibits. A few artists work as art critics for newspapers or magazines or as consultants to foundations or institutional collectors. Other artists teach art classes or conduct workshops in schools or in their own studios. Some artists also hold full-time or part-time jobs unrelated to the art field and pursue fine art as a hobby or second career.

Usually, fine artists specialize in one or two art forms, such as painting, illustrating, sketching, sculpting, printmaking, and restoring. *Painters, illustrators, cartoonists, and sketch artists* work with two-dimensional art forms, using shading, perspective, and color to produce realistic scenes or abstractions.

Illustrators typically create pictures for books, magazines, and other publications and for commercial products such as textiles, wrapping paper, stationery, greeting cards, and calendars. Increasingly, illustrators are working in digital format, preparing work directly on a computer.

Medical and *scientific illustrators* combine drawing skills with knowledge of biology or other sciences. Medical illustrators draw illustrations of human anatomy and surgical procedures. Scientific illustrators draw illustrations of animal and plant life, atomic and molecular structures, and geologic and planetary formations. The illustrations are used in medical and scientific publications and in audiovisual presentations for teaching purposes. Medical illustrators also work for lawyers, producing exhibits for court cases.

Cartoonists draw political, advertising, social, and sports cartoons. Some cartoonists work with others who create the idea or story and write the captions. Most cartoonists have comic, critical, or dramatic talents in addition to drawing skills.

Sketch artists create likenesses of subjects with pencil, charcoal, or pastels. Sketches are used by law enforcement agencies to assist in identifying suspects, by the news media to depict courtroom scenes, and by individual patrons for their own enjoyment.

Sculptors design three-dimensional artworks, either by molding and joining materials such as clay, glass, wire, plastic, fabric, or metal or by cutting and carving forms from a block of plaster, wood, or stone. Some sculptors combine various materials to create mixed-media installations. Some incorporate light, sound, and motion into their works.

Printmakers create printed images from designs cut or etched into wood, stone, or metal. After creating the design, the artist inks the surface of the woodblock, stone, or plate and uses a printing press to roll the image onto paper or fabric. Some make prints by pressing the inked surface onto paper by hand or by graphically encoding and processing data, using a computer. The digitized images are then printed on paper with the use of a computer printer.

Painting restorers preserve and restore damaged and faded paintings. They apply solvents and cleaning agents to clean the surfaces of the paintings, they reconstruct or retouch damaged areas, and they apply preservatives to protect the paintings. Restoration is highly detailed work and usually is reserved for experts in the field.

Multi-media artists and animators work primarily in motion picture and video industries, advertising, and computer systems design services. They draw by hand and use computers to create the large series of pictures that form the animated images or special effects seen in movies, television programs, and computer games. Some draw storyboards for television commercials, movies, and animated features. Storyboards present television commercials in a series of scenes similar to a comic strip and allow an advertising agency to evaluate commercials proposed by the company doing the advertising. Storyboards also serve as guides to placing actors and cameras on the television or motion picture set and to other details that need to be taken care of during the production of commercials.

Working Conditions

Many artists work in fine- or commercial-art studios located in office buildings, warehouses, or lofts. Others work in private studios in their homes. Some fine artists share studio space, where they also may exhibit their work. Studio surroundings usually are well lighted and ventilated; however, fine artists may be exposed to fumes from glue, paint, ink, and other materials and to dust or other residue from filings, splattered paint, or spilled fluids. Artists who sit at drafting tables or who use computers for extended periods may experience back pain, eyestrain, or fatigue.

Artists employed by publishing companies, advertising agencies, and design firms generally work a standard workweek. During busy periods, they may work overtime to meet deadlines. Self-employed artists can set their own hours, but may spend much time and effort selling their artwork to potential customers or clients and building a reputation.

Training, Other Qualifications, and Advancement

Postsecondary training is recommended for all artist specialties. Although formal training is not strictly required, it is very difficult to become skilled enough to make a living without some training. Many colleges and universities offer programs leading to the bachelor's or master's degree in fine arts. Courses usually include core subjects such as English, social science, and natural science in addition to art history and studio art.

Independent schools of art and design also offer postsecondary studio training in the craft, fine, and multi-media arts leading to a certificate in the specialty or to an associate's or bachelor's degree in fine arts. Typically, these programs focus more intensively on studio work than do the academic programs in a university setting. The National Association of Schools of Art and Design accredits about 250 postsecondary institutions with programs in art and design; most award a degree in art.

Formal educational programs in art also provide training in computer techniques. Computers are used widely in the visual arts, and knowledge and training in computer graphics and other visual display software are critical elements of many jobs in these fields.

Medical illustrators must have both a demonstrated artistic ability and a detailed knowledge of living organisms, surgical and medical procedures, and human and animal anatomy. A bachelor's degree combining art and premedical courses usually is required. However, most medical illustrators also choose to pursue a master's degree in medical illustration. This degree is offered in five accredited schools in the United States.

Art directors usually begin as entry-level artists in advertising, publishing, design, and motion picture production firms. Artists are promoted to art director after demonstrating artistic and leadership abilities. Some art schools offer coursework in art direction as part of postsecondary training. Depending on the scope of their responsibilities, some art directors also may pursue a degree in art administration, which teaches nonartistic skills such as project management and communication.

Those who want to teach fine arts at public elementary or secondary schools must have a teaching certificate in addition to a bachelor's degree. An advanced degree in fine arts or arts administration is necessary for management or administrative positions in government or in foundations or for teaching in colleges and universities.

Evidence of appropriate talent and skill, displayed in an artist's portfolio, is an important factor used by art directors, clients, and others in deciding whether to hire an individual or to contract out work. The portfolio is a collection of handmade, computer-generated, photographic, or printed samples of the artist's best work. Assembling a successful portfolio requires skills usually developed through postsecondary training in art or visual communications. Internships also provide excellent opportunities for artists to develop and enhance their portfolios.

Artists hired by firms often start with relatively routine work. While doing this work, however, they may observe and practice their skills on the side. Many artists freelance on a part-time basis while continuing to hold a full-time job until they are established. Others freelance part time while still in school to develop experience and to build a portfolio of published work.

Freelance artists try to develop a set of clients who regularly contract for work. Some freelance artists are widely recognized for their skill in specialties such as cartooning or children's book illustration. These artists may earn high incomes and can choose the type of work they do.

Craft and fine artists advance professionally as their work circulates and as they establish a reputation for a particular style. Many of the most successful artists continually develop new ideas, and their work often evolves over time.

Employment

Artists held about 208,000 jobs in 2004. Sixty-three percent were self-employed. Employment was distributed as follows:

Multi-media artists and animators 94,000
Art directors 71,000
Fine artists, including painters, sculptors,
   and illustrators 29,000
Artists and related workers, all other 8,500
Craft artists 6,100

Of the artists who were not self-employed, many worked in advertising and related services; newspaper, periodical, book, and software publishers; motion picture and video industries; specialized design services; and computer systems design and related services. Some self-employed artists offered their services to advertising agencies, design firms, publishing houses, and other businesses on a contract or freelance basis.

Job Outlook

Employment of artists and related workers is expected to grow about as fast as average for all occupations through the year 2014. However, the competition for jobs is expected to be keen for both salaried and freelance jobs in all specialties because the number of qualified workers exceeds the number of available openings. Also, because the arts attract many talented people with creative ability, the number of aspiring artists continues to grow. Employers in all industries should be able to choose from among the most qualified candidates.

Art directors work in a variety of industries, such as advertising, public relations, publishing, and design firms. Despite an expanding number of opportunities, they should experience keen competition for the available openings.

Craft and fine artists work mostly on a freelance or commission basis and may find it difficult to earn a living solely by selling their artwork. Only the most successful craft and fine artists receive major commissions for their work. Competition among artists for

the privilege of being shown in galleries is expected to remain acute, and grants from sponsors such as private foundations, state and local arts councils, and the National Endowment for the Arts should remain competitive. Nonetheless, studios, galleries, and individual clients are always on the lookout for artists who display outstanding talent, creativity, and style. Among craft and fine artists, talented individuals who have developed a mastery of artistic techniques and skills will have the best job prospects.

The growth in computer graphics packages and stock art Web sites is making it easier for writers, publishers, and art directors to create their own illustrations. As the use of this technology grows, there will be fewer opportunities for illustrators. One exception is the small number of medical illustrators, who will be in greater demand to illustrate journal articles and books as medical research continues to grow.

Salaried cartoonists will have fewer job opportunities because many newspapers and magazines are increasingly relying on freelance work. In addition, many cartoonists are opting to post their work on political Web sites and online publications. As online posting of cartoons increases, many are creating animated or interactive images to satisfy readers' demands for more sophisticated cartoons.

Multi-media artists and animators should have better job opportunities than other artists, but still will experience competition. Demand for these workers will increase as consumers continue to demand more realistic video games, movie and television special effects, and 3-D animated movies. Additional job openings will arise from an increasing demand for Web site development and for computer graphics adaptation from the growing number of mobile technologies. Job opportunities for animators of lower-technology, two-dimensional television cartoons could be hampered as these jobs continue to be outsourced overseas.

Earnings

Median annual earnings of salaried art directors were $63,840 in May 2004. The middle 50 percent earned between $47,890 and $88,120. The lowest 10 percent earned less than $35,500, and the highest 10 percent earned more than $123,320. Median annual earnings were $66,900 in advertising and related services.

Median annual earnings of salaried craft artists were $23,520 in May 2004. The middle 50 percent earned between $17,950 and $32,980. The lowest 10 percent earned less than $14,740, and the highest 10 percent earned more than $44,490.

Median annual earnings of salaried fine artists, including painters, sculptors, and illustrators, were $38,060 in May 2004. The middle 50 percent earned between $25,990 and $51,730. The lowest 10 percent earned less than $17,390, and the highest 10 percent earned more than $68,860. According to the Association of Medical Illustrators, the median earnings in 2005 for salaried medical illustrators were $59,000.

Median annual earnings of salaried multi-media artists and animators were $50,360 in May 2004. The middle 50 percent earned between $37,980 and $70,730. The lowest 10 percent earned less than $29,030, and the highest 10 percent earned more than $94,260. Median annual earnings were $67,390 in motion picture and video industries and $46,810 in advertising and related services.

Earnings for self-employed artists vary widely. Some charge only a nominal fee while they gain experience and build a reputation for their work. Others, such as well-established freelance fine artists and illustrators, can earn more than salaried artists. Many, however, find it difficult to rely solely on income earned from selling paintings or other works of art. Like other self-employed workers, freelance artists must provide their own benefits.

Related Occupations

Other workers who apply art skills include architects, except landscape and naval; archivists, curators, and museum technicians; commercial and industrial designers; fashion designers; floral designers; graphic designers; interior designers; jewelers and precious stone and metal workers; landscape architects; photographers; and woodworkers. Some workers who use computers extensively, including computer software engineers and desktop publishers, may require art skills.

Sources of Additional Information

For general information about art and design and a list of accredited college-level programs, contact

▸ National Association of Schools of Art and Design, 11250 Roger Bacon Dr., Suite 21, Reston, VA 20190-5248. Internet: http://nasad.arts-accredit.org

For information on careers in the craft arts and for a list of schools and workshops, contact

▸ American Craft Council Library, 72 Spring St., 6th Floor, New York, NY 10012-4019. Internet: http://www.craftcouncil.org

For information on careers in illustration, contact

▸ Society of Illustrators, 128 E. 63rd St., New York, NY 10021-7303. Internet: http://www.societyillustrators.org

For information on careers in medical illustration, contact

▸ Association of Medical Illustrators, 245 First St., Suite 1800, Cambridge, MA 02142. Internet: http://www.ami.org

For information on workshops, scholarships, internships, and competitions for art students interested in advertising careers, contact

▸ Art Directors Club, 106 W. 29th St., New York, NY 10001. Internet: http://www.adcglobal.org

Computer Support Specialists and Systems Administrators

(O*NET 15-1041.00, 15-1071.00, and 15-1071.01)

Significant Points

■ Rapid job growth is projected over the 2004–2014 period.

■ There are many paths of entry to these occupations.

■ Job prospects should be best for college graduates who are up to date with the latest skills and technologies; certifications and practical experience are essential for persons without degrees.

Nature of the Work

In the last decade, computers have become an integral part of everyday life, used for a variety of reasons at home, in the workplace, and at schools. Of course, almost every computer user encounters a problem occasionally, whether it is the disaster of a crashing hard drive or the annoyance of a forgotten password. The explosive use of computers has created a high demand for specialists to provide advice to users as well as for day-to-day administration, maintenance, and support of computer systems and networks.

Computer support specialists provide technical assistance, support, and advice to customers and other users. This occupational group includes *technical support specialists* and *help-desk technicians*. These troubleshooters interpret problems and provide technical support for hardware, software, and systems. They answer telephone calls, analyze problems by using automated diagnostic programs, and resolve recurring difficulties. Support specialists may work either within a company that uses computer systems or directly for a computer hardware or software vendor. Increasingly, these specialists work for help-desk or support services firms, for which they provide computer support to clients on a contract basis.

Technical support specialists answer telephone calls from their organizations' computer users and may run automatic diagnostics programs to resolve problems. Working on monitors, keyboards, printers, and mice, they install, modify, clean, and repair computer hardware and software. They also may write training manuals and train computer users in how to use new computer hardware and software. In addition, technical support specialists oversee the daily performance of their company's computer systems and evaluate software programs with regard to their usefulness.

Help-desk technicians assist computer users with the inevitable hardware and software questions that are not addressed in a product's instruction manual. Help-desk technicians field telephone calls and e-mail messages from customers who are seeking guidance on technical problems. In responding to these requests for guidance, help-desk technicians must listen carefully to the customer, ask questions to diagnose the nature of the problem, and then patiently walk the customer through the problem-solving steps.

Help-desk technicians deal directly with customer issues, and companies value them as a source of feedback on their products. These technicians are consulted for information about what gives customers the most trouble as well as other customer concerns. Most computer support specialists start out at the help desk.

Network administrators and *computer systems administrators* design, install, and support an organization's local area network (LAN), wide area network (WAN), network segment, Internet, or intranet system. They provide day-to-day onsite administrative support for software users in a variety of work environments, including professional offices, small businesses, government, and large corporations. They maintain network hardware and software, analyze problems, and monitor the network to ensure its availability to system users. These workers gather data to identify customer needs and then use the information to identify, interpret, and evaluate system and network requirements. Administrators also may plan, coordinate, and implement network security measures.

Systems administrators are the information technology employees responsible for the efficient use of networks by organizations. They ensure that the design of an organization's computer site allows all of the components, including computers, the network, and software, to fit together and work properly. Furthermore, they monitor and adjust the performance of existing networks and continually survey the current computer site to determine future network needs. Administrators also troubleshoot problems reported by users and by automated network monitoring systems and make recommendations for enhancements in the implementation of future servers and networks.

In some organizations, *computer security specialists* may plan, coordinate, and implement the organization's information security. These workers may be called upon to educate users about computer security, install security software, monitor the network for security breaches, respond to cyber attacks, and, in some cases, gather data and evidence to be used in prosecuting cyber crime. The responsibilities of computer security specialists have increased in recent years, as there has been a large increase in the number of cyber attacks on data and networks. This and other growing specialty occupations reflect an increasing emphasis on client-server applications, the expansion of Internet and intranet applications, and the demand for more end-user support.

Working Conditions

Computer support specialists and systems administrators normally work in well-lighted, comfortable offices or computer laboratories. They usually work about 40 hours a week, but that may include being "on call" via pager or telephone for rotating evening or weekend work if the employer requires computer support over extended hours. Overtime may be necessary when unexpected technical problems arise. Like other workers who type on a keyboard for long periods, computer support specialists and systems administrators are susceptible to eyestrain, back discomfort, and hand and wrist problems such as carpal tunnel syndrome.

Due to the heavy emphasis on helping all types of computer users, computer support specialists and systems administrators constantly interact with customers and fellow employees as they answer questions and give valuable advice. Those who work as consultants are away from their offices much of the time, sometimes spending months working in a client's office.

As computer networks expand, more computer support specialists and systems administrators may be able to connect to a customer's computer remotely, using modems, laptops, e-mail, and the Internet, to provide technical support to computer users. This capability would reduce or eliminate travel to the customer's workplace. Systems administrators also can administer and configure networks and servers remotely, although this practice is not as common as it is among computer support specialists.

Training, Other Qualifications, and Advancement

Due to the wide range of skills required, there are many paths of entry to a job as a computer support specialist or systems administrator. While there is no universally accepted way to prepare for a job as a computer support specialist, many employers prefer to hire persons with some formal college education. A bachelor's degree in computer science or information systems is a prerequisite for some

jobs; however, other jobs may require only a computer-related associate's degree. For systems administrators, many employers seek applicants with bachelor's degrees, although not necessarily in a computer-related field.

A number of companies are becoming more flexible about requiring a college degree for support positions. However, certification and practical experience demonstrating these skills will be essential for applicants without a degree. The completion of a certification training program, offered by a variety of vendors and product makers, may help some people to qualify for entry-level positions. Relevant computer experience may substitute for formal education.

Beginning computer support specialists usually work for organizations that deal directly with customers or in-house users. Then they may advance into more responsible positions in which they use what they have learned from customers to improve the design and efficiency of future products. Job promotions usually depend more on performance than on formal education. Eventually, some computer support specialists become applications developers, designing products rather than assisting users. Computer support specialists at hardware and software companies often enjoy great upward mobility; advancement sometimes comes within months of one's initial employment.

Entry-level network and computer systems administrators are involved in routine maintenance and monitoring of computer systems, typically working behind the scenes in an organization. After gaining experience and expertise, they often are able to advance into more senior-level positions in which they take on more responsibilities. For example, senior network and computer systems administrators may present recommendations to management on matters related to a company's network. They also may translate the needs of an organization into a set of technical requirements based on the available technology. As with support specialists, administrators may become software engineers, actually involved in the designing of the system or network and not just its day-to-day administration.

Persons interested in becoming a computer support specialist or systems administrator must have strong problem-solving, analytical, and communication skills because troubleshooting and helping others are vital parts of the job. The constant interaction with other computer personnel, customers, and employees requires computer support specialists and systems administrators to communicate effectively on paper, via e-mail, or in person. Strong writing skills are useful in preparing manuals for employees and customers.

As technology continues to improve, computer support specialists and systems administrators must keep their skills current and acquire new ones. Many continuing education programs are provided by employers, hardware and software vendors, colleges and universities, and private training institutions. Professional development seminars offered by computing services firms also can enhance one's skills and advancement opportunities.

Employment

Computer support specialists and systems administrators held about 797,000 jobs in 2004. Of these, approximately 518,000 were computer support specialists and around 278,000 were network and computer systems administrators. Although they worked in a wide range of industries, about 23 percent of all computer support specialists and systems administrators were employed in professional, scientific, and technical services industries, principally computer systems design and related services. Other organizations that employed substantial numbers of these workers include administrative and support services companies; banks; government agencies; insurance companies; educational institutions; and wholesale and retail vendors of computers, office equipment, appliances, and home electronic equipment. Many computer support specialists worked for manufacturers of computers, semiconductors, and other electronic components.

Employers of computer support specialists and systems administrators range from startup companies to established industry leaders. With the continued development of the Internet, telecommunications, and e-mail, industries not typically associated with computers—such as construction—increasingly need computer workers. Small and large firms across all industries are expanding or developing computer systems, creating an immediate need for computer support specialists and systems administrators.

Job Outlook

Job prospects should be best for college graduates who are up to date with the latest skills and technologies, particularly if they have supplemented their formal education with some relevant work experience. Employers will continue to seek computer specialists who possess a strong background in fundamental computer skills combined with good interpersonal and communication skills. Due to the demand for computer support specialists and systems administrators over the next decade, those who have strong computer skills but do not have a bachelor's degree should continue to qualify for some entry-level positions. However, certifications and practical experience are essential for persons without degrees.

Employment of computer support specialists is expected to increase faster than the average for all occupations through 2014 as organizations continue to adopt increasingly sophisticated technology and integrate it into their systems. Job growth will continue to be driven by the ongoing expansion of the computer system design and related services industry, which is projected to remain one of the fastest-growing industries in the U.S. economy. Growth will not be as explosive as during the previous decade, however, as the information technology industry matures and some of these jobs are increasingly outsourced overseas.

Job growth among computer support specialists reflects the rapid pace of improved technology. As computers and software become more complex, support specialists will be needed to provide technical assistance to customers and other users. New mobile technologies, such as wireless Internet access, will continue to create a demand for these workers to familiarize and educate computer users. Consulting opportunities for computer support specialists also should continue to grow as businesses increasingly need help managing, upgrading, and customizing ever more complex computer systems. However, growth in employment of support specialists may be tempered somewhat as firms continue to cut costs by shifting more routine work abroad to countries where workers are highly skilled and labor costs are lower. Physical location is not as important for computer support specialists as it is for others because these

workers can provide assistance remotely and support services can be provided around the clock.

Employment of systems administrators is expected to increase much faster than the average for all occupations as firms continue to invest heavily in securing computer networks. Companies are looking for workers who are knowledgeable about the function and administration of networks. Such employees have become increasingly hard to find as systems administration has moved from being a separate function within corporations to one that forms a crucial element of business in an increasingly high-technology economy. Also, demand for computer security specialists will grow as businesses and government continue to invest heavily in "cyber security," protecting vital computer networks and electronic infrastructures from attack. The information security field is expected to generate many opportunities over the next decade as firms across all industries place a high priority on safeguarding their data and systems.

The growth of electronic commerce means that more establishments use the Internet to conduct their business online. This growth translates into a need for information technology specialists who can help organizations use technology to communicate with employees, clients, and consumers. Growth in these areas also is expected to fuel demand for specialists who are knowledgeable about network, data, and communications security.

Earnings

Median annual earnings of computer support specialists were $40,430 in May 2004. The middle 50 percent earned between $30,980 and $53,010. The lowest 10 percent earned less than $24,190, and the highest 10 percent earned more than $69,110. Median annual earnings in the industries employing the largest numbers of computer support specialists in May 2004 were as follows:

Software publishers	$44,890
Management of companies and enterprises	42,780
Computer systems design and related services	42,750
Colleges, universities, and professional schools	37,940
Elementary and secondary schools	35,500

Median annual earnings of network and computer systems administrators were $58,190 in May 2004. The middle 50 percent earned between $46,260 and $73,620. The lowest 10 percent earned less than $37,100, and the highest 10 percent earned more than $91,300. Median annual earnings in the industries employing the largest numbers of network and computer systems administrators in May 2004 were as follows:

Wired telecommunications carriers	$65,120
Computer systems design and related services	63,710
Management of companies and enterprises	61,600
Elementary and secondary schools	51,420
Colleges, universities, and professional schools	51,170

According to Robert Half International, starting salaries in 2005 ranged from $26,250 to $53,750 for help-desk and technical support staff and from $44,500 to $63,250 for more senior technical support specialists. For systems administrators, starting salaries in 2005 ranged from $47,250 to $70,500.

Related Occupations

Other computer specialists include computer programmers, computer software engineers, computer systems analysts, and computer scientists and database administrators.

Sources of Additional Information

For additional information about a career as a computer support specialist, contact the following organizations:

▸ Association of Computer Support Specialists, 333 Mamaroneck Ave., #129, White Plains, NY 10605. Internet: http://www.acss.org

▸ Association of Support Professionals, 122 Barnard Ave., Watertown, MA 02472.

For additional information about a career as a systems administrator, contact

▸ System Administrators Guild, 2560 9th St., Suite 215, Berkeley, CA 94710. Internet: http://www.sage.org

Further information about computer careers is available from

▸ National Workforce Center for Emerging Technologies, 3000 Landerholm Circle SE, Bellevue, WA 98007. Internet: http://www.nwcet.org

Interpreters and Translators

(O*NET 27-3091.00)

Significant Points

■ Fifteen percent of these workers are self-employed.

■ Work is often sporadic, and many interpreters and translators work part time.

■ Although training requirements can vary, most interpreters and translators have a bachelor's degree.

■ Job outlook varies by specialty and language combination.

Nature of the Work

Interpreters and translators enable the cross-cultural communication necessary in today's society by converting one language into another. However, these language specialists do more than simply translate words—they relay concepts and ideas between languages. They must thoroughly understand the subject matter in which they work so that they are able to convert information from one language, known as the source language, into another, the target language. In addition, they must remain sensitive to the cultures associated with their languages of expertise.

Interpreters and translators are often discussed together because they share some common traits. For example, both need a special ability, known as language combination. This enables them to be fluent in at least two languages—a native, or active, language and a secondary, or passive, language; a small number of interpreters and translators are fluent in two or more passive languages. Their active language is the one that they know best and into which they

interpret or translate, and their passive language is one of which they have nearly perfect knowledge.

Although some people do both, interpretation and translation are different professions. Each requires a distinct set of skills and aptitudes, and most people are better suited for one or the other. While interpreters often work into and from both languages, translators generally work only into their active language.

Interpreters convert one spoken language into another—or, in the case of sign-language interpreters, between spoken communication and sign language. This requires interpreters to pay attention carefully, understand what is communicated in both languages, and express thoughts and ideas clearly. Strong research and analytical skills, mental dexterity, and an exceptional memory also are important.

The first part of an interpreter's work begins before arriving at the jobsite. The interpreter must become familiar with the subject matter that the speakers will discuss, a task that may involve research to create a list of common words and phrases associated with the topic. Next, the interpreter usually travels to the location where his or her services are needed. Physical presence may not be required for some work, such as telephone interpretation. But it is usually important that the interpreter see the communicators in order to hear and observe the person speaking and to relay the message to the other party.

There are two types of interpretation: simultaneous and consecutive. Simultaneous interpretation requires interpreters to listen and speak (or sign) at the same time. In simultaneous interpretation, the interpreter begins to convey a sentence being spoken while the speaker is still talking. Ideally, simultaneous interpreters should be so familiar with a subject that they are able to anticipate the end of the speaker's sentence. Because they need a high degree of concentration, simultaneous interpreters work in pairs, with each interpreting for 20- to 30-minute segments. This type of interpretation is required at international conferences and is sometimes used in the courts.

In contrast to simultaneous interpretation's immediacy, consecutive interpretation begins only after the speaker has verbalized a group of words or sentences. Consecutive interpreters often take notes while listening to the speakers, so they must develop some type of note-taking or shorthand system. This form of interpretation is used most often for person-to-person communication, during which the interpreter sits near both parties.

Translators convert written materials from one language into another. They must have excellent writing and analytical ability. And because the documents that they translate must be as flawless as possible, they also need good editing skills.

Translators' assignments may vary in length, writing style, and subject matter. When they first receive text to convert into another language, translators usually read it in its entirety to get an idea of the subject. Next, they identify and look up any unfamiliar words. Multiple additional readings are usually needed before translators begin to actually write and finalize the translation. Translators also might do additional research on the subject matter if they are unclear about anything in the text. They consult with the text's originator or issuing agency to clarify unclear or unfamiliar ideas, words, or acronyms.

Translating involves more than replacing a word with its equivalent in another language; sentences and ideas must be manipulated to flow with the same coherence as those in the source document so that the translation reads as though it originated in the target language. Translators also must bear in mind any cultural references that may need to be explained to the intended audience, such as colloquialisms, slang, and other expressions that do not translate literally. Some subjects may be more difficult than others to translate because words or passages may have multiple meanings that make several translations possible. Not surprisingly, translated work often goes through multiple revisions before final text is submitted.

The way in which translators do their jobs has changed with advancements in technology. Today, nearly all translation work is done on a computer, and most assignments are received and submitted electronically. This enables translators to work from almost anywhere, and a large percentage of them work from home. The Internet provides advanced research capabilities and valuable language resources, such as specialized dictionaries and glossaries. In some cases, use of machine-assisted translation—including memory tools that provide comparisons of previous translations with current work—helps save time and reduce repetition.

The services of interpreters and translators are needed in a number of subject areas. While these workers may not completely specialize in a particular field or industry, many do focus on one area of expertise. Some of the most common areas are described below; however, interpreters and translators also may work in a variety of other areas, including business, social services, or entertainment.

Conference interpreters work at conferences that involve non-English-speaking attendees. This work includes international business and diplomacy, although conference interpreters also may interpret for any organization that works with foreign language speakers. Employers prefer high-level interpreters who have the ability to translate from at least two passive languages into one active (native) language—for example, the ability to interpret from Spanish and French into English. For some positions, such as those with the United Nations, this qualification is mandatory.

Much of the interpreting performed at conferences is simultaneous; however, at some meetings with a small number of attendees, consecutive interpreting also may be used. Usually, interpreters sit in soundproof booths, listening to the speakers through headphones and interpreting into a microphone what is said. The interpreted speech is then relayed to the listener through headsets. When interpreting is needed for only one or two people, the interpreter generally sits behind or next to the attendee and whispers a translation of the proceedings.

Guide or escort interpreters accompany either U.S. visitors abroad or foreign visitors in the United States to ensure that they are able to communicate during their stay. These specialists interpret on a variety of subjects, both on an informal basis and on a professional level. Most of their interpretation is consecutive, and work is generally shared by two interpreters when the assignment requires more than an 8-hour day. Frequent travel, often for days or weeks at a time, is common, an aspect of the job that some find particularly appealing.

Judiciary interpreters and translators help people appearing in court who are unable or unwilling to communicate in English. These workers must remain detached from the content of their work and not alter or modify the meaning or tone of what is said. Legal translators must be thoroughly familiar with the language and functions of the U.S. judicial system, as well as other countries' legal systems. Court interpreters work in a variety of legal settings, such as attorney-client meetings, preliminary hearings, depositions, trials, and arraignments. Success as a court interpreter requires an understanding of both legal terminology and colloquial language. In addition to interpreting what is said, court interpreters also may be required to translate written documents and read them aloud, also known as sight translation.

Literary translators adapt written literature from one language into another. They may translate any number of documents, including journal articles, books, poetry, and short stories. Literary translation is related to creative writing; literary translators must create a new text in the target language that reproduces the content and style of the original. Whenever possible, literary translators work closely with authors in order to best capture their intended meanings and literary characteristics.

This type of work often is done as a sideline by university professors; however, opportunities exist for well-established literary translators. As is the case with writers, finding a publisher and maintaining a network of contacts in the publishing industry is a critical part of the job. Most aspiring literary translators begin by submitting a short sample of their work in the hope that it will be printed and give them recognition. For example, after receiving permission from the author, they might submit to a publishing house a previously unpublished short work, such as a poem or essay.

Localization translators constitute a relatively recent and rapidly expanding specialty. Localization involves the complete adaptation of a product for use in a different language and culture. At its earlier stages, this work dealt primarily with software localization, but the specialty has expanded to include the adaptation of Internet sites and products in manufacturing and other business sectors.

Translators working in localization need a solid grasp of the languages to be translated, a thorough understanding of technical concepts and vocabulary, and a high degree of knowledge about the intended target audience or users of the product. The goal of these specialists is for the product to appear as if it were originally manufactured in the country where it will be sold and supported. Because software often is involved, it is not uncommon for people who work in this area of translation to have a strong background in computer science or computer-related work experience.

Providing language services to health care patients with limited English proficiency is the realm of *medical interpreters and translators*. Medical interpreters help patients to communicate with doctors, nurses, and other medical staff. Translators working in this specialty primarily convert patient materials and informational brochures, issued by hospitals and medical facilities, into the desired language. Medical interpreters need a strong grasp of medical and colloquial terminology in both languages, along with cultural sensitivity regarding how the patient receives the information. They must remain detached but aware of the patient's feelings and pain.

Sign language interpreters facilitate communication between people who are deaf or hard of hearing and people who can hear. Sign language interpreters must be fluent in English and in American Sign

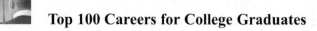

Language (ASL), which combines signing, fingerspelling, and specific body language. ASL has its own grammatical rules, sentence structure, idioms, historical contexts, and cultural nuances. Sign language interpreting, like foreign language interpreting, involves more than simply replacing a word of spoken English with a sign representing that word.

Most sign language interpreters either interpret, aiding communication between English and ASL, or transliterate, facilitating communication between English and contact signing—a form of signing that uses a more English language–based word order. Some interpreters specialize in oral interpreting for deaf or hard-of-hearing persons who lip-read instead of sign. Other specialties include tactile signing, which is interpreting for persons who are blind as well as deaf by making manual signs into a person's hands; cued speech; and signing exact English.

Self-employed and freelance interpreters and translators need general business skills to successfully manage their finances and careers. They must set prices for their work, bill customers, keep financial records, and market their services to attract new business and build their client base.

Working Conditions

Working environments of interpreters and translators vary. Interpreters work in a variety of settings, such as hospitals, courtrooms, and conference centers. They are required to travel to the site—whether it is in a neighboring town or on the other side of the world—where their services are needed. Interpreters who work over the telephone generally work on call, often in call centers in urban areas, and keep to a standard 5-day, 40-hour workweek. Interpreters for deaf students in schools usually work in a school setting for 9 months out of the year. Translators usually work alone, and they must frequently perform under pressure of deadlines and tight schedules. Many translators choose to work at home; however, technology allows translators to work from virtually anywhere.

Because many interpreters and translators freelance, their schedules are often erratic, with extensive periods of no work interspersed with others requiring long, irregular hours. For those who freelance, a significant amount of time must be dedicated to looking for jobs. In addition, freelancers must manage their own finances, and payment for their services may not always be prompt. Freelancing, however, offers variety and flexibility and allows many workers to choose which jobs to accept or decline.

The number of work-related accidents in these occupations is relatively low. The work can be stressful and exhausting, and translation can be lonesome or dull. However, interpreters and translators may use their irregular schedules to pursue other interests, such as traveling, dabbling in a hobby, or working a second job. Many interpreters and translators enjoy what they do and value the ability to control their schedules and workloads.

Training, Other Qualifications, and Advancement

The educational backgrounds of interpreters and translators vary. Knowing a language in addition to a native language is essential.

Although it is not necessary to have been raised bilingual to succeed, many interpreters and translators grew up speaking two languages.

In high school, students can prepare for these careers by taking a broad range of courses that include English writing and comprehension, foreign languages, and basic computer proficiency. Other helpful pursuits include spending time abroad, engaging in comparable forms of direct contact with foreign cultures, and reading extensively on a variety of subjects in English and at least one other language.

Beyond high school, there are many educational options. Although a bachelor's degree is often required, interpreters and translators note that it is acceptable to major in something other than a language. However, specialized training in how to do the work is generally required. A number of formal programs in interpreting and translation are available at colleges nationwide and through nonuniversity training programs, conferences, and courses. Many people who work as conference interpreters or in more technical areas—such as localization, engineering, or finance—have master's degrees, while those working in the community as court or medical interpreters or translators are more likely to complete job-specific training programs.

There is currently no universal form of certification required of all interpreters and translators in the United States, but there are a variety of different tests that workers can voluntarily take to demonstrate proficiency. The American Translators Association provides accreditation in more than 24 language combinations for its members; other options include a certification program offered by The Translators and Interpreters Guild. Many interpreters are not certified. Federal courts have certification for Spanish, Navaho, and Haitian Creole interpreters, and many state and municipal courts offer their own forms of certification. The National Association of Judiciary Interpreters and Translators also offers certification for court interpreting.

The U.S. Department of State has a three-test series for interpreters, including simple consecutive interpreting (for escort work), simultaneous interpreting (for court or seminar work), and conference-level interpreting (for international conferences). These tests are not referred to directly as certification, but successful completion often indicates that a person has an adequate level of skill to work in the field.

The National Association of the Deaf and the Registry of Interpreters for the Deaf (RID) jointly offer certification for general sign interpreters. In addition, RID offers specialty tests in legal interpreting, speech reading, and deaf-to-deaf interpreting—which includes interpreting between deaf speakers with different native languages and from ASL to tactile signing.

Experience is an essential part of a successful career in either interpreting or translation. In fact, many agencies or companies use only the services of people who have worked in the field for 3 to 5 years or who have a degree in translation studies or both.

A good way for translators to learn firsthand about the profession is to start out working in-house for a company; however, such jobs are not very numerous. Persons seeking to enter interpreter or translator jobs should begin by getting experience whatever way they can—even if it means doing informal or unpaid work. All translation can be used as examples for potential clients, even translation done as practice. Mentoring relationships and internships are other ways to build skills and confidence. Escort interpreting may offer an opportunity for inexperienced candidates to work alongside a more seasoned interpreter. Interpreters might also find it easier to break into areas with particularly high demand for language services, such as court or medical interpretation. Once interpreters and translators have gained sufficient experience, they may then move up to more difficult or prestigious assignments, may seek certification, may be given editorial responsibility, or may eventually manage or start their own translation agency.

Employment

Interpreters and translators held about 31,000 jobs in 2004. However, the actual number of interpreters and translators is probably significantly higher because many work in the occupation only sporadically. Interpreters and translators are employed in a variety of industries, reflecting the diversity of employment options in the field. About 9,900 worked in public and private educational institutions, such as schools, colleges, and universities. About 4,100 worked in health care, many of which worked for hospitals. Another 3,400 worked in other areas of government, such as federal, state and local courts. Other employers of interpreters and translators include publishing companies, telephone companies, airlines, and interpreting and translating agencies.

About 4,600 interpreters and translators are self-employed. To find work, these interpreters and translators may submit resumes to many different employment agencies and then wait to be contacted when an agency matches their skills with a job. After establishing a few regular clients, interpreters and translators may receive enough work from a few clients to stay busy, and they often hear of subsequent jobs by word of mouth or through referrals from existing clients. Many who freelance in the occupation work only part time, relying on other sources of income to supplement earnings from interpreting or translation.

Job Outlook

Employment of interpreters and translators is projected to increase faster than the average for all occupations over the 2004–2014 period, reflecting strong growth in the industries employing interpreters and translators. Higher demand for interpreters and translators in recent years has resulted directly from the broadening of international ties and the increase in the number of foreign-language speakers in the United States. Both of these trends are expected to continue, contributing to relatively rapid growth in the number of jobs for interpreters and translators. Demand will remain strong for translators of the languages referred to as "PFIGS"—Portuguese, French, Italian, German, and Spanish—and the principal Asian languages—Chinese, Japanese, and Korean. In addition, current events and changing political environments, often difficult to foresee, will increase the need for persons who can work with other languages. For example, homeland security needs are expected to drive increasing demand for interpreters and translators of Middle Eastern and North African languages, primarily in federal government agencies.

Technology has made the work of interpreters and translators easier. However, technology is not likely to have a negative impact on employment of interpreters and translators because such innovations are incapable of producing work comparable with work produced by these professionals.

Urban areas, especially those in California; New York; and Washington, DC, provide the largest numbers of employment possibilities, especially for interpreters; however, as the immigrant population spreads into more rural areas, jobs in smaller communities will become more widely available.

Job prospects for interpreters and translators vary by specialty. In particular, there should be strong demand for specialists in localization, driven by imports and exports; the expansion of the Internet; and demand in other technical areas, such as medicine or law. Rapid employment growth among interpreters and translators in health services industries will be fueled by the implementation of relatively recent guidelines regarding compliance with Title VI of the Civil Rights Act, which require all health care providers receiving federal aid to provide language services to non-English speakers. Similarly, the Americans with Disabilities Act and other laws, such as the Rehabilitation Act, mandate that, in certain situations, an interpreter must be available for people who are deaf or hard of hearing. Given the shortage of interpreters and translators meeting the desired skill level of employers, interpreters for the deaf will continue to have favorable employment prospects. On the other hand, job growth is expected to be limited for both conference interpreters and literary translators.

Earnings

Salaried interpreters and translators had median hourly earnings of $16.28 in May 2004. The middle 50 percent earned between $12.40 and $21.09. The lowest 10 percent earned less than $9.67, and the highest 10 percent earned more than $27.45.

Earnings depend on language, subject matter, skill, experience, education, certification, and type of employer, and salaries of interpreters and translators can vary widely. Interpreters and translators with language skills for which there is a greater demand, or for which there are relatively few people with the skills, often have higher earnings. Interpreters and translators with specialized expertise, such as those working in software localization, also generally command higher rates. Individuals classified as language specialists for the federal government earned an average of $71,625 annually in 2005. Limited information suggests that some highly skilled interpreters and translators—for example, high-level conference interpreters—working full time can earn more than $100,000 annually.

For those who are not salaried, earnings may fluctuate, depending on the availability of work. Furthermore, freelancers do not have any employer-paid benefits. Freelance interpreters usually earn an hourly rate, whereas translators who freelance typically earn a rate per word or per hour.

Related Occupations

Interpreters and translators use their multilingual skills, as do teachers of languages. These include teachers—preschool, kindergarten, elementary, middle, and secondary; teachers—postsecondary; teachers—special education; teachers—adult literacy and remedial education; and teachers—self-enrichment education. The work of interpreters, particularly guide or escort interpreters, can be likened to that of tour and travel guides in that they accompany individuals or groups on tours or to places of interest.

The work of translators is similar to that of writers and editors in that they communicate information and ideas through the written word and prepare texts for publication or dissemination. Furthermore, interpreters or translators working in a legal or health care environment are required to have a knowledge of terms and concepts that is similar to that of professionals working in these fields, such as court reporters or medical transcriptionists.

Sources of Additional Information

Organizations dedicated to these professions can provide valuable advice and guidance for people interested in learning more about interpretation and translation. The language services division of local hospitals or courthouses also may have information about available opportunities.

For general career information, contact the organizations listed here:

▸ American Translators Association, 225 Reinekers Ln., Suite 590, Alexandria, VA 22314. Internet: http://www.atanet.org

▸ The Translators and Interpreters Guild, 962 Wayne Ave., Suite 500, Silver Spring, MD 20910. Internet: http://www.ttig.org

▸ U.S. Department of State, Office of Language Services, Suite 1400 SA-1, Department of State, Washington, DC 20520.

For more detailed information by specialty, contact the association affiliated with that subject area:

▸ National Association of Judiciary Interpreters and Translators, 603 Stewart St., Suite 610, Seattle, WA 98101. Internet: http://www.najit.org

▸ American Literary Translators Association, The University of Texas at Dallas, Box 830688 Mail Station J051, Richardson, TX 75083-0688. Internet: http://www.literarytranslators.org

▸ Localization Industry Standards Association, 7 Route du Monastère-CH-1173, Féchy, Switzerland. Internet: http://www.lisa.org

▸ Registry of Interpreters for the Deaf, 333 Commerce St., Alexandria, VA 22314. Internet: http://www.rid.org

Musicians, Singers, and Related Workers

(O*NET 27-2041.01, 27-2041.02, 27-2041.03, 27-2042.01, and 27-2042.02)

Significant Points

■ Part-time schedules and intermittent unemployment are common; many musicians supplement their income with earnings from other sources.

■ Aspiring musicians begin studying an instrument or training their voices at an early age.

■ Competition for jobs is keen; those who can play several instruments and perform a wide range of musical styles should enjoy the best job prospects.

Nature of the Work

Musicians, singers, and related workers play musical instruments; sing, compose or arrange music; or conduct groups in instrumental or vocal performances. They may perform solo or as part of a group. Musicians, singers, and related workers entertain live audiences in nightclubs, concert halls, and theaters featuring opera, musical theater, or dance. Many of these entertainers play for live audiences; others perform exclusively for recording or production studios. Regardless of the setting, musicians, singers, and related workers spend considerable time practicing alone and with their bands, orchestras, or other musical ensembles.

Musicians often gain their reputation or professional standing by exhibiting a high level of professionalism and proficiency in a particular kind of music or performance. However, those who learn several related instruments and who can perform equally well in several musical styles have better employment opportunities. Instrumental musicians, for example, may play in a symphony orchestra, rock group, or jazz combo one night; appear in another ensemble the next; and work in a studio band the following day. Some play a variety of string, brass, woodwind, or percussion instruments or electronic synthesizers.

Singers interpret music and text, using their knowledge of voice production, melody, and harmony. They sing character parts or perform in their own individual style. Singers are often classified according to their voice range—soprano, contralto, tenor, baritone, or bass—or by the type of music they sing, such as opera, rock, popular, folk, rap, or country and western.

Music directors conduct, direct, plan, and lead instrumental or vocal performances by musical groups, such as orchestras, choirs, and glee clubs. *Conductors* lead instrumental music groups, such as symphony orchestras, dance bands, show bands, and various popular ensembles. These leaders audition and select musicians, choose the music most appropriate for their talents and abilities, and direct rehearsals and performances. Choral directors lead choirs and glee clubs, sometimes working with a band or an orchestra conductor. Directors audition and select singers and lead them at rehearsals and performances to achieve harmony, rhythm, tempo, shading, and other desired musical effects.

Composers create original music such as symphonies, operas, sonatas, radio and television jingles, film scores, and popular songs. They transcribe ideas into musical notation, using harmony, rhythm, melody, and tonal structure. Although most composers and songwriters practice their craft on instruments and transcribe the notes with pen and paper, some use computer software to compose and edit their music.

Arrangers transcribe and adapt musical compositions to a particular style for orchestras, bands, choral groups, or individuals. Components of music—including tempo, volume, and the mix of instruments needed—are arranged to express the composer's message. While some arrangers write directly into a musical composition, others use computer software to make changes.

Working Conditions

Musicians typically perform at night and on weekends. They spend much additional time practicing or in rehearsal. Full-time musicians with long-term employment contracts, such as those with symphony orchestras or television and film production companies, enjoy steady work and less travel. Nightclub, solo, or recital musicians frequently travel to perform in a variety of local settings and may tour nationally or internationally. Because many musicians find only part-time or intermittent work, experiencing unemployment between engagements, they often supplement their income with other types of jobs. The stress of constantly looking for work leads many musicians to accept permanent, full-time jobs in other occupations while working only part time as musicians.

Most instrumental musicians work closely with a variety of other people, including their colleagues, agents, employers, sponsors, and audiences. Although they usually work indoors, some perform outdoors for parades, concerts, and festivals. In some nightclubs and restaurants, smoke and odors may be present and lighting and ventilation may be poor.

Training, Other Qualifications, and Advancement

Aspiring musicians begin studying an instrument at an early age. They may gain valuable experience playing in a school or community band or an orchestra or with a group of friends. Singers usually start training when their voices mature. Participation in school musicals or choirs often provides good early training and experience.

Musicians need extensive and prolonged training and practice to acquire the necessary skills, knowledge, and ability to interpret music at a professional level. Like other artists, musicians and singers continually strive to stretch themselves—exploring different forms of music. Formal training may be obtained through private study with an accomplished musician, in a college or university music program, or in a music conservatory. For university or conservatory study, an audition generally is necessary. The National Association of Schools of Music accredits more than 600 college-level programs in music. Courses typically include music theory, music interpretation, composition, conducting, and performance in a particular instrument or in voice. Music directors, composers, conductors, and arrangers need considerable related work experience or advanced training in these subjects.

Many colleges, universities, and music conservatories grant bachelor's or higher degrees in music. A master's or doctoral degree usually is required to teach advanced music courses in colleges and universities; a bachelor's degree may be sufficient to teach basic courses. A degree in music education qualifies graduates for a state certificate to teach music in public elementary or secondary schools. Musicians who do not meet public school music education requirements may teach in private schools and recreation associations or instruct individual students in private sessions.

Musicians must be knowledgeable about a broad range of musical styles but keenly aware of the form that interests them most. Having a broader range of interest, knowledge, and training can help expand employment opportunities and musical abilities. Voice training and private instrumental lessons, taken especially when the individual is young, also help develop technique and enhance one's performance.

Young persons considering careers in music should have musical talent, versatility, creativity, poise, and a good stage presence.

Because quality performance requires constant study and practice, self-discipline is vital. To sustain a career as a musician or singer, performers must achieve a level of performing excellence and be counted on to be on their game whenever they perform. Moreover, musicians who play in concerts or in nightclubs and those who tour must have physical stamina to endure frequent travel and an irregular performance schedule. Because musicians and singers always must make their performances look effortless, preparation and practice are important. Musicians and singers also must be prepared to face the anxiety of intermittent employment and of rejection when auditioning for work.

Advancement for musicians usually means becoming better known, finding work more easily, and performing for higher earnings. Successful musicians often rely on agents or managers to find them performing engagements, negotiate contracts, and develop their careers.

Employment

Musicians, singers, and related workers held about 249,000 jobs in 2004. Around 40 percent worked part time; almost half were self-employed. Many found jobs in cities in which entertainment and recording activities are concentrated, such as New York, Los Angeles, Las Vegas, Chicago, and Nashville.

Musicians, singers, and related workers are employed in a variety of settings. Of those who earn a wage or salary, almost two-thirds were employed by religious organizations and almost one-fourth by performing arts companies such as professional orchestras, small chamber music groups, opera companies, musical theater companies, and ballet troupes. Musicians and singers also perform in nightclubs and restaurants and for weddings and other events. Well-known musicians and groups may perform in concerts, appear on radio and television broadcasts, and make recordings and music videos. The Armed Forces also offer careers in their bands and smaller musical groups.

Job Outlook

Competition for jobs for musicians, singers, and related workers is expected to be keen. The vast number of persons with the desire to perform will continue to greatly exceed the number of openings. Talent alone is no guarantee of success: Many people start out to become musicians or singers but leave the profession because they find the work difficult, the discipline demanding, and the long periods of intermittent unemployment unendurable.

Overall employment of musicians, singers, and related workers is expected to grow about as fast as the average for all occupations through 2014. Most new wage and salary jobs for musicians will arise in religious organizations. Slower-than-average growth is expected for self-employed musicians, who generally perform in nightclubs, concert tours, and other venues. Growth in demand for musicians will generate a number of job opportunities, and many openings also will arise from the need to replace those who leave the field each year because they are unable to make a living solely as musicians or for other reasons.

Earnings

Median hourly earnings of musicians and singers were $17.85 in May 2004. The middle 50 percent earned between $9.68 and $30.75. The lowest 10 percent earned less than $6.47, and the highest 10 percent earned more than $53.59. Median hourly earnings were $20.70 in performing arts companies and $12.17 in religious organizations. Annual earnings data for musicians and singers were not available because of the wide variation in the number of hours worked by musicians and singers and the short-term nature of many jobs, which may last for 1 day or 1 week; it is extremely rare for musicians and singers to have guaranteed employment that exceeds 3 to 6 months.

Median annual earnings of salaried music directors and composers were $34,570 in May 2004. The middle 50 percent earned between $24,040 and $51,770. The lowest 10 percent earned less than $15,960, and the highest 10 percent earned more than $75,380.

Yearly earnings typically reflect the number of gigs a freelance musician or singer played or the number of hours and weeks of salaried contract work, in addition to a performer's professional reputation and setting: Performers who can fill large concert halls, arenas, or outdoor stadiums generally command higher pay than those who perform in local clubs. Soloists or headliners usually receive higher earnings than band members or opening acts. The most successful musicians earn performance or recording fees that far exceed the median earnings.

According to the American Federation of Musicians, weekly minimum salaries in major orchestras ranged from about $700 to $2,080 during the 2004–2005 performing season. Each orchestra works out a separate contract with its local union, but individual musicians may negotiate higher salaries. Top orchestras have a season ranging from 24 to 52 weeks, with 18 orchestras reporting 52-week contracts. In regional orchestras, minimum salaries are often less because fewer performances are scheduled. Regional orchestra musicians often are paid for their services without any guarantee of future employment. Community orchestras often have even more limited levels of funding and offer salaries that are much lower for seasons of shorter duration.

Although musicians employed by some symphony orchestras work under master wage agreements, which guarantee a season's work up to 52 weeks, many other musicians face relatively long periods of unemployment between jobs. Even when employed, many musicians and singers work part time in unrelated occupations. Thus, their earnings usually are lower than earnings in many other occupations. Moreover, because they may not work steadily for one employer, some performers cannot qualify for unemployment compensation, and few have typical benefits such as sick leave or paid vacations. For these reasons, many musicians give private lessons or take jobs unrelated to music to supplement their earnings as performers.

Many musicians belong to a local of the American Federation of Musicians. Professional singers who perform live often belong to a branch of the American Guild of Musical Artists; those who record for the broadcast industries may belong to the American Federation of Television and Radio Artists.

Related Occupations

Musical instrument repairers and tuners (part of precision instrument and equipment repairers) require technical knowledge of musical instruments. Others whose work involves the performing arts include actors, producers, and directors; announcers; and dancers and choreographers.

Sources of Additional Information

For general information about music and music teacher education and a list of accredited college-level programs, contact

▸ National Association of Schools of Music, 11250 Roger Bacon Dr., Suite 21, Reston, VA 20190. Internet: http://nasm.arts-accredit.org

Nuclear Medicine Technologists

(O*NET 29-2033.00)

Significant Points

■ About 7 out of 10 work in hospitals.

■ Nuclear medicine technology programs range in length from 1 to 4 years and lead to a certificate, an associate degree, or a bachelor's degree.

■ Faster-than-average growth will arise from an increase in the number of middle-aged and elderly persons, who are the primary users of diagnostic procedures.

■ The number of job openings each year will be relatively low because the occupation is small; technologists who also are trained in other diagnostic methods, such as radiologic technology or diagnostic medical sonography, will have the best prospects.

Nature of the Work

Diagnostic imaging embraces several procedures that aid in diagnosing ailments, the most familiar being the X ray. Another increasingly common diagnostic imaging method, called magnetic resonance imaging (MRI), uses giant magnets and radio waves, rather than radiation, to create an image. In nuclear medicine, radionuclides—unstable atoms that emit radiation spontaneously—are used to diagnose and treat disease. Radionuclides are purified and compounded to form radiopharmaceuticals. Nuclear medicine technologists administer radiopharmaceuticals to patients and then monitor the characteristics and functions of tissues or organs in which the drugs localize. Abnormal areas show higher-than-expected or lower-than-expected concentrations of radioactivity. Nuclear medicine differs from other diagnostic imaging technologies because it determines the presence of disease on the basis of biological changes rather than changes in organ structure.

Nuclear medicine technologists operate cameras that detect and map the radioactive drug in a patient's body to create diagnostic images.

After explaining test procedures to patients, technologists prepare a dosage of the radiopharmaceutical and administer it by mouth, injection, inhalation, or other means. They position patients and start a gamma scintillation camera, or "scanner," which creates images of the distribution of a radiopharmaceutical as it localizes in, and emits signals from, the patient's body. The images are produced on a computer screen or on film for a physician to interpret.

When preparing radiopharmaceuticals, technologists adhere to safety standards that keep the radiation dose to workers and patients as low as possible. Technologists keep patient records and record the amount and type of radionuclides that they receive, use, and discard.

Radiologic technologists and technicians and cardiovascular technologists and technicians also operate diagnostic imaging equipment, but their equipment creates images by means of a different technology.

Nuclear medicine technologists also perform radioimmunoassay studies that assess the behavior of a radioactive substance inside the body. For example, technologists may add radioactive substances to blood or serum to determine levels of hormones or of therapeutic drugs in the body. Most nuclear medicine studies, such as cardiac function studies, are processed with the aid of a computer.

Working Conditions

Nuclear medicine technologists generally work a 40-hour week, perhaps including evening or weekend hours, in departments that operate on an extended schedule. Opportunities for part-time and shift work also are available. In addition, technologists in hospitals may have on-call duty on a rotational basis.

Physical stamina is important because technologists are on their feet much of the day and may lift or turn disabled patients.

Although the potential for radiation exposure exists in this field, it is kept to a minimum by the use of shielded syringes, gloves, and other protective devices and by adherence to strict radiation safety guidelines. The amount of radiation in a nuclear medicine procedure is comparable to that received during a diagnostic X-ray procedure. Technologists also wear badges that measure radiation levels. Because of safety programs, badge measurements rarely exceed established safety levels.

Training, Other Qualifications, and Advancement

Many employers and an increasing number of states require certification or licensure. Aspiring nuclear medicine technologists should check the requirements of the state in which they plan to work. Certification is available from the American Registry of Radiologic Technologists and from the Nuclear Medicine Technology Certification Board. Some workers receive certification from both agencies. Nuclear medicine technologists must meet the minimum federal standards on the administration of radioactive drugs and the operation of radiation detection equipment.

Nuclear medicine technology programs range in length from 1 to 4 years and lead to a certificate, an associate degree, or a bachelor's degree. Generally, certificate programs are offered in hospitals, associate degree programs in community colleges, and bachelor's degree programs in 4-year colleges and universities. Courses cover the physical sciences, biological effects of radiation exposure, radiation protection and procedures, the use of radiopharmaceuticals, imaging techniques, and computer applications.

One-year certificate programs are for health professionals who already possess an associate degree—especially radiologic technologists and diagnostic medical sonographers—but who wish to specialize in nuclear medicine. The programs also attract medical technologists, registered nurses, and others who wish to change fields or specialize. Others interested in nuclear medicine technology have three options: a 2-year certificate program, a 2-year associate degree program, or a 4-year bachelor's degree program.

The Joint Review Committee on Education Programs in Nuclear Medicine Technology accredits most formal training programs in nuclear medicine technology. In 2005, there were 100 accredited programs in the continental United States and Puerto Rico.

Nuclear medicine technologists should be sensitive to patients' physical and psychological needs. They must pay attention to detail, follow instructions, and work as part of a team. In addition, operating complicated equipment requires mechanical ability and manual dexterity.

Technologists may advance to supervisor, then to chief technologist, and, finally, to department administrator or director. Some technologists specialize in a clinical area such as nuclear cardiology or computer analysis or leave patient care to take positions in research laboratories. Some become instructors in, or directors of, nuclear medicine technology programs, a step that usually requires a bachelor's or master's degree in the subject. Others leave the occupation to work as sales or training representatives for medical equipment and radiopharmaceutical manufacturing firms or as radiation safety officers in regulatory agencies or hospitals.

Employment

Nuclear medicine technologists held about 18,000 jobs in 2004. About 7 out of 10 were in hospitals—private and government. Most of the rest were in offices of physicians or in medical and diagnostic laboratories, including diagnostic imaging centers.

Job Outlook

Employment of nuclear medicine technologists is expected to grow faster than the average for all occupations through the year 2014. Growth will arise from technological advancement; the development of new nuclear medicine treatments; and an increase in the number of middle-aged and older persons, who are the primary users of diagnostic procedures, including nuclear medicine tests. However, the number of openings each year will be relatively low because the occupation is small. Technologists who also are trained in other diagnostic methods, such as radiologic technology or diagnostic medical sonography, will have the best prospects.

Technological innovations may increase the diagnostic uses of nuclear medicine. One example is the use of radiopharmaceuticals in combination with monoclonal antibodies to detect cancer at far earlier stages than is customary today and without resorting to surgery. Another is the use of radionuclides to examine the heart's ability to pump blood. New nuclear medical imaging technologies, including positron emission tomography (PET) and single photon emission computed tomography (SPECT), are expected to be used increasingly and to contribute further to employment growth. The wider use of nuclear medical imaging to observe metabolic and biochemical changes during neurology, cardiology, and oncology procedures also will spur demand for nuclear medicine technologists.

Nonetheless, cost considerations will affect the speed with which new applications of nuclear medicine grow. Some promising nuclear medicine procedures, such as positron emission tomography, are extremely costly, and hospitals contemplating these procedures will have to consider equipment costs, reimbursement policies, and the number of potential users.

Earnings

Median annual earnings of nuclear medicine technologists were $56,450 in May 2004. The middle 50 percent earned between $48,720 and $67,460. The lowest 10 percent earned less than $41,800, and the highest 10 percent earned more than $80,300. Median annual earnings of nuclear medicine technologists in May 2004 were $54,920 in general medical and surgical hospitals.

Related Occupations

Nuclear medical technologists operate sophisticated equipment to help physicians and other health practitioners diagnose and treat patients. Cardiovascular technologists and technicians, clinical laboratory technologists and technicians, diagnostic medical sonographers, radiation therapists, radiologic technologists and technicians, and respiratory therapists perform similar functions.

Sources of Additional Information

Additional information on a career as a nuclear medicine technologist is available from

▶ Society of Nuclear Medicine Technologists, 1850 Samuel Morse Dr., Reston, VA 20190-5316. Internet: http://www.snm.org

For career information, send a stamped, self-addressed, business-size envelope with your request to

▶ American Society of Radiologic Technologists, 15000 Central Ave. SE, Albuquerque, NM 87123-3917. Internet: http://www.asrt.org

For a list of accredited programs in nuclear medicine technology, write to

▶ Joint Review Committee on Educational Programs in Nuclear Medicine Technology, 1716 Black Point Rd., P.O. Box 1149, Polson, MT 59860-1149. Internet: http://www.jrcnmt.org

Information on certification is available from

▶ American Registry of Radiologic Technologists, 1255 Northland Dr., St. Paul, MN 55120-1155. Internet: http://www.arrt.org

▶ Nuclear Medicine Technology Certification Board, 2970 Clairmont Rd., Suite 935, Atlanta, GA 30329-4421. Internet: http://www.nmtcb.org

Occupational Health and Safety Specialists and Technicians

(O*NET 29-9011.00 and 29-9012.00)

Significant Points

■ About 2 out of 5 specialists work in federal, state, and local government agencies that enforce rules on safety, health, and the environment.

■ Many employers, including the federal government, require a bachelor's degree in occupational health, safety, or a related field for some specialist positions.

■ Projected average employment growth reflects a balance of continuing public demand for a safe and healthy work environment against the desire for smaller government and fewer regulations.

Nature of the Work

Occupational health and safety specialists and technicians, also known as *safety and health practitioners* or *occupational health and safety inspectors*, help prevent harm to workers, property, the environment, and the general public. They promote occupational health and safety within organizations in many ways, such as by advising management on how to increase worker productivity through raising morale and reducing absenteeism, turnover, and equipment downtime while securing savings on insurance premiums, workers' compensation benefits, and litigation expenses. (Industrial engineers, including health and safety, have similar goals. See the description of engineers elsewhere in this book.)

Occupational health and safety specialists analyze work environments and design programs to control, eliminate, and prevent disease or injury caused by chemical, physical, radiological, and biological agents or ergonomic factors that involve the impact of equipment design on a worker's comfort or fatigue. They may conduct inspections and inform the management of a business which areas may not be in compliance with state and federal laws or employer policies in order to gain their support for addressing these areas. They advise management on the cost and effectiveness of safety and health programs.

Occupational health and safety technicians collect data on work environments for analysis by occupational health and safety specialists. Usually working under the supervision of specialists, they help implement and evaluate programs designed to limit risks to workers.

The specific responsibilities of occupational health and safety specialists and technicians vary by industry, workplace, and types of hazards affecting employees. In most settings, they initially focus on identifying hazardous conditions and practices. Sometimes they develop methods to predict hazards from experience, historical data, workplace analysis, and other information sources. Then they identify potential hazards in systems, equipment, products, facilities, or processes planned for use in the future. For example, they might uncover patterns in injury data that implicate a specific cause such as system failure, human error, incomplete or faulty decision making, or a weakness in existing policies or practices. After reviewing the causes or effects of hazards, they evaluate the probability and severity of accidents or exposures to hazardous materials that may result. Then they identify where controls need to be implemented to reduce or eliminate hazards and advise if a new program or practice is required. As necessary, they conduct training sessions for management, supervisors, and workers on health and safety practices and regulations to promote an understanding of a new or existing process. After implementation, they may monitor and evaluate the program's progress, making additional suggestions when needed.

To ensure the machinery and equipment meet appropriate safety regulations, occupational health and safety specialists and technicians may examine and test machinery and equipment, such as lifting devices, machine guards, or scaffolding. They may check that personal protective equipment, such as masks, respirators, protective eyewear, or hardhats, is being used in workplaces according to regulations. They also check that hazardous materials are stored correctly. They test and identify work areas for potential accident and health hazards, such as toxic vapors, mold, mildew, and explosive gas-air mixtures, and help implement appropriate control measures, such as adjustments to ventilation systems. Their survey of the workplace might involve talking with workers and observing their work as well as inspecting elements in their work environment such as lighting, tools, and equipment.

To measure and control hazardous substances, such as the noise or radiation levels, occupational health and safety specialists and technicians prepare and calibrate scientific equipment. They must properly collect and handle samples of dust, gases, vapors, and other potentially toxic materials to ensure personal safety and accurate test results.

If an injury or illness occurs, occupational health and safety specialists and technicians help investigate unsafe working conditions, study possible causes, and recommend remedial action. Some occupational health and safety specialists and technicians assist with the rehabilitation of workers after accidents and injuries and make sure they return to work successfully.

Frequent communication with management may be necessary to report on the status of occupational health and safety programs. Consultation with engineers or physicians also may be required.

Occupational health and safety specialists and technicians prepare reports, including accident reports, Occupational Safety and Health Administration record-keeping forms, observations, analysis of contaminants, and recommendations for control and correction of hazards. They may prepare documents to be used in legal proceedings and give testimony in court proceedings. Those who develop expertise in certain areas may develop occupational health and safety systems, including policies, procedures, and manuals.

Specialists and technicians that concentrate in particular areas include environmental protection officers, ergonomists, health physicists, industrial hygienists, and mine examiners. Environmental protection officers evaluate and coordinate programs that impact the environment, such as the storage and handling of hazardous waste or monitoring the cleanup of contaminated soil or water.

Ergonomists help ensure that the work environment allows employees to maximize their comfort, safety, and productivity. Health physicists help protect people and the environment from hazardous radiation exposure by monitoring the manufacture, handling, and disposal of radioactive material. Industrial hygienists examine the workplace for health hazards, such as worker exposure to lead, asbestos, pesticides, or communicable diseases. Mine examiners are technicians who inspect mines for proper air flow and health hazards such as the buildup of methane or other noxious gases.

Working Conditions

Occupational health and safety specialists and technicians work with many different people in a variety of environments. Their jobs often involve considerable fieldwork, and some travel frequently. Many occupational health and safety specialists and technicians work long and often irregular hours.

Occupational health and safety specialists and technicians may be exposed to many of the same physically strenuous conditions and hazards as industrial employees, and the work may be performed in unpleasant, stressful, and dangerous working conditions. They may find themselves in an adversarial role if the management of an organization disagrees with the recommendations for ensuring a safe working environment.

Training, Other Qualifications, and Advancement

All occupational health and safety specialists and technicians are trained in the applicable laws or inspection procedures through some combination of classroom and on-the-job training. Awards and degrees in programs related to occupational safety and health include 1-year certificates, associate degrees, bachelor's degrees, and graduate degrees. The Accreditation Board for Engineering and Technology (ABET) accredits health physics, industrial hygiene, and safety programs in addition to engineering programs. Many employers, including the federal government, require a bachelor's degree in occupational health; safety; or a related field, such as engineering, biology, or chemistry, for some specialist positions. Many industrial hygiene programs result in a master's degree. Experience as an occupational health and safety professional is also a prerequisite for many positions. Advancement to senior specialist positions is likely to require an advanced degree and substantial experience in several areas of practice.

In general, people who want to enter this occupation should be responsible and like detailed work. Occupational health and safety specialists and technicians should be able to communicate well. Recommended high school courses include English, mathematics, chemistry, biology, and physics.

Certification is available through the Board of Certified Safety Professionals (BCSP) and the American Board of Industrial Hygiene (ABIH). The BCSP offers the Certified Safety Professional (CSP) credential, while the ABIH offers the Certified Industrial Hygienist (CIH) and Certified Associate Industrial Hygienist (CAIH) credentials. Also, the Council on Certification of Health, Environmental, and Safety Technologists, a joint effort between the BCSP and ABIH, awards the Occupational Health and Safety Technologist

(OHST) and Construction Health and Safety Technician (CHST) credentials. Requirements for the OHST and CHST credentials are less stringent than those for the CSP, CIH, or CAIH credentials. Once education and experience requirements have been met, certification may be obtained through an examination. Continuing education is required for recertification. Although voluntary, many employers encourage certification.

Federal government occupational health and safety specialists and technicians whose job performance is satisfactory advance through their career ladder to a specified full-performance level. For positions above this level, usually supervisory positions, advancement is competitive and based on agency needs and individual merit. Advancement opportunities in state and local governments and the private sector are often similar to those in the federal government.

Research or related teaching positions at the college level require advanced education.

Employment

Occupational health and safety specialists held about 40,000 jobs in 2004. While the majority of jobs were spread throughout the private sector, about 2 out of 5 specialists worked for government agencies. Local governments employed 19 percent, state governments employed 18 percent, and the federal government employed 4 percent. Other occupational health and safety specialists were employed in manufacturing firms; private general medical and surgical hospitals; management, scientific, and technical consulting services; management of companies and enterprises; support activities for mining; research and development in the physical, engineering, and life sciences; private colleges, universities, and professional schools; and electric power generation, transmission, and distribution. Some were self-employed.

Occupational health and safety technicians held about 12,000 jobs in 2004. Nearly 3 out of 10 technicians worked in government agencies. Local governments employed 13 percent, state governments employed 7 percent, and the federal government employed 9 percent. Other occupational health and safety technicians were employed in manufacturing firms; private general medical and surgical hospitals; private colleges, universities, and professional schools; employment services; management, scientific, and technical consulting services; testing laboratories for architectural, engineering, and related services; research and development in the physical, engineering, and life sciences; and electric power generation, transmission, and distribution.

Within the federal government, most jobs are as Occupational Safety and Health Administration (OSHA) inspectors, who enforce U.S. Department of Labor regulations that ensure adequate safety principles, practices, and techniques are applied in workplaces. Employers may be fined for violation of OSHA standards. Within the U.S. Department of Health and Human Services, occupational health and safety specialists working for the National Institute of Occupational Safety and Health (NIOSH) provide private companies with an avenue to evaluate the health and safety of their employees without the risk of being fined. Most large government agencies also employ occupational health and safety specialists and technicians who work to protect agency employees.

Most private companies either employ their own occupational health and safety personnel or contract with occupational health and safety professionals to ensure the safety of their workers and compliance with federal, state, and local government agencies that enforce rules on safety, health, and the environment.

Job Outlook

Employment of occupational health and safety specialists and technicians is expected to grow about as fast as average for all occupations through 2014, reflecting a balance of continuing public demand for a safe and healthy work environment against the desire for smaller government and fewer regulations. Since the September 11, 2001, attacks, emergency preparedness has become a greater focus for the public and private sectors and for occupational health and safety specialists and technicians. Additional job openings will arise from the need to replace those who transfer to other occupations, retire, or leave for other reasons. In private industry, employment growth will reflect industry growth and the continuing self-enforcement of government and company regulations and policies.

Employment of occupational health and safety specialists and technicians in the private sector is somewhat affected by general economic fluctuations. Federal, state, and local governments, which employ about 2 out of 5 of all specialists and technicians, provide considerable job security; workers are less likely to be affected by changes in the economy.

Earnings

Median annual earnings of occupational health and safety specialists were $51,570 in May 2004. The middle 50 percent earned between $39,580 and $65,370. The lowest 10 percent earned less than $30,590, and the highest 10 percent earned more than $79,530. Median annual earnings of occupational health and safety specialists in May 2004 were $48,710 in local government and $44,400 in state government.

Median annual earnings of occupational health and safety technicians were $42,130 in May 2004. The middle 50 percent earned between $29,900 and $56,640. The lowest 10 percent earned less than $22,860, and the highest 10 percent earned more than $70,460.

Most occupational health and safety specialists and technicians work in large private firms or for federal, state, and local governments, most of which generally offer more generous benefits than smaller firms.

Related Occupations

Occupational health and safety specialists and technicians help to ensure that laws and regulations are obeyed. Others who enforce laws and regulations include agricultural inspectors, construction and building inspectors, correctional officers, financial examiners, fire inspectors, police and detectives, and transportation inspectors.

Sources of Additional Information

Information about jobs in federal, state, and local governments and in private industry is available from state employment service offices.

For information on a career as an industrial hygienist, including a list of colleges and universities offering industrial hygiene and related degrees, contact

▶ American Industrial Hygiene Association, 2700 Prosperity Ave., Suite 250, Fairfax, VA 22031. Internet: http://www.aiha.org

For information on the Certified Industrial Hygienist or Certified Associate Industrial Hygienist credential, contact

▶ American Board of Industrial Hygiene, 6015 West St. Joseph Hwy., Suite 102, Lansing, MI 48917. Internet: http://www.abih.org

For more information on professions in safety, a comprehensive list of colleges and universities offering safety and related degrees, and applications for scholarships, contact

▶ American Society of Safety Engineers, 1800 E Oakton St., Des Plaines, IL 60018. Internet: http://www.asse.org

For more information on professions in safety, a list of programs in safety and related academic fields, and the Certified Safety Professional credential, contact

▶ Board of Certified Safety Professionals, 208 Burwash Ave., Savoy, IL 61874. Internet: http://www.bcsp.org

For information on the Occupational Health and Safety Technologist and Construction Health and Safety Technician credentials, contact

▶ Council on Certification of Health, Environmental, and Safety Technologists, 208 Burwash Ave., Savoy, IL 61874. Internet: http://www.cchest.org

For information on a career as a health physicist, contact

▶ Health Physics Society, 1313 Dolley Madison Blvd., Suite 402, McLean, VA 22101. Internet: http://www.hps.org

For additional career information, contact

▶ U.S. Department of Health and Human Services, Center for Disease Control and Prevention, National Institute of Occupational Safety and Health, Hubert H. Humphrey Bldg., 200 Independence Ave. SW, Room 715H, Washington, DC 20201. Internet: http://www.cdc.gov/niosh

▶ U.S. Department of Labor, Occupational Safety and Health Administration, Office of Communication, 200 Constitution Ave. NW, Washington, DC 20210. Internet: http://www.osha.gov

Information on obtaining positions as occupational health and safety specialists and technicians with the federal government is available from the Office of Personnel Management through USAJOBS, the federal government's official employment information system. This resource for locating and applying for job opportunities can be accessed through the Internet at http://www.usajobs.opm.gov or through an interactive voice response telephone system at (703) 724-1850 or TDD (978) 461-8404. These numbers are not toll free, and charges may result.

Paralegals and Legal Assistants

(O*NET 23-2011.00)

Significant Points

■ About 7 out of 10 work for law firms; others work for corporate legal departments and government agencies.

■ Most entrants have an associate's degree in paralegal studies or a bachelor's degree coupled with a certificate in paralegal studies.

■ Employment is projected to grow much faster than average as employers try to reduce costs by hiring paralegals to perform tasks formerly carried out by lawyers.

■ Competition for jobs should continue; experienced, formally trained paralegals should have the best employment opportunities.

Nature of the Work

While lawyers assume ultimate responsibility for legal work, they often delegate many of their tasks to paralegals. In fact, *paralegals*—also called *legal assistants*—are continuing to assume a growing range of tasks in the nation's legal offices and perform many of the same tasks as lawyers. Nevertheless, they are still explicitly prohibited from carrying out duties that are considered to be the practice of law, such as setting legal fees, giving legal advice, and presenting cases in court.

One of a paralegal's most important tasks is helping lawyers prepare for closings, hearings, trials, and corporate meetings. Paralegals investigate the facts of cases and ensure that all relevant information is considered. They also identify appropriate laws, judicial decisions, legal articles, and other materials that are relevant to assigned cases. After they analyze and organize the information, paralegals may prepare written reports that attorneys use in determining how cases should be handled. Should attorneys decide to file lawsuits on behalf of clients, paralegals may help prepare the legal arguments, draft pleadings and motions to be filed with the court, obtain affidavits, and assist attorneys during trials. Paralegals also organize and track files of all important case documents and make them available and easily accessible to attorneys.

In addition to this preparatory work, paralegals perform a number of other vital functions. For example, they help draft contracts, mortgages, separation agreements, and instruments of trust. They also may assist in preparing tax returns and planning estates. Some paralegals coordinate the activities of other law office employees and maintain financial office records. Various additional tasks may differ, depending on the employer.

Paralegals are found in all types of organizations, but most are employed by law firms, corporate legal departments, and various government offices. In these organizations, they can work in many different areas of the law, including litigation, personal injury, corporate law, criminal law, employee benefits, intellectual property, labor law, bankruptcy, immigration, family law, and real estate. As the law has become more complex, paralegals have responded by becoming more specialized. Within specialties, functions often are broken down further so that paralegals may deal with a specific area. For example, paralegals specializing in labor law may concentrate exclusively on employee benefits.

The duties of paralegals also differ widely with the type of organization in which they are employed. Paralegals who work for corporations often assist attorneys with employee contracts, shareholder agreements, stock-option plans, and employee benefit plans. They also may help prepare and file annual financial reports, maintain corporate minutes,' record resolutions, and prepare forms to secure loans for the corporation. Paralegals often monitor and review government regulations to ensure that the corporation is aware of new requirements and is operating within the law. Increasingly, experienced paralegals are assuming additional supervisory responsibilities such as overseeing team projects and serving as a communications link between the team and the corporation.

The duties of paralegals who work in the public sector usually vary within each agency. In general, paralegals analyze legal material for internal use, maintain reference files, conduct research for attorneys, and collect and analyze evidence for agency hearings. They may prepare informative or explanatory material on laws, agency regulations, and agency policy for general use by the agency and the public. Paralegals employed in community legal-service projects help the poor, the aged, and others who are in need of legal assistance. They file forms, conduct research, prepare documents, and, when authorized by law, may represent clients at administrative hearings.

Paralegals in small and medium-size law firms usually perform a variety of duties that require a general knowledge of the law. For example, they may research judicial decisions on improper police arrests or help prepare a mortgage contract. Paralegals employed by large law firms, government agencies, and corporations, however, are more likely to specialize in one aspect of the law.

Familiarity with computer use and technical knowledge have become essential to paralegal work. Computer software packages and the Internet are used to search legal literature stored in computer databases and on CD-ROM. In litigation involving many supporting documents, paralegals usually use computer databases to retrieve, organize, and index various materials. Imaging software allows paralegals to scan documents directly into a database, while billing programs help them to track hours billed to clients. Computer software packages also are used to perform tax computations and explore the consequences of various tax strategies for clients.

Working Conditions

Paralegals employed by corporations and government usually work a standard 40-hour week. Although most paralegals work year round, some are temporarily employed during busy times of the year and then are released when the workload diminishes. Paralegals who work for law firms sometimes work very long hours when they are under pressure to meet deadlines. Some law firms reward such loyalty with bonuses and additional time off.

These workers handle many routine assignments, particularly when they are inexperienced. As they gain experience, paralegals usually assume more varied tasks with additional responsibility. Paralegals

do most of their work at desks in offices and law libraries. Occasionally, they travel to gather information and perform other duties.

Training, Other Qualifications, and Advancement

There are several ways to become a paralegal. The most common is through a community college paralegal program that leads to an associate's degree. The other common method of entry, mainly for those who already have a college degree, is through a program that leads to a certification in paralegal studies. A small number of schools also offer bachelor's and master's degrees in paralegal studies. Some employers train paralegals on the job, hiring college graduates with no legal experience or promoting experienced legal secretaries. Other entrants have experience in a technical field that is useful to law firms, such as a background in tax preparation for tax and estate practice or in criminal justice, nursing, or health administration for personal injury practice.

An estimated 1,000 colleges and universities, law schools, and proprietary schools offer formal paralegal training programs. Approximately 260 paralegal programs are approved by the American Bar Association (ABA). Although many programs do not require such approval, graduation from an ABA-approved program can enhance one's employment opportunities. The requirements for admission to these programs vary. Some require certain college courses or a bachelor's degree, others accept high school graduates or those with legal experience, and a few schools require standardized tests and personal interviews.

Paralegal programs include 2-year associate degree's programs, 4-year bachelor's degree programs, and certificate programs that can take only a few months to complete. Most certificate programs provide intensive and, in some cases, specialized paralegal training for individuals who already hold college degrees, while associate's and bachelor's degree programs usually combine paralegal training with courses in other academic subjects. The quality of paralegal training programs varies; the better programs usually include job placement services. Programs generally offer courses introducing students to the legal applications of computers, including how to perform legal research on the Internet. Many paralegal training programs also offer an internship in which students gain practical experience by working for several months in a private law firm, the office of a public defender or attorney general, a bank, a corporate legal department, a legal aid organization, or a government agency. Experience gained in internships is an asset when one is seeking a job after graduation. Prospective students should examine the experiences of recent graduates before enrolling in a paralegal program.

Although most employers do not require certification, earning a voluntary certificate from a professional society may offer advantages in the labor market. The National Association of Legal Assistants (NALA), for example, has established standards for certification requiring various combinations of education and experience. Paralegals who meet these standards are eligible to take a 2-day examination, given three times each year at several regional testing centers. Those who pass this examination may use the Certified Legal Assistant (CLA) designation. The NALA also offers an advanced paralegal certification for those who want to specialize in other areas of the law. In addition, the Paralegal Advanced Competency Exam, administered through the National Federation of Paralegal Associations, offers professional recognition to paralegals with a bachelor's degree and at least 2 years of experience. Those who pass this examination may use the Registered Paralegal (RP) designation.

Paralegals must be able to document and present their findings and opinions to their supervising attorney. They need to understand legal terminology and have good research and investigative skills. Familiarity with the operation and applications of computers in legal research and litigation support also is important. Paralegals should stay informed of new developments in the laws that affect their area of practice. Participation in continuing legal education seminars allows paralegals to maintain and expand their knowledge of the law.

Because paralegals frequently deal with the public, they should be courteous and uphold the ethical standards of the legal profession. The National Association of Legal Assistants, the National Federation of Paralegal Associations, and a few states have established ethical guidelines for paralegals to follow.

Paralegals usually are given more responsibilities and require less supervision as they gain work experience. Experienced paralegals who work in large law firms, corporate legal departments, or government agencies may supervise and delegate assignments to other paralegals and clerical staff. Advancement opportunities also include promotion to managerial and other law-related positions within the firm or corporate legal department. However, some paralegals find it easier to move to another law firm when seeking increased responsibility or advancement.

Employment

Paralegals and legal assistants held about 224,000 jobs in 2004. Private law firms employed 7 out of 10 paralegals and legal assistants; most of the remainder worked for corporate legal departments and various levels of government. Within the federal government, the U.S. Department of Justice is the largest employer, followed by the Social Security Administration and the U.S. Department of the Treasury. A small number of paralegals own their own businesses and work as freelance legal assistants, contracting their services to attorneys or corporate legal departments.

Job Outlook

Employment for paralegals and legal assistants is projected to grow much faster than average for all occupations through 2014. Employers are trying to reduce costs and increase the availability and efficiency of legal services by hiring paralegals to perform tasks formerly carried out by lawyers. Besides new jobs created by employment growth, additional job openings will arise as people leave the occupation. Despite projections of rapid employment growth, competition for jobs should continue as many people seek to go into this profession; however, experienced, formally trained paralegals should have the best employment opportunities.

Private law firms will continue to be the largest employers of paralegals, but a growing array of other organizations, such as corporate legal departments, insurance companies, real estate and title

insurance firms, and banks hire paralegals. Corporations in particular are boosting their in-house legal departments to cut costs. Demand for paralegals also is expected to grow as an expanding population increasingly requires legal services, especially in areas such as intellectual property, health care, international law, elder issues, criminal law, and environmental law. Paralegals who specialize in areas such as real estate, bankruptcy, medical malpractice, and product liability should have ample employment opportunities. The growth of prepaid legal plans also should contribute to the demand for legal services. Paralegal employment is expected to increase as organizations presently employing paralegals assign them a growing range of tasks and as paralegals are increasingly employed in small and medium-size establishments. A growing number of experienced paralegals are expected to establish their own businesses.

Job opportunities for paralegals will expand in the public sector as well. Community legal-service programs, which provide assistance to the poor, elderly, minorities, and middle-income families, will employ additional paralegals to minimize expenses and serve the most people. Federal, state, and local government agencies; consumer organizations; and the courts also should continue to hire paralegals in increasing numbers.

To a limited extent, paralegal jobs are affected by the business cycle. During recessions, demand declines for some discretionary legal services, such as planning estates, drafting wills, and handling real estate transactions. Corporations are less inclined to initiate certain types of litigation when falling sales and profits lead to fiscal belt tightening. As a result, full-time paralegals employed in offices adversely affected by a recession may be laid off or have their work hours reduced. However, during recessions, corporations and individuals are more likely to face other problems that require legal assistance, such as bankruptcies, foreclosures, and divorces. Paralegals, who provide many of the same legal services as lawyers at a lower cost, tend to fare relatively better in difficult economic conditions.

Earnings

Earnings of paralegals and legal assistants vary greatly. Salaries depend on education, training, experience, the type and size of employer, and the geographic location of the job. In general, paralegals who work for large law firms or in large metropolitan areas earn more than those who work for smaller firms or in less populated regions. In addition to earning a salary, many paralegals receive bonuses. In May 2004, full-time wage and salary paralegals and legal assistants had median annual earnings, including bonuses, of $39,130. The middle 50 percent earned between $31,040 and $49,950. The top 10 percent earned more than $61,390, while the bottom 10 percent earned less than $25,360. Median annual earnings in the industries employing the largest numbers of paralegals in May 2004 were as follows:

Federal government	$59,370
Local government	38,260
Legal services	37,870
State government	34,910

Related Occupations

Among the other occupations that call for a specialized understanding of the law and the legal system, but do not require the extensive training of a lawyer, are law clerks; title examiners, abstractors, and searchers; claims adjusters, appraisers, examiners, and investigators; and occupational health and safety specialists and technicians.

Sources of Additional Information

General information on a career as a paralegal can be obtained from

▸ Standing Committee on Paralegals, American Bar Association, 321 North Clark St., Chicago, IL 60610. Internet: http://www.abanet.org/legalservices/paralegals

For information on the Certified Legal Assistant exam, schools that offer training programs in a specific state, and standards and guidelines for paralegals, contact

▸ National Association of Legal Assistants, Inc., 1516 South Boston St., Suite 200, Tulsa, OK 74119. Internet: http://www.nala.org

Information on a career as a paralegal, schools that offer training programs, job postings for paralegals, the Paralegal Advanced Competency Exam, and local paralegal associations can be obtained from

▸ National Federation of Paralegal Associations, 2517 Eastlake Ave. East, Suite 200, Seattle, WA 98102. Internet: http://www.paralegals.org

Information on paralegal training programs, including the pamphlet *How to Choose a Paralegal Education Program*, may be obtained from

▸ American Association for Paralegal Education, 19 Mantua Rd., Mt. Royal, NJ 08061. Internet: http://www.aafpe.org

Information on obtaining positions as occupational health and safety specialists and technicians with the federal government is available from the Office of Personnel Management through USAJOBS, the federal government's official employment information system. This resource for locating and applying for job opportunities can be accessed through the Internet at http://www.usajobs.opm.gov or through an interactive voice response telephone system at (703) 724-1850 or TDD (978) 461-8404. These numbers are not toll free, and charges may result.

Police and Detectives

(O*NET 33-1012.00, 33-3021.01, 33-3021.02, 33-3021.03, 33-3021.04, 33-3021.05, 33-3031.00, 33-3051.01, 33-3051.02, 33-3051.03, and 33-3052.00)

Significant Points

■ Police and detective work can be dangerous and stressful.

■ Competition should remain keen for higher-paying jobs with state and federal agencies and police departments in affluent areas; opportunities will be better in local and special police departments that offer relatively low salaries or in urban communities where the crime rate is relatively high.

■ Applicants with college training in police science or military police experience should have the best opportunities.

Nature of the Work

People depend on police officers and detectives to protect their lives and property. Law enforcement officers, some of whom are state or federal special agents or inspectors, perform these duties in a variety of ways, depending on the size and type of their organization. In most jurisdictions, they are expected to exercise authority when necessary, whether on or off duty.

Uniformed police officers have general law enforcement duties, including maintaining regular patrols and responding to calls for service. They may direct traffic at the scene of an accident, investigate a burglary, or give first aid to an accident victim. In large police departments, officers usually are assigned to a specific type of duty. Many urban police agencies are involved in community policing—a practice in which an officer builds relationships with the citizens of local neighborhoods and mobilizes the public to help fight crime.

Police agencies are usually organized into geographic districts, with uniformed officers assigned to patrol a specific area, such as part of the business district or outlying residential neighborhoods. Officers may work alone, but in large agencies, they often patrol with a partner. While on patrol, officers attempt to become thoroughly familiar with their patrol area and remain alert for anything unusual. Suspicious circumstances and hazards to public safety are investigated or noted, and officers are dispatched to individual calls for assistance within their district. During their shift, they may identify, pursue, and arrest suspected criminals; resolve problems within the community; and enforce traffic laws.

Public college and university police forces, public school district police, and agencies serving transportation systems and facilities are examples of special police agencies. These agencies have special geographic jurisdictions and enforcement responsibilities in the United States. Most sworn personnel in special agencies are uniformed officers; a smaller number are investigators.

Some police officers specialize in such diverse fields as chemical and microscopic analysis, training and firearms instruction, or handwriting and fingerprint identification. Others work with special units, such as horseback, bicycle, motorcycle, or harbor patrol; canine corps; special weapons and tactics (SWAT); or emergency response teams. A few local and special law enforcement officers primarily perform jail-related duties or work in courts. Regardless of job duties or location, police officers and detectives at all levels must write reports and maintain meticulous records that will be needed if they testify in court.

Sheriffs and deputy sheriffs enforce the law on the county level. Sheriffs are usually elected to their posts and perform duties similar to those of a local or county police chief. Sheriffs' departments tend to be relatively small, most having fewer than 50 sworn officers. Deputy sheriffs have law enforcement duties similar to those of officers in urban police departments. Police and sheriffs' deputies who provide security in city and county courts are sometimes called bailiffs.

State police officers (sometimes called *state troopers* or *highway patrol officers*) arrest criminals statewide and patrol highways to enforce motor vehicle laws and regulations. State police officers are best known for issuing traffic citations to motorists. At the scene of accidents, they may direct traffic, give first aid, and call for emergency equipment. They also write reports used to determine the cause of the accident. State police officers are frequently called upon to render assistance to other law enforcement agencies, especially those in rural areas or small towns.

State law enforcement agencies operate in every state except Hawaii. Most full-time sworn personnel are uniformed officers who regularly patrol and respond to calls for service. Others work as investigators, perform court-related duties, or carry out administrative or other assignments.

Detectives are plainclothes investigators who gather facts and collect evidence for criminal cases. Some are assigned to interagency task forces to combat specific types of crime. They conduct interviews, examine records, observe the activities of suspects, and participate in raids or arrests. Detectives and state and federal agents and inspectors usually specialize in investigating one of a wide variety of violations, such as homicide or fraud. They are assigned cases on a rotating basis and work on them until an arrest and conviction occurs or until the case is dropped.

Fish and game wardens enforce fishing, hunting, and boating laws. They patrol hunting and fishing areas, conduct search and rescue operations, investigate complaints and accidents, and aid in prosecuting court cases.

The federal government maintains a high profile in many areas of law enforcement. *Federal Bureau of Investigation (FBI) agents* are the government's principal investigators, and they are responsible for investigating violations of more than 200 categories of federal law and conducting sensitive national security investigations. Agents may conduct surveillance, monitor court-authorized wiretaps, examine business records, investigate white-collar crime, or participate in sensitive undercover assignments. The FBI investigates organized crime, public corruption, financial crime, fraud against the government, bribery, copyright infringement, civil rights violations, bank robbery, extortion, kidnapping, air piracy, terrorism, espionage, interstate criminal activity, drug trafficking, and other violations of federal statutes.

U.S. Drug Enforcement Administration (DEA) agents enforce laws and regulations relating to illegal drugs. Not only is the DEA the lead agency for domestic enforcement of federal drug laws, it also has sole responsibility for coordinating and pursuing U.S. drug investigations abroad. Agents may conduct complex criminal investigations, carry out surveillance of criminals, and infiltrate illicit drug organizations using undercover techniques.

U.S. marshals and deputy marshals protect the federal courts and ensure the effective operation of the judicial system. They provide protection for the federal judiciary, transport federal prisoners, protect federal witnesses, and manage assets seized from criminal enterprises. They enjoy the widest jurisdiction of any federal law enforcement agency and are involved to some degree in nearly all federal law enforcement efforts. In addition, U.S. marshals pursue and arrest federal fugitives.

Bureau of Alcohol, Tobacco, Firearms, and Explosives agents regulate and investigate violations of federal firearms and explosives laws as well as federal alcohol and tobacco tax regulations.

The U.S. Department of State *Bureau of Diplomatic Security special agents* are engaged in the battle against terrorism. Overseas, they advise ambassadors on all security matters and manage a complex range of security programs designed to protect personnel, facilities, and information. In the United States, they investigate passport and visa fraud, conduct personnel security investigations, issue security clearances, and protect the Secretary of State and a number of foreign dignitaries. They also train foreign civilian police and administer a counter-terrorism reward program.

The *Department of Homeland Security* employs numerous law enforcement officers under several different agencies, including *Customs and Border Protection, Immigration and Customs Enforcement,* and the *U.S. Secret Service. U.S. Border Patrol agents* protect more than 8,000 miles of international land and water boundaries. Their missions are to detect and prevent the smuggling and unlawful entry of undocumented foreign nationals into the United States; to apprehend those persons violating the immigration laws; and to interdict contraband, such as narcotics.

Immigration inspectors interview and examine people seeking entrance to the United States and its territories. They inspect passports to determine whether people are legally eligible to enter the United States. Immigration inspectors also prepare reports, maintain records, and process applications and petitions for immigration or temporary residence in the United States.

Customs inspectors enforce laws governing imports and exports by inspecting cargo, baggage, and articles worn or carried by people, vessels, vehicles, trains, and aircraft entering or leaving the United States. These inspectors examine, count, weigh, gauge, measure, and sample commercial and noncommercial cargoes entering and leaving the United States. Customs inspectors seize prohibited or smuggled articles; intercept contraband; and apprehend, search, detain, and arrest violators of U.S. laws. *Customs agents* investigate violations, such as narcotics smuggling, money laundering, child pornography, and customs fraud, and they enforce the Arms Export Control Act. During domestic and foreign investigations, they develop and use informants; conduct physical and electronic surveillance; and examine records from importers and exporters, banks, couriers, and manufacturers. They conduct interviews, serve on joint task forces with other agencies, and get and execute search warrants.

Federal Air Marshals provide air security by fighting attacks targeting U.S. airports, passengers, and crews. They disguise themselves as ordinary passengers and board flights of U.S. air carriers to locations worldwide.

U.S. Secret Service special agents protect the President, Vice President, and their immediate families; Presidential candidates; former Presidents; and foreign dignitaries visiting the United States. Secret Service agents also investigate counterfeiting, forgery of government checks or bonds, and fraudulent use of credit cards.

Other federal agencies employ police and special agents with sworn arrest powers and the authority to carry firearms. These agencies include the Postal Service, the Bureau of Indian Affairs Office of Law Enforcement, the Forest Service, and the National Park Service.

Working Conditions

Police and detective work can be very dangerous and stressful. In addition to the obvious dangers of confrontations with criminals, police officers and detectives need to be constantly alert and ready to deal appropriately with a number of other threatening situations. Many law enforcement officers witness death and suffering resulting from accidents and criminal behavior. A career in law enforcement may take a toll on their private lives.

Uniformed officers, detectives, agents, and inspectors are usually scheduled to work 40-hour weeks, but paid overtime is common. Shift work is necessary because protection must be provided around the clock. Junior officers frequently work weekends, holidays, and nights. Police officers and detectives are required to work at any time their services are needed and may work long hours during investigations. In most jurisdictions, whether on or off duty, officers are expected to be armed and to exercise their authority whenever necessary.

The jobs of some federal agents such as U.S. Secret Service and DEA special agents require extensive travel, often on very short notice. They may relocate a number of times over the course of their careers. Some special agents in agencies such as the U.S. Border Patrol work outdoors in rugged terrain for long periods and in all kinds of weather.

Training, Other Qualifications, and Advancement

Civil service regulations govern the appointment of police and detectives in most states, large municipalities, and special police agencies, as well as in many smaller jurisdictions. Candidates must be U.S. citizens, usually must be at least 20 years of age, and must meet rigorous physical and personal qualifications. In the federal government, candidates must be at least 21 years of age but less than 37 years of age at the time of appointment. Physical examinations for entrance into law enforcement often include tests of vision, hearing, strength, and agility. Eligibility for appointment usually depends on performance in competitive written examinations and previous education and experience. In larger departments, where the majority of law enforcement jobs are found, applicants usually must have at least a high school education, and some departments require a year or two of college coursework. Federal and state agencies typically require a college degree. Candidates should enjoy working with people and meeting the public.

Because personal characteristics such as honesty, sound judgment, integrity, and a sense of responsibility are especially important in law enforcement, candidates are interviewed by senior officers, and their character traits and backgrounds are investigated. In some agencies, candidates are interviewed by a psychiatrist or a psychologist or given a personality test. Most applicants are subjected to lie detector examinations or drug testing. Some agencies subject sworn personnel to random drug testing as a condition of continuing employment.

Before their first assignments, officers usually go through a period of training. In state and large local departments, recruits get training in their agency's police academy, often for 12 to 14 weeks. In small agencies, recruits often attend a regional or state academy. Training includes classroom instruction in constitutional law and civil rights, state laws and local ordinances, and accident investigation. Recruits also receive training and supervised experience in patrol, traffic control, use of firearms, self-defense, first aid, and emergency response.

Police departments in some large cities hire high school graduates who are still in their teens as police cadets or trainees. They do clerical work and attend classes, usually for 1 to 2 years, at which point they reach the minimum age requirement and may be appointed to the regular force.

Police officers usually become eligible for promotion after a probationary period ranging from 6 months to 3 years. In a large department, promotion may enable an officer to become a detective or to specialize in one type of police work, such as working with juveniles. Promotions to corporal, sergeant, lieutenant, and captain usually are made according to a candidate's position on a promotion list as determined by scores on a written examination and on-the-job performance.

Most states require at least two years of college study to qualify as a fish and game warden. Applicants must pass written and physical examinations and vision, hearing, psychological, and drug tests similar to those taken by other law enforcement officers. Once hired, officers attend a training academy lasting from 3 to 12 months, sometimes followed by further training in the field.

To be considered for appointment as an FBI agent, an applicant must be a graduate of an accredited law school or a college graduate with one of the following: a major in accounting, electrical engineering, or information technology; fluency in a foreign language; or three years of related full-time work experience. All new agents undergo 18 weeks of training at the FBI Academy on the U.S. Marine Corps base in Quantico, Virginia.

Applicants for special agent jobs with the U.S. Secret Service and the Bureau of Alcohol, Tobacco, and Firearms must have a bachelor's degree, a minimum of three years' related work experience, or a combination of education and experience. Prospective special agents undergo 11 weeks of initial criminal investigation training at the Federal Law Enforcement Training Center in Glynco, Georgia, and another 17 weeks of specialized training with their particular agencies.

Applicants for special agent jobs with the DEA must have a college degree with at least a 2.95 grade point average or specialized skills or work experience, such as foreign language fluency, technical skills, law enforcement experience, or accounting experience. DEA special agents undergo 14 weeks of specialized training at the FBI Academy in Quantico, Virginia.

U.S. Border Patrol agents must be U.S. citizens, be younger than 37 years of age at the time of appointment, possess a valid driver's license, and pass a three-part examination on reasoning and language skills. A bachelor's degree or previous work experience that demonstrates the ability to handle stressful situations, make decisions, and take charge is required for a position as a Border Patrol agent. Applicants may qualify through a combination of education and work experience.

Postal inspectors must have a bachelor's degree and 1 year of related work experience. It is desirable that they have one of several professional certifications, such as that of certified public accountant. They also must pass a background investigation, meet certain health requirements, undergo a drug screening test, possess a valid state driver's license, and be a U.S. citizen between 21 and 36 years of age when hired.

Law enforcement agencies are encouraging applicants to take post-secondary school training in law enforcement-related subjects. Many entry-level applicants for police jobs have completed some formal postsecondary education, and a significant number are college graduates. Many junior colleges, colleges, and universities offer programs in law enforcement or administration of justice. Other courses helpful in preparing for a career in law enforcement include accounting, finance, electrical engineering, computer science, and foreign languages. Physical education and sports are helpful in developing the competitiveness, stamina, and agility needed for many law enforcement positions. Knowledge of a foreign language is an asset in many federal agencies and urban departments.

Continuing training helps police officers, detectives, and special agents improve their job performance. Through police department academies, regional centers for public safety employees established by the states, and federal agency training centers, instructors provide annual training in self-defense tactics, firearms, use-of-force policies, sensitivity and communications skills, crowd-control techniques, relevant legal developments, and advances in law enforcement equipment. Many agencies pay all or part of the tuition for officers to work toward degrees in criminal justice, police science, administration of justice, or public administration and pay higher salaries to those who earn such a degree.

Employment

Police and detectives held about 842,000 jobs in 2004. About 80 percent were employed by local governments. State police agencies employed about 12 percent, and various federal agencies employed about 6 percent. A small proportion worked for educational services, rail transportation, and contract investigation and security services.

According to the U.S. Bureau of Justice Statistics, police and detectives employed by local governments primarily worked in cities with more than 25,000 inhabitants. Some cities have very large police forces, while thousands of small communities employ fewer than 25 officers each.

Job Outlook

The opportunity for public service through law enforcement work is attractive to many because the job is challenging and involves much personal responsibility. Furthermore, law enforcement officers in many agencies may retire with a pension after 25 or 30 years of service, allowing them to pursue a second career while still in their 40s or 50s. Because of relatively attractive salaries and benefits, the number of qualified candidates exceeds the number of job openings in federal law enforcement agencies and in most state police departments, resulting in increased hiring standards and selectivity by employers. Competition should remain keen for higher-paying jobs with state and federal agencies and police departments in more affluent areas. Opportunities will be better in local and special police departments, especially in departments that offer relatively low salaries or in urban communities where the crime rate is relatively high. Applicants with college training in police science, military police experience, or both should have the best opportunities.

Employment of police and detectives is expected to grow about as fast as the average for all occupations through 2014. A more

security-conscious society and concern about drug-related crimes should contribute to the increasing demand for police services. However, employment growth will be hindered by reductions in federal hiring grants to local police departments and by expectations of low crime rates by the general public.

The level of government spending determines the level of employment for police and detectives. The number of job opportunities, therefore, can vary from year to year and from place to place. Layoffs, on the other hand, are rare because retirements enable most staffing cuts to be handled through attrition. Trained law enforcement officers who lose their jobs because of budget cuts usually have little difficulty finding jobs with other agencies. The need to replace workers who retire, transfer to other occupations, or stop working for other reasons will be the source of many job openings.

Earnings

Police and sheriff's patrol officers had median annual earnings of $45,210 in May 2004. The middle 50 percent earned between $34,410 and $56,360. The lowest 10 percent earned less than $26,910, and the highest 10 percent earned more than $68,880. Median annual earnings were $44,750 in federal government, $48,980 in state government, and $45,010 in local government.

In May 2004, median annual earnings of police and detective supervisors were $64,430. The middle 50 percent earned between $49,370 and $80,510. The lowest 10 percent earned less than $36,690, and the highest 10 percent earned more than $96,950. Median annual earnings were $86,030 in federal government, $62,300 in state government, and $63,590 in local government.

In May 2004, median annual earnings of detectives and criminal investigators were $53,990. The middle 50 percent earned between $40,690 and $72,280. The lowest 10 percent earned less than $32,180, and the highest 10 percent earned more than $86,010. Median annual earnings were $75,700 in federal government, $46,670 in state government, and $49,650 in local government.

Federal law provides special salary rates to federal employees who serve in law enforcement. Additionally, federal special agents and inspectors receive law enforcement availability pay (LEAP)—equal to 25 percent of the agent's grade and step—awarded because of the large amount of overtime that these agents are expected to work. For example, in 2005, FBI agents entered federal service as GS-10 employees on the pay scale at a base salary of $42,548, yet they earned about $53,185 a year with availability pay. They could advance to the GS-13 grade level in field nonsupervisory assignments at a base salary of $64,478, which was worth $80,597 with availability pay. FBI supervisory, management, and executive positions in grades GS-14 and GS-15 paid a base salary of about $76,193 and $89,625 a year, respectively, which amounted to $95,241 or $112,031 per year including availability pay. Salaries were slightly higher in selected areas where the prevailing local pay level was higher. Because federal agents may be eligible for a special law enforcement benefits package, applicants should ask their recruiter for more information.

According to the International City-County Management Association's annual Police and Fire Personnel, Salaries, and Expenditures Survey, average salaries for sworn full-time positions in 2004 were as follows:

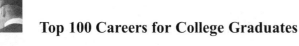

	Minimum annual base salary	Maximum annual base salary
Police chief	$72,924	$92,983
Deputy chief	61,110	76,994
Police captain	60,908	75,497
Police lieutenant	56,115	67,580
Police sergeant	49,895	59,454
Police corporal	41,793	51,661

Total earnings for local, state, and special police and detectives frequently exceed the stated salary because of payments for overtime, which can be significant. In addition to the common benefits—paid vacation, sick leave, and medical and life insurance—most police and sheriffs' departments provide officers with special allowances for uniforms. Because police officers usually are covered by liberal pension plans, many retire at half pay after 25 or 30 years of service.

Related Occupations

Police and detectives maintain law and order, collect evidence and information, and conduct investigations and surveillance. Workers in related occupations include correctional officers, private detectives and investigators, and security guards and gaming surveillance officers.

Sources of Additional Information

Information about entrance requirements may be obtained from federal, state, and local law enforcement agencies.

For general information about sheriffs and to learn more about the National Sheriffs' Association scholarship, contact

▷ National Sheriffs' Association, 1450 Duke St., Alexandria, VA 22314. Internet: http://www.sheriffs.org

Information about qualifications for employment as a FBI Special Agent is available from the nearest state FBI office. The address and phone number are listed in the local telephone directory. Internet: http://www.fbi.gov

Information on career opportunities, qualifications, and training for U.S. Secret Service Special Agents is available from the Secret Service Personnel Division at (202) 406-5800, (888) 813-8777, or (888) 813-USSS. Internet: http://www.treas.gov/usss

Information about qualifications for employment as a DEA Special Agent is available from the nearest DEA office, or call (800) DEA-4288. Internet: http://www.usdoj.gov/dea

Information about career opportunities, qualifications, and training to become a deputy marshal is available from

▷ U.S. Marshals Service, Human Resources Division—Law Enforcement Recruiting, Washington, DC 20530-1000. Internet: http://www.usmarshals.gov

For information on operations and career opportunities in the U.S. Bureau of Alcohol, Tobacco, Firearms, and Explosives operations, contact

▷ U.S. Bureau of Alcohol, Tobacco, Firearms, and Explosives Personnel Division, 650 Massachusetts Ave. NW, Room 4100, Washington, DC 20226. Internet: http://www.atf.treas.gov

Information about careers in U.S. Customs and Border Protection is available from

▷ U.S. Customs and Border Protection, 1300 Pennsylvania Ave. NW, Washington, DC 20229. Internet: http://www.cbp.gov

Information about law enforcement agencies within the Department of Homeland Security is available from

▷ U.S. Department of Homeland Security, Washington, DC 20528. Internet: http://www.dhs.gov

Purchasing Managers, Buyers, and Purchasing Agents

(O*NET 11-3061.00, 13-1021.00, 13-1022.00, and 13-1023.00)

Significant Points

■ Forty-three percent are employed in wholesale trade or manufacturing establishments.

■ Some firms promote qualified employees to these positions, while other employers recruit college graduates; regardless of academic preparation, new employees need 1 to 5 years to learn the specifics of their employer's business.

■ Overall employment growth is expected to be slower than average.

■ Opportunities should be best for those with a college degree.

Nature of the Work

Purchasing managers, buyers, and purchasing agents make up a key component of a firm's supply chain. They buy the goods and services the company or institution needs either to resell to customers or for the establishment's own use. *Wholesale and retail buyers* purchase goods for resale, such as clothing or electronics, and *purchasing agents* buy goods and services for use by their own company or organization such as raw materials for manufacturing or office supplies. *Purchasing agents and buyers of farm products* purchase goods such as grain, Christmas trees, and tobacco for further processing or resale. Purchasing professionals consider price, quality, availability, reliability, and technical support when choosing suppliers and merchandise. They try to get the best deal for their company, meaning the highest-quality goods and services at the lowest possible cost to their companies. In order to accomplish these tasks successfully, purchasing managers, buyers, and purchasing agents study sales records and inventory levels of current stock, identify foreign and domestic suppliers, and keep abreast of changes affecting both the supply of, and demand for, needed products and materials.

In large industrial organizations, a distinction often is drawn between the work of a buyer or purchasing agent and that of a *purchasing manager*. Purchasing agents commonly focus on routine purchasing tasks, often specializing in a commodity or group of related commodities, such as steel, lumber, cotton, grains, fabricated metal products, or petroleum products. Purchasing agents usually track market conditions, price trends, and futures markets. Purchasing managers usually handle the more complex or critical purchases and may supervise a group of purchasing agents handling other goods and services. Whether a person is titled purchasing manager, buyer, or purchasing agent depends more on specific industry and employer practices than on specific job duties.

Purchasing specialists employed by government agencies or manufacturing firms usually are called *purchasing directors, managers, or agents* or *contract specialists*. These workers acquire materials, parts, machines, supplies, services, and other inputs to the production of a final product. Some purchasing managers specialize in negotiating and supervising supply contracts and are called contract or supply managers. Purchasing agents and managers obtain items ranging from raw materials, fabricated parts, machinery, and office supplies to construction services and airline tickets. Often, purchasing specialists in government place solicitations for services and accept bids and offers through the Internet. Government purchasing agents and managers must follow strict laws and regulations in their work in order to avoid any appearance of impropriety. To be effective, purchasing specialists must have a working technical knowledge of the goods or services to be purchased.

Purchasing specialists who buy finished goods for resale are employed by wholesale and retail establishments, where they commonly are known as *buyers* or *merchandise managers*. Wholesale and retail buyers are an integral part of a complex system of distribution and merchandising that caters to the vast array of consumer needs and desires. Wholesale buyers purchase goods directly from manufacturers or from other wholesale firms for resale to retail firms, commercial establishments, institutions, and other organizations. In retail firms, buyers purchase goods from wholesale firms or directly from manufacturers for resale to the public. Buyers largely determine which products their establishment will sell. Therefore, it is essential that they have the ability to predict what will appeal to consumers. They must constantly stay informed of the latest trends because failure to do so could jeopardize profits and the reputation of their company. They keep track of inventories and sales levels through computer software that is linked to the store's cash registers. Buyers also follow ads in newspapers and other media to check competitors' sales activities, and they watch general economic conditions to anticipate consumer buying patterns. Buyers working for large and medium-sized firms usually specialize in acquiring one or two lines of merchandise, whereas buyers working for small stores may purchase the establishment's complete inventory.

The use of private-label merchandise and the consolidation of buying departments have increased the responsibilities of retail buyers. Private-label merchandise, produced for a particular retailer, requires buyers to work closely with vendors to develop and obtain the desired product. The downsizing and consolidation of buying departments increases the demands placed on buyers because, although the amount of work remains unchanged, there are fewer people to accomplish it. The result is an increase in the workloads and levels of responsibility for all.

Many merchandise managers assist in the planning and implementation of sales promotion programs. Working with merchandise executives, they determine the nature of the sale and purchase items accordingly. Merchandise managers may work with advertising personnel to create an ad campaign. For example, they may determine in which media the advertisement will be placed—newspapers, direct mail, television, or some combination of all three. In addition,

merchandise managers often visit the selling floor to ensure that goods are properly displayed. Buyers stay in constant contact with store and department managers to find out what products are selling well and which items the customers are demanding to be added to the product line. Often, assistant buyers are responsible for placing orders and checking shipments.

Evaluating suppliers is one of the most critical functions of a purchasing manager, buyer, or purchasing agent. Many firms now run on a lean manufacturing schedule and use just-in-time inventories, so any delays in the supply chain can shut down production and cost the firm its customers and reputation. Purchasing professionals use many resources to find out all they can about potential suppliers. The Internet has become an effective tool in searching catalogs, trade journals, and industry and company publications and directories. Purchasing professionals will attend meetings, trade shows, and conferences to learn of new industry trends and make contacts with suppliers. Purchasing managers, agents, and buyers will usually interview prospective suppliers and visit their plants and distribution centers to asses their capabilities. It is important to make certain that the supplier is capable of delivering the desired goods or services on time and in the correct quantities without sacrificing quality. Once all of the necessary information on suppliers is gathered, orders are placed and contracts are awarded to those suppliers who meet the purchaser's needs. Most of the transaction process is now automated using electronic purchasing systems that link the supplier and firms together through the Internet.

Purchasing professionals can gain instant access to the specifications for thousands of commodities, inventory records, and their customers' purchase records to avoid overpaying for goods and to avoid shortages of popular goods or surpluses of goods that do not sell as well. These systems permit faster selection, customization, and ordering of products, and they allow buyers to concentrate on the qualitative and analytical aspects of the job. Long-term contracts are an important strategy of purchasing professionals because they allow purchasers to consolidate their supply bases around fewer suppliers. In today's global economy, purchasing managers, buyers, and purchasing agents should expect to deal with foreign suppliers, which may require travel to other countries, and to be familiar with other cultures and languages.

Changing business practices have altered the traditional roles of purchasing or supply management specialists in many industries. For example, manufacturing companies increasingly involve workers in this occupation at most stages of product development because of their ability to forecast a part's or material's cost, availability, and suitability for its intended purpose. Furthermore, potential problems with the supply of materials may be avoided by consulting the purchasing department in the early stages of product design.

Purchasing specialists often work closely with other employees in their own organization when deciding on purchases, an arrangement sometimes called team buying. For example, before submitting an order, they may discuss the design of custom-made products with company design engineers, talk about problems involving the quality of purchased goods with quality assurance engineers and production supervisors, or mention shipment problems to managers in the receiving department.

Working Conditions

Most purchasing managers, buyers, and purchasing agents work in comfortable offices. They frequently work more than the standard 40-hour week because of special sales, conferences, or production deadlines. Evening and weekend work also is common before holiday and back-to-school seasons for those working in retail trade. Consequently, many retail firms discourage the use of vacation time during peak periods.

Buyers and merchandise managers often work under great pressure. Because wholesale and retail stores are so competitive, buyers need physical stamina to keep up with the fast-paced nature of their work.

Many purchasing managers, buyers, and purchasing agents travel at least several days a month. Purchasers for worldwide manufacturing companies and large retailers, as well as buyers of high fashion, may travel outside the United States.

Training, Other Qualifications, and Advancement

Qualified persons may begin as trainees, purchasing clerks, expediters, junior buyers, or assistant buyers. Retail and wholesale firms prefer to hire applicants who have a college degree and who are familiar with the merchandise they sell and with wholesaling and retailing practices. Some retail firms promote qualified employees to assistant buyer positions; others recruit and train college graduates as assistant buyers. Most employers use a combination of methods.

Educational requirements tend to vary with the size of the organization. Large stores and distributors prefer applicants who have completed a bachelor's degree program with a business emphasis. Many manufacturing firms put yet a greater emphasis on formal training, preferring applicants with a bachelor's or master's degree in engineering, business, economics, or one of the applied sciences. A master's degree is essential for advancement to many top-level purchasing manager jobs.

Regardless of academic preparation, new employees must learn the specifics of their employers' business. Training periods vary in length, with most lasting 1 to 5 years. In wholesale and retail establishments, most trainees begin by selling merchandise, supervising sales workers, checking invoices on material received, and keeping track of stock. As they progress, retail trainees are given increased buying-related responsibilities.

In manufacturing, new purchasing employees often are enrolled in company training programs and spend a considerable amount of time learning about their firm's operations and purchasing practices. They work with experienced purchasers to learn about commodities, prices, suppliers, and markets. In addition, they may be assigned to the production planning department to learn about the material requirements system and the inventory system the company uses to keep production and replenishment functions working smoothly.

Purchasing managers, buyers, and purchasing agents must know how to use both word processing and spreadsheet software, as well as the Internet. Other important qualities include the ability to analyze technical data in suppliers' proposals; good communication, negotiation, and mathematical skills; knowledge of supply-chain management; and the ability to perform financial analyses.

Persons who wish to become wholesale or retail buyers should be good at planning and decisionmaking and have an interest in merchandising. Anticipating consumer preferences and ensuring that goods are in stock when they are needed requires resourcefulness, good judgment, and self-confidence. Buyers must be able to make decisions quickly and to take risks. Marketing skills and the ability to identify products that will sell also are very important. Employers often look for leadership ability, too, because buyers spend a large portion of their time supervising assistant buyers and dealing with manufacturers' representatives and store executives.

Experienced buyers may advance by moving to a department that manages a larger volume or by becoming a merchandise manager. Others may go to work in sales for a manufacturer or wholesaler.

An experienced purchasing agent or buyer may become an assistant purchasing manager in charge of a group of purchasing professionals before advancing to purchasing manager, supply manager, or director of materials management. At the top levels, duties may overlap with other management functions, such as production, planning, logistics, and marketing.

Regardless of industry, continuing education is essential for advancement. Many purchasers participate in seminars offered by professional societies and take college courses in supply management. Professional certification is becoming increasingly important, especially for those just entering the occupation.

In private industry, recognized marks of experience and professional competence are the Accredited Purchasing Practitioner (APP) and Certified Purchasing Manager (CPM) designations, conferred by the Institute for Supply Management, and the Certified Purchasing Professional (CPP) and Certified Professional Purchasing Manager (CPPM) designations, conferred by the American Purchasing Society. In federal, state, and local government, the indications of professional competence are Certified Professional Public Buyer (CPPB) and Certified Public Purchasing Officer (CPPO), conferred by the National Institute of Governmental Purchasing. Most of these certifications are awarded only after work-related experience and education requirements are met and written or oral exams are successfully completed.

Employment

Purchasing managers, buyers, and purchasing agents held about 520,000 jobs in 2004. Forty-three percent worked in the wholesale trade and manufacturing industries, and another twelve percent worked in retail trade. The remainder worked mostly in service establishments, such as hospitals, or different levels of government. A small number were self-employed.

The following tabulation shows the distribution of employment by occupational specialty:

Purchasing agents, except wholesale, retail,
 and farm products 273,000
Wholesale and retail buyers, except
 farm products 156,000
Purchasing managers 75,000
Purchasing agents and buyers, farm products..........16,000

Job Outlook

Overall employment of purchasing managers, buyers, and purchasing agents is expected to grow slower than the average for all occupations through the year 2014. Offsetting some declines for purchasing workers in the manufacturing sector will be increases in the services sector. Companies in the services sector, which have typically made purchases on an ad hoc basis, are beginning to realize that centralized purchasing offices may be more efficient. Also, many purchasing agents are now charged with procuring services that were traditionally done in-house in the past, such as computer and IT (information technology) support, in addition to traditionally contracted services such as advertising. Demand for purchasing workers will be limited by improving software, which has eliminated much of the paperwork involved in ordering and procuring supplies, and also by the growing number of purchases being made electronically through the internet and electronic data interchange (EDI). Despite slower-than-average growth, some job openings will result from the need to replace workers who transfer to other occupations or leave the labor force.

Employment of purchasing managers is expected to grow more slowly than average. The use of the Internet to conduct electronic commerce has made information easier to obtain, thus increasing the productivity of purchasing managers. The Internet also allows both large and small companies to bid on contracts. Exclusive supply contracts and long-term contracting have allowed companies to negotiate with fewer suppliers less frequently.

Employment of wholesale and retail buyers, except farm products, also is projected to grow more slowly than average. In the retail industry, mergers and acquisitions have caused buying departments to consolidate. In addition, larger retail stores are eliminating local buying departments and centralizing them at their headquarters.

Employment of purchasing agents, except wholesale, retail, and farm products, is expected to increase more slowly than average, limited by the increased globalization of the U.S. economy. As more materials and supplies come from abroad, firms have begun to outsource more of their purchasing duties to foreign purchasing agents who are located closer to the foreign suppliers of goods and materials they will need. This trend is expected to continue, but it will likely be limited to routine transactions, with complex and critical purchases still being handled in-house.

Finally, employment of purchasing agents and buyers, farm products, also is projected to increase more slowly than average as overall growth in agricultural industries decreases and retailers in the grocery-related industries consolidate.

Persons who have a bachelor's degree in business should have the best chance of obtaining a buyer position in wholesale or retail trade or within government. A bachelor's degree, combined with industry experience and knowledge of a technical field, will be an advantage for those interested in working for a manufacturing or industrial company. Government agencies and larger companies usually require a master's degree in business or public administration for top-level purchasing positions.

Earnings

Median annual earnings of purchasing managers were $72,450 in May 2004. The middle 50 percent earned between $54,150 and $94,970 a year. The lowest 10 percent earned less than $41,300, and the highest 10 percent earned more than $121,600 a year.

Median annual earnings for purchasing agents and buyers, farm products, were $43,720 in May 2004. The middle 50 percent earned between $33,100 and $59,420 a year. The lowest 10 percent earned less than $25,260, and the highest 10 percent earned more than $82,330 a year.

Median annual earnings for wholesale and retail buyers, except farm products, were $42,230 in May 2004. The middle 50 percent earned between $31,550 and $57,010 a year. The lowest 10 percent earned less than $24,380, and the highest 10 percent earned more than $79,340 a year. Median annual earnings in the industries employing the largest numbers of wholesale and retail buyers, except farm products, in May 2004 were

Management of companies and enterprises	$49,770
Grocery and related product wholesalers	43,910
Wholesale electronic markets and agents and brokers	43,860
Building material and supplies dealers	35,850
Grocery stores	32,790

Median annual earnings for purchasing agents, except wholesale, retail, and farm products, were $47,680 in May 2004. The middle 50 percent earned between $36,760 and $62,600 a year. The lowest 10 percent earned less than $29,640, and the highest 10 percent earned more than $79,710 a year. Median annual earnings in the industries employing the largest numbers of purchasing agents, except wholesale, retail, and farm products, in May 2004 were

Federal executive branch and United States Postal Service	$63,940
Aerospace product and parts manufacturing	55,820
Management of companies and enterprises	53,750
Local government	44,730
General medical and surgical hospitals	37,090

Purchasing managers, buyers, and purchasing agents receive the same benefits package as other workers, including vacations, sick leave, life and health insurance, and pension plans. In addition to receiving standard benefits, retail buyers often earn cash bonuses based on their performance and may receive discounts on merchandise bought from their employer.

Related Occupations

Workers in other occupations who need a knowledge of marketing and the ability to assess consumer demand include those in advertising, marketing, promotions, public relations, and sales managers; food service managers; insurance sales agents; lodging managers; sales engineers; and sales representatives, wholesale and manufacturing.

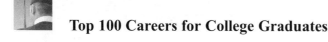

Sources of Additional Information

Further information about education, training, employment, and certification for purchasing careers is available from

▶ American Purchasing Society, North Island Center, Suite 203, 8 East Galena Blvd., Aurora, IL 60506.

▶ Institute for Supply Management, P.O. Box 22160, Tempe, AZ 85285-2160. Internet: http://www.ism.ws

▶ National Institute of Governmental Purchasing, Inc., 151 Spring St., Suite 300, Herndon, VA 20170-5223. Internet: http://www.nigp.org

Radiologic Technologists and Technicians

(O*NET 29-2034.01 and 29-2034.02)

Significant Points

■ Job opportunities are expected to be favorable; some employers report difficulty hiring sufficient numbers of radiologic technologists and technicians.

■ Formal training programs in radiography range in length from 1 to 4 years and lead to a certificate, an associate degree, or a bachelor's degree.

■ Although hospitals will remain the primary employer, a greater number of new jobs will be found in physicians' offices and diagnostic imaging centers.

Nature of the Work

Radiologic technologists and technicians take X rays and administer nonradioactive materials into patients' bloodstreams for diagnostic purposes. Some specialize in diagnostic imaging technologies, such as computerized tomography (CT) and magnetic resonance imaging (MRI).

In addition to radiologic technologists and technicians, others who conduct diagnostic imaging procedures include cardiovascular technologists and technicians and nuclear medicine technologists.

Radiologic technologists and technicians, also referred to as *radiographers,* produce X-ray films (radiographs) of parts of the human body for use in diagnosing medical problems. They prepare patients for radiologic examinations by explaining the procedure, removing articles such as jewelry, through which X rays cannot pass, and positioning patients so that the parts of the body can be appropriately radiographed. To prevent unnecessary exposure to radiation, these workers surround the exposed area with radiation protection devices, such as lead shields, or limit the size of the X-ray beam. Radiographers position radiographic equipment at the correct angle and height over the appropriate area of a patient's body. Using instruments similar to a measuring tape, they may measure the thickness of the section to be radiographed and set controls on the X-ray machine to produce radiographs of the appropriate density, detail, and contrast. They place the X-ray film under the part of the patient's body to be examined and make the exposure. They then remove the film and develop it.

Experienced radiographers may perform more complex imaging procedures. For fluoroscopies, radiographers prepare a solution of contrast medium for the patient to drink, allowing the radiologist (a physician who interprets radiographs) to see soft tissues in the body. Some radiographers, called *CT technologists,* operate CT scanners to produce cross-sectional images of patients. Radiographers who operate machines that use strong magnets and radio waves, rather than radiation, to create an image are called *MRI technologists.*

Radiologic technologists and technicians must follow physicians' orders precisely and conform to regulations concerning the use of radiation to protect themselves, their patients, and their co-workers from unnecessary exposure.

In addition to preparing patients and operating equipment, radiologic technologists and technicians keep patient records and adjust and maintain equipment. They also may prepare work schedules, evaluate purchases of equipment, or manage a radiology department.

Working Conditions

Most full-time radiologic technologists and technicians work about 40 hours a week. They may, however, have evening, weekend, or on-call hours. Opportunities for part-time and shift work also are available.

Physical stamina is important, because technologists and technicians are on their feet for long periods and may lift or turn disabled patients. Technologists and technicians work at diagnostic machines, but also may perform some procedures at patients' bedsides. Some travel to patients in large vans equipped with sophisticated diagnostic equipment.

Although radiation hazards exist in this occupation, they are minimized by the use of lead aprons, gloves, and other shielding devices, as well as by instruments monitoring exposure to radiation. Technologists and technicians wear badges measuring radiation levels in the radiation area, and detailed records are kept on their cumulative lifetime dose.

Training, Other Qualifications, and Advancement

Preparation for this profession is offered in hospitals, colleges and universities, vocational-technical institutes, and the U.S. Armed Forces. Hospitals, which employ most radiologic technologists and technicians, prefer to hire those with formal training.

Formal training programs in radiography range in length from 1 to 4 years and lead to a certificate, an associate degree, or a bachelor's degree. Two-year associate degree programs are most prevalent.

Some 1-year certificate programs are available for experienced radiographers or individuals from other health occupations, such as medical technologists and registered nurses, who want to change fields or specialize in CT or MRI. A bachelor's or master's degree in one of the radiologic technologies is desirable for supervisory, administrative, or teaching positions.

The Joint Review Committee on Education in Radiologic Technology accredits most formal training programs for the field. The committee accredited 606 radiography programs in 2005. Radiography programs require, at a minimum, a high school diploma or the equivalent. High school courses in mathematics, physics, chemistry, and biology are helpful. The programs provide both classroom and clinical instruction in anatomy and physiology, patient care procedures, radiation physics, radiation protection, principles of imaging, medical terminology, positioning of patients, medical ethics, radiobiology, and pathology.

Federal legislation protects the public from the hazards of unnecessary exposure to medical and dental radiation by ensuring that operators of radiologic equipment are properly trained. Under this legislation, the federal government sets voluntary standards that the states may use for accrediting training programs and certifying individuals who engage in medical or dental radiography.

In 2005, 38 states certified radiologic technologists and technicians. Certification, which is voluntary, is offered by the American Registry of Radiologic Technologists. To be eligible for certification, technologists generally must graduate from an accredited program and pass an examination. Many employers prefer to hire certified radiographers. To be recertified, radiographers must complete 24 hours of continuing education every two years.

Radiologic technologists and technicians should be sensitive to patients' physical and psychological needs. They must pay attention to detail, follow instructions, and work as part of a team. In addition, operating complicated equipment requires mechanical ability and manual dexterity.

With experience and additional training, staff technologists may become specialists, performing CT scanning, angiography, and magnetic resonance imaging. Experienced technologists also may be promoted to supervisor, chief radiologic technologist, and, ultimately, department administrator or director. Depending on the institution, courses or a master's degree in business or health administration may be necessary for the director's position. Some technologists progress by leaving the occupation to become instructors or directors in radiologic technology programs; others take jobs as sales representatives or instructors with equipment manufacturers.

Employment

Radiologic technologists and technicians held about 182,000 jobs in 2004. More than half of all jobs were in hospitals. Most of the rest were in offices of physicians; medical and diagnostic laboratories, including diagnostic imaging centers; and outpatient care centers.

Job Outlook

Job opportunities are expected to be favorable. Some employers report difficulty hiring sufficient numbers of radiologic technologists and technicians. Imbalances between the demand for, and supply of, radiologic technologists and technicians should spur efforts to attract and retain qualified workers, such as improved compensation and working conditions. Radiologic technologists who also are experienced in more complex diagnostic imaging procedures, such as CT and MRI, will have better employment opportunities, brought about as employers seek to control costs by using multiskilled employees.

Employment of radiologic technologists and technicians is expected to grow faster than the average for all occupations through 2014 as

the population grows and ages, increasing the demand for diagnostic imaging. Although health care providers are enthusiastic about the clinical benefits of new technologies, the extent to which they are adopted depends largely on cost and reimbursement considerations. For example, digital imaging technology can improve the quality of the images and the efficiency of the procedure, but remains expensive. Some promising new technologies may not come into widespread use because they are too expensive and third-party payers may not be willing to pay for their use.

Hospitals will remain the principal employer of radiologic technologists and technicians. However, a greater number of new jobs will be found in offices of physicians and diagnostic imaging centers. Health facilities such as these are expected to grow rapidly through 2014 due to the strong shift toward outpatient care encouraged by third-party payers and made possible by technological advances that permit more procedures to be performed outside the hospital. Some job openings also will arise from the need to replace technologists and technicians who leave the occupation.

Earnings

Median annual earnings of radiologic technologists and technicians were $43,350 in May 2004. The middle 50 percent earned between $36,170 and $52,430. The lowest 10 percent earned less than $30,020, and the highest 10 percent earned more than $60,210. Median annual earnings in the industries employing the largest numbers of radiologic technologists and technicians in May 2004 were

Medical and diagnostic laboratories	$46,620
General medical and surgical hospitals	43,960
Offices of physicians	40,290

Related Occupations

Radiologic technologists and technicians operate sophisticated equipment to help physicians, dentists, and other health practitioners diagnose and treat patients. Workers in related occupations include cardiovascular technologists and technicians, clinical laboratory technologists and technicians, diagnostic medical sonographers, nuclear medicine technologists, radiation therapists, and respiratory therapists.

Sources of Additional Information

For career information, send a stamped, self-addressed business-size envelope with your request to

▸ American Society of Radiologic Technologists, 15000 Central Ave. SE, Albuquerque, NM 87123-3917. Internet: http://www.asrt.org

For the current list of accredited education programs in radiography, write to

▸ Joint Review Committee on Education in Radiologic Technology, 20 N. Wacker Dr., Suite 2850, Chicago, IL 60606-3182. Internet: http://www.jrcert.org

For information on certification, contact

▸ American Registry of Radiologic Technologists, 1255 Northland Dr., St. Paul, MN 55120-1155. Internet: http://www.arrt.org

Real Estate Brokers and Sales Agents

(O*NET 41-9021.00 and 41-9022.00)

Significant Points

- Real estate brokers and sales agents often work evenings and weekends and usually are on call to suit the needs of clients.

- A license is required in every state and the District of Columbia.

- Although gaining a job may be relatively easy, beginning workers may face competition from well-established, more experienced agents and brokers in obtaining listings and in closing an adequate number of sales.

- Employment is sensitive to swings in the economy, especially interest rates; during periods of declining economic activity and increasing interest rates, the volume of sales and the resulting demand for sales workers fall.

Nature of the Work

One of the most complex and significant financial events in peoples' lives is the purchase or sale of a home or investment property. Because of this complexity and significance, people typically seek the help of real estate brokers and sales agents when buying or selling real estate.

Real estate brokers and sales agents have a thorough knowledge of the real estate market in their communities. They know which neighborhoods will best fit clients' needs and budgets. They are familiar with local zoning and tax laws and know where to obtain financing. Agents and brokers also act as intermediaries in price negotiations between buyers and sellers.

Real estate agents usually are independent sales workers who provide their services to a licensed real estate broker on a contract basis. In return, the broker pays the agent a portion of the commission earned from the agent's sale of the property. Brokers are independent businesspeople who sell real estate owned by others; they also may rent or manage properties for a fee. When selling real estate, brokers arrange for title searches and for meetings between buyers and sellers during which the details of the transactions are agreed upon and the new owners take possession of the property. A broker may help to arrange favorable financing from a lender for the prospective buyer; often, this makes the difference between success and failure in closing a sale. In some cases, brokers and agents assume primary responsibility for closing sales; in others, lawyers or lenders do. Brokers supervise agents who may have many of the same job duties. Brokers also supervise their own offices, advertise properties, and handle other business matters. Some combine other types of work, such as selling insurance or practicing law, with their real estate business.

Besides making sales, agents and brokers must have properties to sell. Consequently, they spend a significant amount of time obtaining listings—agreements by owners to place properties for sale with the firm. When listing a property for sale, agents and brokers

compare the listed property with similar properties that recently sold in order to determine a competitive market price for the property. Once the property is sold, both the agent who sold it and the agent who obtained the listing receive a portion of the commission. Thus, agents who sell a property that they themselves have listed can increase their commission.

Most real estate brokers and sales agents sell residential property. A small number—usually employed in large or specialized firms—sell commercial, industrial, agricultural, or other types of real estate. Every specialty requires knowledge of that particular type of property and clientele. Selling or leasing business property requires an understanding of leasing practices, business trends, and the location of the property. Agents who sell or lease industrial properties must know about the region's transportation, utilities, and labor supply. Whatever the type of property, the agent or broker must know how to meet the client's particular requirements.

Before showing residential properties to potential buyers, agents meet with them to get a feeling for the type of home the buyers would like. In this prequalifying phase, the agent determines how much the buyers can afford to spend. In addition, the agent and the buyer usually sign a loyalty contract that states that the agent will be the only one to show houses to buyers. An agent or broker then generates lists of properties for sale, their location and description, and available sources of financing. In some cases, agents and brokers use computers to give buyers a virtual tour of properties in which they are interested. With a computer, buyers can view interior and exterior images or floor plans without leaving the real estate office.

Agents may meet several times with prospective buyers to discuss and visit available properties. Agents identify and emphasize the most pertinent selling points. To a young family looking for a house, they may emphasize the convenient floor plan, the area's low crime rate, and the proximity to schools and shopping centers. To a potential investor, they may point out the tax advantages of owning a rental property and the ease of finding a renter. If bargaining over price becomes necessary, agents must follow their client's instructions carefully and may have to present counteroffers in order to get the best possible price.

Once both parties have signed the contract, the real estate broker or agent must make sure that all special terms of the contract are met before the closing date. For example, the agent must make sure that the mandated and agreed-upon inspections, including that of the home and termite and radon inspections, take place. Also, if the seller agrees to any repairs, the broker or agent must see that they are made. Increasingly, brokers and agents are handling environmental problems as well by making sure that the properties they sell meet environmental regulations. For example, they may be responsible for dealing with lead paint on the walls. While loan officers, attorneys, or other persons handle many details, the agent must ensure that they are carried out.

Working Conditions

Advances in telecommunications and the ability to retrieve data about properties over the Internet allow many real estate brokers and sales agents to work out of their homes instead of real estate offices. Even with this convenience, much of the time of these workers is spent away from their desks—showing properties to customers, analyzing properties for sale, meeting with prospective clients, or researching the state of the market.

Agents and brokers often work more than a standard 40-hour week. They usually work evenings and weekends and are always on call to suit the needs of clients. Although the hours are long and frequently irregular, most agents and brokers have the freedom to determine their own schedule. Consequently, they can arrange their work so that they can have time off when they want it. Business usually is slower during the winter season.

Training, Other Qualifications, and Advancement

In every state and the District of Columbia, real estate brokers and sales agents must be licensed. Prospective agents must be high school graduates, be at least 18 years old, and pass a written test. The examination—more comprehensive for brokers than for agents—includes questions on basic real estate transactions and laws affecting the sale of property. Most states require candidates for the general sales license to complete between 30 and 90 hours of classroom instruction. Those seeking a broker's license need between 60 and 90 hours of formal training and a specific amount of experience selling real estate, usually 1 to 3 years. Some states waive the experience requirements for the broker's license for applicants who have a bachelor's degree in real estate.

State licenses typically must be renewed every 1 or 2 years; usually, no examination needs to be taken. However, many states require continuing education for license renewals. Prospective agents and brokers should contact the real estate licensing commission of the state in which they wish to work in order to verify the exact licensing requirements.

As real estate transactions have become more legally complex, many firms have turned to college graduates to fill positions. A large number of agents and brokers have some college training. College courses in real estate, finance, business administration, statistics, economics, law, and English are helpful. For those who intend to start their own company, business courses such as marketing and accounting are as significant as courses in real estate or finance.

Personality traits are equally as important as one's academic background. Brokers look for applicants who possess a pleasant personality, are honest, and present a neat appearance. Maturity, good judgment, trustworthiness, and enthusiasm for the job are required in order to encourage prospective customers in this highly competitive field. Agents should be well organized; be detail oriented; and have a good memory for names, faces, and business particulars.

Those interested in jobs as real estate agents often begin in their own communities. Their knowledge of local neighborhoods is a clear advantage. Under the direction of an experienced agent, beginners learn the practical aspects of the job, including the use of computers to locate or list available properties and identify sources of financing.

Many firms offer formal training programs for both beginners and experienced agents. Larger firms usually offer more extensive programs than smaller firms. More than a thousand universities, colleges, and junior colleges offer courses in real estate. At some, a student can earn an associate's or bachelor's degree with a major in real estate; several offer advanced degrees. Many local real estate associations that are members of the National Association of Realtors sponsor courses covering the fundamentals and legal aspects of the field. Advanced courses in mortgage financing, property development and management, and other subjects also are available.

Advancement opportunities for agents may take the form of higher rates of commission. As agents gain knowledge and expertise, they become more efficient in closing a greater number of transactions and increase their earnings. In many large firms, experienced agents can advance to sales manager or general manager. Persons who have received their broker's license may open their own offices. Others with experience and training in estimating property value may become real estate appraisers, and people familiar with operating and maintaining rental properties may become property managers. Experienced agents and brokers with a thorough knowledge of business conditions and property values in their localities may enter mortgage financing or real estate investment counseling.

Employment

In 2004, real estate brokers and sales agents held about 460,000 jobs; real estate sales agents held approximately 24 percent of these jobs. Many worked part time, combining their real estate activities with other careers. About 6 out of 10 real estate agents and brokers were self-employed. Real estate is sold in all areas, but employment is concentrated in large urban areas and in rapidly growing communities.

Most real estate firms are relatively small; indeed, some are one-person businesses. By contrast, some large real estate firms have several hundred agents operating out of numerous branch offices. Many brokers have franchise agreements with national or regional real estate organizations. Under this type of arrangement, the broker pays a fee in exchange for the privilege of using the more widely known name of the parent organization. Although franchised brokers often receive help in training sales staff and running their offices, they bear the ultimate responsibility for the success or failure of their firms.

Real estate brokers and sales agents are older, on average, than most other workers. Historically, many homemakers and retired persons were attracted to real estate sales by the flexible and part-time work schedules characteristic of the field. These individuals could enter, leave, and later return to the occupation, depending on the strength of the real estate market, their family responsibilities, or other personal circumstances. Recently, however, the attractiveness of part-time real estate work has declined as increasingly complex legal and technological requirements are raising startup costs associated with becoming an agent.

Job Outlook

Employment of real estate brokers and sales agents is expected to grow about as fast as the average for all occupations through the year 2014 because of the increasing housing needs of a growing population, as well as the perception that real estate is a good investment. Relatively low interest rates should continue to stimulate sales of real estate, resulting in the need for more agents and brokers. In addition, a large number of job openings will arise each

year from the need to replace workers who transfer to other occupations or leave the labor force. However, job growth will be somewhat limited by the increasing use of technology, which is improving the productivity of agents and brokers. For example, prospective customers often can perform their own searches for properties that meet their criteria by accessing real estate information on the Internet. The increasing use of technology is likely to be more detrimental to part-time or temporary real estate agents than to full-time agents because part-time agents generally are not able to compete with full-time agents who have invested in new technology. Changing legal requirements, such as disclosure laws, also may dissuade some who are not serious about practicing full time from continuing to work part time.

This occupation is relatively easy to enter and is attractive because of its flexible working conditions; the high interest in, and familiarity with, local real estate markets that entrants often have; and the potential for high earnings. Therefore, although gaining a job as a real estate agent or broker may be relatively easy, beginning agents and brokers may face competition from their well-established, more experienced counterparts in obtaining listings and in closing an adequate number of sales. Well-trained, ambitious people who enjoy selling—particularly those with extensive social and business connections in their communities—should have the best chance for success.

Employment of real estate brokers and sales agents often is sensitive to swings in the economy, especially interest rates. During periods of declining economic activity and increasing interest rates, the volume of sales and the resulting demand for sales workers falls. As a result, the earnings of agents and brokers decline, and many work fewer hours or leave the occupation altogether.

Earnings

The median annual earnings of salaried real estate sales agents, including commissions, were $35,670 in May 2004. The middle 50 percent earned between $23,500 and $58,110 a year. The lowest 10 percent earned less than $17,600, and the highest 10 percent earned more than $92,770. Median annual earnings in the industries employing the largest number of real estate sales agents in May 2004 were as follows:

Residential building construction $54,770

Offices of real estate agents and brokers................37,970

Activities related to real estate 32,460

Lessors of real estate 25,840

Median annual earnings of salaried real estate brokers, including commission, were $58,720 in May 2004. The middle 50 percent earned between $33,480 and $99,820 a year. Median annual earning of real estate brokers were $61,550 in offices of real estate agents and brokers and $44,920 in activities related to real estate.

Commissions on sales are the main source of earnings of real estate agents and brokers. The rate of commission varies according to whatever the agent and broker agree on, the type of property, and its value. The percentage paid on the sale of farm and commercial properties or unimproved land is typically higher than the percentage paid for selling a home.

Commissions may be divided among several agents and brokers. When the property is sold, the broker or agent who obtained the listing usually shares the commission with the broker or agent who made the sale and with the firm that employs each of them. Although an agent's share varies greatly from one firm to another, often it is about half of the total amount received by the firm. Agents who both list and sell a property maximize their commission.

Income usually increases as an agent gains experience, but individual motivation, economic conditions, and the type and location of the property also affect earnings. Sales workers who are active in community organizations and in local real estate associations can broaden their contacts and increase their earnings. A beginner's earnings often are irregular because a few weeks or even months may go by without a sale. Although some brokers allow an agent to draw against future earnings from a special account, the practice is not common with new employees. The beginner, therefore, should have enough money to live for about 6 months or until commissions increase.

Related Occupations

Selling expensive items such as homes requires maturity, tact, and a sense of responsibility. Other sales workers who find these character traits important in their work include insurance sales agents; retail salespersons; sales representatives, wholesale and manufacturing; and securities, commodities, and financial services sales agents. Although not involving sales, the work of property, real estate, and community association managers, as well as appraisers and assessors of real estate, requires an understanding of real estate.

Sources of Additional Information

Information on licensing requirements for real estate brokers and sales agents is available from most local real estate organizations or from the state real estate commission or board.

More information about opportunities in real estate is available on the Internet site of the following organization:

▶ National Association of Realtors. Internet: http://www.realtor.org

Registered Nurses

(O*NET 29-1111.00)

Significant Points

■ Registered nurses constitute the largest health care occupation, with 2.4 million jobs.

■ About 3 out of 5 jobs are in hospitals.

■ The three major educational paths to registered nursing are a bachelor's degree, an associate degree, and a diploma from an approved nursing program.

■ Registered nurses are projected to create the second-largest number of new jobs among all occupations; job opportunities in most specialties and employment settings are expected to be excellent, with some employers reporting difficulty in attracting and retaining enough RNs.

Nature of the Work

Registered nurses (RNs), regardless of specialty or work setting, perform basic duties that include treating patients, educating patients and the public about various medical conditions, and providing advice and emotional support to patients' family members. RNs record patients' medical histories and symptoms, help to perform diagnostic tests and analyze results, operate medical machinery, administer treatment and medications, and help with patient follow-up and rehabilitation.

RNs teach patients and their families how to manage their illness or injury, including post-treatment home care needs, diet and exercise programs, and self-administration of medication and physical therapy. Some RNs also are trained to provide grief counseling to family members of critically ill patients. RNs work to promote general health by educating the public on various warning signs and symptoms of disease and where to go for help. RNs also might run general health screening or immunization clinics, blood drives, and public seminars on various conditions.

RNs can specialize in one or more patient care specialties. The most common specialties can be divided into roughly four categories—by work setting or type of treatment; disease, ailment, or condition; organ or body system type; or population. RNs may combine specialties from more than one area—for example, pediatric oncology or cardiac emergency—depending on personal interest and employer needs.

RNs may specialize by work setting or by type of care provided. For example, *ambulatory care nurses* treat patients with a variety of illnesses and injuries on an outpatient basis, either in physicians' offices or in clinics. Some ambulatory care nurses are involved in telehealth, providing care and advice through electronic communications media such as videoconferencing or the Internet. *Critical care nurses* work in critical or intensive care hospital units and provide care to patients with cardiovascular, respiratory, or pulmonary failure. *Emergency,* or *trauma, nurses* work in hospital emergency departments and treat patients with life-threatening conditions caused by accidents, heart attacks, and strokes. Some emergency nurses are flight nurses, who provide medical care to patients who must be flown by helicopter to the nearest medical facility. *Holistic nurses* provide care such as acupuncture, massage therapy and aromatherapy, and biofeedback, which are meant to treat patients' mental and spiritual health in addition to their physical health. *Home health care nurses* provide at-home care for patients who are recovering from surgery, accidents, and childbirth. *Hospice and palliative care nurses* provide care for, and help ease the pain of, terminally ill patients outside of hospitals. *Infusion nurses* administer medications, fluids, and blood to patients through injections into patients' veins. *Long-term care nurses* provide medical services on a recurring basis to patients with chronic physical or mental disorders. *Medical-surgical nurses* provide basic medical care to a variety of patients in all health settings. *Occupational health nurses* provide treatment for job-related injuries and illnesses and help employers to detect workplace hazards and implement health and safety standards. *Perianesthesia nurses* provide preoperative and postoperative care to patients undergoing anesthesia during surgery. *Perioperative nurses* assist surgeons by selecting and handling instruments, controlling bleeding, and suturing incisions. Some of these nurses also can specialize in plastic and reconstructive surgery. *Psychiatric*

nurses treat patients with personality and mood disorders. *Radiologic nurses* provide care to patients undergoing diagnostic radiation procedures such as ultrasounds and magnetic resonance imaging. *Rehabilitation nurses* care for patients with temporary and permanent disabilities. *Transplant nurses* care for both transplant recipients and living donors and monitor signs of organ rejection.

RNs specializing in a particular disease, ailment, or condition are employed in virtually all work settings, including physicians' offices, outpatient treatment facilities, home health care agencies, and hospitals. For instance, *addictions nurses* treat patients seeking help with alcohol, drug, and tobacco addictions. *Developmental disabilities nurses* provide care for patients with physical, mental, or behavioral disabilities; care may include help with feeding, controlling bodily functions, and sitting or standing independently. *Diabetes management nurses* help diabetics to manage their disease by teaching them proper nutrition and showing them how to test blood sugar levels and administer insulin injections. *Genetics nurses* provide early detection screenings and treatment of patients with genetic disorders, including cystic fibrosis and Huntington's disease. *HIV/AIDS nurses* care for patients diagnosed with HIV and AIDS. *Oncology nurses* care for patients with various types of cancer and may administer radiation and chemotherapies. Finally, *wound, ostomy, and continence nurses* treat patients with wounds caused by traumatic injury, ulcers, or arterial disease; provide postoperative care for patients with openings that allow for alternative methods of bodily waste elimination; and treat patients with urinary and fecal incontinence.

RNs specializing in treatment of a particular organ or body system usually are employed in specialty physicians' offices or outpatient care facilities, although some are employed in hospital specialty or critical care units. For example, *cardiac and vascular nurses* treat patients with coronary heart disease and those who have had heart surgery, providing services such as postoperative rehabilitation. *Dermatology nurses* treat patients with disorders of the skin, such as skin cancer and psoriasis. *Gastroenterology nurses* treat patients with digestive and intestinal disorders, including ulcers, acid reflux disease, and abdominal bleeding. Some nurses in this field also specialize in endoscopic procedures, which look inside the gastrointestinal tract using a tube equipped with a light and a camera that can capture images of diseased tissue. *Gynecology nurses* provide care to women with disorders of the reproductive system, including endometriosis, cancer, and sexually transmitted diseases. *Nephrology nurses* care for patients with kidney disease caused by diabetes, hypertension, or substance abuse. *Neuroscience nurses* care for patients with dysfunctions of the nervous system, including brain and spinal cord injuries and seizures. *Ophthalmic nurses* provide care to patients with disorders of the eyes, including blindness and glaucoma, and to patients undergoing eye surgery. *Orthopedic nurses* care for patients with muscular and skeletal problems, including arthritis, bone fractures, and muscular dystrophy. *Otorhinolaryngology nurses* care for patients with ear, nose, and throat disorders, such as cleft palates, allergies, and sinus disorders. *Respiratory nurses* provide care to patients with respiratory disorders such as asthma, tuberculosis, and cystic fibrosis. *Urology nurses* care for patients with disorders of the kidneys, urinary tract, and male reproductive organs, including infections, kidney and bladder stones, and cancers.

Finally, RNs may specialize by providing preventive and acute care in all health care settings to various segments of the population, including newborns (neonatology), children and adolescents (pediatrics), adults, and the elderly (gerontology or geriatrics). RNs also may provide basic health care to patients outside of health care settings in such venues as correctional facilities, schools, summer camps, and the military. Some RNs travel around the United States and abroad providing care to patients in areas with shortages of medical professionals.

Most RNs work as staff nurses, providing critical health care services along with physicians, surgeons, and other health care practitioners. However, some RNs choose to become advanced practice nurses, who often are considered primary health care practitioners and work independently or in collaboration with physicians. For example, *clinical nurse specialists* provide direct patient care and expert consultations in one of many of the nursing specialties listed above. *Nurse anesthetists* administer anesthesia, monitor patient's vital signs during surgery, and provide post-anesthesia care. *Nurse-midwives* provide primary care to women, including gynecological exams, family planning advice, prenatal care, assistance in labor and delivery, and neonatal care. *Nurse practitioners* provide basic preventive health care to patients and increasingly serve as primary and specialty care providers in mainly medically underserved areas. The most common areas of specialty for nurse practitioners are family practice, adult practice, women's health, pediatrics, acute care, and gerontology; however, there are many other specialties. In most states, advanced practice nurses can prescribe medications.

Some nurses have jobs that require little or no direct patient contact. Most of these positions still require an active RN license. *Case managers* ensure that all of the medical needs of patients with severe injuries and illnesses are met, including the type, location, and duration of treatment. *Forensics nurses* combine nursing with law enforcement by treating and investigating victims of sexual assault, child abuse, or accidental death. *Infection control nurses* identify, track, and control infectious outbreaks in health care facilities; develop methods of outbreak prevention and biological terrorism responses; and staff immunization clinics. *Legal nurse consultants* assist lawyers in medical cases by interviewing patients and witnesses, organizing medical records, determining damages and costs, locating evidence, and educating lawyers about medical issues. *Nurse administrators* supervise nursing staff, establish work schedules and budgets, and maintain medical supply inventories. *Nurse educators* teach student nurses and also provide continuing education for RNs. *Nurse informaticists* collect, store, and analyze nursing data in order to improve efficiency, reduce risk, and improve patient care. RNs also may work as health care consultants, public policy advisors, pharmaceutical and medical supply researchers and salespersons, and medical writers and editors.

Working Conditions

Most RNs work in well-lighted, comfortable health care facilities. Home health and public health nurses travel to patients' homes, schools, community centers, and other sites. RNs may spend considerable time walking and standing. Patients in hospitals and nursing care facilities require 24-hour care; consequently, nurses in these institutions may work nights, weekends, and holidays. RNs also

may be on call—available to work on short notice. Nurses who work in office settings are more likely to work regular business hours. About 23 percent of RNs worked part time in 2004, and 7 percent held more than one job.

Nursing has its hazards, especially in hospitals, nursing care facilities, and clinics, where nurses may care for individuals with infectious diseases. RNs must observe rigid, standardized guidelines to guard against disease and other dangers, such as those posed by radiation, accidental needle sticks, chemicals used to sterilize instruments, and anesthetics. In addition, they are vulnerable to back injury when moving patients, shocks from electrical equipment, and hazards posed by compressed gases. RNs who work with critically ill patients also may suffer emotional strain from observing patient suffering and from close personal contact with patients' families.

Training, Other Qualifications, and Advancement

In all states and the District of Columbia, students must graduate from an approved nursing program and pass a national licensing examination, known as the NCLEX-RN, in order to obtain a nursing license. Nurses may be licensed in more than one state, either by examination or by the endorsement of a license issued by another state. Currently 18 states participate in the Nurse Licensure Compact Agreement, which allows nurses to practice in member states without recertifying. All states require periodic renewal of licenses, which may involve continuing education.

There are three major educational paths to registered nursing: A bachelor's of science degree in nursing (BSN), an associate degree in nursing (ADN), and a diploma. BSN programs, offered by colleges and universities, take about 4 years to complete. In 2004, 674 nursing programs offered degrees at the bachelor's level. ADN programs, offered by community and junior colleges, take about 2 to 3 years to complete. About 846 RN programs in 2004 granted associate degrees. Diploma programs, administered in hospitals, last about 3 years. Only 69 programs offered diplomas in 2004. Generally, licensed graduates of any of the three types of educational programs qualify for entry-level positions as staff nurses.

Many RNs with an ADN or diploma later enter bachelor's programs to prepare for a broader scope of nursing practice. Often, they can find a staff nurse position and then take advantage of tuition reimbursement benefits to work toward a BSN by completing an RN-to-BSN program. In 2004, there were 600 RN-to-BSN programs in the United States. Accelerated master's degree programs in nursing also are available. These programs combine 1 year of an accelerated BSN program with 2 years of graduate study. In 2004, there were 137 RN-to-MSN programs.

Accelerated BSN programs also are available for individuals who have a bachelor's or higher degree in another field and who are interested in moving into nursing. In 2004, more than 165 of these programs were available. Accelerated BSN programs last 12 to 18 months and provide the fastest route to a BSN for individuals who already hold a degree.

Individuals considering nursing should carefully weigh the advantages and disadvantages of enrolling in a BSN program, because if they do, their advancement opportunities usually are broader. In fact, some career paths are open only to nurses with a bachelor's or master's degree. A bachelor's degree often is necessary for administrative positions and is a prerequisite for admission to graduate nursing programs in research, consulting, and teaching and all four advanced practice nursing specialties—clinical nurse specialists, nurse anesthetists, nurse-midwives, and nurse practitioners. Individuals who complete a bachelor's receive more training in areas such as communication, leadership, and critical thinking, all of which are becoming more important as nursing care becomes more complex. Additionally, bachelor's degree programs offer more clinical experience in nonhospital settings. In 2004, 417 nursing schools offered master's degrees, 93 offered doctoral degrees, and 46 offered accelerated BSN-to-doctoral programs.

All four advanced practice nursing specialties require at least a master's degree. Most programs last about 2 years and require a BSN degree, and some programs require at least 1 to 2 years of clinical experience as an RN for admission. In 2004, there were 329 master's and post-master's programs offered for nurse practitioners, 218 master's and post-master's programs for clinical nurse specialists, 92 programs for nurse anesthetists, and 45 programs for nurse-midwives. Upon completion of a program, most advanced practice nurses become nationally certified in their area of specialty. In some states, certification in a specialty is required in order to practice that specialty.

All nursing education programs include classroom instruction and supervised clinical experience in hospitals and other health care facilities. Students take courses in anatomy, physiology, microbiology, chemistry, nutrition, psychology and other behavioral sciences, and nursing. Coursework also includes the liberal arts for ADN and BSN students.

Supervised clinical experience is provided in hospital departments such as pediatrics, psychiatry, maternity, and surgery. A growing number of programs include clinical experience in nursing care facilities, public health departments, home health agencies, and ambulatory clinics.

Nurses should be caring, sympathetic, responsible, and detail oriented. They must be able to direct or supervise others, correctly assess patients' conditions, and determine when consultation is required. They need emotional stability to cope with human suffering, emergencies, and other stresses.

Some RNs start their careers as licensed practical nurses or nursing aides and then go back to school to receive their RN degree. Most RNs begin as staff nurses, and with experience and good performance often are promoted to more responsible positions. In management, nurses can advance to assistant head nurse or head nurse and, from there, to assistant director, director, and vice president. Increasingly, management-level nursing positions require a graduate or an advanced degree in nursing or health services administration. They also require leadership, negotiation skills, and good judgment.

Some nurses move into the business side of health care. Their nursing expertise and experience on a health care team equip them to manage ambulatory, acute, home-based, and chronic care. Employers—including hospitals, insurance companies, pharmaceutical manufacturers, and managed care organizations, among others—need RNs for health planning and development, marketing, consulting, policy development, and quality assurance. Other nurses work as college and university faculty or conduct research.

Foreign-educated nurses wishing to work in the United States must obtain a work visa. Applicants are required to undergo a review of their education and licensing credentials and pass a nursing certification and English proficiency exam, both conducted by the Commission on Graduates of Foreign Nursing Schools. (The commission is an immigration-neutral, nonprofit organization that is recognized internationally as an authority on credentials evaluation in the health care field.) Applicants from Australia, Canada (except Quebec), Ireland, New Zealand, and the United Kingdom are exempt from the language proficiency exam. In addition to these national requirements, most states have their own requirements.

Employment

As the largest health care occupation, registered nurses held about 2.4 million jobs in 2004. About 3 out of 5 jobs were in hospitals, in inpatient and outpatient departments. Others worked in offices of physicians, nursing care facilities, home health care services, employment services, government agencies, and outpatient care centers. The remainder worked mostly in social assistance agencies and educational services, public and private. About 1 in 4 RNs worked part time.

Job Outlook

Job opportunities for RNs in all specialties are expected to be excellent. Employment of registered nurses is expected to grow much faster than average for all occupations through 2014, and, because the occupation is very large, many new jobs will result. In fact, registered nurses are projected to create the second-largest number of new jobs among all occupations. Thousands of job openings also will result from the need to replace experienced nurses who leave the occupation, especially as the median age of the registered nurse population continues to rise.

Much-faster-than-average growth will be driven by technological advances in patient care, which permit a greater number of medical problems to be treated, and by an increasing emphasis on preventive care. In addition, the number of older people, who are much more likely than younger people to need nursing care, is projected to grow rapidly.

Employers in some parts of the country and in certain employment settings are reporting difficulty in attracting and retaining an adequate number of RNs, primarily because of an aging RN workforce and a lack of younger workers to fill positions. Enrollments in nursing programs at all levels have increased more rapidly in the past couple of years as students seek jobs with stable employment. However, many qualified applicants are being turned away because of a shortage of nursing faculty to teach classes. The need for nursing faculty will only increase as a large number of instructors nears retirement. Many employers also are relying on foreign-educated nurses to fill open positions.

Even though employment opportunities for all nursing specialties are expected to be excellent, they can vary by employment setting. For example, employment is expected to grow more slowly in hospitals—which comprise health care's largest industry—than in most other health care industries. While the intensity of nursing care is likely to increase, requiring more nurses per patient, the number of inpatients (those who remain in the hospital for more than 24 hours) is not likely to grow by much. Patients are being discharged earlier, and more procedures are being done on an outpatient basis, both inside and outside hospitals. Rapid growth is expected in hospital outpatient facilities, such as those providing same-day surgery, rehabilitation, and chemotherapy.

Despite the slower employment growth in hospitals, job opportunities should still be excellent because of the relatively high turnover of hospital nurses. RNs working in hospitals frequently work overtime and night and weekend shifts and also treat seriously ill and injured patients, all of which can contribute to stress and burnout. Hospital departments in which these working conditions occur most frequently—critical care units, emergency departments, and operating rooms—generally will have more job openings than other departments.

To attract and retain qualified nurses, hospitals may offer signing bonuses, family-friendly work schedules, or subsidized training. A growing number of hospitals also are experimenting with online bidding to fill open shifts, in which nurses can volunteer to fill open shifts at premium wages. This can decrease the amount of mandatory overtime that nurses are required to work.

More and more sophisticated procedures, once performed only in hospitals, are being performed in physicians' offices and in outpatient care centers, such as freestanding ambulatory surgical and emergency centers. Accordingly, employment is expected to grow much faster than average in these places as health care in general expands. However, RNs may face greater competition for these positions because they generally offer regular working hours and more comfortable working environments.

Employment in nursing care facilities is expected to grow faster than average because of increases in the number of elderly, many of whom require long-term care. In addition, the financial pressure on hospitals to discharge patients as soon as possible should produce more admissions to nursing care facilities. Job growth also is expected in units that provide specialized long-term rehabilitation for stroke and head injury patients, as well as units that treat Alzheimer's victims.

Employment in home health care is expected to increase rapidly in response to the growing number of older persons with functional disabilities, consumer preference for care in the home, and technological advances that make it possible to bring increasingly complex treatments into the home. The type of care demanded will require nurses who are able to perform complex procedures.

Generally, RNs with at least a bachelor's degree will have better job prospects than those without a bachelor's. In addition, all four advanced practice specialties—clinical nurse specialists, nurse practitioners, midwives, and anesthetists—will be in high demand, particularly in medically underserved areas such as inner cities and rural areas. Relative to physicians, these RNs increasingly serve as lower-cost primary care providers.

Earnings

Median annual earnings of registered nurses were $52,330 in May 2004. The middle 50 percent earned between $43,370 and $63,360. The lowest 10 percent earned less than $37,300, and the highest 10 percent earned more than $74,760. Median annual earnings in the

industries employing the largest numbers of registered nurses in May 2004 were as follows:

Employment services	$63,170
General medical and surgical hospitals	53,450
Home health care services	48,990
Offices of physicians	48,250
Nursing care facilities	48,220

Many employers offer flexible work schedules, child care, educational benefits, and bonuses.

Related Occupations

Workers in other health care occupations with responsibilities and duties related to those of registered nurses are cardiovascular technologists and technicians; diagnostic medical sonographers; dietitians and nutritionists; emergency medical technicians and paramedics; licensed practical and licensed vocational nurses; massage therapists; medical and health services managers; nursing, psychiatric, and home health aides; occupational therapists; physical therapists; physician assistants; physicians and surgeons; radiologic technologists and technicians; respiratory therapists; and surgical technologists.

Sources of Additional Information

For information on a career as a registered nurse and nursing education, contact

▸ National League for Nursing, 61 Broadway, New York, NY 10006. Internet: http://www.nln.org

For information on nursing career options; financial aid; and listings of BSN, graduate, and accelerated nursing programs, contact

▸ American Association of Colleges of Nursing, 1 Dupont Circle NW, Suite 530, Washington, DC 20036. Internet: http://www.aacn.nche.edu

For additional information on registered nurses, including credentialing, contact

▸ American Nurses Association, 8515 Georgia Ave., Suite 400, Silver Spring, MD 20910. Internet: http://nursingworld.org

For information on the NCLEX-RN exam and a list of individual states' boards of nursing, contact

▸ National Council of State Boards of Nursing, 111 E. Wacker Dr., Suite 2900, Chicago, IL 60611. Internet: http://www.ncsbn.org

For information on obtaining U.S. certification and work visas for foreign-educated nurses, contact

▸ Commission on Graduates of Foreign Nursing Schools, 3600 Market St., Suite 400, Philadelphia, PA 19104. Internet: http://www.cgfns.org

For a list of accredited clinical nurse specialist programs, contact

▸ National Association of Clinical Nurse Specialists, 2090 Linglestown Rd., Suite 107, Harrisburg, PA 17110. Internet: http://www.nacns.org/cnsdirectory.shtml

For information on nurse anesthetists, including a list of accredited programs, contact

▸ American Association of Nurse Anesthetists, 222 Prospect Ave., Park Ridge, IL 60068.

For information on nurse-midwives, including a list of accredited programs, contact

▸ American College of Nurse-Midwives, 8403 Colesville Rd., Suite 1550, Silver Spring, MD 20910. Internet: http://www.midwife.org

For information on nurse practitioners, including a list of accredited programs, contact

▸ American Academy of Nurse Practitioners, P.O. Box 12846, Austin, TX 78711. Internet: http://www.aanp.org

Respiratory Therapists

(O*NET 29-1126.00 and 29-2054.00)

Significant Points

■ Job opportunities will be very good, especially for therapists with cardiopulmonary care skills or experience working with infants.

■ All states (except Alaska and Hawaii), the District of Columbia, and Puerto Rico require respiratory therapists to obtain a license.

■ Hospitals will continue to employ the vast majority of respiratory therapists, but a growing number of therapists will work in other settings.

Nature of the Work

Respiratory therapists and *respiratory therapy technicians*—also known as *respiratory care practitioners*—evaluate, treat, and care for patients with breathing or other cardiopulmonary disorders. Practicing under the direction of a physician, respiratory therapists assume primary responsibility for all respiratory care therapeutic treatments and diagnostic procedures, including the supervision of respiratory therapy technicians. Respiratory therapy technicians follow specific, well-defined respiratory care procedures under the direction of respiratory therapists and physicians. In clinical practice, many of the daily duties of therapists and technicians overlap; furthermore, the two have the same education and training requirements. However, therapists generally have greater responsibility than technicians. For example, respiratory therapists will consult with physicians and other health care staff to help develop and modify individual patient care plans. Respiratory therapists also are more likely to provide complex therapy requiring considerable independent judgment, such as caring for patients on life support in intensive-care units of hospitals. In this description, the term *respiratory therapists* includes both respiratory therapists and respiratory therapy technicians.

Respiratory therapists evaluate and treat all types of patients, ranging from premature infants whose lungs are not fully developed to elderly people whose lungs are diseased. Respiratory therapists provide temporary relief to patients with chronic asthma or emphysema, as well as emergency care to patients who are victims of a heart attack, stroke, drowning, or shock.

To evaluate patients, respiratory therapists interview them, perform limited physical examinations, and conduct diagnostic tests. For example, respiratory therapists test patients' breathing capacity and determine the concentration of oxygen and other gases in patients' blood. They also measure patients' pH, which indicates the acidity or alkalinity of the blood. To evaluate a patient's lung capacity, respiratory therapists have the patient breathe into an instrument that measures the volume and flow of oxygen during inhalation and exhalation. By comparing the reading with the norm for the patient's age, height, weight, and sex, respiratory therapists can provide information that helps determine whether the patient has any lung deficiencies. To analyze oxygen, carbon dioxide, and pH levels, therapists draw an arterial blood sample, place it in a blood gas analyzer, and relay the results to a physician, who then may make treatment decisions.

To treat patients, respiratory therapists use oxygen or oxygen mixtures, chest physiotherapy, and aerosol medications. When a patient has difficulty getting enough oxygen into his or her blood, therapists increase the patient's concentration of oxygen by placing an oxygen mask or nasal cannula on the patient and set the oxygen flow at the level prescribed by a physician. Therapists also connect patients who cannot breathe on their own to ventilators that deliver pressurized oxygen into the lungs. The therapists insert a tube into the patient's trachea, or windpipe; connect the tube to the ventilator; and set the rate, volume, and oxygen concentration of the oxygen mixture entering the patient's lungs.

Therapists perform regular assessments of patients and equipment. If the patient appears to be having difficulty breathing or if the oxygen, carbon dioxide, or pH level of the blood is abnormal, therapists change the ventilator setting according to the doctor's orders or check the equipment for mechanical problems. In home care, therapists teach patients and their families to use ventilators and other life-support systems. In addition, therapists visit patients several times a month to inspect and clean equipment and to ensure its proper use. Therapists also make emergency visits if equipment problems arise.

Respiratory therapists perform chest physiotherapy on patients to remove mucus from their lungs and make it easier for them to breathe. For example, during surgery, anesthesia depresses respiration, so chest physiotherapy may be prescribed to help get the patient's lungs back to normal and to prevent congestion. Chest physiotherapy also helps patients suffering from lung diseases, such as cystic fibrosis, that cause mucus to collect in the lungs. Therapists place patients in positions that help drain mucus and then vibrate the patients' rib cages and instruct the patients to cough.

Respiratory therapists also administer aerosols—liquid medications suspended in a gas that forms a mist which is inhaled—and teach patients how to inhale the aerosol properly to ensure its effectiveness.

In some hospitals, therapists perform tasks that fall outside their traditional role. Therapists' tasks are expanding into areas such as pulmonary rehabilitation, smoking cessation counseling, disease prevention, case management, and polysomnography—the diagnosis of breathing disorders during sleep, such as apnea. Respiratory therapists also increasingly treat critical care patients, either as part of surface and air transport teams or as part of rapid-response teams in hospitals.

Working Conditions

Respiratory therapists generally work between 35 and 40 hours a week. Because hospitals operate around the clock, therapists may work evenings, nights, or weekends. They spend long periods standing and walking between patients' rooms. In an emergency, therapists work under a great deal of stress. Respiratory therapists employed in home health care must travel frequently to the homes of patients.

Respiratory therapists are trained to work with hazardous gases stored under pressure. Adherence to safety precautions and regular maintenance and testing of equipment minimize the risk of injury. As in many other health occupations, respiratory therapists run the risk of catching an infectious disease, but carefully following proper procedures minimizes this risk.

Training, Other Qualifications, and Advancement

Formal training is necessary for entry into this field. Training is offered at the postsecondary level by colleges and universities, medical schools, vocational-technical institutes, and the Armed Forces. An associate's degree is required for entry into the field. Most programs award associate's or bachelor's degrees and prepare graduates for jobs as advanced respiratory therapists. A limited number of associate's degree programs lead to jobs as entry-level respiratory therapists. According to the Commission on Accreditation of Allied Health Education Programs (CAAHEP), 51 entry-level and 329 advanced respiratory therapy programs were accredited in the United States, including Puerto Rico, in 2005.

Among the areas of study in respiratory therapy are human anatomy and physiology, pathophysiology, chemistry, physics, microbiology, pharmacology, and mathematics. Other courses deal with therapeutic and diagnostic procedures and tests, equipment, patient assessment, cardiopulmonary resuscitation, the application of clinical practice guidelines, patient care outside of hospitals, cardiac and pulmonary rehabilitation, respiratory health promotion and disease prevention, and medical recordkeeping and reimbursement.

The National Board for Respiratory Care (NBRC) offers certification and registration to graduates of programs accredited by CAAHEP or the Committee on Accreditation for Respiratory Care (CoARC). Two credentials are awarded to respiratory therapists who satisfy the requirements: Registered Respiratory Therapist (RRT) and Certified Respiratory Therapist (CRT). Graduates from accredited entry-level or advanced-level programs in respiratory therapy may take the CRT examination. CRTs who were graduated from advanced-level programs and who meet additional experience requirements can take two separate examinations leading to the award of the RRT credential.

All states (except Alaska and Hawaii), the District of Columbia, and Puerto Rico require respiratory therapists to obtain a license. Passing the CRT exam qualifies respiratory therapists for state licenses. Also, most employers require respiratory therapists to maintain a cardiopulmonary resuscitation (CPR) certification. Supervisory positions and intensive-care specialties usually require the RRT or at least RRT eligibility.

Therapists should be sensitive to patients' physical and psychological needs. Respiratory care practitioners must pay attention to detail, follow instructions, and work as part of a team. In addition, operating advanced equipment requires proficiency with computers.

High school students interested in a career in respiratory care should take courses in health, biology, mathematics, chemistry, and physics. Respiratory care involves basic mathematical problem solving and an understanding of chemical and physical principles. For example, respiratory care workers must be able to compute dosages of medication and calculate gas concentrations.

Respiratory therapists advance in clinical practice by moving from general care to the care of critically ill patients who have significant problems in other organ systems, such as the heart or kidneys. Respiratory therapists, especially those with bachelor's or master's degrees, also may advance to supervisory or managerial positions in a respiratory therapy department. Respiratory therapists in home health care and equipment rental firms may become branch managers. Some respiratory therapists advance by moving into teaching positions.

Employment

Respiratory therapists held about 118,000 jobs in 2004. More than 4 out of 5 jobs were in hospital departments of respiratory care, anesthesiology, or pulmonary medicine. Most of the remaining jobs were in offices of physicians or other health practitioners, consumer-goods rental firms that supply respiratory equipment for home use, nursing care facilities, and home health care services. Holding a second job is relatively common for respiratory therapists. About 13 percent held another job, compared with 5 percent of workers in all occupations.

Job Outlook

Job opportunities are expected to be very good, especially for respiratory therapists with cardiopulmonary care skills or experience working with infants. Employment of respiratory therapists is expected to increase faster than average for all occupations through the year 2014 because of substantial growth in the numbers of the middle-aged and elderly population—a development that will heighten the incidence of cardiopulmonary disease—and because of the expanding role of respiratory therapists in the early detection of pulmonary disorders, case management, disease prevention, and emergency care.

Older Americans suffer most from respiratory ailments and cardiopulmonary diseases such as pneumonia, chronic bronchitis, emphysema, and heart disease. As their numbers increase, the need for respiratory therapists will increase as well. In addition, advances in inhalable medications and in the treatment of lung transplant patients, heart attack and accident victims, and premature infants (many of whom are dependent on a ventilator during part of their treatment) will increase the demand for the services of respiratory care practitioners.

Although hospitals will continue to employ the vast majority of therapists, a growing number can expect to work outside of hospitals in home health care services, offices of physicians or other health practitioners, or consumer-goods rental firms.

Earnings

Median annual earnings of respiratory therapists were $43,140 in May 2004. The middle 50 percent earned between $37,650 and $50,860. The lowest 10 percent earned less than $32,220, and the highest 10 percent earned more than $57,580. In general medical and surgical hospitals, median annual earnings of respiratory therapists were $43,140 in May 2004.

Median annual earnings of respiratory therapy technicians were $36,740 in May 2004. The middle 50 percent earned between $30,490 and $43,830. The lowest 10 percent earned less than $24,640, and the highest 10 percent earned more than $52,280. Median annual earnings of respiratory therapy technicians employed in general medical and surgical hospitals were $36,990 in May 2004.

Related Occupations

Under the supervision of a physician, respiratory therapists administer respiratory care and life support to patients with heart and lung difficulties. Other workers who care for, treat, or train people to improve their physical condition include registered nurses, occupational therapists, physical therapists, and radiation therapists.

Sources of Additional Information

Information concerning a career in respiratory care is available from

▸ American Association for Respiratory Care, 9425 N. MacArthur Blvd., Suite 100, Irving, TX 75063-4706. Internet: http://www.aarc.org

For a list of accredited educational programs for respiratory care practitioners, contact either of the following organizations:

▸ Commission on Accreditation for Allied Health Education Programs, 35 East Wacker Dr., Suite 1970, Chicago, IL 60601. Internet: http://www.caahep.org

Information on gaining credentials in respiratory care and a list of state licensing agencies can be obtained from

▸ National Board for Respiratory Care, Inc., 8310 Nieman Rd., Lenexa, KS 66214-1579. Internet: http://www.nbrc.org

Sales Representatives, Wholesale and Manufacturing

(O*NET 41-4011.01, 41-4011.02, 41-4011.03, 41-4011.04, 41-4011.05, 41-4011.06, and 41-4012.00)

Significant Points

■ Employment opportunities will be best for those with a college degree, the appropriate knowledge or technical expertise, and the personal traits necessary for successful selling. Job prospects for wholesale sales representatives will be better than those for manufacturing sales representatives, particularly in small firms.

■ Earnings of sales representatives usually are based on a combination of salary and commissions.

Nature of the Work

Sales representatives are an important part of manufacturers' and wholesalers' success. Regardless of the type of product they sell, their primary duties are to interest wholesale and retail buyers and purchasing agents in their merchandise and to address clients' questions and concerns. Sales representatives represent one or several manufacturers or wholesale distributors by selling one product or a complementary line of products. Sales representatives demonstrate their products and advise clients on how using these products can reduce costs and increase sales. They market their company's products to manufacturers, wholesale and retail establishments, construction contractors, government agencies, and other institutions.

Depending on where they work, sales representatives have different job titles. Those employed directly by a manufacturer or wholesaler often are called *sales representatives. Manufacturers' agents* or *manufacturers' representatives* are self-employed sales workers or independent firms who contract their services to all types of manufacturing companies. Many of these titles, however, are used interchangeably.

Sales representatives spend much of their time traveling to and visiting with prospective buyers and current clients. During a sales call, they discuss the client's needs and suggest how their merchandise or services can meet those needs. They may show samples or catalogs that describe items their company stocks and inform customers about prices, availability, and ways in which their products can save money and boost productivity. Because a vast number of manufacturers and wholesalers sell similar products, sales representatives must emphasize any unique qualities of their products and services. Manufacturers' agents or manufacturers' representatives might sell several complementary products made by different manufacturers and, thus, take a broad approach to their customers' business. Sales representatives may help install new equipment and train employees in its use. They also take orders and resolve any problems with or complaints about the merchandise.

Obtaining new accounts is an important part of the job. Sales representatives follow leads from other clients, track advertisements in trade journals, participate in trade shows and conferences, and may visit potential clients unannounced. In addition, they may spend time meeting with and entertaining prospective clients during evenings and weekends.

In a process that can take several months, sales representatives present their product to a customer and negotiate the sale. Aided by a laptop computer connected to the Internet, or other telecommunications device, they can make a persuasive audiovisual sales pitch and often can answer technical and nontechnical questions immediately.

Frequently, sales representatives who lack technical expertise work as a team with a technical expert. In this arrangement, the technical expert—sometimes a sales engineer—attends the sales presentation to explain the product and answer questions or concerns. The sales representative makes the preliminary contact with customers, introduces the company's product, and closes the sale. The representative is then able to spend more time maintaining and soliciting accounts and less time acquiring technical knowledge. After the sale, representatives may make follow-up visits to ensure that the equipment is functioning properly and may even help train customers' employees to operate and maintain new equipment. Those selling consumer goods often suggest how and where merchandise should be displayed. Working with retailers, they may help arrange promotional programs, store displays, and advertising.

Sales representatives have several duties beyond selling products. They analyze sales statistics; prepare reports; and handle administrative duties, such as filing expense account reports, scheduling appointments, and making travel plans. They read about new and existing products and monitor the sales, prices, and products of their competitors.

Manufacturers' agents who operate a sales agency also must manage their business. This requires organizational and general business skills as well as knowledge of accounting, marketing, and administration.

Working Conditions

Some sales representatives have large territories and travel considerably. Because a sales region may cover several states, representatives may be away from home for several days or weeks at a time. Others work near their home base and travel mostly by car. Because of the nature of the work and the amount of travel, sales representatives may work more than 40 hours per week.

Although the hours are long and often irregular, most sales representatives have the freedom to determine their own schedule. Sales representatives often are on their feet for long periods and may carry heavy sample products, necessitating some physical stamina.

Dealing with different types of people can be stimulating but demanding. Sales representatives often face competition from representatives of other companies. Companies usually set goals or quotas that representatives are expected to meet. Because their earnings depend on commissions, manufacturers' agents are also under the added pressure to maintain and expand their clientele.

Training, Other Qualifications, and Advancement

The background needed for sales jobs varies by product line and market. Many employers hire individuals with previous sales experience who lack a college degree, but they increasingly prefer or require a bachelor's degree because job requirements have become more technical and analytical. Nevertheless, for some consumer products, factors such as sales ability, personality, and familiarity with brands are more important than educational background. On the other hand, firms selling complex, technical products may require a technical degree in addition to some sales experience. Many sales representatives attend seminars in sales techniques or take courses in marketing, economics, communication, or even a foreign language to provide the extra edge needed to make sales. In general, companies are looking for the best and brightest individuals who have the personality and desire to sell. Sales representatives need to be familiar with computer technology, as computers are increasingly used in the workplace to place and track orders and to monitor inventory levels.

Many companies have formal training programs for beginning sales representatives lasting up to 2 years. However, most businesses are accelerating these programs to reduce costs and expedite the returns from training. In some programs, trainees rotate among jobs in plants and offices to learn all phases of production, installation, and distribution of the product. In others, trainees take formal classroom instruction at the plant, followed by on-the-job training under the supervision of a field sales manager.

New workers may get training by accompanying experienced workers on their sales calls. As they gain familiarity with the firm's products and clients, the new workers are given increasing responsibility until they are eventually assigned their own territory. As businesses experience greater competition, increased pressure is placed upon sales representatives to produce sales.

Sales representatives stay abreast of new products and the changing needs of their customers in a variety of ways. They attend trade shows at which new products and technologies are showcased. They also attend conferences and conventions to meet other sales representatives and clients and discuss new product developments. In addition, the entire sales force may participate in company-sponsored meetings to review sales performance, product development, sales goals, and profitability.

There are many certifications designed to raise standards and develop the skills of sales representatives, wholesale and manufacturing. A few examples are the Certified Professional Manufacturers' Representative, the Certified Sales Professional, and the Certified National Pharmaceutical Representative. Certification may involve completion of formal training and passing an examination.

Those who want to become sales representatives should be goal-oriented, persuasive, and able to work well both independently and as part of a team. A pleasant personality and appearance, the ability to communicate well with people, and problem-solving skills are highly valued. Patience and perseverance also are key to completing a sale, which can take several months.

Frequently, promotion takes the form of an assignment to a larger account or territory where commissions are likely to be greater. Experienced sales representatives may move into jobs as sales trainers, who instruct new employees on selling techniques and on company policies and procedures. Those who have good sales records and leadership ability may advance to higher-level positions such as sales supervisor, district manager, or vice president of sales. In addition to advancement opportunities within a firm, some manufacturers' agents go into business for themselves. Others find opportunities in purchasing, advertising, or marketing research.

Employment

Manufacturers' and wholesale sales representatives held about 1.9 million jobs in 2004. About half of all salaried representatives worked in wholesale trade. Others were employed in manufacturing, retail trade, information, and construction. Because of the diversity of products and services sold, employment opportunities are available in every part of the country in a wide range of industries.

In addition to those working directly for a firm, many sales representatives are self-employed manufacturers' agents. They often form small sales firms and work for a straight commission based on the value of their own sales. Usually, however, manufacturers' agents gain experience and recognition with a manufacturer or wholesaler before becoming self-employed.

Job Outlook

Employment of sales representatives, wholesale and manufacturing, is expected to grow about as fast as the average for all occupations through the year 2014, primarily because of continued growth in the variety and number of goods to be sold. Also, many job openings will result from the need to replace workers who transfer to other occupations or leave the labor force.

Prospective customers require sales workers to demonstrate or illustrate the particulars of a good or service. Computer technology makes sales representatives more effective and productive, for example, by allowing them to provide accurate and current information to customers during sales presentations.

Job prospects for sales representatives, wholesale and manufacturing, will be best for persons with the appropriate knowledge or technical expertise as well as the personal traits necessary for successful selling. Opportunities will be better for wholesale sales representatives than for manufacturing sales representatives because manufacturers are expected to continue contracting out sales duties to independent agents rather than using in-house or direct selling personnel. Agents are paid only if they sell, a practice that reduces the overhead cost to their clients. Also, by using an agent who usually contracts his or her services to more than one company, companies can share costs with the other companies involved with that agent. As their customers and manufacturers continue to merge with other companies, independent agents and other wholesale trade firms will, in response, also merge with each other to better serve their clients. Although the demand for independent sales agents will increase over the 2004–2014 projection period, the supply is expected to remain stable, or possibly decline, because of the difficulties associated with self-employment. This factor could lead to many opportunities for sales representatives to start their own independent sales agencies.

Those interested in this occupation should keep in mind that direct selling opportunities in manufacturing are likely to be best for products for which there is strong demand. Furthermore, jobs will be most plentiful in small wholesale and manufacturing firms because a growing number of these companies will rely on agents to market their products as a way to control their costs and expand their customer base.

Employment opportunities and earnings may fluctuate from year to year because sales are affected by changing economic conditions, legislative issues, and consumer preferences.

Earnings

Compensation methods vary significantly by the type of firm and the product sold. Most employers use a combination of salary and commissions or salary plus bonus. Commissions usually are based on the amount of sales, whereas bonuses may depend on individual performance, on the performance of all sales workers in the group or district, or on the company's performance.

Median annual earnings of sales representatives, wholesale and manufacturing, technical and scientific products, were $58,580, including commissions, in May 2004. The middle 50 percent earned between $41,660 and $84,480 a year. The lowest 10 percent earned

less than $30,270, and the highest 10 percent earned more than $114,540 a year. Median annual earnings in the industries employing the largest numbers of sales representatives, technical and scientific products, in May 2004 were as follows:

Computer systems design and related services	......$70,220
Wholesale electronic markets and agents and brokers	65,990
Drugs and druggists' sundries merchant wholesalers	60,130
Professional and commercial equipment and supplies merchant wholesalers	59,080
Electrical and electronic goods merchant wholesalers	52,870

Median annual earnings of sales representatives, wholesale and manufacturing, except technical and scientific products, were $45,400, including commission, in May 2004. The middle 50 percent earned between $32,640 and $65,260 a year. The lowest 10 percent earned less than $24,070, and the highest 10 percent earned more than $92,740 a year. Median annual earnings in the industries employing the largest numbers of sales representatives, except technical and scientific products, in May 2004 were as follows:

Wholesale electronic markets and agents and brokers	....$50,680
Machinery, equipment, and supplies merchant wholesalers	46,030
Professional and commercial equipment and supplies merchant wholesalers	45,320
Grocery and related product wholesalers	44,210
Miscellaneous nondurable goods merchant wholesalers	40,240

In addition to their earnings, sales representatives usually are reimbursed for expenses such as transportation costs, meals, hotels, and entertaining customers. They often receive benefits such as health and life insurance, pension plan, vacation and sick leave, personal use of a company car, and frequent flyer mileage. Some companies offer incentives such as free vacation trips or gifts for outstanding sales workers.

Unlike those working directly for a manufacturer or wholesaler, manufacturers' agents are paid strictly on commission and usually are not reimbursed for expenses. Depending on the type of product or products they are selling, their experience in the field, and the number of clients they have, they can earn significantly more or less than those working in direct sales.

Related Occupations

Sales representatives, wholesale and manufacturing, must have sales ability and knowledge of the products they sell. Other occupations that require similar skills include advertising, marketing, promotions, public relations, and sales managers; insurance sales agents; purchasing managers, buyers, and purchasing agents; real estate brokers and sales agents; retail salespersons; sales engineers; and securities, commodities, and financial services sales agents.

Sources of Additional Information

Information on careers for manufacturers' representatives and agents is available from

▸ Manufacturers' Agents National Association, One Spectrum Pointe, Suite 150, Lake Forest, CA 92630. Internet: http://www.manaonline.org

▸ Manufacturers' Representatives Educational Research Foundation, P.O. Box 247, Geneva, IL 60134. Internet: http://www.mrerf.org

Surveyors, Cartographers, Photogrammetrists, and Surveying Technicians

(O*NET 17-1021.00, 17-1022.00, 17-3031.01, and 17-3031.02)

Significant Points

■ About 2 out of 3 jobs are in architectural, engineering, and related services.

■ Opportunities will be best for surveyors, cartographers, and photogrammetrists who have a bachelor's degree and strong technical skills.

■ Applicants for jobs as technicians may face competition.

Nature of the Work

Surveyors, cartographers, and photogrammetrists are responsible for measuring and mapping the earth's surface. Traditionally, *surveyors* establish official land, airspace, and water boundaries. They write descriptions of land for deeds, leases, and other legal documents; define airspace for airports; and take measurements of construction and mineral sites. Other surveyors provide data relevant to the shape, contour, location, elevation, or dimension of land or land features. *Cartographers* compile geographic, political, and cultural information and prepare maps of large areas. *Photogrammetrists* measure and analyze aerial photographs that are subsequently used to prepare detailed maps and drawings. *Surveying and mapping technicians* assist these professionals in their duties by collecting data in the field and using it to calculate mapmaking information for use in performing computations and computer-aided drafting.

Surveyors measure distances, directions, and angles between points and elevations of points, lines, and contours on, above, and below the earth's surface. In the field, they select known survey reference points and determine the precise location of important features in the survey area. Surveyors research legal records, look for evidence of previous boundaries, and analyze the data to determine the location of boundary lines. They also record the results of surveys; verify the accuracy of data; and prepare plots, maps, and reports. Surveyors who establish boundaries must be licensed by the state in which they work. Surveyors are sometimes called to provide expert testimony in court cases concerning matters pertaining to surveying.

Cartographers measure, map, and chart the earth's surface. Their work involves everything from performing geographical research and compiling data to actually producing maps. Cartographers collect, analyze, and interpret both spatial data—such as latitude,

longitude, elevation, and distance—and nonspatial data—for example, population density, land-use patterns, annual precipitation levels, and demographic characteristics. Their maps may give both physical and social characteristics of the land. They prepare maps in either digital or graphic form, using information provided by geodetic surveys, aerial photographs, and satellite data.

Photogrammetrists prepare detailed maps and drawings from aerial photographs, usually of areas that are inaccessible, difficult, or more costly to survey by other methods. *Map editors* develop and verify the contents of maps, using aerial photographs and other reference sources. Some states require photogrammetrists to be licensed as surveyors.

Some surveyors perform specialized functions closer to those of cartographers than to those of traditional surveyors. For example, *geodetic surveyors* use high-accuracy techniques, including satellite observations (remote sensing), to measure large areas of the earth's surface. *Geophysical prospecting surveyors* mark sites for subsurface exploration, usually in relation to petroleum. *Marine or hydrographic surveyors* survey harbors, rivers, and other bodies of water to determine shorelines, the topography of the bottom, water depth, and other features.

There is more to surveying and cartography than meets the eye. Chains, transits, theodolites, and plumb lines have given way to cutting-edge technology such as the Global Positioning System (GPS), laptops, and robotic total stations as the preferred tools of surveyors. Advanced computer software known as Geographic Information Systems (GIS) has become an invaluable tool to booth surveyors and cartographers.

Surveyors are able to use GPS to locate reference points with a high degree of precision. To use this system, a surveyor places a satellite signal receiver—a small instrument mounted on a tripod—on a desired point and another receiver on a point for which the geographic position is known. The receiver simultaneously collects information from several satellites to establish a precise position. The receiver also can be placed in a vehicle for tracing out road systems. Because receivers now come in different sizes and shapes, and because the cost of receivers has fallen, much more surveying work can be done with GPS. Surveyors then must interpret and check the results produced by the new technology.

Fieldwork is done by a survey party that gathers the information needed by the surveyor. A typical survey party consists of a party chief and one or more surveying technicians and helpers. The party chief, who may be either a surveyor or a senior surveying technician, leads day-to-day work activities. Surveying technicians assist the party chief by adjusting and operating surveying instruments such as the total station, which measures and records angles and distances simultaneously. Surveying technicians or assistants position and hold the vertical rods, or targets, that the operator sights on to measure angles, distances, or elevations. In addition, they may hold measuring tapes if electronic distance-measuring equipment is not used. Surveying technicians compile notes, make sketches, and enter the data obtained from surveying instruments into computers either in the field or at the office. Survey parties also may include laborers or helpers who perform less-skilled duties, such as clearing brush from sight lines, driving stakes, or carrying equipment.

GIS software is capable of assembling, integrating, analyzing, and displaying data identified according to location and compiled from previous surveys and mappings. GIS software has become an important tool of both surveyors and cartographers. A GIS typically is used to handle maps that combine information that is useful for environmental studies, geology, engineering, planning, business marketing, and other disciplines. As more of these systems are developed, a new type of mapping scientist is emerging from the older specialties of photogrammetrist and cartographer: The *geographic information specialist* combines the functions of mapping science and surveying into a broader field concerned with the collection and analysis of geographic data.

Working Conditions

Surveyors and surveying technicians usually work an 8-hour day, 5 days a week, and may spend a lot of time outdoors. Sometimes they work longer hours during the summer, when weather and light conditions are most suitable for fieldwork. Seasonal demands for longer hours are related to demand for specific surveying services. For example, construction-related work may be limited during times of inclement weather and aerial photography is most effective when the leaves are off the trees.

Surveyors and technicians engage in active, sometimes strenuous, work. They often stand for long periods, walk considerable distances, and climb hills with heavy packs of instruments and other equipment. They also can be exposed to all types of weather. Traveling is sometimes part of the job, and land surveyors and technicians may commute long distances, stay away from home overnight, or temporarily relocate near a survey site.

Although surveyors can spend considerable time indoors while planning surveys, searching court records for deed information, analyzing data, and preparing reports and maps, cartographers and photogrammetrists spend virtually all of their time in offices using computers and seldom visit the sites they are mapping.

Training, Other Qualifications, and Advancement

Most people prepare for a career as a licensed surveyor by combining postsecondary school courses in surveying with extensive on-the-job training. However, as technology advances, a 4-year college degree is increasingly becoming a prerequisite. A number of universities now offer 4-year programs leading to a bachelor's degree in surveying. Junior and community colleges, technical institutes, and vocational schools offer 1-year, 2-year, and 3-year programs in both surveying and surveying technology.

All 50 states and all U.S. territories license surveyors. For licensure, most state licensing boards require that individuals pass a written examination given by the National Council of Examiners for Engineering and Surveying (NCEES). Most states also require surveyors to pass a written examination prepared by the state licensing board. In addition, candidates must meet varying standards of formal education and work experience in the field.

In the past, many with little formal training in surveying started as members of survey crews and worked their way up to become licensed surveyors. Currently, the route to licensure is most often a combination of 4 years of college followed by passage of the Fundamentals of Surveying Exam. After passing this exam, most

candidates continue to work under the supervision of an experienced surveyor for another 4 years and then take the Principles and Practice of Surveyors Exam for licensure. Specific requirements for training and education vary among the states. An increasing number of states require a bachelor's degree in surveying or in a closely related field, such as civil engineering or forestry (with courses in surveying), regardless of the number of years of experience. Some states require the degree to be from a school accredited by the Accreditation Board for Engineering and Technology (ABET). Many states also have a continuing education requirement.

High school students interested in surveying should take courses in algebra, geometry, trigonometry, drafting, mechanical drawing, and computer science. High school graduates with no formal training in surveying usually start as apprentices. Beginners with postsecondary school training in surveying usually can start as technicians or assistants. With on-the-job experience and formal training in surveying—either in an institutional program or from a correspondence school—workers may advance to senior survey technician and then to party chief and, in some cases, to licensed surveyor (depending on state licensing requirements). However, it is becoming increasingly difficult to gain licensure without a formal education in surveying.

The National Society of Professional Surveyors, a member organization of the American Congress on Surveying and Mapping, has a voluntary certification program for surveying technicians. Technicians are certified at four levels requiring progressive amounts of experience in addition to the passing of written examinations. Although not required for state licensure, many employers require certification for promotion to positions with greater responsibilities.

Surveyors should have the ability to visualize objects, distances, sizes, and abstract forms. They must work with precision and accuracy, because mistakes can be costly. Members of a survey party must be in good physical condition, because they work outdoors and often carry equipment over difficult terrain. They need good eyesight, coordination, and hearing to communicate verbally and manually (using hand signals). Surveying is a cooperative operation, so good interpersonal skills and the ability to work as part of a team are important. Good office skills also are essential, because surveyors must be able to research old deeds and other legal papers and prepare reports that document their work.

Cartographers and photogrammetrists usually have a bachelor's degree in cartography; geography; or a related field such as surveying, engineering, forestry, or a physical science. Although it is possible to enter these positions through previous experience as a photogrammetric or cartographic technician, nowadays most cartographic and photogrammetric technicians have had some specialized postsecondary school training. With the development of GIS, cartographers and photogrammetrists need additional education and stronger technical skills—including more experience with computers—than in the past.

The American Society for Photogrammetry and Remote Sensing has a voluntary certification program for photogrammetrists. To qualify for this professional distinction, individuals must meet work experience standards and pass an oral or a written examination.

Employment

Surveyors, cartographers, photogrammetrists, and surveying technicians held about 131,000 jobs in 2004. The following tabulation shows the distribution of employment by occupational specialty:

Surveying and mapping technicians 65,000

Surveyors 56,000

Cartographers and photogrammetrists....................11,000

The architectural, engineering, and related services industry—including firms that provided surveying and mapping services to other industries on a contract basis—provided 2 out of 3 jobs for these workers. Federal, state, and local governmental agencies provided almost 1 in 6 jobs. Major federal government employers are the U.S. Geological Survey (USGS), the Bureau of Land Management (BLM), the National Geodetic Survey, and the Army Corps of Engineers. Most surveyors in state and local government work for highway departments or urban planning and redevelopment agencies. Construction, mining, and utility companies also employ surveyors, cartographers, photogrammetrists, and surveying technicians. Only a small number were self-employed in 2004.

Job Outlook

Overall employment of surveyors, cartographers, photogrammetrists, and surveying technicians is expected to grow about as fast as average for all occupations through the year 2014. The widespread availability and use of advanced technologies, such as GPS, GIS, and remote sensing, will continue to increase both the accuracy and productivity of these workers, limiting job growth to some extent. However, job openings will continue to arise from the need to replace workers who transfer to other occupations or who leave the labor force altogether. Many of the workers in these occupations are approaching retirement age.

Opportunities for surveyors, cartographers, and photogrammetrists should remain concentrated in architectural, engineering, and related services firms. Areas such as urban planning, emergency preparedness, and natural resource exploration and mapping also should provide employment growth, particularly with regard to producing maps for the management of emergencies and updating maps with the newly available technology. However, employment may fluctuate from year to year as a function of construction activity or with mapping needs for land and resource management.

Opportunities should be stronger for professional surveyors than for surveying and mapping technicians. Advancements in technology, such as total stations and GPS, have made surveying parties smaller than they were in the past. Opportunities for technicians should be available in basic GIS-related data-entry work. However, many persons possess the basic skills needed to qualify for these jobs, so applicants for technician jobs may face competition.

As technologies become more complex, opportunities will be best for surveyors, cartographers, and photogrammetrists who have a bachelor's degree and strong technical skills. Increasing demand for geographic data, as opposed to traditional surveying services, will mean better opportunities for cartographers and photogrammetrists who are involved in the development and use of geographic and land information systems. New technologies, such as GPS and GIS, also may enhance employment opportunities for surveyors and for surveying technicians who have the educational background and who have acquired technical skills that enable them to work with the new systems. At the same time, upgraded licensing requirements will continue to limit opportunities for professional advancement for those without a bachelor's degree.

Earnings

Median annual earnings of cartographers and photogrammetrists were $46,080 in May 2004. The middle 50 percent earned between $35,160 and $59,830. The lowest 10 percent earned less than $28,210 and the highest 10 percent earned more than $74,440.

Median annual earnings of surveyors were $42,980 in May 2004. The middle 50 percent earned between $31,940 and $57,190. The lowest 10 percent earned less than $24,640 and the highest 10 percent earned more than $71,640. Median hourly earnings of surveyors employed in architectural, engineering, and related services were $41,710 in May 2004.

Median annual earnings of surveying and mapping technicians were $30,380 in May 2004. The middle 50 percent earned between $23,600 and $40,100. The lowest 10 percent earned less than $19,140, and the highest 10 percent earned more than $51,070. Median annual earnings of surveying and mapping technicians employed in architectural, engineering, and related services were $28,610 in May 2004, while those employed by local governments had median annual earnings of $34,810.

Related Occupations

Surveying is related to the work of civil engineers, architects, and landscape architects because an accurate survey is the first step in land development and construction projects. Cartography and geodetic surveying are related to the work of environmental scientists and hydrologists and geoscientists, who study the earth's internal composition, surface, and atmosphere. Cartography also is related to the work of geographers and urban and regional planners, who study and decide how the earth's surface is to be used.

Sources of Additional Information

For career information on surveyors, cartographers, photogrammetrists, and surveying technicians, contact

▶ American Congress on Surveying and Mapping, Suite 403, 6 Montgomery Village Ave., Gaithersburg, MD 20879. Internet: http://www.acsm.net

Information about career opportunities, licensure requirements, and the surveying technician certification program is available from

▶ National Society of Professional Surveyors, Suite 403, 6 Montgomery Village Ave., Gaithersburg, MD 20879. Internet: http://www.acsm.net/nsps

For information on a career as a geodetic surveyor, contact

▶ American Association of Geodetic Surveying (AAGS), Suite 403, 6 Montgomery Village Ave., Gaithersburg, MD 20879. Internet: http://www.acsm.net/aags

General information on careers in photogrammetry and remote sensing is available from

▶ ASPRS: Imaging and Geospatial Information Society, 5410 Grosvenor Ln., Suite 210, Bethesda, MD 20814-2160. Internet: http://www.asprs.org

Television, Video, and Motion Picture Camera Operators and Editors

(O*NET 27-4031.00 and 27-4032.00)

Significant Points

■ Workers acquire their skills through on-the-job or formal post-secondary training.

■ Technical expertise, a good eye, imagination, and creativity are essential.

■ Keen competition for job openings is expected because many talented peopled are attracted to the field.

Nature of the Work

Television, video, and motion picture camera operators produce images that tell a story, inform or entertain an audience, or record an event. *Film and video editors* edit soundtracks, film, and video for the motion picture, cable, and broadcast television industries. Some camera operators do their own editing.

Making commercial-quality movies and video programs requires technical expertise and creativity. Producing successful images requires choosing and presenting interesting material, selecting appropriate equipment, and applying a good eye and a steady hand to ensure smooth, natural movement of the camera.

Camera operators use television, video, or motion picture cameras to shoot a wide range of material, including television series, studio programs, news and sporting events, music videos, motion pictures, documentaries, and training sessions. Some camera operators film or videotape private ceremonies and special events, such as weddings and conference program sessions. Those who record images on videotape are often called *videographers*. Many are employed by independent television stations; local affiliate stations of television networks; large cable and television networks; or smaller, independent production companies. *Studio camera operators* work in a broadcast studio and usually videotape their subjects from a fixed position. *News camera operators*, also called *electronic news gathering (ENG) operators*, work as part of a reporting team, following newsworthy events as they unfold. To capture live events, they must anticipate the action and act quickly. ENG operators sometimes edit raw footage on the spot for relay to a television affiliate for broadcast.

Camera operators employed in the entertainment field use motion picture cameras to film movies, television programs, and commercials. Those who film motion pictures also are known as *cinematographers*. Some specialize in filming cartoons or special effects. Cinematographers may be an integral part of the action, using cameras in any of several different mounts. For example, the camera operator can be stationary and shoot whatever passes in front of the lens, or the camera can be mounted on a track, with the camera operator responsible for shooting the scene from different angles or directions. Wider use of digital cameras has enhanced the number of angles and the clarity that a camera operator can provide. Other camera operators sit on cranes and follow the action while crane operators move them into position. *Steadicam operators* mount a harness and carry the camera on their shoulders to provide a clear picture while they move about the action. Camera operators who work in the entertainment field often meet with directors, actors, editors, and camera assistants to discuss ways of filming, editing, and improving scenes.

Working Conditions

Working conditions for camera operators and editors vary considerably. Those employed by television and cable networks and advertising agencies usually work a 5 day, 40 hour week; however, they may work longer hours to meet production schedules. ENG operators often work long, irregular hours and must be available to work on short notice. Camera operators and editors working in motion picture production also may work long, irregular hours.

ENG operators and those who cover major events, such as conventions or sporting events, frequently travel locally and stay overnight or travel to distant places for longer periods. Camera operators filming television programs or motion pictures may travel to film on location.

Some camera operators—especially ENG operators covering accidents, natural disasters, civil unrest, or military conflicts—work in uncomfortable or even dangerous surroundings. Many camera operators must wait long hours in all kinds of weather for an event to take place and must stand or walk for long periods while carrying heavy equipment. ENG operators often work under strict deadlines.

Training, Other Qualifications, and Advancement

Employers usually seek applicants with a good eye, imagination, and creativity, as well as a good technical understanding of how the camera operates. Television, video, and motion picture camera operators and editors usually acquire their skills through on-the-job training or formal postsecondary training at vocational schools, colleges, universities, or photographic institutes. Formal education may be required for some positions.

Many universities, community and junior colleges, vocational-technical institutes, and private trade and technical schools offer courses in camera operation and videography. Basic courses cover equipment, processes, and techniques. Bachelor's degree programs, especially those including business courses, provide a well-rounded education. Film schools also may provide training on the artistic or aesthetic aspects of filmmaking.

Individuals interested in camera operations should subscribe to videographic newsletters and magazines, join audio-video clubs, and seek summer or part-time employment in cable and television networks, motion picture studios, or camera and video stores.

Camera operators in entry-level jobs learn to set up lights, cameras, and other equipment. They may receive routine assignments requiring adjustments to their cameras or decisions on what subject matter to capture. Camera operators in the film and television industries usually are hired for a project on the basis of recommendations from individuals such as producers, directors of photography, and camera assistants from previous projects or through interviews with the producer. ENG and studio camera operators who work for television affiliates usually start in small markets to gain experience.

Camera operators need good eyesight, artistic ability, and hand-eye coordination. They should be patient, accurate, and detail oriented. Camera operators also should have good communication skills and, if needed, the ability to hold a camera by hand for extended periods.

Camera operators who run their own businesses, or freelance, need business skills as well as talent. These individuals must know how to submit bids, write contracts, get permission to shoot on locations that normally are not open to the public, obtain releases to use film or tape of people, price their services, secure copyright protection for their work, and keep financial records.

With experience, operators may advance to more demanding assignments or to positions with larger or network television stations. Advancement for ENG operators may mean moving to larger media markets. Other camera operators and editors may become directors of photography for movie studios, advertising agencies, or television programs. Some teach at technical schools, film schools, or universities.

Employment

Television, video, and motion picture camera operators held about 28,000 jobs in 2004, and film and video editors held about 20,000. Many are employed by independent television stations, local affiliate stations of television networks or broadcast groups, large cable and television networks, or smaller independent production companies. About 1 in 5 camera operators were self-employed. Some self-employed camera operators contracted with television networks, documentary or independent filmmakers, advertising agencies, or trade show or convention sponsors to work on individual projects for a set fee, often at a daily rate.

Most of the salaried camera operators were employed by television broadcasting stations or motion picture studios. More than half of the salaried film and video editors worked for motion picture studios. Most camera operators and editors worked in large metropolitan areas.

Job Outlook

Television, video, and motion picture camera operators and editors can expect keen competition for job openings because the work is attractive to many people. The number of individuals interested in positions as videographers and movie camera operators usually is much greater than the number of openings. Those who succeed in landing a salaried job or attracting enough work to earn a living by freelancing are likely to be the most creative and highly motivated people, able to adapt to rapidly changing technologies and adept at operating a business. Related work experience or job-related training also can benefit prospective camera operators.

Employment of camera operators and editors is expected to grow about as fast as the average for all occupations through 2014. Rapid expansion of the entertainment market, especially motion picture production and distribution, will spur growth of camera operators. In addition, computer and Internet services will provide new outlets for interactive productions. Growth will be tempered, however, by the increased off-shore production of motion pictures. Camera operators will be needed to film made-for-the-Internet broadcasts, such as live music videos, digital movies, sports features, and general information or entertainment programming. These images can be delivered directly into the home either on compact discs or as streaming video over the Internet. Job growth in radio and television broadcasting will be tempered by the use of robocams and Parkervision systems for studio broadcasts; cameras in these systems are automated and under the control of a single person working either on the studio floor or in a director's booth.

Earnings

Median annual earnings for television, video, and motion picture camera operators were $37,610 in May 2004. The middle 50 percent earned between $22,640 and $56,400. The lowest 10 percent earned less than $15,730, and the highest 10 percent earned more than $76,100. Median annual earnings were $48,900 in the motion picture and video industries and $29,560 in radio and television broadcasting.

Median annual earnings for film and video editors were $43,590 in May 2004. The middle 50 percent earned between $29,310 and $63,890. The lowest 10 percent earned less than $21,710, and the highest 10 percent earned more than $93,950. Median annual earnings were $44,710 in the motion picture and video industries, which employed the largest numbers of film and video editors.

Many camera operators who work in film or video are freelancers, whose earnings tend to fluctuate each year. Because most freelance camera operators purchase their own equipment, they incur considerable expense acquiring and maintaining cameras and accessories. Some camera operators belong to unions, including the International Alliance of Theatrical Stage Employees and the National Association of Broadcast Employees and Technicians.

Related Occupations

Related arts and media occupations include artists and related workers; broadcast and sound engineering technicians; and radio operators, designers, and photographers.

Sources of Additional Information

For information about careers as a camera operator, contact

▸ International Cinematographer's Guild, 80 Eighth Ave., 14th Floor, New York, NY 10011.

▸ National Association of Broadcast Employees and Technicians, 501 Third St. NW, 6th Floor, Washington, DC 20001. Internet: http://www.nabetcwa.org/

Information about career and employment opportunities for camera operators and film and video editors also is available from local offices of state employment service agencies, local offices of the relevant trade unions, and local television and film production companies that employ these workers.

QUICK
JOB SEARCH

Seven Steps to Getting a Good Job in Less Time

The Complete Text of a Results-Oriented Minibook by Michael Farr

Millions of job seekers have found better jobs faster using the techniques in the *Quick Job Search*. So can you! The *Quick Job Search* covers the essential steps proven to cut job search time in half and is used widely by job search programs throughout North America. Topics include how to identify your key skills, define your ideal job, write a great resume quickly, use the most effective job search methods, get more interviews, and much more.

If you completed "Using the Job-Match Grid to Choose a Career" earlier in this book, the activities in this section will complement those efforts by helping you to define other skills you possess, focus your resume, and get a job quickly.

While it is a section in this book, the *Quick Job Search* is available from JIST Publishing as a separate booklet and in an expanded form as *Seven-Step Job Search*.

Quick Job Search Is Short, But It May Be All You Need

While *Quick Job Search* is short, it covers the basics on how to explore career options and conduct an effective job search. While these topics can seem complex, I have found some simple truths about looking for a job:

- If you are going to work, you might as well look for what you really want to do and are good at.

- If you are looking for a job, you might as well use techniques that will reduce the time it takes to find one—and that help you get a better job than you might otherwise.

That's what I emphasize in *Quick Job Search*.

Trust Me—Do the Worksheets. I know you will resist completing the worksheets. But trust me. They are worth your time. Doing them will give you a better sense of what you are good at, what you want to do, and how to go about getting it. You will also most likely get more interviews and present yourself better. Is this worth giving up a night of TV? Yes, I think so.

Once you finish this minibook and its activities, you will have spent more time planning your career than most people do. And you will know more than the average job seeker about finding a job.

Why Such a Short Book? I've taught job seeking skills for many years, and I've written longer and more detailed books than this one. Yet I have often been asked to tell someone, in a few minutes or hours, the most important things they should do in their career planning or job search. Instructors and counselors also ask the same question because they have only a short time to spend with folks they're trying to help. I've given this a lot of thought, and the seven topics in this book are the ones I think are most important to know.

This minibook is short enough to scan in a morning and conduct a more effective job search that afternoon. Granted, doing all the activities would take more time, but they will prepare you far better than scanning the book. Of course, you can learn more about all the topics it covers, but this minibook, *Quick Job Search,* may be all you need.

You can't just read about getting a job. The best way to get a job is to go out and get interviews! And the best way to get interviews is to make a job out of getting a job.

After many years of experience, I have identified just seven basic things you need to do that make a big difference in your job search. Each will be covered and expanded on in this minibook.

1. Identify your key skills.

2. Define your ideal job.

3. Learn the two most effective job search methods.

4. Create a superior resume and a portfolio.

5. Organize your time to get two interviews a day.

6. Dramatically improve your interviewing skills.

7. Follow up on all leads.

So, without further delay, let's get started!

STEP 1: Identify Your Key Skills and Develop a "Skills Language" to Describe Yourself

One survey of employers found that about 90 percent of the people they interviewed might have the required job skills, but they could not describe those skills and thereby prove that they could do the job they sought. They could not answer the basic question "Why should I hire you?"

Knowing and describing your skills is essential to doing well in interviews. This same knowledge is important to help you decide what type of job you will enjoy and do well. For these reasons, I consider identifying your skills a necessary part of a successful career plan or job search.

The Three Types of Skills

Most people think of their skills as job-related skills, such as using a computer. But we all have other types of skills that are important for success on a job—and that are important to employers. The following triangle arranges skills in three groups, and I think that this is a very useful way to consider skills.

Let's look at these three types of skills—self-management, transferable, and job-related—and identify those that are most important to you.

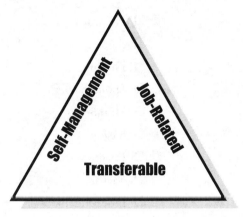

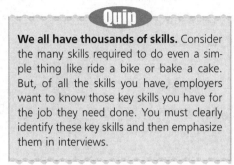

Quip

We all have thousands of skills. Consider the many skills required to do even a simple thing like ride a bike or bake a cake. But, of all the skills you have, employers want to know those key skills you have for the job they need done. You must clearly identify these key skills and then emphasize them in interviews.

Self-Management Skills

To begin identifying your skills, answer the question in the box that follows.

YOUR GOOD WORKER TRAITS

Write down three things about yourself that you think make you a good worker. Think about what an employer might like about you or the way you work.

1. _____

2. _____

3. _____

You just wrote down the most important things for an employer to know about you! They describe your basic personality and your ability to adapt to new environments. They are some of the most important skills to emphasize in interviews, yet most job seekers don't realize their importance—and don't mention them.

Review the Self-Management Skills Checklist that follows and put a check mark beside any skills you have. The key self-management skills listed first cover abilities that employers find particularly important. If one or more of the key self-management skills apply to you, mentioning them in interviews can help you greatly.

SELF-MANAGEMENT SKILLS CHECKLIST

Following are the key self-management skills that employers value highly. Place a check by those you already have.

- ❏ Have good attendance
- ❏ Get work done on time
- ❏ Am honest
- ❏ Get along with supervisor

- ❏ Arrive on time
- ❏ Get along with co-workers
- ❏ Follow instructions
- ❏ Am hard working/productive

(continued)

(continued)

Place a check by other self-management skills you have.

❑ Ambitious	❑ Discreet	❑ Helpful
❑ Mature	❑ Physically strong	❑ Sincere
❑ Assertive	❑ Eager	❑ Humble
❑ Methodical	❑ Practical	❑ Spontaneous
❑ Capable	❑ Efficient	❑ Humorous
❑ Modest	❑ Problem-solving	❑ Steady
❑ Cheerful	❑ Energetic	❑ Imaginative
❑ Motivated	❑ Proud of work	❑ Tactful
❑ Competent	❑ Enthusiastic	❑ Independent
❑ Natural	❑ Quick to learn	❑ Team player
❑ Conscientious	❑ Expressive	❑ Industrious
❑ Open-minded	❑ Reliable	❑ Tenacious
❑ Creative	❑ Flexible	❑ Informal
❑ Optimistic	❑ Resourceful	❑ Thrifty
❑ Culturally tolerant	❑ Formal	❑ Intelligent
❑ Original	❑ Responsible	❑ Trustworthy
❑ Decisive	❑ Friendly	❑ Intuitive
❑ Patient	❑ Results-oriented	❑ Versatile
❑ Dependable	❑ Good-natured	❑ Loyal
❑ Persistent	❑ Self-confident	❑ Well-organized

List the other self-management skills you have that have not been mentioned but you think are important to include.

_____

_____

_____

After you finish checking the list, circle the five skills you feel are most important and write them in the box that follows.

YOUR TOP FIVE SELF-MANAGEMENT SKILLS

1. _____

2. _____

3. _____

4. _____

5. _____

Note When thinking about their skills, some people find it helpful to complete the Essential Job Search Data Worksheet that starts on page 364. It organizes skills and accomplishments from previous jobs and other life experiences. Take a look at it and decide whether to complete it now or later.

Transferable Skills

We all have skills that can transfer from one job or career to another. For example, the ability to organize events could be used in a variety of jobs and may be essential for success in certain occupations. Your mission is to find a job that requires the skills you have and enjoy using.

Quip

It's not bragging if it's true. Using your new skills language may be uncomfortable at first, but employers need to learn about your skills. So practice saying positive things about the skills you have for the job. If you don't, who will?

TRANSFERABLE SKILLS CHECKLIST

Following are the key transferable skills that employers value highly. Place a check by those you already have. You may have used them in a previous job or in some non-work setting.

- ❏ Managing money/budgets
- ❏ Speaking in public
- ❏ Managing people
- ❏ Organizing/managing projects
- ❏ Meeting deadlines

- ❏ Using computers
- ❏ Meeting the public
- ❏ Writing well
- ❏ Negotiating

Place a check by the skills you have for working with data.

- ❏ Analyzing data
- ❏ Counting/taking inventory
- ❏ Auditing/checking for accuracy
- ❏ Investigating
- ❏ Budgeting
- ❏ Keeping financial records
- ❏ Calculating/computing

- ❏ Observing/inspecting
- ❏ Classifying data
- ❏ Paying attention to details
- ❏ Comparing/evaluating
- ❏ Researching/locating information
- ❏ Compiling/recording facts
- ❏ Synthesizing

Place a check by the skills you have for working with people.

- ❏ Administering
- ❏ Counseling people
- ❏ Being diplomatic
- ❏ Demonstrating

- ❏ Being kind
- ❏ Having insight
- ❏ Being outgoing
- ❏ Helping others

- ❏ Being patient
- ❏ Instructing others
- ❏ Being pleasant
- ❏ Interviewing people

(continued)

(continued)

- ❏ Being sensitive
- ❏ Listening
- ❏ Being sociable
- ❏ Persuading

- ❏ Being tactful
- ❏ Supervising
- ❏ Being tough
- ❏ Tolerating

- ❏ Caring for others
- ❏ Trusting
- ❏ Coaching
- ❏ Understanding
- ❏ Confronting others

Place a check by your skills in working with words and ideas.

- ❏ Being articulate
- ❏ Creating new ideas
- ❏ Being ingenious
- ❏ Designing
- ❏ Being inventive
- ❏ Editing

- ❏ Being logical
- ❏ Remembering information
- ❏ Communicating verbally
- ❏ Speaking publicly
- ❏ Corresponding with others
- ❏ Writing clearly

Place a check by the leadership skills you have.

- ❏ Being competitive
- ❏ Mediating problems
- ❏ Delegating
- ❏ Motivating people
- ❏ Directing others
- ❏ Motivating yourself
- ❏ Getting results
- ❏ Negotiating agreements

- ❏ Having self-confidence
- ❏ Planning events
- ❏ Influencing others
- ❏ Running meetings
- ❏ Making decisions
- ❏ Solving problems
- ❏ Making explanations
- ❏ Taking risks

Place a check by your creative or artistic skills.

- ❏ Appreciating music
- ❏ Expressing yourself
- ❏ Being artistic
- ❏ Performing/acting

- ❏ Dancing
- ❏ Playing instruments
- ❏ Drawing
- ❏ Presenting artistic ideas

Place a check by your skills for working with things.

- ❏ Assembling things
- ❏ Driving or operating vehicles
- ❏ Building things

- ❏ Operating tools/machines
- ❏ Constructing or repairing things

Add the other transferable skills you have that have not been mentioned but you think are important to include.

_____

_____

_____

When you are finished, circle the five transferable skills you feel are most important for you to use in your next job and list them below.

YOUR TOP FIVE TRANSFERABLE SKILLS

1. _____

2. _____

3. _____

4. _____

5. _____

Job-Related Skills

Job content or job-related skills are those you need to do a particular occupation. A carpenter, for example, needs to know how to use various tools. Before you select job-related skills to emphasize, you must first have a clear idea of the jobs you want. So let's put off developing your job-related skills list until you have defined the job you want—the topic that is covered next.

STEP 2: Define Your Ideal Job

Too many people look for a job without clearly knowing what they are looking for. Before you go out seeking a job, I suggest that you first define exactly what you want—not *just a job* but *the job*.

Most people think that a job objective is the same as a job title, but it isn't. You need to consider other elements of what makes a job satisfying for you. Then, later, you can decide what that job is called and what industry it might be in. You can compromise on what you consider your ideal job later if you need to.

EIGHT FACTORS TO CONSIDER IN DEFINING YOUR IDEAL JOB

As you try to define your ideal job, consider the following eight important questions. When you know what you want, your task then becomes finding a position that is as close to your ideal job as possible.

1. **What skills do you want to use?** From the skills lists in Step 1, select the top five skills that you enjoy using and most want to use in your next job.

   a._____

   b._____

   c._____

   d._____

   e._____

(continued)

(continued)

2. **What type of special knowledge do you have?** Perhaps you know how to fix radios, keep accounting records, or cook food. Write down the things you know from schooling, training, hobbies, family experiences, and other sources. One or more of these knowledge areas could make you a very special applicant in the right setting._____

_____

_____

3. **With what types of people do you prefer to work?** Do you like to work with competitive people, or do you prefer hardworking folks, creative personalities, relaxed people, or some other types?_____

_____

_____

4. **What type of work environment do you prefer?** Do you want to work inside, outside, in a quiet place, in a busy place, or in a clean or messy place; or do you want to have a window with a nice view? List the types of environments you prefer._____

_____

_____

5. **Where do you want your next job to be located—in what city or region?** If you are open to living and working anywhere, what would your ideal community be like? Near a bus line? Close to a childcare center?_____

_____

_____

6. **What benefits or income do you hope to have in your next job?** Many people will take less money or fewer benefits if they like a job in other ways—or if they need a job quickly to survive. Think about the minimum you would take as well as what you would eventually like to earn. Your next job will probably pay somewhere in between._____

_____

_____

7. **How much and what types of responsibility are you willing to accept?** Usually, the more money you want to make, the more responsibility you must accept. Do you want to work by yourself, be part of a group, or be in charge? If you want to be in charge, how many people are you willing to supervise?

_____

_____

8. **What values are important or have meaning to you?** Do you have important values you would prefer to include in considering the work you do? For example, some people want to work to help others, clean up the environment, build structures, make machines work, gain power or prestige, or care for animals or plants. Think about what is important to you and how you might include this in your next job._____

_____

_____

_____

Is It Possible to Find Your Ideal Job?

Can you find a job that meets all the criteria you just defined? Perhaps. Some people do. The harder you look, the more likely you are to find it. But you will likely need to compromise, so it is useful to know what is *most* important to include in your next job. Go back over your responses to the eight factors and mark a few of those that you would most like to have or include in your ideal job.

FACTORS I WANT IN MY IDEAL JOB

Write a brief description of your ideal job. Don't worry about a job title, or whether you have the experience, or other practical matters yet._____

_____

_____

_____

How Can You Explore Specific Job Titles and Industries?

You might find your ideal job in an occupation you haven't considered yet. And, even if you are sure of the occupation you want, it may be in an industry that is unfamiliar to you. This combination of occupation and industry forms the basis for your job search, and you should consider a variety of options.

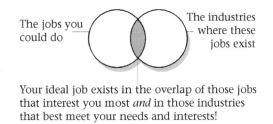

The jobs you could do

The industries where these jobs exist

Your ideal job exists in the overlap of those jobs that interest you most *and* in those industries that best meet your needs and interests!

There are thousands of job titles, and many jobs are highly specialized, employing just a few people. While one of these more specialized jobs may be just what you want, most work falls within more general job titles that employ large numbers of people.

The list of job titles that follows was based on a list developed by the U.S. Department of Labor. It contains approximately 270 major jobs that employ about 90 percent of the U.S. workforce.

The job titles are organized within 16 major groupings called interest areas, presented in bold type. These groupings will help you quickly identify fields most likely to interest you. Job titles are presented in regular type within these groupings.

Begin with the interest areas that appeal to you most, and underline any job title that interests you. (Don't worry for now about whether you have the experience or credentials to do these jobs.) Then quickly review the remaining interest areas, underlining any job titles there that interest you. Note that some job titles are listed more than once because they fit into more than one interest area. When you have gone through all 16 interest areas, go back and circle the 5 to 10 job titles that interest you most. These are the ones you will want to research in more detail.

1. **Agriculture and Natural Resources:** Agricultural and Food Scientists; Agricultural Workers; Biological Scientists; Conservation Scientists and Foresters; Engineers; Farmers, Ranchers, and Agricultural Managers; Fishers and Fishing Vessel Operators; Forest, Conservation, and Logging Workers; Grounds Maintenance Workers; Material Moving Occupations; Pest Control Workers; Purchasing Managers, Buyers, and Purchasing Agents; Science Technicians.

2. **Architecture and Construction:** Architects, except Landscape and Naval; Boilermakers; Brickmasons, Blockmasons, and Stonemasons; Carpenters; Carpet, Floor, and Tile Installers and Finishers; Cement Masons, Concrete Finishers, Segmental Pavers, and Terrazzo Workers; Construction and Building Inspectors; Construction Equipment Operators; Construction Laborers; Construction Managers; Drafters; Drywall Installers, Ceiling Tile Installers, and Tapers; Electrical and Electronics Installers and Repairers; Electricians; Elevator Installers and Repairers; Glaziers; Hazardous Materials Removal Workers; Heating, Air-Conditioning, and Refrigeration Mechanics and Installers; Home Appliance Repairers; Insulation Workers; Landscape Architects; Line Installers and Repairers; Maintenance and Repair Workers, General; Material Moving Occupations; Painters and Paperhangers; Pipelayers, Plumbers, Pipefitters, and Steamfitters; Plasterers and Stucco Masons; Radio and Telecommunications Equipment Installers and Repairers; Roofers; Sheet Metal Workers; Structural and Reinforcing Iron and Metal Workers; Surveyors, Cartographers, Photogrammetrists, and Surveying Technicians.

3. **Arts and Communication:** Actors, Producers, and Directors; Advertising, Marketing, Promotions, Public Relations, and Sales Managers; Air Traffic Controllers; Announcers; Artists and Related Workers; Barbers, Cosmetologists, and Other Personal Appearance Workers; Broadcast and Sound Engineering Technicians and Radio Operators; Commercial and Industrial Designers; Communications Equipment Operators; Dancers and Choreographers; Dispatchers; Fashion Designers; Floral Designers; Graphic Designers; Interior Designers; Interpreters and Translators; Musicians, Singers, and Related Workers; News Analysts, Reporters, and Correspondents; Photographers; Photographic Process Workers and Processing Machine Operators; Precision Instrument and Equipment Repairers; Public Relations Specialists; Television, Video, and Motion Picture Camera Operators and Editors; Writers and Editors.

4. **Business and Administration:** Accountants and Auditors; Administrative Services Managers; Billing and Posting Clerks and Machine Operators; Bookkeeping, Accounting, and Auditing Clerks; Brokerage Clerks; Budget Analysts; Building Cleaning Workers; Communications Equipment Operators; Data Entry and Information Processing Workers; Engineering Technicians; File Clerks; Human Resources Assistants, except Payroll and Timekeeping; Human Resources, Training, and Labor Relations Managers

and Specialists; Management Analysts; Meeting and Convention Planners; Meter Readers, Utilities; Office and Administrative Support Worker Supervisors and Managers; Office Clerks, General; Operations Research Analysts; Payroll and Timekeeping Clerks; Postal Service Workers; Procurement Clerks; Production, Planning, and Expediting Clerks; Secretaries and Administrative Assistants; Shipping, Receiving, and Traffic Clerks; Stock Clerks and Order Fillers; Top Executives; Weighers, Measurers, Checkers, and Samplers, Recordkeeping.

5. **Education and Training:** Archivists, Curators, and Museum Technicians; Counselors; Education Administrators; Fitness Workers; Instructional Coordinators; Librarians; Library Assistants, Clerical; Library Technicians; Teacher Assistants; Teachers—Adult Literacy and Remedial Education; Teachers—Postsecondary; Teachers—Preschool, Kindergarten, Elementary, Middle, and Secondary; Teachers—Self-Enrichment Education; Teachers—Special Education.

6. **Finance and Insurance:** Advertising Sales Agents; Appraisers and Assessors of Real Estate; Bill and Account Collectors; Claims Adjusters, Appraisers, Examiners, and Investigators; Cost Estimators; Credit Authorizers, Checkers, and Clerks; Financial Analysts and Personal Financial Advisors; Financial Managers; Insurance Sales Agents; Insurance Underwriters; Interviewers; Loan Officers; Market and Survey Researchers; Securities, Commodities, and Financial Services Sales Agents; Tellers.

7. **Government and Public Administration:** Agricultural Workers; Court Reporters; Fire Fighting Occupations; Inspectors, Testers, Sorters, Samplers, and Weighers; Occupational Health and Safety Specialists and Technicians; Police and Detectives; Science Technicians; Tax Examiners, Collectors, and Revenue Agents; Top Executives; Urban and Regional Planners.

8. **Health Science:** Agricultural Workers; Animal Care and Service Workers; Athletic Trainers; Audiologists; Cardiovascular Technologists and Technicians; Chiropractors; Clinical Laboratory Technologists and Technicians; Dental Assistants; Dental Hygienists; Dentists; Diagnostic Medical Sonographers; Dietitians and Nutritionists; Licensed Practical and Licensed Vocational Nurses; Massage Therapists; Medical and Health Services Managers; Medical Assistants; Medical Records and Health Information Technicians; Medical Transcriptionists; Nuclear Medicine Technologists; Nursing, Psychiatric, and Home Health Aides; Occupational Therapist Assistants and Aides; Occupational Therapists; Opticians, Dispensing; Optometrists; Pharmacists; Pharmacy Aides; Pharmacy Technicians; Physical Therapist Assistants and Aides; Physical Therapists; Physician Assistants; Physicians and Surgeons; Podiatrists; Radiation Therapists; Radiologic Technologists and Technicians; Recreational Therapists; Registered Nurses; Respiratory Therapists; Science Technicians; Speech-Language Pathologists; Surgical Technologists; Veterinarians; Veterinary Technologists and Technicians.

9. **Hospitality, Tourism, and Recreation:** Athletes, Coaches, Umpires, and Related Workers; Barbers, Cosmetologists, and Other Personal Appearance Workers; Building Cleaning Workers; Chefs, Cooks, and Food Preparation Workers; Flight Attendants; Food and Beverage Serving and Related Workers; Food Processing Occupations; Food Service Managers; Gaming Services Occupations; Hotel, Motel, and Resort Desk Clerks; Lodging Managers; Recreation Workers; Reservation and Transportation Ticket Agents and Travel Clerks; Travel Agents.

10. **Human Service:** Child Care Workers; Counselors; Interviewers; Personal and Home Care Aides; Probation Officers and Correctional Treatment Specialists; Psychologists; Social and Human Service Assistants; Social Workers.

(continued)

(continued)

11. **Information Technology:** Coin, Vending, and Amusement Machine Servicers and Repairers; Computer and Information Systems Managers; Computer Operators; Computer Programmers; Computer Scientists and Database Administrators; Computer Software Engineers; Computer Support Specialists and Systems Administrators; Computer Systems Analysts; Computer, Automated Teller, and Office Machine Repairers.

12. **Law and Public Safety:** Correctional Officers; Emergency Medical Technicians and Paramedics; Fire Fighting Occupations; Job Opportunities in the Armed Forces; Judges, Magistrates, and Other Judicial Workers; Lawyers; Paralegals and Legal Assistants; Police and Detectives; Private Detectives and Investigators; Science Technicians; Security Guards and Gaming Surveillance Officers.

13. **Manufacturing:** Agricultural Workers; Aircraft and Avionics Equipment Mechanics and Service Technicians; Assemblers and Fabricators; Automotive Body and Related Repairers; Automotive Service Technicians and Mechanics; Bookbinders and Bindery Workers; Computer Control Programmers and Operators; Desktop Publishers; Diesel Service Technicians and Mechanics; Electrical and Electronics Installers and Repairers; Electronic Home Entertainment Equipment Installers and Repairers; Food Processing Occupations; Heavy Vehicle and Mobile Equipment Service Technicians and Mechanics; Home Appliance Repairers; Industrial Machinery Mechanics and Maintenance Workers; Industrial Production Managers; Inspectors, Testers, Sorters, Samplers, and Weighers; Jewelers and Precious Stone and Metal Workers; Machine Setters, Operators, and Tenders—Metal and Plastic; Machinists; Material Moving Occupations; Medical, Dental, and Ophthalmic Laboratory Technicians; Millwrights; Painting and Coating Workers, except Construction and Maintenance; Photographic Process Workers and Processing Machine Operators; Power Plant Operators, Distributors, and Dispatchers; Precision Instrument and Equipment Repairers; Prepress Technicians and Workers; Printing Machine Operators; Radio and Telecommunications Equipment Installers and Repairers; Semiconductor Processors; Small Engine Mechanics; Stationary Engineers and Boiler Operators; Textile, Apparel, and Furnishings Occupations; Tool and Die Makers; Water and Liquid Waste Treatment Plant and System Operators; Water Transportation Occupations; Welding, Soldering, and Brazing Workers; Woodworkers.

14. **Retail and Wholesale Sales and Service:** Advertising, Marketing, Promotions, Public Relations, and Sales Managers; Cashiers; Counter and Rental Clerks; Customer Service Representatives; Demonstrators, Product Promoters, and Models; Funeral Directors; Order Clerks; Property, Real Estate, and Community Association Managers; Purchasing Managers, Buyers, and Purchasing Agents; Real Estate Brokers and Sales Agents; Receptionists and Information Clerks; Retail Salespersons; Sales Engineers; Sales Representatives, Wholesale and Manufacturing; Sales Worker Supervisors.

15. **Scientific Research, Engineering, and Mathematics:** Actuaries; Atmospheric Scientists; Biological Scientists; Chemists and Materials Scientists; Drafters; Economists; Engineering and Natural Sciences Managers; Engineering Technicians; Engineers; Environmental Scientists and Hydrologists; Geoscientists; Mathematicians; Medical Scientists; Photographers; Physicists and Astronomers; Psychologists; Science Technicians; Social Scientists, Other; Statisticians; Surveyors, Cartographers, Photogrammetrists, and Surveying Technicians.

16. **Transportation, Distribution, and Logistics:** Aircraft Pilots and Flight Engineers; Bus Drivers; Cargo and Freight Agents; Couriers and Messengers; Material Moving Occupations; Postal Service Workers; Rail Transportation Occupations; Taxi Drivers and Chauffeurs; Truck Drivers and Driver/Sales Workers; Water Transportation Occupations.

> Note
>
> *You can find thorough descriptions for the job titles in the preceding list in the* Occupational Outlook Handbook, *published by the U.S. Department of Labor. Its descriptions include information on earnings, training and education needed to hold specific jobs, working conditions, advancement opportunities, projected growth, and sources for additional information. Most libraries have this book.*
>
> *You also can find descriptions of these jobs on the Internet. Go to www.bls.gov/oco/.*
>
> *The* New Guide for Occupational Exploration, *Fourth Edition, also provides more information on the interest areas used in this list. This book is published by JIST Works and describes about 1,000 major jobs, arranged within groupings of related jobs.*
>
> *Finally, "A Short List of Additional Resources" at the end of this minibook gives you resources for more job information.*

CONSIDER MAJOR INDUSTRIES

What industry you work in is often as important as the career field. For example, some industries pay much better than others, and others may simply be more interesting to you. A book titled *40 Best Fields for Your Career* contains very helpful reviews for each of the major industries mentioned in the following list. Many libraries and bookstores carry this book, as well as the U.S. Department of Labor's *Career Guide to Industries*, or you can find the information on the Internet at www.CareerOINK.com or at www.bls.gov/oco/cg/.

Underline industries that interest you, and then learn more about the opportunities they present. Jobs in most careers are available in a variety of industries, so consider what industries fit you best and focus your job search in these.

Agriculture and natural resources: Agriculture, forestry, and fishing; mining; oil and gas extraction.

Manufacturing, construction, and utilities: Aerospace product and parts manufacturing; chemical manufacturing, except drugs; computer and electronic product manufacturing; construction; food manufacturing; machinery manufacturing; motor vehicle and parts manufacturing; pharmaceutical and medicine manufacturing; printing; steel manufacturing; textile, textile products, and apparel manufacturing; utilities.

Trade: Automobile dealers, clothing, accessories, and general merchandise stores; grocery stores; wholesale trade.

Transportation: Air transportation; truck transportation and warehousing.

Information: Broadcasting; Internet service providers, Web search portals, and data processing services; motion picture and video industries; publishing, except software; software publishing; telecommunications.

Financial activities: Banking; insurance; securities, commodities, and other investments.

Professional and business services: Advertising and public relations; computer systems design and related services; employment services; management, scientific, and technical consulting services; scientific research and development services.

Education, health care, and social services: Child daycare services; educational services; health care; social assistance, except child care.

(continued)

(continued)

> **Leisure and hospitality:** Art, entertainment, and recreation; food services and drinking places; hotels and other accommodations.
>
> **Government and advocacy, grantmaking, and civic organizations:** Advocacy, grantmaking, and civic organizations; federal government; state and local government, except education and health care.

THE TOP JOBS AND INDUSTRIES THAT INTEREST YOU

Go back over the lists of job titles and industries. For numbers 1 and 2 below, list the jobs that interest you most. Then select the industries that interest you most, and list them below in number 3. These are the jobs and industries you should research most carefully. Your ideal job is likely to be found in some combination of these jobs and industries, or in more specialized but related jobs and industries.

1. The five job titles that interest you most

   a._____

   b._____

   c._____

   d._____

   e._____

2. The five next most interesting job titles

   a._____

   b._____

   c._____

   d._____

   e._____

3. The industries that interest you most

   a._____

   b._____

   c._____

   d._____

   e._____

Is Self-Employment or Starting a Business an Option?

More than one in 10 workers are self-employed or own their own businesses. If these options interest you, consider them as well. Talk to people in similar roles to gather information and look for books and Web sites that provide information on options that are similar to those that interest you. A book titled *Best Jobs for the 21st*

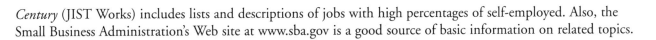

Century (JIST Works) includes lists and descriptions of jobs with high percentages of self-employed. Also, the Small Business Administration's Web site at www.sba.gov is a good source of basic information on related topics.

SELF-EMPLOYMENT AREAS OF INTEREST

In the following space, write your current interest in self-employment or starting a business in an area related to your general job objective.

_____

_____

_____

Can You Identify Your Job-Related Skills Now That You've Defined Your Ideal Job?

Earlier, I suggested that you should first define the job you want and then identify key job-related skills you have that support your ability to do that job. These are the job-related skills to emphasize in interviews.

So, now that you have determined your ideal job, you can pinpoint the job-related skills it requires. If you haven't done so, complete the Essential Job Search Data Worksheet on pages 364–368. Completing it will give you specific skills and accomplishments to highlight.

Yes, completing that worksheet requires time, but doing so will help you clearly define key skills to emphasize in interviews—when what you say matters so much. People who complete that worksheet will do better in their interviews than those who don't. After you complete the Essential Job Search Data Worksheet, you are ready to list your top five job-related skills.

> **Quip**
>
> **It's a hassle, but...** Completing the Essential Job Search Data Worksheet that starts on page 364 will help you define what you are good at—and remember examples of when you did things well. This information will help you define your ideal job and will be of great value in interviews. Look at the worksheet now, and promise to do it later today.

YOUR TOP FIVE JOB-RELATED SKILLS

List the top five job-related skills you think are most important. Include the job-related skills you have that you would most like to use in your next job.

1. _____

2. _____

3. _____

4. _____

5. _____

STEP 3: Use the Most Effective Methods to Find a Job in Less Time

Employer surveys have found that most employers don't advertise their job openings. They most often hire people they already know, people who find out about the jobs through word of mouth, or people who happen to be in the right place at the right time. Although luck plays a part in finding job openings, you can use the tips in this step to increase your luck.

Let's look at the job search methods that people use. The U.S. Department of Labor conducts a regular survey of unemployed people actively looking for work. Following are the results of their most recent findings.

Percentage of Unemployed People Who Use Various Job Search Methods

- Contacted employer directly: 62.7%
- Sent out resumes/filled out applications: 54.5%
- Contacted public employment agency: 19.9%
- Placed or answered help wanted ads: 16.4%
- Contacted friends or relatives: 18%
- Contacted private employment agency: 7.7%
- Used other active search methods: 11.8%

Source: U.S. Department of Labor, Current Population Survey

N o t e *This step covers a number of job search methods. Most of the material is presented as information, with a few interactive activities. While each topic is short and reasonably interesting, taking a break now and then will help you absorb it all.*

The survey shows that most people use more than one job search technique. For example, one person might read want ads, fill out applications, and ask friends for job leads. Others might send out resumes, contact everyone they know through previous jobs, and sign up at employment agencies.

But the survey covered only seven job search methods and asked only whether the job seeker did or did not use each method. The survey did not cover Internet job searches, nor did it ask whether a method actually worked in getting job offers.

Unfortunately, there hasn't been much conclusive recent research on the effectiveness of various job search methods. Most of what we know is based on older research and the observations of people who work directly with job seekers, such as professional resume writers and career counselors. I'll share what we do know about the effectiveness of job search methods in the content that follows.

Quip

Your job search objective. Almost everyone finds a job eventually, so your objective should be to find a good job in less time. The job search methods I emphasize in this minibook will help you do just that.

Get the Most Out of Less Effective Job Search Methods

The truth is that every job search method works for someone. But experience and research show that some methods are more effective than others are. Your task in the job search is to spend more of your time using more effective methods—and increase the effectiveness of all the methods you use.

So let's start by looking at some traditional job search methods and how you can increase their effectiveness. Only about one-third of all job seekers get their jobs using one of these methods, but you should still consider using them to some extent in your search. Later in the step, you'll read about the most effective methods, the ones you should devote the most time to in your search.

Newspaper and Internet Help Wanted Ads

Most jobs are never advertised, and only about 16 percent of all people get their jobs through the want ads. Everyone who reads the paper knows about these openings, so competition is fierce for the few advertised jobs.

The Internet also lists many job openings. But, as happens with newspaper ads, enormous numbers of people view these postings. Many job seekers make direct contact with employers via a company's Web site. Some people do get jobs through the bigger sites, so go ahead and apply. Just be sure to spend most of your time using more effective methods.

Filling Out Applications

Most employers require job seekers to complete an application form. Applications are designed to collect negative information, and employers use applications to screen people out. If, for example, your training or work history is not the best, you will often never get an interview, even if you can do the job.

Completing applications is a more effective approach for young and entry-level job seekers. The reason is that there is a shortage of workers for the relatively low-paying jobs typically sought by less-experienced job seekers. As a result, when trying to fill those positions, employers are more willing to accept a lack of experience or fewer job skills. Even so, you will get better results by filling out the application, if asked to do so, and then requesting an interview with the person in charge.

When you complete an application, make it neat and error-free, and do not include anything that could get you screened out. If necessary, leave a problem section blank. You can always explain situations in an interview.

Employment Agencies

There are three types of employment agencies. One is operated by the government and is free. The others, private employment agencies and temp agencies, are run as for-profit businesses and charge a fee to either you or an employer. Following are the advantages and disadvantages to using each.

The government employment service and One-Stop centers. Each state and province has a network of local offices to pay unemployment compensation, provide job leads, and offer other services—at no charge to you or to employers. The service's name varies by region. It may be called Job Service, Department of Labor, Unemployment Office, Workforce Development, or another name. Many of these offices are now also online, and some even require their users to sign up with a login and password to search for job leads and use other services on the Internet.

The Employment and Training Administration Web site at www.doleta.gov/uses gives you information on the programs provided by the government employment service, plus links to other useful sites. Canada's government employment Web site is at www.jobbank.gc.ca.

The government employment service lists only 5 to 10 percent of the available openings nationally, and only about 6 percent of all job seekers get their jobs there. Even so, visit your local office early in your job search. Find out whether you qualify for unemployment compensation and learn more about its services. Look into it—the price is right.

Private employment agencies. Private employment agencies are businesses that charge a fee either to you or to the employer who hires you. Fees can be from less than one month's pay to 15 percent or more of your annual salary. You will often see these agencies' ads in the help wanted section of the newspaper. Many have Web sites.

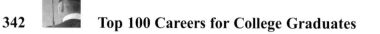

Be careful about using fee-based employment agencies. Recent research indicates that more people use and bene-fit from fee-based agencies than in the past. However, relatively few people who register with private agencies get a job through them.

If you use a private employment agency, ask for interviews with the employers who agree to pay the agency's fee. Do not sign an exclusive agreement or be pressured into accepting a job. Also, continue to actively look for your own leads. You can find these agencies in the phone book's yellow pages, and many state- or province-government Web sites offer lists of the private employment agencies in their states.

Temporary agencies. Temporary agencies offer jobs that last from several days to many months. They charge the employer an hourly fee, and then pay you a bit less and keep the difference. You pay no direct fee to the agency. Many private employment agencies now provide temporary jobs as well.

Temp agencies have grown rapidly for good reason. They provide employers with short-term help, and employ-ers often use them to find people they might want to hire later. If the employers are dissatisfied, they can just ask the agency for different temp workers.

Temp agencies can help you survive between jobs and get experience in different work settings. Temp jobs pro-vide a very good option while you look for long-term work, and you might get a job offer while working in a temp job. Holding a temporary job might even lead to a regular job with the same or a similar employer.

School and Other Employment Services

Only a small percentage of job seekers use school and other special employment services, probably because few job seekers have the service available to them. If you are a student or graduate, find out about any employment services at your school. Some schools provide free career counseling, resume-writing help, referrals to job open-ings, career interest tests, reference materials, Web sites listing job openings, and other services. Special career programs work with veterans, people with disabilities, welfare recipients, union members, professional groups, and many others. So check out these services and consider using them.

Mailing Versus Posting Resumes on the Internet

Many job search experts used to suggest that sending out lots of resumes was a great technique. That advice probably helped sell their resume books, but mailing resumes to people you do not know was never an effective approach. It very rarely works. A recent survey of 1,500 successful job seekers showed that only 2 percent found their positions through sending an unsolicited resume. The same is true for the Internet.

Although mailing your resume to strangers doesn't make much sense, posting it on the Internet might because

- It doesn't take much time.

- Many employers have the potential of finding your resume.

- You can post your resume on niche sites that attract only employers in your field.

- Your Internet resume is easily updated, allowing you to post your current accomplishments.

- You can easily link your resume to projects and Web sites that highlight your accomplishments.

Job searching on the Internet has its limitations, just like other methods. I'll cover resumes in more detail later and provide tips on using the Internet throughout this minibook.

Use the Two Job Search Methods That Work Best

The fact is that most jobs are not advertised, so how do *you* find them? The same way that about two-thirds of all job seekers do: networking with people you know (which I call making warm contacts) and directly

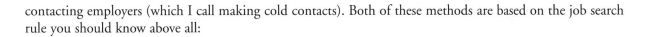
contacting employers (which I call making cold contacts). Both of these methods are based on the job search rule you should know above all:

> **The Most Important Job Search Rule:** Don't wait until the job opens before contacting the employer!

Employers fill most jobs with people they meet before a job is formally open. The trick is to meet people who can hire you before a job is formally available. Instead of asking whether the employer has any jobs open, I suggest that you say, *"I realize you may not have any openings now, but I would still like to talk to you about the possibility of future openings."*

Most Effective Job Search Method 1: Develop a Network of Contacts in Five Easy Stages

Studies find that 60 percent of all people located their jobs through a lead provided by a friend, a relative, or an acquaintance. That makes the people you know your number one source of job leads—more effective than all the traditional methods combined! Developing and using your contacts is called *networking,* and here's how it works:

1. **Make lists of people you know.** Make a thorough list of anyone you are friendly with. Then make a separate list of all your relatives. These two lists alone often add up to 25 to 100 people or more. Next, think of other groups of people that you have something in common with, such as former co-workers or classmates, members of your social or sports groups, members of your professional association, former employers, neighbors, and other groups. You might not know many of these people personally or well, but most will help you if you ask them.

2. **Contact each person in your list in a systematic way.** Obviously, some people will be more helpful than others, but any one of them might help you find a job lead.

3. **Present yourself well.** Begin with your friends and relatives. Call and tell them you are looking for a job and need their help. Be as clear as possible about the type of employment you want and the skills and qualifications you have. Look at the sample JIST Card and phone script later in this step for good presentation ideas.

4. **Ask your contacts for leads.** It is possible that your contacts will know of a job opening that interests you. If so, get the details and get right on it! More likely, however, they will not, so you should ask each person the Three Magic Networking Questions.

> **Quip**
>
> **Most jobs are never advertised because employers don't need to advertise or don't want to.** Employers trust people referred to them by someone they know far more than they trust strangers. And most jobs are filled by referrals and people that the employer knows, eliminating the need to advertise. So, your job search must involve more than looking at ads.

The Three Magic Networking Questions

- **Do you know of any openings for a person with my skills?**

  If the answer is "No" (which it usually is), then ask...

- **Do you know of someone else who might know of such an opening? If your contact does, get that name and ask for another one.**

  If he or she doesn't, ask...

(continued)

(continued)

> ● **Do you know of anyone who might know of someone else who might know of a job opening?**
>
> *Another good way to ask this is* "Do you know someone who knows lots of people?" *If all else fails, this will usually get you a name.*

5. **Contact these referrals and ask them the same questions.** From each person you contact, try to get two names of other people you might contact. Doing this consistently can extend your network of acquaintances by hundreds of people. Eventually, one of these people will hire you or refer you to someone who will!

If you are persistent in following these five steps, networking might be the only job search method you need. It works.

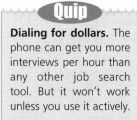

> **Quip**
>
> **Dialing for dollars.** The phone can get you more interviews per hour than any other job search tool. But it won't work unless you use it actively.

> **Quip**
>
> **The phone book's yellow pages provide the most complete, up-to-date listing of potential job search targets you can get.** It organizes them into categories that are very useful for job seekers. Just find a category that interests you, evaluate each listing, and then contact employers that interest you. All it takes is a 30-second phone call. Ask to speak with the hiring authority.

Most Effective Job Search Method 2: Contact Employers Directly

It takes more courage, but making direct contact with employers is a very effective job search technique. I call these cold contacts because people you don't know in advance will need to warm up to your inquiries. Two basic techniques for making cold contacts follow.

Use the yellow pages to find potential employers. Begin by looking at the index in the front of your phone book's yellow pages. For each entry, ask yourself, *"Would an organization of this kind need a person with my skills?"* If you answer *"Yes,"* then that organization or business type is a possible target. You can also rate "Yes" entries based on your interest, writing a "1" next to those that seem very interesting, a "2" next to those that you are not sure of, and a "3" next to those that aren't interesting at all.

Next, select a type of organization that got a "Yes" response and turn to that section of the yellow pages. Call each organization listed there and ask to speak to the person who is most likely to hire or supervise you—typically the manager of the business or a department head—not the personnel or human resources manager. A sample telephone script is included later in this section to give you ideas about what to say.

You can easily adapt this approach for use on the Internet by using sites such as www.yellowpages.com to get contacts anywhere in the world, or you can find phone and e-mail contacts on an employer's own Web site.

Drop in without an appointment. Another effective cold contact method is to just walk into a business or organization that interests you and ask to speak to the person in charge. Although dropping in is particularly effective in small businesses, it also works surprisingly well in larger ones. Remember to ask for an interview even if there are no openings now. If your timing is inconvenient, ask for a better time to come back for an interview.

Most Jobs Are with Small Employers

Businesses and organizations with fewer than 250 employees employ about 72 percent of all U.S. workers. Small organizations are also the source for around 75 percent of the new jobs created each year. They are simply too important to overlook in your job search! Many of them don't have personnel departments, which makes direct contacts even easier and more effective.

Create a Powerful Job Search Tool—the JIST Card®

Look at the sample cards that follow—they are JIST Cards, and they get results. Computer printed or even neatly written on a 3-by-5–inch card, JIST Cards include the essential information employers want to know.

A JIST Card Is a Mini Resume

JIST Cards have been used by thousands of job search programs and millions of people. Employers like their direct and timesaving format, and they have been proven as an effective tool to get job leads. Attach one to your resume. Give them to friends, relatives, and other contacts and ask them to pass them along to others who might know of an opening. Enclose them in thank-you notes after interviews. Leave one with employers as a business card. However you get them in circulation, you may be surprised at how well they work.

You can easily create JIST Cards on a computer and print them on card stock you can buy at any office supply store. Or have a few hundred printed cheaply by a local quick print shop. While they are often done as 3-by-5 cards, they can be printed in any size or format.

Sandy Nolan

Position: General Office/Clerical

Cell phone: (512) 232-9213

Email: snolan@aol.com

More than two years of work experience plus one year of training in office practices. Type 55 wpm, trained in word processing, post general ledger, have good interpersonal skills, and get along with most people. Can meet deadlines and handle pressure well.

Willing to work any hours.

Organized, honest, reliable, and hardworking.

Richard Straightarrow   **Home: (602) 253-9678**
                                             Message: (602) 257-6643
                                             E-mail: RSS@email.com

Objective: Electronics installation, maintenance, and sales

Four years of work experience plus a two-year A.S. degree in Electronics Engineering Technology. Managed a $360,000/year business while going to school full time, with grades in the top 25%. Familiar with all major electronic diagnostic and repair equipment. Hands-on experience with medical, consumer, communication, and industrial electronics equipment and applications. Good problem-solving and communication skills. Customer service oriented.

Willing to do what it takes to get the job done.

Self motivated, dependable, learn quickly.

A JIST Card Can Lead to an Effective Phone Script

The phone is an essential job search tool that can get you more interviews per hour than any other job search tool. But the technique won't work unless you use it actively throughout your search. After you have created your JIST Card, you can use it as the basis for a phone script to make warm or cold calls. Revise your JIST Card content so that it sounds natural when spoken, and then edit it until you can read it out loud in about 30 seconds. The sample phone script that follows is based on the content of a JIST Card. Use it to help you modify your own JIST Card into a phone script.

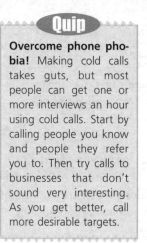

Quip

Overcome phone phobia! Making cold calls takes guts, but most people can get one or more interviews an hour using cold calls. Start by calling people you know and people they refer you to. Then try calls to businesses that don't sound very interesting. As you get better, call more desirable targets.

"Hello. My name is Pam Nykanen. I am interested in a position in hotel management. I have four years' experience in sales, catering, and accounting with a 300-room hotel. I also have an associate degree in hotel management, plus one year of experience with the Brady Culinary Institute. During my employment, I helped double revenues from meetings and conferences and increased bar revenues by 46 percent. I have good problem-solving skills and am good with people. I am also well-organized, hardworking, and detail-oriented. When may I come in for an interview?"

With your script in hand, make some practice calls to warm or cold contacts. If making cold calls, contact the person most likely to supervise you. Then present your script just as you practiced it—without stopping.

Although the sample script assumes that you are calling someone you don't know, you can change it to address warm contacts and referrals. Making cold calls takes courage but works very well for many who are willing to do it.

Use the Internet in Your Job Search

The Internet has limitations as a job search tool. While many have used it to get job leads, it has not worked well for far more. Too many assume they can simply add their resume to resume databases, and employers will line up to hire them. Just like the older approach of sending out lots of resumes, good things sometimes happen, but not often.

I recommend two points that apply to all job search methods, including using the Internet:

- It is unwise to rely on just one or two methods in conducting your job search.

- It is essential that you use an active rather than a passive approach in your job search.

Use More Than One Job Search Method

I encourage you to use the Internet in your job search, but I suggest that you use it along with other techniques. Use the same sorts of job search techniques online as you do offline, including contacting employers directly and building up a network of personal contacts that can help you with your search.

Tips to Increase Your Effectiveness in Internet Job Searches

The following tips can increase the effectiveness of using the Internet in your job search:

- **Be as specific as possible in the job you seek.** This is important in using any job search method, and it's even more important in using the Internet in your job search. The Internet is enormous, so it is essential to be as focused as possible in your search. Narrow your job title or titles to be as specific as possible. Limit your search to specific industries or areas of specialization. Locate and use specialized job banks in your area of interest.

- **Have reasonable expectations.** Success on the Internet is more likely if you understand its limitations and strengths. For example, employers trying to find someone with skills in high demand, such as nurses, are more likely to use the Internet to recruit job candidates.

- **Limit your geographic options.** If you don't want to move or would move only to certain areas, state this preference on your resume and restrict your search to those areas. Many Internet sites allow you to view or search for only those jobs that meet your location criteria.

- **Create an electronic resume.** With few exceptions, resumes submitted on the Internet end up as simple text files with no graphic elements. Employers search databases of many resumes for those that include key words or meet other searchable criteria. So create a simple text resume for Internet use and include words that are likely to be used by employers searching for someone with your abilities. (See Step 4 for more on creating an electronic resume.)

- **Get your resume into the major resume databases.** Most Internet employment sites let you add your resume for free and then charge employers to advertise openings or to search for candidates. Although adding your resume to these databases is not likely to result in job offers, doing so allows you to use your stored resume to easily apply for positions that are posted at these sites. These easy-to-use sites often provide all sorts of useful information for job seekers.

- **Make direct contacts.** Visit the Web sites of organizations that interest you and learn more about them. Many post openings, allow you to apply online, offer information on benefits and work environment, or even provide access to staff who can answer your questions. Even if they don't, you can always search the site or e-mail a request for the name of the person in charge of the work that interests you and then communicate with that person directly.

- **Network.** You can network online, too, finding names and e-mail addresses of potential employer contacts or of other people who might know someone with job openings. Look at and participate in interest groups, professional association sites, alumni sites, chat rooms, e-mail discussion lists, and employer sites—these are just some of the many creative ways to network and interact with people via the Internet.

Check Out Career-Specific Sites First

Thousands of Internet sites provide lists of job openings and information on careers or education. Many have links to other sites that they recommend. Service providers such as America Online (www.aol.com) and the Microsoft Network (www.msn.com) have partnered with sites such as Careerbuilder.com to include career information and job listings plus links to other sites. Also check out www.jist.com and www.CareerOINK.com. Two additional career-related sites are Riley Guide at www.rileyguide.com and Monster.com at www.monster.com.

STEP 4: Write a Simple Resume Now and a Better One Later

Sending out resumes and waiting for responses is not an effective job-seeking technique. But, many employers *will* ask you for a resume, and it can be a useful tool in your job search. I suggest that you begin with a simple resume you can complete quickly. I've seen too many people spend weeks working on a resume when they could have been out getting interviews instead. If you want a better resume, you can work on it on weekends and evenings. So let's begin with the basics.

Tips for Creating a Superior Resume

The following tips make sense for any resume format:

- **Write it yourself.** It's okay to look at other resumes for ideas, but write yours yourself. Doing so will force you to organize your thoughts and background.

- **Make it error-free.** One spelling or grammar error will create a negative impressionist (see what I mean?). Get someone else to review your final draft for any errors. Then review it again because these rascals have a way of slipping in.

- **Make it look good.** Poor copy quality, cheap paper, bad type quality, or anything else that creates a poor appearance will turn off employers to even the best resume content. Get professional help with design and printing if necessary. Many professional resume writers and even print shops offer writing and desktop design services if you need help.

- **Be brief, be relevant.** Many good resumes fit on one page, and few justify more than two. Include only the most important points. Use short sentences and action words. If it doesn't relate to and support the job objective, cut it!

- **Be honest.** Don't overstate your qualifications. If you end up getting a job you can't handle, who does it help? And a lie can result in your being fired later.

- **Be positive.** Emphasize your accomplishments and results. A resume is no place to be too humble or to display your faults.

- **Be specific.** Instead of saying, "I am good with people," say, "I supervised four people in the warehouse and increased productivity by 30 percent." Use numbers whenever possible, such as the number of people served, percentage of sales increase, or amount of dollars saved.

You should also know that everyone feels that he or she is a resume expert. Whatever you do, someone will tell you that it's wrong. Remember that a resume is simply a job search tool.

You should never delay or slow down your job search because your resume is not good enough. The best approach is to create a simple and acceptable resume as quickly as possible and then use it. As time permits, create a better one if you feel you must.

Avoid the resume pile. Resume experts often suggest that a dynamite resume will jump out of the pile. This is old-fashioned advice. It assumes that you are applying to large organizations and for advertised jobs. Today most jobs are with small employers and are not advertised. To avoid joining that stack of resumes in the first place, look for job openings that others overlook.

Writing Chronological Resumes

Most resumes use a chronological format where the most recent experience is listed first, followed by each previous job. This arrangement works fine for someone with work experience in several similar jobs, but not as well for those with limited experience or for career changers.

Look at the two resumes for Judith Jones that follow. Both use the chronological approach.

The first resume would work fine for most job search needs. It could be completed in about an hour.

Notice that the second one includes some improvements. The first resume is good, but most employers would like the additional positive information in the improved resume.

Basic Chronological Resume Example

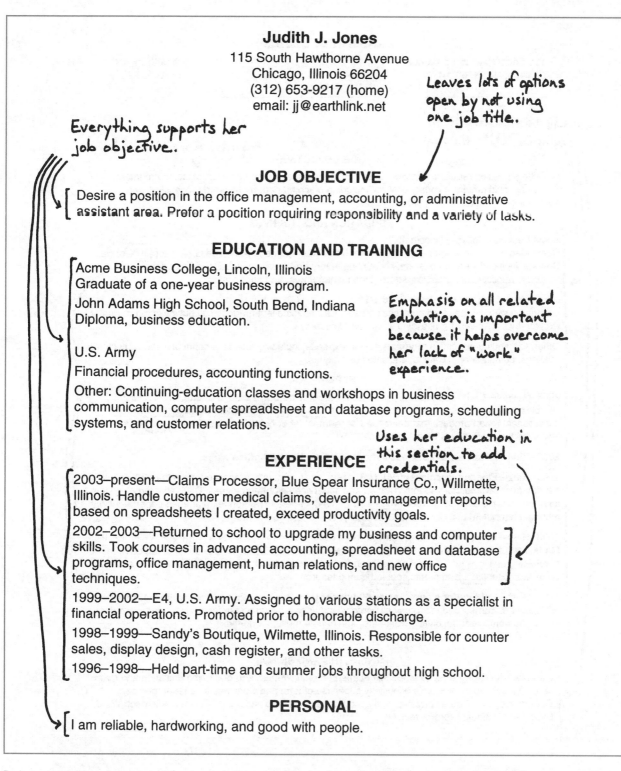

Judith J. Jones

115 South Hawthorne Avenue
Chicago, Illinois 66204
(312) 653-9217 (home)
email: jj@earthlink.net

Everything supports her job objective.

Leaves lots of options open by not using one job title.

JOB OBJECTIVE

Desire a position in the office management, accounting, or administrative assistant area. Prefer a position requiring responsibility and a variety of tasks.

EDUCATION AND TRAINING

Acme Business College, Lincoln, Illinois
Graduate of a one-year business program.

John Adams High School, South Bend, Indiana
Diploma, business education.

U.S. Army
Financial procedures, accounting functions.

Other: Continuing-education classes and workshops in business communication, computer spreadsheet and database programs, scheduling systems, and customer relations.

Emphasis on all related education is important because it helps overcome her lack of "work" experience.

EXPERIENCE

Uses her education in this section to add credentials.

2003–present—Claims Processor, Blue Spear Insurance Co., Willmette, Illinois. Handle customer medical claims, develop management reports based on spreadsheets I created, exceed productivity goals.

2002–2003—Returned to school to upgrade my business and computer skills. Took courses in advanced accounting, spreadsheet and database programs, office management, human relations, and new office techniques.

1999–2002—E4, U.S. Army. Assigned to various stations as a specialist in financial operations. Promoted prior to honorable discharge.

1998–1999—Sandy's Boutique, Wilmette, Illinois. Responsible for counter sales, display design, cash register, and other tasks.

1996–1998—Held part-time and summer jobs throughout high school.

PERSONAL

I am reliable, hardworking, and good with people.

I give some tips you can use when you write your simple chronological resume. Use the preceding resume as your guide.

Improved Chronological Resume Example

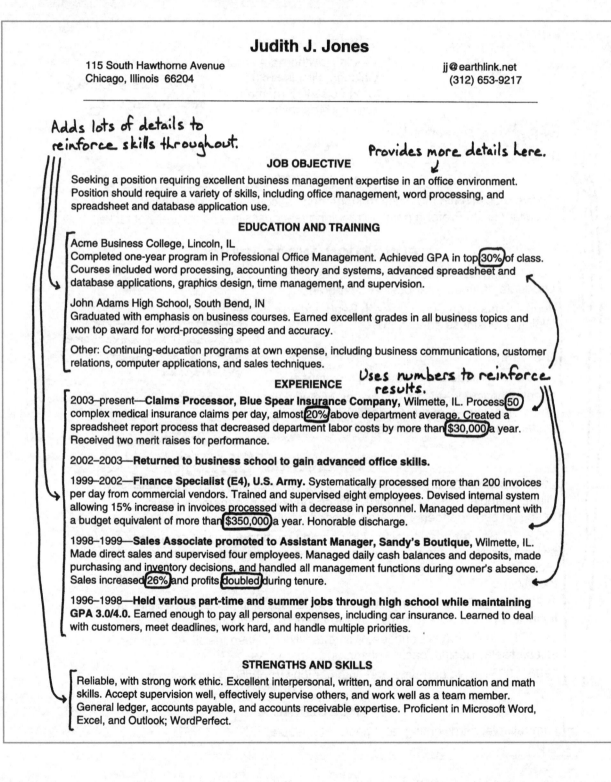

Judith J. Jones

115 South Hawthorne Avenue
Chicago, Illinois 66204

jj@earthlink.net
(312) 653-9217

Adds lots of details to reinforce skills throughout.

Provides more details here.

JOB OBJECTIVE

Seeking a position requiring excellent business management expertise in an office environment. Position should require a variety of skills, including office management, word processing, and spreadsheet and database application use.

EDUCATION AND TRAINING

Acme Business College, Lincoln, IL
Completed one-year program in Professional Office Management. Achieved GPA in top 30% of class. Courses included word processing, accounting theory and systems, advanced spreadsheet and database applications, graphics design, time management, and supervision.

John Adams High School, South Bend, IN
Graduated with emphasis on business courses. Earned excellent grades in all business topics and won top award for word-processing speed and accuracy.

Other: Continuing-education programs at own expense, including business communications, customer relations, computer applications, and sales techniques.

EXPERIENCE

Uses numbers to reinforce results.

2003–present—**Claims Processor, Blue Spear Insurance Company**, Wilmette, IL. Process 50 complex medical insurance claims per day, almost 20% above department average. Created a spreadsheet report process that decreased department labor costs by more than $30,000 a year. Received two merit raises for performance.

2002–2003—**Returned to business school to gain advanced office skills.**

1999–2002—**Finance Specialist (E4), U.S. Army.** Systematically processed more than 200 invoices per day from commercial vendors. Trained and supervised eight employees. Devised internal system allowing 15% increase in invoices processed with a decrease in personnel. Managed department with a budget equivalent of more than $350,000 a year. Honorable discharge.

1998–1999—**Sales Associate promoted to Assistant Manager, Sandy's Boutique**, Wilmette, IL. Made direct sales and supervised four employees. Managed daily cash balances and deposits, made purchasing and inventory decisions, and handled all management functions during owner's absence. Sales increased 26% and profits doubled during tenure.

1996–1998—**Held various part-time and summer jobs through high school while maintaining GPA 3.0/4.0.** Earned enough to pay all personal expenses, including car insurance. Learned to deal with customers, meet deadlines, work hard, and handle multiple priorities.

STRENGTHS AND SKILLS

Reliable, with strong work ethic. Excellent interpersonal, written, and oral communication and math skills. Accept supervision well, effectively supervise others, and work well as a team member. General ledger, accounts payable, and accounts receivable expertise. Proficient in Microsoft Word, Excel, and Outlook; WordPerfect.

Tips for Writing a Simple Chronological Resume

Follow these tips as you write a basic chronological resume:

- **Name.** Use your formal name (not a nickname).

- **Address and contact information.** Avoid abbreviations in your address and include your ZIP code. If you may move, use a friend's address or include a forwarding address. Most employers will not write to you, so provide reliable phone numbers and other contact options. Always include your area code in your phone number because you never know where your resume might travel. Make sure that you have an answering machine or voice mail, and record a professional-sounding message. Include alternative ways to reach you, such as a cell phone and e-mail address.

- **Job objective.** You should almost always have one, even if it is general. Notice how Judith Jones keeps her options open with her broad job objective in her basic resume on page 349. Writing "secretary" or "clerical" might limit her from being considered for other jobs.

- **Education and training.** Include any training or education you've had that supports your job objective. If you did not finish a formal degree or program, list what you did complete and emphasize accomplishments. If your experience is not strong, add details here such as related courses and extracurricular activities. In the two examples, Judith Jones puts her business schooling in both the education and experience sections. Doing this fills a job gap and allows her to present her training as equal to work experience.

- **Previous experience.** Include the basics such as employer name, job title, dates employed, and responsibilities—but emphasize specific skills, results, accomplishments, superior performance, and so on.

- **Personal data.** Do not include irrelevant details such as height, weight, and marital status or a photo. Current laws do not allow an employer to base hiring decisions on these points. Providing this information can cause some employers to toss your resume. You can include information about hobbies or leisure activities in a special section that directly supports your job objective. The first sample includes a Personal section in which Judith lists some of her strengths, which are often not included in a resume.

- **References.** Make sure that each reference will make nice comments about you and ask each to write a letter of recommendation that you can give to employers. You do not need to list your references on your resume. List them on a separate page and give it to employers who ask. If your references are particularly good, however, you can mention this somewhere—the last section is often a good place.

When you have a simple, errorless, and eye-pleasing resume, get on with your job search. There is no reason to delay! If you want to create a better resume in your spare time (evenings or weekends), use the name and contact information you currently have and improve the other sections of the resume.

Tips for an Improved Chronological Resume

Use these tips to improve your simple resume:

- **Job objective.** A poorly written job objective can limit the jobs an employer might consider you for. Think of the skills you have and the types of jobs you want to do; describe them in general terms. Instead of using a narrow job title such as "restaurant manager," you might write "manage a small to mid-sized business."

- **Education and training.** New graduates should emphasize their recent training and education more than those with a few years of related work experience would. A more detailed education and training section might include specific courses you took, and activities or accomplishments that support your job objective or reinforce your key skills. Include other details that reflect how hard you work, such as working your way through school or handling family responsibilities.

- **Skills and accomplishments.** Include those that support your ability to do well in the job you seek now. Even small details count. Maybe your attendance was perfect, you met a tight deadline, or you did the work of others during vacations. Be specific and include numbers—even if you have to estimate them. Judith's improved chronological resume example features more accomplishments and skills. Notice the impact of the numbers to reinforce results.

- **Job titles.** Past job titles may not accurately reflect what you did. For example, your job title may have been "cashier," but you also opened the store, trained new staff, and covered for the boss on vacations. Perhaps "head cashier and assistant manager" would be more accurate. Check with your previous employer if you are not sure.

(continued)

(continued)

- **Promotions.** If you were promoted or got good evaluations, say so—"cashier, promoted to assistant manager," for example. You can list a promotion to a more responsible job as a separate job if doing so results in a stronger resume.
- **Gaps in employment and other problem areas.** Employee turnover is expensive, so few employers want to hire people who won't stay or who won't work out. Gaps in employment, jobs held for short periods, or a lack of direction in the jobs you've held are all concerns for employers. So consider your situation and try to give an explanation of a problem area. Here are a few examples:

2007—Continued my education at...	2006 to present—Self-employed as barn painter and...
2007—Traveled extensively throughout...	2006—Took year off to have first child

Use entire years to avoid displaying employment gaps you can't explain easily. If you had a few months of unemployment at the beginning of 2006 and then began a job in mid-2006, for example, you can list the job as "2006 to 2007."

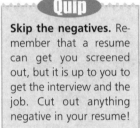

Skip the negatives. Remember that a resume can get you screened out, but it is up to you to get the interview and the job. Cut out anything negative in your resume!

Writing Skills and Combination Resumes

The skills resume emphasizes your most important skills, supported by specific examples of how you have used them. This type of resume allows you to use any part of your life history to support your ability to do the job you want.

While skills resumes can be very effective, creating them requires more work. And some employers don't like them because they can hide a job seeker's faults (such as job gaps, lack of formal education, or little related work experience) better than can a chronological resume. Still, a skills resume may make sense for you.

Look over the sample resumes that follow for ideas. Notice that one resume includes elements of a skills *and* a chronological resume. This so-called combination resume makes sense if your previous job history or education and training are positive.

More Resume Examples

Find resume layout and presentation ideas in the four samples that follow.

The chronological resume sample on page 353 focuses on accomplishments through the use of numbers. While Jon's resume does not say so, it is obvious that he works hard and that he gets results.

The skills resume on page 354 is for a recent high school graduate whose only work experience was at a school office!

The combination resume on page 355 emphasizes Grant's relevant education and transferable skills because he has little work experience in the field.

The electronic resume on page 356 is appropriate for scanning or e-mail submission. It has a plain format that is easily read by scanners. It also has lots of key words that increase its chances of being selected when an employer searches a database.

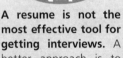

A resume is not the most effective tool for getting interviews. A better approach is to make direct contact with those who hire or supervise people with your skills and ask them for an interview, even if no openings exist now. Then send a resume.

Use the information from your completed Essential Job Search Data Worksheet to write your resume.

The Chronological Resume to Emphasize Results

This simple chronological resume has few but carefully chosen words. It has an effective summary at the beginning, and every word supports his job objective.

Jon Feder

2140 Beach Road
Pompano Beach, Florida 20000

Phone: (222) 333-4444
E-mail: jfeder@com.com

Objective:

Management position in a major hotel

He emphasizes results!

Summary of Experience:

Three years of experience in sales, catering banquet services, and guest relations in a 75 room hotel. Doubled sales revenues from conferences and meetings. Increased dining room and bar revenues by 40%. Won prestigious national and local awards for increased productivity and services.

Experience:

Beachcomber Hotel, Pompano Beach, Florida
Assistant Manager
20XX to Present

Notice his use of numbers to increase the impact of the statements.

- Oversee a staff of 24, including dining room and bar, housekeeping, and public relations operations.
- Introduced new menus and increased dining room revenues by 40%. Awarded *Saveur* magazine's prestigious first place Hotel Cuisine award as a result of my selection of chefs.
- Attracted 58% more bar patrons by implementing Friday night Jazz at the Beach.

Beachcombers' Suites, Hollywood Beach, Florida
Sales and Public Relations
20XX to 20XX

Bullets here and above improve readability and emphasize key points.

- Doubled venues per month from weddings, conferences, and meetings.
- Chosen Chamber of Commerce Newcomer of the Year 20XX for the increase in business within the community.

Education:

Associate Degree in Hotel Management from Sullivan Technical Institute
Certificate in Travel Management from Phoenix University

While Jon had only a few years of related work experience, he used this resume to help him land a very responsible job in a large resort hotel.

The Skills Resume for Those with Limited Work Experience

In this skills resume, each skill directly supports the job objective of this recent high school graduate with very limited work experience.

Catalina A. Garcia
2340 N. Delaware Street · Denver, Colorado 81613
Home: (413) 643-2173 (Leave Message)
Cell phone: (413) 345-2189
E-mail: cagarcia@net.net

Position Desired
Office assistant in a fast-paced business

Note her key skills.

Support for her key skills comes from her activities: school, clubs, and volunteer work.

Skills and Abilities

Communications
Excellent written and verbal presentation skills. Use proper grammar and have a good speaking voice.

Interpersonal
Able to get along well with all types of people. Accept supervision. Received positive evaluation from previous supervisors.

Flexible
Willing to try new things and am interested in improving efficiency on assigned tasks.

Notice the emphasis on adaptive skills.

Attention to Detail
Maintained confidential student records accurately and efficiently. Uploaded 500 student records in one day without errors.

Hard Working
Worked 30 hours per week throughout high school and maintained above-average grades.

She makes good use of numbers.

This statement is very strong.

Student Contact
Cordially dealt with as many as 150 students a day in Dean's office.

Dependable
Never absent or tardy in four years.

Awards
English Department Student of the Year, April 20XX
20XX Outstanding Student Newspaper, Newspaper Association of America

Education
Denver North High School. Took advanced English and communication classes. Member of student newspaper staff and FCCLA for four years. Graduated in top 30% of class.

Other
Girls' basketball team for four years. This taught me discipline, teamwork, how to follow instructions, and hard work. I am ambitious, outgoing, reliable, and willing to work.

Catalina's resume makes it clear that she is talented and hard working.

The Combination Resume for Those Changing Careers

Grant just finished computer programming school and has no work experience in the field. After listing the topics covered in the course, he summarized his employment experience, specifying that he earned promotions quickly. This would be attractive to any employer.

Grant Thomas

717 Carlin Court • Mendelein, IL 60000 • (555) 555-3333
E-mail: gthomas@com.com

Profile

- Outstanding student and tutor
- Winner of international computer software design competition three years
- Capable of being self-directed and independent, but also a team player
- Effective communicator, both orally and written
- Creative problem solver

Education and Training

M.S. in Software Engineering, Massachusetts Institute of Technology, Cambridge, MA
B.S. in Computer Engineering, California State University, Fullerton, CA
A rigorous education that focuses on topics such as

He includes important information that specifies topics he studied.

- Structure and interpretation of computer programs
- Circuits and electronics
- Signals and systems
- Computation structures
- Microelectronic devices and circuits
- Computer system engineering
- Computer language engineering
- Mathematics for computer science
- Analog electronics laboratory
- Digital systems laboratory

The work experiences support the job objective.

Highlights of Experience and Abilities

- Develop, create, and modify general computer applications software.
- Analyze user needs and develop software solutions.
- Confer with system analysts, computer programmers, and others.
- Modify existing software to correct errors.
- Coordinate software system installation and monitor equipment functioning to ensure specifications are met.
- Supervise work of programmers and technicians.
- Train customers and employees to use new and modified software.

Employment History

Software Specialist, First Rate Computers, Mendelein, IL 20XX – Present
- Technician and Customer and Employee Trainer throughout high school
- Promoted to software specialist and worked as a full-time telecommuting employee while completing the B.S. and M.S. degrees

References available on request

The Electronic Resume

William Brown
409 S. Maish Road
Phoenix, AZ 50000

Because this electronic format is to be scanned or e-mailed, it has no bold, bullets, or italics.

Phone message: (300) 444-5567

E-mail: wbrown@email.com

OBJECTIVE

The many key words ensure that the employers' computer searches will select this resume.

Store management career track in car audio store

==
SUMMARY OF SKILLS

Strategic planning, time management, team building,
leadership, problem solving, quality customer service,
conflict resolution, increasing productivity, confident,
outgoing, high performing, aggressive sales

==
EXPERIENCE   *Note the results statements and numbers used below.*

Total of three years in sales

* SHIFT SUPERVISOR, Tech World, Audio Department, Phoenix,
AZ, April 20XX to present: Promoted to Shift Supervisor of
nine salespeople in three months. Responsible for strategic
planning, time management, team building, leadership,
problem solving, quality customer service, conflict
resolution, and increasing productivity. Highest-selling
team for three years.

* AUDIO SALESPERSON, Tech World, Audio Department, Phoenix,
AZ, January 20XX to April 20XX: Arranged display, organized
stockroom, sales to customers, and tracked inventory.
Highest-selling staff member for three months.

==
EDUCATION AND TRAINING

Phoenix High School, top 40% of class

Additional training: Team Building, Franklin Time Management
seminar, Team Building seminar

==
OTHER

* Installed audio systems in 10 cars: family, friends, and
my own.

* Member of United States Autosound Association (USAA)

Use a Career Portfolio to Support Your Resume

Your resume is impressive, but there is another way that you can show prospective employers evidence of who you are and what you can do—a career portfolio.

What Is a Career Portfolio?

Unlike a resume, a career portfolio is a collection of documents that can include a variety of items. Here are some items you may want to place in your portfolio:

- Resume
- School transcripts
- Summary of skills
- Credentials, such as diplomas and certificates of recognition
- Reference letters from school officials and instructors, former employers, or co-workers
- List of accomplishments: Describe hobbies and interests that are not directly related to your job objective and are not included on your resume.
- Examples of your work: Depending on your situation, you can include samples of your art, photographs of a project, audiotapes, videotapes, images of Web pages you developed, and other media that can provide examples of your work.

Place each item on a separate page when you assemble your career portfolio.

Create a Digital Portfolio

A digital portfolio, also known as an electronic portfolio, contains all the information from your career portfolio in an electronic format. This material is then copied onto a CD-ROM or published on a Web site. With a digital portfolio, you can present your skills to a greater number of people than you can your paper career portfolio.

YOUR CAREER PORTFOLIO

On the following lines, list the items you want to include in your career portfolio. Think specifically of those items that show your skills, education, and personal accomplishments.

_____

_____

_____

_____

_____

_____

_____

_____

_____

STEP 5: Redefine What Counts as an Interview, and Then Get Two a Day

The average job seeker gets about five interviews a month—fewer than two a week. Yet many job seekers use the methods in this *Quick Job Search* to get two interviews a day. Getting two interviews a day equals 10 a week and 40 a month. That's 800 percent more interviews than the average job seeker gets. Who do you think will get a job offer quicker?

However, getting two interviews a day is nearly impossible unless you redefine what counts as an interview. If you define an interview in a different way, getting two a day is quite possible.

The New Definition of an Interview: Any face-to-face contact with someone who has the authority to hire or supervise a person with your skills—even if no opening exists at the time you talk with them.

If you use this new definition, it becomes *much* easier to get interviews. You can now interview with all sorts of potential employers, not just those who have job openings now. While most other job seekers look for advertised or actual openings, you can get interviews before a job opens up or before it is advertised and widely known. You will be considered for jobs that may soon be created but that others will not know about. And, of course, you can also interview for existing openings just as everyone else does.

Spending as much time as possible on your job search and setting a job search schedule are important parts of this Step.

Make Your Search a Full-Time Job

Job seekers average fewer than 15 hours a week looking for work. On average, unemployment lasts three or more months, with some people out of work far longer (for example, older workers and higher earners). My many years of experience researching job seeking indicate that the more time you spend on your job search each week, the less time you will likely remain unemployed.

Of course, using the more effective job search methods presented in this minibook also helps. Many job search programs that teach job seekers my basic approach of using more effective methods and spending more time looking have proven that these seekers often find a job in half the average time. More importantly, many job seekers also find better jobs using these methods.

So, if you are unemployed and looking for a full-time job, you should plan to look on a full-time basis. It just makes sense to do so, although many do not, or they start out well but quickly get discouraged. Most job seekers simply don't have a structured plan—they have no idea what they are going to do next Thursday. The plan that follows will show you how to structure your job search like a job.

Decide How Much Time You Will Spend Looking for Work Each Week and Day

First and most importantly, decide how many hours you are willing to spend each week on your job search. You should spend a minimum of 25 hours a week on hard-core job search activities with no goofing around. The following worksheet walks you through a simple but effective process to set a job search schedule for each week.

PLAN YOUR JOB SEARCH WEEK

1. How many hours are you willing to spend each week looking for a job?_____

2. Which days of the week will you spend looking for a job?_____

3. How many hours will you look each day?_____

4. At what times will you begin and end your job search on each of these days?_____

_____

Create a Specific Daily Job Search Schedule

Having a specific daily schedule is essential because most job seekers find it hard to stay productive each day. The sample daily schedule that follows is the result of years of research into what schedule gets the best results. I tested many schedules in job search programs I ran, and this particular schedule worked best.

Consider using a schedule like this sample daily schedule. Why? Because it works.

A Sample Daily Schedule That Works

Time	Activity
7–8 a.m.	Get up, shower, dress, eat breakfast
8–8:15 a.m.	Organize work space, review schedule for today's interviews and promised follow-ups, check e-mail, update schedule as needed
8:15–9 a.m.	Review old leads for follow-up needed today; develop new leads from want ads, yellow pages, the Internet, warm contact lists, and other sources; complete daily contact list
9–10 a.m.	Make phone calls and set up interviews
10–10:15 a.m.	Take a break
10:15–11 a.m.	Make more phone calls, set up more interviews
11 a.m.–Noon	Send follow-up notes and do other office activities as needed
Noon–1 p.m.	Lunch break, relax
1–3 p.m.	Go on interviews, make cold contacts in the field
Evening	Read job search books, make calls to warm contacts not reachable during the day, work on a better resume, spend time with friends and family, exercise, relax

If you are not accustomed to using a daily schedule book or electronic planner, promise yourself to get a good one tomorrow. Choose one that allows for each day's plan on an hourly basis, plus daily to-do lists. Record your daily schedule in advance, and then add interviews as they come. Get used to carrying your planner with you and use it!

You can find a variety of computer programs or pocket-sized electronic schedulers to help organize your job search. If you don't use electronic tools, a simple schedule book and other paper systems will work just fine.

STEP 6: Dramatically Improve Your Interviewing Skills

Interviews are where the job search action is. You have to get them; then you have to do well in them. According to surveys of employers, most job seekers do not effectively present the skills they have to do the job. Even worse, most job seekers can't answer one or more problem questions.

This lack of performance in interviews is one reason why employers will often hire a job seeker who does well in the interview over someone with better credentials. The good news is that you can do simple things to dramatically improve your interviewing skills. This section will emphasize interviewing tips and techniques that make the most difference.

Your First Impression May Be the Only One You Make

Some research suggests that if the interviewer forms a negative impression in the first five minutes of an interview, your chances of getting a job offer approach zero. I know from experience that many job seekers can create a lasting negative impression within seconds.

Tips for Interviewing

Because a positive first impression is so important, I share these suggestions to help you get off to a good start:

- **Make a good impression before you arrive.** Your resume, e-mails, applications, and other written correspondence create an impression before the interview, so make them professional and error-free.
- **Do some homework on the organization before you go.** You can often get information on a business and on industry trends from the Internet or a library.
- **Dress and groom the same way the interviewer is likely to be dressed—but cleaner!** Employer surveys find that almost half of all people's dress or grooming creates an initial negative impression. So this is a big problem. If necessary, get advice on your interviewing outfits from someone who dresses well. Pay close attention to your grooming, too—little things do count.
- **Be early.** Leave in plenty of time to be a few minutes early to an interview.
- **Be friendly and respectful with the receptionist.** Doing otherwise will often get back to the interviewer and result in a quick rejection.
- **Follow the interviewer's lead in the first few minutes.** It's often informal small talk but very important for that person to see how you interact. This is a good time to make a positive comment on the organization or even something you see in the office.
- **Understand that a traditional interview is not a friendly exchange.** In a traditional interview situation, there is a job opening, and you will be one of several applicants for it. In this setting, the employer's task is to eliminate all applicants but one. The interviewer's questions are designed to elicit information that can be used to screen you out. And your objective is to avoid getting screened out. It's hardly an open and honest interaction, is it?

  Setting up interviews before an opening exists eliminates the stress of a traditional interview. In pre-interviews, employers are not trying to screen you out, and you are not trying to keep them from finding out stuff about you. Having said that, knowing how to answer questions that might be asked in a traditional interview is good preparation for any interview you face.
- **Be prepared to answer the tough interview questions.** Your answers to a few key problem questions may determine whether you get a job offer. There are simply too many possible interview questions to cover one by one. Instead, 10 basic questions cover variations of most other interview questions. So, if you can learn to answer the Top 10 Problem Interview Questions well, you will know how to answer most others.
- **Be prepared for the most important interview question of all.** "Why should I hire you?" is the most important question of all to answer well. Do you have a convincing argument why someone should hire you over someone else? If you don't, you probably won't get that job you really want. So think carefully about why someone should hire you and practice your response. Then make sure you communicate this in the interview, even if the interviewer never asks the question in a clear way.

Top 10 Problem Interview Questions

1. Why should I hire you?
2. Why don't you tell me about yourself?
3. What are your major strengths?
4. What are your major weaknesses?
5. What sort of pay do you expect to receive?
6. How does your previous experience relate to the jobs we have here?
7. What are your plans for the future?
8. What will your former employer (or references) say about you?
9. Why are you looking for this type of position, and why here?
10. Why don't you tell me about your personal situation?

Follow the Three-Step Process for Answering Interview Questions

I've developed a three-step process for answering interview questions. I know this might seem too simple, but the three-step process is easy to remember and can help you create a good answer to most interview questions. The technique has worked for thousands of people, so consider trying it.

1. **Understand what is really being asked.**

   Most questions are designed to find out about your self-management skills and personality, but interviewers are rarely this blunt. The employer's *real* question is often one or more of the following:

   - Can I depend on you?

   - Are you easy to get along with?

   - Are you a good worker?

   - Do you have the experience and training to do the job if we hire you?

   - Are you likely to stay on the job for a reasonable period of time and be productive?

   Ultimately, if you don't convince the employer that you will stay and be a good worker, it won't matter if you have the best credentials—he or she won't hire you.

2. **Answer the question briefly in a nondamaging way.** Present the facts of your particular work experience as advantages, not disadvantages. Many interview questions encourage you to provide negative information. One classic question I included in my list of Top 10 Problem Interview Questions was "What are your major weaknesses?" This is obviously a trick question, and many people are just not prepared for it.

   A good response is to mention something that is not very damaging, such as *"I have been told that I am a perfectionist, sometimes not delegating as effectively as I might."*

   But your answer is not complete until you continue with the next step.

3. **Answer the real question by presenting your related skills.** Base your answer on the key skills you have that support the job, and give examples to support these skills. For example, an employer might say to a recent graduate, *"We were looking for someone with more experience in this field. Why should we consider you?"* Here is one possible answer:

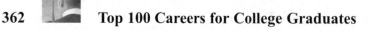
"I'm sure there are people who have more experience, but I do have more than six years of work experience, including three years of advanced training and hands-on experience using the latest methods and techniques. Because my training is recent, I am open to new ideas and am used to working hard and learning quickly."

In the previous example (about your need to delegate), a good skills statement might be

"I've been working on this problem and have learned to let my staff do more, making sure that they have good training and supervision. I've found that their performance improves, and it frees me up to do other things."

Whatever your situation, learn to answer questions that present you well. It's essential to communicate your skills during an interview, and the three-step process can help you answer problem questions and dramatically improve your responses. It works!

How to Earn a Thousand Dollars a Minute

What do you do when the employer asks, "How much money would it take to get you to join our company?"

Tips on Negotiating Pay

Remember these few essential tips when it comes time to negotiate your pay:

- **The Number 1 Salary Negotiation Rule: The person who names a specific amount first loses.**
- **The only time to negotiate is after you have been offered the job.** Employers want to know how much you want to be paid so that they can eliminate you from consideration. They figure if you want too much, you won't be happy with their job and won't stay. And if you will take too little, they may think you don't have enough experience. So never discuss your salary expectations until an employer offers you the job.
- **If pressed, speak in terms of wide pay ranges.** If you are pushed to reveal your pay expectations early in an interview, ask the interviewer what the normal pay range is for this job. Interviewers will often tell you, and you can say that you would consider offers in this range.

  If you are forced to be more specific, speak in terms of a wide pay range. If you figure that the company will likely pay from $20,000 to $25,000 a year, for example, say that you would consider "any fair offer in the low to mid-twenties." This statement covers the employer's range and goes a bit higher. If all else fails, tell the interviewer that you would consider any reasonable offer.

  For this tip to work, you must know in advance what the job is likely to pay. You can get this information by asking people who do similar work, or from a variety of books and Internet sources of career information.
- **If you want the job, you should say so.** This is no time to be playing games.
- **Don't say "no" too quickly.** Never, ever turn down a job offer during an interview! Instead, thank the interviewer for the offer and ask to consider the offer overnight. You can turn it down tomorrow, saying how much you appreciate the offer and asking to be considered for other jobs that pay better or whatever. And it is okay to ask for additional pay or other concessions. But if you simply can't accept the offer, say why and ask the interviewer to keep you in mind for future opportunities. You just never know.

STEP 7: Follow Up on all Job Leads

It's a fact: People who follow up with potential employers and with others in their network get jobs more quickly than those who do not.

Thank-You Notes Make a Difference

Although thank-you notes can be e-mailed, most people appreciate and are more impressed by a mailed note. Here are some tips about mailed thank-you notes that you can easily adapt to e-mail use:

- You can handwrite or type thank-you notes on quality paper and matching envelopes.
- Keep the notes simple, neat, and error-free.
- Make sure to include a few copies of your JIST Card in the envelope.

Here is an example of a simple thank-you note.

April 5, XXXX

Mr. Kijek,

Thanks so much for your willingness to see me next Wednesday at 9 a.m. I know that I am one of many who are interested in working with your organization. I appreciate the opportunity to meet you and learn more about the position.

I've enclosed a JIST Card that presents the basics of my skills for this job and will bring my resume to the interview. Please call me if you have any questions at all.

Sincerely,

Bruce Vernon

Use Job Lead Cards to Follow Up

If you use contact management software, use it to schedule follow-up activities. But the simple paper system I describe here can work very well or can be adapted for setting up your contact management software.

- Use a simple 3-by-5–inch card to record essential information about each person in your network.
- Buy a 3-by-5–inch card file box and tabs for each day of the month.
- File the cards under the date you want to contact the person.
- Follow through by contacting the person on that date.

I've found that staying in touch with a good contact every other week can pay off big. Here's a sample card to give you ideas about creating your own.

```
ORGANIZATION: _Mutual Health Insurance_____
CONTACT PERSON: _Anna Tomey_____    PHONE: _317-355-0216____
SOURCE OF LEAD: _Aunt Ruth_____
NOTES: _4/10 Called. Anna on vacation. Call back 4/15. 4/15 Interview set_
    _4/20 at 1:30. 4/20 Anna showed me around. They use the same computers_
    _we used in school! (Friendly people.) Sent thank-you note and JIST_
    _Card, call back 5/1. 5/1 Second interview 5/8 at 9 a.m.!_
```

In Closing

This is a short book, but it may be all you need to get a better job in less time. I hope this will be true for you, and I wish you well in your search. Remember this: You won't get a job offer because someone knocks on your door and offers one. Job seeking does involve luck, but you are more likely to have good luck if you are out getting interviews.

I'll close this minibook with a few final tips:

- **Approach your job search as if it were a job itself.** Create and stick to a daily schedule, and spend at least 25 hours a week looking.

- **Follow up on each lead you generate and ask each contact for referrals.**

- **Set out each day to schedule at least two interviews.** Remember the new definition of an interview—an interview includes talking to potential employers who don't have an opening now.

- **Send out lots of thank-you notes and JIST Cards.**

- **When you want the job, tell the employer that you want it and why you should be hired over everyone else.**

Don't get discouraged. There are lots of jobs out there, and someone needs an employee with your skills—your job is to find that someone.

I wish you luck in your job search and in your life.

ESSENTIAL JOB SEARCH DATA WORKSHEET

Take some time to complete this worksheet carefully. It will help you write your resume and answer interview questions. You can also photocopy it and take it with you to help complete applications and as a reference throughout your job search. Use an erasable pen or pencil to allow for corrections. Whenever possible, emphasize skills and accomplishments that support your ability to do the job you want. Use extra sheets as needed.

Your name_____

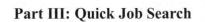
Date completed_____

Job objective_____

Key Accomplishments

List three accomplishments that best prove your ability to do the kind of job you want.

1. _____

2. _____

3. _____

Education and Training

Name of high school(s) and specific years attended_____

Subjects related to job objective_____

_____

Related extracurricular activities/hobbies/leisure activities_____

_____

Accomplishments/things you did well_____

_____

Specific things you can do as a result_____

_____

Schools you attended after high school, specific years attended, and degrees/certificates earned_____

_____

Courses related to job objective_____

_____

Related extracurricular activities/hobbies/leisure activities_____

_____

Accomplishments/things you did well_____

_____

Specific things you can do as a result_____

_____

Other Training

Include formal or informal learning, workshops, military training, skills you learned on the job or from hobbies—anything that will help support your job objective. Include specific dates, certificates earned, or other details as needed._____

_____

(continued)

(continued)

Work and Volunteer History

List your most recent job first, followed by each previous job. Military experience, unpaid or volunteer work, and work in a family business should be included here, too. If needed, use additional sheets to cover *all* significant paid or unpaid work experiences. Emphasize details that will help support your new job objective. Include numbers to support what you did: the number of people served over one or more years, number of transactions processed, percentage of sales increased, total inventory value you were responsible for, payroll of the staff you supervised, total budget responsible for, and so on. Emphasize results you achieved, using numbers to support them whenever possible. Mentioning these things on your resume and in an interview will help you get the job you want.

Job 1

Dates employed _____

Name of organization _____

Supervisor's name and job title _____

Address _____

Phone number/e-mail address/Web site _____

What did you accomplish and do well? _____

_____

Things you learned; skills you developed or used _____

_____

Raises, promotions, positive evaluations, awards _____

_____

Computer software, hardware, and other equipment you used _____

_____

Other details that might support your job objective _____

_____

Job 2

Dates employed _____

Name of organization _____

Supervisor's name and job title _____

Address _____

Phone number/e-mail address/Web site _____

What did you accomplish and do well? _____

_____

Things you learned; skills you developed or used _____

_____

Raises, promotions, positive evaluations, awards_____

_____

Computer software, hardware, and other equipment you used_____

_____

Other details that might support your job objective_____

_____

Job 3

Dates employed_____

Name of organization_____

Supervisor's name and job title_____

Address_____

Phone number/e-mail address/Web site_____

What did you accomplish and do well?_____

_____

Things you learned; skills you developed or used_____

_____

Raises, promotions, positive evaluations, awards_____

_____

Computer software, hardware, and other equipment you used_____

_____

Other details that might support your job objective_____

_____

References

Think of people who know your work well and will be positive about your work and character. Past supervisors are best. Contact them and tell them what type of job you want and your qualifications, and ask what they will say about you if contacted by a potential employer. Some employers will not provide references by phone, so ask them for a letter of reference in advance. If a past employer may say negative things, negotiate what they will say or get written references from others you worked with there.

Reference name_____

Position or title_____

Relationship to you_____

Contact information (complete address, phone number, e-mail address)_____

_____

(continued)

(continued)

Reference name_____

Position or title_____

Relationship to you_____

Contact information (complete address, phone number, e-mail address)_____

_____

Reference name_____

Position or title_____

Relationship to you_____

Contact information (complete address, phone number, e-mail address)_____

_____

A Short List of Additional Resources

Thousands of books and countless Internet sites provide information on career subjects. Space limitations do not permit me to describe the many good resources available, so I list here some of the most useful ones. Because this is my list, I've included books I've written or that JIST publishes. You should be able to find these and many other resources at libraries, bookstores, and Web bookselling sites.

Resume and Cover Letter Books

My books. *The Quick Resume & Cover Letter Book* is one of the top-selling resume books at various large bookstore chains. It is very simple to follow, is inexpensive, has good design, and has good sample resumes written by professional resume writers. For more in-depth but still quick help, check out my two books in the *Help in a Hurry* series: *Same-Day Resume* (with advice on creating a simple resume in an hour and a better one later) and *15-Minute Cover Letter,* co-authored with Louise Kursmark (offering sample cover letters and tips for writing them fast and effectively).

Other books published by JIST. The following titles include many sample resumes written by professional resume writers, as well as good advice: *Amazing Resumes* by Jim Bright and Joanne Earl; *Cover Letter Magic* by Wendy S. Enelow and Louise M. Kursmark; the entire *Expert Resumes* series by Enelow and Kursmark; *Federal Resume Guidebook* by Kathryn Kraemer Troutman; *Gallery of Best Resumes, Gallery of Best Cover Letters,* and other books by David F. Noble; and *Résumé Magic* by Susan Britton Whitcomb.

Job Search and Interviewing Books

My books. You may want to check out my two books in the *Help in a Hurry* series: *Seven-Step Job Search* (even more tips and step-by-step guidance to cut your job search time in half) and *Next-Day Job Interview* (quick tips for preparing for a job interview at the last minute). *The Very Quick Job Search* is a thorough book with detailed advice and a "quick" section of key tips you can finish in a few hours. *Getting the Job You Really Want* includes many in-the-book activities and good career decision-making and job search advice.

Other books published by JIST. Titles include *Inside Secrets of Finding a Teaching Job* by Warner, Bryan, and Warner; *Insider's Guide to Finding a Job* by Wendy S. Enelow and Shelly Goldman; *Job Search Handbook for People with Disabilities* by Daniel J. Ryan; *Job Search Magic* and *Interview Magic* by Susan Britton Whitcomb; *Ultimate Job Search* by Richard H. Beatty; and *Over-40 Job Search Guide* by Gail Geary.

Books with Information on Jobs

The primary reference books. The *Occupational Outlook Handbook* is the source of job titles listed in this book. Published by the U.S. Department of Labor and updated every other year, the *OOH* covers about 90 percent of the workforce. The *O*NET Dictionary of Occupational Titles* book has descriptions for more than 1,000 jobs based on the O*NET (Occupational Information Network) database developed by the Department of Labor. The *Enhanced Occupational Outlook Handbook* includes the *OOH* descriptions plus more than 7,000 additional descriptions of related jobs from the O*NET and other sources. The *New Guide for Occupational Exploration* allows you to explore major jobs based on your interests.

Other books published by JIST. Here are a few good books that include job descriptions and helpful details on career options: *Overnight Career Choice, Best Jobs for the 21st Century, 50 Best Jobs for Your Personality, 40 Best Fields for Your Career, 200 Best Jobs for College Graduates,* and *300 Best Jobs Without a Four-Year Degree.*

Internet Resources

There are too many Web sites to list, but here are a few places you can start. A book by Anne Wolfinger titled *Best Career and Education Web Sites* gives unbiased reviews of the most helpful sites and ideas on how to use them. *Job Seeker's Online Goldmine,* by Janet Wall, lists the extensive free online job search tools from government and other sources. This book's job descriptions also include Internet addresses for related organizations. And www.jist.com lists recommended sites for career, education, and related topics, along with comments on each. Be aware that some Web sites provide poor advice, so ask your librarian, instructor, or counselor for suggestions on those best for your needs.

Other Resources

Libraries. Most libraries have the books mentioned here, as well as many other resources. Many also provide Internet access so that you can research online information. Ask the librarian for help finding what you need.

People. People who hold the jobs that interest you are one of the best career information sources. Ask them what they like and don't like about their work, how they got started, and the education or training needed. Most people are helpful and will give advice you can't get any other way.

Career Counseling. A good vocational counselor can help you explore career options. Take advantage of this service if it is available to you! Also consider a career-planning course or program, which will encourage you to be more thorough in your thinking.

Sample Resumes for Some of the Top Careers for College Graduates

If you read the previous information, you know that I believe you should not depend on a resume alone in your job search. Even so, you will most likely need one, and you should have a good one.

Unlike some career authors, I do not preach that there is only one right way to do a resume. I encourage you to be an individual and to do what you think will work well for you. But I also know that some resumes are clearly better than others. The following pages contain some resumes that you can use as examples when preparing your own resume.

Each resume was written by a professional resume writer who is a member of one or more professional associations. These writers are highly qualified and hold various credentials. Most will provide help (for a fee) and welcome your contacting them (although this is not a personal endorsement).

The resumes appear in books published by JIST Works, including the following:

- *Best Resumes for College Students and New Grads* by Louise M. Kursmark

- *Expert Resumes for Computer and Web Jobs* by Louise M. Kursmark

- *Expert Resumes for Health Care Careers* by Wendy S. Enelow and Louise M. Kursmark

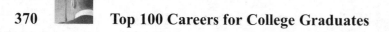
- *Expert Resumes for Teachers and Educators* by Wendy S. Enelow and Louise M. Kursmark

- *Gallery of Best Resumes* by David F. Noble

Contact Information for Resume Contributors

The following professional resume writers contributed resumes to this section. Their names are listed in alphabetical order. Each entry indicates which resume that person contributed.

Ann Baehr
Best Resumes of New York
East Islip, NY 11730
Phone: (631) 224-9300
Fax: (916) 314-6871
E-mail: resumesbest@earthlink.net
Web site: www.e-bestresumes.com
or www.nyresumewriter.com
Resume on pages 381–382

Janet L. Beckstrom, CPRW
Owner, Word Crafter
1717 Montclair Ave.
Flint, MI 48503
Toll-free: 800-351-9818
Fax: (810) 232-9257
E-mail: wordcrafter@voyager.net
Resume on page 383

Kristin Coleman
Career Services
44 Hillcrest Dr.
Poughkeepsie, NY 12603
Phone: (845) 452-8274
Fax: (845) 452-7789
E-mail:
kristincoleman44@yahoo.com
Resume on page 384

**Laura A. DeCarlo, MCD, CCM,
CERW, JCTC, CECC, CCMC**
President, A Competitive Edge
Career Service
1665 Clover Circle
Melbourne, FL 32935
Phone: (321) 752-0880
Toll-free: (800) 715-3442
Fax: (321) 752-7513
E-mail: getanedge@aol.com
Web site:
www.anexecutiveedge.com
Resume on page 373

Michele Haffner, CPRW, JCTC
Advanced Resume Services
1314 W. Paradise Ct.
Glendale, WI 53209
Phone: (414) 247-1677
Fax: (414) 247-1808
E-mail:
michele@resumeservices.com
www.resumeservices.com
Resume on pages 385–386

**Jennifer Rushton Keraijen,
CARW, CEIC**
Certified Advanced Resume Writer
Level 14, 309 Kent St.
Sydney NSW 2000, Australia
Phone: 61 2 9994 8050
E-mail: info@keraijen.com.au
Web site: www.keraijen.com.au
Resume on pages 377–378

Jeanne Knight, JCTC, CCMC
Career and Job Search Coach
P.O. Box 760828
Melrose, MA 02176
Phone: (617) 968-7747
E-mail: jeanne@careerdesigns.biz
Web site: www.careerdesigns.biz
Resume on page 374

**Myriam-Rose Kohn, CPRW,
IJCTC, CCM, CCMC, CEIP,
CPBS**
President, JEDA Enterprises
27201 Tourney Rd., Ste. 201
Valencia, CA 91355-1857
Phone: (661) 253-0801
Toll-free: (800) 600-JEDA
Fax: (661) 253-0744
E-mail: myriam-rose
@jedaenterprises.com

Web site:
http://jedaenterprises.com/
Resume on pages 371–372

Diana C. LeGere
Executive Director, Writing Flair
P.O. Box 634
Colonial Heights, VA 23834
Phone: (804) 720-7236
E-mail: DianaLeGere@aol.com
www.dianalegere.com
Resume on pages 375–376

**Sharon Pierce-Williams, M.Ed.,
CPRW**
President, The Resume.Doc
609 Lincolnshire Ln.
Findlay, OH 45840
Phone: (419) 422-0228
Fax: (419) 425-1185
E-mail:
Sharon@TheResumeDoc.com
Web Site:
www.TheResumeDoc.com
Resume on pages 379–380

**Janice Shepherd, CPRW, JCTC,
CEIP**
Write On Career Keys
Bellingham, WA 98226-4260
Phone: (360) 738-7958
Fax: (360) 738-1189
E-mail:
Janis@writeoncareerkeys.com
Web site:
www.writeoncareerkeys.com
Resume on page 387

Architects, Except Landscape and Naval

LINDA A. BUILDER
Licensed Architect

1227 Oak Avenue
Lantern, Texas 77391

331 271-9952
facsimile: 331 271-9953

ARCHITECT / PROJECT MANAGER with experience in the planning, design, and construction of diverse project renovations (major and minor) and architecture projects such as institutional, recreational, and health care facilities. Extensive background in **urbanism** and all infrastructure directing all project phases, from design through completion of construction, coordinating the efforts of contractors; architectural, engineering, and landscaping consultants; and government agencies. Excellent technical qualifications complement an **innate sense of creativity** in the design of aesthetically attractive, architecturally strong, and utilitarian space. Highly organized and proficient in AutoCAD. Meticulous, detail-oriented, perfectionist; work well under pressure.

AREAS OF PROFICIENCY

Experienced in all phases of design from program definition through working drawing; expertise in
- Construction estimating, cost analysis, feasibility studies, and project budgeting;
- Negotiation and contract administration;
- Inspection and supervision of construction.

► Solid design and construction experience in commercial projects, including landscaping, office buildings, schools, churches, hotels, and restaurants.

► Established a **regional reputation** for excellence and developed a loyal following. Highly successful for project profitability and investor ROI.

► Strong **management skills,** including personnel and project scheduling, employee and subcontractor supervision, budgeting and finance, problem solving, client relations, and quality control.

► Seasoned **sales and marketing skills.** Demonstrated ability to gain trust and confidence of prospects. Personable and highly ethical.

► Proven **communications ability** that is straightforward, honest, and articulate, yet tactful and diplomatic. Sincere sensitivity to unique needs and aspirations of all segments of a community. Active listening and consultation skills with talent for respecting and responding to divergent opinions and interests. Strength in blending idealism with political reality, and devising new methods to improve procedural and system efficiency.

► Computer literate: Microsoft PowerPoint, Adobe PageMaker, CorelDRAW, Harvard Graphics.

► Fully bilingual: Spanish and English.

CAREER HIGHLIGHTS

ARCHITECT
Planin Consultores, S.A., Caracas, Venezuela

1999   Designed, drafted, and supervised the building project for the new Emergency area for Adults and Pediatrics at the Hospital Clinico de Caracas.

1997   Remodeled living quarters on the second floor of the Caracas Hospital (4 models).

(continued)

(continued)

LINDA A. BUILDER   Page 2

1996   Designed individual family units for private owner.
        Participated in all project phases from initial client contact and presentation through
        conceptual design; production of contract documents; interface with engineers and
        outside planning consultants; and development of interiors, finishes, and specifications.

1996   Key member of design team responsible for the renovation of the Adult Emergency area
        at the Public (County) Hospital in Caracas (Hospital Universitario de Caracas). While
        work was in progress, intervened and adjusted the specifications to improve production.

ARCHITECT
G.P. Arquitectura, S.A., Valencia, Venezuela

1998   Assigned as architect in charge for the Main Control Room project at the Energia
        Eléctrica (Electrical Energy) of Venezuela (ENELVEN / CAUJARITO), approximately
        1000 mt2.

1996   Designed and drafted the remodeling of the main offices at the Investment Bank of
        Welles Orvitz. Served as director of field operations. Reviewed project specifications,
        researched previous designs, and prepared designs for customer presentation and
        approval. Maintained in-house library of design materials and references.

ARCHITECT
Faculty of Architecture, University of Apure, Cabimas, Venezuela

1992–1995   Supervising Architect on several relocation projects, among which were the communities
             of *El Hornito* (252 acres, $300 million budget, 325 houses from 7 different models,
             church, elementary school, community center, clinic, and fishing processing center) and
             Villa Hermosa.

Reviewed development proposals for adherence to county zoning and other ordinances,
and aesthetically based design guidelines. Dealt with

- zoning administration
- site plan review and approval
- subdivision regulation
- wastewater distribution
- design ordinance administration
- economic development
- historic preservation
- environmental impact and planning
- policy analysis
- community development
- stormwater drainage
- surface hydrology
- parking lot design
- environmental impact
- public relations
- urban redevelopment
- administrative management

Directed and facilitated the design and construction of new development projects
and improvements to transportation facilities, streets, sidewalks, and utility systems.
Coordinated/supervised an interdisciplinary team of professional consultants and
construction inspectors to meet individual project time and cost objectives. Analyzed
impediments to project goals; quickly identified and implemented solutions.

Prepared graphic files for inspection and critical path schedules; analyzed construction
schedules from contractors. Monitored project construction daily and represented the
interests of client at progress meetings. Prepared design revisions when required by
unknown field conditions. Analyzed requirements of plans and specifications to deny or
justify claims by contractors for extra work. Facilitated public involvement in planning
decisions by communicating merits of project(s), which in turn promoted community good
will and continued support. Explained or modified construction activity to respond to
public concern. Assisted with final project designs and construction drawings.

Computer Software Engineers

TANYA KIRKPATRICK

578 14th Street, #3
Tampa, FL 33609

(813) 967-1408
tanya.kirk@browsenet.com

PROGRAMMER / SOFTWARE ENGINEER

PROFILE OF QUALIFICATIONS

Cited as *"a keen technical intellect who consistently makes the grade through innovation and the perfect eye for finding coding flaws."* - Jerry Drake, Director

- Results-oriented software engineer who adapts easily to requirements in mainframe and PC application development.
- Consistently commended for ability to work as a team member or independently while achieving critical deadlines. Strong project leader.
- Recognized for performance and project contributions. Consistently achieve highest rating in annual evaluations for top 2% of total company personnel.

TECHNICAL APPLICATIONS

- Programming Languages: C, C++, COBOL, SQL, CICS, Lotus Notes application development, FORTRAN, C-Shell, Java, HSPICE and Matlab.
- Platforms: Windows NT, Unix, OS/2, Windows 95 and Windows 98.
- Software: MS Word, Excel, PowerPoint and Access; various other programs.
- Experienced in developing Graphical User Interfaces (GUIs).

EDUCATION & TRAINING

B.S. in Computer Information Systems, University of South Florida, Tampa, FL
- Courses: **Coding for Tomorrow, Java, SQL and Images, Copyrights and the Web**

PROFESSIONAL EXPERIENCE

Senior Programmer, Carco Corporation, Orlando, FL - 1994 to Present
Performed multifaceted programming and analysis from code development through acceptance testing on a number of projects.

- Developed special applications in C++ to customize office business systems.
  - Enhanced existing software subsystems to accommodate new requirements.

- Developed a graphical user interface (GUI) for an analog design automation tool in a Unix environment.

  - Interface communicated with a range of C programs to transfer input parameters provided by user and to display programs' output on the screen.

Software Analyst and Programmer I, Carco Corporation, Orlando, FL - 1992 to 1994

- Analyzed all company-designed software programs for Y2K compliance.
- Led a consulting team in the analysis of customer operating systems and software applications. Made suggestions for software changes and customization to existing programs.

Engineers

SEAN L. STEEPER

17 Woodcliff Road
Westboro, MA 01581

Home: 333-333-3333
slsteeper@hotmail.com

INDUSTRIAL ENGINEER
New Product Design • Manufacturing Process Redesign • Project Management

EDUCATION

University of Massachusetts ~ Amherst, MA
B.S. Industrial Engineering ~ Graduated with Honors ~ May 2003

RELEVANT COURSEWORK

Engineering Design • Systems Engineering • Computer Integrated Manufacturing • Production Systems
Production Engineering • Operations Research • Oral and Visual Communications
Industrial Psychology • Ergonomics • Quality Management

ACADEMIC PROJECTS

- Researched and recommended alternative methods for coating coronary stents for a leading manufacturer of cardiovascular products. Designed and manufactured prototype for spray-coating each stent, as opposed to the current practice of dipping them, which resulted in a 25% reduction in defects.
- Designed a facility and assembly-line layout to optimize production for an electronics products company.
- Generated a comprehensive Safety and Development Plan for a medical devices company.
- Created an ergonomically efficient material-handling trolley.

ENGINEERING EXPERIENCE

ABC Cardiovascular, Amherst, MA   5/02–10/02
Industrial Engineer, Co–Op

- Designed, developed, and implemented a unique device for facilitating the movement of coronary stent and catheter products from one workstation to another, resulting in a 20% decrease in scrapped product.
- Revised and simplified the Standard Operating Procedure for a label-printing machine that included detailed, easy-to-follow troubleshooting procedures and digital photographs.
- Analyzed production reports associated with a crimping machine and successfully identified one product that was consistently more prone to defects than others. Recommended machine adjustments to alleviate defects.
- Optimized floor space by rearranging and redesigning four production cells within a tightly constricted space.
- Member of a team to prepare for a critical FDA audit. Ensured machines were fully validated and safety guards were properly and securely in place.

ADDITIONAL EXPERIENCE

Albright Roofing and Painting, Framingham, MA   9/03–Present
Construction Laborer—Contribute to roofing and home painting projects.

Dunmore Plastering, Southboro, MA   Summers 01 and 03
Plasters Foreman—Organized and monitored building materials and inventory levels.

Independently Employed, Amherst, MA   1/99–5/01
Agricultural Contractor—Performed agricultural contract work for farmers.

Librarians

MICHAEL MILLER

458 North Western Avenue, Salt Lake City, UT 84117 • Phone (801) 277-5555
E-mail: mmiller237@hotlink.com

INFORMATION SERVICES LIBRARIAN

PROFILE

Articulate, organized Librarian with more than 10 years of experience in all facets of Library Science–related work. Expertise in utilizing the World Wide Web as a tool for research and analysis. Skilled instructor of various workshops including The World Wide Web, The Internet, Electronic Databases, and Bibliographic Software. Excellent presentation skills. Advanced computer literacy.

TECHNICAL SKILLS

- Microsoft Office (Word, Excel, and PowerPoint) • WordPerfect, Lotus Notes
- NOTIS Library System • Arc View, Photoshop, FrontPage, UNIX, HTML
- Internet • Voyager Library System • Verity Search Engine
- LEXIS/NEXIS, OCLC

EDUCATION

Master of Library Science, University of Utah (1999)
Graduate coursework in Sociology, University of Phoenix (1997–1998)
Bachelor of Science in Sociology, Utah College (1996)
  - Dean's List
  - Received Dawson Scholarship (1989)
School of Library & Information Science, Catholic University (1993)

SPECIAL PROJECTS AND ACCOMPLISHMENTS

- Achieved Above and Beyond Peer Recognition Award for Library Service (1997).
- Presenter at Utah State Library Conference for University of Utah College faculty (2000). Topic: Integrating Technology into the Classroom via the Internet.
- Presenter at Utah Educational Research Association Annual Conference (1999).
- Spearheaded retrospective conversion of U.S. government documents for University of Utah Acquisitions Department.
- Pioneered Rio Grande Learning Center for homeless mothers. Managed and directed resource selection, furniture, and computer needs, and gathered potential funding resources for materials.

(continued)

MICHAEL MILLER   Page 2

PROFESSIONAL EXPERIENCE

Salt Lake City Main Library, Salt Lake City, UT   1999–2005
INTERNET LIBRARIAN
- Collaborated with instructors in teaching specialized topics. Prepared and delivered workshops.
- Coordinated reference queries via phone and e-mail.
- Managed and directed website development for several websites including creation of intellectual content of SLC Library web pages.
- Wrote documentation for Rio Grande Learning Center and facilitated operation.
- Oversaw support staff in departmental area.

Alderman Library, University of Utah, Salt Lake City, UT   1998–1999
REFERENCE LIBRARIAN
- Administered direction and answers to reference questions.
- Created Alderman Library website and consulted on development of web-based tutorials.
- Prepared study aids and bibliographies.

Huntsman Library, Provo University, Provo, UT   1996–1998
REFERENCE LIBRARIAN
- Maintained e-mail inquiries in reference to cancer.
- Updated and coordinated cancer reference materials and catalog files.
- Troubleshot and maintained library equipment.

Science/Engineering Library, University of Utah, Salt Lake City, UT   1994–1995
REFERENCE PRACTICUM
- Utilized print, electronic medium, and online resources to assist patrons with reference questions.
- Conducted on-site instruction for use of various reference resources.
- Oversaw archives, periodicals, and circulation.

Cabal Library, Virginia Commonwealth University, Richmond, VA   1993–1994
REFERENCE LIBRARIAN/WEEKEND COORDINATOR
- Trained and supervised student employees in Circulation/Reserve Department.
- Coordinated workflow, shelving, and circulation.
- Handled billing procedures.

PROFESSIONAL AFFILIATIONS

- American Library Association
- Utah Library Association
- Task Force member, Salt Lake City Library and Information Network (2001)

Physicians and Surgeons

MICHELLE JONES, M.D.

98 Ben Franklin Drive
P.O. Box 219
Cherry Hill, New Jersey 07896   mjones@aol.com

Home: (609) 654–1040
Cell: (609) 654–5809
Home Fax: (609) 654–1755

HEALTHCARE PHYSICIAN

Senior Medical Resident in Internal Medicine with extensive knowledge of community medical diagnostic and patient care services in various settings, including inpatient and outpatient clinics, and government/private hospitals and clinics. Strong understanding of current principles, methods, and procedures for the delivery of medical evaluation, diagnosis, and treatment in women's healthcare, including rotation in OB/GYN. Outstanding interpersonal and cross-cultural communication skills: Fluent in English, Romanian, and French, combined with a basic command of Hungarian.

- ☑ Obstetrics/gynecology
- ☑ General surgery
- ☑ Internal medicine
- ☑ Infectious diseases
- ☑ Hospital medical service
- ☑ Private practice experience

- ☑ Pediatrics
- ☑ Outpatient clinic/office
- ☑ Emergency room experience
- ☑ Rheumatology
- ☑ Urology
- ☑ Nursing home/rehab/long-term care

- ☑ Cardiology
- ☑ Orthodontic
- ☑ Neurology
- ☑ Pulmonary
- ☑ Vascular
- ☑ Psychiatry/behavioral/substance abuse

EDUCATION

Institute of Medicine & Pharmacy — New York
Doctor of Medicine (*1998*)
Class Rank: Top 8%

Institute of Medicine — Hungary
Doctor of Medicine (*1991*)
Class Rank: Top 10%

Certifications:
Advanced Cardiac Life Support (ACLS)
Basic Life Support (BLS)
Advanced Trauma Life Support (ATLS)
American Board of Internal Medicine (ABIM)

Professional Licenses:
Doctor of Medicine (MD) — New Jersey
Doctor of Medicine (MD) — California

PROFESSIONAL EXPERIENCE

CLIFTON MEDICAL CENTER — Clifton, New Jersey   Oct 1998–Present
Attending Physician/Staff
Reporting directly to Chief of Medical Service and Chief of Staff M.D for 140-bed medical center providing hospital, outpatient clinic, rehabilitation unit, and nursing home services. Scope of responsibilities includes health care; supervising/teaching rounds; teaching clinic; supervising on-call residents; and working with residents on Internal Medicine Residency Program.

- Provide and manage direct patient care, including physical examinations, evaluations, assessments, diagnoses, and treatment.

(continued)

(continued)

MICHELLE JONES, M.D.   Page 2 of 2

Professional Experience, Continued

- Train and supervise residents and on-call residents engaged in specialty activities and procedures, including emergency room on-call duties, inpatient area, outpatient clinic, nursing home/rehabilitation and long-term care/hospice unit, and off-site outpatient clinics.
- Effectively manage ER, medical floor inpatients, emergencies in ICU/CCU, and all in-house medical residents while on call as attending Medical Officer of the day.
- Frequently function as acting Chief Resident, directing and coordinating the patient care activities of nursing and support staff.
- Collaborate with residents on Internal Medicine Residency Program.

MEDICINE ASSOCIATES OF BLOOMFIELD — Bloomfield, New Jersey   Jan 1999–Jan 2001
Associate Physician
Reported directly to partner physicians while supervising a staff of 4 for small private practice. Scope of responsibilities included providing internal medicine; daily office functions; managing in-hospital patients; and managing patients at several local nursing homes and personal care homes.

- Developed and implemented patient management plans, recorded progress notes, and assisted in provision of continuity of care.
- Managed in-hospital patients at 3 local hospitals; provided appropriate patient education explaining the necessity, preparation, nature, and anticipated effects of scheduled procedures to the patient.
- Managed patients at several local nursing homes and personal care homes; examined patients, performed comprehensive physical examinations, and compiled patient medical data, including health history and results of physical examination; and prescribed pharmaceuticals, other medications, and treatment regimens as appropriate to assessed medical conditions.

PROFESSIONAL AFFILIATIONS

Member, American Medical Association (AMA)
Member, American Society of Internal Medicine (now called the American College
of Physicians — American Society of Internal Medicine, ACP — ASIM)

PUBLICATIONS

*The Use of a Correction Factor for the Calculation of Suprarenal Outputs as a Function of
Arterial Pressure,* diploma thesis, 1982.

Baucht, J., and Jones, M., "The Use of a Correction Factor for the Calculation of
Suprarenal Outputs as a Function of Arterial Pressure," presented at and published in
the proceedings of The National Symposium of Physiology, New York, August 16–18,
Vol. 1, 2:20–24, 1981.

RESEARCH

Determination by E-testing of sensitivity of gram-negative microorganisms to
Levoflaxacin, sponsored by Baxter Pharmaceuticals (submitted for publication).

Measurement of adrenal blood flow in an experiment model.
Advisor: Dr. James Baucht

REFERENCES AVAILABLE UPON REQUEST

Police and Detectives

CHARLES WILSON

2158 Hampton Lane, Cincinnati, OH 45219
513.426.9568
cwilson@ci.cincinnati.oh.us

CAREER PROFILE

A results-oriented, high-energy LAW ENFORCEMENT LIEUTENANT with 20+ years of progressively responsible experience in the Public Service area. Highly developed administrative and analytical skills as evidenced by the ability to continuously improve division operations. Qualified by:

Investigative Techniques	DEA Certification	Evidence Collection
Police Media Relations	Supervision & Training	Emergency Response
Conflict Resolution	Search & Seizure	Technical Surveillance
Protection Programs	Defense Management	Professional Development

PROFESSIONAL EXPERIENCE

CINCINNATI POLICE DEPARTMENT, Cincinnati, OH   1984–Present

Lieutenant of Detective Division, 1997–Present
Lieutenant of Patrol Division, 1996–1997
Sergeant of Patrol Division, 1994–1996
Detective Division—Forensics, 1992–1994
Field Training Officer, 1989–1992
Patrol Officer, 1984–1989
Prior police experience in various security positions, 1981–1984

KEY ACCOMPLISHMENTS

- Supervise seven investigators assigned 330+ cases per year who gather and analyze sufficient evidence in major crime cases, resulting in an average solvability rate of 40%.

- Supervised three-year investigation of a major drug enterprise leading to the seizure of 200 kilos of cocaine and the indictment of 40+ individuals on state and federal charges.

- Increased charge rate 10% due to advanced investigative techniques and technology training.

- Redesigned police department schedules to allow for 100 hours per year of in-service training for all officers in the department.

- Modernized Detective Division's infrastructure by purchasing new computers and reconfiguring office space to allow for increased communications.

- Equipped cruisers with laptop computers and CAD-RMS (Computer-Aided Dispatch—Records Management System) software, increasing report-writing efficiency and reducing paperwork 80% for Patrol Division officers.

- Led Patrol Division with 50 drunk-driving arrests, accounting for 10% of total arrests.

- Updated forensic lab equipment and coordinated training for all officers, leading to increased evidence-collection capabilities for the police department.

- "Police Officer of the Month" presented by the Cincinnati Police Department—October 1993.

(continued)

CHARLES WILSON

2158 Hampton Lane, Cincinnati, OH 45219
513.426.9568
cwilson@ci.cincinnati.oh.us

Page 2

EDUCATION

UNIVERSITY of CINCINNATI, Cincinnati, OH
Bachelor of Arts Degree
Major: Criminal Justice
GPA: 4.0 Anticipated Graduation: 2004

TERRA COMMUNITY COLLEGE, Fremont, OH
Associate in Law Enforcement Degree
GPA: 3.84 *Magna Cum Laude*
Distinguished Alumni Award, 2001

NORTHWESTERN UNIVERSITY TRAFFIC INSTITUTE, Evanston, IL
School of Police Staff and Command (19 semester hours)

FEDERAL BUREAU of INVESTIGATION NATIONAL ACADEMY, Quantico, VA
Criminal Justice Education (17 semester hours)

OHIO PEACE OFFICER TRAINING COUNCIL (386 hours), Fremont, OH—**Top Honors**

PROFESSIONAL DEVELOPMENT

FBI U.S. Department of Justice, Media Relations for the Law Enforcement Executive,
    Quantico, VA—2001
Crime Stoppers Annual Training Conference, Pueblo, CO—2001
Combating Violent Crimes in the 21st Century Information Sharing Conference, MAGLOCLEN,
    Cleveland, OH—2000
FBI Hostile School Environment: Causes and Solutions Conference, Cleveland, OH—1999
Exploring Economic, Electronic and Financial Crimes in Our Society Information Sharing
    Conference, MAGLOCLEN, Atlantic City, NY—1999
Crime Stoppers International Conference, Gillette, WY—1998
Crime Trends in America, MAGLOCLEN, Pittsburgh, PA—1998

AFFILIATIONS & LEADERSHIP

Board of Crime Stoppers of Cincinnati, **Law Enforcement Coordinator/Liaison,** 1997–Present
Benevolent Protective Order of the Elks #75, **Chairman of Youth Activities,** 2001–Present
Free and Accepted Masons of Ohio—32nd Degree, 2002
Fraternal Order of Police Lodge #20 Member, **President,** 1989–1990

CONTINUING EDUCATION

Ohio Department of Health, Alcohol Testing, Approval & Permit Program, Senior Operator Permit
Search and Seizure Update, Cincinnati Academy (16 hours)
The Dispatch Institute: Liability and Public Image Concerns in Public Safety Telecommunications
Laws of Arrest, Search & Seizure, Firearms Training (50 hours)
Ohio Peace Officer Training Council, Evidence Technician (40 hours)
Lucas County Coroner Forensic Medical Sciences, Evidence Related to Blood (8 hours)
Front-Line Effective Police Supervision Skills (14 hours)
Defensive Tactics Training (16 hours)
Public Safety Training, Saving Our Own Lives (16 hours)
FBI U.S. Department of Justice DEA, Basic Narcotics and Dangerous Drug Law Enforcement (80 hours)

Psychologists

NANCY JOHNSON
SCHOOL PSYCHOLOGIST

555 Peachtree Road
Hauppauge, NY 55555
(555) 000-0000

EDUCATION / CERTIFICATIONS

Master of Arts, School Psychology, 2004—GPA 3.9/4.0
ST. JAMES COLLEGE, Buffalo, NY

Bachelor of Arts, Psychology, 2000—GPA 3.2/4.0
STATE UNIVERSITY OF NEW YORK AT BINGHAMTON, Binghamton, NY

New York State Provisional Certification, School Psychologist
New York State Initial Educator Certification, School Psychologist

PROFILE

Qualified school psychologist bringing a range of professional experience in the counseling and teaching of general and special education students throughout inner-city schools, group residency, and private day-care settings. Bring strong skills in areas of assessment, intervention, and prevention; program development and implementation; and a proactive approach towards promoting a home/school connection and awareness of supportive services and resources. Computer proficient: MS Office/Internet.

PROFESSIONAL EXPERIENCE

School Psychologist, Henry Hudson Public School District, Lakeview, NY   2000–present
  Blake Elementary School, Pre-Kindergarten–Sixth Grade, 2003–present
  Hillside Elementary School, Pre-Kindergarten–Third Grade, 2002–present
  Special Education Summer School Program, 2002
  James Elementary School, Pre-Kindergarten–Sixth Grade, 2000–2001
  Consultation Center, 2000–2001

- Perform evaluations and screenings to assess students' academic skills, learning aptitudes, emotional development, social skills, learning environments, and school climate, and determine eligibility for special education services to the Planning and Placement Team.

- Conduct counseling sessions to address issues affecting students' academic performance, social behavior, and mental health, and to develop tolerance, understanding, and appreciation for diversity.

- Administer/evaluate academic programs and behavioral management systems through Functional Behavioral Assessments, Behavioral Intervention Plans, and Individualized Education Plans.

- Provide teachers with student-tailored academic and behavioral management strategies designed to reduce students' risk of failure at a preventative level.

- Observe preschool-aged children in playgroup sessions, and consult with parents to obtain developmental and social histories.

- Keep students and parents current on important topics, community resources, and upcoming programs and events through Web page access, bulletin board postings, and pamphlets.

— continued —

(continued)

Nancy Johnson

Page 2

School Psychologist, Henry Hudson Public School District, continued

- Co-facilitate a school-wide program providing third- through sixth-grade students with positive social and behavioral skills through role model students, motivational speakers, and community resources.
- Collaborate with the Family Support Team on the development of strategies designed to improve students' reading levels and to promote parental involvement in the Success For All program.
- Attend monthly staff meetings, professional development workshops, and school-wide activities.

School Psychologist Intern, Lexington Central School District, Landon, NY   1999–2000
    Shawnee Middle School, New Spring, NY
    Lake Grove Middle School, Bloomington, NY

- Provided individual and group counseling and crisis-intervention services; consulted on academic, behavioral, and organizational issues; and developed behavioral strategies for the classroom.
- Conducted achievement and cognitive testing, and assessed emotional/social adjustment.
- Presented results of students with different handicapping conditions to the Committee on Special Education, and developed and implemented Individualized Education Plans.

Counseling Practicum, Pinkerton School District, Fishkill, NY   1999

- Worked closely with students, parents, and professional teams to identify and resolve a broad range of issues directly impacting students' academic and social performance.
- Devised and presented counseling summaries on students' progress and future recommendations.

Residential Counselor, St. Mary's Youth Center, Fishkill, NY   1998

- Supervised residential housing units provided to homeless youth, aged 16–21.
- Performed intake and exit evaluations, conducted on-site visitations to observe living conditions, and ensured full compliance with mandatory health and safety regulations.
- Collaborated with community representatives to provide clients with supportive services in areas of financial assistance, education, work and life skills, housing, childcare, and substance abuse.

Counselor, Kids Town, Fishkill, NY   1998

- Coordinated and directed group activities for youth day camp and nursery programs.
- Integrated recreational activities to create an environment conducive to learning and social growth for a multicultural population of students of varying ages and learning disabilities.

Pre-School Teacher, Fishkill Developmental Center, Fishkill, NY   1996–1998

- Implemented behavior reinforcement programs, performed formal evaluations, and collaborated with school psychologist and parents to identify and resolve problems.
- Co-taught individualized lessons and life skills within an integrated classroom environment.
- Adapted educational materials to facilitate the learning process at an appropriate pace.

PROFESSIONAL AFFILIATIONS

Member, New York Association of School Psychologists
Member, National Association of School Psychologists

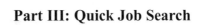

Respiratory Therapists

ANGELA P. CARDOVA, CRT

1834 Highlands Dr.
Novi, MI 48375

248-555-3729
cardova@msn.com

PROFILE

✓ Over 8 years as Respiratory Therapist.
✓ Adult and pediatric care provider at emergency, critical, and subacute levels. Strong patient-assessment skills.
✓ Additional experience in home-care settings.

HIGHLIGHTS OF CLINICAL SKILLS

✓ Basic respiratory therapy
✓ Ventilator set-up and management (including high-frequency oscillator ventilators)
✓ Nasal CPAP therapy
✓ Arterial blood gas sampling and analysis

✓ Oxygen therapy
✓ Pulmonary function testing
✓ Extubation
✓ Weaning
✓ Protocol-driven therapy

CERTIFICATIONS

✓ Certified Respiratory Therapist/Registry-eligible (NBRC)   ✓ BCLS (American Heart Assoc.)

EMPLOYMENT HISTORY

Respiratory Therapist: MERCY HOSPITAL • Livonia, Michigan   2002–Present
 • Set up respiratory and related equipment in homes of recently discharged patients. Equipment includes:
  ✓ Oxygen concentrator   ✓ Nebulizer compressor   ✓ Air compressor
  ✓ Liquid oxygen   ✓ Apnea monitor   ✓ Suction machine
  ✓ Oxygen conserving device   ✓ Ultrasonic nebulizer   ✓ CPAP fitting and set-up
 • Perform respiratory assessments.
 • Verify health benefits; maintain familiarity with Medicare guidelines.

Polysomnography Technician: OAKDALE HEALTH SYSTEM • Ypsilanti, Michigan   2001–2002
 • Prepared for and monitored patients during sleep studies for evaluation of obstructive sleep apnea and other sleeping disorders.

Respiratory Therapist
HALMARK HOME HEALTH CARE CENTERS • Centerline, Michigan   1998–1999
ST. JOSEPH MERCY HOSPITAL • Ann Arbor, Michigan   1995–1998

EDUCATION

AAS in Respiratory Care: GRAND VALLEY STATE UNIVERSITY • Grand Rapids, Michigan   1995
Certified Medical Assistant Program: CLEARY COLLEGE • Ypsilanti, Michigan   1990

ACCOMPLISHMENTS

✓ Collaborated with other students to reactivate Zeta Phi Beta Sorority chapter at Grand Valley State University. Served as Chapter President for one year.

References available on request.

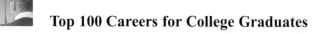

Teachers—Preschool, Kindergarten, Elementary, Middle, and Secondary

GRACE TAYLOR

76 Columbia Street
Frankfort, NY 13340

Home 315.249.2309
Mobile 315.890.1276

EXPERIENCED ELEMENTARY TEACHER

Energetic and dedicated teacher with a solid foundation in subject matter instruction (particularly science) and active involvement in creating change. Offering an optimistic attitude and a strong commitment to shaping reflective, self-directed learners who think critically and creatively. Experienced with the most up-to-date instructional methodologies and exposed to a variety of collaborative teaching approaches. Excellent knowledge of the needs of students requiring remedial reading instruction. Continuously strive to enhance the educational environment and promote school unity.

- Character Education
- Two-Year Looping Program
- Differentiated Classroom

- Technology Integration
- Enrichment Programs
- Authentic Assessments

- Diversity Curriculum
- Curriculum Mapping
- Departmentalization

HIGHLIGHTS OF QUALIFICATIONS

→ Experienced with a full range of exceptional children from high-needs remedial students to highly advanced enrichment students. Proven ability to ease the transition of bilingual students into the mainstream school system.

→ Actively engaged in sharing new models of learning and collaborating with other educators to promote innovation and exemplary practices. Continuously seek professional development to expand and reaffirm classroom techniques.

→ Involved in educational improvement initiatives (i.e., Micro Society) that focus on building classroom and school-wide cultures of "thinking" by fostering the attitudes, values, and skills that support good critical and creative thinking.

→ Able to recognize and develop students' multiple intellectual strengths, adapting instruction to individual differences, cultural backgrounds, and developmental levels. Also able to assess their work in ways that promote further learning.

→ Possess useful current insights to make sound educational judgments, focus standards, and respond to state frameworks to strengthen teaching and learning of both general education and special education.

TEACHING EXPERIENCE

Mohawk Central School District, *Mohawk, NY*   **1997 to Present**
(Middle-class suburban community and the largest school district in Herkimer County, with a student population of 9,350)

<u>Fisher Elementary</u>   **6th Grade**—*2000 to Present (Tenured 2000)*   **5th Grade**—*1997 to 2000*

Implement district programs in 4th through 6th grade school. Strive to shape classroom and instruction materials to help students develop valuable thinking skills and encourage a deeper understanding of concepts within and across disciplines. Curriculum marked by diversity of education practices and innovative approaches to learning.

- Rewrote the district's science curriculum and piloted the use of science kits for the district.
- Serve as 6th Grade Yearbook Advisor and as Head Coordinator for the annual science fair.
- Rewrote the English/Language Arts curriculum to align district program and assessments to state frameworks.
- Coordinator for 6th grade activities, school-wide fairs, and field trips.
- Member of various leadership teams involved with curriculum restructuring.

EDUCATION & CREDENTIALS

<u>**M.S. Elementary Education; Emphasis: Reading**</u>
Marist College, Poughkeepsie, NY

<u>**B.A. Social Science and Elementary Education**</u>
Marist College, Poughkeepsie, NY

Teachers—Postsecondary

SHARON C. BRAXTON

sharoncbraxton@aol.com

2501 West Summit Avenue
Milwaukee, Wisconsin 54443

Home (414) 563-2341
Facsimile (414) 563-3242

OBJECTIVE: To Obtain an Adjunct Faculty Position Teaching Criminal Justice

A highly organized and capable teacher and facilitator with several years of experience developing and implementing instructional programs. Extensive background presenting within multi-cultural, inclusionary, and regular classrooms. Excellent interpersonal and written communication skills. MA in Public Service with undergraduate degrees in Criminal Justice and Education. Demonstrated expertise in the following areas:

- Curriculum Design & Development
- Instructional Materials
- Research, Analysis & Presentation
- Teacher Training & Leadership
- Interdisciplinary Teams

- Classroom Management
- Interactive & Multimedia Instruction
- Diagnostic Evaluation & Program Planning
- Educational Administration
- Special Events Planning & Management

PROFESSIONAL EXPERIENCE

Milwaukee Public Schools — Milwaukee, Wisconsin   1989 to Present

SPECIAL EDUCATION TEACHER

Develop curricula and lesson plans for multicultural learning-disabled, behaviorally disabled, or cognitively disabled children within an inclusionary setting. Adapt materials to meet individual needs, and teach split classes in language arts and reading. Create and implement Individualized Education Plans (IEPs) providing interpersonal and written counsel to students and parents/guardians. Consult with psychologists, social workers, parents/guardians, and students to establish behavior plans including techniques for improvements and appropriate consequences for repeated misbehavior. Direct referrals to alternative educational programs. Review and analyze ADA regulations to ensure programs comply with current laws.

Accomplishments
- Recognized by staff, faculty, and students as an exceptionally competent professional who mentors new staff and cares deeply about the students.
- Selected to participate on curriculum/program analysis and development teams for educational programs at all age levels.
- Selected to evaluate and apply new, assistive learning programs within the classroom, including specialized computers with speech synthesis and interactive software.

(continued)

PROFESSIONAL EXPERIENCE (continued)

University of Wisconsin Milwaukee — Milwaukee, Wisconsin   1999 to Present

EDITORIAL ADMINISTRATIVE ASSISTANT

Assist editor (Professor John Kindberg) of the *Teaching Special Education Professional Journal* with pre- and post-publication activities. Solicit throughout professional community for articles. Receive articles and submit manuscripts for peer review. Prepare journal for publication.

EDUCATION

MASTER OF ARTS IN PUBLIC SERVICE (specialty Administration of Justice)   2004
    Marquette University — Milwaukee, Wisconsin

BACHELOR OF SCIENCE IN CRIMINAL JUSTICE (National Dean's List 1995)   1999
    University of Wisconsin — Milwaukee, Wisconsin

BACHELOR OF ARTS IN EDUCATION   1982
    Mississippi State University, Jackson, Mississippi

TECHNOLOGY SKILLS

Proficient with Microsoft Word, Excel, and PowerPoint — Windows and Macintosh

COMMUNITY ACTIVITIES

Black Women's Network — Co-Chair & Committee Head for Annual Recognition Award Dinner
Miss Black Wisconsin Scholarship Pageant — Recruiter & Mentor for program participants
St. Cecilia's-Lakeside — Tutor & Mentor for underprivileged children

PUBLICATIONS AND RESEARCH PROJECTS

- "The Impact of the Use of Advanced Technology in the Criminal Justice System," August 2004. Independent Research Project.
- "Pseudofamilies in Prison: Advantages and Disadvantages," June 2004. Correctional Management and Policy Analysis.
- "Project S.T.O.R. (Schools Teaching Options for Reconciliation) Proposed Evaluation," May 2004. Research, Program Planning, and Evaluation in Criminal Justice.
- "The State of Incarceration: Where We Are Today," July 2003. Independent Research Project.

Veterinarians

Mary Wiggley, D.V.M.

6399 Bonnett Drive
Lingham, WA 90028
(333) 447-3353
e-mail: mwdvm@hotmail.com

PROFESSIONAL QUALIFICATIONS

Highly motivated, practice-oriented recent graduate with great interest in personal and practice growth. Team player with special interest in high-quality feline medicine and surgery. Use outstanding communication skills to provide clients with professional and compassionate care. Pursue continuing education to remain current in feline medicine. Intend to pursue ABVP Diplomat Certification.

Licensed to practice Veterinary Medicine in the State of Washington—current

PC skills—word processing, spreadsheet, data entry, and AVIMARK software

Member—AVMA, AAFP, and VIN

PROFESSIONAL EXPERIENCE

Associate Veterinarian, Memorial Cat Clinic, Lingham, WA   2005–present

- Examine feline patients, perform diagnostic tests, create treatment plans, estimate costs, and counsel clients.

- Perform routine surgeries including spays, neuters, abscesses, dentals, and C-sections.

- Rotate with other veterinary clinics to handle weekend and off-hours emergencies.

"... you see sick animals and their families every day and yet I feel like Rico got 'special' treatment ... I couldn't be more pleased or comfortable with the way things were handled."

"...deeply moved by your depth of understanding for our grief ...."

"Thank you for all your caring and concern ... we appreciate you!"

" ... really appreciated all the extra special treatment you gave Frosty ...."

"Thank you warmly for your thoughtfulness and care with Sugar .... Life is full of beautiful people and you are a part of that." Excerpts from client notes to Dr. Wiggley

---

EDUCATION

Continuing Education—VIN classes

D.V.M., Washington State University College of Veterinary Medicine, Pullman, 2005

Pre-Veterinary Medicine/Zoology, Washington State University College of Science, 1998–2000

B.S., Animal Science, Oregon State University, Corvallis, OR, 1985

OTHER EMPLOYMENT

Technician, Fab 4 & 5, Corvallis, OR, 1988–1998

Part IV

Important Trends in Jobs and Industries

In putting this section together, my objective was to give you a quick review of major labor market trends. To accomplish this, I included three excellent articles that originally appeared in U.S. Department of Labor publications.

The first article is "Tomorrow's Jobs." It provides a superb—and short—review of the major trends that will affect your career in the years to come. Read it for ideas on selecting a career path for the long term.

The second article is "Employment Trends in Major Industries." While you may not have thought much about it, the industry you work in is just as important as your occupational choice. This great article will help you learn about major trends affecting various industries.

The third article, "Job Outlook for College Graduates," discusses the benefits a college education brings to jobseekers. The article covers job growth, earnings, and job openings, among other topics. The article can help you focus on promising careers in many industries.

Tomorrow's Jobs

Making informed career decisions requires reliable information about opportunities in the future. Opportunities result from the relationships between the population, the labor force, and the demand for goods and services.

Population ultimately limits the size of the labor force—individuals working or looking for work—which constrains how much can be produced. Demand for various goods and services determines employment in the industries providing them. Occupational employment opportunities, in turn, result from demand for skills needed within specific industries. Opportunities for medical assistants and other healthcare occupations, for example, have surged in response to rapid growth in demand for health services.

Examining the past and projecting changes in these relationships is the foundation of the U.S. Department of Labor's Occupational Outlook Program. "Tomorrow's Jobs" presents highlights of Bureau of Labor Statistics projections of the labor force and occupational and industry employment that can help guide your career plans.

Population

Population trends affect employment opportunities in a number of ways. Changes in population influence the demand for goods and services. For example, a growing and aging population has increased the demand for health services. Equally important, population changes produce corresponding changes in the size and demographic composition of the labor force.

The U.S. civilian noninstitutional population is expected to increase by 23.9 million over the 2004–2014 period, at a slower rate of growth than during both the 1994–2004 and 1984–1994 periods (Chart 1). Continued growth will mean more consumers of goods and services, spurring demand for workers in a wide range of occupations and industries. The effects of population growth on various occupations will differ. The differences are partially accounted for by the age distribution of the future population.

The youth population, aged 16 to 24, will grow 2.9 percent over the 2004–2014 period. As the baby boomers

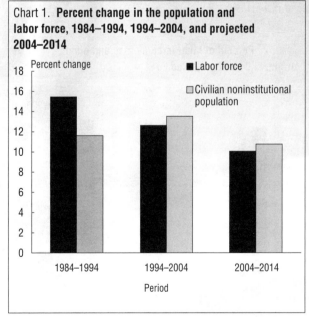

Chart 1. **Percent change in the population and labor force, 1984–1994, 1994–2004, and projected 2004–2014**

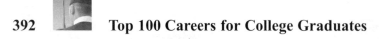

continue to age, the group aged 55 to 64 will increase by 36 percent or 10.4 million persons, more than any other group. The group aged 35 to 44 will decrease in size, reflecting the birth dearth following the baby boom generation.

Minorities and immigrants will constitute a larger share of the U.S. population in 2014. The number of Hispanics is projected to continue to grow much faster than those of all other racial and ethnic groups.

Labor Force

Population is the single most important factor in determining the size and composition of the labor force—that is, people who are either working or looking for work. The civilian labor force is projected to increase by 14.7 million, or 10 percent, to 162.1 million over the 2004–2014 period.

The U.S. workforce will become more diverse by 2014. White, non-Hispanic persons will continue to make up a decreasing share of the labor force, falling from 70 percent in 2004 to 65.6 percent in 2014 (Chart 2). However, despite relatively slow growth, white, non-Hispanics will remain the largest group in the labor force in 2014. Asians are projected to account for an increasing share of the labor force by 2014, growing from 4.3 to 5.1 percent. Hispanics are projected to be the fastest growing of the four labor force groups, growing by 33.7 percent. By 2014, Hispanics will continue to constitute a larger proportion of the labor force than will blacks, whose share will grow from 11.3 percent to 12.0 percent.

The numbers of men and women in the labor force will grow, but the number of women will grow at a faster rate than the number of men. The male labor force is projected to grow by 9.1 percent from 2004 to 2014, compared with 10.9 percent for women. As a result, men's share of the labor force is expected to decrease from 53.6 to 53.2 percent, while women's share is expected to increase from 46.4 to 46.8 percent.

The youth labor force, aged 16 to 24, is expected to slightly decrease its share of the labor force to 13.7 percent by 2014. The primary working age group, between 25 and 54 years old, is projected to decline from 69.3 percent of the labor force in 2004 to 65.2 percent by 2014. Workers 55 and older, on the other hand, are projected to increase from 15.6 percent to 21.2 percent of the labor force between 2004 and 2014, due to the aging of the baby-boom generation (Chart 3).

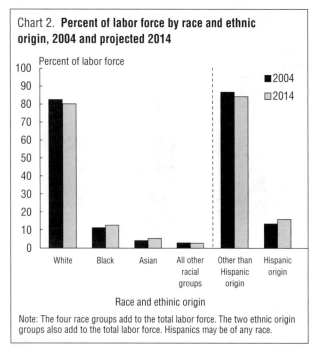

Chart 2. **Percent of labor force by race and ethnic origin, 2004 and projected 2014**

Note: The four race groups add to the total labor force. The two ethnic origin groups also add to the total labor force. Hispanics may be of any race.

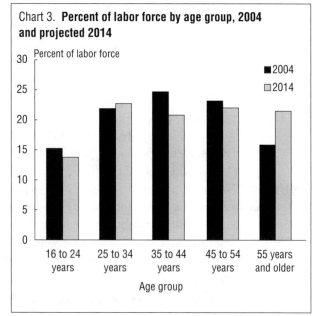

Chart 3. **Percent of labor force by age group, 2004 and projected 2014**

Employment

Total employment is expected to increase from 145.6 million in 2004 to 164.5 million in 2014, or by 13 percent. The 18.9 million jobs that will be added by 2014 will not be evenly distributed across major industrial and occupational groups. Changes in consumer demand, technology, and many other factors will contribute to the continually changing employment structure in the U.S. economy.

The following two sections examine projected employment change from both industrial and occupational perspectives. The industrial profile is discussed in terms of primary wage and salary employment. Primary employment excludes secondary jobs for those who hold multiple jobs. The exception is employment in agriculture, which includes self-employed and unpaid family workers in addition to wage and salary workers.

The occupational profile is viewed in terms of total employment—including primary and secondary jobs for wage and salary, self-employed, and unpaid family workers. Of the nearly 146 million jobs in the U.S. economy in 2004, wage and salary workers accounted for 133.5 million; self-employed workers accounted for 12.1 million; and unpaid family workers accounted for about 141,000. Secondary employment accounted for 1.7 million jobs. Self-employed workers held 9 out of 10 secondary jobs; wage and salary workers held most of the remainder.

Industry

Service-providing industries. The long-term shift from goods-producing to service-providing employment is expected to continue. Service-providing industries are expected to account for approximately 18.7 million of the 18.9 million new wage and salary jobs generated over the 2004–2014 period (Chart 4).

Education and health services. This industry supersector is projected to grow faster, 30.6 percent, and add more jobs than any other industry supersector. About 3 out of every 10 new jobs created in the U.S. economy will be in either the healthcare and social assistance or private educational services sectors.

Healthcare and social assistance—including private hospitals, nursing and residential care facilities, and individual and family services—will grow by 30.3 percent and add 4.3 million new jobs. Employment growth will be driven by increasing demand for healthcare and social assistance because of an aging population and longer life expectancies. Also, as more women enter the labor force, demand for childcare services is expected to grow. Private educational services will grow by 32.5 percent and add 898,000 new jobs through 2014. Rising student enrollments at all levels of education will create demand for educational services.

Professional and business services. This industry supersector, which includes some of the fastest-growing industries in the U.S. economy, will grow by 27.8 percent and add more than 4.5 million new jobs.

Employment in administrative and support and waste management and remediation services will grow by 31 percent and add 2.5 million new jobs to the economy by 2014. The fastest-growing industry in this sector will be employment services, which will grow by 45.5 percent and will contribute almost two-thirds of all new jobs in

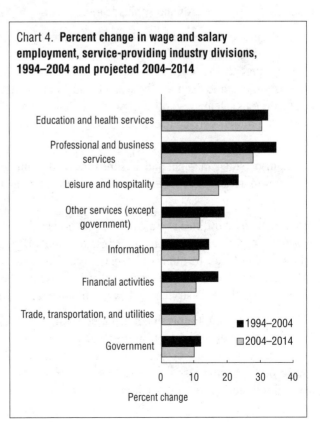

Chart 4. **Percent change in wage and salary employment, service-providing industry divisions, 1994–2004 and projected 2004–2014**

administrative and support and waste management and remediation services. Employment services ranks among the fastest-growing industries in the nation and is expected to be among those that provide the most new jobs.

Employment in professional, scientific, and technical services will grow by 28.4 percent and add 1.9 million new jobs by 2014. Employment in computer systems design and related services will grow by 39.5 percent and add almost one-fourth of all new jobs in professional, scientific, and technical services. Employment growth will be driven by the increasing reliance of businesses on information technology and the continuing importance of maintaining system and network security. Management, scientific, and technical consulting services also will grow very rapidly, by 60.5 percent, spurred by the increased use of new technology and computer software and the growing complexity of business.

Management of companies and enterprises will grow by 10.6 percent and add 182,000 new jobs.

Information. Employment in the information supersector is expected to increase by 11.6 percent, adding 364,000 jobs by 2014. Information contains some of the fast-growing computer-related industries such as software publishers; Internet publishing and broadcasting; and Internet service providers, Web search portals, and data processing services. Employment in these industries is expected to grow by 67.6 percent, 43.5 percent, and 27.8 percent, respectively. The information supersector also includes telecommunications; broadcasting; and newspaper, periodical, book, and directory publishers. Increased demand for residential and business land-line and wireless services, cable service, high-speed Internet connections, and software will fuel job growth among these industries.

Leisure and hospitality. Overall employment will grow by 17.7 percent. Arts, entertainment, and recreation will grow by 25 percent and add 460,000 new jobs by 2014. Most of these new job openings will come from the amusement, gambling, and recreation sector. Job growth will stem from public participation in arts, entertainment, and recreation activities—reflecting increasing incomes, leisure time, and awareness of the health benefits of physical fitness.

Accommodation and food services is expected to grow by 16.5 percent and add 1.8 million new jobs through 2014. Job growth will be concentrated in food services and drinking places, reflecting increases in population, dual-income families, and dining sophistication.

Trade, transportation, and utilities. Overall employment in this industry supersector will grow by 10.3 percent between 2004 and 2014. Transportation and warehousing is expected to increase by 506,000 jobs, or by 11.9 percent through 2014. Truck transportation will grow by 9.6 percent, adding 129,000 new jobs, while rail transportation is projected to decline. The warehousing and storage sector is projected to grow rapidly at 24.8 percent, adding 138,000 jobs. Demand for truck transportation and warehousing services will expand as many manufacturers concentrate on their core competencies and contract out their product transportation and storage functions.

Employment in retail trade is expected to increase by 11 percent, from 15 million to 16.7 million. Increases in population, personal income, and leisure time will contribute to employment growth in this industry, as consumers demand more goods. Wholesale trade is expected to increase by 8.4 percent, growing from 5.7 million to 6.1 million jobs.

Employment in utilities is projected to decrease by 1.3 percent through 2014. Despite increased output, employment in electric power generation, transmission, and distribution and natural gas distribution is expected to decline through 2014 due to improved technology that increases worker productivity. However, employment in water, sewage, and other systems is expected to increase 21 percent by 2014. Jobs are not easily eliminated by technological gains in this industry because water treatment and waste disposal are very labor-intensive activities.

Financial activities. Employment is projected to grow 10.5 percent over the 2004–2014 period. Real estate and rental and leasing is expected to grow by 16.9 percent and add 353,000 jobs by 2014. Growth will be due, in part, to increased demand for housing as the population grows. The fastest-growing industry in the financial activities supersector will be activities related to real estate, which will grow by 32.1 percent, reflecting the housing boom that persists throughout most of the nation.

Finance and insurance is expected to increase by 496,000 jobs, or 8.3 percent, by 2014. Employment in securities, commodity contracts, and other financial investments and related activities is expected to grow 15.8 percent by 2014, reflecting the increased number of baby boomers in their peak savings years, the growth of tax-favorable retirement plans, and the globalization of the securities markets. Employment in credit intermediation and related services, including banks, will grow by 5.4 percent and add about one-third of all new jobs within finance and insurance. Insurance carriers and related activities is expected to grow by 9.5 percent and add 215,000 new jobs by 2014. The number of jobs within agencies, brokerages, and other insurance-related activities is expected to grow about 19.4 percent, as many insurance carriers downsize their sales staffs and as agents set up their own businesses.

Government. Between 2004 and 2014, government employment, including that in public education and hospitals, is expected to increase by 10 percent, from 21.6 million to 23.8 million jobs. Growth in government employment will be fueled by growth in state and local educational services and the shift of responsibilities from the federal government to the state and local governments. Local government educational services is projected to increase 10 percent, adding 783,000 jobs. State government educational services is projected to grow by 19.6 percent, adding 442,000 jobs. Federal government employment, including the postal service, is expected to increase by only 1.6 percent as the federal government continues to contract out many government jobs to private companies.

Other services (except government). Employment will grow by 14 percent. More than 1 out of every 4 new jobs in this supersector will be in religious organizations, which is expected to grow by 11.9 percent. Other automotive repair and maintenance will be the fastest-growing industry at 30.7 percent. Also included among other services is personal care services, which is expected to increase by 19.5 percent.

Goods-producing industries. Employment in the goods-producing industries has been relatively stagnant since the early 1980s. Overall, this sector is expected to decline 0.4 percent over the 2004–2014 period. Although employment is expected to decline or increase more slowly than in the service-providing industries, projected growth among goods-producing industries varies considerably (Chart 5).

Construction. Employment in construction is expected to increase by 11.4 percent, from 7 million to 7.8 million. Demand for new housing and an increase in road, bridge, and tunnel construction will account for the bulk of job growth in this supersector.

Manufacturing. Employment change in manufacturing will vary by individual industry, but overall employment in this supersector will decline by 5.4 percent or 777,000 jobs. For example, employment in transportation equipment manufacturing is expected to grow by 95,000 jobs. Due to an aging population and increasing life expectancies, pharmaceutical and medicine manufacturing is expected to grow by 26.1 percent and add 76,000 jobs through 2014. However, productivity gains, job automation, and international competition will adversely affect employment in many other manufacturing industries. Employment in textile mills and apparel manufacturing will decline by 119,000 and 170,000 jobs, respectively. Employment in computer and electronic product manufacturing also will decline by 94,000 jobs through 2014.

Agriculture, forestry, fishing, and hunting. Overall employment in agriculture, forestry, fishing, and hunting is expected to decrease by 5.2 percent. Employment is expected to continue to decline due to advancements in technology. The only industry within this supersector

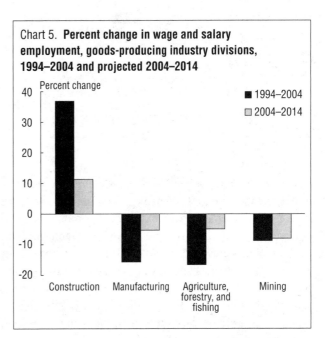

Chart 5. **Percent change in wage and salary employment, goods-producing industry divisions, 1994–2004 and projected 2004–2014**

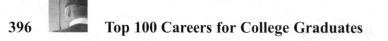

expected to grow is support activities for agriculture and forestry, which includes farm labor contractors and farm management services. This industry is expected to grow by 18.2 percent and add 19,000 new jobs.

Mining. Employment in mining is expected to decrease 8.8 percent, or by some 46,000 jobs, by 2014. Employment in coal mining and metal ore mining is expected to decline by 23.3 percent and 29.3 percent, respectively. Employment in oil and gas extraction also is projected to decline by 13.1 percent through 2014. Employment decreases in these industries are attributable mainly to technology gains that boost worker productivity, growing international competition, restricted access to federal lands, and strict environmental regulations that require cleaning of burning fuels.

Occupation

Expansion of service-providing industries is expected to continue, creating demand for many occupations. However, projected job growth varies among major occupational groups (Chart 6).

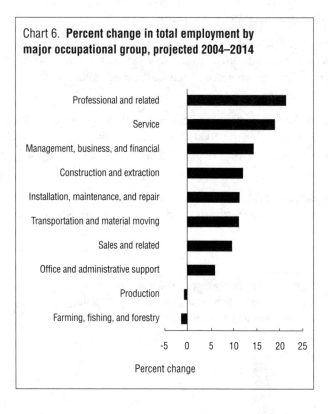

Chart 6. **Percent change in total employment by major occupational group, projected 2004–2014**

Professional and related occupations. Professional and related occupations will grow the fastest and add more new jobs than any other major occupational group. Over the 2004–2014 period, a 21.2-percent increase in the number of professional and related jobs is projected, which translates into 6 million new jobs. Professional and related workers perform a wide variety of duties, and are employed throughout private industry and government. About three-quarters of the job growth will come from three groups of professional occupations—computer and mathematical occupations; healthcare practitioners and technical occupations; and education, training, and library occupations—which will add 4.5 million jobs combined.

Service occupations. Service workers perform services for the public. Employment in service occupations is projected to increase by 5.3 million, or 19 percent, the second largest numerical gain and second highest rate of growth among the major occupational groups. Food preparation and serving related occupations are expected to add the most jobs among the service occupations, 1.7 million by 2014. However, healthcare support occupations are expected to grow the fastest, 33.3 percent, adding 1.2 million new jobs.

Management, business, and financial occupations. Workers in management, business, and financial occupations plan and direct the activities of business, government, and other organizations. Their employment is expected to increase by 2.2 million, or 14.4 percent, by 2014. Among managers, the numbers of preschool and childcare center/program educational administrators and of computer and information systems managers will grow the fastest, by 27.9 percent and 25.9 percent, respectively. General and operations managers will add the most new jobs, 308,000, by 2014. Farmers and ranchers are the only workers in this major occupational group whose numbers are expected to decline, losing 155,000 jobs. Among business and financial occupations, accountants and auditors and management analysts will add the most jobs, 386,000 combined. Employment, recruitment, and placement specialists and personal financial advisors will be the fastest-growing occupations in this group, with job increases of 30.5 percent and 25.9 percent, respectively.

Construction and extraction occupations. Construction and extraction workers construct new residential and commercial buildings, and also work in mines, quarries, and oil and gas fields. Employment of these workers is expected to grow 12 percent, adding 931,000 new jobs. Construction trades and related workers will account for more than three-fourths of these new jobs, 699,000, by 2014. Many extraction occupations will decline, reflecting overall employment losses in the mining and oil and gas extraction industries.

Installation, maintenance, and repair occupations. Workers in installation, maintenance, and repair occupations install new equipment and maintain and repair older equipment. These occupations will add 657,000 jobs by 2014, growing by 11.4 percent. Automotive service technicians and mechanics and general maintenance and repair workers will account for half of all new installation, maintenance, and repair jobs. The fastest growth rate will be among security and fire alarm systems installers, an occupation that is expected to grow 21.7 percent over the 2004–2014 period.

Transportation and material moving occupations. Transportation and material moving workers transport people and materials by land, sea, or air. The number of these workers should grow 11.1 percent, accounting for 1.1 million additional jobs by 2014. Among transportation occupations, motor vehicle operators will add the most jobs, 629,000. Material moving occupations will grow 8.3 percent and will add 405,000 jobs. Rail transportation occupations are the only group in which employment is projected to decline, by 1.1 percent, through 2014.

Sales and related occupations. Sales and related workers transfer goods and services among businesses and consumers. Sales and related occupations are expected to add 1.5 million new jobs by 2014, growing by 9.6 percent. The majority of these jobs will be among retail salespersons and cashiers, occupations that will add 849,000 jobs combined.

Office and administrative support occupations. Office and administrative support workers perform the day-to-day activities of the office, such as preparing and filing documents, dealing with the public, and distributing information. Employment in these occupations is expected to grow by 5.8 percent, adding 1.4 million new jobs by 2014. Customer service representatives will add the most new jobs, 471,000. Desktop publishers will be among the fastest-growing occupations in this group, increasing by 23.2 percent over the decade. However, due to rising productivity and increased automation, office and administrative support occupations also account for 11 of the 20 occupations with the largest employment declines.

Farming, fishing, and forestry occupations. Farming, fishing, and forestry workers cultivate plants, breed and raise livestock, and catch animals. These occupations will decline 1.3 percent and lose 13,000 jobs by 2014. Agricultural workers, including farmworkers and laborers, accounted for the overwhelming majority of new jobs in this group. The number of fishing and hunting workers is expected to decline, by 16.6 percent, while the number of logging workers is expected to increase by less than 1 percent.

Production occupations. Production workers are employed mainly in manufacturing, where they assemble goods and operate plants. Production occupations are expected to decline less than 1 percent, losing 79,000 jobs by 2014. Jobs will be created for many production occupations, including food processing workers; machinists; and welders, cutters, solderers, and brazers. Textile, apparel, and furnishings occupations, as well as assemblers and fabricators, will account for much of the job losses among production occupations.

Among all occupations in the economy, computer and healthcare occupations are expected to grow the fastest over the projection period (Chart 7). In fact, healthcare occupations make up 12 of the 20 fastest-growing occupations, while computer occupations account for 5 out of the 20 fastest-growing occupations in the economy. In addition to high growth rates, these 17 computer and healthcare occupations combined will add more than 1.8 million new jobs. High growth rates among computer and healthcare occupations reflect projected rapid growth in the computer and data processing and health services industries.

The 20 occupations listed in Chart 8 will account for 7.1 million jobs combined, over the 2004–2014 period. The occupations with the largest numerical increases cover a wider range of occupational categories than do those occupations with the fastest growth rates. Health occupations will account for some of these increases in employment,

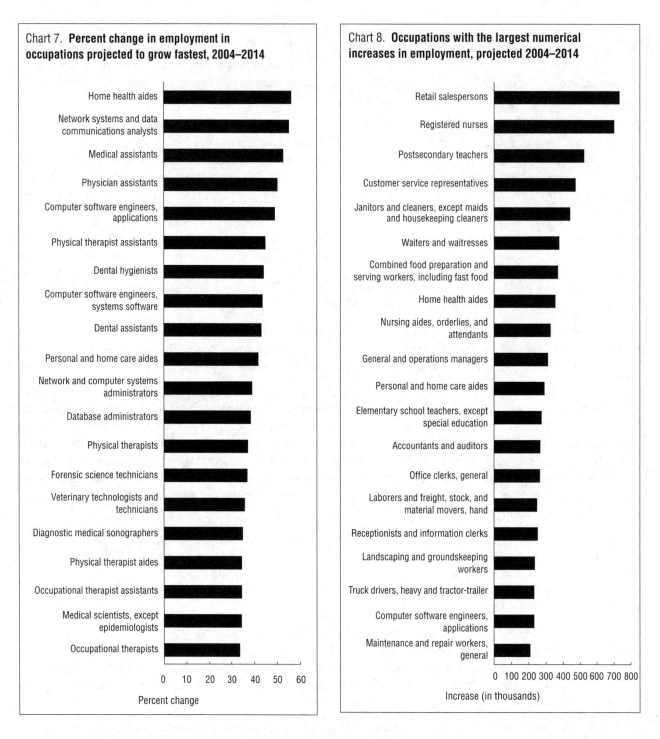

Chart 7. **Percent change in employment in occupations projected to grow fastest, 2004–2014**

Home health aides
Network systems and data communications analysts
Medical assistants
Physician assistants
Computer software engineers, applications
Physical therapist assistants
Dental hygienists
Computer software engineers, systems software
Dental assistants
Personal and home care aides
Network and computer systems administrators
Database administrators
Physical therapists
Forensic science technicians
Veterinary technologists and technicians
Diagnostic medical sonographers
Physical therapist aides
Occupational therapist assistants
Medical scientists, except epidemiologists
Occupational therapists

0   10   20   30   40   50   60
Percent change

Chart 8. **Occupations with the largest numerical increases in employment, projected 2004–2014**

Retail salespersons
Registered nurses
Postsecondary teachers
Customer service representatives
Janitors and cleaners, except maids and housekeeping cleaners
Waiters and waitresses
Combined food preparation and serving workers, including fast food
Home health aides
Nursing aides, orderlies, and attendants
General and operations managers
Personal and home care aides
Elementary school teachers, except special education
Accountants and auditors
Office clerks, general
Laborers and freight, stock, and material movers, hand
Receptionists and information clerks
Landscaping and groundskeeping workers
Truck drivers, heavy and tractor-trailer
Computer software engineers, applications
Maintenance and repair workers, general

0 100 200 300 400 500 600 700 800
Increase (in thousands)

as well as occupations in education, sales, transportation, office and administrative support, and food service. Many of these occupations are very large, and will create more new jobs than will those with high growth rates. Only 3 out of the 20 fastest-growing occupations—home health aides, personal and home care aides, and computer software application engineers—also are projected to be among the 20 occupations with the largest numerical increases in employment.

Declining occupational employment stems from declining industry employment, technological advancements, changes in business practices, and other factors. For example, increased productivity and farm consolidations are expected to result in a decline of 155,000 farmers and ranchers over the 2004–2014 period (Chart 9).

The majority of the 20 occupations with the largest numerical decreases are office and administrative support and production occupations, which are affected by increasing plant and factory automation and the implementation of office technology that reduces the needs for these workers. For example, employment of word processors and typists is expected to decline due to the proliferation of personal computers, which allows other workers to perform duties formerly assigned to word processors and typists.

Education and Training

Among the 20 fastest-growing occupations, a bachelor's or associate degree is the most significant source of postsecondary education or training for 12 of them—network systems and data communications analysts; physician assistants; computer software engineers, applications; physical therapist assistants; dental hygienists; computer software engineers, systems software; network and computer systems administrators; database administrators; forensic science technicians; veterinary technologists and technicians; diagnostic medical sonographers; and occupational therapists assistants.

On-the-job training is the most significant source of postsecondary education or training for another 5 of the 20 fastest-growing occupations—physical therapist aides, medical assistants, home health aides, dental assistants, and personal and home care aides.

In contrast, on-the-job training is the most significant source of postsecondary education or training for 13 of the 20 occupations with the largest numerical increases; 6 of these 20 occupations have an associate or higher degree as the most significant source of postsecondary education or training. On-the-job training also is the most significant source of postsecondary education or training for all 20 of the occupations with the largest numerical decreases.

Chart 9. **Job declines in occupations with the largest numerical decreases in employment, projected 2004–2014**

Occupation	Decrease (in thousands)
Farmers and ranchers	
Stock clerks and order fillers	
Sewing machine operators	
File clerks	
Order clerks	
Mail clerks and mail machine operators, except postal service	
Computer operators	
Secretaries, except legal, medical, and executive	
Cutting, punching, and press machine setters, operators, and tenders, metal and plastic	
Telemarketers	
Word processors and typists	
Credit authorizers, checkers, and clerks	
Machine feeders and offbearers	
Textile knitting and weaving machine setters, operators, and tenders	
Textile winding, twisting, and drawing out machine setters, operators, and tenders	
Meter readers, utilities	
Office machine operators, except computer	
Extruding and drawing machine setters, operators, and tenders, metal and plastic	
Switchboard operators, including answering services	
Door-to-door sales workers, news and street vendors, and related workers	

-200   -150   -100   -50   0

Decrease (in thousands)

Total Job Openings

Job openings stem from both employment growth and replacement needs (Chart 10). Replacement needs arise as workers leave occupations. Some transfer to other occupations while others retire, return to school, or quit to assume household responsibilities. Replacement needs are projected to account for more than 60 percent of the

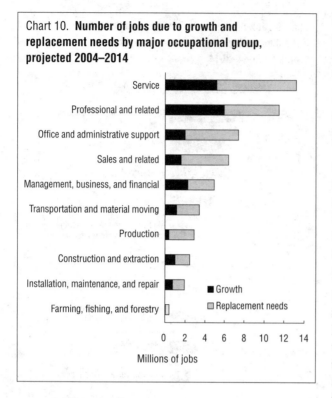

Chart 10. **Number of jobs due to growth and replacement needs by major occupational group, projected 2004–2014**

approximately 55 million job openings between 2004 and 2014. Thus, even occupations projected to experience slower-than-average growth or to decline in employment still may offer many job openings.

Professional and related occupations are projected to grow faster and add more jobs than any other major occupational group, with 6 million new jobs by 2014. Three-fourths of the job growth in professional and related occupations is expected among computer and mathematical occupations; healthcare practitioners and technical occupations; and education, training, and library occupations. With 5.5 million job openings due to replacement needs, professional and related occupations are the only major group projected to generate more openings from job growth than from replacement needs.

Service occupations are projected to have the largest number of total job openings, 13.2 million, reflecting high replacement needs. A large number of replacements will be necessary as young workers leave food preparation and service occupations. Replacement needs generally are greatest in the largest occupations and in those with relatively low pay or limited training requirements.

Office automation will significantly affect many individual office and administrative support occupations. Overall, these occupations are projected to grow more slowly than average, while some are projected to decline. Office and administrative support occupations are projected to create 7.5 million job openings over the 2004–2014 period, ranking third behind service and professional and related occupations.

Farming, fishing, and forestry occupations are projected to have the fewest job openings, approximately 286,000. Because job growth is expected to be slow, and levels of retirement and job turnover high, more than 95 percent of these projected job openings are due to replacement needs.

Editor's Note: This section, with minor changes, came from the *Occupational Outlook Handbook* and was written by the U.S. Department of Labor staff. Much of this section uses 2004 data, the most recent available at press time. By the time it is carefully collected and analyzed, data used by the U.S. Department of Labor is typically several years old. Because market trends tend to be gradual, this delay does not affect the material's usefulness.

Employment Trends in Major Industries

The U.S. economy can be broken down into numerous industries, each with its own set of characteristics. The Department of Labor has identified 45 industries that account for three-quarters of all workers. This section provides an overview of these industries and the economy as a whole.

Nature of the Industry

Industries are defined by the processes they use to produce goods and services. Workers in the United States produce and provide a wide variety of products and services and, as a result, the types of industries in the U.S. economy range widely—from agriculture, forestry, and fishing to aerospace manufacturing. Each industry has a unique combination of occupations, production techniques, inputs and outputs, and business characteristics. Understanding the nature of industries that interest you is important because it is this unique combination that determines working conditions, educational requirements, and the job outlook.

Industries consist of many different places of work, called establishments. Establishments are physical locations in which people work, such as the branch office of a bank, a gasoline service station, a school, a department store, or a plant that manufactures machinery. Establishments range from large factories and corporate office complexes employing thousands of workers to small community stores, restaurants, professional offices, and service businesses employing only a few workers. Establishments should not be confused with companies or corporations, which are legal entities. Thus, a company or corporation may have a single establishment or more than one establishment. Establishments that use the same or similar processes to produce goods or services are organized together into industries. Industries are, in turn, organized together into industry groups such as Information and Trade. These are further organized into industry subsectors and then ultimately into industry sectors. For the purposes of labor market analysis, the Bureau of Labor Statistics organizes industry sectors into industry supersectors. A company or corporation could own establishments classified in more than one industry, industry sector, or even industry supersector.

Each industry subsector is made up of a number of industry groups, which are, as mentioned, determined by differences in production processes. An easily recognized example of these distinctions is in the food manufacturing subsector, which is made up of industry groups that produce meat products, preserved fruits and vegetables, bakery items, and dairy products, among others. Each of these industry groups requires workers with varying skills and employs unique production techniques. Another example of these distinctions is found in utilities, which employs workers in establishments that provide electricity, natural gas, and water.

There are slightly more than 8 million private business establishments in the United States. Business establishments in the United States are predominantly small; 59.9 percent of all establishments employed fewer than 5 workers.

However, the medium-sized to large establishments employ a greater proportion of all workers. For example, establishments that employed 50 or more workers accounted for only 4.6 percent of all establishments, yet employed 56.3 percent of all workers. The large establishments—those with more than 500 workers—accounted for only 0.2 percent of all establishments, but employed 17.3 percent of all workers. Table 1 presents the percent distribution of employment according to establishment size.

The average size of these establishments varies widely across industries. Most establishments in the construction, wholesale trade, retail trade, finance and insurance, real estate and rental and leasing, and professional, scientific, and technical services industries are small, averaging fewer than 20 employees per establishment. However, wide differences within industries can exist. Hospitals, for example, employ an average of 724.9 workers, while physicians' offices employ an average of 10.1. Similarly, although there is an average of 14.3 employees per establishment for all of retail trade, department stores employ an average of 124.1 people but jewelry stores employ an average of only 5.8.

Establishment size can play a role in the characteristics of each job. Large establishments generally offer workers greater occupational mobility and advancement potential, whereas small establishments may provide their employees with broader experience by requiring them to assume a wider range of responsibilities. Also, small establishments are distributed throughout the nation—every locality has a few small businesses. Large establishments, in contrast, employ more workers and are less common, but they play a much more prominent role in the economies of the areas in which they are located.

Table 1. Percent distribution of nongovernment establishments and employment by establishment size

Establishment size (number of workers)	Establishments	Employment
Total	100.0	100.0
1 to 4	59.9	6.8
5 to 9	16.9	8.4
10 to 19	11.1	11.2
20 to 49	7.6	17.3
50 to 99	2.6	13.3
100 to 249	1.4	16.4
250 to 499	0.4	9.3
500 to 999	0.1	6.6
1,000 or more	0.1	10.7

Working Conditions

Just as the goods and services produced in each industry are different, working conditions vary significantly among industries. In some industries, the work setting is quiet, temperature-controlled, and virtually hazard-free, while other industries are characterized by noisy, uncomfortable, and sometimes dangerous work environments. Some industries require long workweeks and shift work, but standard 40-hour workweeks are common in many other industries. In still other industries, a lot of the jobs can be seasonal, requiring long hours during busy periods and abbreviated schedules during slower months. Production processes, establishment size, and the physical location of work usually determine these varying conditions.

One of the most telling indicators of working conditions is an industry's injury and illness rate. Overexertion, being struck by an object, and falls on the same level are among the most common incidents causing work-related injury or illness. In 2003, approximately 5.0 million nonfatal injuries and illnesses were reported across the various nongovernment industries. Among major industry divisions, manufacturing and construction tied for the highest rate of injury and illness—6.8 cases for every 100 full-time workers—while financial activities had the lowest rate—1.7 cases. About 5,700 work-related fatalities were reported in 2004; the most common events resulting in fatal injuries were transportation incidents, contact with objects and equipment, assaults and violent acts, and falls.

Work schedules are another important reflection of working conditions, and the operational requirements of each industry lead to large differences in hours worked and in part-time versus full-time status. In food services and drinking places, for example, fully 41.1 percent of employees worked part time in 2005 compared with only 1.7 percent in motor vehicles and motor vehicle equipment manufacturing. Table 2 presents industries having relatively high and low percentages of part-time workers.

Table 2. Part-time workers as a percent of total employment, selected industries

Industry	Percent part-time
All industries	17.4
Many part-time workers	
Food services and drinking places	41.1
Grocery stores	35.3
Clothing, accessory, and general merchandise stores	33.8
Arts, entertainment, and recreation	32.0
Child day care services	28.7
Motion picture and video industries	27.1
Social assistance	24.6
Educational services	21.9
Few part-time workers	
Pharmaceutical and medicine manufacturing	3.6
Utilities	3.2
Oil and gas extraction	3.2
Computer and electronic product manufacturing	2.8
Steel manufacturing	2.4
Mining	2.3
Aerospace product and parts manufacturing	1.9
Motor vehicles and parts manufacturing	1.7

The low proportion of part-time workers in some manufacturing industries often reflects the continuous nature of the production processes that makes it difficult to adapt the volume of production to short-term fluctuations in product demand. Once these processes are begun, it is costly to halt them; machinery must be tended and materials must be moved continuously. For example, the chemical manufacturing industry produces many different chemical products through controlled chemical reactions. These processes require chemical operators to monitor and adjust the flow of materials into and out of the line of production. Because production may continue 24 hours a day, 7 days a week under the watchful eyes of chemical operators who work in shifts, full-time workers are more likely to be employed. Retail trade and service industries, on the other hand, have seasonal cycles marked by various events that affect the hours worked, such as school openings or important holidays. During busy times of the year, longer hours are common, whereas slack periods lead to cutbacks in work hours and shorter workweeks. Jobs in these industries are generally appealing to students and others who desire flexible, part-time schedules.

Employment

The total number of jobs in the United States in 2004 was 145.6 million. This included 12.1 million self-employed workers, 141,000 unpaid workers in family businesses, and 133.5 million wage and salary jobs—including primary and secondary job holders. The total number of jobs is projected to increase to 164.5 million by 2014, and wage and salary jobs are projected to account for more than 152.1 million of them.

As shown in table 3, wage and salary jobs are the vast majority of all jobs, but they are not evenly divided among the various industries. Education, health, and social services had the largest number of jobs in 2004 with almost 28 million. Manufacturing, construction, and utilities had almost 21.9 million jobs, including 14.3 million manufacturing and 7.0 million construction jobs. The trade supersector was nearly as large, with about 20.7 million jobs, followed by professional and business services with 16.4 million jobs in 2004. Among the 45 industries, wage and salary employment ranged from only 156,200 in steel manufacturing to over 13 million in health services. The three largest industries—education services, health services, and food services and drinking places—together accounted for 34.7 million jobs, over one-quarter of the nation's wage and salary employment.

Table 3. Wage and salary employment, 2004, and projected change, 2004–14 (Employment in thousands)

Industry	2004		2014		2004–2014	
	Employment	Percent distribution	Employment	Percent distribution	Percent change	Employment change
All industries	133,478	100.0	152,093	100.0	13.9	18,615
Agriculture and natural resources	1,672	1.3	1,567	1.0	–6.3	–105
Agriculture, forestry, and fishing	1,149	0.9	1,090	0.7	–5.2	–60
Mining	207	0.2	180	0.1	–12.9	–27
Oil and gas extraction	316	0.2	297	0.2	–6.1	–19
Manufacturing, construction, and utilities	21,864	16.4	21,872	14.4	0.0	8
Aerospace product and parts manufacturing	444	0.3	480	0.3	8.2	36
Chemical manufacturing, except drugs	596	0.5	510	0.3	–14.4	–86
Computer and electronic product manufacturing	1,326	1.0	1,232	0.8	–7.1	–94
Construction	6,964	5.2	7,757	5.1	11.4	792
Food manufacturing	1,498	1.1	1,555	1.0	3.8	57
Machinery manufacturing	1,142	0.9	995	0.7	–12.8	–146
Motor vehicle and parts manufacturing	1,109	0.8	1,171	0.8	5.6	62
Pharmaceutical and medicine manufacturing	291	0.2	367	0.2	26.1	76
Printing	665	0.5	600	0.4	–9.8	–65
Steel manufacturing	156	0.1	135	0.1	–13.4	–21
Textile, textile product, and apparel manufacturing	701	0.5	380	0.2	–44.6	–321
Utilities	570	0.4	563	0.4	–1.3	–8
Trade	20,689	15.5	22,814	15.0	10.3	2,125
Automobile dealers	1,254	0.9	1,407	0.9	12.2	153
Clothing, accessory, and general merchandise stores	4,205	3.1	4,628	3.0	10.1	423
Grocery stores	2,447	1.8	2,607	1.7	6.6	160
Wholesale trade	5,655	4.2	6,131	4.0	8.4	476
Transportation	4,250	3.2	4,756	3.1	11.9	506
Air transportation	515	0.4	560	0.4	8.8	45
Truck transportation and warehousing	1,907	1.4	2,174	1.4	14.0	267

| Industry | 2004 | | 2014 | | 2004–2014 | |
	Employment	Percent distribution	Employment	Percent distribution	Percent change	Employment change
Information	3,138	2.4	3,502	2.3	11.6	364
Broadcasting	327	0.2	362	0.2	10.7	35
Motion picture and video industries	368	0.3	430	0.3	17.1	63
Publishing, except software	671	0.5	715	0.5	6.5	44
Software publishers	239	0.2	400	0.3	67.6	161
Telecommunications	1,043	0.8	975	0.6	–6.5	–68
Internet service providers, Web search portals, and data processing services	388	0.3	496	0.3	27.8	108
Financial activities	8,052	6.0	8,901	5.9	10.5	849
Banking	1,783	1.3	1,751	1.2	–1.8	–31
Insurance	2,260	1.7	2,476	1.6	9.5	215
Securities, commodities, and other investments	767	0.6	888	0.6	15.8	121
Professional and business services	16,414	12.3	20,980	13.8	27.8	4,566
Advertising and public relations services	425	0.3	520	0.3	22.4	95
Computer systems design and related services	1,147	0.9	1,600	1.1	39.5	453
Employment services	3,470	2.6	5,050	3.3	45.5	1,580
Management, scientific, and technical consulting services	779	0.6	1,250	0.8	60.5	471
Scientific research and development services	548	0.4	613	0.4	11.9	65
Education, health, and social services	27,973	21.0	34,399	22.6	23.0	6,426
Child day care services	767	0.6	1,062	0.7	38.4	295
Educational services	12,778	9.6	14,901	9.8	16.6	2,123
Health services	13,062	9.8	16,626	10.9	27.3	3,564
Social assistance, except child day care	1,365	1.0	1,810	1.2	32.6	445
Leisure and hospitality	12,479	9.3	14,694	9.7	17.7	2,215
Arts, entertainment, and recreation	1,833	1.4	2,293	1.5	25.1	460
Food services and drinking places	8,850	6.6	10,301	6.8	16.4	1,451
Hotels and other accommodations	1,796	1.3	2,100	1.4	16.9	304
Government and advocacy, grantmaking, and civic organizations	11,047	8.3	12,170	8.0	10.2	1,123
Advocacy, grantmaking, and civic organizations	1,231	0.9	1,410	0.9	14.5	179
Federal government	1,943	1.5	1,993	1.3	2.5	50
State and local government, except education and health	7,872	5.9	8,767	5.8	11.4	895

Note: May not add to totals due to omission of industries not covered.

Although workers of all ages are employed in each industry, certain industries tend to possess workers of distinct age groups. For the previously mentioned reasons, retail trade employs a relatively high proportion of younger

workers to fill part-time and temporary positions. The manufacturing sector, on the other hand, has a relatively high median age because many jobs in the sector require a number of years to learn and perfect specialized skills that do not easily transfer to other firms. Also, manufacturing employment has been declining, providing fewer opportunities for younger workers to get jobs. As a result, one-fourth of the workers in retail trade were 24 years of age or younger in 2004, compared with only 8.2 percent of workers in manufacturing. Table 4 contrasts the age distribution of workers in all industries with the distributions in five very different industries.

Table 4. Percent distribution of wage and salary workers by age group, selected industries

Industry	Age group			
	16 to 24	25 to 44	45 to 64	65 and older
All industries	14	47	36	4
Computer systems design and related services	7	63	29	1
Educational services	9	42	45	3
Food services and drinking places	44	39	15	2
Telecommunications	8	56	34	2
Utilities	5	43	50	2

Employment in some industries is concentrated in one region of the country. Such industries often are located near a source of raw or unfinished materials upon which the industry relies. For example, oil and gas extraction jobs are concentrated in Texas, Louisiana, and Oklahoma; many textile mills and products manufacturing jobs are found in North Carolina, South Carolina, and Georgia; and a significant proportion of motor vehicle manufacturing jobs are located in Michigan and Ohio. On the other hand, some industries—such as grocery stores and educational services—have jobs distributed throughout the nation, reflecting the general population density.

Occupations in the Industry

The occupations found in each industry depend on the types of services provided or goods produced. For example, because construction companies require skilled trades workers to build and renovate buildings, these companies employ large numbers of carpenters, electricians, plumbers, painters, and sheet metal workers. Other occupations common to construction include construction equipment operators and mechanics, installers, and repairers. Retail trade, on the other hand, displays and sells manufactured goods to consumers. As a result, retail trade employs numerous retail salespersons and other workers, including more than three-fourths of all cashiers. Table 5 shows the industry sectors and the occupational groups that predominate in each.

Table 5. Industry sectors and their largest occupational group

Industry sector	Largest occupational group	Percent of industry wage and salary jobs
Agriculture, forestry, fishing, and hunting	Farming, fishing, and forestry occupations	61.1
Mining	Construction and extraction occupations	33.3
Construction	Construction and extraction occupations	66.2
Manufacturing	Production occupations	52.1
Wholesale trade	Sales and related occupations	24.7
Retail trade	Sales and related occupations	52.5
Transportation and warehousing	Transportation and material moving occupations	56.0
Utilities	Installation, maintenance, and repair occupations	25.6
Information	Professional and related occupations	29.1
Finance and insurance	Office and administrative support occupations	51.4
Real estate and rental and leasing	Sales and related occupations	22.7

Industry sector	Largest occupational group	Percent of industry wage and salary jobs
Professional, scientific, and technical services	Professional and related occupations	42.6
Management of companies and enterprises	Office and administrative support occupations	33.6
Administrative and support and waste management and remediation services	Office and administrative support occupations	23.2
Educational services, private	Professional and related occupations	59.6
Health care and social assistance	Professional and related occupations	42.6
Arts, entertainment, and recreation	Service occupations	57.2
Accommodation and food services	Service occupations	84.0
Government	Professional and related occupations	43.7

The occupational distribution clearly is influenced by the structure of its industries, yet there are many occupations, such as general managers or secretaries, that are found in all industries. In fact, some of the largest occupations in the U.S. economy are dispersed across many industries. For example, the group of professional and related occupations is among the largest in the nation while also experiencing the fastest growth rate. (See table 6.) Other large occupational groups include service occupations; office and administrative support occupations; sales and related occupations; and management, business, and financial occupations.

Table 6. Total employment and projected change by broad occupational group, 2004–14 (Employment in thousands)

Occupational group	Employment, 2004	Percent change, 2004–2014
Total, all occupations	145,612	13.0
Professional and related occupations	28,544	21.2
Service occupations	27,673	19.0
Office and administrative support occupations	23,907	5.8
Sales and related occupations	15,330	9.6
Management, business, and financial occupations	14,987	14.4
Production occupations	10,562	−0.1
Transportation and material moving occupations	10,098	11.1
Construction and extraction occupations	7,738	12.0
Installation, maintenance, and repair occupations	5,747	11.4
Farming, fishing, and forestry occupations	1,026	−1.3

Training and Advancement

Workers prepare for employment in many ways, but the most fundamental form of job training in the United States is a high school education. Better than 88 percent of the nation's workforce possessed a high school diploma or its equivalent in 2004. However, many occupations require more training, so growing numbers of workers pursue additional training or education after high school. In 2004, 28.7 percent of the nation's workforce reported having completed some college or an associate's degree as their highest level of education, while an additional 29.5 percent continued in their studies and attained a bachelor's or higher degree. In addition to these types of formal education, other sources of qualifying training include formal company-provided training, apprenticeships, informal on-the-job training, correspondence courses, Armed Forces vocational training, and non-work-related training.

The unique combination of training required to succeed in each industry is determined largely by the industry's production process and the mix of occupations it requires. For example, manufacturing employs many machine operators who generally need little formal education after high school, but sometimes complete considerable on-the-job training. In contrast, the educational services industry employs many types of teachers, most of whom require a bachelor's or higher degree. Training requirements by industry sector are shown in table 7.

Table 7. Percent distribution of workers by highest grade completed or degree received, by industry sector

Industry sector	High school diploma or less	Some college or associate degree	Bachelor's or higher degree
All industries	41.6	28.7	29.5
Agriculture, forestry, fishing, and hunting	64.3	21.4	14.2
Mining	60.4	21.8	17.8
Construction	64.7	24.5	10.8
Manufacturing	51.5	25.1	23.4
Wholesale trade	42.7	29.0	28.3
Retail trade	50.6	32.3	17.1
Transportation and warehousing	52.6	31.7	15.6
Utilities	38.7	34.1	27.0
Information	26.7	31.3	42.0
Finance and insurance	24.9	31.6	43.4
Real estate and rental and leasing	36.2	31.7	32.2
Professional, scientific, and technical services	14.4	25.1	60.6
Administrative and support and waste management services	55.3	28.4	16.3
Educational services	17.8	19.0	63.2
Health care and social assistance	30.6	34.8	34.7
Arts, entertainment, and recreation	39.5	31.8	28.6
Accommodation and food services	60.7	28.4	11.0

Persons with no more than a high school diploma accounted for about 64.7 percent of all workers in construction; 64.3 in agriculture, forestry, fishing, and hunting; 60.7 percent in accommodation and food services; 60.4 percent in mining; 51.5 percent in manufacturing; and 50.6 in retail trade. On the other hand, those who had acquired a bachelor's or higher degree accounted for 63.2 percent of all workers in private educational services; 60.6 percent in professional, scientific, and technical services; 43.4 percent in finance and insurance; and 42.0 percent in information.

Education and training also are important factors in the variety of advancement paths found in different industries. Each industry has some unique advancement paths, but workers who complete additional on-the-job training or education generally help their chances of being promoted. In much of the manufacturing sector, for example, production workers who receive training in management and computer skills increase their likelihood of being promoted to supervisory positions. Other factors that impact advancement and that may figure prominently in industries include the size of the establishments, institutionalized career tracks, and the mix of occupations. As a result, persons who seek jobs in particular industries should be aware of how these advancement paths and other factors may later shape their careers.

Earnings

Like other characteristics, earnings differ by industry, the result of a highly complicated process that reflects a number of factors. For example, earnings may vary due to the nature of occupations in the industry, average hours worked, geographical location, workers' average age, educational requirements, profits, and the degree of union representation of the workforce. In general, wages are highest in metropolitan areas to compensate for the higher cost of living. Also, as would be expected, industries that employ a large proportion of unskilled minimum-wage or part-time workers tend to have lower earnings.

The difference in earnings between the industries of software publishers and of food services and drinking places illustrates how various characteristics of industries can result in great differences in earnings. In software publishers, earnings of all wage and salary workers averaged $1,342 a week in 2004, while in food service and drinking places, earnings of all wage and salary workers averaged only $194 weekly. The difference is large primarily because software publishing establishments employ more higher-skilled, full-time workers, while food services and drinking places employ many lower-skilled workers on a part-time basis. In addition, most workers in software publishing are paid an annual salary, while many workers in food service and drinking places are paid a low hourly wage that is supplemented with money the workers receive as tips. Table 8 highlights the industries with the highest and lowest average weekly earnings.

Table 8. Average weekly earnings of production or nonsupervisory workers on private nonfarm payrolls, selected industries

Industry	Earnings
All industries	$529
Industries with high earnings	
Software publishers	1,342
Computer systems design and related services	1,136
Aerospace product and parts manufacturing	1,019
Scientific research and development services	1,006
Motor vehicle and parts manufacturing	925
Mining	909
Industries with low earnings	
Food manufacturing	510
Grocery stores	332
Arts, entertainment, and recreation	313
Hotels and other accommodations	302
Child day care services	299
Food services and drinking places	194

Employee benefits, once a minor addition to wages and salaries, continue to grow in diversity and cost. In addition to traditional benefits—paid vacations, life and health insurance, and pensions—many employers now offer various benefits to accommodate the needs of a changing labor force. Such benefits sometimes include childcare; employee assistance programs that provide counseling for personal problems; and wellness programs that encourage exercise, stress management, and self-improvement. Benefits vary among occupational groups, full- and part-time workers, public and private sector workers, regions, unionized and nonunionized workers, and small and large establishments. Data indicate that full-time workers and those in medium-sized and large establishments—those with 100 or more workers—usually receive better benefits than do part-time workers and those in smaller establishments.

Union representation of the workforce varies widely by industry, and it also may play a role in determining earnings and benefits. In 2004, about 13.8 percent of workers throughout the nation were union members or covered by union contracts. As table 9 demonstrates, union affiliation of workers varies widely by industry. Fully 50.0 percent of the workers in air transportation were union members, the highest rate of all the industries, followed by 37.6 percent in educational services, and 33.0 percent in iron and steel mills and steel product manufacturing. Industries with the lowest unionization rate include computer systems design and related services, 1.3 percent; food services and drinking places, 1.7 percent; and advertising and related services, 1.7 percent.

Table 9. Union members and other workers covered by union contracts as a percent of total employment, selected industries

Industry	Percent union members or covered by union contract
All industries 13.8	
Industries with high unionization rates	
Air transportation 50.0	
Educational services 37.6	
Iron and steel mills and steel product manufacturing...................33.0	
Motor vehicles and motor vehicle equipment manufacturing 30.2	
Industries with low unionization rates	
Banking and related activities 1.9	
Advertising and related services 1.7	
Food services and drinking places...1.7	
Computer systems design and related services 1.3	

Outlook

Total employment in the United States is projected to increase by about 14 percent over the 2004–2014 period. Employment growth, however, is only one source of job openings. The total number of openings in any industry also depends on the industry's current employment level and its need to replace workers who leave their jobs. Throughout the economy, replacement needs will create more job openings than will employment growth. Employment size is a major determinant of job openings—larger industries generally have larger numbers of workers who must be replaced and provide more openings. The occupational composition of an industry is another factor. Industries with high concentrations of professional, technical, and other jobs that require more formal education—occupations in which workers tend to leave their jobs less frequently—generally have fewer openings resulting from replacement needs. On the other hand, more replacement openings generally occur in industries with high concentrations of service, laborer, and other jobs that require little formal education and have lower wages because workers in these jobs are more likely to leave their occupations.

Employment growth is determined largely by changes in the demand for the goods and services provided by an industry, worker productivity, and foreign competition. Each industry is affected by a different set of variables that determines the number and composition of jobs that will be available. Even within an industry, employment may grow at different rates in different occupations. For example, changes in technology, production methods, and business practices in an industry might eliminate some jobs, while creating others. Some industries may be growing rapidly overall, yet opportunities for workers in occupations within those industries could be stagnant or even declining because they are adversely affected by technological change. Similarly, employment of some occupations may be declining in the economy as a whole, yet may be increasing in a rapidly growing industry.

Employment growth rates over the next decade will vary widely among industries. Agriculture and natural resources is the only sector in which all of the industries are expected to experience employment declines. Consolidation of farm land, increasing worker productivity, and depletion of wild fish stocks should continue to decrease employment in agriculture, forestry, and fishing. Employment in mining is expected to decline due to labor-saving technology while jobs in oil and gas extraction are expected to decrease with the continued reliance on foreign sources of energy.

Employment in manufacturing, construction, and utilities is expected to remain nearly unchanged as growth in construction is partially offset by declines in utilities and selected manufacturing industries. Growth in construction employment will stem from new factory construction as existing facilities are modernized; from new school construction, reflecting growth in the school-age population; and from infrastructure improvements, such as road and bridge construction. Employment declines are expected in chemical manufacturing, except drugs; machinery manufacturing; computer and electronic product manufacturing; printing; steel manufacturing; and textile, textile product, and apparel manufacturing. Textile, textile product, and apparel manufacturing is projected to lose about 321,200 jobs over the 2004–2014 period—more than any other manufacturing industry—due primarily to increasing imports replacing domestic products.

Employment gains are expected in some manufacturing industries. Small employment gains in food manufacturing are expected, as a growing and ever more diverse population increases the demand for manufactured food products. Employment growth in pharmaceutical and medicine manufacturing is expected, as sales of pharmaceuticals increase with growth in the population, particularly among the elderly, and with the introduction of new medicines to the market. Both food and pharmaceutical and medicine manufacturing also have growing export markets. Aerospace product and parts manufacturing and motor vehicle and parts manufacturing are both expected to have modest employment increases.

Growth in overall employment will result primarily from growth in service-providing industries over the 2004–2014 period, almost all of which are expected to have increasing employment. Job growth is expected to be led by health services and educational services, with large numbers of new jobs also in employment services, food services and drinking places, state and local government, and wholesale trade. When combined, these sectors will account for almost half of all new wage and salary jobs across the nation. Employment growth is expected in many other service-providing industries, but they will result in far fewer numbers of new jobs.

Health services will account for the most new wage and salary jobs, about 3.6 million over the 2004–2014 period. Population growth, advances in medical technologies that increase the number of treatable diseases, and a growing share of the population in older age groups will drive employment growth. Offices of physicians, the largest health care industry group, is expected to account for about 760,000 of these new jobs as patients seek more healthcare outside of the traditional inpatient hospital setting.

The educational services industry is expected to grow by nearly 17 percent over the 2004–2014 period, adding about 2.1 million new jobs. A growing emphasis on improving education and making it available to more children and young adults will be the primary factors contributing to employment growth. Employment growth at all levels of education is expected, particularly at the postsecondary level, as children of the baby boomers continue to reach college age, and as more adults pursue continuing education to enhance or update their skills.

Employment in one of the nation's fastest-growing industries—employment services—is expected to increase by more than 45 percent, adding another 1.6 million jobs over the 2004–2014 period. Employment will increase, particularly in temporary help services and professional employer organizations, as businesses seek new ways to make their workforces more specialized and responsive to changes in demand.

The food services and drinking places industry is expected to add almost 1.5 million new jobs over the 2004–2014 projection period. Increases in population, dual-income families, and dining sophistication will contribute to job growth. In addition, the increasing diversity of the population will contribute to job growth in food services and drinking places that offer a wider variety of ethnic foods and drinks.

Over 890,000 new jobs are expected to arise in state and local government, adding more than 11 percent over the 2004–2014 period. Job growth will result primarily from growth in the population and its demand for public services. Additional job growth will result as state and local governments continue to receive greater responsibility for administering federally funded programs from the federal government.

Wholesale trade is expected to add almost 480,000 new jobs over the coming decade, reflecting growth both in trade and in the overall economy. Most new jobs will be for sales representatives at the wholesale and manufacturing levels. However, industry consolidation and the growth of electronic commerce using the Internet are expected to limit job growth to 8.4 percent over the 2004–2014 period, less than the 14 percent projected for all industries.

Continual changes in the economy have far-reaching and complex effects on employment in industries. Job seekers should be aware of these changes, keeping alert for developments that can affect job opportunities in industries and the variety of occupations that are found in each industry.

Editor's Note: The preceding article was adapted from the Career Guide to Industries, *a publication of the U.S. Department of Labor. A book titled* 40 Best Fields for Your Career *(JIST Publishing) includes information from the* Career Guide to Industries *plus useful "best fields" lists and other helpful insights.*

Job Outlook for College Graduates

You've heard it again and again: Having a college degree leads to higher earnings and more career opportunities. But is it true?

For the most part, it is. When it comes to paychecks and prospects, conventional wisdom is right. On average, college graduates earn more money, experience less unemployment, and have a wider variety of career options than other workers do. A college degree also makes it easier to enter many of the fastest-growing, highest-paying occupations. In some occupations, in fact, having a degree is the only way to get your start.

According to statistics and projections from the U.S. Bureau of Labor Statistics (BLS), college graduates will continue to have bright prospects. Data consistently show that workers who have a bachelor's or graduate degree have higher earnings and lower unemployment than workers who have less education. And between 2002 and 2012, more than 14 million job openings are projected to be filled by workers who have a bachelor's or graduate degree and who are entering an occupation for the first time.

A college education can be costly, of course, in terms of both time and money. But the rewards can be bigger than the sacrifices if a degree helps you to qualify for occupations that interest you.

Keep reading to learn about the benefits of having a college degree and the demand for college graduates. You'll also find out which occupations are expected to offer the most job openings for people who are entering them for the first time. Many of these occupations employ workers who have more education than a bachelor's degree. A box beginning on page 418 shows which occupations usually offer the biggest financial rewards for getting a graduate degree.

In this article, a college graduate is defined as a person who has a bachelor's, master's, or doctoral (Ph.D.) degree or a professional degree, such as one in law or medicine.

College Graduates: In Demand and Doing Well

More people are going to college now than ever before, in part because of the career advantages that a college degree confers. College-educated workers' higher earnings and lower unemployment are good reasons to go to college, and these benefits are also evidence of the demand for college graduates. Higher earnings show that employers are willing to pay more to have college graduates work for them. And lower unemployment means that college graduates are more likely to find a job when they want one.

413

More People Going to College

The number of people who have a college degree has been increasing steadily. According to Current Population Survey data, the number of people age 25 and older who have a college degree grew from 35 million to 52 million between 1992 and 2004, an increase of almost 50 percent. By mid-2004, nearly 28 percent of people aged 25 and older had a bachelor's or graduate degree. (See chart 1.)

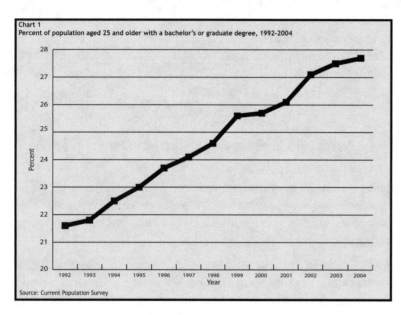

Chart 1
Percent of population aged 25 and older with a bachelor's or graduate degree, 1992-2004

Source: Current Population Survey

Higher Earnings, Lower Unemployment

As a whole, college-educated workers earn more money than workers who have less education. In 2003, workers who had a bachelor's degree had median weekly earnings of $900, compared with $554 a week for high school graduates—that's a difference of $346 per week, or a 62 percent jump in median earnings. (Median earnings show that half of the workers in the educational category earned more than that amount and half earned less.)

For workers who had a master's, doctoral, or professional degree, median earnings were even higher. In addition to earning more money, workers who had more education were also less likely to be unemployed. Chart 2 shows the median earnings and unemployment rates for workers at various levels of educational attainment. Taken together, higher earnings and more regular employment amount to large differences in income over a lifetime.

Higher earnings for workers who have a college degree are part of a long-term trend. Even when adjusted for inflation, the wages of college-educated workers have been rising over the past decade. (See chart 3.) Moreover, the earnings for college-educated workers have been increasing faster than the earnings for workers who do not have a bachelor's degree.

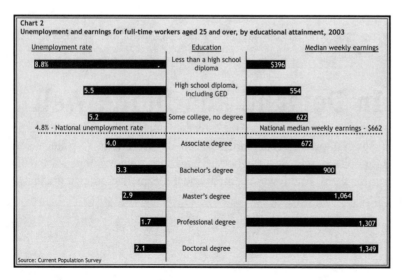

Chart 2
Unemployment and earnings for full-time workers aged 25 and over, by educational attainment, 2003

Unemployment rate	Education	Median weekly earnings
8.8%	Less than a high school diploma	$396
5.5	High school diploma, including GED	554
5.2	Some college, no degree	622
4.8% - National unemployment rate		National median weekly earnings - $662
4.0	Associate degree	672
3.3	Bachelor's degree	900
2.9	Master's degree	1,064
1.7	Professional degree	1,307
2.1	Doctoral degree	1,349

Source: Current Population Survey

The Trouble with Averages

Statistics about college graduates paint a rosy—and numerically accurate—picture of overall employment. But the data are based on college graduates as a whole. For every graduate who earns more than the median, another earns less. And while unemployment rates are low overall, many college graduates sometimes have trouble finding work, especially if they wait for the type of job they want.

The career prospects of individuals depend on many factors besides having a college degree. These factors include the local job market, the type of degree they have, their level of experience and skill, and the occupation they are trying to enter.

Openings and Where They Will Be

Between 2002 and 2012, BLS projects 56 million job openings for workers who are entering an occupation for the first time. Of these, at least 14 million are expected to be filled by college-educated workers. More than half of these openings are expected to come from the need to fill newly created jobs.

The remaining openings for college-educated workers are projected to come from the need to replace workers who leave an occupation permanently. With many of today's college-educated workers poised to retire, replacement needs are expected to be great, especially in large occupations.

In some occupations, most workers have bachelor's or graduate degrees. In other occupations, education levels are more varied.

Many of the occupations that are expected to have the most openings for college graduates are in the business, computers and engineering, education, counseling, and healthcare fields.

"Pure-College" Occupations

For this analysis, it is assumed that each future job opening will be for a college-educated worker. In these "pure-college" occupations, at least 60 percent of current workers aged 25–44 have a bachelor's or graduate degree, fewer than 20 percent have a high school diploma or less education, and fewer than 20 percent have some college courses but less education than a

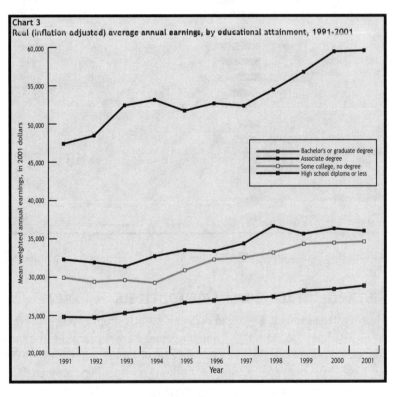

Chart 3
Real (inflation adjusted) average annual earnings, by educational attainment, 1991–2001

bachelor's degree. Even if some workers do not have a bachelor's or graduate degree, all openings are counted as being for college-educated workers because that most accurately reflects the job market new workers face. (For more about the methods used to count job openings, see the section beginning on page 420.)

BLS projects that pure-college occupations will provide about 6.8 million openings over the 2002–2012 decade for college graduates who are entering an occupation for the first time. Chart 4 shows the 20 pure-college occupations expected to provide the most openings during the projections decade. Like nearly all pure-college occupations, all but one of the occupations on the chart have earnings above $27,380, the 2002 median for all workers.

Despite high numbers of job openings, jobseekers can face strong competition when trying to enter some occupations, such as public relations specialists or management analysts. Because these occupations offer high earnings and prestige and because workers can qualify with many different college majors, the number of qualified workers who want these jobs could be greater than the number of openings. Analyses of job competition are possible for a few occupations, ones for which there is anecdotal evidence or for which other data exist. To qualify for many of the occupations shown in chart 4, workers need more than a bachelor's degree. In three of the occupations—lawyers, physicians and surgeons, and pharmacists—a professional degree is required. Similarly, physical therapists now train for their occupation only in a master's or doctoral degree program.

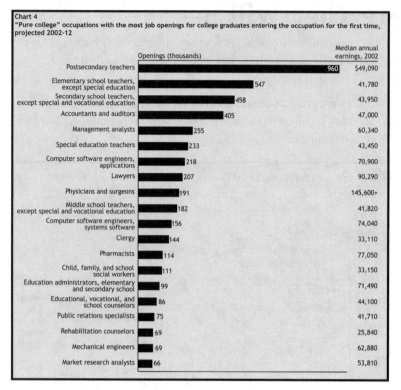

Chart 4
"Pure college" occupations with the most job openings for college graduates entering the occupation for the first time, projected 2002-12

	Openings (thousands)	Median annual earnings, 2002
Postsecondary teachers	960	$49,090
Elementary school teachers, except special education	547	41,780
Secondary school teachers, except special and vocational education	458	43,950
Accountants and auditors	405	47,000
Management analysts	255	60,340
Special education teachers	233	43,450
Computer software engineers, applications	218	70,900
Lawyers	207	90,290
Physicians and surgeons	191	145,600+
Middle school teachers, except special and vocational education	182	41,820
Computer software engineers, systems software	156	74,040
Clergy	144	33,110
Pharmacists	114	77,050
Child, family, and school social workers	111	33,150
Education administrators, elementary and secondary school	99	71,490
Educational, vocational, and school counselors	86	44,100
Public relations specialists	75	41,710
Rehabilitation counselors	69	25,840
Mechanical engineers	69	62,880
Market research analysts	66	53,810

In other occupations, educational requirements are more flexible. About one-fourth of management analysts have a master's degree, for example, but many analysts do not have education beyond a bachelor's degree. Schoolteachers, too, often have a graduate degree, but many teachers earn that degree after they begin their careers; while employed, they take graduate-level courses to gain skills, qualify for higher salaries, and maintain certification. In many occupations, employment and advancement opportunities improve with attainment of a graduate degree, even when one is not required for career entry.

Education level often determines the type of work a person can do within an occupation. Psychologists, for example, usually need a doctoral degree to do independent, clinical work, but some school psychologists do not need this level of education. Social workers can get some jobs with a bachelor's degree, but to work in a clinical setting, they often need a graduate degree.

"Mixed-Education" Occupations

Many college graduates work in occupations that employ workers who have a variety of education levels. Over the 2002–2012 decade, about 23 million openings are projected to be in occupations in which the number of college-educated workers is significant—20 percent or more—but for which college is not the only level of education workers have. For example, of the 1.1 million job openings projected for registered nurses, more than 650,000 are projected to be filled by bachelor's or graduate degree holders based on current educational attainment patterns. Overall, of the 23 million job openings in these "mixed-education" occupations, BLS expects 7.5 million to be filled by college graduates.

Chart 5 shows the mixed-education occupations that are expected to provide the most openings over the projections decade for college graduates who are entering an occupation for the first time. In several of these occupations, such as registered nurses, police and sheriff's patrol officers, and wholesale and manufacturing sales representatives, the education levels of workers have been rising. When hiring workers, some employers prefer their new employees to be college graduates, even though many existing workers do not have a degree.

Sometimes, as is often the case for preschool teachers and social and human service assistants, having a degree benefits workers beyond helping them get the job. It may qualify workers to take on more complex tasks in the occupation, for example, or increase workers' opportunities for advancement and responsibility.

In other occupations—such as retail salespersons and customer service representatives—workers from every education level are represented even though most qualify after a few weeks or months of on-the-job training. A degree is not required, and many college graduates choose these occupations for reasons unrelated to education or training, such as plentiful opportunities or flexible hours.

Mixed-education occupations make it difficult to measure with certainty the demand for college graduates. Defining a college-level occupation is highly subjective. Some openings in an occupation might require a degree; for other openings, a degree might be useful; and for still other openings, a degree might not make much of a difference.

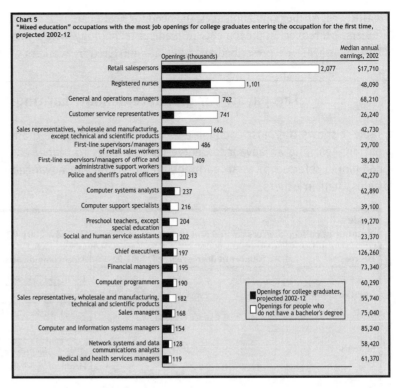

Chart 5
"Mixed education" occupations with the most job openings for college graduates entering the occupation for the first time, projected 2002-12

Occupation	Openings (thousands)	Median annual earnings, 2002
Retail salespersons	2,077	$17,710
Registered nurses	1,101	48,090
General and operations managers	762	68,210
Customer service representatives	741	26,240
Sales representatives, wholesale and manufacturing, except technical and scientific products	662	42,730
First-line supervisors/managers of retail sales workers	486	29,700
First-line supervisors/managers of office and administrative support workers	409	38,820
Police and sheriff's patrol officers	313	42,270
Computer systems analysts	237	62,890
Computer support specialists	216	39,100
Preschool teachers, except special education	204	19,270
Social and human service assistants	202	23,370
Chief executives	197	126,260
Financial managers	195	73,340
Computer programmers	190	60,290
Sales representatives, wholesale and manufacturing, technical and scientific products	182	55,740
Sales managers	168	75,040
Computer and information systems managers	154	85,240
Network systems and data communications analysts	128	58,420
Medical and health services managers	119	61,370

■ Openings for college graduates, projected 2002-12
□ Openings for people who do not have a bachelor's degree

Occupations with Increasing Demand: Trends and Themes

As a whole, occupations that employ mostly college graduates are expected to gain new jobs faster than other types of occupations. Between 2002 and 2012, pure-college occupations are projected to grow 22 percent overall, considerably faster than the 15-percent average growth projected for all occupations. Eighteen of the 20 pure-college occupations in chart 4 are projected to grow faster than the 15-percent average for all occupations.

Looking at job growth is important because occupations that are gaining jobs quickly are, in effect, showing rapidly increasing demand for workers. Some of the economic trends that are creating growth in pure-college and mixed-education occupations are described in this section by career field.

Business, finance, and sales. The growing complexity of business is expected to increase the demand for college graduates in business and financial occupations. More workers will be needed to manage rising personal incomes, increased regulation of financial activity, and growing competition among businesses.

Sales occupations are expected to grow along with the overall economy. Although numerous workers in these occupations do not have a college degree, many others do. Having a degree is especially valued in occupations involving sales of complex scientific or technical products.

Computers and engineering. The demand for new products and new technology is expected to continue to drive growth in computer and engineering occupations. Occupations in emerging engineering specialties, including biotechnology and environmental engineering, are expected to gain jobs rapidly over the projections decade. However, these specialties are expected to remain small and provide fewer openings than larger engineering specialties, such as mechanical and computer engineering.

Counseling, social service, and psychology. Numerous social trends are projected to increase the number of counselors, social workers, and psychologists needed over the 2002–2012 decade. More schools are hiring trained counselors. At the same time, more people are seeking counseling for family problems, substance abuse, and mental disorders. And to ease overcrowding at prisons, many offenders are being sent instead to rehabilitation facilities, where counselors, social workers, and psychologists are employed to assist them.

Education. Most opportunities in the field of education will come from the need to replace the many teachers and administrators who are expected to retire over the 2002–2012 decade. But additional positions are projected because of efforts to reduce class sizes and because of increasing enrollments at colleges and universities.

Healthcare. As the population ages, the need for healthcare will increase, fueling the need for more healthcare practitioners. Moreover, improvements in medical technology will create more medical and rehabilitative treatments. Those treatments are prescribed and often administered by workers who have a college degree.

The payoff for graduate school: Earnings premiums by degree

Table 1 shows the most common areas of study for college graduates by academic degree. In many occupations, earning an advanced degree usually leads to higher earnings. This difference in earnings is commonly referred to as an earnings premium. But an advanced degree is worth more in some career fields than in others.

Table 1
Number of college degrees earned and most common areas of study, 2001-02

Degree	Number of degrees earned, 2001-02	Most common areas of study
Bachelor's	1,375,000	Business management and administrative services
		Education
		Social sciences and history
Master's	491,000	Education
		Business management and administrative services
		Health professions and related sciences
Doctoral	45,000	Education
		Engineering
		Psychology
		Biological and life sciences
Professional	82,000	Law and legal studies
		Health professions and related sciences
		Theological studies and religious vocations
Total	1,993,000	

Source: National Center for Education Statistics, U.S. Department of Education

Table 2 shows how much more money was earned in various occupations by workers who have an advanced degree compared with workers who have a bachelor's degree. Data are reported only for occupations in which 10,000 or more workers held a bachelor's degree and another 10,000 or more workers held a graduate or professional degree. The information in the table is based on 2000, 2001, 2002, and 2003 data from the Current Population Survey. The data from these 4 years were averaged to increase statistical reliability by increasing the number of workers surveyed.

For most occupations, having an advanced degree increased median earnings—and the higher the degree, the larger the earnings premium. On average, having a master's degree increased earnings by 21 percent over a bachelor's degree. Among occupations for which there were reliable data, almost all offered an increase in median earnings for workers who have a master's degree. Physical therapists and network and communications systems administrators were exceptions, perhaps because many of the workers who have an advanced degree in these occupations were recent entrants and so earned less.

Earnings premiums were highest in occupations that usually require an advanced degree. Psychologists have the highest earnings premium of any occupation, with master's degree holders earning 78 percent and doctoral degree holders earning 132 percent more than bachelor's degree holders. Many jobs in this field require a doctorate.

Table 2							
Employment and median earnings by occupation and educational attainment, 2000-03							
	Median weekly earnings				Earnings premiums (percent)		
Occupation	Bachelor's degree	Master's degree	Professional degree	Doctoral degree	Master's over bachelor's	Professional over bachelor's	Doctoral over master's
Total, all occupations	$838	$1,016	$1,240	$1,280	21%	48%	26%
Accountants and auditors	868	1,078	1,053		24	21	
Actors, producers, and directors	917	1,072			17		
Architects, except naval	1,049	1,066			2		
Athletes, coaches, umpires, and related workers	740	745			1		
Chief executives	1,657	1,765	1,664	1,907	7	0.4	8
Clergy	702	731	865	895	4	23	22
Clinical laboratory technologists and technicians	766	856			12		
Compliance officers, except agriculture, construction, health and safety, and transportation	960	1,090			14		
Computer and information systems managers	1,415	1,640			16		
Computer and mathematical occupations	1,080	1,237	1,326	1,442	15	23	17
Computer programmers	1,037	1,141			10		
Computer scientists and systems analysts	1,099	1,201			9		
Computer software engineers	1,201	1,363		1,579	13		16
Computer support specialists	847	996			18		
Database administrators	1,158	1,368			18		
Network and computer systems administrators	1,069	1,012			-5		
Network systems and data communications analysts	1,026	1,171			14		
Operations research analysts	1,058	1,140			8		
Counselors, social workers, and other community and social service specialists	630	820	946	926	30	50	13
Counselors	614	819			33		
Social workers	622	813			31		
Designers	769	970			26		
Dietitians and nutritionists	646	766			19		
Editors	769	965			25		
Education administrators	765	1,136	1,297	1,392	48	70	23
Elementary and middle school teachers	683	888	871	1159	30	28	31

In addition, education-related occupations paid higher-than-average earnings premiums for both master's and doctoral degrees.

Occupations such as management analysts, counselors, social workers, biological scientists, and market and survey researchers also paid higher-than-average premiums for a graduate degree.

(continued)

(continued)

The financial benefits of advanced degrees might be understated in many occupations because newer workers are more likely to have an advanced degree, and these workers might earn less because they have less experience. The occupation of pharmacist, for example, averages some of the lowest earnings premiums for advanced degrees. In part, this is because new pharmacists now need a professional degree, so the workers who have a bachelor's degree almost always have more experience than other workers do.

Overall, occupations that provide above-average earnings premiums for advanced degrees are usually those in which most workers have at least a bachelor's degree. Earnings premiums are the highest in occupations that value advanced degrees. If a bachelor's degree is the most education that is required in an occupation, earning an advanced degree will not always increase median earnings significantly.

How These Numbers Were Developed

There are many ways to measure job outlook by education, and each method has both strengths and limitations. This analysis focuses on future job openings because job openings show how many new workers will be able to enter an occupation.

Deciding which job openings will be filled by college graduates was more complicated. Counselors and jobseekers often ask which occupations are "college level." But answering that question is difficult because workers in most occupations come from many different educational backgrounds. This analysis used the education levels of current workers as an objective way to account for this variation.

Like any analysis based on projections and estimates, however, this one has limitations to its accuracy. Understanding these limitations will help readers to better use the results.

Methods Used

To estimate the demand for college graduates between 2002 and 2012, BLS analysts got specific. First, they projected the number of job openings for workers entering each of more than 500 occupations over the decade. Next, analysts estimated how many of those openings would be filled by college graduates.

Measuring job openings. Job openings come from two sources: the need to fill newly created jobs and the need to replace workers who retire or leave an occupation permanently for other reasons.

To estimate the number of newly created jobs, analysts projected how much each occupation would grow or decline between 2002 and 2012. An occupation might gain jobs for many reasons. Sometimes, the demand for a specific good or service creates the need for additional workers in an occupation, such as when an increased use of computer software creates a greater need for software engineers. The way a good or service is provided can also lead to more jobs in an occupation. Rather than relying solely on teachers and administrators to guide and educate students, for example, more schools are hiring counselors and psychologists, creating more openings for those workers. In the same way, a decrease in the demand for a good or service or a change in production methods can reduce the number of jobs and openings in an occupation.

The second source of job openings is replacement needs. To estimate how many workers will need to be replaced during the projections decade, BLS analysts studied the ages of current workers and the length of time that workers in each occupation usually remain. In occupations that require high levels of training, workers tend to stay longer. In other occupations, especially those that have shorter training periods, workers tend to leave or retire more quickly.

Job openings for college graduates. After analysts projected the number of job openings for workers entering an occupation, they estimated how many of those openings would be for college graduates. Using information from 2000, 2001, and 2002 Current Population Survey data, analysts classified current workers' educational attainment into one of three categories: a high school diploma or less, some college but no bachelor's or graduate degree, or a bachelor's or graduate degree. If at least 20 percent of workers in an occupation belonged to a given educational category, that level was deemed significant. Expected openings were divided among each of these significant education categories according to how common each category was.

For example, the occupation of administrative services managers includes workers in each educational category: About 23 percent have a high school diploma or less, 37 percent have some college coursework or an associate degree but no bachelor's degree, and 41 percent have a bachelor's or graduate degree. Projected openings were divided among the education categories using those percentages.

For some occupations, a bachelor's or graduate degree was the only education level common enough to be significant. At least 60 percent of workers in the occupation were college graduates, and fewer than 20 percent of workers belonged to the other two educational categories. In these 115 pure-college occupations, every projected opening was considered to be for a college graduate.

In addition to using the three educational attainment categories, this article provides specific information about the types of degrees commonly required in some occupations. This type of information comes from the occupational analyses conducted for the *Occupational Outlook Handbook.*

Earnings data. This analysis uses earnings data from two surveys: the Current Population Survey and the Occupational Employment Statistics survey. Earnings data from the Current Population Survey, which includes information about workers' education levels, were used to compare earnings by education. Earnings data from the Occupational Employment Statistics survey, which is more comprehensive, provide median earnings for an occupation as a whole.

The two surveys are different. The Current Population Survey is a household survey that asks workers themselves to give earnings, occupational, and other types of information; it includes self-employed workers. The Occupational Employment Statistics survey, an establishment survey, asks employers to provide earnings and occupational information about their workers; it does not include the self-employed.

Limitations of the Data

To measure job openings for college graduates, BLS analysts needed to make assumptions about the future. First, analysts assumed that the education levels in each occupation would remain roughly the same over the 2002–2012 decade. In reality, the educational characteristics of some occupations change over time. Many occupations—such as registered nurses and police officers—have had a gradual increase in the number of workers who have a bachelor's degree.

Analysts also ignored education levels that were uncommon in an occupation; as stated previously, at least 20 percent of workers in an occupation had to have a given level of education for it to be considered significant. So, for example, even though almost 17 percent of engineering technicians have a college degree, none of that occupation's projected openings were counted as openings for college graduates.

Another limitation of this study is that it focuses on the number of job openings projected in an occupation. But job openings give only a partial view of the prospects that workers can expect. The number of people who will compete for those openings is also important. For most occupations, however, BLS analysts do not have enough information to analyze the competition for jobs.

Finally, the accuracy of this study is limited by its use of survey data. Surveys are always subject to some error because not every worker is counted and because the information gathered is sometimes incorrect. In addition, the education levels of many occupations could not be determined with statistical accuracy because the number of workers surveyed was too small. In those cases, analysts substituted the education levels of similar occupations or groups of occupations that had larger numbers of workers.

Even with its assumptions and limitations, however, there is evidence that estimating future job openings using the analysis described here produces accurate results. When existing jobs are separated into educational categories in such a way, the results closely match current numbers.

For More Information

This article shows expected job openings in only a few of the occupations available to workers who have a college degree. To compare the expected job openings in every occupation studied, see the 2004–2005 *Occupational Projections and Training Data* bulletin, which also explains in detail the methods used in this analysis. The bulletin is available online at www.bls.gov/emp/optd/home.htm and is available for sale by calling the Superintendent of Documents toll-free at (866) 572-1800.

To learn more about the occupations described in this article and in the bulletin, see the 2006–2007 *Occupational Outlook Handbook*. The *Handbook* describes the job outlook, education and training requirements, and job duties of nearly 270 occupations and is available in many libraries and career centers and online at www.bls.gov/oco.

BLS is not the only organization that gathers data on the demand and earnings for college graduates. Associations, both professional ones for specific occupations and general ones like the National Association of Colleges and Employers, often do surveys on employers' hiring needs, workers' education levels, and workers' earnings. Find contact information for these associations in the *Occupational Outlook Handbook* or at your local library.

If you are considering college, the U.S. Department of Education provides additional information and assistance, including information about financial aid. Most college students receive some form of financial aid through programs administered by the Department of Education. The Department provides applications for grants and loans; lists resources for finding scholarships; and maintains a searchable database of colleges and universities by location, available majors, enrollment, and other characteristics. Call the financial aid hotline toll-free at (800) 4FED-AID (433-3243); write the Federal Student Aid Information Center, P.O. Box 84, Washington, DC 20044-0084; or visit online at www.studentaid.ed.gov.

Projections and education statistics are a few of the factors to consider when deciding on a career. Other considerations, including working conditions, personal interests and strengths, and local labor market conditions, are also important. Career centers and labor market information offices can help you explore these matters. Find your local one-stop career center and labor market information office by visiting America's Service Locator online at www.servicelocator.org or by calling the U.S. Department of Labor's toll-free career hotline, (877) US2-JOBS (872-5627).

A job search is about more than job outlook. Choosing an occupation that is projected to have many opportunities can ease your way into employment—but in the end, it takes only one job opening to begin finding career satisfaction.

From the **Occupational Outlook Quarterly** *by the U.S. Department of Labor. Written by Jill N. Lacey and Olivia Crosby, economists in the Office of Occupational Statistics and Employment Projections.*

Index